ARTHURIAN STUDIES XXVI

Publications of the Institute of Germanic Studies
Volume 53

CHRÉTIEN DE TROYES
AND THE GERMAN MIDDLE AGES

The pre-eminent role of Chrétien de Troyes in the formation of
Arthurian romance is reflected in the swift and brilliant response of
German courtly poets to his works. Within a few years of their
composition, *Erec et Enide* and *Yvain* were adapted for German
audiences by Hartmann von Aue, initiating the tradition of
Arthurian romance in his country, while Chrétien's unfinished
Grail-story was taken up and brought to a triumphant conclusion
in *Parzival*, composed by the most influential of medieval German
authors of romance, Wolfram von Eschenbach. Chrétien's *Cligés*
and *Lancelot*, by contrast, had a much less distinct impact in
Germany, a circumstance which reveals significant differences in
the literary configurations east and west of the Rhine and in the
expectations of French and German courtly audiences.

The papers contained in this volume are a selection from those
given at an international symposium held at the University of
London's Institute of Germanic Studies which brought together
distinguished specialists in medieval German, French and comparative literature. The contributors explore diverse aspects of
Chrétien's reception in Germany, relating his works and those of
his German adaptors to their historical, social, intellectual and
artistic contexts and tracing the interplay of creative personalities,
literary traditions and cultural preoccupations which were involved in the process of accommodating the French romances to
their new German setting. Marked by a heightened awareness of
the inherent ambiguity of Chrétien's works and a refreshing
openness to the varied possibilities of literary adaptation, the
individual studies exemplify an appropriately wide range of critical
approaches and emphases. Collectively they underline the rich-
ness both of Chrétien's work and of the imaginative responses
which it evoked and present a vivid picture of medieval romance in
the period of its first flowering in France and Germany.

ARTHURIAN STUDIES
ISSN 0261-9814

Previously published volumes in this series
are listed at the back of this book

Publications of the Institute of Germanic Studies
ISSN 0076-0811

CHRÉTIEN DE TROYES
AND THE GERMAN MIDDLE AGES

PAPERS FROM AN INTERNATIONAL SYMPOSIUM

EDITED WITH AN INTRODUCTION BY

Martin H. Jones   and   Roy Wisbey

D. S. BREWER

INSTITUTE OF GERMANIC STUDIES

First published 1993 by
D. S. Brewer, Cambridge and by
The Institute of Germanic Studies, University of London

D. S. Brewer is an imprint of Boydell & Brewer Ltd
PO Box 9, Woodbridge, Suffolk IP12 3DF, UK
and of Boydell & Brewer Inc.
PO Box 41026, Rochester, NY 14604, USA

D. S. Brewer ISBN 0 85991 356 2
The Institute of Germanic Studies ISBN 0 85457 160 4

British Library Cataloguing-in-Publication Data
Chretien De Troyes and the German Middle Ages: Papers from an International
Symposium. – (Arthurian Studies Series, ISSN 0261-9814; Vol. 26)
 I. Jones, Martin H. II. Wisbey, Roy
 III. Series
 841.1
 ISBN 0-85991-356-2

Library of Congress Cataloging-in-Publication Data
Chrétien de Troyes and the German Middle Ages : papers from an international symposium
/ edited with an introduction by Martin H. Jones and Roy Wisbey.
  p. cm. – (Arthurian studies ; 26) (Publications of the Institute of Germanic Studies ; 53)
Includes bibliographical references and index.
 ISBN 0-85991-356-2 (alk. paper)
 1. Court epic, German–History and criticism–Congresses. 2. German poetry–Middle High
German, 1050–1500–History and criticism–Congresses. 3. Chrétien, de Troye, 12th cent.–
Influence–Congresses. 4. Arthurian romances–History and criticism–Congresses. I. Jones,
Martin H., 1944– . II. Wisbey, R. A. (Roy Albert), 1929– . III. Series. IV. Series: Publications
(University of London. Institute of Germanic Studies) ; 53.
PT203.C49 1993
831'.209–dc20   92–34156

Printed in Great Britain by
St Edmundsbury Press Ltd, Bury St Edmunds, Suffolk

Contents

Introduction

From 19 to 22 April 1988 some fifty scholars from Western Europe, North America, South Africa, and the (then) U.S.S.R. gathered in London, at our invitation, for a symposium on the subject which forms the title of this volume. The University of London's Institute of Germanic Studies provided the setting for our deliberations over the four days, during which time twenty-six papers were delivered. Each of the papers was given in one of the three conference languages, English, French, or German, and frequently the discussions following the papers were conducted in more than one of these languages simultaneously. The trilingual character of the occasion itself is reflected in the contributions to the volume. As befits a symposium, the academic programme was punctuated by opportunities to exchange ideas and deepen acquaintance over food and drink, including most notably receptions at the Embassy of the Federal Republic of Germany and the Institute of Germanic Studies and a conference dinner at King's College London. For a variety of reasons it was not possible to include in this volume all the papers presented at the symposium, but the majority – nineteen of the twenty-six – are to be found here. These were submitted to us subsequently, many in a substantially revised form which bears testimony to the value of the lively discussions in an atmosphere of friendly collegiality which accompanied our proceedings.

The initial steps in the organization of the symposium were taken in March 1987, when invitations to attend and contribute papers were circulated. From the outset we hoped to secure the participation of qualified scholars in fields outside that of medieval German literature, where inevitably the bulk of the work on Chrétien's reception in Germany has taken place. In the event we were fortunate to be able to include Romance scholars and – with generous support by the British Council – a comparativist in our programme and in the contributions to this volume. Such widening of the framework of discussion seemed to us appropriate to the stage which the study of Chrétien's influence on medieval German literature had reached. This we regarded as offering the possibility of a new openness and plurality of approach following a period in which debate had been dominated – and polarized – by the claims arising from the excessively narrow view of the possibilities of literary reception associated with the concept of 'l'adaptation courtoise'.

It was, therefore, in no way our purpose to seek to impose on speakers and contributors a rigid conception of their task. Nor would such an imposition have been feasible, given the diversity of issues raised by the impact of Chrétien's five major romances in Germany.

The papers are arranged, as far as is practicable, according to the generally agreed chronology of Chrétien's romances; a contribution concerning *Guillaume d'Angleterre*, which not all scholars would attribute to Chrétien, has been placed after consideration of the works of undoubted authenticity. The same order is observed for the summaries of the individual contributions which, in view of the polyglot nature of the volume, we have provided in this introduction. We hope that these extended summaries, interspersed with occasional explanatory comment, will be of service to those who do not read with ease all the languages represented here.

E.M. Meletinsky opens the volume with a study which points to the structural unity of Chrétien's works and, without any assumption of reciprocal influence, to striking correspondences between them and medieval romances from Persia, Georgia, and even Japan. In Chrétien he finds a well-defined synchronic (and, in the last instance, mutually balancing) system of complementary oppositions: sexual love versus love as compassion, conjugal love versus adulterous love, secular chivalry versus Christian chivalry. Such simultaneous parallelisms and antinomies exist within and between individual romances by Chrétien, and prove to be matched by dichotomies of composition which they share, e.g. achievement of initial success followed by a 'tragic' loss of equilibrium, then its restoration through trials in the form of chivalrous exploits under the inspiration of love. This second phase, with its interiorization, represents a distinctive moral advance of the romance beyond the simple tale with supernatural features (first phase). The Tristan story displays the same twofold structure (heroic tale followed by interior conflict), but without the harmonious solution of the crisis, indeed with a destructive outcome. Despite evident differences, typological parallels exist between *Tristan et Iseult* and Gorgâni's *Wîs and Râmîn* (representing the first phase in the Persian romance), and between Nizâmî's *Khosrau and Shirin* and Chrétien, representing the second, 'classical', phase of medieval romance. Works of the latter kind end in harmony, and with the reconciliation of the 'interior' with the 'social'. Although in the Japanese *Genji* of the eleventh century linear personal development has been replaced under Buddhist influence by a cyclical model, the work contains an element of harmonisation showing that it too belongs to the 'classical' phase of romance.

In his contribution, Michael Batts is concerned with the implications, for medieval authors and modern scholarship alike, of the fact that, in the twelfth and thirteenth centuries, literary virtuosity was demonstrated by the skilful reworking and reinterpretation of existing sources, rather than in the treatment of 'materiam [. . .] novam et inusitatam' (Geoffrey of Vinsauf). This situation has resulted, not only in an undue preoccupation with sources, but in a transference to adaptations, for instance those of Chrétien's works by Hartmann, of the intuitive feeling that the 'translated' version is inferior to the 'original'. Close textual comparison has led scholarship, also, to concentrate on divergences of the adaptation from its source, rather than on the new whole as an independent entity. Batts argues that qualitative comparisons between original and translation are not only of doubtful value (p. 12), but also lead to untenable, absolute value-judgements, a process which opens the door to nationalist prejudice and stereotype, of which earlier French and German literary histories yield copious illustrations.

A series of papers concerned with Hartmann's adaptations of Chrétien's *Erec et Enide* and *Yvain* is opened by Silvia Ranawake, who focuses on the issue of the heroes' guilt. This she sees as residing precisely in the omission which in each case immediately precipitates the crisis: Erec's neglect of his duties as ruler, and Yvain/Iwein's failure to return to Laudine at the appointed time. Hartmann presents these omissions – Erec's *verligen* and Iwein's *versitzen* – differently from Chrétien. Their significance is widened in that they are not merely offences against the codes of chivalry (*Erec et Enide*) and courtly love (*Yvain*) but indications of a fundamental failure on the heroes' part to fulfil the personal and social responsibilities they have assumed. Developing hints already present in Chrétien, Hartmann depicts both *verligen* and *versitzen* in terms which suggest an analogy with the sin of *acedia*; aspects of each hero's behaviour are paralleled by various manifestations of sloth: Erec's preoccupation with ease (*gemach*), for example, and Iwein's self-reproach and sense of guilt which make him despair of regaining Laudine's favour. While a strict equation of the heroes' failures, which lie in the sphere of personal and social relations, with *acedia*, a spiritual sin, is not intended, a neat separation between the secular and religious is not possible in Hartmann's romances. In both works the climax shows the hero as the antitype of the slothful sinner, the tireless soldier of Christ (p. 33), facing danger with joyful trust and fortitude, espousing the cause of compassion and justice, and proving fitness for a kingship whose duties are prescribed by God. The religious analogy proves relevant also in evaluating the overall course of the heroes' stories. These are not to be read as accounts of personal immaturity overcome in a process of growing understanding, but rather as the exemplification of innate human frailty which, like sin, can manifest itself in any person and to which the appropriate response is the resolve to atone and seek rehabilitation. If at the end of the works Erec and Iwein are seen to have advanced from the condition in which they first appeared, this is the result not of a learning or maturing process but of the grace which has made it possible for them to do the works which confirm their vocation to lordship.

The paper by W.H. Jackson reviews the status of knighthood in the social reality of twelfth-century Germany, focusing on Hartmann's adaptation of Chrétien's *Erec et Enide*. He concludes that the idealistic connotations of Hartmann's version have led previous research to underestimate the extent of its social concreteness (p. 38). The term *ritters name*, it is argued, reflects a social category entitling its members to privileged treatment, a process attested historically from the mid-twelfth century in Germany, in addition to indicating desirable standards of ethical behaviour, a juxtaposition not unconnected with 'the cultural importance and self-awareness of lordly courts' in the period (pp. 42–43). It is in the twelfth century, too, that the term *ritter* assumes dominance over the (simple) *kneht*, the latter becoming firmly subordinated to the former. Hartmann's *Erec* is found to correspond in this respect to the hierarchy of *chevalier* and *serjant/ escuiier* in Chrétien's *Erec et Enide*, as well as to German legal and historical sources of the time, while the archaism *guoter kneht* becomes the fast diminishing alternative to *ritter*, owing its survival – one may add – not merely to its place in standing rhymes, but to its role within epic formulae as such. From the *Kaiserchronik* onwards, moreover, *ritter*, even in the lower echelons of the *ministeriales*, proves to be differentiated increasingly from other groups (*rustici, mercatores*) as a distinct social category.

In the first of two contributions devoted to the heroine of Chrétien's *Erec et Enide* and Hartmann's *Erec*, Bernard Willson examines the qualities of character demonstrated during the adventures shared with Erec which prove her fitness to be his wife. In both works the heroine evinces a degree of loyalty and constancy which transcends the expectations of Erec with his conventional demand that she show him the obedience of a dutiful wife. Hartmann, however, emphasizes that Enite's acts of disobedience in defying the prohibition of speech when Erec's life is in danger – at one level acts of *untriuwe* and *unstæte* – are evidence of *triuwe* and *stæte* of a higher order to which she attains through the enabling power of God, released in response to her prayers at the moments of crisis. This religious dimension in the heroine's portrayal, at best only latent in Chrétien's version, is vital to Hartmann's view of her as the embodiment of a selfless, measureless love which partakes of the nature of *caritas* itself. Whereas Enide's trials in Chrétien prove that she loves her husband perfectly, Hartmann's Enite is shown to be the very epitome of 'Christian wifehood' – *ein rehtez wîp* – who, with God's help, fulfils her part in a way that underlines the sacramental nature of marriage.

Karen Pratt's approach to Enide/Enite is via a sympathetic, but detached survey of feminist readings of the two works, intended to exemplify the value of viewing works by male authors from a 'somewhat oblique' female standpoint. Chrétien's treatment proves to be polysemic, leaving the way free for a dissenting, perhaps deliberately subversive view, and presenting 'a highly ambiguous image of woman'. His narrator is seen as non-intrusive, rarely expressing moral value judgements, and preferring to demonstrate the problematic nature of the relationship between Erec and Enide through an ironic discrepancy between words and actions. Chrétien's treatment of gender roles is found to be complex and ambivalent: Enide's catalytic 'parole' is justified by the facts, but leads to punishment and even self-criticism. Chrétien's narrator offers little guidance between divergent readings, yet inappropriate silence (or speech) is a key theme of the work. Hartmann, by contrast, invents 'a more authoritarian narrator' whose 'message is less open to challenge', and who does not hesitate to provide firm narratorial guidance, reflecting Hartmann's own more complete identification with the ideology of his audience (p. 69). His Enite conforms to the author's own ideal of *wîplîcher site*, *triuwe* and *güete*, in the interests of which almost all the ironic ambiguities of his source have been suppressed. In proposing a model of the 'good woman' whose love supports the male in 'his royal duties and knightly pursuits' (p. 83), Hartmann, instead of encouraging debate like Chrétien, has reinforced the traditional stereotypes of a patriarchal society.

Martin Jones devotes himself to the depiction of Erec, by both Chrétien and Hartmann, 'as a representative of chivalry and as a fighting man' (p. 85). Erec's temporary withdrawal from knightly activity following his marriage and return to Karnant raises questions about his physical and mental preparedness for combat, questions which the series of encounters culminating in the first confrontation with King Guivret/Guivreiz are designed to resolve, albeit with a different emphasis in each author. In Chrétien, Erec is charged with *recreantise*, i.e. his military prowess and even his courage is publicly placed in doubt. In Hartmann, Erec's *verligen* refers to a more general personal and social degeneration, making Erec unfit to rule. Erec's abandonment of tourneying, with the consequent loss of 'vreude' at his court, reflects a problem of mentality ('sîn muot'), that is of his whole attitude to chivalry. Hartmann sees himself as entitled to exercise his artistic independence in combat scenes, more than doubling the number of encounters contained in his source, but in some instances omitting, telescoping and truncating Chrétien's accounts. Chrétien's descriptions of Erec's combats owe much to French epic tradition, although he shapes the convention to his purpose of depicting Erec's courage and effectiveness as a fighting man. Hartmann too demonstrably inherits a literary tradition where sword-play is concerned, although he makes restrained use of it. Yet, unlike Chrétien, he stands, in Germany, at or near the beginning of a narrative convention serving to portray lance attacks. This allows him to project a new and less violent model of knighthood. In Hartmann's reshaping of Chrétien, Guivreiz is Erec's first truly worthy opponent after he leaves Karnant, an opponent who continually seeks *âventiure* (combat experience), as a means of ensuring mental hardness and preparedness – as Shakespeare's Henry V tells his nobles before the battle of Agincourt: 'All things are ready, if our minds be so' (IV.3.71). Erec's ambiguous performance in this combat illustrates the effect which the *verligen* of the Karnant episode has had upon his confidence and psychological readiness for action, and points to Enite's role in his restoration to the full status of knighthood, a pre-condition of his later kingship.

Daniel Rocher sets himself the task of evaluating the reception of *Cligés* in Germany. He begins by questioning the conventional perception of Chrétien's work as a Byzantine rather than an Arthurian romance, and as an anti-Tristan polemic. He points out that three-quarters of the action is located in Western Europe, mainly in Arthur's lands, and only its last portion can be described as Byzantine; furthermore, while the anti-Tristan thesis finds support in the bulk of the work, in its last quarter there is a dramatic change of tack as the experience of Cligés and Fenice mimics that of Tristan and Isold in many respects. The ambiguities of Chrétien's work may provide at least a partial explanation for the paucity of evidence for the one German version of *Cligés* that is certainly known to have been made, that by Ulrich von Türheim (Rocher considers the possibility of there having been also an earlier version by Konrad Fleck). Exiguously preserved in three separate sets of fragments (remarkably all of the same manuscript), the tendency of Ulrich's adaptation, in so far as it can be discerned with any assurance, is towards conformity with conventional moral standards. Though his work was praised by Rudolf von Ems in *Willehalm von Orlens*, Ulrich's attempt to counteract the morally suspect character of Chrétien's conclusion may not have been found persuasive by German audiences; their preference was for works of unambiguous intent, such as Rudolf's *Willehalm*, whose anti-Tristan stance may indeed have been inspired by reaction to *Cligés*.

Why is it that the figure of Lancelot, so prominent in the contemporary European and North American context, hardly features in the present-day German revival of Arthurian subject-matter? In his penetrating analysis of the Lancelot tradition, Walter Blank traces the problem back to its roots in the failure of medieval Germany to give to Lancelot the status and elevated literary treatments which caused Parzival and Tristan to fire the imagination of Richard Wagner. In Germany, King Arthur provides a supranational embodiment of feudal rule, but more local, political aspirations towards a utopian future in which justice and peace would reign supreme are transferred to the Grail story, overwhelmingly represented, in weight of preserved manuscripts, by Wolfram. The Lancelot perspective, on the other hand, is a grimly negative one, foreboding coming disaster. Nor can Lancelot find acceptance in Germany as the canonic exemplar of an absolute, forbidden love, a role pre-empted unchallengeably by Tristan. In the religious sphere, the dominance of Parzival leaves no room for competing figures like Lancelot or Galahad. The German Prose-Lancelot, with its untraditional form, comes too late to affect this outcome.

Klaus Grubmüller re-examines the view, represented above all by Kurt Ruh, that, in his *Lanzelet*, Ulrich von Zatzikhoven – like his Anglo-Norman source – interacted with Chrétien's Arthurian romances and set up his own counter-model. Grubmüller, by contrast, argues that Ulrich's *Lanzelet*, despite features in common (individual episodes, role stereotypes, constellations of figures, motifs), came into being independently of Chrétien – he considers it unlikely that Ulrich simply chose to disregard works of such a high profile. The structure of *Lanzelet* does not reflect the compositional principles associated with Chrétien, while its themes and ethos also diverge, albeit without any hint of deliberate opposition to a canonic model. Archaic, mythical elements appear, in a form suggesting derivation from an earlier substratum; King Arthur himself resumes the role as an active monarch familiar to us from Geoffrey of Monmouth and Wace. Moreover, the adulterous relationship between Lancelot and the Queen, characteristic of Chrétien's *Chevalier de la Charrette*, is missing here. With a sidelong glance at research on the pre-history of the heroic epic, Grubmüller concludes that Lanzelet and its source is rooted in an Arthurian legend existing, as we know, before Chrétien and surviving after him, in short, that there was an 'Artussage vor und außerhalb der Dichtung' (p. 149).

Tony Hunt takes as his starting point the instability introduced by recent scholarship – not least by his own – into the interpretation of Chrétien, and the implications of this for the understanding of Hartmann's Arthurian romances. How does the German author react to what is seen as 'the *ludic* nature of [French] courtly culture' with its attendant 'irony, dialectic and scepticism' (p. 151)? A pointer is sought in the methods used by Hartmann to remodel the love relationship in *Yvain*. The first device, of which research has long been aware in principle, is the omission of passages – four examples are discussed here – in which Chrétien presents women or love itself in a dubious or ambiguous light, for instance by suggesting a distinction between *amor* and amorousness. Little heeded, by contrast, is Hartmann's use of a further technique, employed in glossed school books of the period, in which the letter of the text is retained, but is reinterpreted in advance by a commentary which predisposes the audience to see the content from a new angle (p. 163). Eight illustrations of this device of anticipation ('Vorwegnahme') are given. They show that, even where blocks of source text are taken over relatively unchanged – on this matter see the remarks of Michael Batts, below pp. 11–12 – they are infused with new meaning through the different context provided. Hartmann emerges as an authoritative narrator (a view anticipated in this volume by Karen Pratt). He conducts his audience through the uncertain terrain of Chrétien's tale, removing the worst obstacles from their path, always keeping before them his conviction that moral qualities like compassion, *stæte*, *triuwe* and womanly *güete* are inseparable from the pursuit of love, chivalry and honour.

In her contribution Wiebke Freytag is concerned to establish to what extent vernacular poetry, in this case Hartmann's *Iwein* in particular, seeks to conform to the expectation of the school-trained *litterati* of the time that literature should have an ethical import, with the purpose of *correctio morum*, and employ appropriate means for its presentation, including the tools of logic. While Chrétien betrays, through occasional formulations, an acquaintance with scholastic discourse, Hartmann draws on his knowledge of philosophical ethics, specifically of discussion concerning the nature of the good, to provide a framework for the interpretation of his whole work. The prologue to *Iwein*, with its opening *sententia* on *rehte güete* and its exemplification in King Arthur, is seen to reflect with particular clarity Boethius's notion of the *verum bonum* and its use by medieval school authors, and possibly to derive from a sentence of Cicero's *Paradoxa Stoicorum*. Discourse about the nature of the good is not restricted, however, to statements in the narrator's voice, but is conducted also by the characters of the work. This is exemplified above all in a detailed analysis of the exchanges between Keie and the Queen in the opening episode of the work. Good, identified with Guinevere, is shown here to triumph over evil, represented by Keie, both using weapons from the armoury of dialectic and logical rhetoric to maintain their positions. With sophistic arguments and fallacies, Keie seeks to discredit Kalogrenant, while the Queen employs syllogism and topic arguments to establish that Keie's *site* of abusing the best and praising the worst is unharmful to others but probably harmful to him. By the arguments which the Queen skilfully applies Keie is made to appear as one who exemplifies *ex negativo* the *sententia* with which the work opens. Hartmann emerges from this account as one who shares the learning of the *litterati* and their perception of the function and formal requirements of literature; that learning does not, however, substitute for poetic imagination but rather feeds it creatively.

Michael Curschmann favours a dating in the 1220s for the unprecedented Rodenegg Iwein picture cycle. This allows him to entertain the possibility that, given the close ties between Aquileia and Brixen, Thomasin's *Der welsche Gast* may have fostered in the German-speaking region about Rodenegg 'the general sanction of *aventiure* as (indirect) purveyor of (partial) truth' (p. 225). In other words, the work may have lent 'quasi-official authorization' to the view that courtly romance may embody icons of exemplarity which, like figures of scripture, can be responsibly depicted in paintings for the edification of those unable to read. This, in turn, could explain how an artist or artists trained in an ecclesiastical workshop might justify participation in such work. The *ministeriales* of Rodenegg, on the other hand, as members of a new class of nobles, could seize the opportunity to further their own aspirations by identifying themselves publicly and socially through these pictorial representations with the new models of action and behaviour offered by Chrétien and Hartmann, just as earlier generations of the nobility had traded on associations with the literary traditions of the (oral) heroic epic.

René Pérennec aims to stimulate new ways of thinking about the relationship between an adaptation and its source (see Batts, above) in his essay entitled 'Wolfram von Eschenbach before the *Conte du Graal*'. Having established by reference to *Willehalm* that Wolfram's narrative stance is typically confrontational, presenting the material of the source from contrary and provocative points of view, he turns to consider how Wolfram met the challenge posed by the Grail utopia in Chrétien's last romance. Although intended by Chrétien to represent something beyond the traditional world of chivalry and its preoccupation with love and adventure, the utopian concept was not clearly differentiated from that world and resisted realization in narrative form. Wolfram, too, did not give it concrete shape, but his characteristic 'agonistic' approach facilitated criticism of conventional notions of love and combat which served to imply the transcendent nature of the indescribable Grail utopia. The initial impetus for the composition of the Gahmuret books is also traced back to this objective: taken together with the existing Gawan episodes, the prehistory created a graded series of narrative parts providing a perspective on the story of Parzival with its focus in the Grail. A possible consequence of Wolfram's style of adaptation is that his work makes more explicit polarities contained in his source, which may help to explain the existence of equally well-founded but divergent interpretations of the work. Furthermore, Wolfram's sensitivity to Chrétien's text may have caused him to pick up 'vibrations' present there which were then magnified in his version (the Ither-theme is cited as an example), so that *Parzival* can in some respects serve as a commentary on the *Conte du Graal*.

Adrian Stevens employs Mikhail Bakhtin's concept of heteroglossia to illuminate Wolfram's introduction of non-literary registers into his *Parzival*, a procedure which offends against the rigorous selectivity demanded by rhetorical conventions of decorum (pp. 245–47). Chrétien is quite distinct from Wolfram, the one a *literatus*, steeped in the clerical traditions of the trivium, the other defiantly *illiteratus*. The contrast is pointed by detailed analysis of the nocturnal scene where Blancheflur/ Condwiramurs appears at the bedside of the young hero. In Chrétien, the surface of the sophisticated clerical narrative conceals a figurative and improper Ovidian sub-text, which the reader or audience is left to decode in private complicity with the author. In Wolfram, there is not even an implied breach of feminine propriety. By a descent into vulgarity in commenting on the action, Wolfram reveals directly the gulf between himself and his audience on the one hand and the innocence of the young couple on the other. 'A fallen narrator tells the idealised story of his protagonists in a fallen world' (p. 253).

In his complementary, yet – in accordance with his theme – heterogeneous study of this same episode, in which Perceval/Parzival wins the hand of Blancheflur/Condwiramurs, Arthur Groos brings further concepts of Bakhtin into play. Old and new insights as to the divergences of Wolfram's narrative from that of Chrétien, come to life within an approach which detects limited 'dialogic or polyphonic' potential in Chrétien's narrative, but credits Wolfram with a comprehensive 'dialogic imagination', creating discourse between narrator and protagonists, organizing and orchestrating interconnections between characters and episodes, articulating 'chronotopic' interrelationships in space and time. *Parzival* proves, finally, to embody a 'pervasive intertextual dynamic' (interacting particularly with Hartmann's *Erec*), and to be a variegated, pluralistic unity that, unlike Chrétien's work, subsumes even historiographical and scientific discourse (pp. 274–75).

Timothy McFarland concerns himself with the creative inversion whereby the Clinschor of *Parzival* becomes a priest who has turned to necromancy, and with the possibility that Wolfram's treatment of this narrative complex is yet another reflection in his work of the contemporary aristocratic scene. Gawan is shown to have an advantage over Chrétien's Gauvain (and to some extent over Wolfram's audience, as well as over Parzival at Munsalvaesche), in being better informed about the nature of the supreme challenge facing him at the enchanted 'other-world' castle, and even, possibly, about the identity of the royal ladies imprisoned there, as well as about the lordship of Clinschor. In the *Conte du Graal* and *Parzival* alike, fuller knowledge about the situation at the castle is imparted only after the adventure itself has taken place. Wolfram's Gawan has yet to learn, not who the royal ladies are – as in the narrative climax to Chrétien's version of the episode – 'but the reason why they are in the castle at all' (p. 283). In *Parzival*, it is Orgeluse who first associates Clinschor with 'nigromanzî' and 'zouber' (617, 12–13), significantly in a political, courtly context. In a double process of gradual disclosure, Wolfram displaces surprise at the kinship relationships away from Gawan to the imprisoned ladies and King Arthur. For Gawan and for the reader, Arnive's revelations, absent from Chrétien, are what provide the main narrative tension here. Demonic sorcery, as opposed to natural magic, is invoked as one of the sources of misfortune in the courtly world. The many structural and thematic parallels (in addition to significant differences) between the Parzival and Gawan stories, including the human misery experienced in the castle episodes which are common to both, thus need to be supplemented by a further insight. In a reversal of the pattern familiar from the religious and social history of late Roman antiquity, the 'Augustinian' view of the fall of man (represented here by Munsalvaesche) as a sufficient explanation of the evil in the world, weakens, and a growing belief in sorcery (Schastel Marveile) gains ground as an alternative explanation of the sufferings of mankind. In *Parzival*, Wolfram contrives the defeat of sorcery, but its role in the work perhaps indicates its growing currency in high courtly and clerical circles of his time.

Jean-Marc Pastré examines the depiction of female characters by Chrétien, Hartmann, and Wolfram, with reference more generally to the art of portraiture in the twelfth and thirteenth centuries. Hartmann's portraits of Enite and Laudine display a 'functional schematism' (p. 299), in accordance with which details of a person's appearance are described not for their intrinsic beauty but for their significance in narrative terms. Chrétien's portraits of these women, by contrast, are both functional and ornamental in nature, reflecting in their detailed attention to physical beauty a genuine aesthetic of portraiture. In depicting his central female characters, women whose virtue is beyond reproach, Wolfram adopts a style which is similar to that of Hartmann, except for his reference to the expressive quality of the eyes and to radiant beauty; Wolfram shares with Gottfried the distinction of being the first to use these motifs in German literature. On the other hand, for characters such as Jeschute and Antikonie, who are involved in erotically charged situations, he employs an extended range of details, giving prominence to features – lips, teeth, breasts, hips, waist, arms, hands – which, while often present in Latin and French portraits, had rarely received mention in German texts previously. The differences observed between French and German authors in portraiture are associated with wider aesthetic contrasts between the two countries: just as Gothic superseded Romanesque architecture earlier in France than in the Empire, so French poets adopted a style of portraiture which rendered physical beauty in precise detail already in the second half of the twelfth century, while a shift in that direction was not evident in Germany until Wolfram and Gottfried. In addition, French portraits give evidence of an 'aesthetic optimism' (p. 308), describing feminine beauty for its own sake, whereas in the German context graphic depictions of women's physical appearance are associated with sensuality and seductiveness.

Volker Honemann comes down on the side of those who consider *Guillaume d'Angleterre* to be a work of Chrétien de Troyes, and places it in the context of a series of thematically related texts deriving from about the eighth to the late thirteenth century. The texts considered are principally the Latin Eustachius legend, *Guillaume d'Angleterre* (before 1170?), the *Gute Frau* (c.1235), and *Wilhelm von Wenden* by Ulrich von Etzenbach (c.1289–90). The Eustachius theme is both powerful and poignant: a family accepts exile on religious grounds, with consequent loss of high status and years of hardship, experienced in separation. Eventually, the family is reunited, after recognition scenes embodying many traditional narrative elements. This study compares the works thematically, not seeking to establish interdependences, but showing how the individual authors, each working within a particular religious, literary and socio-historical framework, draw on this complex of material, which was readily accessible, shaping it in order to satisfy their own specific intentions and the expectations of their audiences. In one case (the *Gute Frau*), this includes a striking female success story (p. 323): the wife rises above her tribulations in exile to become the (chaste) queen of France.

Our readers will, we hope, conclude that Chrétien, too, has risen triumphantly above any potential adversities of his 'exile' in a receptive Germany. Certainly, Chrétien would be gratified, if hardly surprised, to find ample confirmation in this volume that the proud boast he made in the prologue to *Erec et Enide* about the survival of his work had itself stood the test of time. Yet the very diversity and (as we now see more acutely) ambiguity of his *œuvre* ruled out in advance any expectation that the results of our symposium would be unilinear or clear-cut, least of all that they might be capable of reduction, for the purposes of this introduction, to a unifying, final *sententia*. Nevertheless, a string of mutually supportive generalities could – if we were to usurp the function of our reviewers yet further – be abstracted from the summaries we have provided, for there is indeed much common ground between the approaches represented, not only in the shared aspiration to scrupulous standards of interpretation, but, for instance, in a sustained effort to relate the works discussed to their historical, social, intellectual, and artistic context. As the more myopic aspects of the editors' labours recede, they are left not only with a much sharpened focus on innumerable passages in the texts of Chrétien and his German adaptors, but also with a vivifying sense of having been in the presence of some powerful and impressive literary interactions, in a cultural setting of great importance. May this sense convey itself to others.

Editorial Note and Acknowledgements

No one who has been active in Chrétien studies will be unaware of the problems posed by the lack of a fully satisfactory critical edition of his works. Under the circumstances we regarded it as untenable to require our contributors to refer uniformly to a single edition among those available for each of Chrétien's romances. References are, therefore, to the editions of the contributors' own choice; these are clearly indicated in the footnotes. Similarly, we have not standardized the form of his name throughout the volume, allowing Chrétien to coexist with Chrestien (and even with Kristian in some older references). The position with editions of the major German authors of the period is less parlous, though here too we believed it right to respect authors' preferences for either Lachmann's or Leitzmann's *Parzival* and for editions of Hartmann's works other than the latest ones available. Again, the footnotes provide the necessary guidance for readers.

In matters of presentation we have conformed, as far as possible, to the recommendations of the *MHRA Style Book*, fourth edition (London, 1991). The abbreviations of periodical titles, series, and standard reference works (listed on pp. xxiii–iv) follow the conventions of *Die Deutsche Literatur des Mittelalters: Verfasserlexikon*, ed. by Kurt Ruh and others, 2nd edn (Berlin/New York, 1977–).

Other unavoidable commitments have held back completion of the present volume, although this delay has allowed us to receive important contributions which the original time scale would have excluded. An additional burden – the submission of the entire edited text in machine-readable form – was accepted by the editors in return for a major reduction in the print subsidy required. At considerable hidden cost, the volume thus appears without financial support from the contributors, or from outside bodies, and with the assistance only of a subvention from residual conference funds, supplemented by our Department. Martin Jones assumed responsibility for the arduous and time-consuming task of preparing the text on disk, an operation in which he was aided by the Computing Centre of King's College London, where certain of the contributions were scanned on an Optical Character Recognition device. A grant from the College's School of Humanities enabled him to enlist secretarial support in the later stages of preparation. The necessary computing facilities were provided by the Department of German. We are indebted to Achim Timmermann for compiling the index in a remarkably short space of time.

In addition to acknowledging this assistance in the production of the text, we wish to express our thanks to the staff of the Institute of Germanic Studies for ensuring the smooth running of the symposium, and to Cultural Counsellor Herr Georg von Neubronner for inviting participants to a reception held at the Embassy of the Federal Republic of Germany. We are grateful to Boydell & Brewer and to the Publications Committee of the Institute of Germanic Studies for accepting the volume for inclusion in their respective series. We thank Dr Richard Barber at Boydell & Brewer, and our contributors, for their forebearance during the protracted gestation of the volume: 'dâ wider und in lange/ daz herze was getrüebet,/ sô wart nû vreude güebet' (Hartmann, *Erec*, 9661–63).

Martin H. Jones   Roy Wisbey

Department of German
King's College London
February 1992

List of Contributors

MICHAEL BATTS	University of Vancouver
WALTER BLANK	University of Freiburg
MICHAEL CURSCHMANN	Princeton University
WIEBKE FREYTAG	University of Hamburg
ARTHUR GROOS	Cornell University
KLAUS GRUBMÜLLER	University of Göttingen
VOLKER HONEMANN	University of Münster
TONY HUNT	University of Oxford
WILLIAM HENRY JACKSON	University of St. Andrews
MARTIN H. JONES	King's College London
TIMOTHY McFARLAND	University College London
E.M. MELETINSKY	University of Moscow
JEAN-MARC PASTRÉ	University of Rouen
RENÉ PÉRENNEC	University of Tours
KAREN PRATT	Goldsmiths' College London
SILVIA RANAWAKE	Queen Mary and Westfield College London
DANIEL ROCHER	University of Aix-en-Provence
ADRIAN STEVENS	University College London
BERNARD WILLSON	University of Leicester

Abbreviations

ABäG	*Amsterdamer Beiträge zur älteren Germanistik*
AfdA	*Anzeiger für deutsches Altertum und deutsche Literatur*
ATB	Altdeutsche Textbibliothek
BBSIA	*Bulletin Bibliographique de la Société Internationale Arthurienne*
BHL	*Bibliotheca hagiographica latina, I–II*
Bibl.d.ges.dt.Nat.-Lit.	Bibliothek der gesamten deutschen National-Literatur von der ältesten bis auf die neuere Zeit
CFMA	Les Classiques Français du Moyen Âge
CSEL	Corpus scriptorum ecclesiasticorum latinorum
DTM	Deutsche Texte des Mittelalters
DVjs	*Deutsche Vierteljahresschrift für Literaturwissenschaft und Geistesgeschichte*
Et. Germ.	*Études Germaniques*
Euph.	*Euphorion. Zeitschrift für Literaturgeschichte*
GAG	Göppinger Arbeiten zur Germanistik
GLL	*German Life and Letters*
GQ	*German Quarterly*
GR	*Germanic Review*
GRM	*Germanisch-romanische Monatsschrift*
HZ	*Historische Zeitschrift*
Leuv. Bijdr.	*Leuvense Bijdragen*
MGH	Monumenta Germaniae Historica
MLN	*Modern Language Notes*
MSD	*Denkmäler deutscher Poesie und Prosa*, ed. by K. Müllenhoff and W. Scherer, 3rd edn (Berlin, 1892)
MTU	Münchener Texte und Untersuchungen zur deutschen Literatur des Mittelalters
Neoph.	*Neophilologus*
NF	Neue Folge
PBB (Tüb.)	*Beiträge zur Geschichte der deutschen Sprache und Literatur* (Tübingen)

PL	Patrologia Latina, ed. by J. P. Migne (Paris, 1878–90)
QF	Quellen und Forschungen zur Sprach- und Kulturgeschichte der germanischen Völker
Reclam UB	Reclam Universal-Bibliothek
SATF	Société des Anciens Textes Français
StLV	Bibliothek des Stuttgarter Litterarischen Vereins
WdF	Wege der Forschung
WW	*Wirkendes Wort*
ZfdA	*Zeitschrift für deutsches Altertum und deutsche Literatur*
ZfdPh	*Zeitschrift für deutsche Philologie*
ZfromPh	*Zeitschrift für romanische Philologie*

L'œuvre de Chrétien de Troyes dans une perspective comparatiste

E. M. MELETINSKY

Les romans 'bretons' de Chrétien de Troyes représentent la forme typique du roman courtois au stade classique de son développement. Leur structure est assez universelle et il existe un certain parallélisme entre ces romans bretons de Chrétien et les romans (ou épopées romanesques) d'autres pays. L'influence de l'œuvre de Chrétien ne s'étendait qu'au cadre européen, en particulier en l'Allemagne où Hartmann von Aue et Wolfram von Eschenbach traduisaient ses romans le plus souvent en renforçant l'originalité stylistique et en approfondissant des aspects éthiques et religieux de manière plus abstraite. L'influence réciproque du roman médiéval français et oriental est exclue, mais par exemple le parallélisme de Chrétien et Nizâmî, ainsi que le parallélisme de *Tristan et Iseult* et *Wîs et Râmîn* (par Gorgâni) est frappant. Ce parallélisme, contrairement à l'hypothèse de Gallais et d'autres d'une soi-disant influence orientale sur le roman courtois, est évidemment d'ordre typologique. Un parallélisme existe, quoique moins frappant, entre le roman courtois français et l'œuvre romanesque en Géorgie, au Japon, etc.

Mais avant d'analyser la nature commune du roman médiéval, il est nécéssaire de révéler l'unité profonde des romans bretons de Chrétien lui-même.

Ces romans sont généralement envisagés dans une perspective diachronique, comme un cheminement créatif zigzagant, dicté en partie par les commandes de grands personnages, tels que Marie de France ou Philippe d'Alsace.

Cependant l'approche consistant à y voir un système synchronique bien défini, dont les différents éléments se complètent et se reflètent l'un l'autre comme dans un jeu de miroirs, est bien plus productive. Les romans bretons de Chrétien de Troyes s'inscrivent dans les rapports de la distribution complémentaire et forment un système paradigmatique uni. C'est dans ce cadre que se manifeste leur sens commun et, au-delà,

1

l'idée de *mesure*, qui est très chère à Chrétien. Dans tous les romans bretons Chrétien varie la collision de l'amour et de la chevalerie, précisée à l'aide d'oppositions supplémentaires: amour sexuel et courtois vs. amour-compassion (éros vs. agape) et amour conjugal vs. amour adultère et chevalerie profane formaliste vs. chevalerie véritable chrétienne. L'opposition principale amour/chevalerie est manifestée partout et Chrétien de Troyes proclame toujours l'équilibre, l'harmonie de ces deux éléments.

L'amour conjugal (en principe préféré) est célébré dans *Erec et Enide*, dans *Yvain ou le chevalier au lion*, implicitement aussi dans *Le Conte du Graal*, tandis que l'amour adultère dans le goût provençal est chanté (non sans une certaine ironie) dans *Lancelot ou le chevalier de la charrette*. L'amour courtois (avec la coincidence dans une seule personne de la dame et de la femme) et la chevalerie mondaine se manifestent dans les romans *Erec* et *Yvain* et l'amour chrétien, c'est à dire l'amour-compassion dans *Le Conte du Graal*.

Partout dans le point culminant, au moment de crise, le héros rompt l'équilibre entre *amour* et *chevalerie*; puis cet équilibre se rétablit progressivement et le personnage du héros se fait réintégrer dans son unité. De cette manière Erec rompt l'équilibre en faveur de l'amour et Yvain en faveur de la chevalerie, Lancelot semble à première vue le rompre en faveur de la chevalerie (quand il hésite devant la charrette du nain) mais au fond il le rompt en faveur de l'amour (soumission à la dame au point de feindre la défaite dans un tournoi, etc.). Perceval au début agit à l'avantage de la chevalerie (quand il abandonne sa mère et Blanchefleur), à la fin (cette fin est réalisée complètement chez Wolfram von Eschenbach) il agit en faveur de l'amour, mais d'un amour-compassion chrétien.

Erec et *Yvain* s'inscrivent dans ces rapports de la distribution complémentaire, l'un étant pratiquement le reflet inversé de l'autre. Leur comparaison donne une idée de l'importance de la mesure dans l'éthique de Chrétien. L'histoire de la littérature contient un certain nombre de rapports de ce genre, par exemple *Le Jaloux d'Estrémadure* et *Le Curieux extravagant* de Cervantès ou *Le Procès* et *Le Château* de Kafka. Erec fait d'Enide, une 'Cendrillon', la reine de son domaine, Yvain, au contraire, reçoit le domaine grâce au mariage avec Laudine. Erec lâchement oublie la chevalerie pour un amour, tandis qu'Yvain tout au contraire abandonne sa femme-dame pour des aventures chevale-resques. Conformément Erec voyage en compagnie d'Enide, Yvain rôde au début tout seul et puis accompagné par un lion et 'excommunié' par Laudine, etc.

L'antinomie-complémentarité, que nous avons notée entre *Erec* et *Yvain* existe aussi entre *Lancelot* et *Perceval* (*Le Conte du Graal*), quoique de façon moins évidente – ce qui s'explique par le fait que *Perceval* s'oppose non seulement à *Lancelot*, mais aux trois autres romans dans leur ensemble, car le roman sur Perceval est éclairé par un idéal nouveau. L'opposition de la miséricorde chrétienne à l'amour courtois et au courage chevaleresque de caste représente un progrès dans la vision du monde du poète et fait de ce roman une œuvre infiniment plus complexe, tant sur le plan paradigmatique, que sur le plan syntagmatique. Au début de *Lancelot* et de *Perceval* nous voyons une intrusion à la cour du roi Arthur du chevalier hostile (Méléagant ou le Chevalier Rouge), suivie de la quête. Comme nous le savons, Lancelot préfère l'amour et Perceval la chevalerie. Lancelot et Perceval tous les deux sont opposés de différents côtés à Gauvain comme à un chevalier 'normal'. Un élément de folie chez Lancelot exprime la passion, la soi-disant sottise de Perceval cache sa naïveté au début et peut-être sa sainteté à la fin supposée.

C'est ainsi que les romans bretons de Chrétien se situent dans les rapports de la distribution complémentaire (parallélisme et antinomie simultanément), mais comme un tout ils forment le système uni et le sens commun. Ce sens commun se manifeste surtout sur le plan syntagmatique, dans leur composition commune.

On peut présenter cette composition comme une certaine dichotomie syntagmatique, dont chaque partie à son tour se divise en deux chaînons. Seul *Le Conte du Graal* contient un prologue sur l'enfance de Perceval et son arrivée à la cour d'Arthur (en ce qui concerne *Lancelot* un pareil prologue n'existe qu'en légendes et n'est pas utilisé dans le roman). Mais plus loin:

Ia. L'argument servant de nœud à l'action de la première partie par l'entrée en scène de 'l'agresseur', qui vient à la cour d'Arthur et/ou par la déclaration de 'la tâche difficile' dans le genre du conte merveilleux (la fontaine magique, l'offenseur disparu, la reine enlevée). Notons que toutes les deux variantes correspondent aux deux variantes du même chaînon dans le schéma syntagmatique de V.Y. Propp: agression d'antagoniste/manque.

Ib. Les premiers exploits merveilleux et la conquête de la dame (Enide, Laudine, la reine, Blanchefleur) et/ou le royaume (Yvain et, en perspective, Perceval – le futur seigneur du château Graal), c'est à dire qu'ils atteignent le but du héros du conte. On peut aussi attribuer au conte 'la sottise' de Perceval, la folie de Lancelot (et à une autre étape – d'Yvain). Le passage de la première partie, celle du 'conte', à la seconde (romanesque au sens propre) est accompli grâce à l'intériorisation du conflit, qui sert de nœud à l'action romanesque principale.

IIa. Un 'raté' dans la biographie héroïque par suite de la violation d'équilibre entre 'amour' et 'chevalerie', entre personne 'intérieure' et personne 'sociale' du héros. C'est sa faute 'tragique'. Au stade de la crise la complémentarité des romans bretons de Chrétien se manifeste: Erec et Yvain dépassent tous les deux la mesure, mais d'une manière inverse (l'un oublie des exploits, l'autre abandonne la femme-dame). Lancelot, quoiqu'il accomplit des exploits pour la dame-reine, manque formellement à ses devoirs chevaleresques (il monte la charrette du nain) et courtois (il hésite un moment devant la charrette et fait soi-disant 'offense' à sa dame) tandis que Perceval agit selon l'étiquette chevaleresque formelle et il lui manque de la compassion pour le roi-pêcheur malade.

IIb. La tâche de l'action principale de la seconde partie – c'est la solution du conflit, l'harmonisation de l'antinomie, la réintégration sociale de la personne achevée du héros. Pour cela le chevalier passe une épreuve difficile, qui contient non seulement des exploits chevale-resques mais aussi une initiation morale du chevalier et de la dame de telle manière que des exploits chevaleresques doivent être inspirés par l'amour. C'est une conception courtoise, qui garantit l'harmonisation. Parmi ces exploits nous trouvons aussi des actions d'éclats de la valeur sociale, 'épique', par exemple la conquête par Erec de *joie de la cort* ou l'affranchissement par Yvain des couturières captives (soi-disant *pesme avanture*); comparer la libération des captifs par Lancelot et la perspec-tive pour Perceval d'acquérir et de recevoir sous son empire le royaume merveilleux de Graal, après une série d'exploits chevaleresques et une pénitence religieuse. L'existence de la composition dichotomique des romans de Chrétien était notée par plusieurs chercheurs (Kellermann, Bezzola, Jackson. Bezzola la trouvait aussi dans le roman grec, Jackson dans l'épopée française ou allemande; Frappier insistait sur la trichotomie).

A mon avis, la dichotomie décrite est propre à Chrétien et au roman courtois en général (mais pas à une épopée héroïque ou roman grec). Cette dichotomie est le résultat d'un certain dédoublement de la fable grâce à l'intériorisation jusqu'à une solution harmonisante.

Une séparation logique des épisodes de la valeur sociale transforme la dichotomie en 'triptyche'.

La dichotomie syntagmatique des romans bretons de Chrétien reflète deux phases successives de la formation du roman courtois; au début c'est un pas de l'épopée héroïque vers le conte merveilleux (ce 'pas' ou cette 'marche' correspond à la première partie de la narration, qui ressemble à un conte), puis un second pas vers le tableau des collisions intérieures romanesques (avec la mise en valeur de l'expérience de la poésie lyrique et des conceptions courtoises de l'amour).

Cependant il ne faut pas oublier que le roman courtois breton lui-même passe par deux étapes et que les romans de Chrétien de Troyes correspondent à la deuxième étape ('classique') tandis que la première étape est bien présentée par les romans sur Tristan et Iseult. Nous trouvons là la même dichotomie (le conte héroïque et puis le conflit romanesque intérieur), mais sans solution de la crise, sans la fin harmonieuse. Tristan n'est un héros de l'épopée ou du conte qu'au début du roman; l'amour pour Iseult apporte un élement destructif, asocial, chaotique. La découverte de 'l'homme intérieur' est exprimée par la passion individuelle pour un objet sexuel irremplaçable, comme une conduite adultère, comme un péché contre le roi et vieux parent. Notons que la métaphysique de l'amour est décrite dans *Tristan et Iseult* à l'aide d'un mythème archaïque ('Frazerien') de vieux roi-père impuissant physiquement, qui doit céder son pouvoir à son jeune héritier. Les traces du même mythème, nous les trouvons dans *Le Conte du Graal* (l'image du roi-pêcheur blessé) et aussi dans la littérature orientale, mais avec un arrangement soufi et non courtois.

Dans ces romans sur Tristan et Iseult (malgré un élément courtois dans la version de Thomas) l'harmonisation n'a pas lieu et le conflit mène à la fin tragique. C'est seulement dans la version allemande de Gottfried von Straßburg que l'harmonisation se réalise d'une manière paradoxale, parce que cet auteur a beaucoup d'estimation pour le sentiment libre, plus que pour les valeurs courtoises et les vertus chrétiennes. Il existe (nous l'avons déjà noté) un parallélisme typologique frappant entre l'œuvre romanesque française et orientale. Un des parallèles les plus évidents, c'est l'épopée romanesque persane *Wîs et Râmîn* de Gorgâni pour *Tristan et Iseult* (la première étape d'évolution du genre), l'œuvre romanesque de Nizâmî (surtout *Khosrau et Shirin*) pour les romans bretons de Chrétien de Troyes (l'étape classique du roman médiéval).

Comme Béroul ou Thomas, Gorgâni nous montre la merveille de la passion fatale individuelle pour un objet irremplaçable ainsi qu'un adultère avec la femme du roi – proche parent aîné, la rupture entre le personnel et le social dans la personne du héros, etc. Ici, comme dans la fable de Tristan, on utilise le mythème frazerien, dont nous avons parlé plus haut. Quelques motifs concrets coïncident d'une manière vraiment frappante, tels que la tentative avortée du héros de s'éprendre d'une autre femme, la tolérance du roi envers les amants, le proxénétisme de la servante, qui, en outre, remplace une fois l'héroïne au lit nuptial. On peut comparer le philtre dans *Tristan et Iseult* avec l'objet magique, frappant le vieux Moubad d'impuissance sexuelle. La composition des deux œuvres coïncide à l'exception du prologue et de l'epilogue. Le happy end de *Wîs et Râmîn* n'est que le résultat de la mort accidentelle de Moubad.

En principe, la différence entre les romans français et persans (surtout le prologue) provient de ce que le héros occidental est toujours chevalier tandis que le héros oriental est plutôt roi ou prince. Le prince doit devenir un roi juste, c'est pourquoi l'heroïsme militaire dans le roman oriental joue un moindre rôle. Naturellement en Orient n'existe pas le culte de la dame.

Ce n'est pas par hasard que Chrétien et Nizâmî ont pour point de départ et pour objet de 'polémique' *Tristan et Iseult* et *Wîs et Râmîn*. Les deux auteurs représentent le stade classique du roman médiéval et dans la seconde partie de la narration ils peignent la crise et puis la reconciliation du héros avec l'héroïne, de l'amour avec la chevalerie ou la sagesse royale, de l'être 'intérieur' avec l'être 'social', etc. d'une manière harmonisante. Ce thème est applicable à *Laïla et Majnûn* sous certaines réserves. Ici la situation caractéristique de la première étape du développement du roman (Béroul, Thomas, Gorgâni) paraît se répéter et même s'approfondir, dans la mesure que la démence amoureuse de Keis fait de lui un mauvais continuateur de la tribu (principe 'épique') et l'isole de la société; le destin des amants reste tragique jusqu'à la fin. Néanmoins, contrairement à ce qui se passe dans les romans de Gorgâni et de Thomas, l'harmonisation se fait à travers la conception panthéiste soufie de l'amour et de la poésie, la folie amoureuse de Keis apparaît comme un don divin, un facteur non de ruine, mais de création, une source d'inspiration poétique, qui a une valeur sociale (on retrouve dans l'interprétation du sujet de Tristan et Iseult par Gottfried von Straßburg certains éléments de cette approche). L'extatisme amoureux de Keis nous rappelle, entre autres, ceux d'Yvain et de Lancelot. *Laïla et Majnûn* forme avec *Khosrau et Shirin* une 'paire' complémentaire bien définie: Khosrau est détourné de l'amour par les réalités concrètes de sa condition princière, et Keis, au contraire, sacrifie le côté matériel et social de la vie pour la folie amoureuse, grâce à l'amour Khosrau va devenir un monarque juste, et, par contre, l'amour va entraîner Keis dans un renoncement mystique au monde, etc.

En même temps la structure de *Khosrau et Shirin* est presque identique à la structure des romans bretons de Chrétien. Après le prologue sur la naissance et la jeunesse de Khosrau (comparez avec *Le Conte du Graal*) commence la première partie de la narration (I) dans le goût de conte ou du roman grec. Khosrau et Shirin, tous les deux tombent amoureux l'un de l'autre, sans se voir, et longtemps ne peuvent se rencontrer par suite des obstacles extérieurs. Finalement ils se rencontrent et peuvent se réunir, alors le but du conte est atteint. Mais dans la deuxième partie (II), proprement romanesque, ainsi que dans les romans de Chrétien, a lieu une intériorisation du conflit et commence l'initiation morale du héros, qui surmonte maintenant des obstacles intérieurs. Le conflit est double et nous rappelle les deux variantes de Chrétien, celles d'Erec et d'Yvain. Khosrau oublie son devoir du Shah, et Shirin, comme Enide, le lui rappelle (le prince s'exclame en ce moment que l'amour et le royaume ne peuvent s'accommoder), mais un peu plus tard, occupé d'affaires d'État, il oublie son amour (comme Yvain et Perceval) et même tente à se consoler avec une autre (comme Tristan et Râmîn sans succès). Ce double conflit 'à la Chrétien' doit être résolu, et Nizâmî développe un processus pénible d'harmonisation des relations de Khosrau et Shirin et de leur heureuse réunion. Ce processus est accompagné de la profonde transformation du caractère du héros de telle manière que la conception du haut amour (non courtoise, mais soufie) devient une prémisse idéologique de l'harmonisation. L'amour pour Shirin, plein d'abnégation, aide Khosrau à être un shah sage et juste (comme l'amour inspire les héros de Chrétien à accomplir des exploits chevaleresques). *Khosrau et Shirin* a la fin double. Dans un épisode supplémentaire (qui, soit dit en passant, nous rappelle le mythème frazerien) le fils du shah tue son père pour usurper le trône et la belle Shirin, Khosrau meurt en silence pour ne pas réveiller sa bien aimée Shirin! C'est le triomphe de l'amour haut et 'de l'éducation sentimentale' du prince oriental. La combinaison des deux déviations de la norme et de la mesure, et aussi des deux fins – heureuse et malheureuse, enrichissent le contenu de ce roman en vers. On peut aussi comparer *Le Conte du Graal* de Chrétien et *Iskandar-nâma* de Nizâmî! En principe le dernier est plus proche du roman didactique, ce qui est propre à la pensée islamique. En qualité de résumé on peut dire que la comparaison des romans (français et persans) aide à manifester des traits relevants du roman courtois européen/épopée romanesque du Proche Orient.

Dans un poème (roman en vers) géorgien *Vepkhis Tkaosani* de Rustaveli il y a stylisation à la manière persane, mais des élements orientaux et occidentaux se mêlent dans cette œuvre célèbre: l'idéal soufi et l'idéal courtois se sont rapprochés, le culte de la dame-femme est lié à la folie amoureuse nécéssaire pour le chevalier, mais le chevalier amoureux s'appelle 'mijnun', c'est-à-dire Majnûn d'après Nizâmî. Grâce à la formalisation du code chevaleresque et aux traditions vivantes de l'épopée héroïque, le roman de Rustaveli ignore la dichotomie de Chrétien ou de Nizâmî. Les éléments du conte, du roman, de l'épopée héroïque sont réunis dans la même œuvre. Les obstacles surmontés par le héros ne sont qu'extérieurs. L'amour pour la dame (la fiancée) du chevalier immédiatement l'amène à accomplir des exploits héroïques, sans conflit et sans 'rupture' entre un homme 'intérieur' et 'social'.

Tout au contraire, le roman japonais du commencement du XIe siècle *Genji monogatari* de Murasaki Shikibu est privé d'élément héroïque; toutes les aventures du prince Genji sont d'ordre amoureux. Il ne s'agit pas de vaillance chevaleresque, mais ses sentiments personnels sont en conflit avec ses obligations sociales, l'amour-passion est fatal, il apporte le chaos et menace un ordre social, comme dans les romans sur Tristan ou Râmîn. L'amour d'empereur-père de Genji pour sa mère est une folie, les passions de Genji ont un caractère incestueux (l'amour pour la concubine de son père ou pour les filles de ses vieilles maîtresses) ou, du moins, ils violent l'exogamie ou endogamie, la hierarchie sociale, etc. L'œuvre de Murasaki commence comme un conte et se développe comme un roman psychologique analysant les contradictions intérieures de l'âme et de la société, mais la dichotomie formelle est absente; le passage du conte au vrai roman (accompagné même de parodies des contes) est tout à fait progressif. Cela s'explique par le modèle cyclique d'ordre bouddhique et s'oppose au modèle linéaire chrétien du roman occidental; l'histoire de Genji retrace non seulement la formation d'un héros (comme en Occident), mais le cycle d'une vie, de la naissance à l'épanouissement et au déclin, un cycle qui se répète partiellement chez ses proches descendants et héritiers. Si le héros de Chrétien et même Nizâmî arrive à travers l'expérience des épreuves de la vie à surmonter ses fautes et devenir un 'sauveur' pour les autres, Genji, même après avoir dominé ses erreurs de jeunesse, est obligé jusqu'à sa mort d'en observer les fatales conséquences, de subir le Karma bouddhique. Le Karma régit la composition du roman; l'adultère incestueux avec la femme de son père est châtié par un adultère commis par sa propre femme, le fils d'un autre deviendra son héritier; la répétition forme un cercle vicieux.

Le modèle cyclique mène à l'utilisation des symboles saisonniers en partie liés avec le calendrier naturel et rituel (comparez avec le rôle des fêtes saisonnières à la cour d'Arthur dans le roman breton).

Néanmoins l'harmonisation se fait dans ce roman grâce à l'idée bouddhique de 'mono no avare' ('le charme des choses'); on apprécie de rares moments et de rares tableaux, qui sont vraiment très beaux, qui apparaissent devant nos yeux pour nous donner de la joie sublime et pour s'éclipser et ensuite se dissoudre dans le torrent infini de la vie cosmique. Ainsi ce roman japonais, si original, appartient au stade classique du roman médiéval.

National Perspectives on Originality and Translation: Chrétien de Troyes and Hartmann von Aue

MICHAEL BATTS

It is generally recognized that authors of the twelfth and thirteenth centuries confined themselves to a limited body of material, which was worked and re-worked, translated, and adapted, to meet the needs of varying audiences and different generations. It is also generally recognized that the re-working of existing sources was not solely a matter of convenience, or even of preference, but the outcome of an attitude towards literature which is in contrast to our own. Briefly this may be described as an attitude which saw no particular virtue in originality or suspense. As Geoffrey of Vinsauf put it in his *Documentum de modo et arte dictandi et versificandi*: 'And in the degree that it is more difficult so also it is more praiseworthy to treat such material well, namely, common and familiar material, than to treat other material, namely, new and unusual.' ('Et quanto difficilius, tanto laudabilius est bene tractare materiam talem, scilicet communem et usitatam, quam materiam aliam, scilicet novam et inusitatam'.)[1]

Given that literary works recounted what was true, one could not – or should not – invent tales, and one did not attempt to conceal from readers or the audience what was going to happen in the end. This attitude is by and large as true for the courtly epics as it is for the heroic epics, the major differences being the naming of the author in the courtly epics and the anonymity of the author and more frequent references to the outcome of the story in heroic epics. Both, however, assume a degree of familiarity on the part of the audience with the basic material.

The study of sources is consequently a major activity of medievalists. Great efforts have been made and still are made to identify specific

---

[1] Geoffrey of Vinsauf, *'Documentum de modo et arte dictandi et versificandi': (Instruction in the Method and Art of Speaking and Versifying)*, trans. by Roger P. Parr (Milwaukee, 1968), p. 85, para. 132.

sources, or even specific manuscripts, from which a given author may have worked; and to determine why or how this particular source rather than another came to be used. The concern of the scholar is partly, of course, the verification of the supposedly genuine article among the various manuscripts of the derived text, much as Jakob Püterich von Reichertshausen searched for a reliable text of *Titurel*, having dismissed, so he claims, 30 or more as *un*reliable – 'wol dreissig Titurelen/ hab ich gesehen: der kheiner nit was rechte'.[2] These are certainly ideas which an author like Gottfried von Strassburg would have appreciated, for he claims to have spared no effort to find the true source for his work – which for him was Thomas of Britain:

> Als *der* von Tristande seit,
> die rihte und die warheit
> begunde ich sere suochen
> in beider hande buochen
> walschen und latinen
> und begunde mich des pinen,
> daz ich in *siner* rihte
> rihte dise tihte.[3]

However, there is a considerable difference between an author selecting a source on which to base a new version, in order to undeceive the audience which may have been reading wrong versions, and a critic subsequently judging that version in relation to its source.

The essential problem with the concept of translation is the implied derogation; no matter how much one may approve of a translated work, there is always the underlying feeling that the text is unoriginal, that translations are *sui generis* derivative and therefore in some way inferior. No matter how thoroughly we may accept as axiomatic that all literary works are in some way or another – at least in the High Middle Ages – translations and adaptations, it is virtually impossible to avoid using the act of translation itself as a basis for judgments. Statements such as: 'Die Abhängigkeit der deutschen Litteratur von den Franzosen ist nie so gross gewesen wie damals' in Hirsch's literary history,[4] or Scherer's introductory comment on Hartmann: 'Denn auch Hartmann ist ein bloßer Übersetzer wie Veldeke',[5] inevitably suggest a degree of inferiority in relation to the original.

---

[2] *Der Ehrenbrief des Jakob Püterich von Reichertshausen an die Erzherzogin Mechthild*, ed. by A. Goette (dissertation, Strassburg, 1899), ll. 142: 6–7.

[3] Gottfried von Strassburg, *Tristan und Isold*, ed. by Friedrich Ranke (Berlin, 1949), ll. 155–62. (Emphasis by M.B.)

[4] Franz Wilhelm Hirsch, *Geschichte der deutschen Litteratur von ihren Anfängen bis auf die neueste Zeit* (Leipzig, 1883), p. 163.

[5] Wilhelm Scherer, *Geschichte der deutschen Litteratur* (Berlin, 1883), p. 161.

Part of the problem lies, of course, in the fact that the philologically legitimate desire to identify the source leads to a detailed comparison of the texts of the supposed source and the derivate. And that almost inexorably, it seems, leads to textual comparisons that are literary, rather than strictly linguistic or historical. Such philological analyses then provide a basis for critics who preface their discussion with the assertion that the works to be evaluated are *only* translations. The classic example of this approach is provided by Golther, in whose history of early German literature in Kürschner's *Deutsche National-Litteratur*[6] discussion of German literature from the mid-twelfth century – 'Soweit es sich um den Inhalt handelt, kann fast nur von einer *Übersetzungslitteratur* die Rede sein' (p. 111) – is prefaced by a seventy-five page description of *Old French* literature. While few critics go as far as that, some do provide a general description of specific French poets, such as Chrétien de Troyes, and almost all of them insist on the necessity of comparing the derivate with the source for the purposes of evaluation. 'Die mittelhochdeutsche Literaturgeschichte hat', as Golther puts it in his later work, 'zunächst danach zu fragen, wie Hartmann seine Aufgabe löste' (p. 193) – that is, how did he handle the task of translation?

These comparisons lead on the one hand to a concentration on the substance of the story, on the 'Stoff', since it is there that the differences immediately manifest themselves. On the other hand, the emphasis on those aspects of the story that are different produces a tendency to pay too much attention to these passages when interpreting the work. The most striking example of this fallacy is Gottfried's *Tristan*, where the reflective digressions (*excursus*) have received attention out of all proportion to their function within the text, simply because they are – supposedly – Gottfried's own contribution and – again supposedly – for that reason of particular significance to the understanding of the poem. Occasionally some differentiation is made, as when de Boor remarks: 'Wichtiger als die stofflichen Variationen sind uns die Abweichungen in der Erfassung und Deutung des Stoffes; denn darin liegt Hartmanns Eigenes'[7] – but he still concentrates on 'Abweichungen'. However, if it is agreed that the medieval poet consciously and deliberately used existing material and transferred this into his own language, adapting it *wherever necessary* to his own devices, there is no logical reason for

---

6 Wolfgang Golther, *Geschichte der deutschen Litteratur*, vol. I: *Von den ersten Anfängen bis zum Ausgang des Mittelalters* (Stuttgart, 1892; a later version, cited below, appeared in the Epochen der deutschen Literatur series under the title *Die deutsche Dichtung im Mittelalter 800 bis 1500* (Stuttgart, 1912)).
7 Helmut de Boor and Richard Newald, *Geschichte der deutschen Literatur von den Anfängen bis zur Gegenwart*, vol. II: Helmut de Boor, *Die höfische Literatur: Vorbereitung, Blüte, Ausklang 1170–1250*, 4th edn (München, 1960), p. 69.

assuming that that which is translated without overt change is any less the author's own than that which deviates from the original.

Other and more general conclusions are also drawn in a similar manner. If, for example, derivate A is longer than B, that is, it has passages that are lacking in B, then this may be interpreted as indicative of a later and (therefore) less original work. Alternatively, it can be argued that passages are eliminated over time and that therefore the *longer* work is the more original. This line of argument is perhaps most familiar in connection with the priorities of the manuscripts A – B – C, respectively C – B – A, of the *Nibelungenlied*. In the case of Hartmann, this kind of divergence can be interpreted in different ways. While there is general agreement, for example, that in *Erec* Hartmann does not follow his source closely, the conclusions that are drawn from this simple fact vary widely: Golther argues that Hartmann is not yet competent as a translator and consequently forced to paraphrase; Biese says that he is here 'freier und selbständiger als in einigen der späteren Werke';[8] Suchier writes that Hartmann translated *Erec* 'mit großer Freiheit, dann, wohl weil diese von Kritikern übel vermerkt sein mochte, den *Yvain* mit engerem Anschluß an das Original'.[9] There is no basis in fact for any of these suppositions.

Qualitative comparisons between original and translation are of doubtful value, not least because of the absence of a *tertium comparationis*, the lack of an absolute mean or benchmark against which the two works being compared may be measured. Compared with source A in one language, derivate B in another language may, for example, be more wordy; and of course A is then less wordy than B. But that means nothing, if one has no standard by which to define brevity or turgidity. The relative wordiness or non-wordiness of either is irrelevant, since they belong in totally different contexts. If there is to be any measure of 'quality' in such an aspect of a translated work, then this must be the context in which it appears, that is to say, in relation to other works in the same language and genre.

In the case of Chrétien de Troyes and Hartmann von Aue this can lead to the type of argument where on the basis of comparison Hartmann is found to be more wordy, more intellectual, more ethical, or whatever, than Chrétien. At this point Hartmann ceases to be relatively more x *or* y and becomes instead simply x *or* y, that is, not wordier than Chrétien, but simply wordy, or even wordy by design. A simple example from Ehrismann exemplifies this tendency. In connection with *Erec* he writes on one page: 'Die Erweiterungen beruhen oft auf technischen Gründen,

[8] Alfred Biese, *Deutsche Literaturgeschichte*, 3 vols (München, 1907–11), I, 93.
[9] Hermann Suchier and Adolf Birch-Hirschfeld, *Geschichte der französischen Litteratur von den ältesten Zeiten bis zur Gegenwart* (Leipzig/Wien, 1900), p. 143.

es war eben häufig leichter, einen fremden Ausdruck zu umschreiben und zu dehnen als ihn genau wiederzugeben.' On the following page, however, we read: 'Durch das Übersetzungs*prinzip* der Erweiterung erhält der Vortrag ein langsameres Tempo.'[10] What was previously necessity has become a principle, something on which to base our interpretation, which otherwise lacks a solid foundation, that is, lacks a source of comparison.

It seems in fact inevitable that evaluations of medieval German works are based to some extent on the relationship of the translation to the original, and the absence of an established original becomes a source of concern. Becker, for example, recently wrote in commenting on *Der arme Heinrich*: 'Da wir Hartmanns Quelle nicht kennen, es sei denn, daß er sehr selbständig gestaltet hat, können wir das Werk nur aus sich selbst bewerten' – the tone of regret is unmistakable.[11] In the case of Hartmann von Aue, who himself speaks of translating, the relationship of his work to the source is perhaps of greater importance than elsewhere, since he is credited with having, through his versions of Chrétien de Troyes, introduced the Arthurian epic material into German. Consequently very few general interpretations of Hartmann's work pass over the question of how he treated his sources. Looking back over the long history of these comparisons, however, it becomes evident that the evaluation of the derivate and its source has not been conditioned solely by the kind of problem I have outlined above. This is particularly – and understandably – the case in general histories of literature, and my intention in the following is to document one special factor in the assessment of the relative value of original and translation, namely, national sentiment.

In the first place it must be noted that translation *per se* is not rejected out of hand as inappropriate where translations from the French language are concerned, as was on occasion the case with translations from the classical languages. Heinrich von Veldeke's translation of the *Aeneid*, for example, could (regardless of its French source) be rejected as unsatisfactory solely on the grounds that one could not adequately convey a work in Latin through any other language, and this concept underlies Adelung's evaluation of the Middle High German poets: 'Unmöglich würden sie die Arbeiten der Alten so haben verunstalten können, wenn sie im mindesten Geschmack und Empfindung des Schönen gehabt hätten.'[12] This attitude was of course later reversed, and by the early nineteenth century, especially after the contribution of the

---

[10] Gustav Ehrismann, *Geschichte der deutschen Literatur bis zum Ausgang des Mittelalters*, vol. II, 2, i (München, 1927; repr. 1959), pp. 163–64. (Emphasis by M.B.)
[11] Henrik Becker, *Bausteine zur deutschen Literaturgeschichte* (Halle, 1957), p. 104.
[12] Johann Christoph Adelung, *Umständliches Lehrgebäude der deutschen Sprache zur Erläuterung der deutschen Sprachlehre für Schulen* (Leipzig, 1782), p. 54.

Romantics, the German language was seen as capable of adequately rendering *any* work from *any* language. Much more problematic is the question of the status of original and translation in the context of their own and the 'other' literature.

In French histories of French literature Chrétien is seen as highly original and creative, although the degree of originality vis-à-vis his sources cannot be addressed directly. He is assumed to have had a variety of oral sources which his genius adapted to the new courtly style. According to Jasinski, Chrétien's works 'charment par leurs évocations brillantes, leur psychologie délicate, leur merveilleux souriant et secrètement ému, l'idéal raffiné qui s'exalte en eux';[13] Guth writes: 'Chrétien de Troyes parfume de toute la finesse française et de toutes les grâces de notre psychologie le merveilleux breton.'[14] The Larousse *Littérature française* speaks of his 'exaltation des valeurs humaines', 'le sens du mystère et du destin', 'l'habileté de la composition', and so forth.[15] In general his art is summed up perhaps in the two words 'profondeur' and 'finesse'.

German histories of French literature are also quite positive about Chrétien, but only one of these that I have seen enters into any lengthy discussion of his possible sources, that by Suchier-Hirschfeld (1900). It comes to no firm conclusion about the sources, but does stress the great qualities of Chrétien's work, summed up in the phrase 'psychologische Vertiefung [. . .] [und] stilistisches Geschick' (p. 143). Neubert writes: 'Chrestiens Erzählungskunst versteht es in bisher unerreichbarer Eindruckskraft, die reichen wechselvollen äußeren Erlebnisse mit der die Handlung wesentlich bestimmenden seelischen Eigenart seiner Gestalten zu einer ungetrübten Harmonie zu verschmelzen. Die Voraussetzungen dazu wurden durch die große dichterische Erfindungskraft, [. . .] seine psychologische Feinfühligkeit, die glänzende Kunst des Aufbaus seiner Romane [. . .] gewährleistet.'[16] Not unexpectedly, however, such works sometimes also make reference to Hartmann. Theisen, for example, points out that Hartmann adapted Chrétien 'ohne sein Vorbild zu erreichen'.[17] It is clear where the interest of these critics lies.

The subsequent history of any work – for most medievalists at least – is naturally of less interest than the pre-history. It is consequently in histories of German literature that most references to the sources are to be found. Here the French critics argue that Hartmann is a poor

---

13   René Jasinski, *Histoire de la littérature française*, 2 vols (Paris, 1947), I, 30.

14   Paul Guth, *Histoire de la littérature française*, 2 vols (Paris, 1967), I, 25.

15   *Littérature française* (Paris, 1967), vol. I, 20–21.

16   Fritz Neubert, *Geschichte der französischen Literatur* (Tübingen, 1949), p. 24.

17   Josef Theisen, *Geschichte der französischen Literatur*, Sprache und Literatur, 11 (Stuttgart, 1964), p. 16.

imitation of Chrétien. Chuquet, for example, writes: 'Que Hartmann ait avec raison adouci ou accusé certains traits et pallié heureusement quelques invraisemblances de Chrestien, ce sont là menus details; encore, lorsqu'il remanie le texte français, commet-il souvent des maladresses, et pour les réflexions de son cru [. . .] elles n'ont que peu d'importance.'[18] Bossert writes: 'Hartmann ne montre pas la vivacité de Chrestien de Troyes; mais il est plus soigneux, plus réfléchi. Il cherche davantage à enchaîner les faits, à les expliquer, à les motiver. Il a des scrupules qui sont presque déplacés en pareille matière. On dirait qu'il veut mettre de la logique dans l'extravagance et faire rentrer le merveilleux dans les limites du naturel.'[19] Tonnelat claims that Hartmann followed Chrétien 'pas à pas'. 'Sa part d'invention est nulle en ce qui concerne la matière traitée. Tout au plus a-t-il introduit ça et là quelques détails qui rendent plus vraisemblable ou plus logique l'enchaînement des motifs essentiels. Son récit est plus ordonné que celui de Chrétien de Troyes; mais il n'en a pas l'allure entraînante, ni la verve drue, ni la force expressive.'[20]

German critics spend a good deal of time on the comparison between Hartmann and Chrétien and deduce on the whole that Hartmann has taken a work that lacks refinement and improved it, primarily by removing various faults of propriety and by giving it a greater depth of feeling. The expression of the differences varies widely, from the simplistic statement of Koberstein: 'Iwein [. . .] beruht auf dem Chevalier au lion des Chrétien de Troyes, der indess dem Deutschen nur den rohen Stoff gab',[21] to lengthy comparisons in the florid style favoured by Gervinus[22] and Scherer. I shall therefore quote *in toto* a relatively short example from a popular coffee-table type of literary history from the last quarter of the nineteenth century.[23] Leixner writes: 'Trotz aller Anlehnung an Chrétien zeigt sich auch in Einzelheiten der sittliche Geist des Deutschen, besonders in den eingeschobenen Betrachtungen. Man fühlt, daß Hartmann inniger und ehrlicher empfindet als der Franzose, und daß sein religiöser Sinn nicht wie bei diesem nur Formsache sei. Mit feinem Gefühl hat er auch manchen verletzenden Zug des Urbildes gemildert oder ganz getilgt.'

What is important here is the use of the words 'der Deutsche' und 'der Franzose' (cf. Guth quoted above), for Leixner is clearly implying that

18 Arthur Maxime Chuquet, *Littérature allemande* (Paris, 1909), p. 33.
19 Adolphe Bossert, *Histoire de la littérature allemande* (Paris, 1909), p. 56.
20 Ernest Tonnelat, *Histoire de la littérature française des origines au xviie siècle* (Paris, 1923), p. 64.
21 August Koberstein, *Grundriß zur Geschichte der deutschen National-Litteratur* (Leipzig, 1827), p. 169.
22 Georg Gottfried Gervinus, *Geschichte der poetischen National-Literatur der Deutschen*, 4th edn (Leipzig, 1853), vol. I.
23 Otto von Leixner, *Geschichte der deutschen Litteratur* (Leipzig, 1880), p. 50.

these characteristics are, as it were, typical for the authors by virtue of their nationality. The terms are anachronistic, of course, inasmuch as there was neither a France nor a Germany at the time, but their use nevertheless suggests an identification with the present. In other words, these works are an exemplification of typical German 'Sittlichkeit' and typical French 'Frivolität' – characteristics which are not necessarily cited in order to 'put down' the French, although there is deliberate criticism enough to be found, for example, in Hirsch, who claims that the Arthurian stories 'entsprachen ganz der laxen Anschauung über eheliche Treue, welche der romanischen Welt bis heute eigen geblieben ist' (p. 162).

The evaluations of Hartmann's versions of Chrétien must in fact be looked at in a wider context, that is to say, with the more general pronouncements of the critics in mind, in particular their pronounce-ments about the characteristics of the Celts and the French. Gervinus's judgement on Hartmann, for example, is based primarily on his antagonistic attitude towards the Celtic people. 'Die Trümmer der absinkenden Poesie einer abgesunkenen und obscuren Nation' – the Arthurian material – provided stories, according to him, 'ohne innere Bedeutung', where 'der Inhalt uns abstößt', etc. The story of *Iwein*, is in part of a 'Gemeinheit, [. . .] die auch die Kunst des Chretien von Troyes und das Wenige, was Hartmann's Eigenthum dabei ist, nicht ganz verdecken konnte' (p. 371). Lindemann even tells us something of his sources for the character of the Celts: 'Die vorhin nach Cäsar bezeichneten Eigenthümlichkeiten des keltischen Volkscharacters [. . .] mögen nun die Eigenthümlichkeiten der keltischen Nationalsagen erklären.'[24] The evaluation of Hartmann is thus coloured – and Gervinus and Lindemann are by no means the only examples – by a critical attitude towards the material that has come to Hartmann from an imperfect source – the decadent Celts. By contrast, Gustave Lanson has fulsome praise for the multifarious qualities of the Celts and, conse-quently, less appreciation of Chrétien whom he castigates for his total lack of understanding and perversion of his sources.[25]

Matters are, of course, only made worse for German critics by the fact that Hartmann is translating from the French. For the French are, as everyone knows, superficial, frivolous, lacking in depth of feeling, irreligious, etc. And in case their readers should not be aware of this, many historians of German literature, not only in Germany, but also in England and North America, in fact preface their evaluation of the literature with a discussion of the national characteristics of the

---

[24] Wilhelm Lindemann, *Geschichte der deutschen Literatur von den ältesten Zeiten bis zur Gegenwart* (Freiburg, 1866), vol. I, 118.

[25] Gustave Lanson, *Histoire de la littérature française*, ed. by Paul Tuffrau (Paris, 1952), p. 56.

Germans, the French, and the English. And it is here that one finds those characteristics listed that are then discovered in the works of Chrétien and Hartmann, characteristics that are not (or not necessarily) derived from these and other works, but from general speculations about racial character, the influence of the climate, and so forth, not to mention such suspect sources as Tacitus. Bougeault, for example, cites Tacitus's *Germania* as 'le portrait exact des Germains encore reconnaissable aujourd'hui chez leurs descendants',[26] and other writers repeat endlessly the clichés about the German character, apparently accepting the general idea expressed as follows by Philippi: 'La littérature est l'expression de l'âme du peuple, expression changeante [. . .] mais où il y a quelque chose de permanent comme le caractère de la race.'[27]

And what is this character? 'Cette gravité réfléchie et mélancolique qui caractérise les peuples de l'Allemagne', says Loise;[28] 'cette individualité méditative, cette habitude de creuser dans les mystères les plus cachés de notre être, qui caractérisent [. . .] les Allemands', says Peschier;[29] from Dublin Selss writes: 'The characteristic feature of German authors [. . .] is their more contemplative disposition, as compared to most of their neighbours. [. . .] The German character is earnest, meditative, inclined to be stern.'[30] In general the comparison between French character and German character is summed up as the difference between 'esprit' and 'âme'! Even J.G. Robertson is not above discussing in the earlier versions of his work 'the national characteristics [. . .] of this literature'.[31] He goes on to say that 'the supreme qualities of the French romances of chivalry are those of style [. . .] practical and clear-minded, the French poet deals with facts and concrete ideas. The German poet [. . .] however closely he may translate from the French, [. . .] is never reluctant to enlarge upon his original: not content to describe things as they appear to the outward eye, he reflects upon them, interprets them, and explains them'.

Given, then, that critics had this traditional concept of national characteristics behind them, is it surprising that they then found, when supposedly making an objective comparison of Chrétien's original and Hartmann's translation, that the French work is superficial and the German work deep? 'Die Klassiker des Höfischen Epos in Deutschland

---

[26]   Alfred Bougeault, *Histoire des littératures étrangères, I: Littérature allemande* (Paris, 1876), p. 10.

[27]   J. Philippi, *Histoire de la littérature allemande d'après le Dr. Hermann Kluge* (Paris, 1880), p. ii.

[28]   Ferdinand Loise, *Histoire de la poésie: L'Allemagne dans sa littérature* (Bruxelles, 1873), p. 6.

[29]   Adolphe Peschier, *Histoire de la littérature allemande*, 2 vols (Paris/Genève, 1836), I, 6.

[30]   Albert Maximilian Selss, *A Critical Outline of the Literature of Germany* (London, 1865), pp. 19–20.

[31]   John G. Robertson, *A History of German Literature* (Edinburgh, 1902), pp. xxiv–xxvi.

haben sich von der Frivolität der Franzosen verhältnismäßig freigehalten', says O.E. Lessing,[32] or, as Koch puts it, Hartmann's works are 'Übersetzungen [. . .] aber unabhängig davon selbständige deutsche Dichtungen, die ihre Vorlage erweitern nicht nur, sondern vor allem veredeln, im seelischen und ethischen Sinne vertiefen, von der Oberfläche des Lebens zum Wesen vorstoßen'[33] – and so on and so forth.

Whatever one may think of the possibility of comparing original and translation and whatever one may derive from such a comparison about the qualities of the poet Chrétien and the poet Hartmann, it must be obvious that in comparisons of the kind that I have quoted – and which could be extended almost indefinitely – there is, to put it in the mildest of terms, a certain lack of objectivity. It is only natural, I suppose, that a French critic will find more to praise in Chrétien than in his translator Hartmann, and that a German critic will find more to praise in Hartmann than in his source Chrétien. But the nature of these comparisons and the context in which they are placed make it evident that the critics are basing themselves on national stereotypes rather than on close textual analysis. Comparisons of this type are therefore used – for whatever reason – to reinforce the stereotypes and to encourage the reader to accept them as valid. While contemporary histories of literature no longer treat their readers to an analysis of racial characteristics, national stereotypes die hard, and it seems legitimate to ask whether source studies are not still (inevitably?) influenced by such traditional preconceptions.

---

[32] O.E. Lessing, *Geschichte der deutschen Literatur* (Dresden, 1921), p. 49.
[33] Franz Koch, *Geschichte deutscher Dichtung* (Hamburg, 1937), pp. 65–66.

verligen *und* versitzen:
Das Versäumnis des Helden und
die Sünde der Trägheit in
den Artusromanen Hartmanns von Aue

SILVIA RANAWAKE

Die Krise des Helden in Hartmanns Artusromanen und ihren französischen Vorlagen wird jeweils herbeigeführt durch ein Versäumnis. Erek 'verliegt' sich, er vernachlässigt seine Ritterpflichten, Iwein 'versitzt', versäumt einen wichtigen Termin. Nun versagen aber beide Helden so plötzlich und unerklärlich – gerade haben sie sich als ausgezeichnete Ritter bewährt –, daß man des öfteren versucht hat, über das 'bloße' Versäumnis hinaus zu einer 'eigentlichen' Schuld vorzustoßen.

Für den Erekroman kann man sich für diesen Interpretationsansatz auf Chrétien und Hartmann selbst berufen – oder zumindest scheint es so. Als Erklärung für die Verwandlung eines ehrgeizigen jungen Ritters in einen königlichen Müßiggänger tischen beide Erzähler ein seit der Antike gängiges Klischee auf: Es ist die Liebe zu seiner Frau, die den Helden verweichlicht. Obgleich Chrétien und Hartmann in diesem Punkt übereinstimmen, weichen die romanistische und die germanistische Forschung in den Schlüssen, die sie aus dieser Erklärung ziehen, voneinander ab. Während die Chrétienforschung die *recreantise* des Helden weiterhin als die eigentliche Verfehlung betrachtet, folgern die Hartmanninterpreten aus der Feststellung des Erzählers, Erek habe seine Frau so sehr geliebt, daß er jedes ehrenhafte Tun und Streben aufgegeben habe, schuld an dem Fiasko sei im Grunde Ereks Liebe, oder genauer seine falsche Einstellung zu Liebe und Ehe. Die *minne* des Helden, so heißt es, sei allzu sinnlich, maßlos, egozentrisch, gesellschaftsfeindlich, ja sündhaft, sie durchbreche sowohl die sozialen wie die göttlichen Ordnungen. Das *verligen* selbst spielt demgegenüber in der Hartmannliteratur eine eher untergeordnete Rolle. Es ist nur Folge, Symptom der falschen *minne*.[1]

---

[1] Die folgenden Ausführungen zum Erekroman greifen Überlegungen auf, die ich

19

Nun ist aber in Hartmanns Text nicht von einer maßlosen, einer rein sinnlichen oder gar von einer sündhaften Liebe die Rede. Was die Maßlosigkeit angeht, so verwendet Hartmann den Begriff der *unmâze* überhaupt nicht für den erotischen Bereich,[2] und, was die Sinnlichkeit von Ereks Liebe betrifft, so kürzt der deutsche Autor gerade bei der Schilderung von Ereks *verligen* die erotischen Details der Vorlage:[3] Statt eingehender auf Ereks Liebesleben einzugehen (*EE* 2439–42), schildert Hartmann drastisch-humorvoll Ereks Bequemlichkeit an Hand der täglichen Routine des Königspaares (*E* 2924–53). Hat es doch Erek fertiggebracht, alle Verpflichtungen auf das absolute Minimum zu reduzieren und, abgesehen vom mittäglichen Messebesuch, ausschließlich den leiblichen Genüssen zu frönen: zu schlafen, zu essen und seine Frau zu lieben.

Charakteristisch für Hartmanns Bearbeitung ist die Ausweitung der Thematik der französischen Vorlage. In Chrétiens Roman geht es spezifisch um das Verhältnis von Rittertum und Liebe: Einerseits behandelt Erek seine Ehefrau wie eine Geliebte und findet nur noch am Liebesspiel mit ihr Vergnügen (*EE* 2438–42), andererseits verliert er jedes Interesse an ritterlicher Betätigung (*EE* 2434–37). Auf dem Spiel steht sein Ansehen als Ritter: Man wirft ihm vor, er benehme sich 'recreant' (*EE* 2466), ein Terminus, der besonders für das Aufgeben oder Nachgeben in der militärischen Sphäre gilt.[4]

Für Hartmann hingegen steht nicht allein Ereks Liebe und sein Rittertum zur Diskussion. Die Krise betrifft alle Aspekte seines Lebens, das, allein auf Wohlbehagen ausgerichtet, völlig im *gemach* aufgeht

---

anderorts geäußert habe: 'Erec's *verligen* and the Sin of Sloth', in *Hartmann von Aue: Changing Perspectives: London Hartmann Symposium 1985*, ed. by Timothy McFarland and Silvia Ranawake, GAG, 486 (Göppingen, 1988), pp. 93–115. Dort referierte Literatur und angeführte Belege werden hier nur noch in Auswahl zitiert. Zu Ereks *minne* siehe ebd. S. 93–95 und Anm. 6–9.

[2] Siehe R.A. Boggs, *Hartmann von Aue: Lemmatisierte Konkordanz zum Gesamtwerk*, Indices zur deutschen Literatur, 12–13, 2 Bde. (Nendeln, 1979), I, 460.

[3] Die Kürzung ist umso auffallender, als Hartmann in der Nachfolge Chrétiens Ereks Beziehung zu Enite als Ehe- und Minneverhältnis zugleich gestaltet und demgemäß die erotischen Motive der Vorgeschichte beibehält (*EE* 1483–516, *E* 1484–97; *EE* 2080–108, *E* 1842–86). Vergleiche Ursula Schulze, '*âmîs unde man*. Die zentrale Problematik in Hartmanns *Erec*', *PBB* (Tüb.), 105 (1983), 14–47, (hier S. 39). Stellenangaben nach: Kristian von Troyes, *Erec und Enide*, hg. von Wendelin Foerster, Romanische Bibliothek, 13, 3. Aufl. (Halle (Saale), 1934) (= *EE*); *Erec von Hartmann von Aue*, hg. von Albert Leitzmann, fortgeführt von Ludwig Wolff, 6. Aufl. besorgt von Christoph Cormeau und Kurt Gärtner, ATB, 39 (Tübingen, 1985) (= *E*).

[4] A. Tobler und E. Lommatzsch, *Altfranzösisches Wörterbuch*, Bd. VIII (Wiesbaden, 1971), Sp. 505–07: *recrëant* 'schlapp [. . .], feig, im Kampf unterlegen' (54 Belege, darunter *Yvain* 5539, 5688, 5691, 6281, 6356), charakteristisch etwa die Verbindung 'vaincuz et recrëanz', 'morz o recrëanz'. Die zwei Belege, die einen geistlichen Sinn haben, stammen aus späterer Zeit. (Das Verb *recroire* 'ermüden, abstehen von, aufhören, sich weigern etwas zu tun' hat gegenüber *recrëant* eine breitgefächerte Verwendung.)

('sich vlizzen sîne sinne/ wie er alle sîne sache/ wante zuo gemache',
E 2931–33).

Die Bedeutung von *gemach* begrenzt sich nicht auf den sexuellen
Genuß, sondern meint ganz allgemein 'Ruhe, Wohlbehagen, Bequemlichkeit, Annehmlichkeit'. Als Begriff zunächst neutral, kann *gemach* mit
der Scheu vor Anstrengung und mit einem müßigen Leben assoziiert
und damit als der Ehre abträglich betrachtet werden, wie dies Hartmann
dann im Folgenden gestaltet.[5]

Erek läßt sich nicht mehr bei Turnieren sehen, er vernachlässigt seine
königliche repräsentative Rolle, so daß der Glanz seines Hofes erlischt,
er spart den Besuch der Frühmesse aus, kurz, berufliche (Turnier),
gesellschaftliche (Repräsentation) und religiöse (Messebesuch) Verpflichtungen fallen seinem Lebensstil zum Opfer. Diese alle Lebens-
bereiche betreffende Pflichtvergessenheit stellt die ganze soziale und
persönliche Existenz Ereks in Frage.

Die Wiedergabe von Chrétiens *recreant aler* (*EE* 2466) durch den
Ausdruck *sich verligen* (*E* 2971) reflektiert Hartmanns Erweiterung der
höfischen Problemstellung (*amors–armes*) ins Existenzielle; *sich verligen*
trifft nicht nur die konkrete Situation – Erek liegt im Bett, statt seinen
Pflichten nachzukommen;[6] der Ausdruck läßt zudem die Auswirkungen
dieser Pflichtvergessenheit auf das seelische Wohl mitanklingen. Verkörpert doch der Mann im Bett das Hauptlaster der *acedia/tristitia*, der
sündhaften Erschlaffung; *verligen* hat in der Tat auch eine geistliche
Bedeutung: Nach Berthold von Regensburg kann der Christenmensch
'die grôze sælikeit versitzen' oder 'træclîchen verslâfen oder verligen'.[7]
Hartmann unterstreicht diese religiöse Assoziation mit Motiven, die sich
in seiner Quelle noch nicht finden: zum einen Ereks Bequemlichkeit,
seine Überbewertung des *gemaches*, zum anderen Ereks implizierte
Vernachlässigung der Frühmesse – erst nach Mittag erhebt sich das
Paar, um zur Messe zu eilen.[8] Beide Erscheinungen, der übermäßige

---

[5] Georg Friedrich Benecke, Wilhelm Müller, Friedrich Zarncke, *Mittelhochdeutsches
Wörterbuch*, Bd. II, 1 (Leipzig, 1863), Sp. 13a–14a. Zu der in moralischer Hinsicht neutralen
Bedeutung von *gemach* vergleiche 'geistlich gemach' in: *Das Passional: Eine
Legendensammlung des dreizehnten Jahrhunderts*, hg. von Fr. Karl Köpke, Bibl. d. ges. dt.
Nat.-Lit., 32 (Quedlinburg/Leipzig, 1852), S. 402, Z. 57.
[6] Matthias Lexer, *Mittelhochdeutsches Handwörterbuch*, Bd. III (Leipzig, 1878; Neudr.
Stuttgart, 1970), Sp. 164: *verligen* behält die Bedeutung 'durch zu langes Liegen
vernachlässigen' bei, bezieht sich dann aber auch generell auf die Vernachlässigung
sowohl innerweltlicher als auch religiöser Pflichten.
[7] *Berthold von Regensburg: Vollständige Ausgabe seiner Predigten, mit Anmerkungen und
Wörterbuch*, hg. von Franz Pfeiffer, 2 Bde. (Wien, 1862), I, S. 494, Z. 16. Die betreffende
Predigt handelt vom Messebesuch. – Zur Beziehung zwischen Ereks *recreantise* und der
Sünde der *acedia* vergleiche M.B. Ogle, 'The Sloth of Erec', *The Romance Review*, 9 (1918), 1–
20; Glyn S. Burgess, *Chrétien de Troyes: Erec et Enide*, Critical Guides to French Texts, 32
(London, 1984), S. 49: 'To be *recreant* is both to be idle, a victim of sloth or *accidia*, and
incapable of fighting adequately [. . .].'
[8] Zum *verligen* der Frühmesse vergleiche *Das Nibelungenlied* hg. von Helmut de Boor, 18.

Hang zur Bequemlichkeit, *mollities*, und die Schläfrigkeit, *somnolentia*, die den trägen Sünder unter anderem am Besuch des Frühgottes-dienstes hindert, gehören zu den Tochtersünden der *acedia*.[9] Für die Zuhörer Hartmanns, denen *acedia*-Motive aus Predigt und Beichtpraxis bekannt waren, war die damit hergestellte Parallele *verligen* – *acedia* sicher einsichtig.

Die sogenannte Bamberger und die Wessobrunner Beichte, zwei Fassungen eines in Handschriften des 12. Jahrhunderts überlieferten Beichtformulars, mögen dies illustrieren; sie bieten eine ungewöhnlich ausführliche Aufzählung der Tochtersünden der jeweiligen Haupt-laster.[10] So gesteht der Beichtende, nachdem er die Hauptsünde der 'trâgheit' bekannt hat, er habe sich versündigt, indem er unter anderem säumig, nachlässig und müßig gewesen sei ('in sûmigheite', 'in muozzigheite'), indem er nur nach Bequemlichkeit verlangt habe ('in senftigerni'), indem er schläfrig gewesen und sich schlafend versäumt habe ('in slâffigemo muote', 'in virslâffini'), indem er zu lange auf einem bequemen Lager geruht habe ('in senftimo legere') und indem er sich untüchtig verhalten habe ('in aller unfrumigheite').

Ein weiches Bett und langes Schlafen,[11] Bequemlichkeit, Müßiggang und Untüchtigkeit – eine Assoziation zwischen Ereks *verligen* und den Tochtersünden der *acedia* drängt sich auf. Die ehelichen Freuden – 'a sa fame donoiier' (*EE* 2438), 'vrouwen Ênîten minne' (*E* 2930) – ließen sich dann als eine Versuchung verstehen, ganz im *gemach* aufzugehen, sich wie der *otiosus* der *mollities* bzw. der *senftigerne*, Tochtersünde der *acedia*, zu ergeben.[12] Die Liebe zu Enite wäre also eher als das Moment zu betrachten, das die eigentliche Verfehlung auslöst, und weniger als eine aufgrund ihrer Maßlosigkeit an sich schuldhafte Passion.

Es mag zunächst abwegig erscheinen, Iweins Versäumnis mit dem Ereks in einem Atemzug zu nennen, wird Iwein doch sogar als das

---

Aufl. (Wiesbaden, 1965), 1004, 3–4. – Zur Mittagszeit als Stunde der Trägheit (*E* 3013–21) vergleiche Ranawake (wie Anm. 1), S. 101f.

[9] Siegfried Wenzel, *The Sin of Sloth: Acedia in Medieval Thought and Literature* (Chapel Hill, N.C., 1960), S. 83f.

[10] Ausgabe: MSD, Nr. XCI. Zitiert wird die ältere Bamberger Fassung.

[11] Vergleiche die Darstellung der Trägheit in: *Der welsche Gast des Thomasin von Zerclære: Codex palatinus Germanicus 389 der Universitätsbibliothek Heidelberg*, hg. von Friedrich Neumann und Ewald Vetter, Facsimilia Heidelbergensia, 4 (Wiesbaden, 1974), 3 v: Trägheit dargestellt als ein Mann, der sich einredet, es sei noch nicht Tag, während der Trägheitsdämon ihm einflüstert, er solle liegen bleiben ('lige stille'). Vergleiche Thomasins Beschreibung des *otiosus*: 'swer sich an tracheit verlat [. . .], swer zaller vrist mûzzich lit'; siehe Thomasin von Zerclære, *Der welsche Gast*, hg. von F.W. von Kries, GAG, 425, I–IV, 4 Bde. (Göppingen, 1984–85), I, S. 280, Z. 7871 (7233) und 7881 (7243). Dazu auch Wenzel (wie Anm. 9), S. 83f.

[12] Zur *mollities* vergleiche Guilielmus Peraldus, *Summae virtutum ac vitiorum* (Antwerpen, 1587), t. 2, 82c. Die *Summae* entstanden vor 1250, siehe Antoine Dondaine, 'Guillaume Peyraut, vie et œuvres', *Archivum Fratrum Praedicatorum*, 18 (1948), 162–236 (hier S. 187).

Gegenbild Ereks vorgestellt: Dem frischgebackenen Ehemann Iwein rät sein Freund Gawein, er solle sich an Erek ein warnendes Beispiel nehmen und sich nicht bei seiner Ehefrau 'verligen' (*I* 2783–912, vgl. *Y* 2561).[13] Iwein vermeidet dann auch anscheinend Ereks Fehler: Die beiden Freunde 'verligen' sich während ihrer Turnierreise nicht: 'swâ sî turnierens pflâgen,/ des sî niht verlâgen' (*I* 3043f.).

Als aber der Held über der Hektik des Turnierbetriebes (*I* 3051) den von seiner Frau festgesetzten Termin der Rückkehr vergißt, da bezeichnet Chrétien an Hand der juristischen Termini *mantir covant* und *trespasser le terme* (*Y* 2700f.) das Versäumnis als schwerwiegenden Vertragsbruch und Terminverstoß.

Hartmann gibt dies mit den Ausdrücken *sîn gelübede versitzen* und *der jârzal vergezzen* wieder (*I* 3055f.). In der Tat kann *versitzen* wie *trespasser* als juristischer Terminus fungieren. Darüber hinaus jedoch besteht bei *versitzen* die Möglichkeit, mit diesem Begriff, den Berthold von Regensburg synonym mit *verligen* zur Bezeichnung der Trägheitssünde verwendet, eine Parallele zwischen Rechtsbruch und religiöser Verfehlung anzudeuten. Die Bamberger und Wessobrunner Beichte rechnen auch Vergeßlichkeit ('agezzil') und das Nicht-Einhalten der rechten Zeit ('uncîtigi') zu den Tochtersünden der *acedia*.[14]

Die sich in *Iwein* andeutende, bereits am Erekroman beobachtete Ausweitung der höfischen Thematik spiegelt sich auch in der Hartmannschen Fassung der gegen den Helden erhobenen Anklage wieder. In der Vorlage richtet sich die Klage gegen Yvain, den heuchlerischen, treulosen Galan, der, statt das Herz seiner Dame in getreuem Gewahrsam zu halten und zu gegebener Zeit zurückzugeben, dieses Herz, an dem ihm nichts lag, unter falschen Vorspiegelungen entwendet und nicht zurückerstattet hat (*Y* 2725–41). Seine Vergeßlichkeit (*Y* 2746) und Unachtsamkeit (*Y* 2753) bilden einen krassen Gegensatz zu der Sehnsucht wahrer Liebender, die schlaflose Nächte damit hinbringen, die Stunden und Tage zu zählen, die sie von der Wiederbegegnung trennen (*Y* 2754–61).

In Hartmanns Version hat Iwein nicht allein die Regeln der höfischen Liebe verletzt. Lunete zeichnet vielmehr ein geradezu erschreckendes Bild von Iweins umfassender Pflichtvergessenheit und Undankbarkeit.

---

[13] Stellenangaben nach: *Iwein: Eine Erzählung von Hartmann von Aue*, hg. von G.F. Benecke und K. Lachmann, neu bearbeitet von Ludwig Wolff, 7. Ausg., 2 Bde. (Berlin, 1968) (= *I*); Kristian von Troyes, *Yvain* (*Der Löwenritter*), hg. von Wendelin Foerster, Romanische Bibliothek, 5, 2. Aufl. (Halle (Saale), 1902) (= *Y*).

[14] Man vergleiche auch Walther von der Vogelweides 'Kreuzlied', das sich der Begriffe *versitzen* und *vergezzen* bedient, um die Trägheitssünde zu bezeichnen: 'Owê wir müezegen liute, wie sîn wir versezzen/ zwischen fröiden an die jâmerlîchen stat!/ aller arebeite heten wir vergezzen,/ [. . .] wol im der ie nâch stæten fröiden ranc!' (13, 19–25). Ausgabe: *Die Gedichte Walthers von der Vogelweide*, hg. von Karl Lachmann, 13., aufgrund der 10. von Carl von Kraus bearbeiteten Ausg. neu hg. von Hugo Kuhn (Berlin, 1965).

Obgleich Laudine ihn unter der Bedingung geheiratet hat, daß er sie und ihr Reich verteidigt, hat er durch sein Versäumnis das Land gefährdet, seine Frau gedemütigt, sich des Meineids schuldig gemacht und Lunete, deren Vermittlung er seine Heirat verdankte, als Ratgeberin diskreditiert. Wie Erek verstößt Iwein damit gegen die Verpflichtungen, die ihm seine Stellung auferlegt. Sein Wortbruch beraubt ihn jeder Glaubwürdigkeit. Er wird ein Ehrloser, dem Lunete das Recht abspricht, Mitglied der Artusrunde zu sein. Ja, sie verbannt ihn aus der Gemeinschaft der höfischen Gesellschaft überhaupt und entzieht ihm damit seine Existenzgrundlage.[15]

Die von Siegfried Wenzel aufgeführten populären Vorstellungen vom Verhalten des trägen Sünders liefern wieder Parallelen zum Fehlverhalten des Helden: so versäumt es der *otiosus*, die ihm anvertrauten Dinge zurückzuerstatten (man vergleiche Chrétiens Ausführungen zum Raub des Herzens) und sein Gelübde zu erfüllen. Es mangelt ihm an Dankbarkeit für die ihm zuteil gewordenen menschlichen und göttlichen Gaben. Der träge Ehemann kümmert sich nicht um seine Haushaltung, ja auch die fehlende eheliche Liebe läßt sich auf die Trägheit zurückführen.[16]

Beide Erzähler gestalten die Reaktion des Helden auf seine Verfehlung und ihre Konsequenzen als einen Anfall von manischer Melancholie ('la rage et la melancolie', *Y* 3005; 'ein zorn unde ein tobesuht', *I* 3233).[17] Hartmann übernimmt zwar nicht den medizinischen Terminus *melancolie* aus der Vorlage, erklärt aber dafür ausdrücklich den ausbrechenden Wahnsinn seines Helden als Minnekrankheit, die als ein Sonderfall der Melancholie galt (*I* 3254–56, vergleiche *I* 3405f.).[18] Wie bei der Verfeh-

---

[15] Siehe Silvia Ranawake, 'Zu Form und Funktion der Ironie bei Hartmann von Aue', *Wolfram-Studien*, 7 (1982), 75–116 (hier S. 99f.).

[16] Wenzel (wie Anm. 9), S. 86f. Zu *acedia* in Chrétiens Yvain-Roman vergleiche: George Hardin Brown, 'Yvain's Sin of Neglect', *Symposium*, 27 (1973), 309–21.

[17] Wolfram Schmitt, 'Der "Wahnsinn" in der Literatur des Mittelalters am Beispiel des *Iwein* Hartmanns von Aue', in *Psychologie in der Mediävistik: Gesammelte Beiträge des Steinheimer Symposiums*, hg. von Jürgen Kühnel u. a., GAG, 431 (1985), S. 197–214. – Heinz-Günter Schmitz, 'Iweins *zorn* und *tobesuht*. Psychologie und Physiologie in mittelhochdeutscher Literatur', in *Sandbjerg 85: Dem Andenken von Heinrich Bach gewidmet*, hg. von Friedhelm Debus und Ernst Dittmer, Kieler Beiträge zur deutschen Sprachgeschichte, 10 (Neumünster, 1986), S. 87–111. Schmitt und Schmitz weisen auf Übereinstimmungen zwischen dem Krankheitsbild Iweins und der Beschreibung der Melancholie hin, wie sie sich in dem exemplarischen Lehrtext der Schule von Salerno, der Schrift 'De melancholia' des Constantinus Africanus, findet, entstanden zwischen 1075 und 1085 als Übersetzung der arabischen Schrift von Ishaq Ibn 'Imran (Schmitt, S. 210); vergleiche Raymond Klibansky, Erwin Panofsky and Fritz Saxl, *Saturn and Melancholy: Studies in the History of Natural Philosophy, Religion and Art* (London, 1964), S. 82–86. – Ausgabe: *Ishaq Ibn 'Imran: Maqala fi-'l-malihuliya (Abhandlung über die Melancholie) und Constantini Africani libri duo de melancholia*. Vergleichende kritische arabisch-lateinische Parallelausgabe, deutsche Übersetzung des arabischen Textes von Karl Garbers (Hamburg, 1977).

[18] Schmitz (wie Anm. 17), S. 101–03 (zur 'Liebesmelancholie'). Vergleiche zur Beziehung zwischen Melancholie und Liebeskrankheit: John Livingston Lowes, 'The Loveres

lung selbst deuten sich in Yvains/Iweins Reaktion Parallelen zum Erscheinungsbild der *acedia* an, denn die Melancholie wurde in engerem Zusammenhang mit der Trägheitssünde gesehen, mit der sie eine Reihe von Symptomen teilt, ein Grund, warum der melancholische Menschentyp als besonders anfällig für die Versuchung der *acedia/tristitia* gehalten wurde.[19] So nennt etwa Konrad von Megenberg 'swærikait', 'trâkheit' und 'klainmüetichait' unter den Anzeichen der Melancholie, drei Zustände, die den Tochtersünden der *acedia, tristitia, torpor* und *pusillanimitas* nahestehen:[20] 'Und wenn diu melancoli ain oberhant nimpt und sich zeucht zuo dem haupt, sô kümpt dem menschen sweigen und betrahten, und swærikait, wainen und trakheit, vorht und sorg und klainmüetichait.'[21]

Chrétiens und Hartmanns Darstellung von Iweins Krankheit stimmt weitgehend mit der Melancholiedefinition Konrads überein. Bei dem Gedanken an das Terminversäumnis überfällt den Helden eine tiefe Trauer (*enuiz, riuwe*), er versinkt in Nachdenken und Schweigen, sitzt da wie ein der Sinne Beraubter (*Y* 2698f., 2702, 2774f., 2781–83; *I* 3090–95).[22] Eine lähmende Niedergeschlagenheit hindert ihn daran, die Katastrophe aufzuhalten. Untätig läßt er es geschehen, daß ihm die Zofe Laudines Ring vom Finger zieht, und versäumt so die letzte Gelegenheit, Reue zu zeigen: 'von herzeleide geschach im daz/ daz erz verdulte und versaz/ daz sîz im ab der hant gewan' (*I* 3197–99).

Von Laudine angeklagt und verstoßen, wird Iwein ein Opfer überwältigender Verlustgefühle, die Selbstverachtung und Menschenscheu mit sich führen (*Y* 2784–803; *I* 3201–26). Eine tiefe Freud- und Hoffnungslosigkeit befällt ihn (*Y* 2780–83, 2791; *I* 3214f.), welche sich bis zum Selbstmordgedanken steigert (*Y* 2790–95; vergleiche *Y* 3531–47 und *I* 3961–4010). Auch diese für die Melancholie typischen Zustände, die schließlich in den Wahnsinn münden, lassen sich parallel mit Erscheinungsformen der Trägheitssünde, wie *tristitia, taedium vitae* und *desperatio*, sehen.[23]

Maladye of Hereos', *Modern Philology*, 11 (1914), 491–546 (hier S. 503f., 527). Zur Liebeskrankheit siehe auch Mary Frances Wack, 'The *Liber de heros morbo* of Johannes Afflacius and its Implications for Medieval Love Conventions', *Speculum*, 62 (1987), 324–44.

[19] Wenzel (wie Anm. 9), S. 191–94: Appendix A, 'Acedia and the Humors'; Klibansky, Panofsky, Saxl (wie Anm. 17), S. 78.

[20] Gregor der Große zählt *torpor* und *pusillanimitas* zu den Tochtersünden der *tristitia*: *Moralia in Job*, XXXI.45 (PL, LXXVI, 620f.).

[21] Konrad von Megenberg, *Das Buch der Natur*, hg. von Franz Pfeiffer (Stuttgart, 1861; Neudr. Hildesheim, 1971), S. 30f.

[22] Vergleiche die Melancholiebeschreibung von Alexander Trallianus (6. Jh.): 'Manche [Kranke] zeigen grosse Abspannung, so dass sie nicht einmal gern sprechen mögen, gerade wie die sogenannten "Stumpfsinnigen".' Übersetzung von Theodor Puschmann: *Alexander von Tralles: Original-Text und Übersetzung*, 2 Bde. (Wien, 1878; Neudr. Amsterdam, 1963), I, 590.

[23] Die drei Sünden gehören zu den schwersten des *acedia*-Komplexes: vergleiche die

Daß trotz der von Chrétien und Hartmann aufgebotenen 'medizinischen' Details hier nicht nur eine Gemütskrankheit anvisiert ist, zeigt die zentrale Rolle, die das Gefühl, den Verlust selbst verschuldet zu haben, für die selbstzerstörerischen Depressionen des Helden spielt (*Y* 2790–95, *I* 3221–24). Derartige Selbstanklagen gehören weniger zum Krankheitsbild der Melancholie als zu der mit der *acedia/tristitia* verbundenen Geistesverfassung. Ein erdrückendes Schuldgefühl ohne den Ausblick auf Gottes Vergebung kann, wie Hartmann dies etwa in seinem *Gregorius*-Prolog erläutert, in die schwerste Sünde des *acedia*-Komplexes, die Verzweiflung an Gottes Gnade (*desperatio, zwîfel*) führen.[24] Iweins übermächtiges Schuldbewußtsein, seine Hoffnungslosigkeit, die ihm den Blick auf die Möglichkeit, Laudines Huld wiederzugewinnen, zunächst verstellt, erinnert an diesen *zwîfel*, eine Analogie, die die Gefahr verdeutlicht, in der Iwein schwebt. Auch nach seiner physischen Heilung bleibt er den Anfechtungen der Verzweiflung ausgesetzt, indem er zunächst angesichts des selbstverschuldeten Verlusts weiterhin den Selbstmord als einzigen Ausweg sieht. Im religiösen Kontext führt die äußerste Hoffnungslosigkeit zum ewigen Untergang. Entsprechend führt Iweins *grôze riuwe* in die Selbstentfremdung (*I* 3509–83)[25] und an den Rand der Selbstvernichtung, von dem ihn erst die Erkenntnis, daß seine Schuld gesühnt werden kann und muß, zurückreißt.

Angesichts dieser von Hartmann betonten Beziehung des *verligens* und *versitzens* zu den Tochtersünden der Trägheit, Wurzel allen Übels, wäre es sicher verfehlt, die Bedeutung der Fahrlässigkeit unserer

Einstufung der Tochtersünden bei Peraldus (wie Anm. 12), 95d, 96b und Wenzel (wie Anm. 9), S. 82. Zur für die *acedia* bezeichnenden Menschenscheu vergleiche den *Tractatus de ordine vitae* aus dem frühen 11. Jahrhundert (Wenzel, ebd., S. 31): 'ac fugere cohortatur de fratrum, cum quibus vivit, societate' (PL, CLXXXIV, 579); zum Selbsthaß die Abhandlung *De quadripartito exercitio cellae* von Adam Scotus (um 1190), 24, 'De taedio' (Wenzel, ebd., S. 33): 'tu tibi oneri es' (PL, CLIII, 841f.).

24 *Gregorius von Hartmann von Aue*, hg. von Hermann Paul, 13. neu bearbeitete Aufl. besorgt von Burghart Wachinger, ATB, 2 (Tübingen, 1984), 162–70.

25 Zu Iweins Identitätsverlust vergleiche Hedda Ragotzky und Barbara Weinmayer, 'Höfischer Roman und soziale Identitätsbildung. Zur soziologischen Deutung des Doppelwegs im *Iwein* Hartmanns von Aue', in *Deutsche Literatur im Mittelalter: Kontakte und Perspektiven: Hugo Kuhn zum Gedenken*, hg. von Christoph Cormeau (Stuttgart, 1979), S. 211–53; Hubertus Fischer, *Ehre, Hof und Abenteuer in Hartmanns 'Iwein': Vorarbeiten zu einer historischen Poetik des höfischen Epos*, Forschungen zur Geschichte der älteren deutschen Literatur, 3 (München, 1983), S. 104–18; Timothy McFarland, 'Narrative Structure and the Renewal of the Hero's Identity in *Iwein*', in *Hartmann von Aue*, GAG, 486 (wie Anm. 1), S. 129–57. Ragotzky und Weinmayer führen Iweins Identitätskrise auf den Verlust der Huld Laudines zurück (S. 225–27), Fischer auf den Verlust des Besitzes und der damit verbundenen Ehre (so auch McFarland, S. 143). Die physisch-psychische Komponente – Gedächtnisverlust als Folge der Melancholie bzw. der *grôzen riuwe* – wird dabei ausgespart, die Selbstanklagen nicht in ihrer Bedeutung gewürdigt. Zur Beeinträchtigung der drei geistigen Fähigkeiten durch die Melancholie siehe Klibansky, Panofsky, Saxl (wie Anm. 17), S. 83.

Artusritter zu verharmlosen. Ereks *verligen* ist nicht nur Nebenprodukt einer fatalen Leidenschaft, Iweins *versitzen* kein bloßer 'technischer Defekt'.[26] Im Gegenteil – Hartmann hat sich gerade bemüht, die umfassende Gefahr, die die geistige Erschlaffung für den Menschen als Individuum wie als Glied der Gesellschaft darstellt, herauszuarbeiten. Es erübrigt sich dann auch nach einer anderen Schuld des Helden zu suchen, etwa die Liebe Ereks als Laster der *concupiscentia* zu brandmarken[27] oder Iwein die Tötung Askalons als eigentliche Verfehlung anzulasten.[28] Nichts spricht dafür, daß mit der Schuld der Helden etwas anderes als ihr *verligen* und *versitzen* gemeint ist.

Sowohl Ereks wie Iweins rehabilitierende Abenteuer sind dann auch eng auf diese Schuld bezogen. Die Entbehrungen der *aventiure*-Fahrt, das *ungemach*, dem Erek sich freiwillig aussetzt, sind dem *gemach* des Karnanter Hoflebens diametral entgegengesetzt: Erek verzichtet auf die Freuden des ehelichen Zusammenlebens (*EE* 3440–44, *E* 3663–67, 3949–58) und darauf, die Bequemlichkeiten einer gastlichen Unterkunft länger als notwendig zu genießen (*EE* 4108f., 4286–89; *E* 4573–79, 4977f.). Iwein ist sich der Gefahr des Sichversäumens voll bewußt (*I* 4308f.; *Y* 4038, *I* 4830–34; *Y* 4086f.; *I* 4884–86) und lehnt es wie Erek ab auszuruhen (*I* 5085–96; *Y* 4588–92, *I* 5466–70; *Y* 5772, 5805, 5810–13, *I* 6877–81), um seinerseits Termine einzuhalten und seinen Verpflichtungen als Beschützer nachzukommen, um Treue und Dankbarkeit zu zeigen und seine Verfehlung wiedergutzumachen.

Am Ende der jeweiligen Aventiurefahrt greift Hartmann noch einmal programmatisch die Trägheitsthematik auf. In *Erec* geschieht dies etwa anläßlich der Schilderung von Ereks Genesung im Schloß von Penefrec. In dieser Schlüsselepisode werden die gegensätzlichen Begriffe *gemach* und *ungemach* zueinander in Beziehung gesetzt. Der rehabilitierte Held darf dankbar allen Komfort genießen, den Penefrec zu bieten hat. Über Chrétien hinausgehend beschreibt Hartmann das Schloß detailliert als Jagdschloß, als Jägerparadies (*E* 7124–87). Für den Erzählzusammenhang besitzen die Jagddetails keine Bedeutung, denn weder Erek noch sein Gastgeber machen von der Möglichkeit zu jagen Gebrauch. Die Funktion des Jagdmotivs ist eine symbolische: die Jagd gilt als Mittel gegen das Laster des Müßigganges.[29] Penefrec symbolisiert die Verbindung eines aktiven mit einem angenehmen Leben. Hier hat *gemach* seine Assoziation mit der Trägheit verloren, so daß für Erek

---

[26] So etwa Peter Wapnewski, *Hartmann von Aue*, 4. Aufl. (Stuttgart, 1969), S. 48 und 67.

[27] Petrus W. Tax, 'Studien zum Symbolischen in Hartmanns *Erec*. Enites Pferd', *ZfdPh*, 82 (1963), 29–44 (hier S. 43f.).

[28] Wapnewski (wie Anm. 26), S. 69.

[29] Marcelle Thiébaux, *The Stag of Love: The Chase in Medieval Literature* (Ithaca/London, 1974), S. 71–78; siehe auch Ranawake, in *Hartmann von Aue*, GAG, 486 (wie Anm. 1), S. 107.

gemach und *ungemach* zu einer höheren Einheit verschmelzen können: das *ungemach* des ritterlichen Daseins wird für ihn zum eigentlichen *gemach*, der Erfüllung dieses Daseins (*E* 7251–59).

Iwein gelingt es am Ende seiner Aventiurefahrt, seine Zeit richtig zu bemessen (*I* 6878–81). Ohne zu eilen, aber auch ohne zu verweilen, erreicht er zur rechten Stunde den Artushof, um sein Wort einzulösen.[30] Das Ordal, Schluß- und Höhepunkt der Abenteuerkette, erlaubt es Iwein, wie er dies einst auf seiner Turnierfahrt angestrebt hatte, seine ritterliche Befähigung vor versammelter Gesellschaft zu erweisen, zugleich aber seine Verpflichtungen als Garant des Rechts, als Beschützer der Schwachen zu erfüllen. Gaweins und Iweins Leben, wie es sich im Ordal darstellt, erscheint als Gegenbild der Trägheit, ein Leben, in dem kein Tag ungenützt verstreicht:

> ir leben was niht verlân
> an deheine müezekheit.
> in was beiden vil leit
> swenne ir tage giengen hin
> daz sî deheinen gewin
> an ir koufe envunden.   (*I* 7182–87)[31]

Es liegt nicht in meiner Absicht, das *verligen* und *versitzen* mit der Sünde der *acedia* gleichzusetzen. Als Sünde beschränkt sich *acedia* trotz ihrer Vielgestaltigkeit auf den religiösen Bereich: Die Sünde der Trägheit war und blieb Trägheit im Dienste Gottes.[32] Bequemlichkeit, Schläfrigkeit, Vergeßlichkeit, Säumigkeit, Undankbarkeit haben im Kontext der Sündenlehre und Beichtpraxis eine andere Bedeutung als in Hartmanns Artusromanen: Man vernachlässigt, verschläft, vergißt es, seine Sünden zu bekennen und zu bereuen, Buße zu tun, seine religiösen Gelübde zu erfüllen, Gott mit Worten und Werken zu dienen.

Erek hingegen versagt in erster Linie in der gesellschaftlichen Sphäre. Iweins gebrochenes Gelübde betrifft gleichfalls persönliche und soziale, nicht religiöse Verpflichtungen. Seine selbstzerstörerische Trauer entspringt nicht dem Zweifel an Gott, sondern dem Zweifel an sich selbst; nicht Gottes Huld, sondern *sîn selbes hulde* und *sîner vrowen hulde* scheint ihm verloren gegangen, und der seiner Verzweiflung entspringende Wahnsinn wird als physisch-psychische,

---

[30] Hartmanns Held braucht sich nicht wie der Chrétiens zu beeilen und ist nicht wie dieser erst im letzten Augenblick zur Stelle; vergleiche *Y* 5805, 5812f., 5889–921.

[31] Daß Gawein in diesem Rechtskampf keine ungerechte Sache vertritt, sondern eine Rechtspartie, die gute Rechtsgründe auf ihrer Seite hat, also sein Rittertum gleichfalls in den Dienst des Rechts stellt, führt Volker Mertens aus: *Laudine: Soziale Problematik im 'Iwein' Hartmanns von Aue*, Beihefte zur Zeitschrift für deutsche Philologie, 3 (Berlin, 1978), S. 100–04.

[32] Wenzel (wie Anm. 9), S. 96.

medikamentös heilbare Krankheit, nicht als Krankheit der Seele dargestellt. Als Iwein Laudine um Vergebung bittet, zieht er zwar selbst die Parallele zwischen seinem Versagen und einer zu büßenden Sünde. Aber es ist eine Parallele keine Gleichsetzung (*Y* 6780-89, *I* 8102-13). Nicht von ungefähr vermeidet es dann Hartmann auch durchaus Ereks *verligen* und Iweins *versitzen* als *trâkheit* oder als *sünde* zu bezeichnen.[33]

Andererseits lassen sich gesellschaftliche und religiöse Sphäre in Hartmanns Artusromanen nicht streng trennen. Für den Ritter und König, der seine Stellung als gottgegeben begreift, bedeutet die Vernachlässigung der Pflichten, die diese Stellung ihm auferlegt, nicht nur den Verlust seines gesellschaftlichen Ansehens. Sie bedroht auch das Heil der Seele: 'verlegeniu müezekheit/ ist gote und der werlte leit' (*I* 7171f.), so konstatiert Hartmann programmatisch anläßlich Iweins letzten Kampfes.

Nirgends ist das Ineinandergreifen der gesellschaftlichen und der religiösen Sphäre eindrucksvoller geschildert als im Schlußteil der beiden Romane. Die Apotheose des Helden, der seine *verlegene müezekheit* abgebüßt hat, vollzieht sich in der Hochstilisierung des Artusritters zum Antityp des trägen Sünders, zum unermüdlichen Soldaten Christi. Gegen jede Form der *acedia* – sündhafte Niederge- schlagenheit, Wankelmut, Kleinmut, unrechte Angst – ist er gefeit. Lächelnd, ein fröhliches Lied singend (*E* 8154-58), begegnet Erek den Warnungen und Klagen der Bewohner Brandigans, die bereits seinen sicheren Tod voraussehen, eine Verkörperung der *laetitia spiritualis* und der *fortitudo*, derjenigen Tugenden, die das Laster der Trägheit zu überwinden imstande sind.[34] Fröhlich läßt auch Iwein bei seinem Einritt in die Burg zum schlimmen Abenteuer Drohungen und Schmähungen des Pförtners über sich ergehen (*I* 6278-82). Die unerschütterliche Zuversicht beider Helden ist letztlich in ihrem Gottvertrauen begründet. Während der träge Sünder, dem es an diesem Vertrauen mangelt, dem Aberglauben anheimfällt, der *abtrunnide* und *irrigheit*, wie sie Hartmann in einer langen Liste abergläubischer Praktiken schildert, ist der Artusritter über jede Versuchung dieser Art erhaben, da er sein Schicksal ganz Gott anheimgegeben hat (*E* 8119-40). Erek und Iwein lassen es, vor allem gegen Ende des Romans, nicht daran fehlen, Gott sowohl mit Worten als auch mit Werken zu dienen, d. h. in beiden

---

[33] Hartmann gebraucht *trâkheit* nur, um seine Charaktere vom Verdacht eines so schwerwiegenden Fehls in Schutz zu nehmen (*I* 84, 6039).

[34] Hugo Ripelin von Straßburg (vor 1250), *Compendium theologicae veritatis*, lib. III, cap. 18: 'Patet ergo ex his, quod hoc vitium prout vocatur *tristitia*, opponitur laetitiae spirituali [. . .] Sed prout vocatur *acedia*, opponitur fortitudini', hg. unter dem Titel: *B. Alberti Magni Opera omnia*, hg. von Steph. Caes. Aug. Borgnet, Bd. 34 (Paris, 1895), S. 110 (nach Wenzel (wie Anm. 9), S. 55f.).

Sphären Trägheit durchaus zu meiden.[35] Bevor beide in ihr letztes Abenteuer reiten, stehen sie bereits bei Tagesanbruch auf, um eine Messe zu hören, und zwar spezifisch eine Messe zu Ehren des Heiligen Geistes (E 8635–40; Y 5453–56, I 6587–90), der als Spender der geistlichen Freude gilt, die über das Laster der acedia triumphiert.[36]

Beide Artusritter demonstrieren insbesondere in den Kämpfen mit den als Inbegriff der Unbarmherzigkeit geschilderten, riesenhaften Gegnern – Cadocs Peinigern, Harpin, den Riesen des schlimmen Abenteuers –, daß sie fähig und bereit sind, 'gute' Werke, Werke der Nächstenliebe, der pitié/erbermde, zu tun. Bei der Gestaltung dieses Motivs werden Unterschiede in der Konzeption der beiden Chrétienschen Romane deutlich. Für den französischen Erekroman spielt das Thema eine eher untergeordnete Rolle. Obwohl das Cadocabenteuer Erbarmen als Motivation impliziert (EE 4401–04), tritt pitié nicht als Leitbegriff auf. Anders im Yvain, wo der symbolträchtige Kampf für den Löwen, der die eigentliche Aventiurenkette einleitet, durch Yvains pitié motiviert ist (Y 3373f.), womit auch die folgenden Abenteuer unter das Vorzeichen der pitié gestellt werden (Y 3903f., 3942, 4070–75, 4357–59, 5987f.); Erbarmen für hilfsbedürftige Frauen bestimmt neben persönlichen Verpflichtungen die im Dienst von Gott und Recht vollbrachten Befreiungstaten.

Die verschiedene Ausrichtung der Chrétienschen Romane – Erec et Enide noch weitgehend allein durch die höfische innerweltliche Problematik bestimmt, Yvain die religiös-moralische Komponente miteinbeziehend – stellte Hartmann als Bearbeiter vor unterschiedliche Aufgaben. Als er, möglicherweise schon unter dem Eindruck des Yvainromans, versuchte, die religiöse Komponente auch für den Erekroman stärker einzubringen, handelte es sich für ihn oft darum, die religiöse Assoziation durch Zusatz explizit zu machen, wie wir dies etwa an den Ausführungen zum swachen gelouben beobachten konnten. Betonter als Chrétien gestaltet der deutsche Autor deswegen das Cadocabenteuer als Tat des Erbarmens (E 5327–34, 5408, 5429–34). Darüber hinaus versetzt Hartmann seinen Helden in die Lage, sein letztes Abenteuer sowohl mit einem leiblichen als auch mit einem geistigen Werk der Barmherzigkeit zu krönen, das letztere der Grund, aus dem er die Witwen der von Mabonagrin erschlagenen Ritter

---

[35] Zur Definition der acedia als Trägheit im Dienst Gottes und als Widerwillen beim Ausführen guter Werke siehe Wenzel (wie Anm. 9), S. 72 und S. 225, Anm. 19.

[36] Zu gaudium als Frucht des Heiligen Geistes siehe Paulus, Gal. 5. 22ff. (nach Petrus W. Tax, 'Studien zum Symbolischen in Hartmanns Erec. Erecs ritterliche Erhöhung', WW, 13 (1963), 277–88, jetzt in Hartmann von Aue, hg. von Hugo Kuhn und Christoph Cormeau, WdF, 359 (Darmstadt, 1973), S. 287–310 (hier 291f.); vergleiche auch A.E. Schönbach, Über Hartmann von Aue: Drei Bücher Untersuchungen (Graz, 1894), S. 21f.). Das Feuer des heiligen Geistes gilt für Wilhelm Peraldus als Heilmittel gegen die mollicies: Summae (wie Anm. 12), t. 2, S. 82d.

einführt: Hartmanns Erek läßt die Köpfe der Erschlagenen beerdigen –
ein 'leibliches' gutes Werk – und vermag es, beflügelt von *erbermde*, die
verwitweten Damen zu trösten – ein 'geistiges' gutes Werk (*E* 9746–52,
9782–822).[37]

Im *Iwein* bedurfte es solcher Zusätze nicht, da Chrétien Yvains
Befreiungstaten bereits als 'gute', durch *pitié* motivierte Werke gestaltet
hatte, was Hartmann nur zu übernehmen brauchte (*I* 4509, 4740f.,
4905f., 6407–15).[38] Verglichen mit diesen gottgefälligen Taten, mit denen
Iwein sich als wahrer *miles christianus* für die gottgegebene königliche
Aufgabe des Rechtsschutzes qualifiziert erweist,[39] müssen die Turnier-
fahrten, die Iweins *versitzen* herbeiführen, als *müezigiu werc* erscheinen,
allein darauf gerichtet, das Lob der *werlt* zu gewinnen.[40] Auch die
unnütze Tätigkeit stellt, vor allem wenn sie die Erfüllung der von Gott
gebotenen Aufgabe – in Iweins Fall die Erhaltung von Recht und
Frieden – behindert, eine Form der Trägheit dar.[41] Um diesen Aspekt
herauszuarbeiten, schildert Hartmann das abschließende, die Aben-
teuerfahrt Iweins krönende Ordal als Inbegriff der *unmüezekheit*. Die im
Dienste des Rechts kämpfenden Ritter werden anhand einer
breitausgesponnenen Darlehensmetapher mit den guten und getreuen
Dienern des Herrn gleichgesetzt, wie sie die Parabel vom vergrabenen
Talent darstellt (Matth. 25. 14–30). Wie die getreuen Diener sind Iwein
und Gawein gute Wirtschafter, die ihr Gut gegen Zinsen ausleihen; im
Gegensatz zu dem *servus malus et piger* der Parabel (Matth. 25. 27), dem
Inbegriff des trägen Sünders, versäumen sie es also nicht, mit ihrem
Talent zu wuchern:[42]

---

[37] Tax, WdF (wie Anm. 36), S. 301.
[38] Auch wenn man Rudolf Voß beistimmen würde, daß sich Iwein mehr mit seiner
Reputation als mit altruistischen barmherzigen Überlegungen beschäftigt, so läßt sich die
Bedeutung des Motivs in der Harpin- und Pesme-Aventiure nicht leugnen, wie dies
Fischer unternimmt: Rudolf Voß, *Die Artusepik Hartmanns von Aue: Untersuchungen zum
Wirklichkeitsbegriff und zur Ästhetik eines literarischen Genres im Kräftefeld von soziokulturellen
Normen und christlicher Anthropologie*, Literatur und Leben, N.F., 25 (Köln/Wien, 1983),
S. 131f.; Fischer (wie Anm. 25), S. 115–17.
[39] Zum *miles-christianus*-Ideal in Hartmanns Artusromanen vergleiche auch René
Pérennec, *Recherches sur le roman arthurien en vers en Allemagne aux XIIe et XIIIe siècles*, GAG,
393, I–II, 2 Bde. (Göppingen, 1984), I, 142–47.
[40] Vergleiche *Robert [Mannyng] of Brunne: Handlyng Synne (A.D.1303)*, Part I, re-edited by
Frederick J. Furnivall, Early English Text Society, 119 (1901), Z. 4571–620; Turniere werden
im Kapitel über die Sünde der *acedia* für alle Todsünden verantwortlich gemacht (Hinweis
nach Brown (wie Anm. 16), S. 314 und Anm. 22).
[41] Für Hrabanus Maurus gilt derjenige als träger Sünder, der nicht fröhlich seinen
Mitmenschen beisteht und dabei vor allem denen hilft, die unter ungerechter Behandlung
leiden. Statt gute Werke zu tun, treibt er sich unstet umher, stiftet Streit und vergeudet
seine Zeit mit nutzlosen Tätigkeiten. Siehe Wenzel (wie Anm. 9), S. 36f. mit Hinweis auf
Hrabanus Maurus, *De ecclesiastica disciplina* (842–847), lib. III, 'De agone christiano' (PL,
CXII, 1251–53).
[42] Chrétien verwendet die Metapher bereits in seinem *Cligés* (Ausgabe: Wendelin
Foerster, Halle 1884, Z. 4080–87). Zur Auslegung der Parabel als Versinnbildlichung der
Trägheit vergleiche Hrabanus Maurus, *Commentariorum in Matthaeum libri octo*, lib. VII,

> ir leben was niht verlân
> an deheine müezekheit. [. . .]
> si wâren zwêne mære
> karge wehselære
> und entlihen ûz ir varende guot
> ûf einen seltsænen muot.
> sî nâmen wuocher dar an
> sam zwêne werbende man.   (*I* 7182–94)

Unter dem Einsatz des eigenen Lebens gelingt es ihnen, höchsten
Gewinn zu erringen (*I* 7199), indem sie Mühe gegen Ehre tauschen
(*I* 7212f.). Ähnlich wie die getreuen Diener der Parabel zum Lohn mit
Ämtern betraut werden (Matth. 25. 21 und 23),[43] wird Iwein die
freudenvolle Rückkehr ins eigene Reich erleben (*I* 8118–20).

Auch an anderen Werken Hartmanns läßt sich ablesen, wie groß die
Bedeutung war, die der Dichter der *müezekheit* beimaß, als einer
grundlegenden menschlichen Schwäche, die es zu überwinden gilt.
Bereits die *Klage* fordert, daß der *lîp* von der Trägheit lassen muß, damit
ein positives Minneverhältnis möglich wird. Im *Gregorius*-Prolog stellt
Hartmann die Sünde der *acedia* in den Mittelpunkt. Schließlich geht es
im *Armen Heinrich* um die Verpflichtung Gott und den Mitmenschen
gegenüber.

Fassen wir zusammen: In beiden Artusromanen Hartmanns kon-
stituiert das Versäumnis des Helden, das *verligen* und *versitzen*, die
eigentliche Schuld, die es zu büßen gilt, bevor der Artusritter wieder
seine ihm zugewiesene Stellung als Herrscher einnehmen kann. Um die

---

cap. 25: z. B. 'sunt enim plerique in Ecclesia quorum iste servus imaginem tenet, qui
melioris vias vitae aggredi metuunt, et tamen jacere in sui torporis ignavia non
pertimescunt' (PL, CVII, 1091). Der Fehl wird von Hrabanus auch als Sünde der *pigritia*
und *neglegentia* bezeichnet (ebd.). Die Diener der Parabel wurden zwar in den meisten
Fällen als 'Diener am Worte Gottes' verstanden, das anvertraute Gut als das Evangelium,
daneben bildete sich aber auch eine auf alle Menschen bezügliche, moralische Auslegung
heraus, die Gregor der Große im Anschluß an Hieronymus richtungsweisend formulierte
und die vor allem im 12. Jahrhundert öfters aufgegriffen wurde; Gregor analysiert die
Verantwortlichkeit derjenigen, die Gott mit Verstand, Reichtum, einflußreicher Stellung
und beruflichen Kenntnissen und Fähigkeiten ausgestattet hat. Dies sind die 'Talente', die
nach Gregor zum Nutzen der Mitmenschen eingesetzt werden sollen: *XL homiliarum in
evangelia libri duo*, PL, LXXVI, 1075–312 (1109A); siehe Stephen L. Wailes, *Medieval
Allegories of Jesus' Parables* (Berkeley, 1987), S. 192–94.

[43]   In der Version des Lukasevangeliums übergibt der Herr diesen Dienern die Herrschaft
über fünf bzw. zehn Städte (Luk. 19. 17 'eris potestatem habens super decem civitates';
siehe auch Vers 19). Petrus Comestor bezieht dann auch in seinem unveröffentlichten
Werk zu den Evangelien die Betrauung mit den 'Talenten' auf die staatliche Verwaltung,
die Autorität des Haushaltsvorstandes und die persönliche moralische Verantwortung;
siehe Wailes (wie Anm. 42), S. 70, mit Hinweis auf Beryl Smalley, 'Peter Comestor on the
Gospels and His Sources', *Recherches de théologie ancienne et médiévale*, 46 (1979), 84–129
(hier S. 113).

Bedeutung und Tragweite dieses Versäumnisses zu erhellen, gestaltet Hartmann es parallel zur Sünde der *acedia* in ihren verschiedenen Manifestationen, indem er Motive seiner Quelle, die diese Parallelität bereits suggerieren, weiter ausgestaltet und vermehrt und den von seinem Fehl geheilten, rehabilitierten Helden zum Antityp des trägen Sünders, zum *miles christianus* hochstilisiert. Obwohl Hartmann auf diese Weise die religiösen Aspekte stärker betont als Chrétien, hält er doch am gesellschaftlich-sittlichen Charakter des Versagens fest, den er in seiner Quelle vorfand: eine eindeutige Identifikation des *verligens* und *versitzens* mit der Sünde der *acedia* findet auch in Hartmanns Romanen nicht statt.[44] Erst Wolfram von Eschenbach führt im Anschluß an Chrétiens letzten Roman eine derartige Identifikation durch, indem er Parzivals versäumte Frage als Sünde gegen das Gebot der *caritas*, als Unterlassung eines guten Werkes deutet, die hineinführt in die schwerste Tochtersünde der Trägheit, den Verlust des Gottvertrauens, den *zwîfel*.

Auch wenn sich *verligen* und *versitzen* nicht mit der Sünde der *acedia* decken, so bilden doch Hartmanns Hinweise auf die zwischen dem sittlich-gesellschaftlichen und dem religiösen Versäumnis bestehende Analogie einen wesentlichen Bestandteil seines Deutungsangebotes. Analog der Sünde der *acedia* wäre das *verligen* und *versitzen* Manifestation einer in der Gebrechlichkeit des Menschen verankerten, immer präsenten Schwäche. Diese Schwäche offenbart sich plötzlich in einer Situation, die eine Versuchung zum Trägesein darstellt. Eine solche Situation sind Ereks Flitterwochen mit der schönen Enite und Iweins Turnierfahrt mit seinem ehrgeizigen Freund Gawein. Diese Situation vermag es, plötzlich und scheinbar unerklärlich in den Helden eine Desorientierung ihres ganzen Wollens zu bewirken. Die Ausrichtung auf die Bequemlichkeiten des Hof- und Ehelebens, auf die Zerstreuungen der Turnierfahrt führt zum *vergezzen* der an den Helden gestellten Anforderungen, zur Verfehlung, die mühsam gebüßt werden muß. Ebenso plötzlich ist das Maß der Buße, das allein Gott kennt, erfüllt, der Held rehabilitiert.

Eine Versuchung, die von außen an den Menschen herantritt und zu einer Verfehlung führt, die gebüßt werden muß, ist etwas anderes als ein in der Unerfahrenheit der Einzelpersönlichkeit wurzelndes Erkenntnisdefizit, das es in einem Lernprozeß aufzufüllen gilt. Damit wäre ein Interpretationsmodell, das einen Reifeprozeß der Artusritter postuliert, zu revidieren. Ereks Versagen wäre nicht als 'Mangel an

---

[44] Vergleiche zur Herstellung der Beziehungen zwischen dem religiösen und dem weltlichen Bereich, der 'semi-laïcisation' der Begriffe: René Pérennec, 'Un aspect de l'adaptation d'*Erec et Enide* en terre d'Empire: l'analogie entre la carrière du héros et la destinée du chrétien', in *Actes du Colloque des 9 et 10 avril 1976 sur 'L'adaptation courtoise' en littérature médiévale allemande*, hg. von Danielle Buschinger, Université de Picardie, Centre d'Études Médiévales (1976), S. 67–105 (hier besonders S. 75 und 80).

ausreichender Erkenntnis über Situation und ethische Postulate' zu deuten, seine 'schließlich gewonnene Handlungssicherheit' nicht als 'Auswirkung zunehmender Verantwortung'.[45] Auch Iwein muß keinen 'Lernprozeß durchlaufen, der ihn zur Erkenntnis und zur Akzeptierung von übernommener Verantwortung führt'.[46]

Von einem Mangel an Erkenntnis in Bezug auf Ereks und Iweins Versagen spricht Hartmann nicht. Im Gegenteil – kurz bevor die Krise hereinbricht, beweist Erek im Turnier von Tenebroc, daß er nicht *verlegener müezekeit* verfallen will, zeigt Iwein im Kampf mit Keie, daß er sich seiner Aufgaben als Landesverteidiger bewußt ist. Auch eine auf die Krise folgende, langsam zunehmende Erkenntnis der Verfehlung und eine allmählich sich vollziehende Akzeptierung der Verantwortung ist nicht auszumachen. Vielmehr erkennt der Held schlagartig sein Versagen in seiner ganzen Tragweite, und die Stadien der Verfehlung, Buße und Restitution folgen fast übergangslos aufeinander. Das neuzeitliche Menschenbild einer in die Verantwortlichkeit hineinwachsenden Persönlichkeit wird diesen Gegebenheiten nicht gerecht. Es wäre zu ersetzen durch ein Denkmodell, das sich an der mittelalterlichen christlichen Anthropologie orientiert. Menschliche Verfehlung ist nicht Folge individueller sittlicher Unreife, sondern Symptom der menschlichen Schwäche, die jederzeit manifest werden kann. Je vollkommener der Held, an dem die Gebrechlichkeit des Menschen sichtbar wird, je unerwarteter die Bloßstellung, desto eindrücklicher demonstriert der Autor das Faktum potentiellen Versagens als integralen Bestandteil des menschlichen Daseins.[47]

Auch wenn der Aventiurenweg keinen individuellen Reifeprozeß darstellt, so erfahren die höfischen Verhaltensnormen im Verlauf der rehabilitierenden Abenteuer doch eine Differenzierung, eine sittlich-religiöse Vertiefung.[48] Der *miles christianus* der Joie-de-la-Cort-Episode ist ein anderer als der Erek der Vorgeschichte, der Löwenritter, der für Gott und Recht kämpft, ein anderer als der Iwein des Quellenabenteuers.[49] Der Unterschied beruht aber nicht auf der zunächst fehlenden, dann gewonnenen sozialen Kompetenz: Erek ist am Ende ebenso auf seine Ehre bedacht wie in der Vorgeschichte, Iwein beschützt sein Land und liebt seine Frau am Schluß des Romans ebenso wie vor der Krise, und beider Ruhm unterscheidet sich von ihrem ursprünglichen Ansehen quantitativ, nicht qualitativ. Hinzugekommen

---

[45] Christoph Cormeau und Wilhelm Störmer, *Hartmann von Aue: Epoche – Werk – Wirkung* (München, 1985), S. 192.
[46] Mertens (wie Anm. 31), S. 50.
[47] Vergleiche Voß (wie Anm. 38), S. 87.
[48] Silvia Ranawake, Rez. Rudolf Voß, *Die Artusepik Hartmanns von Aue*, Arbitrium (1986), S. 139–44.
[49] Vergleiche McFarland (wie Anm. 25), S. 156f.

ist die sittlich-religiöse Dimension, in *Erec* noch teilweise relativ unverbunden angehängt, in *Iwein* weitgehend integriert. Aber auch dieses Hinzutreten der sittlich-religiösen Komponente impliziert keinen individuellen Reifeprozeß: Der Ritter macht sich nicht auf die Aventiurefahrt, um gute Werke zu tun, sondern die Möglichkeit dazu wird ihm als Gnadengeschenk zuteil. Auf der Suche nach angemessener 'Buße' und Rehabilitation findet er nicht nur das Gesuchte, sondern zugleich die endgültige Bestätigung seiner Erwähltheit zum Herrscheramt. Anhand seiner 'guten Werke' darf er sich als derjenige ausweisen, den der Herr 'über vieles setzen' wird ('super multa te constituam' Matth. 25. 21). Analog zur *felix culpa*, der Schuld, die die Möglichkeit der Erlösung und Erfüllung miteinbegreift, erweist sich der Fall des Helden paradoxerweise zugleich als der erste Schritt auf dem Weg zu seiner letztendlichen Erhöhung. *verligen* und *versitzen* führen über *ungemach* und *riuwe* zur gottgefälligen *unmüezekheit* des sein Amt vorbildlich ausübenden Herrschers.

Aspects of Knighthood in
Hartmann's Adaptations of Chrétien's Romances
and in the Social Context

WILLIAM HENRY JACKSON

I

The romances of Hartmann von Aue occupy a key place in the development of the concept of knighthood in German literature. In the words of Joachim Bumke, it was Hartmann who effected 'den Durchbruch zum neuen Ritterbild', and 'dieser erste Höhenflug adligen Rittertums' took place in Hartmann's *Erec*.[1] More recently Jean Flori has plotted the rising prestige and the developing ideology of knighthood in the Plantagenet domains, Flanders and the surrounding regions, France, and the German empire, reaching the important conclusion that even in the western areas the full articulation of this ideology and the concomitant decisive enhancement of the social prestige of knighthood, whilst having roots that stretch much further back in time, took place in the second half, perhaps even rather in the last third of the twelfth century.[2] Furthermore, Flori ascribes a pioneering role in the literary articulation and in the propagation of this knightly ideology in France to Chrétien de Troyes,[3] whose romances provided the sources for German works which were of central importance in establishing the theme of knighthood in German literature: Hartmann's *Erec*, adapted from Chrétien's *Erec et Enide* in the 1180s or early 1190s, his *Iwein*, adapted from Chrétien's *Yvain* some years later, and Wolfram von Eschenbach's *Parzival*, adapted from Chrétien's *Perceval* after the turn of the century.

---

[1] Joachim Bumke, *Studien zum Ritterbegriff im 12. und 13. Jahrhundert*, Beihefte zum Euphorion, 1, 2nd edn (Heidelberg, 1977), p. 92.
[2] Jean Flori, *L'essor de la chevalerie: XIe–XIIe siècles*, Travaux d'histoire éthico-politique, 46 (Geneva, 1986), pp. 290–338.
[3] Jean Flori, 'Pour une histoire de la chevalerie: l'adoubement chez Chrétien de Troyes', *Romania*, 100 (1979), 21–53; see also Flori's forthcoming book on *chevalerie* in twelfth-century French literature announced in *L'essor*, p. 329, n. 88.

In the light of Flori's researches the time-lag between northern France and the German empire in the emergence of the new cultural model of chivalry shrinks to a few years. Indeed some aspects of the ideological and social enhancement of the *militia* appear in historical sources in the German empire even earlier than in France – thus, according to Flori, it is the German empire that yields the earliest evidence, from about 1100 onwards, of an extension of the ancient royal duty of protection to the knighthood as a whole (*L'essor*, pp. 265–67), and the German laws of 1152 and 1186 underlining social privileges of the *milites* are well in advance of similar provisions in France (*L'essor*, pp. 246–47).

These findings suggest limitations in the conventional wisdom which tends to see the German areas constantly lagging behind France in the development of chivalry and they point to the need for further comparative studies of French and German material in the key period of the late twelfth century, studies in which Chrétien and Hartmann, given the pioneering status of each of these authors in the literary presentation of knighthood, deserve a central place. Nor can literary scholars refer, as a point of orientation for literary studies, to a firm consensus about the position of knighthood in the social reality of twelfth-century Germany, for there are still many unanswered questions here: 'Wie die Realität des Rittertums zu erfassen und zu interpretieren ist, darüber ist [. . .] noch keine Übereinstimmung erzielt worden.'[4] It would go far beyond the scope of a short essay to address all the questions surrounding the topic of knighthood in Chrétien's and Hartmann's works,[5] instead I shall focus on some aspects of knighthood as a social status, especially in Hartmann's adaptation of Chrétien's *Erec et Enide*, taking critical account of Bumke's *Studien zum Ritterbegriff* and René Pérennec's study of German Arthurian romance,[6] and closing with a brief discussion of points of interest for students of Chrétien and Hartmann raised in a recent historical study of the German *ministeriales*.

Pérennec's book is a major contribution to Hartmann scholarship and it analyses the semantics of chivalry in Hartmann's romances more fully than any previous work. However, it may be that in the wake of Bumke's work Pérennec at some points underestimates the degree of social concreteness in Hartmann's presentation of knighthood. In a much quoted sentence at the end of his study Bumke concludes: 'Das adlige Rittertum, von dem die höfische Dichtung erzählt, kann nicht aus Verschiebungen in der Ständeordnung erklärt werden; es ist ein

---

[4] Joachim Bumke, *Höfische Kultur: Literatur und Gesellschaft im hohen Mittelalter*, 2 vols (Munich, 1986), I, 64.
[5] More of these questions will be treated in a book I am preparing on the subject of knighthood in the works of Hartmann von Aue.
[6] René Pérennec, *Recherches sur le roman arthurien en vers en Allemagne aux XIIe et XIIIe siècles*, GAG, 393, I–II, 2 vols (Göppingen, 1984).

Erziehungs- und Bildungsgedanke von weitreichender Bedeutung und
ein Phänomen der Geistesgeschichte viel mehr als der Sozialgeschichte'
(*Studien*, p. 147), and in general Bumke reacted so strongly against an all
too unified view of the 'Ritterstand' as a social reality that he seemed, as
one scholar put it, almost to believe in 'l'inexistence sociale de la
chevalerie même'.[7] Pérennec does not go as far as this, but one senses a
reflex of Bumke's scepticism for instance in his comment that, if
Hartmann tends to go further than Chrétien in endowing the concept of
knighthood with moral connotations, it is perhaps because the word
ritter, lacking a sufficient social support in Germany, had to be linked to
the realm of ideas (Pérennec, I, p. 28); and in his valuable lexical analysis
of the word *ritter* in Hartmann's *Erec* he several times suggests doubt
about its social connotations. We can perhaps reach greater clarity on
this question of the social component of the word *ritter* by considering
three points discussed by Pérennec with reference to Hartmann's
adaptation of Chrétien's *Erec et Enide*: the term *ritters name*, the relation
of the terms *ritter* and *kneht*, and the relation of *ritter* to other social
groups.

II

In two episodes in Hartmann's *Erec*[8] the expression *ritters name* is
connected with a norm of privileged treatment. In an exchange of words
between the count Galoain (unnamed in Hartmann but named in
Chrétien, 3129) and Erec, the count tells Erec that he would be hanged
on the spot were it not for the fact that he is a knight (4179–80: 'wan daz
ir geniezet/ daz ir ritter sît genant'), to which Erec replies:

> 'ir enthöveschet iuch', sprach Êrec,
> 'an mir harte sêre.
> von wem habet ir die lêre
> daz ir scheltet einen man
> der ie ritters namen gewan?
> ir sît an swachem hove erzogen.
> nû schamet iuch: ir habet gelogen.
> ich bin edeler dan ir sît.'   (4197–204)

---

[7] Daniel Rocher, ' "Chevalerie" et littérature "chevaleresque" ', *Et. Germ.*, 21 (1966),
165–79 (p. 179). Bumke himself suggests the possibility of a more substantial social reality
to the phenomenon of knighthood in the *Anhang* to the second edition of his study
(*Studien*, pp. 177–78).
[8] Ed. by Albert Leitzmann, continued by Ludwig Wolff, 6th edn, prepared by Christoph
Cormeau and Kurt Gärtner, ATB, 39 (Tübingen, 1985); for Chrétien's *Erec et Enide* I use the
edition by Wendelin Foerster, Romanische Bibliothek, 13 (Halle, 1934).

Later Hartmann as narrator tells of the cruel treatment of the knight Cadoc by two giants:

> si brâchen vaste ritters reht
> und handelten den guoten kneht,
> und wære er begangen,
> an diebes stat gevangen,
> selher zuht wære ze vil. (5412–16)

And this is followed up by Erec's condemning the giants for their failure to treat Cadoc with the respect that evidently attaches to the condition of knighthood:

> 'hât dirre man ritters namen,
> sô möhtet ir iuch immer schamen
> daz er des niht geniuzet
> und iuch niht bedriuzet
> der grôzen unvuoge.' (5468–72)

The exchange between Galoain and Erec has no precedent in Chrétien's work, whilst the condemnation of the giants' cruel and unseemly treatment of a knight is motivated by Erec's comment in Chrétien:

> 'Granz viltance est de chevalier
> Nu desvestir et puis liier
> Et batre si vilainnemant.' (4413–15)

On the two passages in Hartmann's *Erec* Bumke comments that with the expression *ritters name* Hartmann is thinking 'wohl nicht an Stand und Standesrechte [. . .] sondern an die ethischen Normen der Adelsgesell-schaft' (*Studien*, p. 131, n. 12). However, this explanation seems to introduce a forced contrast; a more natural reading of the passages would call for a 'sowohl . . . als auch' where Bumke has 'nicht . . . sondern'. Pérennec at first concedes that these passages seem to link the designation *ritter* in Hartmann, like *chevalier* in Chrétien, to certain privileges of social status, but then he follows Bumke to cast doubt on this interpretation and to see in the passages rather issues of proper behaviour and of honour (I, pp. 66–67), so that it is not quite clear just how firmly Pérennec does see the word *ritter* as designating a 'catégorie sociale' or 'statut social' (I, p. 67).

It seems to me that here Bumke is led to a forced interpretation and Pérennec to a hesitant one by an exaggerated scepticism about the extent to which the term *ritter* indicates a social category. Bumke's reading of these two passages in *Erec* is part of his general thesis that the knightly terminology of courtly poetry relates more to ethical behaviour than to social status: '*Ritters name* ist in der höfischen Dichtung weniger eine

Standesbezeichnung als ein Zentralbegriff der Herrenethik. Das gilt in noch höherem Maß für die Ausdrücke *ritters ambet*, *ritters leben*, *ritters reht*, die überall den sittlichen Auftrag des Ritternamens meinen' (*Studien*, pp. 131–32). These formulations surely underplay the social resonance of knightly vocabulary, and it would be more accurate to say that *ritters name* is both an indication of social status (a 'Standesbezeichnung') and an ethically or ideologically loaded term which denotes standards of behaviour linked as ideal desiderata to that social status. In other words, the ethical duties are connected with a social group, the ethical dimension of the expression *ritters name*, and of knightly terminology in general, presupposes a social category and cannot properly be understood in isolation from that social category. This double orientation is well illustrated in one of the earliest occurrences of the term *ritters name*, in the *Kaiserchronik*,[9] where those who have *rîteres namen* (8104) are enjoined with the duty of protection (8106–10) and also defined socially as being distinct from merchants and from peasants (8112–15), the wielding of the sword, which is the hallmark of the knightly aristocracy, being explicitly forbidden to peasants (14807–11). The testimony of the *Kaiserchronik* is of great value in indicating social and ethical conceptions in mid-twelfth-century Germany, and here as often in later vernacular texts the ethical component of knightly vocabulary is clearly predicated upon its social meaning. In *König Rother*[10] those who have *ritaris namen* are given preferential treatment by being separated from others and given warhorses, fine clothes and arms, to their intense joy (1331–44) – here it is the material advantage of being a knight that is to the fore.[11] In *Iwein*[12] Hartmann himself strongly emphasises an ethical dimension of *ritters name* when, quite independently of Chrétien, he has Lunete call on Arthur to strip Iwein of *rîters name* (3188) because of his breach of *triuwe* (3167–95). However, even here the ethical condemnation has social connotations, for Lunete's charge takes up the historically recorded practice of imposing the loss of military status and its attendant social privileges as a punishment for serious crime;[13] and

[9] Ed. by Edward Schröder, *MGH, Deutsche Chroniken*, I, i (Hannover, 1892).

[10] Ed. by Theodor Frings and Joachim Kuhnt, Altdeutsche Texte für den akademischen Unterricht, 2 (Halle (Saale), 1954).

[11] On the importance of *König Rother* as evidence that knighthood was associated with a relatively elevated social status around the middle of the twelfth century, see Werner Schröder, 'Zum *ritter*-Bild der frühmittelhochdeutschen Dichter', *GRM*, 53 (1972), 333–51 (pp. 347–50).

[12] Ed. by G.F. Benecke and K. Lachmann, 7th edn, rev. by Ludwig Wolff (Berlin, 1968).

[13] On the history of this practice, see Karl Leyser, 'Early Medieval Canon Law and the Beginnings of Knighthood', in *Institutionen, Kultur und Gesellschaft im Mittelalter: Festschrift für Josef Fleckenstein zum 65. Geburtstag*, ed. by Lutz Fenske, Werner Rösener, Thomas Zotz (Sigmaringen, 1984), pp. 549–66.

indeed Iwein symbolically carries out this sentence upon himself by stealing away from Arthur's retinue and casting off the social forms of knighthood in his stay as 'ein tôre in dem walde' (3260).

The term *ritters name* thus denotes both social status and a complex of ethical values in German texts from the mid-twelfth century onwards. From the use of this term in Hartmann's *Erec* and from lines 4413–15 of Chrétien's *Erec et Enide* it emerges that men who are called *chevalier* or *ritter* can, according to the behavioural norms of both romances, expect a more respectful treatment than other (here unspecified) categories of persons, and this is already a kind of social demarcation and categorization.[14]

Whilst the criterion of social distinction is common to Chrétien and Hartmann in their portrayal of knighthood, the exchange of words between Erec and Galoain in Hartmann's *Erec* (4172–204) is especially revealing for the German author's concerns since it has no correspondence in Chrétien's text, where the two men engage in combat without preliminaries (3571ff.). With regard to the conception of knighthood three points are worth special note in this exchange. Firstly, due to the fabricated story which Enite has told Galoain in Hartmann's work (3843–95), Galoain must believe that Erec is beneath Enite in social rank (see Enite's comment, 3868: 'ichn bin im niht genôzsam') and is an abductor, so that when the count says that it is only the fact of Erec's knighthood that saves him from being hanged (4179–81) he cannot be referring to some moral quality of chivalry, and moreover his readiness to let an abductor of unspecified origins go free merely because he is a knight suggests that the knightly title was connected with privileged treatment even for lesser knights who were below the old, free nobility in rank. Secondly, Erec, in his reply, first reproves Galoain for insulting someone who has *ritters name* (4201) before he points out that he is nobler than the count (4204) – it is as if Hartmann were at least as much concerned to emphasize the deference due to knights in general as to reprove Galoain for impoliteness to the son of a king. And, thirdly, Erec's comment that Galoain is acting in an 'uncourtly' fashion (4197: 'ir enthöveschet iuch'; 4202: 'ir sît an swachem hove erzogen') establishes a suggestive connection between the advocacy of politeness to knights and the institution of the court. It is no mere coincidence that the rise in prestige of knightly terminology and the elaboration of an unprecedentedly broad-ranging ideology of chivalry were paralleled chronologically by a growth in the cultural importance and self-

---

[14] On the Cadoc episode as the expression of a knightly 'Standesprivileg', see also Rudolf Voß, *Die Artusepik Hartmanns von Aue*, Literatur und Leben, N.F., 25 (Cologne/Vienna, 1983), pp. 107–08.

awareness of lordly courts in the twelfth century,[15] rather these developments were intimately connected, with the courts providing focal points for the socialization of knights away from the battlefield, and knights in turn exercising influence on the developing social and cultural forms of the courts, as the lady of the Tegernseer Liebesbriefe (c.1160–1180) points out when she describes the milites (i.e. the ritter) as arbiters of curialitas.[16] Hartmann's independent composition of the exchange between Galoain and Erec seems calculated almost programmatically to express this reciprocal link between respect for knighthood and the prestige of the court.

In the episode of Cadoc's captivity both Chrétien and Hartmann present it as particularly humiliating that a knight should suffer the indignity and the pain of being whipped (Chrétien, 4413–15, Hartmann, 5412–16, 5466–72). Here again the implied norms of the literary works correspond to norms of social reality, for corporal punishments with lash or rod appear time and again in historical sources as dishonouring servile punishments, 'Knechtesstrafen';[17] for instance, in Frederick Barbarossa's disciplinary measures for the army in 1158 a breach of camp discipline is punishable by the forfeiture of arms and exclusion from the army in the case of a knight (miles), whilst a subordinate servus may be shorn, flogged and branded on the cheek.[18] Thus the line which is drawn in Hartmann's Erec between knights and non-knights was not merely taken over by the German author as a poetic borrowing from French romance but also corresponds to social norms (in this case legal norms) in the historical reality of the German empire in the second half of the twelfth century.

---

[15] On the development of court culture in this period, see recently C. Stephen Jaeger, *The Origins of Courtliness: Civilizing Trends and the Formation of Courtly Ideals 939–1210* (Philadelphia, 1985); Bumke, *Höfische Kultur*; and *Höfische Literatur, Hofgesellschaft, höfische Lebensformen um 1200*, ed. by Gert Kaiser and Jan-Dirk Müller, Studia humaniora, 6 (Düsseldorf, 1986).

[16] Text in *Des Minnesangs Frühling*, ed. by Helmut Tervooren and Hugo Moser (Stuttgart 1977–81), vol. III, ii, p. 320; see Peter Ganz, 'curialis/hövesch', in *Höfische Literatur*, ed. by Kaiser and Müller, pp. 39–55 (p. 46).

[17] Wolfgang Schnelbögl, *Die innere Entwicklung der bayerischen Landfrieden des 13. Jahrhunderts*, Deutschrechtliche Beiträge, 13, Heft 2 (Heidelberg, 1932), p. 133. The beating of Iders's dwarf is typical, and carried out with general approval (Hartmann, *Erec*, 1064–77).

[18] Otto von Freising and Rahewin, *Gesta Frederici*, III, 31, ed. by Franz-Josef Schmale, with translation into German by Adolf Schmidt, Ausgewählte Quellen zur deutschen Geschichte des Mittelalters: Freiherr vom Stein-Gedächtnisausgabe, 17 (Darmstadt, 1965), p. 456.

III

The relationship of the terms *ritter* and *kneht* in the twelfth and thirteenth centuries was a complex and dynamic one that raises central questions about the social history of knighthood.[19] It is first of all essential for an understanding of this relationship to distinguish between the simple noun *kneht* and the adjective and noun combination *guoter kneht*, for whereas even great lords in manhood are referred to in a laudatory sense as *guote knehte* still into the thirteenth century, it is only in very exceptional circumstances, such as in relation to God, that such men are described simply as *knehte*.[20] The position was different in England, where *cniht* (the equivalent of German *kneht*) came to dominate over *ridere* and correspond to French *chevalier*, German *ritter*, Latin *miles* in the socially distinctive sense of 'knight'.[21] In German it was *ritter* that assumed dominance over *kneht*, and the twelfth century was the key period in this process. Already Old High German texts contain the three areas of meaning that were to determine the future development of *kneht*: male youth, service and warriordom. From this basis it would not have been surprising if the German *kneht* had followed the upward development of English *cniht*. Instead it was *ritter* that took the upward path, and during the twelfth century the terms *ritter* and *kneht* became increasingly distinct from each other, for just as *kneht* had for long, as a term of subordination, been distinct from *herre*, so it became distinct from and subordinated to *ritter*. A functional hierarchy thus emerges during the twelfth century in German texts, with *ritter* establishing itself in a higher position as the fully armed, mounted warrior, an upper level in lordly retinues, and the noble who has reached manhood and undergone a knighting ritual ('Schwert-leite'), whilst *kneht* remains connected with subordination in its opposition to *herre* and now *ritter*, having the senses of boy, lad, male servant or attendant, ordinary man-at-arms and, in the aristocratic sphere, squire in the sense of youth of kniʒhtly birth who has not yet been knighted.

Hartmann is typical of his time in distinguishing between *ritter* and *knehte* and in according less prestigious, more menial tasks to the latter than the former. For instance, in *Erec* two *knehte* administer a beating at

---

[19] For documentation on most of what follows in this paragraph, see my article 'Zum Verhältnis von *ritter* und *kneht* im 12. und 13. Jahrhundert', in *'Ja muz ich sunder riuwe sin': Festschrift für Karl Stackmann zum 15. Februar 1990*, ed. by Wolfgang Dinkelacker, Ludger Grenzmann, Werner Höver (Göttingen, 1990), pp. 19–35.

[20] See also Bumke, *Studien*, pp. 88–89.

[21] However, usage in the *Anglo-Saxon Chronicle* suggests some resistance to applying the term *cniht* to a prince still *c.*1130 (see Flori, *L'essor*, p. 61).

Erec's command (1065), Galoain's *kneht* (3522, 3542, 3546, 3558) carries food and water for a washing of hands, Oringles's *knehte* (6309) cut branches for a bier, Guivreiz's *knehte* (7080) prepare bivouacs for Erec, Enite, Guivreiz and the knights accompanying them, and time and again the tending of horses appears as the task of a *kneht* (350ff., 3272ff., 3431ff., 3454ff., 4002f., 4103f., 7364f.). By contrast *ritter* ride independently across the lands (5ff., 5649ff.) accompany ladies on social visits of an evening (1389ff.), appear as guests at a prince's wedding feast (2129), and fight in armour, using the aristocratic weapons of sword and lance in serious combats (e.g. 732–950, 4378–438, 9070–315) and in the tournament (2413–807), at which *knaben* appear carrying clubs in a subordinate capacity (2344–50).

This constellation of *ritter* and *kneht* in Hartmann's work corresponds to the elevation in status of *chevalier* above *serjant* and *escuiier* in Chrétien's *Erec et Enide*. Indeed Hartmann's reference to 'ritter unde knehte' at Erec's court (2975) is based on Chrétien's comment: 'Tant fu blasmez de totes janz,/ De chevaliers et de serjanz' (2463–64); and Galoain's servant or squire, who is referred to in Hartmann's text as a *kneht* (3522, 3542, 3546, 3558) and as a *knabe* (3491, 3499, 3510, 3541, 3575) and whom Erec addresses as *knabe* (3559, 3590, 3599), appears in Chrétien's text as an *escuiier(s)* (3124, 3131, 3168, 3170, 3179, 3209, 3216) and a *serjanz* (3165, 3233), and is clearly in neither author's view a knight. However, it is again essential to note that this correspondence of Hartmann and Chrétien on the hierarchy of *ritter* and *kneht* does not indicate that we are dealing solely with a literary borrowing from France, i.e. with a social gradation that would have seemed foreign to Hartmann's German audience, for historical sources in twelfth-century Germany (legal sources and chronicles) also raise the *milites* above *servi*, *famuli*, *armigeri*,[22] so that the social structure within Hartmann's text corresponds on this point to the contemporary German reality.

Whereas Hartmann thus distinguishes *ritter* from *kneht*, he nevertheless applies the term *guoter kneht* precisely to knights; indeed all the named persons whom Hartmann describes as *guote knehte* are also described as *ritter*, so that the term *guoter kneht* appears in his works as an alternative expression for *ritter*.[23] What light does this use of *guoter*

---

[22] Documentation in my article, 'Zum Verhältnis von *ritter* und *kneht*'.
[23] See also Pérennec, I, p. 68. The term *guoter kneht* is applied in *Erec* to Iders (700), Gawein (1629), Erec (3112, 3345, 3679), Cadoc (5413), Guivreiz (6914), Mabonagrin (8386), and amongst other group usages to the knights at Arthur's court (1502, 1615, 1790); in *Iwein* it is applied to Iwein by Gawein (2513, 2901) and to Iwein and Gawein by the narrator (6934, 6940, 7342). It is interesting that in *Iwein* it is always Gawein's presence that prompts the use of the term. (These findings do not mean that *guoter kneht* applied only to knights around 1200, for Thomasin von Zirklære refers to Walther von der Vogelweide as *der guote kneht* (*Der wälsche Gast*, ed. by Heinrich Rückert (Quedlinburg/Leipzig, 1852; repr. Berlin, 1965, l. 11191), and nowhere is Walther documented as a *ritter* or *miles*).

kneht throw on the semantics of *ritter*? Pérennec rightly sees a distinction between *ritter* and *kneht* in his study of the semantics of *ritter* in Hartmann's *Erec* (I, p. 68), but he goes on to suggest that the use of the term *guoter kneht* beside *ritter* to render the concept of knighthood detracts from the clarity of this concept as an indication of social status (I, pp. 70–71). In other words, for Pérennec the conjoint use of *guoter kneht* and *ritter* casts further doubt on the existence of a 'Ritterstand' as a socially defined group in Germany at the time of Hartmann's adapting Chrétien's *Erec et Enide* (I, p. 70). However, a closer look at the evidence suggests, first, that the conjoint use of *ritter* and *guoter kneht* does not indicate some social imprecision of the term *ritter* but shows that *guoter kneht* has become semantically detached from the simple *kneht* (a point which Pérennec himself makes (I, p. 68) without drawing the full conclusion from it), and, second, that *guoter kneht* was in any case being ousted lexically by *ritter* already at the time of Hartmann's writing, which means that we have to place Hartmann's adaptations in their context in a broader semantic process in order to understand the relation of *ritter* and *guoter kneht*.

This last point deserves elaboration. From the earliest occurrences of the word *ritter* it competed with *guoter kneht* in the developing semantic field of knighthood, and Bumke's list of the frequency of occurrence of the terms *ritter*, *helt*, *degen*, *wîgant*, *recke* and *guoter kneht* in works from the middle of the eleventh century to the middle of the thirteenth century (*Studien*, pp. 32–34) provides valuable statistical evidence about the course of this competition. In the three lists printed on pp. 54–55 I have first divided Bumke's list into the four chronological periods *c*.1060–*c*.1170, *c*.1170–*c*.1200, *c*.1200–*c*.1220, *c*.1220–*c*.1250, and I have provided total occurrences of *ritter* and *guoter kneht* and ratios for each of these periods on the basis of Bumke's totals for the individual works. Many datings are of course merely approximate, but this does not affect the overall pattern. I have also taken from Bumke's list a chronological run of the frequency of occurrence of *ritter* and *guoter kneht* in individual texts from the mid-twelfth century to the early thirteenth century, and finally a chronological run of these two terms together with the old heroic terms from the whole period covered by Bumke. These two runs are merely representative selections from Bumke's list, which the reader is urged to consult in full. These lists yield some interesting figures. For about a century from the earliest attestation of *ritter* the term *guoter kneht* has a distinct and fairly steady numerical preponderance with a *ritter* : *guoter kneht* ratio averaging 0.7 : 1. *Guoter kneht* seems very stable in this period, for it appears in 15 of the 16 works which make up this first chronological block in Bumke's complete list, whilst *ritter* appears in 12; and *guoter kneht* is attested more often than *ritter* in 9 of these 16 works, *ritter* more often than *guoter kneht* in only 4 (the earliest being the *Vorauer*

Alexander). The last thirty years or so of the twelfth century bring a remarkable change as the *ritter* : *guoter kneht* ratio moves to 7.9 : 1, and the trend continues in the period *c.*1200–*c.*1220 with a further shift to 35.7 : 1. The position seems to stabilise in the period *c.*1220–*c.*1250 with a ratio of 36.2 : 1, but this figure is skewed by the 55 occurrences of *guoter kneht* in Heinrich von dem Türlin's *Krone* (more than in all the other works *c.*1200–*c.*1250 put together!), and if this erratic work is taken out, the last thirty years or so of Bumke's list produce a *ritter* : *guoter kneht* ratio of 125.8 : 1. An overall pattern thus emerges of *guoter kneht* retreating sharply relative to *ritter* in the decades (given the difficulty of dating many works) from perhaps around 1170 to 1180. In the 62 works from *c.*1170–*c.*1250 *guoter kneht* outnumbers *ritter* in only two works (*Reinhart Fuchs* with 5 *guoter kneht* and 2 *ritter*, *Oberdeutscher Servatius* with 3 *guoter kneht* and 2 *ritter*), *ritter* outnumbers *guoter kneht* in 57. The retreat of *guoter kneht* is further evidenced by the fact that, of the 62 works in Bumke's list *c.*1170–*c.*1250 only 3 lack occurrences of *ritter*, whilst 36 lack occurrences of *guoter kneht*. Such broad-ranging and diverse works as Wolfram's *Parzival* and *Willehalm*, the *Sächsische Weltchronik* and Rudolf von Ems's *Guter Gerhard*, *Willehalm* and *Alexander*, Berthold von Holle's *Demantin* and Ulrich von Liechtenstein's *Frauendienst* have no occurrences of *guoter kneht*, but together amass a staggering 1729 occurrences of *ritter*. A further significant point is that, in the competition with *ritter*, the term *guoter kneht* behaves quite differently from the other heroic terms, for once *ritter* has gained the upper hand over *guoter kneht* in the late twelfth century the term *guoter kneht* becomes a rarity, or is avoided completely, even in works in which the old heroic terms, especially *helt* and *degen*, continue to figure frequently (e.g. in the *Nibelungenlied*, *Parzival*, *Wigalois*, the works of Rudolf von Ems). In other words, what we are witnessing is not a battle between *ritter* and the older heroic terms in general, but quite specifically one between *ritter* and *guoter kneht*, in which *guoter kneht* goes into decline when *ritter* makes its steep ascent.

Hartmann's *œuvre* reflects the key transitional stage in this contest in the last decades of the twelfth century, for the distribution of the 25 occurrences of *guoter kneht* in Hartmann's narrative works shows that he used the term less with the passage of time. Already in *Erec* Hartmann uses *guoter kneht* less often, relative to *ritter*, than was the practice of authors earlier in the century, the *ritter* : *guoter kneht* ratio of 6.7 : 1 in *Erec* (134 *ritter*, 20 *guoter kneht*) closely matching the mean of 7.9 : 1 for the period *c.*1170–*c.*1200; and *guoter kneht* figures even less often in Hartmann's later works, never in *Gregorius* and *Der arme Heinrich* and only 5 times in *Iwein*, where the *ritter* : *guoter kneht* ratio has slipped to 16.6 : 1 (83 *ritter*, 5 *guoter kneht*). Thus 80% of the occurrences of *guoter kneht* in Hartmann's works figure in his first romance, *Erec*. Moreover, of the 20 occurrences in *Erec*, 10 appear in the first quarter of the work (17, 700, 835, 903, 1502, 1615, 1629, 1790, 2070, 2384); of the 25 occurrences of *guoter kneht* in Hartmann's works as a whole 23 are in the rhyme, and the only two internally in the line are in the first third of *Erec* (17, 3112). We thus have a clear pattern of Hartmann using the term *guoter kneht* more often in the opening stages of his first romance than he ever does later. This higher frequency of *guoter kneht* in the early stages of *Erec* surely shows that here Hartmann is still finding his feet stylistically, he is still drawing on an older stylistic tradition to use quite frequently a term which was on the retreat and which he himself will use less often later in the very same work. The appearance of *guoter kneht* in a rhyming position in all its occurrences in Hartmann after line 3112 of *Erec* indicates a major reason why this term survived as long as it did, i.e. its convenience in providing a rhyme (especially with *reht*). Conversely *ritter* is extremely difficult to accommodate in a rhyme,[24] and its prolific use in rhymed poetry from the last decades of the twelfth century onwards despite this encumbrance testifies to the strength of the socio-cultural impetus that was driving this word.

These findings suggest after all some substance in Edward Schröder's view that *guoter kneht* was becoming an archaism before the end of the twelfth century, and more broadly that the developing relations of the terms *ritter* and *kneht* and *ritter* and *guoter kneht* show 'die festigung eines "ritterstandes"' in the second half of the twelfth century.[25] At the very least it seems that already in Hartmann's works the term *guoter kneht* is too clearly detached from the simple *kneht* and too clearly on the retreat for its use conjointly with *ritter* to obscure the social reference of the concept of knighthood.

IV

With regard to the relation of knights to other social categories it is particularly important to note that considerations of social estate ('ständerechtliche Gesichtspunkte') came sharply to the fore during the second half of the twelfth century in the German empire.[26] This was a period of increasingly marked social differentiation, when *milites*/*ritter* appear in sources of the most varied kinds as a group distinguished not

---

[24] See Edmund Wiessner, 'Höfisches Rittertum', in *Deutsche Wortgeschichte*, ed. by Friedrich Maurer and Friedrich Stroh, 2nd edn, 3 vols (Berlin, 1959–60), I, 161; Bumke, *Studien*, p. 22.

[25] Edward Schröder, 'Die Datierung des deutschen Rolandsliedes', *ZfdA*, 65 (1928), 289–96 (p. 295).

[26] Joachim Gernhuber, *Die Landfriedensbewegung in Deutschland bis zum Mainzer Reichslandfrieden von 1235*, Bonner Rechtswissenschaftliche Abhandlungen, 44 (Bonn, 1952), p. 136.

only from *servi, famuli/knehte* but especially (developing earlier tendencies) from peasants (*rustici/gebûre, bûliute*) and also from merchants (*mercatores/koufliute*). This social *ordo* mentality receives a legal sanction already in Barbarossa's first peace law of 1152, which grants different and more generous legal rights to the *miles* (knight) than to the *rusticus* and the *mercator*,[27] and a religious sanction in sermon no. 60 of the *Speculum ecclesiae*, which addresses *riter, chôflute* and *bulute* as different estates,[28] and the triad of knight, peasant and merchant appears in other vernacular texts, for instance in the *Kaiserchronik* (8096–115) and in Heinrich von Veldeke's *Eneide* (12152–53). The legislation of Frederick Barbarossa's reign (1152–1190) was particularly concerned to establish a sharp distinction between knighthood and peasantry,[29] and after the knights had been granted a more privileged legal status than the rustics in 1152, the peace law against arsonists of 1186 went a step further by forbidding the granting of the belt of knighthood to the sons of *rustici*.[30] The high cost of acquiring and maintaining chivalric equipment meant that knighthood had *de facto* long been associated with some material substance, and now *de iure* restrictions of birth status emerge. Thus precisely during the period of Hartmann's literary activity even the lesser knighthood was becoming an increasingly exclusive social group, its ranks closing in the gradual formation of a petty nobility, a 'niederer Adel'.[31] The distinction made between the worlds of knight and peasant in courtly literature from the late twelfth century on is a major cultural reflection of this process. Moreover, a passage in Hartmann's *Gregorius* which the German author introduced quite independently of his French source, matches the historical evidence to indicate that towards the end

[27] MGH, *Constitutiones*, I, no. 140, cap. 10 and 13 (pp. 197–98).
[28] *Speculum Ecclesiae: Eine frühmittelhochdeutsche Predigtsammlung (Cgm. 39)*, ed. by Gert Mellbourn, Lunder Germanistische Forschungen, 12 (Lund/Copenhagen, 1944); on knighthood as a socially distinctive concept in early sermons, see Karl Otto Brogsitter, '*Miles, chevalier* und *ritter*', in *Sprachliche Interferenz: Festschrift für Werner Betz zum 65. Geburtstag*, ed. by Herbert Kolb and others (Tübingen, 1977), pp. 421–35.
[29] Gernhuber, p. 136. On the importance of the demarcation of knights from peasants for the developing class consciousness of knighthood, see Josef Fleckenstein, 'Zur Frage der Abgrenzung von Bauer und Ritter', in *Wort und Begriff 'Bauer'*, ed. by Reinhard Wenskus, Herbert Jankuhn, Klaus Grinda, Abh. d. Ak. d. Wiss. in Göttingen, Philol.-Hist. Kl., 3. Folge, Nr. 89 (Göttingen, 1975), pp. 246–53; Werner Rösener, 'Bauer und Ritter im Hochmittelalter', in *Festschrift Fleckenstein* (see n. 13 above), pp. 665–92.
[30] MGH, *Constitutiones*, I, no. 318, cap. 20 (p. 451). See Eberhard Otto, 'Von der Abschließung des Ritterstandes', *HZ*, 162 (1940), 19–39; Josef Fleckenstein, 'Zum Problem der Abschließung des Ritterstandes', in *Historische Forschungen für Walter Schlesinger*, ed. by Helmut Beumann (Cologne/Vienna, 1974), pp. 252–71.
[31] On this process, see *Herrschaftsstruktur und Ständebildung: Beiträge zur Typologie der österreichischen Länder aus ihren mittelalterlichen Grundlagen*, vol. 1: Peter Feldbauer, *Herren und Ritter* (Munich, 1973), pp. 42ff., 99ff. and passim; *Herrschaft und Stand: Untersuchungen zur Sozialgeschichte im 13. Jahrhundert*, ed. by Josef Fleckenstein, Veröffentlichungen des Max-Planck-Instituts für Geschichte, 51 (Göttingen, 1977), especially the essay by Fleckenstein, 'Die Entstehung des niederen Adels und das Rittertum' (pp. 17–39).

of the twelfth century the status of knighthood was indeed in Germany normally dependent on a certain degree of birth and wealth, as the young Gregorius reveals that he would dearly love to become a knight if only he had the *geburt* and the *guot*.[32]

All this evidence suggests that in Hartmann's view, and on the horizon of expectation of his German audience, knights (*ritter/milites*) formed an actual social category that was distinct from other categories even in legal status, and that was becoming more exclusive as a matter of legal norm. It is true that, as Pérennec points out (I, p. 75), *ritter* are set off against persons belonging to other categories, for instance peasants and merchants, more explicitly in some other works than in Hartmann's *Erec*. However this is not, I think, due to some vagueness in the social reference of the term *ritter* in Hartmann's *Erec*, but to the fact that this romance has a narrower angle of social vision than the other texts we have just considered. Barbarossa's peace laws take into consideration the entire population, sermon no. 60 in the *Speculum ecclesiae* is addressed to all the social estates, and the historical perspectives of the *Kaiserchronik* and Veldeke's *Eneide* are broad enough to allow at least marginal reference to peasants and merchants. Hartmann's *Erec*, however, has a narrower social perspective, the work concentrates exclusively on the knightly hero and his partner, and if knights are not explicitly set off against peasants and merchants, it is because these latter groups are simply never mentioned in the text. And this non-appearance is itself a poetic expression of the social class distinctions which emerge explicitly in the German peace laws of the second half of the twelfth century.

Already Chrétien's *Erec et Enide* focuses sharply on the hero knight and his partner, and Hartmann goes even further in limiting the narrative perspective to the hero and the knightly world. For instance when Erec returns to his homeland of Carnant Chrétien presents a vivid picture with a broad social spectrum of elegant and wealthy clerks (2324–25: 'De jantis clers bien afeitiez,/ Qui bien despandoient lor rantes'; compare 2334, 2340) and influential *borjois* (2327: 'borjois poesteïz', compare 2345, 2389) beside the knights and ladies (2322, compare 2334, 2345, 2389), whilst Hartmann at the corresponding point refers only briefly and generally to king Lac's *mâge unde man* (2894), thus omitting Chrétien's evocation of non-knightly persons. This abbreviation of the social spectrum is all the more striking because Hartmann has just before this passage massively expanded Chrétien's account of the

---

[32] *Gregorius*, ed. by Hermann Paul, 13th edn, rev. by Burghart Wachinger, ATB, 2 (Tübingen, 1984), ll. 1496–1503. On Hartmann's originality in this passage, see W.J. McCann, 'Gregorius's Interview with the Abbot. A Comparative Study', *MLR*, 73 (1978), 82–95.

tournament, which is a central feature of the knightly world.[33] These are characteristic shifts of accent in Hartmann's adaptation of Chrétien's *Erec et Enide*, and they are accompanied by a shift of narrative tone in the attitude of the two authors towards the chivalric hero as Chrétien narrates with greater detachment whilst Hartmann tends to identify more strongly with his hero.[34] As Karl Bertau has seen, this shift has a sociological aspect, for the sense of detachment in Chrétien's presentation of chivalric culture, as in other French romances, probably betrays the perspective of an author who is not himself a knight, but a clerically trained court poet looking at knighthood from the outside and mingling glorification with a note of irony, whilst Hartmann, as a knightly poet, presents in his depiction of knighthood a poetic stylisation of the profession and values of his own social class from more of an inside perspective.[35] The tendency to moralization in the use of knightly vocabulary, which Pérennec impressively describes as a key feature of Hartmann's style in adapting Chrétien's romances (I, pp. 57ff.), should also be seen in this light, as the German author's selectively legitimatory poetic projection of the social category knighthood, which was emerging ever more clearly in the historical sources of the German empire during the second half of the twelfth century, and which finds in the author and *ritter* Hartmann its first decisive spokesman.

V

Already the war-ravaged eleventh century produced a steep increase in the number of *ministeriales* in the armed retinues of German lords, and it has been calculated that by the twelfth century *ministeriales* outnumbered free vassals by some three or four to one in German knighthood.[36] This numerical relation makes study of the *ministeriales*

[33] See my article 'The Tournament in the Works of Hartmann von Aue: Motifs, Style, Functions', in *Hartmann von Aue: Changing Perspectives: London Symposium 1985*, ed. by Timothy McFarland and Silvia Ranawake, GAG, 486 (Göppingen, 1988), pp. 233–51.
[34] See also Karl Bertau, *Deutsche Literatur im europäischen Mittelalter*, 2 vols (Munich, 1972–73), I, 565–66.
[35] Bertau, I, 436. Jaeger (see n. 15 above) also sees the transition from Chrétien to Hartmann (and Wolfram) as a matter of social class, with the German knightly authors internalizing 'a code of behaviour urged on the knightly class by a cleric' (p. 243). In pointing to Hartmann's insider status I do not wish to suggest that he portrays knighthood quite without irony or criticism, rather, as D.H. Green has shown, whilst Hartmann's knightly status gives his work a different social dimension from that of the French romances written by clerical court-poets, the fact of Hartmann's literacy also sets him (like other German knightly authors) apart from the majority of illiterate knights and thus provides for some degree of distance between the German poet and his own class (D.H. Green, *Irony in the Medieval Romance* (Cambridge, 1979), pp. 361–63).
[36] Josef Fleckenstein, 'Vom Rittertum der Stauferzeit am Oberrhein', *Alemannisches Jahrbuch* (1979–80), pp. 21–42 (p. 26).

essential for an understanding of German knighthood, all the more so in our context since Hartmann describes himself as a knight and a *ministerialis* (*Der arme Heinrich*, 1–5: *ritter* and *dienstman*), and it may be useful to close by taking up from Benjamin Arnold's recent study of the German *ministeriales*[37] some observations which may help students of literature by throwing light on the historical context of Chrétien's and Hartmann's treatment of knighthood.

First, with regard to the position within Germany, the sword-bearing aristocracy did not form a homogeneous juridical class in the twelfth century, and Arnold discusses 'the awkward but necessary distinction between knights who were *ministeriales* and knights who were *liberi* [which] continued to be made well into the thirteenth century' (p. 26). But he also points out that the lifestyle, the values and the social privileges of knighthood were common to the various levels of the aristocratic hierarchy, so that 'the high nobility, the free knights, and the *ministeriales* were often viewed as belonging to one knighthood, "the order of knights" as a charter of 1139 put it, including in this *ordo* a duke, two counts, and five prominent *ministeriales* belonging to the archbishop of Cologne' (p. 111); and 'twelfth-century chronicles also assumed that free and unfree knights belonged to one military and social community' (p. 112). Arnold's evidence for this overarching sense of a knighthood linking high nobles and *ministeriales* is drawn mainly from about the middle of the twelfth century onwards, which matches chronologically the various types of evidence adduced earlier in this article to point to the crystallization of knighthood as a distinctive social category in Germany, raised above the mass of the population. Arnold's study of the *ministeriales* thus again suggests that the rise of the term *ritter* as a designation for the heterogeneous and shifting aristocracy of German free nobles and *ministeriales* was not merely a poetic importation from France but is paralleled in the sober language of charters and chronicles in Germany and has roots in the German social soil.

Second, as regards a comparison of Germany and France, Arnold analyses the special legal status of the German *ministeriales*, pointing out that whereas French knights were free men constrained by the contract of vassalage, German *ministeriales* were not free men but bound by hereditary duty to the lord into whose ownership they were born (p. 18). However, it is important not to exaggerate this difference between the French and German secular aristocracies. For one thing, whilst knights were free men in France there were nevertheless marked social distinctions between simple knights and lords (*milites* and *domini*), though interestingly these distinctions between the levels of the French aristocracy seem to have been subject to some erosion in the late twelfth

---

[37] Benjamin Arnold, *German Knighthood 1050–1300* (Oxford, 1985).

century[38] in a process which is remarkably similar to contemporary developments in the position of the *ministeriales* within the German aristocracy. Further, some German *ministeriales* towered above most French free knights in their actual power: most imperial *ministeriales* had retinues of their own knights (Arnold, p. 130), and the famous Wernher of Bolanden had seventeen castles of his own and received 1100 knightly homages (Arnold, p. 129). Service as a *ministerialis* was indeed more a means of social advancement than a burdensome yoke, and even the lesser *ministeriales* came to be reckoned as noblemen during the twelfth century because of the social prestige of the knightly function which was their profession (Arnold, pp. 69–75). This is the broad historical underpinning for Hartmann's associating *ritters name* with social prestige. Arnold himself stresses the common lifestyle which bound the German *ministeriales* into the larger framework of western European chivalry (p. 111), and a perceptive reviewer of Arnold's book further relativises the abstract legal difference between German *ministeriales* and 'western' knights by pointing out that 'in practice there was very little that a free knight could do and a *ministerialis* could not'.[39]

All this is not, of course, to place the least *ministerialis* on a par with the imperial princes and thus deny the many gradations of wealth and legal status that existed within the German aristocracy, nor is it to sweep aside the differences between France and Germany. Indeed it may be that some changes in Hartmann's adaptation of Chrétien's *Erec et Enide* were motivated by the particular situation of the *ministeriales* in the German hierarchy, though it is not the purpose of this article to discuss these. But it seems appropriate in the present state of research into German courtly literature to draw attention also to the essential common features in the social position of knighthood in Chrétien's northern France and Hartmann's southern Germany as an important pragmatic factor in Hartmann's reception of Chrétien's romances, indeed in the German reception of French chivalric poetry in general in the decades around 1200: in France and in Germany knighthood was connected with an expensive military lifestyle; in both areas even the lesser knights enjoyed higher social prestige than the majority of the population; in both areas there was some rapprochement of higher and lower men in knighthood; and in both areas knighthood was becoming associated with a range of social and ideological values that reached beyond the purely military. In France and in Germany these developments seem especially marked in the late twelfth century, so that the emergence of chivalry as a major poetic theme in this period has its place

[38] Georges Duby, 'Situation de la noblesse en France au début du XIIIe siècle', in Georges Duby, *Hommes et structures du moyen âge: Receuil d'articles*, Le savoir historique, 1 (Paris/The Hague, 1973), pp. 343–52.
[39] John Gillingham, review in *English Historical Review*, 101 (1986), 932–33.

in a broader historical process. Nor does it detract from the different but in each case pioneering literary achievements of Chrétien and Hartmann if we remember that knighthood, which is of such unprecedented importance in their works, is – to modify a dictum of Bumke's – at least as much a phenomenon of social history as of the history of ideas.

Material taken from Bumke's list of the frequency of occurrence of *ritter* and the old heroic terms
(*Studien zum Ritterbegriff*, pp. 32–34)

1. Chronological breakdown of Bumke's list

	No. of works	*ritter*	*guoter kneht*	Ratio *ritter* : *guoter kneht*
c.1060–c.1170 (*Wiener Genesis – Graf Rudolf*)	16	77	113	0.7 : 1
c.1170–c.1200 (Eilhart – *Lanzelet*)	23	793	100	7.9 : 1
c.1200–c.1220 (*Nibelungenlied – Flore*)	16	1179	33	35.7 : 1
c.1220–c.1250 (*Walther-Epos* – Liechtenstein, *Frd.*)	23	2570	71	36.2 : 1
c.1220–c.1250 (without Türlin, *Krone*)	22	2013	16	125.8 : 1

2. *ritter/guoter kneht* occurrences in individual works, mid-twelfth century to early thirteenth century

Rolandslied	4/24	Herbort	113/3
Rother	28/27	*Lanzelet*	208/28
Kaiserchronik	10/23	*Nibelungenlied*	170/4
Eilhart	38/20	*Parzival*	372/0
Eneide	59/15	*Willehalm*	89/0
Erec	134/20	Gottfried	64/5
Gregorius	14/0	*Wigalois*	335/2
Armer Heinrich	3/0	Thomasin von	
Iwein	83/5	Zirklære	75/1

3. *ritter*/old heroic terms/*guoter kneht* occurrences, mid-eleventh
to mid-thirteenth century

	ritter	helt	degen	wîgant	recke	guoter kneht
Wiener Genesis	1	5	–	–	1	1
Annolied	–	4	–	–	2	2
Millst. Genesis	3	7	5	3	2	4
Rother	28	99	9	35	27	27
Kaiserchronik	10	102	3	11	6	23
Eneide	59	132	19	39	1	15
Erec	134	1	11	–	–	20
Iwein	83	4	4	–	–	5
Nibelungenlied	170	390	362	2	492	4
Parzival	372	124	65	19	4	–
Gottfried	64	1	–	–	–	5
Wigalois	335	69	29	6	1	2
Sächs. Weltchronik	92	3	–	–	–	–
R. v. Ems, G. Gerhard	59	4	6	6	–	–
R. v. Ems, Willehalm	200	61	128	58	–	–
R. v. Ems, Alexander	76	120	187	91	–	–
Türlin, Krone	557	46	40	10	81	55 (!)
Holle, Demantin	446	128	6	–	–	–
Liechtenstein, Frd.	395	3	6	–	–	–

NOTE: In the above tables, the chronological ordering follows Bumke,
placing works of an author together. Ratios are rounded to the first decimal
point.

The Heroine's Loyalty in Hartmann's and Chrétien's Erec

BERNARD WILLSON

In Hartmann's *Erec*, after the protagonists have been reconciled and the hero is again treating his wife as she should be treated, the narrator says that Erec took Enite on the adventures and was so unkind to her because he wanted to test her. She has now passed that test and he knows 'rehte âne wân' that she is 'ein rehtez wîp'. He has made completely sure of her, like gold that has been cleansed in the crucible. He now knows that she has *triuwe* and *stæte* (6778–91).[1]

In this short passage of fourteen lines the word *reht* occurs three times, one of them as an inflected adjective qualifying *wîp*. The emphatic repetition of this word cannot but be meaningful: it strongly suggests that the function of the test is to validate in Erec's eyes the 'rightness' of Enite's behaviour on the adventures. It also appears to confirm that in Karnant Erec had, or thought he had, grounds for doubting whether Enite possessed the qualities of *triuwe* and *stæte* without which a wife is not a wife, i.e. is not *reht*. If she had already shown those qualities there to Erec's satisfaction there would have been no need for a test. It is only because he has tested her that he knows *rehte* that she is 'ein rehtez wîp'. In other words, this is a very emphatic statement of the fact that on the adventures Enite has, as it were, 'done right' by her wifehood, that is to say, has fulfilled its *reht*, or *ordo*, which is the same thing.[2]

By contrast, Chrétien does not specifically say that Enide was tested so that she could prove to Erec that she had the qualities essential to wifehood. At this point in the narrative *his* Erec addresses Enide as 'ma dolce suer' and says that the test has proved that she loves him perfectly

---

[1] References are to *Erec von Hartmann von Aue*, ed. by Albert Leitzmann, continued by Ludwig Wolff, 6th edn, prepared by Christoph Cormeau and Kurt Gärtner, ATB, 39 (Tübingen, 1985).

[2] See Thomasin von Zirclaria, *Der wälsche Gast*, ed. by Heinrich Rückert with an introduction and index by Friedrich Neumann, Deutsche Neudrucke, Reihe Texte des Mittelalters (Berlin, 1965) for the equation of *reht* and *ordo*: 'daz reht ist über al/ an allen dingen mâze, wâge, zal./ ân reht mac niemen genesen' (12375–77).

(4882–87).[3] There is no mention here of loyalty and constancy or of what might be called, in Hartmann's terms, 'right wifeliness', although Chrétien does, of course, praise Enide's loyalty on a number of occasions.

In the following I hope to show that it is Hartmann's intention to give the clearest possible articulation to what he conceives as *wîbes reht* (if we understand *wîp* in the narrower sense of 'wife' and not in the wider one of 'woman', as Wolfram uses it in the phrase in *Parzival* 4,11) and that he does this by placing a much heavier emphasis than Chrétien on the divine origins and connections of the Christian marriage relationship. There is undoubtedly a direct link between Hartmann's conception of the *reht*, and therefore *ordo*, of wifehood in a Christian marriage and the much more obviously religious character of the German poem, since *ordo* is essentially a religious concept.[4] Hartmann's definition of a 'rehtez wîp' as one who shows *triuwe* and *stæte*, which are arguably the two most meaningful ethical terms in classical Middle High German, is a fundamental constituent of this powerful religious approach, which should hardly surprise us, since what is Christian marriage all about, if not loyalty and constancy?[5]

On the adventures, then, as opposed to in Karnant, Enite proves to Erec's satisfaction that she conforms to the *reht* of a wife, but she does not do so entirely alone. She has a close relationship with God, who becomes deeply involved in her affairs. In the first encounter, with the three robbers, we find her in a state of *zwîvel* (3145) as to how to implement her wifely *triuwe* and *stæte*. She can only warn Erec by speaking to him, but this he has forbidden her to do, and as a would-be dutiful wife she has promised to comply (3103–05). If she breaks her promise and disobeys him she will be showing *untriuwe* and *unstæte*, since Christian tradition requires a wife to submit to the authority of her husband, i.e. *obey* him.[6] But if she does not break her promise and warn Erec she will be showing *untriuwe* and *unstæte* in another way, for she will have made no attempt to save his life, when she could well have done so. This is too big a problem for Enite to solve unaided and so she prays to God for help: 'rîcher got der guote,/ ze dînen genâden suoche ich rât:/ dû weist al eine wiez mir stât' (3149–51). After this prayer, which goes on for eighteen lines, the narrator remarks: 'nû kam der

---

3   References are to *Les Romans de Chrétien de Troyes, I: Erec et Enide*, ed. by Mario Roques, CFMA, 80 (Paris, 1966).

4   See Wisdom 11. 21: 'Sed omnia mensura et numero et pondere disposuisti.'

5   See I Corinthians 7. 10–11: 'His enim qui matrimonio juncti sunt praecipio non ego sed Dominus, uxorem a viro non discedere; quod si discesserit, manere innuptam aut viro suo reconciliari: et vir uxorem ne dimittat.'

6   See Ephesians 5. 22–24: 'Mulieres viris suis subjectae sint sicut Domino. Quoniam vir caput est mulieris, sicut Christus caput est ecclesiae, ipse salvator corporis. Sed ut ecclesia subjecta est Christo, ita et mulieres viris suis in omnibus.'

muot in ir gedanc' (3167), and then articulates the idea that came into her head, namely that Erec's life is worth more than hers. She then warns Erec, which is a sure indication that she has received the advice she prayed for: the idea of sacrificing herself rather than let Erec die is put into her head by God. He helps her resolve her *zwîvel*.[7] In thus speaking to Erec and warning him, she behaves inordinately (i.e. fails to conform to the *ordo* of wifehood) at a lower level, since she disobeys her husband. But at the same time she shows a higher order of *triuwe* and *stæte* than she would have done if she had obeyed him and not spoken, which wholly excuses her lower-level *inordinatio*, since the hierarchical gradualism of the *ordo*-concept requires that a higher 'good' should always take precedence over a lower.[8] Enite's lower-level *inordinatio* is not, however, excused by Erec, who does not yet realise that she is showing a higher, transcendent, order of *triuwe* and *stæte*, which is of divine provenance. In Chrétien the same conflict is of course present and the heroine takes the same decision to warn Erec (2839), showing the same higher order of loyalty, but there is no hint that any help was received from God. Enide simply says: 'Dex [. . .] que porrai dire?' (2829), whereas Hartmann clearly means God to be seen as answering her explicit prayer for advice. Otherwise the prayer is meaningless.

Exactly the same thing happens in the next encounter, with five more robbers. Enite is very concerned when she sees them preparing to attack Erec, but she is sure that if she warns him he will carry out his threat to kill her. But she also believes that if she allows *him* to be killed she will burn in hell for her *untriuwe*, and quite rightly (*rehte*, 3369). So once again she asks God for his advice (3371–73) and again obviously receives it, since she at once begs Erec to listen to her 'durch got' (3380). Chrétien also highlights the heroine's dilemma, but again God is not specifically asked for advice in his version. Nor is there any hint that Enide thinks that disloyalty to one's husband is punishable by eternal damnation, as Hartmann's heroine does. In the German poem the close links between the Christian ethical background and the loyalty and constancy a wife must show in order to be *reht* are much more clearly visible. But Erec still sees Enite's behaviour as *untriuwe* and *unstæte*, which it is, at a lower level, and after defeating the second band of robbers he insults her by calling her a 'wîp vil ungezogen' (3404). Enite's defence is that she has

---

[7] The same thing happens in *Gregorius*: when the hero's mother and the wise man are at a loss to know what to do with the new-born baby, they ask God for his advice, and immediately afterwards the narrator says: 'nû kam in vaste in den muot' (699). See also *Gregorius* 3219, though here God is explicitly named. References are to *Gregorius von Hartmann von Aue*, ed. by Hermann Paul, 13th edn, prepared by Burghart Wachinger, ATB, 2 (Tübingen, 1984).

[8] I have drawn attention to this in earlier publications. See '*Triuwe* and *untriuwe* in Hartmann's *Erec*', GQ, 43 (1970), 5–23 (pp.6ff.), and my Inaugural Lecture, *Love and Order in the Medieval German Courtly Epic* (Leicester, 1973), pp. 12ff.

acted out of *triuwe* (3413ff.), but instead of rewarding her for this *triuwe* he gives her five more horses to look after, thus perverting the *reht* of a *vrouwe*, as he did with the first three horses: '[. . .] wider vrouwen site/ und wider ir reht [. . .]' (3445–46). God, however, who is the essence of order and measure and rightness, knows how to treat a noble lady who shows *triuwe*, and who is also a *wîp* conforming to the essential *reht* of her wifehood, even if Erec does not: God's *hövescheit* (3461), which is fully intended to contrast sharply with the *un*courtly, inordinate behaviour of the hero, sees to it that all eight horses behave impeccably and give her no trouble whatsoever. Chrétien has none of this.

In the next adventure Enite is confronted yet again with the same problem. She needs to speak to Erec about her plan to rescue them from the count (3959ff.), but she is sure that he will not pardon her a third time if she does so. On the other hand, if she does not speak she will lose the dearest husband a woman ever had, since the count will kill him. Only God can help her: 'nû rât mir, herre, rîcher got!/ des enwart mir nie sô nôt' (3981–82). And even though she is terrified, her *triuwe*, manifestly inspired by God once more, in response to her cry for help, commands her to go to Erec and tell him about her stratagem. She does so on her knees at his bedside, a gesture which greatly heightens the religious atmosphere of this episode. In Chrétien's description of the same events Enide's loyalty is strongly stressed: she stays awake all night worrying about Erec's safety, and the narrator comments: 'vers son seignor ot le cuer tandre/ come bone dame et lëax' (3458–59). When she has spoken to him and assured him that, if it please God, who is capable of all good, he won't be killed or captured, the narrator comments further: 'Or ot Erec que bien se prueve/ vers lui sa fame lëaumant' (3480–81). But there is no appeal to God as there is in the German version, where he plays a central role, as the inspiration of Enite's higher order of *triuwe* and *stæte*.

In Hartmann, when Enite hears the count and his men approaching 'mit zornigem muote' (4140), she is forced to break her promise yet again, a promise she has only just 'renewed': 'swie niuwelîch diu guote/ warnen verlobet hæte,/ daz gelübede beleip unstæte,/ wan si zebrach ez dâ zehant,/ als si betwanc der Triuwen bant' (4141–45). Here the apparent paradox which has been inherent in her behaviour all along is expressed in the opposition of *triuwe* and *unstæte*: in spite of having broken her promise Enite is referred to as 'diu guote', because in so doing she implemented her *triuwe* of a higher order, which compelled her to warn Erec of mortal danger. This time Enite is not said to invoke God's aid, but there is no reason to suppose that her higher order of *triuwe* does not come from the same source as before. All that Chrétien says here is that Enide could not help speaking (3542). In Hartmann, however, the opposition of *triuwe* and *unstæte* is again to be seen a little

later, although the two poles of the antithesis (or virtual antithesis) are
separated by at least fifty lines (and probably a lot more, since there is
almost certainly a lacuna after 4317). Erec becomes very angry with Enite
for having disobeyed him so many times, and she vows never to do it
again, but, as the narrator says: 'daz enliez si aber niht stæte' (4267).
Immediately after the lacuna, during which the heroine has clearly
broken her promise yet again and warned Erec of the approach of
Guivreiz, the narrator says: 'dô wart im aber ir triuwe erkant./ als si in
aber gewarnet hâte' (4319–20). Once again Enite has shown *unstaete* at a
lower level to implement her *triuwe* of a higher order. In this case we
cannot be sure whether she called on God for help or not, since the
warning falls within the missing lines of text, but she certainly showed
the same higher order of *triuwe* as on previous occasions when his help
was asked for and received.

Striking evidence of Enite's close relationship with God is to be found
in her highly rhetorical lament for Erec (5743ff.).[9] As she falls on his
'corpse', kisses him, beats her breast, screams, tears her hair and claws
her flesh Enite is again called 'diu guote' (5755), clearly because this lack
of control, though most inordinate and unseemly in a *vrouwe*, patently
demonstrates her wifely *triuwe* to Erec. In other words: the measure and
order of her *triuwe* is its *unmâze*, its *inordinatio*. So violent is this
measureless love for Erec that it perverts her attitude to God, causing
her to turn not *to* him, as she has always done so far, but *against* him:
'vrouwe Ênîte zurnte vaste an got' (5774). Convinced that he is being
unjust to her, she calls on him directly, as she has done in crises before,
but this time reproachfully: he lacks the compassion he is supposed to
have (5781ff.). If she has done anything to harm her husband at any
time, then it is *reht* (5814) that God's *gewalt* should deprive her of him,
but if not he should restore Erec to her. God will be guilty of *unstæte* if he
fails to keep his well-known promise 'daz ein man und sîn wîp/ suln
wesen ein lîp' (5826–27). So she continues: 'ensunder uns niht,/ wan
mir anders geschiht/ von dir ein unrehter gewalt' (5828–30). Here the
divine connections of Christian marriage are patent: it is God's holy
ordinance, instituted by him;[10] it is a union of two persons in one flesh,
and those whom God has joined together man must not put asunder.[11]
If God separates her from Erec he will therefore be breaking his own
commandment! Accordingly, Enite goes on to say, if God really has

---

[9] See Wolfgang Mohr, *Hartmann von Aue: Erec, übersetzt und erläutert*, GAG, 291
(Göppingen, 1980), p. 292: 'Die Klage der Enite ist [. . .] ein sehr bewußt gestaltetes Stück
Rhetorik.'
[10] See Genesis 2. 18: 'Dixit quoque Dominus Deus, non est bonum esse hominem solum;
faciamus ei adjutorem similem sui.'
[11] See Matthew 19. 5–6: 'Et dixit: Propter hoc dimittet homo patrem et matrem et
adhaerebit uxori suae, et erunt duo in carne una. Itaque jam non sunt duo, sed una caro.
Quod ergo Deus conjunxit, homo non separet.'

compassion, he should send hungry wild animals and let one of them devour them both, her and her dead husband, so that their flesh may remain one and undivided, a very graphic, if somewhat gruesome two-in-one image evoking the marriage relationship. 'unser lîp' (5838), very significantly, is in the singular.

In Chrétien, Enide's display of inordinate grief is likewise very prominently featured: she cries, wrings her hands, tears her clothes, her hair and her face, and faints upon Erec's apparently lifeless body, but she does not remonstrate with God, as she does in Hartmann. All she says to God is: 'Ha! Dex, [. . .] biax dolz sire,/ por coi me leisses tu tant vivre?' (4580–81). In Hartmann's story, on the other hand, Enite's chiding of God has a key role to play: inordinate though such behaviour may seem, it is clearly indicative of the essential *reht* and *ordo* of her love for Erec, of her wifehood, and so testifies to the strength, rather than the weakness, of her relationship with God, by whom she and Erec were joined together in one flesh.

But in any case, Enite's anger with God is short-lived. She soon decides that *she* is to blame, not God, for her present situation. He has not been unjust to her. She has indeed done something to harm her husband: she has been disloyal to him ('verrâten', 5945) by heaving the sigh and speaking in Karnant. For this she is sure God will punish her with eternal damnation, which is only right ('von rehte', 5943), because if she hadn't sighed and spoken Erec would still be alive. She is the cause of his apparent death, hardly what one would expect from 'ein rehtez wîp'. She has been a fool, like all those to whom God has given everything they want and need and who then throw it all away by listening to the advice of the devil. Her parents thought they could improve her lot by giving her to a rich king, but as a result she is worse off than before. It is foolish to try and change God's *ordo* and flout his will, and it is now his will that she should be cursed as long as she lives. Then follows the comparison of her situation with that of the linden tree transplanted from bad soil into an orchard. Indeed, throughout the whole passage 5940ff. numerous religious echoes, of paradise and its loss through *superbia*, and the resultant cursing of womankind, may be heard, greatly accentuating the religious tone and atmosphere.[12] In Chrétien, Enide also blames herself for the situation she is in, but there is nothing to suggest that she thinks she will be damned for disloyalty to Erec, no mention of her parents or suggestion that she should not have married a king, nor any of the religious echoes to be heard in Hartmann.

Enite's long monologue, in which she bitterly reproaches God and accuses him of lacking compassion and in which so much stress is placed on Christian marriage and its links with God, provides further

---

12   For example: 5940–48; 5957; 5963–73; 5996–98 and 6031–41.

striking evidence of the profound religiosity inherent in Hartmann's conception of his heroine. As the narrator says, she is very angry with God over her apparent loss of Erec, and she also seems to be unmindful of the help God has already given her, but this does not detract from the closeness and familiarity of her relationship with him, a relationship which continues and is not materially harmed by her reproaches, since she finally turns *to* God again and blames herself, not him, for what has happened to her. Furthermore, God's own attitude to Enite, his deep involvement in her affairs and concern for her welfare and that of her marriage, is shown to have been unaffected by her outburst, since, according to the narrator, he shortly afterwards sends Oringles in the nick of time to prevent her stabbing herself (6115ff.). The count rides through the forest to her salvation ('ir ze heile', 6126). To be sure, Chrétien also sees God's hand in this, his narrator saying that the merciful God caused her to delay her suicide attempt a little (4634–35), which gave Oringle and his suite time to save her. Nevertheless, Hartmann's version has the stronger religious impact, since Chrétien does not say that Oringle has been sent expressly by God to save Enide, whereas in Hartmann this point is made three times, the last time by Oringles himself (6251–52).

In Hartmann's Oringles episode the 'measureless' order of Enite's *triuwe* and *stæte* to Erec continues to receive the strongest possible emphasis. Though recognising the propriety and 'rightness' of Enite's grief for her 'dead' husband, as a sign of wifely *triuwe* in fact (6224 and 6227), Oringles tries to persuade her to moderate her grief. In his view she has done enough mourning and should now marry him. But of course, by its very nature, Enite's *triuwe* cannot be moderated or measured. If she moderates her grief and thereby recovers her self-control it will admittedly be more in keeping with the courtly *ordo* of a noble lady, but it will also be in breach of the Christian ethical *ordo* of her wifehood. In other words, in behaving ordinately as a *wîp* (in the narrower meaning of the word) she behaves inordinately as a *vrouwe*, but of the two it is her wifely *ordo* which is the superior and so must take precedence.

Incensed by her refusal to comply with his wishes, Oringles *forces* her to take part in a marriage service which is carried out with fully ordinate religious ceremonial: 'die herren, die des ambetes phlegent/ daz si die gotes ê gewegent,/ [. . .] bischove und ebbete [. . .]/ und diu pfafheit vil gar' (6336–43). But for Enite this is not a proper and ordinate solemnisation of matrimony, for all its apparent propriety and order, because she considers herself to be still married to Erec, which totally invalidates it. She cannot be joined to Oringles while she is still Erec's wife. She would rather be committed to the earth with her husband than take another man, now or at any time in the future: 'ê erwel ich daz ich der erde/ mit im bevolhen werde./ ich hân immer manne rât/ sît mir in got benomen hât' (6416–19). She is determined that even death shall not part them. Her measureless love for her husband transcends the limits of this earthly life. Chrétien gives less than half the space that Hartmann does to the encounter with Oringle, and there is correspondingly less stress on the marriage relationship as such. The actual marriage ceremony, too, is much less impressively ordinate: only a chaplain officiates.

The foregoing comparison of some parts of the texts of Hartmann's and Chrétien's *Erec* in which the heroine's loyalty as a wife is highlighted confirms that the German poet has infused deeper religious content into the narrative material supplied by Chrétien, as he has, of course, into the story as a whole. He does this, in particular, by placing the strongest emphasis of which he is capable on the two ethical qualities (overlapping in meaning to a very large extent) of *triuwe* and *stæte*, as qualities inseparable from the *ordo* and *reht* of Christian wifehood. As we have seen, the *triuwe* and *stæte* shown by Enite on the adventures are Christian virtues of a much higher order than the *triuwe* and *stæte* she would have shown towards Erec if she had obeyed his command not to speak and had not warned him when his life was in danger. Yet, ironically, the *triuwe* and *stæte* Erec wanted and expected Enite to show towards him on the adventures, in order to prove to his satisfaction that she was 'ein rehtez wîp', were precisely of that lower order: he wanted her to obey his commands, keep the promises she made to him, and submit herself entirely to his authority. As stated earlier, these are all ordinate expressions of wifely *triuwe* and *stæte*, but of a lower order than the *triuwe* and *stæte* actually shown by Enite. As things turned out, those of the lower order would have been quite inadequate to enable Erec to survive even the first adventure. They needed to be transcended.

Hartmann shows very clearly that the transcendently high order of these virtues achieved by Enite is a direct result of her close relationship with God, to which I have frequently referred in this paper. Without his help she could never have reached it. As we saw, God was always ready to help when she called upon him, as she did several times. He helped her overcome her terror of Erec's wrath and warn him of imminent danger, regardless of the consequences to herself. In other words, the *ordo* of Enite's wifehood, the measureless quality of her love for her husband, enjoys the fullest divine support and encouragement. It is essentially God-inspired. This being so, there can be no doubt, as I have claimed elsewhere in earlier publications,[13] that the love she shows for

---

[13] See 'Sin and Redemption in Hartmann's *Erec*', *GR*, 33 (1958), 5–14 (pp. 12–13), and 'Triuwe and untriuwe in Hartmann's *Erec*' (see n. 8 above), p. 17.

Erec on the adventures, as opposed to that at Karnant, is of the nature of *caritas* itself, since the order and measure of *caritas*, love for God and one's neighbour, is without measure. The 'infinite', ineffable, immortal, transcendent and transcendental quality of Enite's *triuwe*, her devoted, self-sacrificial love for Erec, is nothing if not mystical in character. Although it is a secular context, the emotional atmosphere and mood of these passages, especially the lament, are highly religious. Throughout the adventures, when Enite is afflicted with her greatest trials, Hartmann is at pains to leave no room for doubt that God is with her all the way, that he has the success of her marriage relationship with Erec very much at heart, even when she thinks the divinity has deserted her and directs her fury against him.

In this paper I have tried to give concrete textual evidence of Hartmann's much more explicitly religious conception of Enite's wifehood, her ultimate achievement of its Christian *reht* and *ordo* at the highest level. To be sure, Chrétien already provides a firm basis for this strong and emphatic religious approach, not least because his Enide also shows a higher order of loyalty and constancy than Erec expects from her, and in so doing proves the quality of her wifehood. This fundamental element in the structure of the narrative is common to both poets. But the intense religiosity of Hartmann's portrayal of the heroine, its heavy underlining of the essentially sacramental nature, the religious sanctity, of marriage, with all that that implies in the ethical sphere, has been amply demonstrated in the foregoing textual analysis. The poet constantly reminds his audience in all sorts of ways that his protagonists have entered into a lifelong Christian union and that the order of wifely love and loyalty in such a union is an integral part of the order of divine love itself. René Pérennec has rightly said that the spiritualisation and idealisation which characterise Hartmann's adaptation are already latent in Chrétien; he speaks of 'l'arrière-plan religieux à demi voilé dans la source française'.[14] This is very true, but at the same time it cannot be denied that Hartmann has, in the portrayal of Enite at least, capitalised on Chrétien by bringing to full realisation the religious potentialities of his French source in his own individual way, which is a measure of his undoubted poetic imagination and creativity. As Barbara Thoran puts it, Hartmann has 'eine eigene Konzeption dieser Gestalt'.[15]

---

[14] René Pérennec, 'Adaptation et société: l'adaptation par Hartmann d'Aue du roman de Chrétien de Troyes, *Erec et Enide*', *Et. Germ.*, 28 (1973), 289–303 (p. 302).
[15] Barbara Thoran, ' "Diu ir man verrâten hât" – Zum Problem von Enîtes Schuld im *Erec* Hartmanns von Aue', *WW*, 25 (1975), 255–66 (p. 256).

Adapting Enide:
Chrétien, Hartmann, and the Female Reader

KAREN PRATT

One of the more productive lines of research pursued by medievalists in the last twenty years has been the study of women in medieval literature and society.[1] Scholars of both sexes, with varying degrees of indebtedness to the Women's Movement and to feminist criticism, have re-examined the presentation of the female in medieval fiction and the relationship between cultural images of women and the realities of life in the Middle Ages. In particular, the idealised courtly lady, who, we once believed, inspired young knights in combat and poets in their literary pursuits, has been demystified and her pedestal shown in its true light – as an area of highly restricted influence, clearly limited and circumscribed by the needs of fictional heroes and the patriarchal ideology of their creators.[2]

The aim of this paper is to discuss, in the light of feminist critical theory, some recent women's readings of Chrétien's *Erec et Enide* and Hartmann's *Erec* as a prelude to my own analysis of the problem of adapting the figure of Enide.[3] I shall be focusing especially on the narrative strategies employed by Chrétien and Hartmann in their presentation of gender roles within marriage and of a possible ideal of femininity, and in their treatment of the controversial question of female

[1] I should like to thank Professors Curschmann, Groos, Hatto, Pérennec, Ruberg, Willson, and Wynn, and Drs Hunt, Jackson, and Thomas for their helpful reactions to my paper, but in particular Bonnie Krueger, whose advice on feminist critical theory has been invaluable to me in preparing this revised version. I am also grateful to John Gillingham for historical references.
[2] See Andrée Kahn Blumstein, *Misogyny and Idealization in the Courtly Romance* (Bonn, 1977); Joan Ferrante, *Woman as Image in Medieval Literature* (Durham, North Carolina, 1985); *Courtly Ideology and Woman's Place in Medieval French Literature*, ed. by Jane Burns and Roberta Krueger, *Romance Notes*, 25, No. 3 (1985); Penny Schine Gold, *The Lady and the Virgin: Image, Attitude, and Experience in Twelfth-century France* (Chicago, 1985).
[3] For feminist critical theory, see Toril Moi, *Sexual/Textual Politics: Feminist Literary Theory* (London/New York, 1985); Terry Eagleton, *Literary Theory: An Introduction* (Oxford, 1983), Chapter 5; *The New Feminist Criticism*, ed. by Elaine Showalter (London, 1986).

speech. Underlying my approach is Kate Millett's thesis that feminist readers, who do not share the author's androcentrism, can view a work of literature from a somewhat oblique perspective which is potentially in conflict with that of the author, and are thus capable of exposing 'the underlying premises of a work' and of undermining the hierarchical, patriarchal tyranny of a text (Moi, pp. 24–25). As a tool for laying bare the mechanisms of a text, the feminist viewpoint is no less valid than the male-centred approach of much traditional criticism. Indeed, it is particularly useful in that it questions those binary oppositions (male/female; active/passive; strong/weak; subject/object; self/other) char-acteristic of structuralist criticism, whose strong ideological bias is evident beneath its thin veneer of objectivity (see Moi, p. 104). As a model for the twelfth-century reader's reaction to a text the feminist approach is more problematic,[4] since medieval women had not had the benefit of feminism's consciousness-raising and were not as aware of patriarchal conditioning as some (though not all) modern women are. However, it seems likely that some female members of an audience would nevertheless have resisted identification with the prevailing ideology, especially if the text seemed to allow or even invite a dissenting view.

It is my contention that Chrétien's romance is just such a text. Ambiguity, paradox, ironic discrepancy, binary oppositions juxtaposed, but not necessarily resolved, are all recognised hallmarks of Chrétien's style, though they are more frequently identified in his more mature works than in his first Arthurian romance. Together, they render his meaning highly volatile and have led some critics to conclude that his works were designed less to convey an ideological message than to provoke debate.[5] For the female reader, whether contemporary or modern, Chrétien's Enide presents a highly ambiguous image of woman, and the implied author's attitude to his creation has to be sought as much in what the text omits to say, in its 'silences, gaps and contradictions' (Moi, p. 94) as in the overt pronouncements of narrator

---

[4] In a medieval context, the term reader naturally covers listener too. Evidence for the female as reader of medieval romance is to be found in Chrétien's Yvain, 5362–72, where a girl is reading to her parents from a romance. The role of women like Eleanor of Aquitaine and Marie de Champagne as patrons and consumers of courtly literature is more difficult to assess. See John F. Benton, 'The Court of Champagne as a Literary Center', Speculum, 36 (1961), 551–91, and June Hall Martin McCash, 'Marie de Champagne and Eleanor d'Aquitaine', Speculum, 54 (1979), 698–711. The assumption lying behind my use of gender terminology is that a female reader, whether for biological or socio-cultural reasons, is more likely to have a feminine response to a work than a male reader, although socio-cultural factors are no doubt responsible for the potentially divergent responses of medieval and modern women readers.

[5] See Tony Hunt, Yvain, Critical Guides to French Texts, 55 (London, 1986); Peter Haidu, Aesthetic Distance in Chrétien de Troyes: Irony and Comedy in 'Cligès' and 'Perceval' (Geneva, 1968).

or characters.[6] Hartmann, on the other hand, creates a more author-itative text, whose message is less open to challenge and whose meaning is less equivocal. The German adaptor has closed some of the open-endedness of the source by inventing a more authoritarian narrator, who manipulates meaning and the audience's reaction to his story. In general, he explains the behaviour of his protagonists in terms of the (for him unproblematic) binary opposition manlîch and wîplîch. Thus Hartmann's romance smacks of what Jacques Derrida terms phallogocentrism, an attitude which is both 'phallocentric', i.e. male-centred, and 'logocentric', i.e. confident in the ability of language to convey the whole truth and meaning of things. Terry Eagleton maintains that this linguistic 'cocksureness', which is used by 'those who wield sexual and social power' in order to 'maintain their grip' (p. 189), should be contrasted with the fluidity of meaning characteristic of 'semiotic' fiction and associated with some modern women's writing. Similarly, for Hélène Cixous, feminine writing struggles 'to undermine the dominant phallogocentric logic, split open the closure of binary opposition and revel in the pleasures of open-ended textuality' (Moi, p. 108). While it would be rash to claim that Chrétien produced in his Erec et Enide something approaching écriture féminine, the analogy might be instructive, especially in the context of comparison with Hartmann's more phallogocentric discourse.

It is possible that the gaps and contradictions present in Chrétien's work are the result of his being caught between conflicting ideologies, or as Pérennec suggests, of his attempting unsuccessfully to convey a new ideal of 'compagnonnage conjugal' while employing traditional, miso-gynistic stereotypes of female behaviour.[7] It is, however, also possible that the French poet is deliberately employing subversive narrative strategies in order to encourage his audience to question the patriarchal values of twelfth-century aristocratic society. Julia Kristeva considers writing 'in which the hierarchical closure imposed on meaning and language has been opened up to the free play of the signifier' (Moi, p. 172) to be characteristic of marginal groups. It is because women have been marginalised by androcentric society that their writing has become

[6] I owe this point to Moi's summary (p. 94) of Pierre Macherey's approach to the 'ideological determinations' of a text. Thomas Heine, 'Shifting Perspectives: The Narrative Strategy in Hartmann's Erec', Orbis Litterarum, 36 (1981), 95–115, also emphasises the importance of narrative omissions, which leave the reader in a state of bewilderment over Erec's motivations, especially during the 'Probefahrt'. The fact that Heine identifies this technique in Hartmann's romance does not, however, invalidate my own observations which follow, since my concern is with the degree to which the adaptor modified the equivocal nature of his source.

[7] René Pérennec, 'La "Faute" d'Enide: Transgression ou inadéquation entre un projet poétique et des steréotypes de comportement?', in Amour, mariage et transgressions au moyen âge: Actes du Colloque, Université de Picardie, ed. by D. Buschinger and A. Crépin, GAG, 420 (Göppingen, 1984), pp. 153–59.

subversive. However, men on the margins of society are also capable of such discourse. Although Stephen Jaeger has shown that the role of cleric at court was hardly marginal (at least in eleventh-century Germany), Chrétien's less authoritarian, polysemic discourse may well be attributable to the cleric's non-identification or only partial identification with the ideals of his chivalric public and patrons.[8] In contrast, Hartmann, the 'gelehrte Ritter', may well have identified more closely with his audience's ideology and consequently produced a less subversive text, in which the female is largely deproblematised.

Before examining the narrative strategies employed by French poet and German adaptor in their presentation of gender roles, the different approaches adopted by recent female interpreters of the *Erec* material will be surveyed in order to assess their fruitfulness for an analysis of a source and its adaptation.

The historian Penny Gold sets out in *The Lady and the Virgin*[9] to identify medieval views on women as expressed in literary and other types of contemporary document, as well as in iconographical evidence. She finds that the apparent conflict between love and chivalry in Arthurian romance does not represent a power struggle between the sexes, but rather an examination of conflicting desires within the male protagonist, torn between allegiance to men and women. Thus, Chrétien's first extant romance, *Erec et Enide*, is, despite the egalitarian title found in the *Cligés* prologue, androcentric. Enide's role is largely functional, and the hero's attitude towards her ambivalent, for she is both an object of pursuit and a problematic obstacle to Erec's goal. Gold's reading of the text emphasises the heroine's passivity and allows her no active part in the education of the hero.[10] While pointing usefully to the problematic role of the woman, Gold does not accept that this role could be productive and lead to a reassessment of patriarchal values. There is no discussion of Chrétien's narrative technique, simply an analysis of content and especially the psychological dimension of the romance. Indeed, she herself describes her method as follows: 'by examining basic patterns of interaction between men and women in the stories, we could come to an understanding of the complexity of attitudes to women' (p. 68). Gold's reading of *Erec et Enide* is clearly indebted to the early feminist 'Woman as Image' criticism, which concentrated largely on content analysis, uncovering in the deep

[8] See C. Stephen Jaeger, *The Origins of Courtliness* (Philadelphia, 1985), especially p. 165. It was suggested in discussion that whereas Chrétien distanced himself from his audience, Hartmann distanced himself from his source.

[9] See n. 2 above.

[10] Nor does Gold contemplate the possibility that the text might be about the *heroine's* education. This, however, is the view of Sally Mussetter, 'The Education of Chrétien's Enide', *Romanic Review*, 73 (1982), 147–66 and of Penny Sullivan, 'The Education of the Heroine in Chrétien's *Erec et Enide*', *Neophilologus*, 69 (1985), 321–31.

structures of a text the power politics of gender. As such it provides insights into the workings of Hartmann's source, but in its concentration on basic plot structure it is not a sensitive enough tool for the comparative analysis of model and adaptation.

Laurie Finke's paper 'Flesh Made Word: Constructing Sexuality in Chrétien de Troyes'[11] analyses *Erec et Enide* in terms of the power struggle between the sexes and the victory of phallocratic society. She argues that in the bride-winning section, Enide functions as an object of exchange between her father and Erec, and that the sparrowhawk contest is less an exercise in courtship and more an example of male bonding. After all, one result is Yder's reintegration into Arthurian society. Enide is thus 'a vehicle for male interaction',[12] a phenomenon noted by feminists elsewhere.

For Finke the only independent, active, powerful woman in the work is Maboagrain's *amie*, who is dangerous because she has opted out of the male exchange system. Drawing on Lacanian psychoanalysis, Finke identifies in the orchard of Brandigan a symbol of female genitalia and in the heads of the defeated knights, the product of castration. Ultimately, though, Chrétien presents the defeat of this woman-centred system, even going so far as to express patriarchal ideology through Enide's famous speech on the married state (6294–318).[13]

The psychoanalytical approach is further represented by Gertraud Steiner in her study of Hartmann's *Erec*.[14] She makes only fleeting reference to Hartmann's source and indeed, from her perspective, model and adaptation do not differ substantially: 'Der Unterschied zur Chrétienschen Fassung hinsichtlich meines Vorhabens erscheint mir zu gering, um sie eigens zu interpretieren, doch habe ich sie gelegentlich, insbesondere was den Status Enites betrifft, herangezogen' (p. 4). She argues that Erec, in order to exorcise those suppressed desires buried deep in his Unconscious, has to regress into the pre-Oedipal stage where the pleasure principle prevails. This stage, which Lacan calls the Imaginary Order and Kristeva the Semiotic Phase, is always associated with the female or mother figure. Hence it is personified in the shape of Enite. According to Steiner, the theme of the work is 'Enite's Unterdrückung', which forms part of the hero's maturation process.

---

[11] A paper delivered at the Twenty-Second International Congress on Medieval Studies at Kalamazoo, May 1987.

[12] Burns and Krueger (see n. 2 above), 'Introduction', p. 215.

[13] Chrétien's work is referred to in the edition by Wendelin Foerster, *Kristian von Troyes: Erec und Enide*, Romanische Bibliothek, 13 (Halle (Saale), 1934), and Hartmann's work in Hartmann von Aue, *Erec*, ed. by Albert Leitzmann, continued by Ludwig Wolff, 6th edn, prepared by Christoph Cormeau and Kurt Gärtner, ATB, 39 (Tübingen, 1985).

[14] Gertraud Steiner, *Das Abenteuer der Regression: Eine Untersuchung zur phantasmagorischen Wiederkehr der 'verlorenen Zeit' im 'Erec' Hartmanns von Aue*, GAG, 366 (Göppingen, 1983).

Thus she claims that what Hartmann (or more correctly Chrétien before him) has done is to appropriate a female-dominated Celtic pagan myth and modify it to serve the aims of phallocratic, Christian, chivalric society. Ultimately, after a series of therapeutic adventures which demystify the Unknown, the irrational element of the matriarchal, mythic scheme is overcome by the patriarchal, chivalric ethic.[15]

The psychoanalytical approach, while explaining certain cultural archetypes in terms of the male psyche and remaining largely at the level of deep structures, tends to concentrate on the similarities between text and adaptation rather than on those subtle narrative differences through which ideology is often mediated. A more fruitful approach for the analysis of two romances based on the same *matière* is the study of linguistic leitmotifs and recurrent rhyme pairs. This method is combined with the psychoanalytical approach by Jane Burns in her paper 'Lips Unsealed: The Power of the Lady's Voice in *Erec et Enide*'.[16] Beginning with the exordial rhyme pair *teisir/pleisir* (7–8), she traces the association of speaking and sexuality throughout the romance. Burns concludes that Enide's speaking out in bed destroys the pleasure which Erec finds in the passive (and silent) female body and represents a type of sexual emancipation which challenges his virility. Hence his need to test her loyalty as well as to teach her obedience. A parallel case is that of the Count of Limors, who tries to force Enide to be silent, in a passage which significantly contains the pair *pleisir/teisir* (4839–40). While I interpret these rhyme-words as they appear in the prologue rather differently from Burns, I agree that they probably offer an interpretative key to the romance as a whole and I welcome her concentration on leitmotifs and surface, verbal configurations of the text, especially as this is a level at which French poet and German adaptor can invest their material with different meanings. Thus, while Chrétien's repetition of *teisir/pleisir*, *dire* and especially *parole* indicates his concern with the act of speaking, Hartmann's constant use of the ethically charged terms *güete*, *triuwe*, *êre* and *sælde* gives his work an entirely different complexion.

The readings of Chrétien's *Erec et Enide* discussed thus far have identified the French poet as an author who preserves rather than challenges patriarchal values. However, Bonnie Krueger's article 'Love, Honor, and the Exchange of Women in *Yvain*: Some Remarks on the Female Reader'[17] argues that Chrétien, employing a dialectical method,

---

15 Steiner probably over-emphasises the matriarchal nature of Celtic society, which I understand to be the subject of contention amongst Celticists.
16 A paper delivered at the Twenty-Second International Congress on Medieval Studies at Kalamazoo, May 1987.
17 *Romance Notes*, 25, No. 3 (1985), 302–17 (see n. 2 above). On the subject of readers, especially female readers, resisting identification with an androcentric text, see Judith Fetterley, *The Resisting Reader: A Feminist Approach to American Fiction* (Bloomington, 1978),

deliberately juxtaposes and interweaves realistic sexual politics and courtly love casuistry in order both to adopt and undermine romance mystification of sexual tensions. The text remains ideologically ambivalent, allowing members of the audience, with all their preconceptions and social conditioning, to identify with those elements which suit their individual viewpoints. However, she concludes that 'female or male readers who resisted identification and focussed instead on Chrétien's structural paradoxes, may have discovered a *mise en question* of the gender relationships embodied in marriage and chivalry' (p. 317).

Although Chrétien's first extant romance, *Erec et Enide*, is not normally associated with the poet's sophisticated use of dialectic and irony noted elsewhere in his *œuvre*, it is worth examining the work more closely in order to ascertain whether or not this same narrative strategy of simultaneously mystifying and demystifying the relationship between the sexes is indeed present.

Chrétien's mixing of the courtly with the harshly realistic has been noted by Barbara Nelson Sargent-Baur, who sums it up in the opposition *sa feme* or *s'amie*.[18] Her view is that for most of the time Erec treats Enide like a twelfth-century wife, but occasionally she is allowed to play the role of courtly *amie*, though only when it suits Erec. The implication is that this fictional situation reflects the mixed reality of the age: women were mostly obedient wives, but could become *dames* 'on the margin of real life and in its odd moments' (p. 383), which I take to mean within the narrow confines of court amusements. However, this interpretation is undermined by the fact that we are never really *shown* Enide playing this role, though her husband claims that she has done so. As Sargent-Baur herself notices, there is a discrepancy between Erec's words and his actions and this is not elucidated by authorial comment. Indeed, using the terminology of Wayne Booth,[19] she says: 'in his handling of Erec, Chrétien is by no means generous with direct and authoritative *TELLING*; he generally limits himself to *SHOWING* this character in action' (p. 374). Sargent-Baur has thus clearly seen that our interpretation of the romance is complicated by Chrétien's use of a non-intrusive narrative technique. She prefers, however, to resolve the opposition *feme/amie* by arguing that Enide is both, but not simultaneously. Another approach would be to see the unresolved opposition as part of a narrative strategy which aims to question accepted gender roles and provoke debate.

It is now time to define more closely Chrétien's narrative technique.

and for feminist approaches to reading in general, see *Gender and Reading: Essays on Readers, Texts, and Contexts*, ed. by E. Flynn and P. Schweickart (Baltimore/London, 1986).
[18] 'Erec's Enide: "sa feme ou s'amie"?', *Romance Philology*, 33 (1980), 373–87. See also Deborah Nelson, 'Enide: *Amie* or *Femme*?', *Romance Notes*, 21 (1981), 358–63.
[19] Wayne Booth, *The Rhetoric of Fiction*, 2nd edn (Chicago/London, 1983), Chapter 1.

First, it is marked by a paucity of narratorial comment. Occasionally the narrator voices approval of the *courtly* behaviour of hero or heroine, but he rarely intervenes to express *moral* value judgements, especially where the conjugal relationship is concerned. There is, in fact, little overt manipulation of the reader's response through the use of tendentious epithets, Chrétien preferring instead periphrastic expressions which denote social status (*le chevalier*) or relationship (*ses sire, sa feme*). This inclusion of relational rather than ethically charged terms is linked to the French poet's use of restricted viewpoint. As Norris Lacy notes, the first third of the narrative is filtered through Erec, the central section through Enide, and the final section through Erec again, Chrétien thus employing a 'shifting center of consciousness'.[20] An examination of relational terms and of the use of the verb *voir*, which encourages us to see things through the eyes of a protagonist, reveals that viewpoint varies even more frequently than Lacy suggests, but in broad terms his assessment is valid.

The restricted viewpoint technique not only fragments meaning, it also imposes limitations on the omniscience and authority of the narrator. For example, when recounting events through Erec's eyes, the narrator is forced to admit that he does not know what Enide and her mother are working on in the work room: 'Mes ne sai, quel oevre feisoient' (400). Furthermore, he tantalisingly refuses to tell us exactly what Erec's motivations were in leaving Carnant so hurriedly with his wife (6478–87), claiming that this has already been stated. If the narrator is little help in our attempt to interpret Chrétien's romance, what of Booth's 'disguised narrators' – those characters who, through their actions and words, 'tell the audience what it needs to know' (Booth, p. 152)? The problem is that, as we shall see, words can conflict with actions and a character's own interpretation of events may not square with that of another or with the meaning implied by the structure of the plot.

This ironic gap between actions and words is clearly apparent in Chrétien's presentation of the love relationship and in particular of Erec's attitude towards Enide, and is a vital ingredient in the mystification and demystification process. On the whole, Erec behaves like a typical medieval husband.[21] He negotiates with Enide's father for her hand, speaks on her behalf, deciding what she can wear and which

---

[20] See Norris Lacy, 'Narrative point of view and the problem of Erec's motivation', *Kentucky Romance Quarterly*, 18 (1971), 355–62 (p. 356).
[21] On women and marriage, see Eileen Power, *Medieval Women*, ed. by M.M. Postan (London, 1975); Georges Duby, *Le Chevalier, la femme et le prêtre: le mariage dans la France féodale* (Paris, 1981); C.N.L. Brooke, 'Marriage and Society in the Central Middle Ages', in *Marriage and Society: Studies in the Social History of Marriage*, ed. by R.B. Outhwaite (New York, 1982), pp. 17–34; and John Gillingham, 'Love, marriage and politics in the twelfth century', *Forum for Modern Language Studies*, 25 (1989), 292–303.

gifts she can accept (639–76, 1373–78, 1403–06). He expects obedience
and allows her little independent action. After the reconciliation, he
shows Enide more affection and takes her feelings a little more into
account (5833–67), but she is still not asked for her permission or even
her advice when Erec is intending to risk his life in the *joie de la cort*
adventure. Yet shortly beforehand Erec has vowed to return to the role
of *chevalier servant*, which he claims to have played earlier:

> Tot a vostre comandemant
> Vuel estre des or an avant,
> Aussi con j'estoie devant.   (4926–28)[22]

The discrepancy between Erec's avowed behaviour and actual behaviour is striking and alerts the reader, especially a female one, to the
problematic nature of this conjugal relationship. Moreover, Chrétien has
probably deliberately placed words in Erec's mouth which echo
ironically those of his father-in-law at the time the marriage was
arranged:

> Tot a vostre comandemant
> Ma bele fille vos presant.   (675–76)

It is clearly the father's perception of the relationship and not the
husband's which is the more realistic and accurate.

Similarly there is throughout the romance an ironic juxtaposing of the
courtly terms *amie*, *dame* and *drue* as applied to Enide and the uncourtly
treatment of her as a *feme*. Moreover, Chrétien's allusions to the chivalry
topos, whereby a knight's prowess is dependent on the inspiration he
receives from his lady, are equally problematic. On the first occasion,
during the sparrowhawk contest, Erec, on looking at his *amie*,
immediately gains in strength, we are told (911–16). However, Chrétien
then undercuts the topos by saying that Erec also remembers the shame
he suffered at the hands of Yder's dwarf and his promise to the queen to
avenge the dishonour (917–20). The exhortatory monologue which then
ensues deals solely with the question of his honour (921–24). After this
the fight is renewed and we are left wondering about the precise source
of our hero's prowess.

Likewise, when Erec recovers consciousness and attacks the Count of
Limors, he is inspired by 'l'amors qu'a sa fame avoit' (4863). But this is
the second or secondary source of his valour, for in the preceding line
the narrator states that 'ire li done hardemant' (4862). Perhaps Erec is
primarily concerned to protect his property against his male rival, whose

---

[22] Yet during the period of *recreantise* at Carnant there is no suggestion that Enide is
imposing this lifestyle on Erec or that it is the consequence of her *volonté*. She in no way
behaves like Guinevere during the Noauz episode in *Lancelot*.

behaviour and speech convey so faithfully the status and experience of those medieval wives who were victims of male violence (4819–42).[23] Finally, in the *joie de la cort* episode, Erec alludes to the chivalry topos when assuring Enide that the courage her love inspires in him will be enough to secure his victory (5855–59). Yet she is left outside the *vergier*, out of his field of vision and therefore not the active source of inspiration which Lancelot was later to find in Guinevere.

This veneer of *cortoisie* and courtly love, created by words often unsupported by actions, may well be deliberately transparent and designed to encourage a *mise en question* of gender roles both in medieval society and contemporary literature. However, even if this was not the deliberate intention of the author, Chrétien's romance nevertheless invites such a reaction. Enide is clearly not being presented straightforwardly as the lady of the troubadour lyric, and Kathryn Smits is not justified when she follows Hrubý in claiming that in Hartmann's *Erec* 'Chrestiens Troubadourminne wurde durch ein reales Eheverhält-nis ersetzt'.[24] In fact, many of the harsh realities of medieval marriage are already present in Chrétien's portrayal of his eponymous couple, while a closer parallel to the type of love associated with the lyric is to be found in Maboagrain's relationship with his *amie* in the *joie de la cort* adventure. Yet this relationship is not presented as ideal and the episode is clearly designed to demonstrate the merits of marriage over elopement attended by the enslavement of a knight. Here, all the narrative voices harmonise: that of the narrator, the people of Brandigan, Erec, Enide (in her speech on marriage) and Maboagrain. Even his *amie* seems happy to be compensated for her loss of sovereignty by the rediscovery of a long-lost cousin. However, within this harmony it is interesting to note the discrepancies between Maboagrain's account of their story (very much in terms of the *don contraignant* and the female entrapment of the male, 6047–6155) and his lady's version (which stresses her youth and vulnerability when eloping with a knight from a foreign land, 6259–93). Chrétien has at least allowed the female voice to plead her own case, and, by juxtaposing the voices, has underlined the complexities of relations between the sexes and their perception.

A further example of Chrétien's complex and ambiguous treatment of gender roles concerns Enide's famous *parole* and the possible guilt, fault

---

[23] On wife-beating in the Middle Ages, see Frances and Joseph Gies, *Marriage and the Family in the Middle Ages* (New York, 1987), p. 181. On rape see James Brundage, 'Rape and Marriage in Medieval Canon Law', *Revue de Droit Canonique*, 28 (1978), 62–75.

[24] See Kathryn Smits, 'Enite als christliche Ehefrau', in *Interpretation und Edition deutscher Texte des Mittelalters: Festschrift für John Asher zum 60. Geburtstag*, ed. by Kathryn Smits, Werner Besch, and Victor Lange (Berlin, 1981), 13–25 (p. 14, n. 5) and Ursula Schulze, '*âmîs unde man*. Die zentrale Problematik in Hartmanns *Erec*', *PBB* (Tüb.), 105 (1983), 14–47, (p. 15, n. 6).

or flaws one might attach to it. The content of her fateful speech is clearly correct, for Erec is guilty of *recreantise*, and the narrator and Erec himself confirm this.[25] Furthermore, the development of the plot, culminating in the socially useful adventure of the *joie de la cort*, demonstrates that Enide's initial speaking-out, which spurs Erec into action, has been ultimately beneficial not only to Erec, but to society in general. Nevertheless, Enide is punished by Erec and criticised by herself for uttering those momentous words.

Chrétien's narrator offers little guidance in our interpretation of this key event and the non-authoritarian narrative technique gives much scope for divergent readings. It seems to me that Enide's *parole* is most usefully examined within the broader context of the thematic of speech in *Erec et Enide*.[26] The prologue (7–8), rather than promoting silence as a virtue, warns against inappropriate silence, and although these words serve as Chrétien's *causa scribendi*, they may also offer a key to the interpretation of the romance proper. The term *parole*, repeated a number of times, first occurs in connection with the Custom of the White Stag.[27] Here Arthur's *parole* is seen as potentially divisive and dangerous, but the situation is defused by the Queen's (i.e. female) good advice (335ff.). The end of the *premiers vers* not only marks Erec's winning of a bride, it also closes the first chapter of Chrétien's romance on the negative and positive power of words.

When Enide is at last shown speaking, her words are typical of the passive suffering often expressed in female discourse: 'Lasse, con mar m'esmui/ De mon païs' (2496–97).[28] Her lament is not meant for Erec's ears and the narrator makes it clear that misfortune plays an important part in the utterance:

> Qu'il li avint par mescheance
> Que ele dist une parole,

[25] The narrator (2434–37) states unambiguously that Erec was no longer interested in arms or tournaments. I cannot therefore accept Penny Sullivan's view that 'the charge of *recreantise* is made not by the author/narrator, but by Erec's retinue' whose 'accusation is overhasty and slanderous' ('The Education of the Heroine', (n. 10 above), p. 322). Moreover, Erec himself admits to Enide 'droit an eüstes,/ Et cil qui m'an blasment ont droit' (2576–77).

[26] See John Plummer, '*Bien dire* and *bien aprandre* in Chrétien de Troyes' *Erec et Enide*', *Romania*, 95 (1974), 380–94, and A. Castellani, 'La *Parole* d'Enide', *Cultura neolatina*, 18 (1958), 139–49.

[27] Interestingly, the king's speech (*parole*) is associated with Gauvain's displeasure: 'ne plot mie' (39–40). The romance contains several *loci* where the terms *pleisir* and *teisir* are either equated or placed in opposition, thus indicating Chrétien's complex approach to speech.

[28] See Bernard Cerquiglini, 'The Syntax of Discursive Authority: The Example of Feminine Discourse', *Yale French Studies*, 70 (1986), 183–98, who quotes the more appropriate reading of the Guiot manuscript – 'Con mar fui' – in support of his argument (Chrétien de Troyes, *Erec et Enide*, ed. by Mario Roques, CFMA, 80 (Paris, 1973), l. 2492).

> Dont ele se tint puis por fole;
> Mes ele n'i pansoit nul mal.   (2486–89)

Moreover, he stresses the innocence of Enide's intentions and hints in the formulation 'Dont ele se tint puis por fole' that it is *her* subjective view that she has committed *folie* in speaking. The narrator, presenting her as the innocent victim of 'mescheance', does not necessarily share her assessment of her culpability.

It is important that Enide does not willingly repeat the rumours she has heard. Under threat she becomes more bold, but this is hardly arrogance of a kind she then criticises herself for (2589ff.). The verb *oser* and related terms such as *orguel* become something of a leitmotif later (2592–93, 2606–07, 2788, 2794, 2841, 3109, etc.), yet here the narrator tells us just prior to the *parole* that Enide had not *dared* to voice criticism of her husband because she suspected he would take it ill:

> De ceste chose li pesa,
> Mes sanblant feire n'an osa;
> Car ses sire an mal le preïst
> Assez tost, s'ele li deïst.   (2469–72)

Critics seem to be divided over whether Enide is indeed being presumptuous here (especially in 2540–75) or whether Chrétien is pointing to her diffidence and lack of confidence, which need to be overcome before she can be the ideal consort for an ideal ruler.[29] What *is* clear, given Erec's hostile reaction to his wife's revelations, is that she knows her husband very well even at this stage in the relationship. Critical disagreement over Enide's possible pride is again a product of the poet's narrative technique: the narrator does not comment on her *parole*, and the audience is left to draw its own conclusions on the basis of the fragmentary, and sometimes conflicting, evidence provided by the events and the protagonists' reactions to them.

To the female reader/listener, Enide's speech of self-castigation (2589ff.), in which she regrets her words and accuses herself of being arrogant, foolish and foolhardy, seems rather misplaced. Is Chrétien encouraging us to agree with the heroine's assessment of her fault, or is the speech deliberately exaggerated and inappropriate, in order to highlight her innocence as a passive victim of misfortune and of Erec's wrath?[30] Just because the hero and heroine agree that Enide has been too

---

[29] This is the conclusion of Penny Sullivan in 'The Presentation of Enide in the "premiers vers" of Chrétien's *Erec et Enide*', *Medium Aevum*, 52 (1983), 77–89. Yet prior to the crisis the narrator claims that Enide is perfect in every respect (2423–26).

[30] The narrator's comments (2584–88) are difficult of interpretation. Do the reference to *folie* and the ensuing proverb ('Tant grate chievre que mal gist') represent an objective assessment of the situation by the narrator or is he conveying Enide's view? Does the

outspoken (Erec magnanimously forgiving her later for this (4929–31)) does not mean that this is the overall message of the text. On the contrary, woman's speech, as represented by Enide's constant breaking of Erec's prohibition, by her clever use of words or crying out to ward off lecherous counts (3418–19, 4827, 4843, 4853) and by the 'proiiere' which Cadoc's *amie* addresses to Erec (4504), as well as by Guinevere's advice to Arthur, is throughout shown to have positive consequences,[31] while male speech (for example, Maboagrain's rash promise to his *amie* (6056ff.) or his arrogant threats to Erec (5907–14)) or male silence (when Erec fails to identify himself to Guivrez, and Enide has to intervene (5006–25)) can have disastrous results. Through the leitmotifs of *dire*, *parole*, *teisir*, *consoil*, *proiiere* and related terms (often couched in proverbial expressions), the text clearly explores the whole question of appropriate and inappropriate speech. Interestingly, the two central themes of *teisir* and *recroire* appear in combination in the *joie de la cort* episode, in such a way as to suggest provocatively that chivalric failure can be a consequence of silence (5615–19, 5654)![32]

It has been argued by Sally Mussetter that Chrétien is presenting in this romance Enide's education in the arts of grammar, dialectic and rhetoric.[33] While it is difficult to demonstrate with textual evidence Enide's progress in each of the arts of the trivium, it does seem to me that both hero and heroine gradually learn to appreciate the arts of speech, a process set in motion by the female. Having acquired the linguistic tools of learning in the company of his wife, Erec can then go on to acquire the more scientific knowledge of the quadrivium, as symbolised on his coronation robe.

Perhaps this symbolic layer of meaning can further explain the contradictions and discrepancies in the romance. Enide, as philosophical idea, possibly the personification of Philology or Prudence (cf. Martianus Capella and Alan of Lille)[34] or a symbol of the trivium, demands and receives respect. In this guise, it is vital that she speaks. However, in her more literal role as medieval wife she must be very careful how and when she speaks, a problem of which she is aware early

proverb refer to the heroine's initial speaking-out (which has resulted in this deterioration in her situation) or to her present self-beratement (which is making things worse for her)? Again, ambiguity leads to uncertainty in our response.

[31] It is therefore ironic that Chrétien has Enide state in her *planctus* that: 'Ainz teisirs a home ne nut,/ Mes parlers nuist mainte foiee./ Ceste chose ai bien essaiee/ Et esprovee an mainte guise' (4630–33). As was suggested in the previous note, Chrétien's use of proverbial truths often fuels ambiguity and irony rather than producing an unequivocal message. Perhaps he wished his audience to question received wisdom.

[32] The term 'recroire' (5014) also occurs when the narrator is emphasising the stupidity of Erec's refusal to reveal his identity to Guivrez.

[33] See Mussetter (n. 10 above).

[34] See Claude Luttrell, *The Creation of the First Arthurian Romance: A Quest* (London, 1974).

on when she utters her *parole*. Hence the conflicting messages which reach the listener's ears, messages which Hartmann has modified by replacing the Neoplatonic allegory of the source with Christian morality and early scholastic teaching on the roles of the sexes within marriage.[35]

It is now time to examine Hartmann's reading of Chrétien's multi-layered, polysemic romance and his transformation of it into an ideologically less ambiguous work, in which the harmonising narratorial voice leaves little scope for dissent or questioning. The authoritative status of the narrator in Hartmann's *Erec* has already been noted by Harry Jackson, who states that 'predominantly in *Erec* one unambiguous ethical judgement is presented within the work as adequate to assess a given phase of the action, and on the main lines of the action the narrator guides our ethical sympathies firmly in his own voice'.[36] This manipulation is achieved not only by means of direct authorial comment, an intrusive narratorial style (see 241, 3943, 7054–56, 7826–33) and the use of ethically charged epithets and nouns such as *der guote, der degen, der guote kneht, der tugentrîche*, but also by replacing the French narrative's limited, shifting viewpoints with a more omniscient story-teller.[37] For example, whereas Chrétien's audience learns about the sparrowhawk contest only when Enide's father informs Erec of it (557ff.), the German narrator's own omniscient voice divulges this information to us at an earlier point in the story, as Erec enters the town (181ff.). Similarly, while Chrétien's description of the exhausted Erec returning to his wife after fighting the giants shifts from Erec's to Enide's viewpoint (4597ff.), in order to prepare for her reaction, Hartmann relates the event solely from the male perspective, thus fusing viewpoints. The narrator's control over his material is further in evidence where Chrétien's dramatic narration in the present tense is replaced by an account of events in the preterite. This not only imposes a sense of closure and finality on the action, which the more open-ended present tense does not convey. It also gives the impression that the adaptor, unlike his predecessor, knows the outcome of events in advance and divulges this information at will. Finally, while Chrétien's narrator is sometimes unreliable and often to be dissociated from the author, Jackson has shown that in *Erec*, but not in *Iwein*, 'Hartmann the narrator is [. . .] Hartmann the implied poet speaking directly to reader and audience' (p. 81).

Many of the ironic discrepancies, ambiguities and conflicting value systems identified in connection with Chrétien's treatment of gender

---

[35]   See Smits (n. 24 above).
[36]   W.H. Jackson, 'Some Observations on the Status of the Narrator in Hartmann von Aue's *Erec* and *Iwein*', *Forum for Modern Language Studies*, 6 (1970), 65–82 (p. 68).
[37]   This is generally the case, though Hartmann's narrator does affect ignorance concerning the lady's *roc* in ll. 8946ff.

issues have been suppressed in the adaptation. The consequence of these omissions, modifications and the narrator's authoritarian approach is that the reader's independence is compromised. It is therefore not surprising that Eva-Maria Carne, adopting wholesale Hartmann's stereotyped views on the role and nature of women, claims that 'fast alle Frauengestalten Hartmanns sind positive Erscheinungen' and then goes on to say somewhat approvingly that 'Enîte ist zarter und demütiger gezeichnet', while Enide is 'weniger unterwürfig und fromm'.[38] It is indeed true that Enide acts and speaks at times with courage, strength and spirit, while Hartmann's Enite is the embodiment of guête, triuwe, humility, and the passive acceptance of fate or God's will (see 3149ff., 3259ff., 3414ff.).[39] However, to suggest that the German heroine is a more positive figure than Chrétien's is to betray a certain complicity with Hartmann's ideal of femininity, an ideal constantly promoted through the narrator's insistence on wîplîcher site and guête (3445–49, 5762).

Encouraged by this patriarchally conditioned 'positive' view of Enite, Carne then asserts rather romantically: 'In Hartmanns Erec wird das Zusammenwirken von Held und Heldin, eine Nebensache bei Chrétien, zum leitenden Motiv' (p. 147). Yet this view is hardly borne out by the text. The adaptor's main theme seems to me to be Erec's rewinning of sælde and êre after his verligen.[40] These themes are developed often in lengthy passages which concentrate on Erec's activities in male company and in which Enite is either not present or not mentioned. For example, Hartmann's much expanded account of Chrétien's Tenebroc tournament (C: 2135–2262; H: 2378–2807) and Erec's conversation with Ivreins (8520–75). Indeed, Kellermann is surely right when he says: 'Hartmann a centré son roman sur le personnage d'Erec', while 'Chrétien a voulu écrire le roman d'un couple'.[41] This concentration on the hero at the expense of the heroine has been achieved by reducing substantially the problematic of Enide's parole. Hartmann has retained the theme of speaking only insofar as it is necessary to the plot.[42] The whole scene of the parole has been greatly reduced, with indirect speech

---

[38] Eva-Maria Carne, Die Frauengestalten bei Hartmann von Aue (Marburg, 1970), pp. 13 and 147.

[39] Compare Enide's courageous speech to the count of Limors (4844–52) with Enite's less spirited lament which revives Erec (6584–86).

[40] See F.P. Pickering, 'The "Fortune" of Hartmann's Erec', in F.P. Pickering, Essays on Medieval German Literature and Iconography (Cambridge, 1980), pp. 110–29. The view that Hartmann's romance is much more concerned with Erec than with the couple is supported by Silvia Ranawake's study of Erec's sloth in this volume.

[41] See Wilhelm Kellermann, 'L'Adaptation du roman d'Erec et Enide de Chrestien de Troyes par Hartmann von Aue', in Mélanges Jean Frappier, 2 vols (Geneva, 1970), I, pp. 509–22 (pp. 513–14).

[42] Thus Enite, like her French counterpart, saves her husband from Guivreiz's attack by speaking (6946), rouses her husband by shouting, lamenting, etc.

replacing some of the model's direct discourse.[43] Furthermore, the term *parole*, a leitmotif in the model, is replaced in the adaptation by the less specific terms *rede* and *mære*, which are made to refer to the situation in general and the criticisms of Erec's men, as well as to Enite's speech. Later Hartmann suppresses the French heroine's monologue of self-castigation (C: 2782–94), and although in the 'Totenklage' Enite accuses herself of folly ('ich tumbe' 5960) and regrets *die rede*, she uses no term as strong as the French *orguel*, for the German poet does not consider her guilty of pride. This is confirmed when Hartmann has Erec *ask* for forgiveness rather than grant it (6795–99) and the adaptor includes no equivalent here to the French Erec's reference to his wife's offending *parole* (4931). Enite, as an object of desire, is still a problem; as a speaking subject she has been practically deproblematised, hence neutralised, and the narrative can thus concentrate on Erec's rehabilitation.

When Carne claims that, unlike Enite, 'Enide wird von ihrem Stolz geleitet, das harmonische Dasein in Karnant zu stören. Darum fühlt sie sich schuldig und ist bereit, ihre Strafe zu tragen' (p. 147), she has overlooked much of the ambiguity of the source text. While it is true that Chrétien's Enide *feels* guilty, I hope to have shown that there is little objective evidence that she has disrupted their marital harmony through her pride.[44] Carne does not consider the possibility of irony in the 'Vorlage', nor really question the reasons behind Hartmann's almost complete suppression of the motif of pride. He may well have wished to rehabilitate his heroine (in accordance with his own ideals of femininity) and therefore presents her largely as an innocent victim. What he has clearly done though is to remove some of the disturbing, thought-provoking paradoxes from Chrétien's work.

This is not to say that ironic discrepancy is totally absent from Hartmann's work. For example, the adaptor juxtaposes Erec's criticism of Enite along misogynistic lines (he claims that all women are disobedient and perverse, (3242–58)) with Enite's earlier monologue (3149ff.), in which love and loyalty are clearly shown to be behind her disobedience. Kathryn Smits notes that this narrative strategy enables Hartmann to distance himself from Erec's viewpoint.[45] Later, however, when Erec asks for forgiveness for subjecting his wife to so much suffering, Erec's view coalesces with that of the narrator, who frequently shows sympathy for Enite's plight (see 3103–05, 3278–83),

---

[43] See my own discussion of this scene in 'Direct Speech – A Key to the German Adaptor's Art?', in *Medieval Translators and their Craft*, ed. by Jeanette Beer, Studies in Medieval Culture, 25 (Kalamazoo, Michigan, 1989), pp. 213–46.

[44] Marital harmony had already been jeopardised by Erec's excessive devotion to his wife. The narrator makes it quite clear by the use of singular verbs (2434ff.) that it is Erec's behaviour and attitude which are at fault, not the exemplary Enide (see 2402–33).

[45] Smits (n. 24 above), p. 17.

and the conflict between hero and narrator is resolved. Chrétien's
version does not contain such a harmonising of views and is
consequently more ambiguous.[46]

Contradictions and contrasts also appear in the adaptation as
remnants of Chrétien's courtly mystification and demystification of the
love relationship. Hartmann too has the chivalry topos and references to
'âmîen' (468) and 'vriundinne' (200), juxtaposed with Erec's particularly
harsh treatment of Enite as his squire. However, the adaptor suppresses
Erec's problematic reference to himself as a *chevalier servant* and removes
the ambiguity in Chrétien's account of the knight's inspiration during
the sparrowhawk contest (C: 911–24). Hartmann alters the order of
events so that his hero thinks first of the shame inflicted by the dwarf,
then turns his thoughts to Enite. In this way the narrator is able to link
thoughts of love explicitly and unambiguously with the knight's
renewed vigour (930–39), and the idea that women are capable of
inspiring men to great feats is not questioned.

Rather than encouraging debate on gender issues and the role of men
and women within marriage, Hartmann proposes a model of the ideal
couple, in which the male should be supported and aided in his royal
duties and knightly pursuits by the love of a good woman. There is no
suggestion that the woman might contribute actively to the knight's
education; she serves simply as a model of long-suffering, passive
acceptance and loyalty. Thus the heroine's speech is presented as much
less significant in the adaptation than it was in the source, and a similar
fate awaits the utterances of the other problematic female in the text. For
whereas Chrétien has permitted both Maboagrain and his *amie* to
express their views on their relationship, Hartmann has conflated these
two voices, allowing only Mabonagrin to speak on their behalf.
Although the knight does relay his lady's words regarding her sacrifice
(9491–92), her speech loses its force in being reported by a man. Thus
the independent and somewhat conflicting views of male and female are
subsumed in a male-dominated conversation, in which Erec makes the
sort of sweeping remarks about women (9415–42) which occur
frequently in the adaptation (see 3242ff., 3280, 3289, 5103ff., 5760ff.).
Hartmann does allow Enite and the girl to speak together, but their
words are not conveyed to us, not even through indirect speech. We are
merely told that they talked, as women do, about love and suffering:

> und geselleten sich dâ mite
> nâch wîplîchem site. (9710–11)

---

[46] Furthermore, the German narrator tells us authoritatively that Erec had behaved thus
in order to test his wife (6781). When the French Erec says 'Bien vos ai del tot essaiee'
(4921), we are left in doubt as to whether this was his original intention or an attempt by
Erec to rationalise irrational behaviour after the event. Ambiguity prevails.

Thus Hartmann's narrator again exploits his authority in order to reinforce traditional stereotypes of women and to impose on his *matière* a unifying meaning which would appeal to twelfth-century patriarchal society. It is therefore not surprising that even some modern female readers find it difficult to resist the authoritative message the adaptation conveys. Chrétien's romance, however, with its more problematic, speaking women, complicated narrative strategies and multiple layers of meaning is much more subversive, and offers far more scope for the questioning and dissenting female response.

Chrétien, Hartmann, and the Knight as Fighting Man: On Hartmann's Chivalric Adaptation of Erec et Enide

MARTIN H. JONES

It may seem superfluous – indeed, it is in a sense tautological – to speak of 'the knight as fighting man', but our interest in the knightly heroes of medieval romance generally tends to become focused on one or more aspects of chivalry, that complex of social, moral, and religious values which by the late twelfth century had become attached to the knight, with the result that his historically essential character of the mounted warrior whose business is armed conflict receives little direct attention. We know that the knightly hero engages in combat, that it is his principal form of activity, a prime means whereby he interacts with the world around him, but his combats, while they naturally prove his valour and capability in the exercise of arms, are usually examined above all for what they reveal of his standing in terms other than the strictly martial.

In considering the story of Erec as told by Chrétien de Troyes and Hartmann von Aue we are led to view the hero as a knight in both these respects, as a representative of chivalry and as a fighting man. The issues which arise during the period of Erec's regency in his father's country and subsequently are in large measure ones which pertain to the aspirations of chivalry. They concern his relationship to the lady he loves, who is also his wife, the nature of love and marriage and their function in relation to society, the proper goals of chivalric action, the relationship of knighthood to kingship, and the qualities required for Christian kingship. Such matters are the stuff of chivalric romance, at least in its more sophisticated forms, and they are major concerns of this romance in both the versions considered here. But what happens to the newly-wed Erec also creates a point of particular interest in that there is a hiatus in his career as a knight caused by his withdrawal from all forms of chivalric activity. A change comes over him, with the result that he lacks the resolve or fails to see the need to engage in knightly pursuits at all any more and does not even attempt to find a compromise between amatory and martial interests. A question which commands attention, along with others, in the subsquent events is whether Erec has what it takes to be a knight in the sense of being effective as a fighting man. Chrétien and Hartmann deal with this question differently, and it is the purpose of this essay to demonstrate just that, by an examination of the way in which each of them presents events from the time of Erec's departure from court with his wife up to his first combat with King Guivret/Guivreiz.

The theme of Erec's physical and mental preparedness for combat is not strictly confined to this portion of the texts. It is raised already in the first scene involving Erec, where, for reasons which neither of the works makes absolutely clear, he is not equipped to meet the challenge posed by the vicious actions of the dwarf; and the reverberations of the theme are to be detected right through to the Joie de la Cort episode, whose terrors are such as to represent a severe test of any knight's courage. But it is in the sequence of episodes immediately following the crisis in Erec's life that the theme is most insistent, and his first combat with the dwarf-like king of Ireland resolves the doubts about his capacity as a fighting man in so far as it results in a bond of friendship between them, implying Erec's re-integration into the fellowship of knighthood from which he excluded himself during his regency. In order to assess the differences in the way that Chrétien and Hartmann deal with these episodes, it is necessary, first, to examine more closely the terms in which they present Erec's abstention from knightly activity, and, secondly, to make some observations in general on how the two poets depict Erec's actions as a fighting man.[1]

---

[1] References are to the following editions: *Les Romans de Chrétien de Troyes, I: Erec et Enide*, ed. by Mario Roques, CFMA, 80 (Paris, 1977); *Erec von Hartmann von Aue*, ed. by Albert Leitzmann, continued by Ludwig Wolff, 6th edn, prepared by Christoph Cormeau and Kurt Gärtner, ATB, 39 (Tübingen, 1985). The abbreviations *EE* and *E* respectively are used throughout. In view of the questions raised by the new Wolfenbüttel fragments of *Erec*, it should be pointed out that this essay assumes that the Ambraser Heldenbuch preserves Hartmann's text in essence. See Kurt Gärtner, 'Der Text der Wolfenbütteler Erec-Fragmente und seine Bedeutung für die Erec-Forschung', *PBB* (Tüb.), 104 (1982), 207–30 and 359–430, and Eberhard Nellmann, 'Ein zweiter Erec-Roman? Zu den neugefundenen Wolfenbütteler Fragmenten', *ZfdPh*, 101 (1982), 28–78.

I

In Chrétien's account of events at Carnant there is a sharply focused contrast between *amors* and *armes*, Erec's preoccupation with his love for Enide displacing all interest in arms and tournaments:

> Mes tant l'ama Erec d'amors,
> que d'armes mes ne li chaloit,
> ne a tornoiemant n'aloit.
> N'avoit mes soing de tornoier.   (*EE* 2430–33)

Erec still provides for his knights and sends them excellently equipped to tournaments but he does not attend himself (*EE* 2446–54). All the nobles lament the fact that he has no desire to bear arms (*EE* 2455–58), and Enide hears 'chevaliers et [. . .] sergenz' (*EE* 2460) say that he is tired or neglectful of arms and chivalric activity: 'que recreant aloit ses sire/ d'armes et de chevalerie' (*EE* 2462–63). She herself is distressed that the best, most valorous and resolute of knights (*EE* 2495–96) should have renounced 'tote chevalerie' for her sake (*EE* 2500). She is acutely conscious of the universal regret that he has forsaken arms (*EE* 2543) and of his loss of reputation, as everyone mocks him and calls him 'recreant': 'recreant vos apelent tuit' (*EE* 2551).

In this report of society's unanimous view of Erec there falls, for the second time in the episode, the word which has come to stand for Erec's downfall – *recreant*. This word is not limited to the military sphere, signifying one who is weak or cowardly, but can indicate a more general condition of sloth and neglectfulness of responsibilities.[2] In the present context, however, the focus on Erec's withdrawal from all chivalric activity brings the military sense to the fore, so that the charge of *recreantise* concerns his capacity as a fighting man and contains the imputation of cowardice. Certainly this is the sense in which Enide understood the accusation, as is shown by her reflections on her role in the episode at Carnant which follow Erec's victory over the two groups of robber knights. She chides herself for having doubted his courage: she knew then that there was no better knight and she knows it all the more surely now, for she has seen that he fears neither three nor five armed men: 'Bien le savoie. Or le sai

---

[2] See Adolf Tobler and Erhard Lommatzsch, *Altfranzösisches Wörterbuch*, vol. VIII (Wiesbaden, 1971), col. 505: 'recrëant [. . .]: schlapp, schwach, mutlos, feig, im Kampf unterlegen'; also Glyn S. Burgess, *Chrétien de Troyes: Erec et Enide*, Critical Guides to French Texts, 32 (London, 1984), p. 49: 'To be *recreant* is both to be idle, a victim of sloth or *accidia*, and incapable of fighting adequately, because of cowardice or physical weakness. To be *recreant* at the end of a combat, when drained of energy, is a matter for shame and regret [. . .]. To be *recreant* before one begins is a scandal.'

mialz;/ car ge l'ai veü a mes ialz,/ car trois ne cinc armez ne dote' (*EE* 3107–09). She knows that there is no question of Erec having fallen prey to fear of knightly activity and become a coward, but that is the impression which his behaviour made on others, and it is that slur which must be removed by his actions.

No less clearly, though perhaps more discreetly, than in his source Hartmann depicts Erec as absorbed in erotic pleasures on his return home to Karnant (*E* 2929–30, 2935–53), but he presents the change that has come over him as affecting his life more generally than is the case in Chrétien, a fact reflected in his choice of the verb *sich verligen* to describe his condition.[3] In addition to his abstention from chivalric activity – the failure to attend tournaments is again specifically mentioned, Erec is said to be dedicated to a life of ease, *gemach*: 'sich vlizzen sîne sinne/ wie er alle sîne sache/ wante zuo gemache' (*E* 2931–33; cf. 2966–67 and the ironic reference to 'arbeit' in 2946). He avoids all but the most perfunctory appearances in public, emerging from the marital chamber only for mass once and for meals twice daily (*E* 2935–53). His conduct is shown to have a demoralizing and deleterious effect on his court. Knights and squires who had found activities to their liking ('vreude') there previously now desert the court, and its reputation is so poor that no one is drawn to it any more for any 'vreude' that it might afford (*E* 2974–92). The universal opinion is that he is going to ruin – 'des verdirbet unser herre' (*E* 2998). This judgement points to a general personal and social degeneration which makes Erec unfit to rule. His neglect of chivalric activity forms explicitly but one part of this decline, and it touches on Erec's standing specifically as a knight less acutely than does the charge of cowardice that Chrétien's Erec suffers.

Yet we should not fail to be sensitive to the knightly undertones of much of what is described here by Hartmann. Erec's pursuit of the soft life, *gemach*, is a denial of a cardinal condition of the chivalric existence, the readiness constantly to maintain hardiness of body and mind in order to meet the challenge of combat. His failure to participate in tournaments personally, though he makes it possible for knights of his court to do so – Hartmann pointedly praises this in him (*E* 2956–57, 2965), appears in a similar light when juxtaposed with talk of his devotion to *gemach*. The tournament was not only an occasion for the individual to prove his worth and enhance his reputation in the way that Erec does at Arthur's court after his marriage; it was also – and probably its very origins lie in this – a training ground for combat and warfare, so that by avoiding tournaments Erec is turning his back on a prime

---

3   See Silvia Ranawake's contribution in this volume, and her earlier essay: 'Erec's *verligen* and the Sin of Sloth', in *Hartmann von Aue: Changing Perspectives: London Hartmann Symposium 1985*, ed. by Timothy McFarland and Silvia Ranawake, GAG, 486 (Göppingen, 1988), pp. 93–115 (especially pp. 98–100).

opportunity to ensure his continued effectiveness as a knight.[4] The description of his daily round is introduced with the words 'als er nie würde der man' (E 2935) – possibly meaning 'as though he had never become a knight'[5] and a pointer to the significance of the reference to the mass which follows. For elsewhere in *Erec* knights attend mass (which is followed by a meal) only before fighting, either in single combat, as when Erec is due to confront Iders (E 662–68) and later Mabonagrin (E 8635–47), or in the tournament (E 2540–43).[6] In the light of the earlier allusions to the mass in the text, the description of his lying with Enite until the bell summons them, of how they rise in leisurely fashion (E 2941 'vil müezeclîche'; cf. the emended reading of the fifth and earlier editions: 'vil unmüezeclîche'), then walk, hand in hand, to the chapel, the service being followed by a quick meal and a swift retreat to bed, is a further telling comment on the extent to which Erec has distanced himself from the knightly life, a point reinforced by the irony of 'diz was sîn meistiu arbeit' (E 2946). Finally, the *vreude* which is said to be lacking at Karnant as a consequence of the change in Erec's behaviour (E 2977, 2989, 2992) may well contain an allusion specifically to his failure to stage chivalric events there himself, as well as more generally to the demoralized atmosphere of the court under his direction. Imain, we are

---

[4] The fact that in both texts the tournament is the one form of chivalric activity which Erec is specifically said to have neglected, rather than some more obviously grievous dereliction of lordly duty such as the failure to maintain the country's security, is at once an indication of the central place which tourneying had come to occupy in courtly life by this time and an encouragement to consider whether its significance does not extend beyond the winning of reputation, important though that certainly was, as we see in the tournament after Erec's marriage. The motive of material gain, which was in reality a considerable factor in the popularity of the tournament and to which Hartmann alludes (E 2613–20), does not appear to be pertinent here. In addition to the aspect of training, to which attention has been drawn, it is noteworthy that for Hartmann the tournament is an activity which Erec would otherwise have shared with his companions (E 2963–64), emphasizing his withdrawal from the knightly fraternity. It goes without saying that Erec's neglect of tourneying after excelling in it at Arthur's court underlines the change in his style of life when he returns home.

[5] It is difficult to see what other meaning might attach to these words, especially in the light of the preceding verses (E 2924ff.). For examples of 'man werden' in the sense of 'to become a knight', see Georg Friedrich Benecke, Wilhelm Müller and Friedrich Zarncke, *Mittelhochdeutsches Wörterbuch*, II, 1 (Leipzig, 1863; repr. Stuttgart, 1990), pp. 30–31 Although there was no strict correlation between attaining the age of majority and dubbing to knighthood, the latter act was taken to mark the end of the period of dependent youthfulness and the assumption of personal responsibility. See Elsbet Orth, 'Formen und Funktionen der Rittererhebung', in *Curialitas: Studien zu Grundfragen der höfisch-ritterlichen Kultur*, ed. by Josef Fleckenstein, Veröffentlichungen des Max-Planck-Instituts für Geschichte, 100 (Göttingen, 1990), pp. 128–70 (pp. 154–56).

[6] Erec attends church before entering upon the second day of the tournament, though it is not specified that the service is a mass (E 2487–92); he eats on that day after mass has been attended by the other knights (E 2544). The only references to mass in *Iwein* occur in similar circumstances: *Iwein: Eine Erzählung von Hartmann von Aue*, ed. by G.F. Benecke and K. Lachmann, revised by Ludwig Wolff, 7th edn, 2 vols (Berlin, 1968), I, ll. 4820–24, 6587ff.

told, arranges the sparrow-hawk contest annually 'ze vreuden sîner lantdiet' (E 192), and the demand from guests at Erec's wedding for a tournament to mark the occasion is supported by the remark 'sît si durch vreude wæren komen/ ze Britanje in ir lant' (E 2227–28). Because Erec does not make such provision, no one is attracted to his court: 'in [= his court] endorfte ûz vremden landen/ durch vreude niemen suochen' (E 2991–92).

What emerges, then, as a subtext in Hartmann's account of Erec's life at Karnant is the description of one who no longer has any understanding of the ethos of knighthood, of what is required in order to maintain excellence in the profession of arms.[7] It is a problem of mentality which is exposed here rather than a question of prowess, as in the case of Chrétien's Erec; it is the fact that 'sîn muot' can no longer be described as 'ritterlîch' since Erec has returned to Karnant (E 2925) that represents the challenge in the next stage of his progress as a fighting man.

II

In one of the few direct comparisons of combat descriptions specifically in Erec et Enide and Erec, Werner Richter commented: 'Hartmann hat ja in allem, was Kampf und Turnier betrifft, seine Chrétiensche Vorlage nur als Anregung benutzt. Chrétien ist viel ausführlicher als Hartmann. Von den einzelnen Gängen des Kampfes stimmt kein einziger so recht in beiden Werken überein.'[8] In its stress on Hartmann's independence from his source this assessment is assuredly accurate. He is not bound to Chrétien even in the number of combats he attributes to Erec: in the tournament he adds more than thirty encounters to the three which Chrétien records, bringing the total for the work as a whole to over fifty as against the twenty in Erec et Enide;[9] on the other hand, he later consolidates the attacks of several of the robbers, described individually by Chrétien, into one summary account (E 3392–99), and he removes the figure of Galoain's seneschal and with him one whole combat. In the combat with Iders, Hartmann describes six jousts as against the one which Chrétien's Erec fights, resulting in an almost sixfold expansion of this first phase of the encounter, while in the ensuing sword fight much of the action is couched in metaphors of gambling and commercial

---

7   An implication of this observation is that active participation in chivalry is a condition of successful lordship, a principle which is otherwise maintained in both versions of the story.
8   Werner Richter, Der Lanzelet des Ulrich von Zazikhoven, Deutsche Forschungen, 27 (Frankfurt a.M., 1934), p. 104.
9   The figure for Erec et Enide excludes only Erec's actions in the mêlée (EE 2186–94) and his attack on Oringles.

exchange which have the effect of 'deconcretizing'[10] the passage of arms and adding a kind of interpretative gloss to it. Details are moved from one combat in Chrétien to another combat in Hartmann: the motif of the breaking of a sword in the course of combat is transferred, together with other features, from Chrétien's account of the first combat with Guivret to the Mabonagrin combat in *Erec*.[11] In other cases details are introduced and used to link combats, as with Hartmann's description of the horses being set back on their hocks by the force of the knights' collision in both the Iders and the first Guivreiz combats (E 774–76, 4390–92).[12] The list of such changes is almost endless, confirming that Richter was right to emphasize that Hartmann went his own way in his depiction of combat.

However, Richter's claim that Chrétien is much more detailed than Hartmann specifically in his combat descriptions requires a certain qualification.[13] It is necessary to ask in what regard he is more detailed. If one is looking for a circumstantial description of the way that knights close with one another for the joust, with attention paid to the correct handling of shield and lance and the means of controlling the horse in the gallop, then one must turn to Hartmann's account of Erec's combat with Mabonagrin (E 9070–97) and not to Chrétien's work, where nothing comparable can be found. On the other hand, and this is presumably what Richter had in mind, it is the case that Chrétien is significantly more graphic than Hartmann when it comes to describing the exchange of blows, whether by lance or sword, and the damaging effect which these weapons have on armour and body. For example, in the longest of the three sword fights depicted by Chrétien, that between Erec and Yders, there are five distinct phases as attacks simultaneously by both knights alternate with attacks by only one of them, and in each of these phases we are told of the blows sustained by their equipment – helms, shields, hauberks – and by various parts of their bodies – necks, shoulders, thighs, and skulls – and of the wounds from which blood flows profusely. By contrast, in Hartmann's account of that incident, which is no shorter, there is reference only to the damage sustained by helms (twice) and a shield (once) and none at all to wounds and the shedding of blood, and even the blow which brings Erec victory, graphically visualized by Chrétien, is not described at all (EE 875–988, E 833–950). Furthermore, in Chrétien's accounts of lance attacks, which

---

[10] I use this word in imitation of Pérennec's term 'déconcrétisation' to describe the phenomenon: René Pérennec, *Recherches sur le roman arthurien en vers en Allemagne aux XIIe et XIIIe siècles*, GAG, 393, I–II, 2 vols (Göppingen, 1984), I, 8ff.

[11] On the significance of this change, see Gärtner (see n. 1 above), p. 411.

[12] See Jean Fourquet, 'Hartmann d'Aue et l'adaptation courtoise: Histoire d'une invention de détail', *Et. Germ.*, 27 (1972), 333–40, and Gärtner (see n. 1 above), pp. 395–96.

[13] That Chrétien's descriptions are in general more detailed and 'realistic' than Hartmann's is a commonplace in comparisons of the two poets which does not require documentation.

far outnumber the sword attacks, occurring in all but two of the combats which he describes, shields are split asunder, hauberks torn, and bodies pierced, sometimes in gruesome fashion, while Hartmann only exceptionally goes beyond a reference to the impact of the lances and the unhorsing of one or both of the combatants.

Looking more closely at Chrétien's technique in the description of Erec's combats, it is evident that he is indebted to the conventions of the epic tradition, as exemplified above all in the *chansons de geste* but also in the *romans d'antiquité* which preceded him.[14] This debt is very striking in the case of the lance attack, which constitutes, as just indicated, the predominant form of fighting in the work and is of particular interest in the present context, since it makes up the bulk of the evidence of Erec's fighting in the events following the crisis at Carnant.

In his study of the narrative art of the *chanson de geste*, Jean Rychner identified a scheme of seven elements, to each of which attaches a range of formulaic expressions, constituting what he called the 'motif' of the lance attack in the epic.[15] Subsequent analysis of the scheme suggests that one of Rychner's elements should be removed,[16] leaving six which occur in the following order:

1. Spurring the horse
2. Striking the opponent
3. Shattering his shield
4. Breaking or piercing his hauberk
5. Thrusting the lance into his body or just grazing it
6. Knocking him down from his horse, usually lifeless.

[14] Chrétien's dependence on the *chansons de geste* in this regard has been commented on, with varying emphases, on several occasions, though the detail of it has not been worked out, nor has account always been taken of the differences between his practice in *Erec et Enide* and in his later works. See S. Heinimann, 'Zur stilgeschichtlichen Stellung Chrétiens', in *Mélanges de linguistique et de littérature romanes à la mémoire d'István Frank*, Annales Universitatis Saraviensis, 6 (Saarbrücken, 1957), pp. 235–50 (p. 240); Renate Hitze, *Studien zu Sprache und Stil der Kampfschilderungen in den chansons de geste*, Kölner Romanistische Arbeiten, N.F., Heft 33 (Geneva/Paris, 1965), pp. 146–48; Alois Wolf, 'Die "adaptation courtoise": Kritische Anmerkungen zu einem neuen Dogma', *GRM*, 27 (1977), 257–83 (p. 267); Katalin Halász, *Structures narratives chez Chrétien de Troyes*, Studia Romanica Universitatis Debreceniensis de Ludovico Kossuth nominatae, Series Litteraria, Fasc. VII (Debrecen, 1980), pp. 62–63. Detailed information on combat descriptions in the *chansons de geste* is to be found above all in Hitze, but see also Otto Clausnitzer, *Die Kampfschilderungen in den ältesten chansons de geste: Ein Beitrag zur Entstehungsgeschichte der altfranzösischen Heldendichtung* (dissertation, Halle, 1926), pp. 66–86, 92–101. Viktor Schroedter, *Der Wortschatz Kristians von Troyes bezüglich der Ausdrücke der Kampfschilderung* (dissertation, Leipzig, 1907) includes parallels from the works of Wace and the *romans d'antiquité*.

[15] Jean Rychner, *La chanson de geste: Essai sur l'art épique des jongleurs* (Geneva/Lille, 1955), pp. 126–29, 139–48.

[16] See the two articles by Edward A. Heinemann: 'Composition stylisée et technique littéraire dans la *Chanson de Roland*', *Romania*, 94 (1973), 1–28, and 'La place de l'élément "brandir la lance" dans la structure du motif de l'attaque à la lance', *Romania*, 95 (1974), 105–13.

To illustrate how the scheme is realized in practice in a *chanson de geste*, a *roman d'antiquité*, and Chrétien, three combat descriptions, drawn from *La Chanson de Roland*, *Eneas*, and *Erec et Enide*, are set out below and marked to show the incidence of the six elements.[17]

Sun cheval brochet, laiset curre a esforz,	1
Vait le ferir li quens quanque il pout.	2
L'escut li freint e l'osberc li desclot,	3, 4
Trenchet le piz, si li briset les os,	5
Tute l'eschine li desevret del dos,	5
Od sun espiét l'anme li getet fors;	
Enpeint le ben, fait li brandir le cors,	
Pleine sa hanste del cheval l'abat mort,	6
En dous meitiez li ad brisét le col.	5

(*La Chanson de Roland* 1197–1205)[18]

Il a devant soi mis l'escu,	
l'uns vers l'autre point lo cheval,	1
si s'antrefierent li vasal.	2
Lausus lo fiert an l'escu halt,	2
desor la bocle. Ce qui chalt?	
Unques la lance n'i antra,	(3)
il nel fandi n'il nel perça.	
Eneas ravoit lui feru	2
o grant vigor desor l'escu,	
qu'il li a frait et peçoié,	3
l'auberc rompu et desmaillié.	4
Lez le costé desoz l'aiselle	
li a conduite l'alemelle,	
il ne lo tocha giens el cors,	(5)
mais de la selle l'a mis fors;	6
par som la coe del destrier	
lo trebucha jus el gravier.	

(*Eneas* 5884–900)[19]

Lors torne l'escu et la lance,	
contre le chevalier se lance;	
cil le voit venir, si l'escrie.	
Quant Erec l'ot, si le desfie;	

---

[17] A number in brackets indicates that the element concerned is represented by the negation of the action which it describes.

[18] *La Chanson de Roland*, ed. by F. Whitehead (Oxford, 1978).

[19] *Eneas: Roman du XIIe siècle*, ed. by J.-J. Salverda de Grave, CFMA, 44 and 62, 2 vols (Paris, 1973 and 1968).

andui poignent, si s'antre vienent,   1
les lances esloigniees tienent;
mes cil a a Erec failli,   (2)
et Erec a lui maubailli
que bien le sot droit anvaïr.
Sor l'escu fiert de tel aïr   2
que d'un chief en autre le fant,   3
ne li haubers ne li desfant:
en mi le piz le fraint et ront,   4
et de la lance li repont
pié et demi dedanz le cors.   5
Au retrere a son cop estors,
et cil cheï; morir l'estut,   6
car li glaives el cuer li but.   5

(*EE* 2853–70)

Clearly the descriptions drawn from the romances are somewhat longer than that from the *Roland* but most of the expansion can be explained by the change from the paratactic, formulaic style of the epic to the more supple hypotaxis of the romances, and by the fact that in the romance examples the actions of both combatants are described, whereas the *Roland* focuses exclusively on Roland. The emphasis remains the same in all three instances, lying firmly on the destructive and wounding path of the lance in the clash of combatants, in preference to other aspects of the performance of the lance attack which can be highlighted, such as the management of arms and horse in the approach to the joust, as exemplified by the Mabonagrin combat in Hartmann.

Chrétien does not reproduce the epic scheme for the lance attack slavishly. There is only one other example like that cited above in which all six elements of the motif are represented,[20] and variation in detail is a notable feature of his combat descriptions in *Erec et Enide*.[21] Yet throughout the work we can detect the influence of the scheme, with its focus on the penetrating and wounding force of the lance as a recurrent feature. In Chrétien's later works, with the partial exception of *Cligés*, this influence is much less in evidence. No other work has an example of the lance attack realized in all particulars of the scheme, and frequently the descriptions cover only the charge and the thrust of the lance, which, if the shaft does not splinter, kills the opponent outright or

[20] Rychner (see n. 15 above) notes that not all the elements of his scheme are present in every instance in the *chansons de geste*: 'L'un ou l'autre de ces éléments manque souvent' (p. 141).
[21] Roques (see n. 1 above) draws attention to 'la diversité des combats d'Érec' (pp. XXV–XXVI, n. 1).

unhorses him wounded.[22] Descriptions which give some of the further detail of the epic scheme are not numerous, and where they do occur, as for example in Lancelot's final combat with Meleagant,[23] Yvain's combat with Esclados,[24] and some of Gauvain's combats in *Perceval*,[25] it is possible to see that the epic style has been chosen for a purpose. This last point may be held to be valid for Chrétien's use of the motif in *Erec et Enide* as well, in preference to the possible alternative explanation that his debt to the *chansons de geste* and *romans d'antiquité* arises from the fact that this was his first chivalric romance when he was still under the shadow of these predecessors. For it is very much to Chrétien's purpose to depict Erec as an effective fighting man both before and after his period of *recreantise*, and there could scarcely be a better way to do that than to portray his fighting in a manner reminiscent of the epic.

The realization that, in his combat descriptions, Chrétien stands in a literary tradition whose conventions he exploits for his own purposes raises the question as to whether Hartmann, who avoids the kind of emphases that Chrétien places, was in a comparable position in relation to his own literature. The short answer to that question is that he both was and was not. He was *not* in a comparable position when it came to the depiction of the lance attack, for, quite in contrast to what we have observed for France in the twelfth century, there is no evidence from German texts of that time for the existence of any pattern of description which could be called a convention or on which a tradition could be founded.[26] There are relatively few texts of a date earlier than Erec that

[22] Halász (see n. 14 above) comments on the progressive reduction in the space given to describing 'l'échange de coups' in the works following *Erec et Enide* (pp. 49–50, 61). Though the full epic scheme for the lance attack does not occur in *Cligés*, severe woundings are not uncommon. The prominence of scenes of warfare in this work accounts for the traces of the epic manner here.
[23] *Les Romans de Chrétien de Troyes, III: Le Chevalier de la Charrete*, ed. by Mario Roques, CFMA, 86 (Paris, 1978), ll. 7010–38.
[24] Chrestien de Troyes, *Yvain (Le Chevalier au lion)*, ed. by T.B.W. Reid (Manchester, 1942, repr. 1967), ll. 815–23.
[25] Chrétien de Troyes, *Le Roman de Perceval ou le Conte du Graal*, ed. by William Roach, Textes Littéraires Français, 71, 2nd edn (Geneva/Paris, 1959), ll. 7347–57, 8392–406.
[26] See Karl Grundmann, *Studien zur Speerkampfschilderung im Mittelhochdeutschen: Ein Beitrag zur Entwicklung des höfischen Stil- und Lebensgefühls*, Universitas Josephi Pilsudski Varsoviensis, Acta Facultatis Litterarum, 3 (Warsaw, 1939), pp. 203–04: 'Mochte nun auch der Schwertkampf auf eine altheimische Tradition zurückblicken, [. . .] so ist die Speerkampfschilderung eine fast ausschließliche Neuschöpfung der höfischen Zeit.' The formation of a poetic convention will obviously have been consequent upon the military innovation of fighting with the lance in couched position. It is not known precisely when this new combat technique became established in Germany, but it seems to have been later than in the French-speaking world, where the evidence of *La Chanson de Roland* suggests that it was developed by the late eleventh century; see D.J.A. Ross, 'L'originalité de "Turoldus": le maniement de la lance', *Cahiers de Civilisation Médiévale*, 6 (1963), 127–38. Whether this suffices to explain the difference between French and German literary traditions in this particular is uncertain.

have the lance attack, and the descriptions which they give are usually spare, covering only the striking of the opponent and his unhorsing or killing, without any reference to the penetrating path of the lance. Such exceptions as there are – for instance, in Lamprecht's *Alexanderlied* and Eilhart's *Tristrant*[27] – show rather tentative and clumsy attempts to give a more detailed picture of the action, and it was not in fact until Hartmann himself, with his descriptions in the manner of the Mabonagrin encounter in *Erec*, that a pattern which was in any way exemplary for others was created.[28] With the sword attack, however, Hartmann *was* in a position comparable to Chrétien's, in so far as there were well-established conventions and a panoply of motifs in German, to a large extent identical with those in French.[29] Hartmann shows awareness of the native German tradition in a number of details which he adds or elaborates beyond Chrétien. In the combat with the second giant, for example, he exchanges the *coup épique* with which Chrétien's hero dispatches his opponent for the motifs of cutting off the giant's leg and decapitation (*EE* 4439–46, *E* 5549–68), and in the Iders and Mabonagrin combats he develops the imagery of sparks and fire created by the knights' swordplay at points where it does not occur in Chrétien (*E* 836, 881–83, 9149–51, 9201–08, 9256–60). Hartmann was, however, inhibited from drawing on this tradition to any great extent by his desire not to identify Erec too closely with the heroic warrior figures of old, an aim evident also in his drastic reduction in the use of the heroic terms for warriors in favour of the new term *ritter*.[30]

It is no doubt for a similar reason that Hartmann judged it inappropriate to imitate the style of combat description in his source and opted for a more restrained mode which placed less emphasis on the wounding and destructive aspects of combat. His objective of establishing the new model of chivalrous knighthood in German literature[31] would not have been served by giving more prominence than was necessary to the violent side of the knight's way of life.

---

[27] *Lamprechts Alexander*, ed. by Karl Kinzel, Germanistische Handbibliothek, 6 (Halle a. S., 1884), Vorau version ll. 537–43, 1249–57 (the Straßburg version provides an interesting comparison with the Vorau in ll. 1727–31); Eilhart von Oberg, *Tristrant*, ed. by Danielle Buschinger, GAG, 202 (Göppingen, 1976), ll. 854–74.

[28] See Grundmann (see n. 26 above), pp. 214–17.

[29] See Leo Wolf, *Der groteske und hyperbolische Stil des mittelhochdeutschen Volksepos*, Palaestra, 25 (Berlin, 1903), pp. 70–85; Friedrich Bode, *Die Kamphesschilderungen* [sic] *in den mittelhochdeutschen Epen* (dissertation, Greifswald, 1909), pp. 179ff.; Hermann Kirchmeier, *Die Darstellung des Zweikampfs im mittelhochdeutschen Heldengedicht* (dissertation, Vienna, 1936), especially pp. 192–213, 230–33, 249–53.

[30] See the frequency lists for the relevant terms in Joachim Bumke, *Studien zum Ritterbegriff im 12. und 13. Jahrhundert*, Beihefte zum Euphorion, 1, 2nd edn (Heidelberg, 1977), pp. 32–34, the essential information from which appears in the third table in William Henry Jackson's contribution to this volume.

[31] See Bumke (as n. 30 above), pp. 92–95, and W.H. Jackson in this volume.

At the end of our examination of the general characteristics of combat description in *Erec et Enide* and *Erec* we have an interesting contrast. On the one side, we find that Chrétien was working within an established tradition, exploiting it for his own ends, which included the association of his hero with existing models of heroic conduct. On the other side, we find that Hartmann, anxious to project an image of the hero as one who embodies the new concept of knighthood, was not committed to the example of a pre-existing tradition; to this extent he had a freer hand than Chrétien and for him each combat was potentially an opportunity to make a new statement about the knight as fighting man.

III

It is in the events which occur in the first three days following Erec's departure from court with Enide/Enite that the issue of his *recreantise* or his *verligen*, in so far as it concerns his capacity as a fighting man, is most directly addressed and is indeed effectively resolved.[32] In both works this initial phase of rehabilitatory adventures leads to a brief reunion of the couple with Arthur's court which serves to mark what has been achieved so far. Erec's standing as a knight is not the only major theme in this portion of the narrative. His relationship with Enide/Enite in particular also comes under close scrutiny, the difficulties between them being indicated by the prohibition on her speaking. In Chrétien the two themes are directly linked when Erec's victory over the robber knights makes Enide realize that she was wrong ever to doubt his courage (*EE* 3097–112). Hartmann omits this scene but establishes a different kind of link between the themes at a later point in the sequence of events. In both works the prohibition on speaking is not repeated after Erec's effectiveness as a knight has been confirmed in the combat with Guivret/Guivreiz.

Chrétien immediately focuses our attention on Erec the fighting man in the magnificent scene of his arming prior to departure from Carnant (*EE* 2620–59). Between that time and his contact with Arthur's court, no fewer than eleven combats take place: groups of three and then of five robber knights assault Erec on the first day, and on the third day he faces challenges from Count Galoain's seneschal, Galoain himself, and Guivret. In each of these instances the initiative is taken by Erec's opponents, who are variously motivated; his role is reactive, the prime point at issue being whether he is capable of withstanding the succession of armed assaults upon him.[33]

[32] There is a different distribution of the events over the three days in the two works but this is not of importance in the present context.
[33] This statement is not meant to exclude the possibility that the episodes are also

The theme of *recreantise* is invoked explicitly in the first and in the last of these incidents. The first of the robber knights tells his companions that if they do not profit from the situation then they will be disgraced, cowardly, and extremely unlucky: 'Se nos ici ne gaaignons,/ honi somes et recreant/ et a mervoilles mescheant' (*EE* 2800–02); it is obvious that none of these epithets will be applicable to Erec if he overcomes them. When Guivret spots Erec passing by, he calls for his arms and it is made clear that he is determined to measure himself in combat with this knight until either he himself tires or Erec does and gives up: 'ou il a lui se lassera/ tant que toz recreanz sera' (*EE* 3679–80).[34] In the event, it is Guivret who must admit himself defeated, though it has to be said that the outcome is settled as much by the misfortune which Guivret suffers in the breaking of his sword as by the prowess which makes Erec a match for him until that moment.

Apart from this one incident, victory comes to Erec clearly by virtue of his superiority in the exercise of arms. Chrétien ensures that this point is made by describing each of the eleven encounters individually. All but one of them include a lance attack,[35] and it is among these instances that we find the two examples of the epic scheme realized in all its particulars. The first of these is the opening combat of the sequence, against the first of the robber knights, which has been given verbatim above; the second is the penultimate combat in the sequence, against Galoain. In the latter encounter both men's shields are pierced but with different results: while not a single link is broken from Erec's hauberk, Galoain, who has no body armour, is severely wounded as more than a yard of Erec's lance is thrust into his side (*EE* 3579–606). Between these two *tours de force*, several other combats are described in considerable detail, incorporating elements of the epic scheme with its emphasis on the lance's impact. For example, the second robber knight in the first group has a quarter of Erec's lance thrust through his body (*EE* 2871–83); the leading man in the second group is struck so powerfully that his shield flies from his neck and his collar-bone is broken (*EE* 3007–15); the next opponent is killed by a blow from Erec's lance, whose sharp tip enters his throat below the chin and cuts through bones and nerves to protrude at the far side of the neck, where warm red blood flows from either side of the wound (*EE* 3016–25); and Galoain's seneschal has the

individually significant in other respects for our understanding of what happens to Erec, but whatever their significance may be, it is predicated on the fact of his gaining victory over his opponents and what they are taken to represent.

[34] Here 'recreanz' does not mean 'cowardly' so much as 'defeated, tired to the point of surrendering', but this does not entirely neutralize the force of the word's repetition at this point.

[35] Erec attacks the last of the eight robber knights only with his sword; sword fighting follows the attack with the lance in the case of the seventh robber knight and in the combat with Guivret.

steel of Erec's strong lance thrust into his body, his shield and hauberk providing no defence (*EE* 3572–78). The final combat in the sequence is that with Guivret, which lasts a whole six hours as a fierce sword fight follows the joust; in the joust itself the leather and wood of their shields are broken and the rings of their hauberks burst apart before their lances penetrate their bodies as far as their entrails (*EE* 3756–68).

There can no doubt about the nature of Chrétien's strategy in this portion of the narrative. It is to load the dense series of combats which occur here with particularly strong epic associations, so that Erec's courage and competence as a fighting man are seen to be vindicated by his appearing in the mould of the epic heroes.

While this is the most striking way in which Chrétien shows Erec's rehabilitation as a fighting man being effected in this sequence of events, it is not the only one. In the succession of opponents he faces there is a social grading, rising from the robber knights via the count's seneschal and the count to King Guivret, in whom Erec, son of King Lac, has finally to deal with one who is his social equal. The encounter with Guivret is also a match of equals in knightly prowess, the outcome being settled by luck rather than by superior skill or strength, and in contrast to the earlier incidents it leads to friendship between the two men. This, as indicated earlier, is to be taken as signalling Erec's re-integration into the fellowship of knighthood, to which he made himself a stranger at Carnant, and this step is shortly confirmed by his contact with Arthur's court. Guivret plays an important role in marking Erec's status in knightly terms, and it is worth considering what his actions represent.

Unlike those who have previously attacked Erec, Guivret is not motivated by covetousness of a material or sexual kind in challenging him to fight but seeks rather to compete with him to see which of them is the hardier knight (*EE* 3667–80). It is a moot point whether this is to be regarded as mindless aggression or as a legitimate way of maintaining the combat fitness and reputation which underpin Guivret's lordship.[36] There is no indication that he regularly pits himself against knights in this way, but he does pride himself on exercising authority over all his neighbours and being feared by them (*EE* 3849–55), and presumably such fierceness as he displays here, or at least the threat of it, helps him to keep up that status. Guivret is a model of kingship to the extent that this dominance over others ensures the security of his country, and a

---

[36] Burgess (see n. 2 above) reflects the opposing views without attempting to reconcile them, when he describes Guivret as 'in several respects [. . .] the perfect king' (p. 66) and as one who 'clearly adopts the right approach for a knight' (p. 67), yet goes on to criticize 'his entire ethic of chivalry' (p. 67). Donald Maddox, *Structure and Sacring: The Systematic Kingdom in Chrétien's 'Erec et Enide'*, French Forum Monographs, 8 (Lexington, 1978), p. 67 refers to the 'self-determined dynamism displayed by the knight-king Guivrez', seeing him as embodying the values of chivalry and monarchy.

contrast with the inactive Erec of the Carnant episode suggests itself, leading us to wonder how long the country would remain safe under the regency of a lord who has become *recreant*.

There is possibly an allusion to tourneying in the reference to Guivret having seen Erec pass in front of 'ses lices' (*EE* 3676),[37] and this might be intended to place what he does here on a par with that activity, which Erec avoided during his regency at Carnant. Were that the case, then Guivret's action in challenging Erec would be seen to relate to an aspect of the knight's existence in which Erec has been deficient and which needs to be reinstated in his life. This would in turn imply that Guivret's conduct is to be judged in a positive rather than a negative light. This is a speculative line of argument, but it has the virtue of suggesting that the ethic which Guivret embodies is appropriate for Erec, in that effective kingship is seen to be founded upon active knighthood, a point which he lost sight of at Carnant and which is affirmed by subsequent events, culminating in Erec's coronation; it also possibly hints at a nexus of ideas which are more fully developed in Hartmann's account of this episode.

Some of the changes which Hartmann makes in recounting events between the departure of Erec and Enite from Karnant and their reunion with Arthur's court have already been mentioned, in particular the reduction of Chrétien's description of the combats with the last four robber knights, which occupies almost fifty verses (*EE* 3016–63), to a summary account of only eight verses (*E* 3392–99), and the removal entirely of the combat with Galoain's seneschal. These changes are typical of his treatment of the combats throughout this section.[38] With the sole exception of the encounter with Guivreiz, the description of each of the remaining combats is reduced in length, and the last of the robbers in the first group is simply ignored. With the abbreviations and excisions there is lost virtually all the detailed description of the damage and wounds inflicted by the lance which marks Chrétien's account. One example will suffice to illustrate this, the combat with the first of the robbers, which is the longest of those that remain; it can be compared with the corresponding incident in Chrétien (*EE* 2853–70), which has been cited above:

> den schilt er dô ze halse nam.
> als im Êrec nâhen kam,

---

[37]   Burgess (see n. 2 above) renders 'lices' by 'the palisades, wooden bars which surround the tournament field' (p. 67), and the word is translated as 'lists' in *Chrétien de Troyes: Arthurian Romances*, trans., with an introduction and notes, by D.D.R. Owen (London, 1987), p. 49.
[38]   See Ernst Scheunemann, *Artushof und Abenteuer: Zeichnung höfischen Daseins in Hartmanns Erec* (Breslau, 1937; repr. Darmstadt, 1973), pp. 41–42.

daz ros nam er mit den sporn.
er sprach: 'herre, ir habet verlorn
beide lîp unde guot.'
Êrec durch sînen grimmen muot
im dehein antwurt enbôt
und stach in von dem rosse tôt.   (E 3216–23)

In place of Chrétien's eighteen verses of detailed description, there are just eight verses, and they tell us no more concerning the passage of arms itself than that the robber raised his shield and spurred his horse and that Erec thrust him dead from his horse. Even in the Guivreiz combat there is little of Chrétien's graphic account of the fighting, Hartmann electing to fill virtually the same number of verses as Chrétien devotes to the incident with matter of a quite different kind.

We have seen that Hartmann had his reasons for playing down the violent side of combat, but equally it was evident that he was quite able, when he chose, to describe a lance attack in detail, only stressing different aspects of it than did Chrétien. The conclusion to be drawn from the changes we have noted is then clear. Hartmann's strategy for demonstrating that Erec has overcome his condition of *verligen* does not depend on the detailed display of the means of gaining victory in combat; it is sufficient that he should be victorious when challenged. The reduction of emphasis on the strictly martial dimension of the events following the Karnant episode is in fact the corollary of Hartmann's different conception of the crisis itself, with the shift from the question of Erec's prowess in Chrétien to one of mentality. The issue for Hartmann is not simply whether Erec is a coward or incompetent in the exercise of arms but whether 'sîn muot' can once again be described as 'ritterlîch'. To see how he has dealt with this issue, particular attention has to be paid to his depiction of the first combat with Guivreiz, which of all the combats after the departure from Karnant is the one in which Hartmann has made the most radical changes in substance.

The episode opens with the narrator commenting that Erec is shortly to endure his hardest test so far; by comparison with what awaits him, everything that has gone before has been a minor hardship – 'ein ringiu arbeit', no more than child's play (E 4268–76). This is no mere topos to stimulate attention. Already the longest and toughest in the sequence of combats in Chrétien, this encounter has been given even greater weight by Hartmann through a number of changes made in the preceding episodes, in addition to the abbreviations and excisions observed above, which in themselves tend towards this effect. Chrétien's knights who live by robbery (cf. EE 2792–93) are downgraded by Hartmann to robbers – the narrator refers to them exclusively as 'roubære', and it is only Enite who on one occasion uses the word 'ritter' of them (*E* 3186). They are described as being poorly armed, as befits robbers, which supplies an explanation of the ease with which Erec is able to overcome them (*E* 3226–34).[39] In the next episode, Hartmann introduces a verbal exchange between Erec and 'Galoain' before they fight in which the count speaks in a manner characterized as 'vil unritterlîch' (*E* 4169), and the fact that he is without armour (this is the case in Chrétien too) is mentioned in the immediate context of his being wounded and overcome by Erec (*E* 4213), as though again to explain the relative ease with which Erec gains the victory. In other words, in Hartmann's account Erec's opponents prior to Guivreiz are in no way worthy ones, neither deserving to be called *ritter* nor armed as befits *ritter*. All the more distinctly then does Guivreiz appear as the first adversary encountered by Erec since leaving Karnant who represents a real challenge for him.

Hartmann continues his account of the episode with a description of Guivreiz which extends over almost forty verses (*E* 4280–318), the burden of it consisting in an elaboration of Chrétien's two-line characterization of Guivret as small of stature but great and bold of heart (*EE* 3665–66). Hartmann stresses that, where the worth of a knight is concerned, what really counts is the heart – 'dâ stât ez allez an' (*E* 4292). A courageous heart gives strength regardless of the physical proportions of the body: were a man twelve fathoms tall, all that flesh would be of no value if his heart were faint and born to cowardice – 'wære sîn herze kranc/ und ûf zageheit geborn' (*E* 4295–96). Such is emphatically not the case with Guivreiz, for he has won fame in many combats, and he has never failed to undertake and excel in chivalric exploits whenever the opportunity to participate in them has arisen: 'dehein ritterschaft er versaz,/ ouch entetez niemen baz,/ swaz er ir bî sînen zîten/ ie mohte errîten' (*E* 4314–17). Indeed, it becomes evident later that he is in the habit of challenging passing knights in the way that he challenges Erec (*E* 4588–603) and also of riding in search of adventure (*E* 7395–99).

It is important to pause and consider what Hartmann has introduced into the episode in these initial verses on Guivreiz, and its relevance to Erec's experience thus far. The figure of Guivreiz, whose corporeal attributes belie his excellence in combat, gives rise to a reflection on the crucial part played by psychological factors in facing the physical challenge of fighting; if the knight is to be effective in the exercise of

---

[39] Pérennec (see n. 10 above), vol. I, pp. 60–61 comments persuasively on the reasons for Enite's reference to 'ritter' in contrast to the narrator's 'roubære'. On the robbers' equipment, see Scheunemann (see n. 38 above), p. 42, and Hans-Christoph Graf von Nayhauss-Cormons-Holub, *Die Bedeutung und Funktion der Kampfszenen für den Abenteuerweg der Helden im 'Erec' und 'Iwein' Hartmanns von Aue* (dissertation, Freiburg, 1967), p. 74.

arms, he has to have the right mental condition, courage ('manheit', E 4280, 4309) as opposed to cowardice ('zageheit', E 4296). With such a right mind, success in combat can be achieved. What is not explicitly stated here but will have been well understood by those with an insight into the psychology of warfare and combat is that practice – training – is necessary to maintain that right mind. Regular participation in chivalric activity such as Guivreiz seeks out is the only way to ensure mental fitness for combat. It is not enough for the knight to be of courageous disposition – he must harden himself mentally through exposure to the challenge of fighting; he cannot allow himself to *versitzen* (E 4314) the opportunity to do so any more than he can afford to *sich verligen* in the way that Erec did at Karnant when he failed to take part in tournaments.[40] Some celebrated observations in this sense on the relationship between training in arms and the psychological dimension of combat are made by the English chronicler Roger of Howden (d. 1201). Writing of the three oldest sons of Henry II of England in 1178, he describes them as being united in the opinion that they had to excel in the exercise of arms, which they knew was only possible through training because the art of war did not come naturally when it was needed if it had not been practised in advance: 'Et erat eis mens una, videlicet, plus cæteris posse in armis: scientes, quod ars bellandi, si non præluditur, cum fuerit necessaria non habetur'. In a passage borrowed from Seneca originally referring to the Roman athlete, Roger expands on the value of training for the knight, stressing that the experience of seeing one's blood flow, feeling one's teeth crack from an opponent's blow, being thrown to the ground, and yet getting up and fighting on courageously is the key to confidence and victory in combat.[41] Hartmann himself shows precisely the same understanding of the importance of training, when he is describing the combat of Iwein and Gawein, those notorious devotees of the tournament, at the end of *Iwein*. These knights

---

[40] See Silvia Ranawake in this volume on the significance of the verbs *versitzen* and *verligen*.

[41] Roger of Howden, *Chronica*, ed. by William Stubbs, Rolls Series, 51, 2 (London, 1869), pp. 166–67 (quotation on p. 166). Henry, Richard, and Geoffrey were all keen practitioners of the tournament, which they had to seek out in France, their father having banned the activity in England. On Roger of Howden's comments and later ones in a similar vein, see Maurice Keen, *Chivalry* (New Haven/London, 1984), p. 86, and Juliet R.V. Barker, *The Tournament in England 1100–1400* (Woodbridge, 1986), pp. 17–18. For a detailed analysis of the passage in Roger's *Chronica*, see Lutz Fenske, 'Der Knappe: Erziehung und Funktion', in *Curialitas*, ed. Fleckenstein (see n. 5 above), pp. 55–127 (pp. 68–70). Fenske summarizes the burden of Roger's comments as follows: 'Gemäß seinem Anliegen richten sich die von ihm vertretenen Anschauungen auf die innere seelische Bereitschaft zum Kampf, auf die Förderung und Stärkung der Kampfmoral, d. h. also auf die psychische Stabilität während des Kampfes und nicht auf die ritterlichen Waffenkünste in ihrem äußeren Erscheinungsbild' (p. 69).

are excellent fighters because they are not doing it for the first time but
have trained for combat from their youth onwards:

> ez was ir unmuoze
> von kinde gewesen ie:
> daz erzeicten sî wol hie.
> ouch sî iu daz vür wâr geseit:
> ez lêret diu gewonheit
> einen zagehaften man
> daz er getar unde kan
> baz vehten danne ein küener degen
> der es ê niht hât gepflegen.
> dô was hie kunst unde kraft:
> sî mohten von rîterschaft
> schuole gehabet hân.   (*Iwein* 6994–7005)

Training not only fosters skill and strength ('kunst unde kraft') but also
confidence and inner resilience, so that even a man who is naturally
timid ('zagehaft') can, through practice in the exercise of arms, acquire
the courage and ability ('getar unde kan') to fight better than a naturally
courageous man who has not undertaken training.[42]

In the light of these remarks it can be seen that Erec's neglect of
chivalric activity, and of tournaments in particular, at Karnant raises
doubts about his psychological fitness for combat; without repeated
exposure to the rigours of fighting it becomes questionable whether he
has any longer the hardiness of mind that is required of a knight. Of
course, the encounters with the robbers and with 'Galoain' have already
provided an answer to that question in so far as Erec has successfully
dealt with their attacks, but Hartmann's awareness of the importance of
having the right mental constitution for combat is such that he does not
leave the matter there. Rather he makes this explicitly an issue when
introducing Guivreiz in order to prepare us for an examination of Erec's
psychological fitness for knighthood in the subsequent course of the
episode.

The combat which follows on the introduction of Guivreiz falls into
two parts, corresponding to the phases of fighting with lance and
sword, but also marked by two different ways in which Erec shows
himself reluctant to fight. In the exchange of words which Hartmann
has introduced prior to the combat (*E* 4324ff.), Guivreiz welcomes

---

[42]   A remarkably similar point about the way in which training in the *scientia militandi* can
compensate for natural timidity is made by Albertus Magnus when comparing the training
of a falcon with that of a fighting man in Book 23, Chapter 13 of his *De animalibus libri
XXVI*, ed. by Hermann Stadler, Beiträge zur Geschichte der Philosophie des Mittelalters:
Texte und Untersuchungen, 15–16, 2 vols (Münster, 1916 and 1920), II, 1468. See Fenske
(see n. 41 above), p. 70, who does not, however, make the comparison with Hartmann.

Erec, then goes on to explain that he takes him to be a knight because of the beauty of the lady accompanying him and because he is well armed like a knight who is seeking 'âventiure' (E 4340). Adventure is what he now offers him, challenging him to defend himself immediately.

In view of Erec's purpose in setting out from Karnant – 'nâch âventiure wâne/ reit der guote kneht Êrec' (E 3111–12), his refusal to accept Guivreiz's challenge to adventure comes as a surprise.[43] His response is described as being spoken 'durch sînen spot' (E 4348: 'in jest', 'jokingly'), a difficult phrase in the context,[44] though it is possible to see Hartmann here suggesting a bantering tone of voice and pointing up the element of pretended – mock(!) – concern for Guivreiz's honour in Erec's initial argument that he should desist from his challenge because he began by greeting him; in seeking to deflect Guivreiz from his purpose, Erec assumes the attitude of one who has to teach Guivreiz manners,[45] a presumption to which Guivreiz does not take kindly and which meets with forthright rejection by him (E 4368–75). Erec's real concern is revealed in the following verses, where he urges Guivreiz to leave him in peace – 'mit gemache' (E 4360), since he has done nothing to him and has suffered such 'arbeit' (E 4363) on his travels that his heart is quite unwilling to accept a challenge to combat: 'daz aller mînes herzen rât/ unwilleclîchen stât' (E 4364–65). The reference here to *gemach* and *arbeit* recalls Erec's preference for the soft life at Karnant, and the mention of the unwillingness of his heart in this situation points very precisely to the consequences which avoidance of the hardship of combat has for the psychological state of the knight – he lacks the mental

[43] Hugo Kuhn, 'Erec', in *Festschrift für Paul Kluckhohn und Hermann Schneider* (Tübingen, 1948), pp. 122–147; repr. in *Hartmann von Aue*, ed. by Hugo Kuhn and Christoph Cormeau, WdF, 359 (Darmstadt, 1973), pp. 17–48 (references are to the reprint) sees in Erec's behaviour in this episode a deliberate rejection of any claim to honour ('Verzicht Erecs auf Ritterehre bis zum Schein des Tölpenhaften', p. 32); this requires Erec's fear (E 4408) to be interpreted as 'gespielte Furcht' (p. 32, n. 42), but it is unclear how this sense can be attributed to words in the narrator's voice. Nellmann (see n. 1 above, p. 62) regards Erec as employing from the start a stratagem to gain the advantage over Guivreiz, but that would imply a serious miscalculation on Erec's part (and certainly not 'taktische [. . .] Überlegenheit'), since he sustains a wound in the side (see also n. 46 below). A careful analysis of the episode, which seeks to come to terms with the ambiguous nature of Erec's role in it, is undertaken by Rudolf Voß, *Die Artusepik Hartmanns von Aue: Untersuchungen zum Wirklichkeitsbegriff und zur Ästhetik eines literarischen Genres im Kräftefeld von soziokulturellen Normen und christlicher Anthropologie* (Cologne/Vienna, 1983), pp. 102–03 and 122. Silvia Ranawake 'Erecs *verligen*' (see n. 3 above) also comments on 'Erec's "untypical" behaviour' here (p. 106, n. 38).
[44] See Scheunemann (see n. 38 above), p. 43, n. 139.
[45] For a different reading of this, with consideration of the possible legal implications of Erec's words, see William Henry Jackson, 'Friedensgesetzgebung und höfischer Roman: Zu Hartmanns *Erec* und *Iwein*', in *Poesie und Gebrauchsliteratur im deutschen Mittelalter: Würzburger Colloquium 1978*, ed. by Volker Honemann and others (Tübingen, 1979), pp. 251–64 (pp. 252–54).

constitution, the right mind, essential to effectiveness when faced with a challenge.

It is then not unnatural that Guivreiz should conclude from Erec's words that he is a coward – 'er ist verzaget' (*E* 4366). Guivreiz is, however, determined not to be diverted and, rejecting Erec's suggestion that his conduct is dishonourable, he insists that Erec look to his defence for the sake of his lady, forcing him thereby, in the terms of his earlier identification of Erec as a knight, to match the pretensions of his appearance with action.

Erec sees that combat is unavoidable and prepares himself for the joust. In doing this, his courage, 'sîn ellen' (*E* 4381), becomes evident, and as the two knights charge together we are told that neither has ever had any part in cowardice, 'zageheit' (*E* 4384). In the transition to the sword fight we learn further that each of them has now been granted what he has long prayed to God for, namely an opponent against whom he can test his mettle (*E* 4399–403). As the combat resumes, however, Erec again conducts himself in a surprising way. Instead of fighting wholeheartedly, exchanging blows with Guivreiz, he attempts only to defend himself with his shield, which, in spite of the skill with which he does so ('mit listen', *E* 4410),[46] leads quickly to his sustaining a wound in his side. The reason given for this tactic is his fear of disgrace and death – 'Êrec fil de roi Lac/ vorhte laster und den tôt' (*E* 4407–08).[47] Once again Guivreiz thinks that he has a coward ('einen zagen', *E* 4420) before him. Here too we can see the effect of Erec's neglect of regular chivalric activity in that he lacks the self-confidence which comes through training and is seized by a disabling fear.[48] The intervention of Enite, who is distraught at the prospect of his being killed, restores Erec's courage, and 'der unverzagete man' (*E* 4430) goes on to gain victory by a show of superior strength and without the assistance of luck in the shape of a broken sword as in Chrétien.

It is apparently a self-contradictory picture of Erec that Hartmann presents here, on the one hand insisting on his courage and his eagerness for just such an encounter, and on the other showing him

[46] The similarity in phrasing between *E* 4409–11 and *E* 5530–31/5534 in the context of the fight with the second giant gives no grounds for arguing that Erec is pursuing a tactic of tiring Guivreiz out by letting him strike him unopposed. In the combat with the giant, Erec allows the blows of the club to fall on his shield so that he has the opportunity to exploit his superior agility and strike the giant's leg (*E* 5529–52). In the Guivreiz combat, Erec's defensive action brings only him disadvantage.

[47] The possibility that Erec might be thought to fear incurring disgrace through the killing of Guivreiz, rather than to fear disgrace and death for himself as the outcome of the encounter, is excluded by his subsequent action in making to kill him (*E* 4439–41). Verses *E* 4407–08 are not discussed in Marianne E. Kalinke, '*vorhte* in Hartmann's *Erec*', *ABäG*, 11 (1976), 67–80.

[48] In *E* 8619–31 Hartmann distinguishes between 'rehtiu vorhte', which is compatible with courage, and 'vorhte' which is 'zagelich'.

inhibited by his state of mind. But the contradictions can be resolved if we see that what Hartmann has done is to translate into action the insight of the Angevin princes, as described by Roger of Howden, that without practice the art of war does not come naturally when it is needed; or to put it another way, Hartmann demonstrates what happens to 'ein küener degen' (*Iwein* 7001) who neglects to train for combat. Erec's loss of the mentality appropriate to the knight in the period at Karnant led him to neglect the practices of knighthood which ensure mental fitness for combat. Now that he again appreciates the need to be active, he is hampered at the crucial moment of confrontation by his lack of psychological preparedness: he is initially unwilling to fight, and then, once he has been provoked into action, he is overcome by fear, until Enite's intervention makes him go onto the offensive.

A question raised by this reading of the first Guivreiz combat is why Hartmann postponed dealing with the issue of Erec's psychological disablement for combat as result of his *verligen* until this point. Logically it belongs earlier in the sequence of encounters following the departure from Karnant, indeed to the opening combat. The answer to this question lies partly in the circumstance, already present in Chrétien and reinforced by Hartmann, that Guivreiz is the first opponent who is fully Erec's equal and therefore qualified to reintegrate him into the fraternity of knighthood through the friendship established between them after the combat. More important than this, however, is the fact that Guivreiz alone among Erec's opponents in this portion of the narrative presents Hartmann with the opportunity to confront Erec with an adversary who is not only worthy of him socially and martially but who also forcefully represents the principle of active knighthood which he neglected at Karnant.[49] Hartmann encapsulates this principle in the concept of *âventiure*, which, in contrast to Chrétien, he explicitly attaches to the figure of Guivreiz and his encounter with Erec. The quest for *âventiure*, that is, for martial challenges of the kind which Guivreiz obliges Erec to accept in this episode, is a regular component of the life of knightly excellence which Guivreiz exemplifies (*E* 4588–603, 7395–99, cf. 4280–318), a means of maintaining his combat fitness as well as his reputation. In the pattern of knightly life evident in the figure of Guivreiz, *âventiure* plays a role similar to that which the tournament ought to have played, but did not, in Erec's life at Karnant. It is, in terms

---

[49] It is possible that Hartmann is here elaborating upon the association between Guivret's challenge and tourneying that was speculatively established in the discussion of Chrétien earlier. Nayhauss-Cormons-Holub (see n. 39 above) interprets the episode as providing evidence that Erec fails to understand 'den Sinn der ritterlichen Kampfethik' (p. 84), but he develops the point in a sense different from that proposed here. See also Wolfgang Harms, *Der Kampf mit dem Freund oder Verwandten in der deutschen Literatur bis um 1300*, Medium Aevum, Philologische Studien, 1 (Munich, 1963), p. 123.

of individual action, the counterpart of the collective action of the tournament, both being forms of training for combat as well as ways of enhancing reputation; both depend on the realization that it is vital to expose oneself to the hardships of armed conflict when there is no compelling necessity to do so, in order that the ability to respond effectively when there is such a necessity is maintained. Guivreiz is motivated by a mentality which prevents him from neglecting (*versitzen*) any opportunity to undertake chivalric action, and through his assumption that Erec shares the same ethos and is likewise seeking *âventiure* (E 4336–40), he shows up the effects which the period of *verligen* has had on Erec's capacity as a fighting man. But Guivreiz's insistence that Erec respond to his challenge and participate in *âventiure* has the further function of setting those effects aside and re-integrating Erec into the estate of knighthood in the fundamental sense that it restores to him the mentality which underpins effective knighthood. Never again does Erec hesitate to accept a challenge. Indeed, as is evident from his responses when he hears the cries of Cadoc's lady, sees (but does not recognize) Guivreiz as he rides to his rescue, and learns of the adventure at Brandigan, he is henceforth far from reluctant to seize opportunities to undertake chivalric action when they present themselves.[50] In the first confrontation with Guivreiz, embodiment of the ethos of active knighthood, Erec is purged of the disabling psychological consequences of his *verligen*, and there is reinstated in him the knightly frame of mind which is a precondition of his accomplishing the tasks which lie ahead of him, leading ultimately to his assumption of the throne in Karnant.[51]

The significance of Erec's combat with Guivreiz is, however, not exhausted in this, for Hartmann assigns an active role to Enite in this incident. In Chrétien's account of the combat Enide is only a spectator, giving evidence of her loyalty to Erec by her distress but not influencing the course of events (EE 3787–94). By contrast, Enite cries out when she sees the side-wound that Erec has sustained, wishing that she might be the one to bear it and voicing her fear of his death (E 4421–28). These words elicit not only an expression of Erec's love for her but also fill him with the courage and strength to overcome his fear of disgrace and death and to defeat Guivreiz.[52] This at one and the same time recalls the

---

50   Though many interpreters take Erec's second combat with Guivreiz to incorporate a qualification of his eagerness to accept challenges, Voß (see n. 43 above) is surely right to point out that he approaches the Brandigan episode without any sign of having learned the need for caution (p. 103). See also Scheunemann (see n. 38 above), p. 42.

51   This is not the place to consider the relevance of this outcome for *Iwein*, but it is at least worth recalling that Gawein advises Iwein not to neglect tourneying now he has the responsibilities of a lord so that he may give evidence of still having 'rîters muot' (*Iwein* 2855).

52   See Ursula Schulze, '*âmîs unde man*. Die zentrale Problematik in Hartmanns *Erec*', PBB

fact that Erec derived strength from Enite in his combat with Iders (*E* 850–59, 935–49) and foreshadows how he will do so again in the combat with Mabonagrin (*E* 9181–87, 9230–31). In these, the two greatest combats which Erec fights, his success depends on Enite, and it is fitting that the Guivreiz combat, which re-affirms his standing as a knight, should incorporate a demonstration of her role in ensuring his effectiveness as a fighting man, and that it should point forward, through the revelation of his regard for her, to their reconciliation.

In his depiction of Erec's encounter with Guivreiz, Hartmann makes particularly fruitful use of the freedom which he enjoyed in the matter of combat description. Confounding normal expectations of the hero's conduct in such a scene to the extent of having him behave in a cowardly manner, he makes of this incident an enactment of the consequences which Erec's *verligen* has for his capacity as a knight and of the process whereby he regains the frame of mind essential for his continued effectiveness as a fighting man. With its focus on the psychological factors which govern performance in combat, the incident presents a resolution of the problem which arises in Karnant in terms matching those in which it was conceived: seen as a problem of the mentality which is associated with a way of life, it is as a reinstatement of the right mind, a 'muot' which is 'ritterlîch', that it is resolved. In contrast to this, Chrétien, conceiving the problem rather as one of individual prowess, uses above all the means of literary association to vindicate Erec's courage, invoking established poetic images of dynamic knighthood to dispel the charge of *recreantise*.

It would be an oversimplification to characterize the different approaches to the theme of the knight as fighting man adopted in the two works as that of the man of letters as against that of the knight which we know Hartmann to have been, especially if such a contrast were taken to imply that Chrétien had no grasp of the chivalric mentality. But it is the case that in remodelling this component of Chrétien's narrative, Hartmann presents the scenes of combat in a way which supports the positive image of knighthood that he wishes to project, and which shows such a keen understanding of the ethos and psychology associated with the profession of arms as to justify the description of his adaptation as chivalric.

(Tüb.), 105 (1983), 14–47 (p. 33), and Norbert Sieverding, *Der ritterliche Kampf bei Hartmann und Wolfram: Seine Bewertung im 'Erec' und 'Iwein' und in den Gahmuret- und Gawan-Büchern des 'Parzival'* (Heidelberg, 1985), p. 47.

Cligés *in Deutschland*

DANIEL ROCHER

Wir meinen wohl alle zu wissen, daß der *Cligés*, der einzige von Chrétien sicher gedichtete und uns überlieferte Roman, der nicht ganz in Artus' 'Wirkungsbereich' spielt, der sogenannte 'byzantinische' Roman Chrétiens, daß dieser Roman also seine Hauptbedeutung im Laufe seiner Polemik gegen den Tristan-Stoff erraten läßt (3105ff., 5199–203, 5249–56):[1] *Cligés* wäre im Grunde ein Anti-Tristan, sozusagen eine Alternativlösung zum Problem: inwiefern darf eine edle Frau den Neffen ihres Manns lieben? Bevor wir uns nun fragen, ob dieses aparte Werk auf dieselbe Art wie die eigentlichen Artusromane Chrétiens in Deutschland rezipiert und bearbeitet worden ist, wäre es doch wohl angebracht, die geläufige Meinung über Beschaffenheit und Bedeutung des französischen Romans nachzuprüfen. Mein eigenes Wiederlesen des Werkes für dieses Kolloquium hat mich jedenfalls eines Besseren belehrt. Zunächst was die Gliederung angeht: nach dem berühmten, inhaltsreichen Prolog, worin Chrétien die Liste seiner bisherigen Werke angibt und die These der doppelten *translatio militiae* und *translatio sapientiae* aus Griechenland nach Rom und von Rom nach Frankreich aufstellt, folgt die Elterngeschichte als erster Teil. Aber dieser erste Teil, die Geschichte von Alexandre und Soredamors, nimmt mehr als 2500 Verse in Anspruch, die Elterngeschichte füllt also mehr als ein Drittel des Romans aus. Das ist sehr zu bedenken, wenn man diese Proportion etwa mit derjenigen der Riwalin/Blanscheflur-Erzählung in Gottfrieds *Tristan* vergleicht: 1500 Zeilen sind es dort, das heißt viel weniger als das Zehntel des unabgeschlossenen Romans, vielleicht das Sechzehntel des ins Auge gefaßten Ganzen. Die Elterngeschichte des *Cligés* spielt nun fast zur Gänze in Artus' Ländern, in England und in der kleinen Bretagne. Der zweite Teil (ca. 1600 Zeilen) ist der Deutschlandfahrt von Alis und Cligés gewidmet, wo beide gemeinsam für Alis, Cligés' Onkel, um Fenice werben (2586–4169). Der dritte Teil (4170–5013, ca. 800 Verse)

---

[1] Zitiert nach: *Les Romans de Chrétien de Troyes, II: Cligés*, hg. von Alexandre Micha, CFMA, 84 (Paris, 1965).

erzählt Cligés' *riterschaft* bei Artus, spielt also auch nicht in Griechenland, sondern wiederum bei Artus, und erst der letzte Teil (5014–6664,
etwa 1600 Verse, genausoviel wie die 'deutsche Epoche' der Erzählung)
spielt in Konstantinopel. Dieser letzte Teil bringt aber auch die meisten
unerhörten Begebenheiten: den angeblichen Tod der Fenice, mit der
greulichen Episode der Ärzte aus Salerno; die Turmidylle; die Entdeckung des Liebespaares durch Bertram; die Flucht, und das Happy-
End. Das ist der eigentliche 'byzantinische', ja orientalisch gefärbte Teil
des Romans, kaum ein Viertel des Ganzen. Anders gesagt, Chrétien hat
den Hauptakzent nicht auf die byzantinische und wenn man will
'spielmännische' Komponente seiner Erzählung gelegt, sondern vielmehr auf die Episoden des westeuropäischen Raums, wo nur 'klassische' Kämpfe und Liebeserlebnisse geschildert werden.

Zweitens, die Thematik: in der Elterngeschichte fallen wohl drei
Hauptmomente auf: die Sozialisierung der Liebeshelden, die Dauer des
Liebesdienstes, die glückliche Beendung dieser Prüfungszeit durch die
Intervention der Königin (Guenièvre, deren Name aber nie genannt
wird). Und dies alles läuft auf dasselbe hinaus: den Triumph der
gesellschaftlichen Interessen und Normen. Alexandre – Alixandre im
Text – ist die beste Stütze von König Artus gegen den Rebellen Angrés
de Guinesores (i.e. Windsor), gegen den Verräter, gegen die
Gefährdung der feudalen Gesellschaft durch das schlimmste Übel: die
untriuwe. Seine Liebesgeschichte mit Soredamors, Gauvains Schwester,
beginnt auf dem Schiff auf der Reise von England in die Bretagne; aber
da gibt es keinen Liebestrank, kein gegenseitiges Geständnis, nur
Leiden und Schweigen. Erst die Königin wird dem ein Ende setzen,
indem sie in einer kurzen Szene den Liebenden entdeckt, daß sie
einander lieben, und sie darauf miteinander vermählt. Faktisch *sind* sie
schon vermählt, bevor sie ein einziges Liebeswort ausgetauscht haben.
Was hat das zu bedeuten, wenn nicht, daß hier die Gesellschaft – von
der Königin vertreten – alles tut und alles bestimmt, nicht die
Liebenden? Und die Gesellschaft interpretiert 'Liebe' natürlich gleich als
'Ehe', d. h. etymologisch 'Gesetz', ihr Gesetz. Kann man sich einen
eklatanteren Gegensatz zur heimlichen Liebe zwischen Riwalin und
Blanscheflur vorstellen, zu ihrer unehelichen Vereinigung und Flucht –
aber auch zu den Anfängen der Liebe zwischen ihrem Sohn Tristan und
Isolde, auf der Fahrt aus Irland nach Cornwall? Die Liebesgeschichte
zweier Generationen scheint hier auf einmal eine kritische Kontrafaktur
zu erhalten! Aber das letzte und beste Wort zu der ganzen Episode hat
der Dichter selbst geprägt, indem er die neue, junge Königin Soredamors (sie ist jetzt Königin, da Artus ihren Mann zum König über sein
'bestes Reich in Wales' erhoben hat) als die 'fierce', d. h. die
Schachkönigin, 'de l'eschaquier don il fu rois', des Schachbretts, auf
dem er als König stand, bezeichnet (2334–35). Kann man deutlicher

sagen, daß Artus' adelige Gesellschaft sie buchstäblich 'in ihren Händen hält'?

Die zwei Motive der stummen Liebe und des Dienstes an der Gesellschaft finden sich wieder im folgenden Teil, in der 'deutschen' Episode: sie werden dort sogar in gesteigerter Form wieder geboten. Nicht nur dient Alexandres Sohn Cligés treu seinem König, sondern er dient getreu einem Untreuen, er dient einem Onkel, der versprochen hatte, nie zu heiraten, damit ihm Cligés auf dem Thron nachfolgen kann (Alis sollte eigentlich die Krone überhaupt nicht tragen) – und Cligés dient ihm, indem er ihm hilft, die ihm nicht zukommende Frau zu erobern, dazu eine Frau, die *er* schon auf den ersten Blick liebt! Aber ebenso stumm wie die Liebe zwischen Alixandre und Soredamors bleibt diejenige zwischen Cligés und Fenice, selbst wenn es Cligés gelingt, die gefangene Fenice aus den Händen sächsischer Ritter zu befreien (3617ff.). Natürlich müssen wir dabei an die Gandin-Episode bei Gottfried denken, wo Tristan Isolde nur scheinbar für Marke, in Wahrheit aber für sich selber zurückgewinnt (und Gottfried läßt uns dabei vermuten, daß sie auf dem Rückweg ihre 'ruowe in den bluomen næmen'[2] – ob es allerdings so in der französischen Quelle stand, ist eine andere Frage). Hier haben wir zugleich eine Überbietung des Motivs der stummen Liebe im ersten Teil und vielleicht eine Kontrafaktur der Tristan-Episode mit umgekehrtem Vorzeichen. Im Gegensatz zu dem, was im ersten Teil durch Guenièvres Vermittlung geschah, interveniert kein Vertreter bzw. keine Vertreterin der Gesellschaft zugunsten der Liebenden, niemand vereinigt sie – aber sie nehmen das hin, und Fenice verantwortet ihre 'Rolle' in der Gesellschaft, indem sie einerseits sich energisch weigert, die Liebesgeschichte zwischen Ysolt und Tristan zu wiederholen, anderseits aber ihre 'meisterin' Thessala zu Hilfe ruft, um der Vereinigung mit Alis zu entgehen. Der Zaubertrank als Mittel *gegen* die Liebe: wie könnte man wiederum ein wirksameres Symbol erfinden oder verwenden zur Veranschaulichung einer Anti-Tristan-These? Ich sage 'verwenden', denn das Rezept kam schon, wie man weiß, in der persischen Erzählung von *Wîs und Râmîn* von Gorgâni vor.

Bei alledem ist bis jetzt kein Konflikt zwischen Onkel und Neffen ausgebrochen, eben weil Cligés' Selbstvergessenheit total ist. Und das geht im dritten Teil so weiter: Cligés verläßt das Land freiwillig, sogar gegen den Wunsch seines Onkels, um sich bei Artus als Ritter zu bewähren, hierin dem letzten Wunsch seines Vaters auf seinem Todesbett folgend. Aber welchem Wunsch, welcher Norm der Umgebung, der Gesellschaft, zu der er gehört, fügt und beugt sich Cligés nicht? Und im vierten Teil – im vierten Teil kippt plötzlich alles um!

---

[2] Gottfried von Straßburg, *Tristan und Isold*, hg. von Friedrich Ranke, 14. Aufl. (Dublin/ Zürich, 1969), V. 13434.

Ende der Fügsamkeit, Ende des Beugens und Verbeugens vor dem Willen der anderen, Ende der Anpassung! Der Keim der Revolte, der paradoxerweise in der 'endormie' schon enthalten war, womit Fenice die Männlichkeit ihres Mannes zum 'Schlafen' gebracht hatte, geht jetzt auf und weckt *sie* zum wahren Leben über einen falschen Tod: dadurch entzieht sich Fenice dem Leben in der Gesellschaft, dem für sie falschen Leben, und wird – wie der Phönix! – zu einem neuen und wahren Leben neugeboren. Cligés und sie entschwinden in den Zauberturm, den der treue Jehan für seinen Herrn gebaut hat, ihre 'fossiure a la gent amant', ihr Paradies auf Erden. Auch hier, wie im Tristan-Roman, nimmt diese Idylle durch die zufällige Entdeckung eines Jägers ein Ende. Allerdings ist *dieser* Jäger weniger glücklich als derjenige Markes, denn er verliert ein Bein dabei! Worauf der Onkel die Wahrheit erfährt, was Fenice unbedingt vermeiden wollte (sie hatte nämlich Cligés erklärt, er würde sie nie besitzen 'wenn Ihr nicht ein Mittel findet, um mich Eurem Onkel solcherweise zu rauben, daß er mich nie wiederfindet, weder mich noch Euch in Verdacht haben kann und nie erfährt, wer das alles verschuldet hat ', 5204–11). Und jetzt weiß er eben alles, er verfolgt sie, der so lange Jahre nicht vorhandene Konflikt mit dem Neffen bricht mit aller Gewalt aus, und Alis stirbt 'com huem forssenez' (6609), im Zustand der Tollwut. Die Liebenden sind in der Zwischenzeit bei König Artus angelangt, was Fenice früher total ablehnte, damit man nicht von ihnen wie von 'Ysolt la Blonde' und 'Tristrant' spräche (5249ff.): es scheint eine absolute Katastrophe zu sein, wo alle früheren guten Vorsätze zunichte gemacht werden, wo die Gesellschaft plötzlich auf der anderen Seite steht, wo Cligés Artus' Ritter gegen sein Vaterland mobilmacht . . ., nur daß alles gut ausgeht! Alis stirbt, nicht die Liebenden; Cligés wird in Konstantinopel zum Kaiser gekrönt und Fenice zur Kaiserin. Aber das Schlußwort, das besagt, daß seit der Zeit jeder Kaiser in Konstantinopel seine Frau eingesperrt hätte, damit sie ihn nicht betrügt wie Fenice ihren Mann, klingt seltsam, wie ein Spott des Dichters über sein eigenes Happy-End und seine Helden. Vielleicht ein anderes Zeichen dieser dichterischen Ironie, dieser 'aesthetic distance' bei Chrétien de Troyes, welche Peter Haidu in seinen Büchern über den Dichter so geistreich herausgearbeitet hat?[3]

Vielleicht wird man denken, daß ich auf Chrétiens *Cligés* viel zuviel Zeit verwendet habe, da mein Thema eigentlich '*Cligés* in Deutschland' sein sollte, vor allem wenn man bedenkt, wie dünn die Spuren der *Cligés*-Rezeption in Deutschland demgegenüber ausfallen. Aber zunächst durfte ein Kolloquium über Chrétiens Rezeption in Deutschland das besondere Problem dieses Romans nicht übergehen. Und andererseits: das *Cligés*-Bild, das ich eben gezeichnet habe, erklärt

---

3 Vor allem Peter Haidu, *Aesthetic Distance in Chrétien de Troyes: Irony and Comedy in*

vielleicht wenigstens zum Teil diese Rarität der deutschen Übertragung, wenn man nicht alles auf Zufälle der Überlieferung zurückführen will. Sicher ist auch Hartmanns *Erec* schlecht überliefert, da die einzige (nicht ganz) vollständige Handschrift, die ihn uns (fast) zur Gänze mitteilt, die Ambraser Handschrift, mehr als drei Jahrhunderte später nieder-geschrieben wurde, und doch wissen wir durch viele Zeugnisse, daß er in seiner Zeit und danach höchst geschätzt und verbreitet war. Die Handschriftsfragmente des deutschen *Cligés*, die in Zürich, Kalocsa und St. Paul im Lavanttal liegen, sind immerhin älter. Die Handschrift, der sie alle angehören, wird auf die Zeit um 1320 datiert. Ich komme gleich darauf zu sprechen. Aber aus der vorigen Analyse möchte ich jedenfalls folgendes Fazit gezogen haben: Chrétiens *Cligés* war zu drei Vierteln kein byzantinischer, sondern ein Artus- und Ritterroman, der in Westeuropa spielte, ein moralisches Anti-Tristan-Modell aufstellte und sich mit dem Tristan-Stoff (in welcher Hypostase auch) heftig ausein-andersetzte, und dies ausführlich und zu wiederholten Malen – und plötzlich schien das alles umzukippen, das letzte Viertel des Werkes all das Vorangehende in den Wind zu schlagen, all die frühere Tugendaus-breitung Lügen zu strafen, und die Tugendbolde Cligés und Fenice als fröhliche Frevler zu entlarven – zu entlarven oder zu feiern? Eher zu feiern, denn der Onkel war schließlich meineidig gewesen, er hatte gegen das Versprechen an seinen Bruder heiraten wollen, deshalb durften Artus, die Griechen und der Autor selbst mit den zynischen Ehebrechern sympathisieren.

Gefeierte Helden, deren Benehmen aber doch die Institution des byzantinischen Harems als Mittel gegen solche 'traison' (6651) rechtfertigt: darf man nicht meinen, daß diese Zwiespältigkeit der Aussage und die wiederholte Umwertung, die im Roman stattfand, die potentiellen ehrlichen deutschen Bearbeiter ein bißchen stutzig machen konnten? Und trotzdem hat es eine wenn nicht gar zwei Bearbeitungen des *Cligés* im deutschen Sprachraum gegeben. Im zweiten Bändchen der Zeitschrift *Armarium*, in Klagenfurt ediert, haben Hans Gröchenig und Peter Hans Pascher 1984 alle schon vorher bekannten Fragmente sowie diejenigen, die P. Pascher erst 1975 in der Bibliothek des Klosters St. Paul im Lavanttal (Kärnten) entdeckt hatte, herausgegeben. Die ersten Fragmente waren von Albert Bachmann im Jahre 1887 in Zürich entdeckt und 1888 im 32. Band der *Zeitschrift für deutsches Altertum* veröffentlicht worden. Diese Fragmente bestehen aus viermal 14 Zeilen, oder genauer gesagt aus achtmal 7 Zeilen auf 4 zweispaltig beschriebe-nen Seiten (zwei Blätter recto verso) plus ein schmaler Streifen mit Anfang und Ende anderer Verse (den Anfang von 36 Zeilen kann man

'*Cligès*' and '*Perceval*' (Genève, 1968); vgl. auch *Lion – queue – coupée: l'écart symbolique chez Chrétien de Troyes* (Genève, 1972).

auf der vollständigen Abbildung in *Armarium* 2 lesen). Die ersten
Fragmente, d. h. die 56 leserlichen Verse, entsprechen dem Anfang des
dritten Teils von Chrétiens *Cligés*, der Abreise Cligés in Artus' Reich.
Die Art, wie er von seinem Onkel Abschied nimmt und ihn um eine
ehrenvolle Ausstattung bittet, entspricht im Grunde durchaus der
Schilderung der Szene bei Chrétien (4186ff.): Alis äußert sein
Mißbehagen wegen der Abfahrt seines Neffen und bietet ihm die
Teilnahme an der Regierung des Reichs an. Wir lesen in der Transkrip-
tion von Gröchenig/Pascher:

> Ich tuon (vielleicht für: ich trag?) swar an din wille leit.
> ob mir chumt meins endes zeit.
> wer haltet dann daz Riche.
> das ist min un dein geliche.
> wan daz ich di chron han.

Chrétien sagte:

> Ja cest congié ne cest otroi
> N'avroiz de moi, qu'il ne me griet,
> Car molt me plest et molt me siet
> Que vos soiez conpainz et sire
> Avoec moi de tot mon empire.   (4188–92)

'Ihr werdet diesen Urlaub von mir nicht bekommen, ohne daß es mir
leid tut, denn es gefällt und es ziemt mir, daß Ihr mit mir mein Reich
teilt und darüber auch Herr seid.' Daß also, wie Eberhard Busse es 1913
in seinem Buch über Ulrich von Türheim wahrhaben wollte, und wie
von Vizkelety 1969 wieder behauptet wurde,[4] Alis bei Ulrich sympathi-
scher und edelmütiger wirkt als bei Chrétien, will mir in diesem
Fragment gar nicht einleuchten. Ulrich – wir werden gleich sehen,
warum Ulrich *von Türheim* – hätte nicht verstanden, daß Chrétien aus
Alis einen Anti-Marke machen wollte? Aber Alis ist kein Anti-Marke! Er
ist zwar meineidig, aber er hat, wie gesagt, keinen Konflikt mit seinem
Neffen und sieht ihn mit großem Bedauern in die Ferne reisen. Wo der –
nach den Zürcher Fragmenten noch unbekannte – deutsche Bearbeiter
von Chrétien dagegen deutlich abweicht, das ist in der darauffolgenden
Szene, worin Cligés von Fenice Abschied nimmt (im Zürcher Fragment
Seiten 1 verso b und 2 recto a und b). Da gestehen offensichtlich Cligés
und Fenice einander ihre Liebe, und es findet ein 'Herzenstausch' statt.
Bei Chrétien trennen sie sich, ohne es gewagt zu haben, sich deutlich zu
äußern (4246–90). Darf man hier aber von einer grundsätzlichen

---

4 Eberhard Kurt Busse, *Ulrich von Türheim* (Berlin, 1913), S. 110ff.; András Vizkelety,
'Neue Fragmente des mhd. Cligès-Epos aus Kalocsa (Ungarn)', *ZfdPh*, 88 (1969), 409–32,
hier S. 418; beide zitiert nach Gröchenig/Pascher, op. cit., S. 16.

Abweichung sprechen? Ich würde nur sagen, daß hier die *fin'amor* besser zu ihrem Recht kommt, daß die zweite Generation ihre Sprache (die Sprache der *fin'amor*) deutlicher spricht als diejenige der Eltern (um mit Peter Haidu zu sprechen[5] – allerdings haben wir die Eltern- geschichte der deutschen Bearbeitung nicht), was im Grunde Chrétiens Auffassung durchaus nicht widerspricht. Soviel für die Zürcher Fragmente. Dann wurden 1966 von Andreas Vizkelety in der Erzdi- özesanbibliothek Kalocsa neue Fragmente *derselben* Handschrift entdeckt und 1969 im 88. Jahrgang der *Zeitschrift für deutsche Philologie* veröffentlicht. Es handelt sich allerdings um sehr schlecht erhaltene und kaum leserliche Reste von zwei Blättern, recto und verso. Christoph Cormeau schrieb mit Recht in *Germanistik*, man könne die Transkription kaum kontrollieren. Es handelt sich um die Szene des falschen Todes Fenices, im letzten Teil des Werkes; dann gibt es einen Dialog mit der Minne (Fragm. 1rb), wo sich der Verfasser aber sehr leserlich nennt: 'Ich ulrich . . . hein', was nur Ulrich von Türheim bezeichnen kann, wie wir gleich bestätigt haben werden. In den folgenden Fragmenten scheint mehrmals von der Jungfrau Maria die Rede zu sein (Fragm. 1 verso b, vv. 23 und 26; 2 recto b, v. 15; ganz deutlich verso a, vv. 11–12 , nach der Transkription von Gröchenig/Pascher, *Armarium* 2, S. 60, 62, 63): dies aber könnte bedeuten, daß der Verfasser, also Ulrich von Türheim, diesem letzten und abenteuerlichen Teil eine gewisse fromme Färbung hätte verleihen wollen, um die Kühnheit des gallischen Autors etwas zu dämpfen. Mehr bin ich jedenfalls nicht imstande, aus den überlieferten Versen zu gewinnen. Die letzte Entdeckung von deutschen *Cligés*- Fragmenten geschah, wie oben gesagt, 1975 in St. Paul im Lavanttal. Das Erstaunliche ist, daß auch diese Fragmente der ersten und einzigen entdeckten Handschrift angehörten. Das Kärntische Fragment besteht aus einem vollständig erhaltenen und vollkommen leserlichen Blatt, zu zwei Spalten mit je 36 Versen beschrieben (die Spalte rb hat aber nur 35 Zeilen, so daß es insgesamt 143 und nicht 144 Verse sind). Diese Verse schildern den ritterlichen Kampf zwischen 'kawein' und 'kliges'. Sie gehören also zum selben Teil der Erzählung wie die Zürcher Fragmente, nämlich dem dritten Teil, mit Cligés' Aufenthalt bei Artus, nur daß *diese* Verse sich diesmal nicht im Anfang, sondern kurz vor dem Schluß dieses Teils befinden. Sie zeigen den Ruhm und 'Preis' von 'kliges' nach dem unentschiedenen Kampf gegen Artus' Prestigeritter, der ihm in Ulrichs Bearbeitung wenn nicht den Sieg, so doch die Überlegenheit zuerkennt. Ulrich erzählt den Kampf und den Triumph Cligés' viel ausführlicher als Chrétien, in 140 Zeilen gegen etwas mehr als 40 bei Chrétien (4883ff.); es ist die typische *amplificatio* durch den deutschen 'höfischen Bearbeiter', wie sie für die Dichter der klassischen (und

---

[5] Haidu, *Aesthetic Distance* (wie Anm. 3), S. 64ff.

vorklassischen) Generation u. a. durch die Arbeiten von Michel Huby nachgewiesen wurde. Artus läßt sich hier auch viel länger bitten, dem erbitterten Kampf ein Ende zu setzen (sonst wäre die *amplificatio* eben unmöglich!). Aber leider erfahren wir nichts mehr aus diesem materiell besten aller erhaltenen Fragmente als eben die völlige Konformität zum Typus. Und deswegen bringt er uns nicht viel weiter in der Deutung der *Cligés*-Rezeption in Deutschland.

Daß Ulrich von Türheim sich in dem Kalocsaer Fragment als den Verfasser nennt, soll uns nicht überraschen, nachdem Rudolf von Ems in seinem *Willehalm von Orlens*, wohl in den 30er Jahren des 13. Jahrhunderts geschrieben, zweimal ein ausgedehntes Lob auf Ulrichs *Clies* (so geschrieben im Donaueschinger Codex, den Victor Junk 1905 herausgab) angestimmt hat (vgl. 2256ff., 4387ff.).[6] Allerdings hat er im *Alexander*, der ungefähr gleichzeitig gedichtet wurde, nochmals Ulrich gelobt (3262–66), doch ohne ein einziges Werk von ihm namhaft zu machen, und dagegen hat er kurz vorher von Konrad Fleck gesagt, er hätte die Geschichte von 'Flôren und Blanscheflûr' erzählt, 'und wie der strengen minne kraft/ Clîesen twanc'.[7] Hat es also denn zwei verschiedene *Cligés*-Bearbeitungen, die eine von Konrad Fleck, die andere von Ulrich von Türheim, in Deutschland gegeben? Hat Ulrich von Türheim etwa das abgebrochene Werk Konrad Flecks vollendet? Das sind die beiden Hypothesen, die Gröchenig/Pascher formulieren. Man darf wohl eine dritte hinzufügen: vielleicht hat Ulrich die Bearbeitung von Konrad Fleck, der ein bißchen älter war, nicht nach seinem Geschmack gefunden und eine verbesserte Fassung geben wollen? Diese dritte Hypothese ist zugegebenermaßen weniger wahrscheinlich, aber wohl auch nicht ganz auszuschließen.

Und ich muß nun auf die Frage zurückkommen, die ich nach der Analyse von Chrétiens Roman gestellt hatte: warum ist die Rezeption des *Cligés* in Deutschland so dünn, bzw. warum ist die Überlieferung so schlecht gewesen? Wir haben gesehen, daß Ulrich in den erhaltenen Fragmenten die höfische Seite aller Gestalten, auch Alis', des meineidigen Onkels, eher betonte, die Minne zwischen Cligés und Fenice früher zum Ausdruck brachte und im letzten Teil eine religiöse Note anklingen ließ. Dies alles bedeutet einen großen Respekt für alle gängigen Normen, diejenigen der Gesellschaft – auch die modische Beliebtheit der *noble passion* – wie die der religiösen Institution. Dieser Respekt mag sehr wohl den (oder die) Bearbeiter vor der 'Umwertung' im letzten Teil, dem Abgleiten des Romans ins Abenteuerliche, zurückschrecken gelassen haben. Ebenso hat Ulrich von Türheim in

---

6   Rudolf von Ems, *Willehalm von Orlens*, hg. von Victor Junk, DTM, 2 (Berlin, 1905).
7   Rudolf von Ems, *Alexander*, hg. von Victor Junk, StLV, 272 und 274, 2 Bde. (Leipzig, 1928 und 1929), Bd. I, V. 3240ff.

seiner Fortsetzung von Gottfrieds *Tristan* den Liebeskult des Meisters nicht verstanden bzw. nicht verstehen wollen. So hat er den Meister 'fortgesetzt', ohne ihm beizupflichten! Vielleicht hat derselbe Ulrich von Türheim den *Cligés* ebenfalls bearbeitet, ohne ihn zu 'verstehen', d. h. ohne ihm bis zum Schluß beizustimmen? Er hätte sich dann an der Zwiespältigkeit eines Werks angestoßen, das das Tristan-Modell gottfriedscher Prägung mehrmals nachdrücklich kritisierte . . ., um es am Ende wieder in Kraft zu setzen! Chrétien, der strenge Kritiker eines Verhältnisses à la Tristan, hatte doch auch zuvor eine Erzählung 'Del roi Marc et d'Ysalt la Blonde' gedichtet, nach dem Prolog des *Cligés* selbst (5)! Vielleicht haben deswegen, wegen so viel Vieldeutigkeit und verwirrender Verwirrung, die ehrlichen Deutschen das verdächtige Werk fallenlassen und ihm einen eindeutigeren Anti-Tristan vorgezogen, etwa den *Willehalm von Orlens*, worin ausgerechnet Rudolf von Ems das ausgedehnte Lob auf Ulrichs *Cligés* anbringt. Helmut Brackert und vor allem Walter Haug haben gezeigt, wie Rudolfs *Willehalm* als eine kritische Kontrafaktur von Gottfrieds *Tristan* gelesen werden konnte und wollte. Haug spricht für den *Willehalm* von 'Bewährung im Ausharren [. . .] Wachsen und Reifen in duldender *triuwe*',[8] von dem Fehlen jedes Gegensatzes zur Gesellschaft: es ist genau das, was wir in den drei ersten, nicht aber im letzten Teil des *Cligés* Chrétiens gefunden haben. Das deutsche Publikum 'erwartete' wohl einen Roman, der entweder ja oder nein zum offiziellen Modell sagte, aber nicht jein. Zum Abschluß schlage ich vor, folgende Tatsachen oder auch Hypothesen ins Auge zu fassen:

(1) Der *Cligés* ist, wie die sonstigen Artusromane Chrétiens (denn er ist schließlich auch einer von denen), in Deutschland doch wohl rezipiert worden aber etwas später als die anderen, vielleicht schon von Konrad Fleck, jedenfalls von Ulrich von Türheim, und zwar bevor Rudolf von Ems seinen *Willehalm von Orlens* und seinen *Alexander* dichtete.

(2) Ulrich von Türheim scheint das Grundschema nicht wesentlich verändert, aber die Konformität mit den moralischen Normen seiner Gesellschaft irgendwie angestrebt zu haben, ja vielleicht gar eine religiöse Garantie für die heikle Episode des angeblichen Todes Fenices.

(3) Aber den blauäugigsten unter seinen Lesern (oder Zuhörern) hat das wohl nicht genügt, und vielleicht ist das einer der Gründe, die die Bearbeitung des *Jehan-und-Blonde*-Romans durch Rudolf von Ems erklären, sowie seine bewußte intertextuelle Kontrastierung zu Gottfrieds *Tristan*.

---

[8] Walter Haug, 'Rudolfs *Willehalm* und Gottfrieds *Tristan*: Kontrafaktur als Kritik', in *Deutsche Literatur des späten Mittelalters: Hamburger Colloquium 1973*, hg. von Wolfgang Harms und L. Peter Johnson (Berlin, 1975), S. 83–98, hier S. 98.

Zu den Schwierigkeiten der Lancelot-Rezeption in Deutschland

WALTER BLANK

Es ist ein Phänomen eigener Art, daß der arthurische Musterritter Lancelot in der deutschen literarischen Tradition der Gegenwart im Unterschied zum europäisch-literarischen Kontext[1] nicht nur keine Zentralfigur darstellt,[2] sondern weitgehend unbekannt ist.[3] Keine zeitlos gültige dichterische Gestaltung hat diese Figur des 'besten Ritters' in unsere Gegenwart herübergerettet. Für den englischen Sprachbereich gilt das nicht in gleicher Weise.[4] Wenn etwa die USA in der Kennedy-Regierung eine Realisierung der universalen Friedensherrschaft von König Artus und Lancelot, dem Hauptrepräsentanten seiner Tafelrunde, erkennen mochten,[5] setzt das eine wache Kenntnis jener Erzählungen und eine aktuelle Identifikation mit diesen mittelalterlichen Figuren voraus. Bei einer so unterschiedlichen Stoffrezeption in

[1] Vgl. Kurt Ruh, 'Lancelot', *DVjs*, 33 (1959), 269–82; mit einem Nachtrag von 1968 wieder in *Der arthurische Roman*, hg. von Kurt Wais, WdF, 157 (Darmstadt, 1970), S. 237–55 (S. 237f.); Ruth Schirmer, *Lancelot und Ginevra: Ein Liebesroman am Artushof: Den Dichtern des Mittelalters nacherzählt* (Zürich, 1961), S. 467.
[2] Hans-Hugo Steinhoff, 'Artusritter und Gralsheld: Zur Bewertung des höfischen Rittertums im *Prosa-Lancelot*', in *The Epic in Medieval Society: Aesthetic and Moral Values*, hg. von Harald Scholler (Tübingen, 1977), S. 271.
[3] *König Artus und seine Tafelrunde: Europäische Dichtung des Mittelalters*, hg. von Karl Langosch, Reclam UB, 9945 (Stuttgart, 1980), S. 613. Daran ändert auch der Popularisierungsversuch von Ruth Schirmer (wie Anm. 1) nichts, so wenig wie die seltenen dramatischen Stoffbearbeitungen von Tankred Dorst: *Merlin* (Frankfurt/M., 1981) oder von Heiner Müller: 'Libretto für Paul Dessaus Oper *Lanzelot* (1969)', *Theater der Zeit*, 25 (1970), Heft 3, 73–80.
[4] Vgl. Raymond H. Thompson, *The Return from Avalon: A Study of the Arthurian Legend in Modern Fiction* (Westport, Connecticut, 1985); Beverly Taylor und Elisabeth Brewer, *The Return of King Arthur: British and American Arthurian Literature Since 1800* (Cambridge, 1983); Stephen R. Reimer, 'The Arthurian Legends in Contemporary English Literature, 1945–1981', *Bulletin of Bibliography*, 38 (1981), 128–38, 149; Ulrich Müller, 'Lanzelot am Broadway und in New Orleans. Zur Rezeption des Lanzelot- und Artus-Stoffes in der zeitgenössischen Literatur und Musik', in *De Poeticis Medii Aevi Quaestiones: Käte Hamburger zum 85. Geburtstag*, hg. von Jürgen Kühnel u. a., GAG, 335 (Göppingen, 1981), S. 351–90.
[5] Vgl. die Ausführungen bei U. Müller (wie Anm. 4).

121

verschiedenen Ländern selbst in der Gegenwart ist daher zu vermuten, daß die Rezeptionsschwierigkeiten in Deutschland an unterschiedlichen nationalen Gegebenheiten oder Prägungen schon im Mittelalter liegen dürften, die einer genaueren Nachfrage wert sind. Die folgende Untersuchung beschränkt sich daher auf die deutsche Lancelot-Rezeption im Mittelalter.

Bei einer solchen Untersuchung steht man methodisch allerdings von Anfang an vor zwei Schwierigkeiten: 1. Bei dieser Fragestellung ist es nicht möglich zu zeigen, daß etwas positiv so und so ist, weil die positive Faktendarstellung hier nur dazu dient aufzuweisen, daß in der Umgebung des Untersuchungsbereichs das erwartete Andere nicht vorliegt, daß also etwas zu Erwartendes fehlt oder ausfällt. Methodisch handelt es sich dabei um eine Art Umkehrschluß, um eine Modifikation des *argumentum e silentio*, das naturgemäß immer der zwingenden Stringenz ermangelt. 2. Noch schwieriger ist es, für dieses Nicht-Dasein auch noch Gründe zu finden, warum diese Nicht-Existenz also sinnvoll oder sogar notwendig so zu konstatieren ist. Ein solches Verfahren führt zwangsläufig zu Hypothesen, die immer den Charakter des Unsicheren haben. Dieser Tatsache bin ich mir wohl bewußt. Trotzdem soll hier versucht werden, einige Überlegungen vorzutragen, die das Phänomen der weitgehenden Ausklammerung Lancelots in Deutschland – hier zunächst eingeschränkt auf das Mittelalter – vielleicht plausibel machen können.

I

Betrachten wir mit dem speziellen Augenmerk auf Deutschland kurz die europäischen Gestaltungen des Lancelot-Stoffes. Eine erste Auffälligkeit ist, daß die nur verhaltene Aufnahme der Lancelot-Geschichte in Deutschland keineswegs ein Phänomen der Neuzeit darstellt, sondern daß dies schon im Mittelalter zu beobachten ist.

In Frankreich waren es die beiden zentralen Gestaltungen des Stoffs, der *Karrenritter* Chrétiens de Troyes[6] (um 1177–81) und der sog. Lancelot-Gral-Zyklus in Prosa[7] (ca. 1215–30), die die Weichen für die gesamten späteren Bearbeitungen gestellt haben. In England ist es nach einer Reihe von Einzelwerken vom 14. bis ins 16. Jahrhundert[8] vor allem

---

[6] *Les Romans de Chrétien de Troyes, III: Le Chevalier de la Charrete*, hg. von Mario Roques, CFMA, 86 (Paris, 1958).

[7] Einzige Gesamtausgabe: *The Vulgate Version of the Arthurian Romances*, hg. von H. Oskar Sommer, 8 Bde. (Washington, D.C., 1908–16); außerdem gibt es eine Reihe neuerer Einzelausgaben der Werke, aufgeführt in *The Arthurian Encyclopedia*, hg. von Norris J. Lacy (New York/London, 1986), S. 614.

[8] Stanzaic *Le Morte Arthur* (14. Jh.); *Lancelot of the Laik* (spätes 15. Jh.); *Sir Lancelot du Lake* (16. Jh.).

Thomas Malorys einprägsamer Gesamtdarstellung *Le Morte Darthur*[9] (1451–1469; gedruckt 1485) zu danken, daß die Figur Lancelots ins 19. und 20. Jahrhundert hinein überliefert wurde und lebendig blieb. Anders in Deutschland. Kennzeichen aller überlieferten Lancelot-Bearbeitungen ist, daß sie Einzelwerke blieben, die isoliert und ohne überzeugende Nachwirkung in der literarischen Landschaft stehen; so Ulrichs von Zatzikhoven *Lanzelet*[10] (nach 1194), so der deutsche Prosa-Lancelot[11] (ca. 1225–50 bzw. Ende 13./Anfang 14. Jh.), und ebenso die beiden späten Bearbeitungen durch Ulrich Fuetrer[12] (Prosa: 1467; strophisch: vor 1484–1487). Warum das so ist, ist zum Teil aus der Problemstellung dieser Werke selbst bzw. aus deren Gestaltung zu erschließen. Gemeinsam ist diesen deutschen Romanen, daß sie Übertragungen oder Bearbeitungen französischer Vorlagen sind. Schon Ulrichs *Lanzelet*, das früheste dieser Werke, hat ein 'welsche[z] buoch'[13] als Vorlage. Doch setzt man aufgrund der Aussage Ulrichs wie der geringen zeitlichen Distanz zwischen Quelle und Übersetzung[14] das Werk Ulrichs inhaltlich im allgemeinen mit dem 'welschen buoch' gleich. Die lange kontrovers diskutierte Frage, ob diese Quelle zeitlich vor oder nach Chrétiens *Karrenritter* anzusetzen sei, wird von der Mehrzahl der Forscher heute dahingehend beantwortet, daß das 'welsche buoch' wohl nach Chrétiens Roman entstanden, inhaltlich aber davon unabhängig sei, auch wenn die Kenntnis des Chrétienschen

---

[9] Sir Thomas Malory, *Le Morte Darthur*, hg. von H. Oskar Sommer (London, 1889–91) nach dem Erstdruck von William Caxton (1485); ders., *The Works*, hg. von E. Vinaver, 2. Aufl., 3 Bde. (Oxford, 1967), überarbeitet 1973. – Deutsche Übersetzung: *Die Geschichten von König Artus und den Rittern seiner Tafelrunde*, übertragen von H. Findeisen auf der Grundlage der Lachmannschen Übersetzung, insel taschenbuch, 239, 4. Aufl., 3 Bde. (Leipzig, 1983).

[10] Ulrich von Zatzikhoven, *Lanzelet: Eine Erzählung*, hg. von K. A. Hahn, mit einem Nachwort und einer Bibliographie von Frederick Norman, Deutsche Neudrucke, Reihe: Texte des Mittelalters (Berlin, 1965).

[11] *Lancelot, nach der Heidelberger Pergamenthandschrift Pal.Germ. 147*, hg. von Reinhold Kluge, DTM, 42/47/63, 3 Bde. (Berlin, 1948/1963/1974).

[12] *Ulrich Füeterers Prosaroman von Lanzelot nach der Donaueschinger Handschrift*, hg. von Arthur Peter, StLV, 175 (Tübingen, 1885). Ulrich Fuetrer, *Lannzilet. (Aus dem 'Buch der Abenteuer'.)* Str. 1–1122, hg. von Karl-Eckhard Lenk, ATB, 102 (Tübingen, 1989). Der hier fehlende Teil des strophischen Lancelot ist bis heute noch nicht ediert.

[13] 'Hûc von Morville/ hiez der selben gîsel ein,/ in des gewalt uns vor erschein/ daz welsche buoch von Lanzelete./ dô twanc in [= Ulrich] lieber vriunde bete,/ daz dise nôt nam an sich/ von Zatzikhoven Uolrich,/ daz er tihten begunde/ in tiutsche, als er kunde,/ diz lange vremde mære/ durch niht wan daz er wære/ in der frumen hulde dester baz.' (Ulrich von Zatzikhoven, *Lanzelet*, hg. von K. A. Hahn (wie Anm. 10), V. 9338ff.)

[14] Carola L. Gottzmann, *Deutsche Artusdichtung*, Bd. I (Frankfurt, 1986), S. 29: 'Die anglonormannische Vorlage könnte entweder noch während der Regentschaft Heinrichs II. (1154–1189) oder kurz danach entstanden sein.' Der zeitliche Abstand beider Werke wäre nur dann größer, wenn sich die Spätdatierung Ulrichs zwischen 1210 und 1220 (J.-M. Pastré, 'L'ornement difficile et la datation du *Lanzelet* d'Ulrich von Zazikhoven', in *Actes du colloque des 14 et 15 janvier 1984 de l'Université de Picardie, Centre d'Études médiévales: Lancelot*, hg. von Danielle Buschinger, GAG, 415 (Göppingen, 1984), S. 149–62 (S. 156)) bestätigen sollte.

Romans vielleicht vorauszusetzen ist.[15] Wichtig ist das bezüglich des zentralen Unterschieds beider. Bei Ulrich gibt es, im Gegensatz zu Chrétien, keine Liebesbeziehung zwischen Lancelot und Ginover, nicht einmal die Form der höfischen Dienst-Minne, geschweige denn eine sexuelle Erfüllung dieser Liebe, auch nicht eine nur einmalige. Ginover ist für Lanzelet bei Ulrich kaum mehr als ein Objekt, bei dessen Befreiung aus der Gefangenschaft er seine ritterlichen Ausnahmequalitäten unter Beweis stellen kann. Außerdem fehlt die Rahmenhandlung, die Tyrannis von Lanzelets Vater Pant, bei Chrétien ganz.

Wie die Minnekonzeption des Helden bei Ulrich zu bestimmen und zu bewerten ist, ist in der Forschung bis heute offen. Übereinstimmung besteht darin, daß das Text-Attribut der 'wîpsælege Lanzelet' kaum geeignet ist, in Ulrichs Roman eine sexuelle Genußmentalität zu entdecken, deren moralische Verwerflichkeit mit Kategorien des 19. Jahrhunderts angeprangert wurde.[16] Die dreifach gesteigerte Liebesbeziehung Lanzelets zunächst zur Tochter des Galagandreis, danach zu Ade und schließlich zum Muster an Treue und Keuschheit, Iblis, ist ohne jeden Bezug zur Liebesproblematik bei Chrétien oder einem der andern bekannten Autoren. Dieser Entwurf ist im gesamten arthurischen Kontext ein Novum.[17] Von der Minnetheorie her nimmt er eine Außenseiterposition ein, die man bestenfalls antipodisch in Beziehung zu Chrétien bringen könnte: dann stünde die Freude-Qualität des liebenden Helden bei Ulrich in klarem Kontrast zum melancholischen Lancelot Chrétiens.[18] Chrétiens wie Ulrichs Position aber, Setzung wie

15 Kurt Ruh, 'Der *Lanzelet* Ulrichs von Zatzikhoven: Modell oder Kompilation?', in *Deutsche Literatur des späten Mittelalters: Hamburger Colloquium 1973*, hg. von Wolfgang Harms und L.Peter Johnson (Berlin, 1975), S. 47–55; wieder abgedruckt in: Kurt Ruh, *Kleine Schriften*, 2 Bde. (Berlin/New York, 1984), I, S. 63–71 (S. 65f.); René Pérennec, 'Artusroman und Familie: ''Daz welsche buoch von Lanzelete'' ', in *Acta Germanica*, 11 (1979), 1–51 (S. 37).

16 So noch Ernst H. Soudek: 'Die hervorstechendste Eigenschaft [. . .] des Helden bei Zatzikhoven ist [. . .] eine ungewöhnliche Leichtfertigkeit in Dingen der Liebe. [. . .] Eigenschaften, die der ethischen Ausrichtung der großen Epiker der mhd. Blütezeit zuwiderlaufen' ('Lancelot und Lanzelet. Zur Verbreitung der Lancelotsage auf deutschem Sprachgebiet', *Studies in German in Memory of Robert L. Kahn, Rice University Studies*, 57,4 (1971), 115–21 (S. 118). Zur Geschichte der moralischen Bewertung von Ulrichs *Lanzelet* vgl. Helga Schüppert, 'Minneszenen und Struktur im *Lanzelet* Ulrichs von Zatzikhoven', in *Würzburger Prosastudien II: Untersuchungen zur Literatur und Sprache des Mittelalters: Kurt Ruh zum 60. Geburtstag*, hg. von Peter Kesting (München, 1975), S. 123–38 (S. 123–126); und die Zusammenstellung der Forschungsliteratur dazu bei John Margetts, 'Eheliche Treue im *Lanzelet* Ulrichs von Zatzikhoven', in *Festschrift für Siegfried Grosse zum 60. Geburtstag*, hg. von Werner Besch u.a., GAG, 423 (Göppingen, 1984), S. 383–400 (S. 386, Anm.4).

17 Vgl. den Aufsatz von K. Ruh, 'Der *Lanzelet* Ulrichs' (wie Anm. 15), der der Forschungsdiskussion wesentlich neue Impulse gab.

18 K. Ruh, 'Lancelot' (wie Anm. 1), S. 247ff.; Alois Wolf, ' ''Ja por les fers ne remanra'' (Chrétiens *Karrenritter* V. 4600): Minnebann, ritterliches Selbstbewußtsein und concordia voluntatum', *Literaturwissenschaftliches Jahrbuch der Görres-Gesellschaft*, NF 20 (1979), S. 31–69 (S. 41f., 50ff.).

mögliche Gegensetzung, bleiben in Deutschland ohne eigene Rezeption. Daraus folgt m. E., daß Chrétiens grundsätzliche Thematik der reinen Dienst-Minne als einer höfischen Qualität, die als Liebe in Konflikt mit den gesellschaftlichen Normen gerät, in Deutschland nicht in Verbindung mit der Figur Lancelots diskutiert wird.

Dieser Feststellung widerspricht scheinbar der Befund im deutschen Prosa-Lancelot. Als deutsche Bearbeitung der drei Hauptbücher des französischen Prosa-Vulgata-Zyklus[19] hat der Prosa-Lancelot die entscheidenden Problembereiche wie auch die Handlungsstruktur seiner Vorlage übernommen: 1. die Kernproblematik der Liebe Lancelots zur Königin, 2. die Utopievorstellung eines arthurischen Friedensreiches und 3. die Verknüpfung des Artusbereichs mit der religiösen Problematik der Gralserlösung und den Fragen nach Sünde und Schuld. Mit dieser Kombination, die quellenmäßig neben Chrétiens *Karrenritter* auch Roberts de Boron Gralzyklus[20] zu integrieren versucht, entsteht ein erzählerisches Spannungsfeld, dessen innere Unvereinbarkeiten, wie sie Fanni Bogdanow noch jüngst einschätzt, letztlich die Sprengung des Ganzen zur Folge haben.[21]

Schon in der Minnekonzeption des französischen Vulgata-Zyklus werden, wie Hans Fromm zeigt,[22] drei unvereinbare Minnekonzepte miteinander verschränkt: der *fin'amors* der Troubadours; der *amour courtois*, der sich in der *aventure* im Dienst einer Dame bewährt; und schließlich die Tristan-Liebe, die die volle Ebenbürtigkeit der Partner verlangt. Wie hier eine 'Lösung' gefunden werden soll, bleibt schon vom Ansatz her fraglich. Diese Spannung steigert sich insbesondere

[19] Alternativ-Bezeichnungen dafür: Lanzelot-Gral-Zyklus; Pseudo-Map-Zyklus. – Die Kernbücher dieses fünfbändigen Zyklus sind: der *Lancelot propre* (oder auch: Prosa-Lancelot) (Buch 3), *Queste del Saint Graal* (4), und *Mort (le roi) Artu* (5). Ihnen sind zwei 'Geschichts'-Bücher vorangestellt, die die Vorgeschichte des Grals und des britischen Königshauses bis zur Inthronisation des Artus berichten: *Estoire del Saint Graal* (oder auch: Grand Saint Graal) (1) und *Estoire de Merlin* (oder: Vulgata-Merlin) (2). – Edition: *The Vulgate Version of the Arthurian Romances*, hg. von H. Oskar Sommer, 8 Bde. (Washington, D.C., 1908–16); außerdem eine Reihe neuerer Einzelausgaben.
[20] Seine Trilogie umfaßt die Bücher *Joseph d'Arimathie* (so die übliche Bezeichnung; ediert wurde es unter dem Titel: *Le Roman de l'Estoire dou Graal*), *Merlin* und (wahrscheinlich) *Perceval* (vielleicht identisch/bearbeitet [?] als der sog. *Didot-Perceval*). – In der originalen Versform sind nur der *Joseph* und die ersten 504 Verse des *Merlin* erhalten. – Edition: Robert de Boron, *Le Roman de l'Estoire dou Graal*, hg. von W.A. Nitze (Paris, 1927). Deutsche Übersetzung: Robert de Boron, *Le Roman du Saint-Graal*, Übers. und eingeleitet von M. Schöler-Beinhauer, Klassische Texte des Romanischen Mittelalters in zweisprachigen Ausgaben, 18 (München, 1981).
[21] Vgl. Fanni Bogdanow: 'In the Vulgate Cycle, the combination of such incompatible themes as that of the Grail and Lancelot's love for Guenevere produced an inevitable clash of ideologies.' (in *The Arthurian Encyclopedia*, hg. von Norris J. Lacy (New York/London, 1986), S. 431).
[22] Hans Fromm, 'Zur Karrenritter-Episode im Prosa-Lancelot. Struktur und Geschichte', in *Medium aevum 'deutsch': Beiträge zur deutschen Literatur des hohen und späten Mittelalters: Festschrift für Kurt Ruh*, hg. von Dietrich Huschenbett u.a. (Tübingen, 1979), S. 69–79 (S. 79).

noch dadurch, daß der nachfolgende Teil III des Prosa-Lancelot[23] mit der Gralserzählung diese Liebe, wie immer sie sich auch konstituieren mag, unter geistlicher Perspektive abwertet und sie letztlich der Schuld am Desaster der ritterlichen Idealwelt zeiht: denn die sündhafte Liebe im Ehebruch Ginovers mit Lancelot verstößt gegen die Normen der Kirche wie der Gesellschaft, außerdem sprengt sie das Gefüge der feudalen Sippenbindung, indem sie Ursache der Fehde der Lot-Sippe mit Gawan gegen die Ban-Sippe mit Lancelot wird, die zum Tod Gawans führt; und letztlich ist die erzwungene Außenseiterposition Lancelots sogar mit schuld am Untergang des Artusreiches.[24] Der Gral dagegen zieht sich in die Jenseits-Dimension zurück, so daß das Ende ein großer Scherbenhaufen ist, auf dem die Rest-Menschheit ohne irdische oder göttliche Hilfe alleingelassen sitzt.

Auch wenn der strukturelle Entwurf dieses riesigen Werks einheitlich ist, wie man seit Jean Frappiers Untersuchungen glaubt,[25] bleibt die Spannung darin unausgleichbar. Daher ist es kein Zufall, daß schon die spätere französische Bearbeitung im Post-Vulgata-Zyklus[26] (ca. 1230–40) die eigentliche Lancelot-Geschichte so weit wie möglich an den Rand drängt und auf diese Weise die Liebesgeschichte als Auslöser der gescheiterten Gralsuche und des Todes von Artus eliminiert. Ähnlich klammert die *Suite du Merlin*[27] (1.Hälfte 13. Jh.) Lancelot überhaupt aus und wendet sich der romantischen Version der Erzählung zu, in der Merlin im Weißdornbusch von der Fee Niniane zu ewiger Liebe eingeschlossen wird und das Schicksal des Artus und seines erstrebten Friedensreichs völlig offen bleibt. Von Artus' Ende ist hier nicht die Rede. Damit bleibt die Hoffnung auf eine Erfüllung der Utopie, im Gegensatz zum Lancelot-Gral-Zyklus, bestehen.

Diese Spannung der französischen Vorlage spiegelt sich auch im deutschen Prosa-Lancelot. Wie die Überlieferungsgeschichte zeigt,[28]

---

23   Entspricht im französischen Zyklus dem Buch 5: *Mort Artu*, im deutschen Prosa-Lancelot dem Bd. III von Kluges Ausgabe.

24   Indem 1. durch den Krieg gegen Lancelot in Frankreich Artus' unehelicher Sohn Mordret in der Zeit der Abwesenheit des Königs von Britannien dessen Herrschaft usurpieren kann, und 2. bei der Entscheidungsschlacht Mordret-Artus der bisher mehrfach als Retter der Artusrunde in Erscheinung getretene Lancelot fehlt.

25   So – in Weiterführung von Frappiers Hypothese – Steinhoff (wie Anm. 2, S. 288) in der Auseinandersetzung mit Rudolf Voß, *Der Prosa-Lancelot*, (Meisenheim, 1970); ähnlich auch U. Ruberg (*AfdA*, 83 (1972), 172–79) und W. Harms (*Leuv.Bijdr.*, 59 (1970), 162–64). – Aber auch Steinhoff verkennt nicht die Spannung, die zwischen dem 'autonomistischen Legitimationsentwurf' Chrétiens und dem 'geistlich orientierten Ritterbild mit deutlich restaurativen Zügen' im Prosa-Lancelot besteht (ebd. S. 288).

26   Fanni Bogdanow, *The Romance of the Grail: A Study of the Structure and Genesis of a Thirteenth-Century Arthurian Prose Romance* (Manchester, 1966).

27   *Merlin*, hg. von Gaston Paris und J. Ulrich, 2 Bde. (Paris, 1886).

28   Hans-Hugo Steinhoff, 'Zur Entstehungsgeschichte des deutschen Prosa-Lancelot', in *Probleme mittelalterlicher Überlieferung und Textkritik: Oxforder Colloquium 1966*, hg. von Peter F. Ganz und Werner Schröder (Berlin, 1968), S. 81–95. Auch K. Ruh konstatiert zwischen

erfolgte die deutsche Bearbeitung in zwei Stufen, wobei der erste Teil nach der Darstellung des Kampfes Lancelots gegen Meleagant zur Befreiung der Königin, d. h. nach der Kernszene bei Chrétien, abbricht und danach eine große Textlücke klafft. Erst in einem zweiten Anlauf rund ein halbes Jahrhundert später folgt die Fortsetzung mit dem Gralsgeschehen und der eindeutig geistlichen Perspektive. Hans-Hugo Steinhoff kommt zu dem Ergebnis: 'Manches spricht für einen vorzeitigen Abbruch des ersten Versuchs, den Lancelot-Zyklus in Deutschland anzusiedeln.' Dieser Abbruch 'ist Mitte des 13. Jhs. nicht undenkbar. [. . .] So wäre es vorstellbar, daß der Torso bis ins angehende 14. Jh. ohne Ergänzung blieb, [. . .] ohne daß es dem Fortsetzer (aus welchen Gründen auch immer) gelang, direkt an die Bruchstelle anzuschließen.'[29] Nimmt man die formalen Überlieferungs-Kriterien neben den genannten werkimmanenten Problem-Spannungen zur unterschiedlichen Wege-Struktur Fromms[30] hinzu, daß nämlich im Prosa-Roman eine zyklisch beeinflußte Geschichtskonzeption neben eine weltanschauliche Programm- und Exempeldichtung des Artusepos tritt, so wird deutlich, daß bereits im Rezeptionsprozeß des französischen Zyklus durch deutsche Prosaisten die innere Dichotomie nur mühsam überbrückt werden kann. Der einheitlichen Konzeption des Prosa-Romans entspricht weder in Frankreich noch in Deutschland eine konsequente und schlüssige Darstellung der angerissenen Probleme, so daß die alte Ambivalenz zwischen Weltverbundenheit und geistlicher Sicht, zwischen der Form des Artusromans und der Geschichtsdichtung permanent als Belastung spürbar ist. Spätestens seit der Mitte des 13. Jahrhunderts weichen französische wie deutsche Bearbeiter daher zunehmend von der vorgezeichneten Linie ab oder unterbrechen zumindest zeitweilig deren Weiterführung. Diese französisch-deutsche Gemeinsamkeit der Zyklus-Rezeption verdient insofern Beachtung, als die Tradierung des Stoffs in England ungebrochen bis ins 15. Jahrhundert weitergeht, vermutlich infolge eines andern literatur-soziologischen Kontexts.

Der deutsche Prosa-Lancelot findet bis in die zweite Hälfte des 15. Jahrhunderts keine weitere Bearbeitung. Erst der Münchner Hofpoet Ulrich Fuetrer hat, vielleicht auf Anregung Püterichs von Reicherts-hausen, um das Jahr 1467 eine verkürzende Version des Romans, ebenfalls in Prosa, vorgelegt.[31] Interessanterweise wendet er sich zwanzig Jahre später noch einmal diesem Stoff zu (vor 1484–1487), um ihn dieses Mal allerdings formal strenger zu behandeln, indem er ihn in

Teil I (Galahot-Teil) und Teil II/III einen Bruch und Widersprüche ('Lancelot', wie Anm. 1, S. 252f.).
29 Steinhoff, 'Entstehungsgeschichte' (wie Anm. 28) S. 89f.
30 Fromm, 'Karrenritter-Episode' (wie Anm. 22), S. 73ff., 89ff.
31 Siehe Anm. 12.

die komplizierte Titurel-Strophe bindet. Inhaltlich arbeitet Fuetrer ganz
in jener Art, die vom späten 15. Jahrhundert bekannt ist: Kürzungen;
Betonung des Faktischen und der Handlung; Unterdrückung von
Charakterbeschreibungen, Emotionen, sinngebenden Zeichen und psy-
chischen Zuständen. In der Minnekonzeption entfällt bei Fuetrer der
Dienst-Gedanke. Lancelots Minnelähmung[32] wie die Eifersucht der
Königin werden zu rein äußerlichen Automatismen ohne inneres
Pendant. Ethische Verhaltensnormen werden zum äußerlichen Ritual.[33]

Bemerkenswerter als diese Beobachtungen aber ist die Tatsache, daß
Fuetrer den Lancelot-Stoff bewußt aus dem Artuskomplex, den er in
seinem Mammutwerk *Buch der Abenteuer*[34] aufarbeitet (1473–84),
ausklammert.[35] Der erste Teil des *Buchs der Abenteuer* orientiert sich für
den Handlungsablauf im wesentlichen an der zusammenhängenden
Geschichte in Wolframs *Parzival* und Albrechts *Jüngerem Titurel*,
ausgeweitet durch Informationen aus dem *Trojanerkrieg* Konrads von
Würzburg, dem verlorengegangenen *Merlin* Albrechts von Scharfen-
berg, der *Krone* Heinrichs von dem Türlin und dem *Lohengrin*. Der
zweite Teil setzt sich aus sieben selbständigen Artusromanen
zusammen,[36] offenbar dem gesamten Rest-Material, das Fuetrer aus
dem Artus-Umfeld greifbar war. An keiner Stelle des riesigen Werks
aber wird der Versuch gemacht, die Lancelot-Figur darin zu integrieren.
Besonders aufschlußreich ist dies bei der näheren Analyse des Merlin-
Stoffs aus dem ersten Teil des *Buchs der Abenteuer*. Denn der Bericht über
Merlin bei Fuetrer reicht exakt so weit, wie er wohl in der Trilogie
Roberts de Boron dargeboten war: mit der Königskrönung Artus'
verschwindet Merlin – im Unterschied zum Vulgata-Zyklus, in dem
Merlin als Artus' Berater bis zu Ende fungiert – ohne Abschied oder
Begründung von der Bildfläche. Mit dieser Quellentradition von Robert

---

[32] Siehe Anm. 18.

[33] Vgl. Susanne Mecklenburg, *Untersuchungen zu Ulrich Füetrers Prosa-Lantzilet*, Magister-
Arbeit, Freiburg i.Br., 1988.

[34] Es gibt davon keine Gesamtausgabe, sondern nur eine größere Zahl von Einzeleditio-
nen. Diese sind aufgeführt bei Kurt Nyholm, 'Ulrich Fuetrer', in *Die deutsche Literatur des
Mittelalters: Verfasserlexikon*, hg. von Kurt Ruh, 2. Aufl., Bd. II (Berlin/New York, 1980), Sp.
1003.

[35] Ich schließe mich hier der Meinung K. Nyholms an, der sowohl den Prosa-Lantzilet
wie auch die spätere Versfassung des Romans als selbständige Werke betrachtet. Danach
war auch der strophische *Lantzilet* nicht als Bestandteil des *Buchs der Abenteuer* geplant (vgl.
Die Gralepen in Ulrich Füetrers Bearbeitung (Buch der Abenteuer), hg. von K. Nyholm, DTM,
57 (Berlin, 1964), S. XXIX, Anm. 3; XXXIIff.). Munz und Fichtner dagegen ordnen in den
Einleitungen zu ihren Editionen den *Lantzilet* dem *Buch der Abenteuer* zu (vgl. *Persibein*, hg.
von R. Munz, ATB, 62 (Tübingen, 1964), S. X; *Trojanerkrieg*, hg. von E.G. Fichtner
(München, 1968), S. 9). Modifizierend will H. Becker, 'Das Epos in der deutschen
Renaissance', *PBB*, 54 (1930), 201–68 (S. 224) den *Lantzilet* als 3.–5. Buch in den Kontext des
Buchs der Abenteuer eingliedern.

[36] *Floreis und Wigoleis, Seifried de Ardemont, Meleranz, Iban, Persibein, Poytislier* und
Flordimar. – K. Nyholm (wie Anm. 34): 'Sämtliche Erzählungen sind Nachdichtungen
älterer Vorlagen.'

her ist aber auch für Fuetrer der Schlüssel gefunden, der Lancelot aus dem Erzählkontext ausschließt. Denn hier wird das Gralsgeschehen ausschließlich mit dem Namen Parzival verknüpft. Und das ist die Linie, an deren Ende Fuetrer steht und der er – hier zeitlich rückwärts betrachtet – folgt: über Albrechts *Jüngeren Titurel* und Wolframs *Parzival* zu Roberts de Boron *Estoire dou Graal* und sogar noch zurück zu Chrétiens *Perceval*. Alle Romane dieses Stranges kennen nur Parzival als Gralserlöser. In der Prosa-Lancelot-Tradition aber ist ursprünglich Lancelot als Erlöserfigur vorgesehen, so daß sich überlieferungsgeschichtlich für den Gralsbereich das Konkurrenzpaar Lancelot–Parzival ergibt. Durch Lancelots fleischliche Sünde aber wird er unfähig zur Gralserlösung, so daß er im Prosa-Lancelot abgelöst wird durch seinen Sohn Galaat, die andere Konkurrenzfigur zu Parzival. Das *Buch der Abenteuer* aber konzentriert sich ganz auf Parzivals Gralsgeschichte und damit auf die für Deutschland dominante Wolfram-Tradition, im Spätmittelalter oft in der 'Fortsetzung' des *Jüngeren Titurel* gelesen. Die Artusgesellschaft[37] ist in diesen Texten aber weder mit der Minne-Ehebruch-Thematik verbunden, noch kommt Lancelot als Protagonist des Artushofes darin überhaupt vor. Und auch die Gralsherrschaft am Ende ist eine andere: der Gral in der Wolfram-Tradition entzieht sich der Menschheit, im Unterschied zum Prosa-Lancelot, nicht, auch wenn er seinen Platz nach Indien verlegt. Von dort aus wirkt er jedoch weiter für die Menschen und ist für sie erfahrbar.

So zeigt sich bei Fuetrer ganz deutlich, daß gegen Ende des 15. Jahrhunderts in Deutschland eine klare Trennung in zwei Stränge erfolgt ist: Auf der einen Seite steht der Lancelot-Strang, der die ritterlich-höfische Dimension einschließlich der innerweltlichen Liebe beschreibt; auf der andern Seite der Parzival-Gral-Strang, der die gesamte höfische Welt vor dem Hintergrund der religiösen Dimension sieht und vor allem ein metaphysisch orientiertes Wertungssystem zugrundelegt. Die Ansätze zur Trennung beider Stränge fallen aber bereits in die Mitte des 13. Jahrhunderts. Die erwähnten inneren Spannungen haben offenbar die Weichen gestellt für eine problemorientierte Figuren-Dichotomie von Lancelot einerseits und Parzival andererseits. Vermutlich erhält die Verknüpfung des Artus mit der positiven Gralsutopie Parzivals in Deutschland den Vorzug gegenüber der Katastrophen-Perspektive des Artusreichs in der Lancelot-Tradition.

---

[37] Es ist bemerkenswert, daß sich schon früh auch eine Konkurrenz Lancelot–Gawan abzeichnet. Bereits bei Chrétien wird im *Karrenritter* ein Unterschied zwischen beiden gemacht, wobei der bekannte Gawan als der übliche Artus-Repräsentant gegenüber Lancelot zurücktritt und dieser bei der Befreiung der Königin sowohl die schwierigere Aufgabe löst (Überschreiten der Schwertbrücke), wie er beim Schinderkarren auch die tiefere Liebe zeigt. Vgl. A. Wolf, ' ''Ja por les fers'' ' (wie Anm. 18), S. 43. Im Prosa-Lancelot dann ist das Gefälle von Lancelot zu Gawan sehr deutlich. – In Deutschland

II

Nach dieser knappen Stoff-Übersicht bis ins 15. Jahrhundert stehen wir bei der Frage nach den Gründen für die Lancelot-Zurückweisung in Deutschland. Wie bei Fuetrer schon andeutungsweise erkennbar, ist diese Frage nur im größeren Kontext der europäischen Artus-Gral-Rezeption zu beantworten. Lancelot erscheint dabei einerseits als Ausdruck und Exponent der Maßstäbe setzenden höfisch-arthurischen Welt; andererseits erscheint die Artuswelt vor dem Gral mit seiner religiös-weltanschaulichen Ausrichtung nur von nachgeordneter Bedeutung.

Ein Problem des Artusromans liegt dabei in der jeweiligen Zuordnung der Artusfigur zu einem der beiden Traditionssträge. In der Lancelot-Tradition erhält Artus und seine Runde ihren Glanz durch ihren Musterritter Lancelot. Wenn er fehlt, gibt selbst der König eine meist hilflose Figur ab.[38] Persönlich wird Artus noch stärker in Frage gestellt in seiner Rolle als Hahnrei, der sich mit Lancelot weder im Kampf noch in der Liebe Ginovers messen kann. Konsequent ergibt sich im Ganzen dieses Konzeptes daraus eine Frage nach dem Überleben der Artus-idealität und der Berechtigung der arthurischen Herrschaft. Vor dem Gral dagegen tritt Artus von vornherein ins zweite Glied zurück. Denn Fragen der Sünde und der Erlösung wie auch die zentrale Frage nach der inneren Begründung von Herrschaft und Macht liegen außerhalb seiner Kompetenz. Sie sind selbst diesem personifizierten höfischen Mittelpunkt von einer metaphysischen Instanz vorgegeben. Unmittel-barer Sprecher dieser Instanz ist aber nicht König Artus, sondern nur ein eigens dazu Berufener, der Gralskönig. Auch wenn zwischen diesem und König Artus kein Widerspruch oder eine explizite Wertungsabstufung für den Welt-König vorliegt, ist die Frage einer die innerweltlich bestimmte Artusgesellschaft transzendierenden Ordnung hier doch entscheidend für die Sehweise. Daß dabei national unter-schiedliche Akzente gesetzt werden, hat bezüglich der literarischen Konsequenzen Ulrich Müller angedeutet,[39] dessen Ansatz ich hier für den Lancelot weiterführe. Vergleichen wir daher kurz die unter-schiedlich ausgeprägte literarische Funktion des Artus.

Es ist bekannt, daß der Artus-Mythos in Britannien von Anfang an eine nationalpolitische Bedeutung hatte.[40] Diente König Artus bei

---

dagegen bleibt (außer im Prosa-Lancelot und bei Fuetrer) Gawan der Artus-Repräsentant. Lancelot wird an den Rand gedrängt oder er verschwindet ganz.

38   Das gilt so nicht für den abweichenden *Lanzelet* Ulrichs von Zatzikhoven.
39   Müller, 'Lancelot am Broadway' (wie Anm. 4), bes. S. 362ff.
40   Vgl. W.F. Schirmer, *Die frühen Darstellungen des Artusstoffes* (Köln/Opladen, 1958).

Geoffrey of Monmouth (1135) der dynastischen Begründung und Festigung des anglonormannischen Herrscherhauses, so wurde mit der bei Wace (um 1155) berichteten Entrückung des Artus nach Avalon für Britannien die verbreitete Wiederkehrsage des kommenden Friedenskönigs etabliert, so daß sich jeder regierende englische König in diese Rolle des *rex redivivus* hineinstilisieren konnte. Dieses Verständnis prägt in England die Artus-Literatur bis ins 20. Jahrhundert.[41] Anders in Frankreich. Chrétien tilgte bei der Figur des Artus die national-britische Komponente und schuf statt dessen einen übernationalen Standes-Mythos,[42] eine Konzeption, die im deutschen Artusroman übernommen wurde.

In England fehlt dem Artusroman zunächst die Thematik des Lancelot mit der Liebe zur Königin, ebenso wie die Verbindung des Artus mit dem Gral bzw. Parzival. Statt dessen bleibt die Artus-Perspektive des Königs und Herrschers dominierend, auch später, als Lancelot/Ginevra und der Gralskomplex hinzukommen. In Deutschland dagegen ist die Variante der Wiederkehr eines Friedensfürsten zwar bekannt, aber an andere (historische) Personen als an Artus geknüpft: an Kaiser Barbarossa (im Kyffhäuser) bzw. Kaiser Friedrich II.[43] Dabei ist bemerkenswert, daß mit Friedrichs II. Tod (1250) diese von eschatologischen Ideen getragene Umbildung verstärkt einsetzt und etwa gleichzeitig auch die Lokalisierung der Sage im Kyffhäuserberg in Thüringen, unweit der staufischen Kaiserpfalz Tilleda gelegen, beginnt. Interessant dabei ist,[44] daß der bergentrückte Kaiser zunächst Friedrich II. war. Die Übertragung der Sage auf Kaiser Friedrich I. Barbarossa erfolgte erst im 16. Jahrhundert.[45] Das ist im eschatologisch-politischen Erwartungshorizont ein markanter Unterschied zu Großbritannien. Denn damit ist die national wichtigste Ausgangsfunktion der britischen Artusrezeption in Deutschland personell anderweitig 'besetzt' und entfällt so für König Artus. Wenn dessen Geschichte in Deutschland mit Erfolg erzählt werden soll, muß sie einen andern Begründungszusammenhang erfahren.

Wie steht es vergleichsweise mit der Artus-Perspektive in Frankreich? Hier stellt Chrétien für den Artusroman die Weichen. Dabei ist wichtig,

---

[41] Vgl. die Literatur in Anm. 4.

[42] Müller, 'Lanzelot am Broadway' (wie Anm. 4), S. 364.

[43] Die Ablösung der Artusfigur durch Kaiser Friedrich II. in Italien und Deutschland ist eingehend beschrieben bei Alexander H. Krappe 'Die Sage vom König im Berge', *Mitteilungen der schlesischen Gesellschaft für Volkskunde*, 35 (1935), 76–102 (bes. S. 87ff.). Auf die eschatologisch gesehene Bezugsfigur Friedrich II. und auf die Situation des Reiches in Deutschland bei der Rezeption des Prosa- Lancelot Mitte des 13. Jhs. weist auch Hans Fromm hin ('Karrenritter-Episode' (wie Anm. 22), S. 96, Anm. 26).

[44] Vgl. die Literatur dazu bei Krappe, S. 93 Anm. 1.

[45] Otto Müller, 'Die Kyffhäusersage', in *Auf den Spuren der Staufer*, hg. von Otto Müller (Gerlingen, 1977), S. 133ff. (S. 135).

daß er alle Problemkreise getrennt in eigenen Romanen behandelt. Die nationale Frage (mit der Vorgabe eines britischen Artus) klammert er in seinem Modell des Artusromans völlig aus und überläßt deren Behandlung der Gattung der Chanson de geste mit der dort substituierten kontinentalen oder gar französisch-nationalen Zentralfigur Karl dem Großen. – Den Wunsch nach Erlösung und die religiöse Aufgabe dieser Gesellschaft erörtert Chrétien anhand des Gralsstoffs in seinem letzten, unvollendeten Roman, dem *Perceval*. – Die zentral wichtige höfische Liebesproblematik dagegen entfaltet er im Artusroman trotz der Breite doch differenziert in zwei Aspekten: 1. demonstriert er im *Chevalier de la Charrette* die Gefährdung der höfischen Gesellschaft durch eine illegitime Liebe am Beispiel Lancelot–Ginevra, auch wenn er die konsequente Weiterführung des Problems nach der einmaligen sexuellen Vereinigung der Liebenden abbricht. Der implizite grundsätzliche Konflikt scheint unlösbar. Denn im ständisch-höfischen Sinn ist Lancelot der Ritter der Königin, wodurch die gesellschaftliche Minnedienst-Ideologie des Rittertums hineinkommt. Als aber der Musterritter mit der Liebesvereinigung die Grenze des höfisch Zulässigen überschreitet, indem er nicht nur mit Worten nach der ganzheitlichen Liebe ausgerechnet der Ehefrau des Artus und seiner 'Dienst'-Herrin Ginevra strebt, sondern er dies auch *in actu* vollzieht, wird die Minne in ihrer Überschreitung der Norm zum gesellschaftlichen Problem und die Liebeserfüllung der beiden zum Casus. Wer wird künftig die Oberhand behalten? Die Liebenden oder die Gesellschaft? Chrétien läßt die Frage formal offen, obgleich die Tendenz zur Einhaltung der Standesnorm gegenüber den individuellen Ansprüchen erkennbar ist. König Artus als das Haupt der Gesellschaft garantiert *noch* deren Norm, selbst gegen seinen Musterritter. Aber eine Bestrafung der Normverletzung erfolgt nicht. Auf diese Weise zeigt die Episode trotz ihres Schweigens die beginnende Aushöhlung der Norm. 2. Die andere Seite mit der Betonung auf dem individuellen Glücksanspruch des Liebespaares gegenüber der Gesellschaftsnorm ist das Modell von Tristan und Isolde, das Chrétien eigenwillig modifiziert und gleichzeitig konterkariert im *Cligès*.[46] In beiden Fällen ist das Problem Liebe–Gesellschaft jedoch ein Problem der Sinnhaftigkeit und der innerweltlichen Tragfähigkeit von Standesnormen. Die Frage nach der

---

[46] Modifiziert erscheint mir die Problematik deshalb, da durch die Liebenden, um der Erhaltung der gesellschaftlichen Norm und ihres Ansehens willen, der Tod der Geliebten Fenice inszeniert wird. Damit wird die innere Konsequenz dieser Liebe angesichts der Gesellschaftsverhältnisse gleichsam theatralisch ausgespielt, auch wenn Fenice sich unter ausdrücklicher Ablehnung von Isoldes Beispiel weigert, sich von Cligès entführen zu lassen und dadurch die kaiserliche Gesellschaft von Konstantinopel zu kompromitieren. – Zum genaueren Vergleich siehe: Xenja von Ertzdorff, 'Tristan und Lanzelot. Zur Problematik der Liebe in den höfischen Romanen des 12. und frühen 13. Jahrhunderts', *GRM*, NF 33 (1983), 21–52 (bes. S. 28ff.).

religiösen Bewertung dieses Phänomens ist hier nicht gestellt. Die andern höfischen Romane (*Erec, Yvain*) richten ihre Aufmerksamkeit mehr auf die Dominanz des Spannungsfelds von Ehe und/oder Liebe gegenüber den Herrscherpflichten des Paares und können für unsere Frage hier außer acht bleiben.

Zeitlich nach Chrétien hat dann Robert de Boron trotz seiner Kenntnis von Chrétiens *Perceval* die Artusgeschichte anders akzentuiert und sie in historisierender Form mit dem geistlichen Gralsgeschehen und mit der Figur Percevals verknüpft. Zur Person Lancelots und zur innerweltlichen Standesfrage der Liebe ergibt sich bei ihm keine Beziehung. Erst im französischen Prosa-Lancelot finden wir die Zusammenschau der bei Chrétien wie auch bei Robert noch getrennten Figuren Artus–Lancelot–Perceval und damit auch die Kombination der Fragen nach Herrschaft und Stand (Artusrunde), höfischer oder unhöfischer Liebe (Lancelot) und Erlösung bzw. Sünde (Gral). Damit ist stofflich, strukturell und konzeptionell ein Neues geschaffen.

In Deutschland bleiben die verschiedenen Artus-Stoffe und ihre Probleme, wie bei Chrétien, deutlich getrennt: Eine Tristan-Tradition mit den Autoren Eilhart, Gottfried und Fortsetzern behandelt die Liebe–Gesellschaft–Problematik (wobei das Recht des Einzelnen betont wird). Eine Grals-Tradition mit Wolfram und seinen Nachfolgern verknüpft die Erlösung/Sünde-Problematik mit den Herrschaftsfragen in einem Utopie-Modell, aber ohne nationale Verengung.

Die Lancelot-Tradition als dritter Strang dagegen bleibt seltsam isoliert und ohne eigene Resonanz. Damit ist zunächst und vor allem gemeint, daß die poetische Rezeption des Lancelot-Stoffes durch selbständig übersetzende, bearbeitende oder den Stoff weiterführende Autoren in Deutschland weitgehend ausfällt. So wurde der *Karrenritter* Chrétiens überhaupt nicht ins Deutsche übertragen. Der Prosa-Lancelot hat, wie im Überblick über die Handschriften-Überlieferung schon ausgeführt, zunächst seine eigenen Rezeptionsschwierigkeiten vom Französischen ins Deutsche mit dem Überlieferungs-Bruch um die Mitte des 13. Jahrhunderts. Und kein Späterer außer Ulrich Fuetrer im 15. Jahrhundert hat zu diesem Roman gegriffen, um ihn neu zu bearbeiten. Der *Lanzelet* Ulrichs von Zatzikhoven jedoch ist in jeder Hinsicht ein Sonderfall, sowohl was dessen Quelle angeht, wie auch bezüglich der behandelten Minneproblematik, die ohne Vergleichbares bleibt, auch was die Überlieferung betrifft. Mit nur zwei Handschriften und drei Fragmenten gehört der *Lanzelet* zu den am schwächsten überlieferten mittelalterlichen Romanen überhaupt. Und von einer unmittelbaren poetischen Rezeption oder zumindest direkten Beeinflussung anderer Werke ist bislang nichts bekannt.

Betrachtet man für den Zeitraum vom 13. bis 16. Jahrhundert allein nur die Zahlen für die Handschriften-Überlieferung der mit der

Lancelot-Tradition konkurrierenden Werke, so sprechen diese für sich selbst:[47]

Parzival	86 Hss.	Prosa-Lancelot	10 Hss.
Nibelungenlied	33	Ulrich, Lanzelet	5
Iwein	32	Fuetrer, Prosa-Lancelot	3
Tristan	27	Fuetrer, stroph. Lancelot	3

Vergleicht man die Zahl der deutschen Lancelot-Handschriften mit den rund 100 Handschriften des französischen Prosa-Lancelot-Zyklus, so wirkt der Rezeptions-Unterschied zu Frankreich noch krasser. Eine Deutung dieses Phänomens sehe ich darin, daß der Autor Wolfram für das deutsche Mittelalter eine absolute Ausnahmeerscheinung darstellt. Ist schon die Handschriftenhäufigkeit des *Parzival* etwa dreimal so groß wie die des *Nibelungenliedes*, des *Iwein* und von Gottfrieds *Tristan*, so wird sein Übergewicht noch deutlicher, wenn man auch sein zweites Werk, den *Willehalm*, in die Betrachtung mit einbezieht. Auch die 70 *Willehalm*-Handschriften sind noch mehr als doppelt so viele wie die der genannten Dreiergruppe. Wolframs Einfluß auf die Folgezeit scheint übermächtig, und sein Werk ist, wie diese Zahlen von der rein statistischen Seite her zeigen, für den späten Artusroman in jeder Hinsicht dominant.

Fragt man zusammenfassend nach Gründen für die seltsame Isolation und Wirkungslosigkeit des Lancelot in Deutschland, so ergeben die verschiedenen Gesichtspunkte unserer Sondierungen folgendes Tableau:

1. Artus als national-politische Figur (der *rex britannicus* in England) ist auf dem Kontinent so nicht akzeptabel. Daher gibt Chrétien dieser Figur eine allgemein ständisch-feudalistische Funktion, die idealtypisch überhöht ist. In Deutschland wird die nationale Einigungs- und Friedensfigur in der eschatologischen Endkaiser-Sage auf Friedrich II. gedeutet bzw. später auf die Wiederkehr von Friedrich Barbarossa aus dem Kyffhäuser bezogen. Damit ist diese Funktion personell anders 'besetzt'. König Artus ist in Deutschland, wie bei Chrétien, eine übernationale Statusfigur für die unumschränkte Feudalherrschaft.

2. Die arthurische Reichs- und Herrschaftsidee als abstrakte Vorstellung von einem künftigen Friedensreich ist in Deutschland von Wolframs Konzeption überlagert: seine Gral-Utopie ist eine positive Hoffnung auf eine friedliche Staats- und Herrschaftsstruktur. Der Gral als quasi-göttlicher Garant dieses Reiches[48] wirkt nicht vom Jenseits aus, sondern

---

[47]   Die Zahlen nach B. Schirok, *Parzivalrezeption im Mittelalter* (Darmstadt, 1982), Tabelle S. 57.
[48]   W. Blank, 'Die positive Utopie des Grals. Zu Wolframs Graldarstellung und ihrer

hier auf Erden, konkret im Lande India mit der neuen hierokratischen Modelltypik des Priester-Königs Johannes. Im Unterschied dazu bietet die Lancelot-Geschichte einen deprimierenden Ausblick in ein künftiges Desaster, in dem sich die erstrebte Friedensherrschaft selbst ad absurdum geführt hat und sich eine geistlich überhöhte Friedens- und Erlösungshoffnung durch den Rückzug des Grals ins Jenseits als nicht realisierbar erweist. Insofern steht in Deutschland eine negativ besetzte Lancelot-Artus-Perspektive der durch Wolfram positiv gefüllten Parzival-Gral-Utopie gegenüber, die Artus in einer Ideenverschiebung funktional positiv mit einbindet.

3. Auf der Figurenebene ist die Figur des absolut Liebenden in Deutschland einseitig, aber nachhaltig durch Gottfrieds Gestalt des Tristan 'besetzt'; und dies ungeachtet aller Unterschiede zwischen höfischer Dienst-Minne (Troubadour-Modell; erste Phase der Lancelot-Minne) und der individualistischen, paarbezogenen Tristan-Minne. Die Antwort der eher rückwärts orientierten, standesbestimmten 'Lösung' im Prosa-Lancelot hat offenbar gegenüber dem sich neu her-auskristallisierenden Selbstbehauptungswillen auch in der Liebe nicht mehr genügend Ausstrahlung.

4. Die religiöse Leitfigur in den deutschen Artusromanen ist unbe-stritten Parzival. Durch den nachhaltigen Einfluß Wolframs gibt es für die Konkurrenzfiguren Lancelot bzw. Galaat in diesem Bereich keinen Platz.

5. Ein letzter Gesichtspunkt liegt auf der formalen Ebene: die in der ersten Hälfte des 13. Jahrhunderts noch ungewohnte Prosa (im deutschen Prosa-Lancelot) blieb auf die nachfolgenden Bemühungen um eine angemessene Erzählform offenbar ohne Auswirkung. Wes-halb? War die Prosa zu avantgardistisch? Oder hat die bis dahin tradierte Form-Inhalt-Korrespondenz mit dem durch die Bibel ver-mittelten höheren Wahrheitsanspruch der Prosa eine Rezeptions-barriere vorgeschoben? Warum auch immer, die Prosaform, die im 13. Jahrhundert von dem anonymen Autor bereits so souverän beherrscht wird, findet in der Gattung Artusroman rund zweihundert Jahre lang keine Nachfolge – ein weiteres Zeichen für die isolierte Position dieses Werkes.

Das bedeutet, daß inhaltlich sämtliche für den Lancelot-Gral-Roman relevanten Problemfelder in Deutschland ab ca. 1210 bereits anderweitig 'besetzt' sind. Dabei dominieren sowohl in der Problemorientierung wie in der Gestaltung die beiden Autoren Gottfried von Straßburg und Wolfram von Eschenbach. Ich bin mir bewußt, daß diese 'besetzt'-

Nachwirkung im Mittelalter', in *Sprache, Literatur, Kultur: Studien zu ihrer Geschichte im deutschen Süden und Westen: Festschrift für W. Kleiber*, hg. von A. Greule und U. Ruberg (Stuttgart, 1989), S. 337–53.

Argumentation methodisch schwierig ist. Dennoch sehe ich keine andere Erklärung für das überraschende Ausfallphänomen des Lancelot in Deutschland als genau jene 'besetzt'-Koinzidenz der vier Punkte in der deutschen Artus-Rezeption.

Das bestätigt indirekt auch Heinrich von dem Türlin, der zwischen 1215 und 1240 in seiner Krone[49] versucht hat, gegen das Gralsmonopol Wolframs und seinen Helden Parzival zu opponieren, indem er Gawan den Gral erlösen läßt. Doch bleibt dieser Versuch bei Heinrich begrenzt auf die heilsgeschichtliche Überhöhung des Artusrittertums. Aber selbst sein Anti-Parzival Gawan bleibt eben die exemplarische Tafelrunden-Musterfigur Gawan und wird nicht zu einem geistlichen Lancelot oder einem spirituellen Galaat. Deutschland rezipiert den britisch-französischen Artusstoff also offenkundig nicht nur, sondern setzt in der Auswahl und Weiterbearbeitung auch haltungsmäßig eigene Akzente.

Was hier für das mittelalterliche Deutschland resümiert wurde, gilt unverändert auch für die Neuzeit. Der zentrale 'Schalter' für die Vermittlung der Artusstoffe ins 20. Jahrhundert hinein, Richard Wagner, hat das Thema der Nibelungen, des Tristan und des Parzival mit großer Wirkung neu gestaltet. Der Lancelot fehlt dabei. Für die Gegenwart mag es daher als signifikantes Symptom gelten, daß der Dramatiker Tankred Dorst für seinen Merlin (1981) mit der Zeichnung des Katastrophen-Endes der Artuswelt auf Thomas Malory als Quelle zurückgegriffen hat,[50] genau so wie Heiner Müller für sein Libretto zu Paul Dessaus Oper Lanzelot (1969) eine (stofflich ganz anders geartete) Vorlage des Russen Jewgeni Schwarz[51] bearbeitet. So scheint sich auch im gegenwärtigen Deutschland zu bestätigen, was für das Mittelalter festgestellt wurde: daß die Perspektive einer positiven Utopie als Selektionsmerkmal gegen den Lancelot durchschlägt. Wer aber, wie etwa Dorst, die Katastrophenskizze sucht, muß dafür auf andere Überlieferungen zurückgreifen.[52]

---

49   Heinrich von dem Türlin, Diu Crône, hg. von Gottlob H.F. Scholl, StLV, 27 (Stuttgart, 1852; unveränderter Nachdr. Amsterdam, 1966).
50   Peter von Becker, 'Merlin: Magier und Entertainer. Theater als Phantasiestätte. Ein Werkstatt-Gespräch mit Tankred Dorst', in Theater heute, 1979, H. 4, S. 33–48, hier S. 36.
51   Siehe: Theater der Zeit, 25 (1970), Heft 3, S. 13ff., 73ff.
52   Als bemerkenswertes Nebenergebnis dieser Untersuchung zeigt sich außerdem, daß es in Deutschland – sieht man vom Prosa-Lancelot und Fuetrer ab – im Unterschied zu Großbritannien und Frankreich keine Darstellung des Werdegangs und der Geschichte des Artusreiches gibt, sondern nur eine Darstellung des Artus als Idealtypus in zeitloser Herrschergestaltung und -funktion. Weshalb gestaltet der Artusroman in Deutschland konsequent nur Daten der idealistischen poetischen Fiktion aus und nicht auch die hypothetische Vorgabe der res factae als historia wie in England und Frankreich? – Doch damit ist eine andere Frage gestellt.

Die Konzeption der Artusfigur bei Chrestien und in Ulrichs Lanzelet: Mißverständnis, Kritik oder Selbständigkeit? Ein Diskussionsbeitrag

KLAUS GRUBMÜLLER

Chrestiens Artusromane haben – so nimmt man seit einiger Zeit an[1] – in Deutschland einen etwas abseitigen Kontrahenten erhalten: Ulrich von Zatzikhoven, Dorfpfarrer aus dem Thurgau, habe ein Gegenmodell vorgetragen,[2] einigermaßen wirkungslos zwar (2 Handschriften, 3 Fragmente),[3] aber auch nicht ganz ohne literaturhistorische Registrierung: Rudolf von Ems[4] und Jakob Püterich[5] nennen den Autor, andere, z. B. Heinrich von Freiberg[6] und der Verfasser der *Minneburg*[7] kennen Figuren der Geschichte.[8] Ob diese Signale nun

---

[1] Kurt Ruh, 'Der *Lanzelet* Ulrichs von Zatzikhoven. Modell oder Kompilation?', in *Deutsche Literatur des späten Mittelalters*, hg. von Wolfgang Harms und L. Peter Johnson (Berlin, 1975) S. 47–55; wieder abgedruckt in Kurt Ruh, *Kleine Schriften*, hg. von Volker Mertens, 2 Bde. (Berlin/New York, 1984), I: *Dichtung des Hoch- und Spätmittelalters*, S. 63–71. Die Argumentation ist wiederholt in Kurt Ruh, *Höfische Epik des deutschen Mittelalters II: 'Reinhart Fuchs', 'Lanzelet', Wolfram von Eschenbach, Gottfried von Straßburg* (Berlin, 1980), S. 34–49.

[2] Ulrich von Zatzikhoven, *Lanzelet: Eine Erzählung*, hg. von Karl August Hahn (Frankfurt a.M., 1845). Neudruck: Mit einem Nachwort und einer Bibliographie von Frederick Norman, Deutsche Neudrucke, Reihe Texte des Mittelalters (Berlin, 1965).

[3] Zur Überlieferung vgl. Rosemary Combridge, 'The Problems of a New Edition of Ulrich von Zatzikhovens *Lanzelet*', in *Probleme mittelalterlicher Überlieferung und Textkritik: Oxforder Colloquium 1966*, hg. von Peter F. Ganz und Werner Schröder (Berlin, 1968), S. 67–80.

[4] *Willehalm von Orlens*, hg. von Victor Junk, DTM, 2 (Berlin, 1905), V. 2198f.; *Alexander*, hg. von Victor Junk, StLV, 272 (Leipzig, 1928), V. 3199–204.

[5] *Der Ehrenbrief des Püterich von Reichertshausen*, hg. von Fritz Behrend und Rudolf Wolkan (Weimar, 1920), Str. 102.

[6] *Heinrich von Freiberg*, hg. von Alois Bernt (Halle, 1906), Teil 2, S. 239–48: *Die Ritterfahrt des Johann von Michelsberg*, V. 20.

[7] *Die Minneburg*, hg. von Hans Pyritz, DTM, 43 (Berlin, 1950), V. 3170.

[8] Vgl. weiterhin Norman (wie Anm. 2), S. 290f.; Ruh, Der *Lanzelet* (wie Anm. 1), S. 47; René Pérennec, *Recherches sur le roman arthurien en vers en Allemagne aux XIIe et XIIIe siècles*, GAG, 393, I–II, 2 Bde. (Göppingen, 1984), II: *'Lanzelet', 'Le Conte du Graal', 'Parzival'*, S. 382–84.

damit zu tun haben oder nicht, auf alle Fälle gelte: 'Ulrichs "Lanzelet" [. . .] ist, zumindest der Intention nach, ein neues Modell des Artusromans'.[9] Man braucht sich nicht auf wohlfeile Ironie zurückzuziehen: die Ungleichgewichtigkeit ist schon von Ruh zugestanden: 'Dieses [das Chrestiensche Modell] schuf ein Genie, jenes allenfalls ein Talent'[10] – und hinter Ulrich steht ja auch seine französische Vorlage, von der allgemein und gemäß seiner Beteuerung angenommen wird, er habe sie sehr getreu übersetzt. Diese französische Vorlage, das 'welsche buoch von Lanzelete' (9341), auf das er sich immer wieder beruft und das im anglo-normannischen Gefolge des 'künec von Engellant' (9326), Richard Löwenherz, nach Deutschland gekommen war, zeigt Motivgemeinsamkeiten mit Chrestiens *Erec*, dem *Yvain* und – falls nicht doch Ulrich seine Kenntnis Wolframs zu Veränderungen genutzt hat – auch mit dem *Conte du Graal*. So scheint die literaturhistorische Genealogie eindeutig: Chrestien hat den Artusroman geschaffen, ein unbekannter Anglonormanne hat ihn abgewandelt, Ulrich von Zatzikhoven hat dessen Adaptation ins Deutsche übertragen und vielleicht – mir scheint das eher unwahrscheinlich – ein wenig verändert. Da der neue Romantyp keineswegs – wie man lange geglaubt hat – sich purem Unverständnis für Chrestiens Struktur verdankt, sondern eine gewisse formale Konsequenz zeigt, müsse man einen ernsthaften Gestaltungswillen annehmen und der wäre dann auf Umgestaltung und Gegenentwurf gerichtet: 'Es sieht [. . .] alles darnach aus, daß der Autor im *welschen buoch* Chrétiens Werk, zumindest den 'Erec' und den 'Yvain', reflektierte und ihm sein eigenes Modell entgegensetzte', schreibt Ruh,[11] und an anderer Stelle: 'Der 'Lanzelet' setzt den Artusroman Chrestiens voraus. Nicht nur genealogisch, sondern im Sinn der Konnotation, d. h. daß das arthurische Personal und Bedingungen arthurischen Daseins (Costumes und Ideologie) als Verständnishorizont vorausgesetzt werden.'[12]

Ich blicke auf das Werk und werde meiner Zweifel nicht Herr:

1. Der *Lanzelet* ist gewiß nicht planlos geschrieben, das haben besonders Helga Schüppert,[13] Kurt Ruh (wie Anm. 1) und Walter

---

9 Ruh, 'Der *Lanzelet*' (wie Anm. 1), S. 55.
10 *Höfische Epik II* (wie Anm. 1), S. 34.
11 *Höfische Epik II* (wie Anm. 1), S. 36.
12 'Der *Lanzelet*' (wie Anm. 1), S. 54.
13 'Minneszenen und Struktur im *Lanzelet* Ulrichs von Zatzikhoven', in *Würzburger Prosastudien II: Untersuchungen zur Literatur und Sprache des Mittelalters (Kurt Ruh zum 60. Geburtstag)*, hg. von Peter Kesting, Medium Aevum, 31 (München, 1975), S. 123–38. Vorher schon in ähnlichem Sinne Rosemary Combridge, 'Lanzelet and the Queens', in *Essays in German and Dutch Literature*, hg. von William Douglas Robson-Scott (London, 1973), S. 42–64.

Haug,[14] auf jeweils andere Weise auch René Pérennec,[15] Rodney W. Fisher,[16] James A. Schultz[17] und Barbara Thoran[18] gezeigt. Ganz gleich aber, ob wir – mit Ruh, Haug, Fisher – einen Stationenweg annehmen, der in ununterbrochen aufsteigender Linie unter dem Programm der Identitätsfindung (Namensuche) und Bewährung in Gemeinschaftsleistung zur Herrschaft als erfüllter Lebensform führt (wobei dann die Probleme mit den Frauen[19] eher als ärgerliches Beiwerk verstanden werden müssen), oder ob wir ihn – mit Pérennec, Welz,[20] Thoran – als Panorama eines konservativ-dynastischen Herrschaftsprinzips in einem komplizierten Gewebe von Schemafragmenten, Ironisierungen und archetypischen Konstanten lesen: Chrestiens 'Strukturmodell' ist – natürlich – in keinem Falle wiederholt, und ob es zugrundeliegt, reduziert (Haug), variiert (Thoran), umspielt (Pérennec), konterkariert (Ruh), oder zurückgelassen (Welz) wird, ist eigentlich nur unter einer Voraussetzung leicht zu erkennen: daß nämlich andere Möglichkeiten gar nicht in Betracht kommen, daß jeder Artusroman Chrestien zur Voraussetzung haben müsse.

2. Die im *Lanzelet* vorgeführten Verhaltensweisen, die in ihrer Summe und – je nach der Beantwortung des ersten Punktes – in ihren Konfigurationen das ideologische Programm des Epos ausmachen, stehen – wie immer man sie neu einbinden will – dem Ethos der Chrestienschen Romane eher fern: Wie hier Frauen akkumuliert und vergessen werden ('ab jetzt wird auf Vorrat gearbeitet', kommentiert Bertau[21]), wie – in der Pluris-Episode – miteinander geschaffen (5645: 'wîlent trûric, wîlent vrô') und zugleich die Treue zu einer anderen Frau bewahrt wird, wie Liebe – von Männern und von Frauen – mit Gewalt erzwungen wird, wie man – bei Chrestien und erst recht bei Hartmann war das bekanntlich zum Problem geworden – Männer erschlägt, um Frauen zu erwerben (Galagandreiz, den Burgherrn von Limors, Iweret),

[14] 'Das Land von welchem niemand wiederkehrt': Mythos, Fiktion und Wahrheit in Chrétiens 'Chevalier de la Charrete', im 'Lanzelet' Ulrichs von Zatzikhoven und im 'Lancelot'-Prosaroman, Untersuchungen zur deutschen Literaturgeschichte, 21 (Tübingen, 1978).
[15] Wie Anm. 8; außerdem: 'Artusroman und Familie: "daz welsche buoch von Lanzelete"', Acta Germanica, 11 (1979), 1–51.
[16] 'Ulrich von Zatzikhoven's Lanzelet: In Search of "Sens"', Archiv für das Studium der neueren Sprachen und Literaturen, 217 (1980), 277–92: 'What I would suggest then, is that Ulrich has made some effort to structure the narrative around three peaks, the tournament at Dyofle, the discovery of name and Arthurian affiliations, and the dragon-episode which is designed to prove his absolute superiority even within the Arthurian ranks.' (S. 283).
[17] 'Lanzelet: a flawless hero in a symmetrical world', PBB (Tüb.), 102 (1980), 160–88.
[18] 'Zur Struktur des Lanzelet Ulrichs von Zatzikhoven', ZfdPh, 103 (1984), 52–77.
[19] Dazu vor allem Karl Bertau, Über Literaturgeschichte: Literarischer Kunstcharakter und Geschichte in der höfischen Epik um 1200 (München, 1983), S. 30–41.
[20] Dieter Welz, 'Lanzelet im "schœnen walde": Überlegungen zu Struktur und Sinn des Lanzelet-Romans (mit einem Exkurs im Anhang)', Acta Germanica, 13 (1980), 47–68.
[21] Wie Anm. 19, S. 37.

wie insgesamt auch kriegerische Kampfeskraft als Lebenselement einer Kriegergesellschaft noch robust zur Schau gestellt wird.

3. Ganz ohne Bedeutung ist überhaupt die Radikalisierung und Problematisierung des Minnethemas, die Chrestiens Werke zu einem guten Teil prägen: Die Verankerung von Minne in der Prüfung und Bewährung der Ehegemeinschaft zum einen, die Prüfung der Persönlichkeit in den Anfechtungen durch Passion und Leidenschaft zum anderen. Wo bei Chrestien und seinen Nachfolgern mit großem Ernst die Bindung zu der einen Frau fundiert wird, geht es im *Lanzelet* allenfalls darum, immer noch eine bessere zu finden (auch die Pluris-Episode bestätigt dies: der Königin gelingt es eben nicht, die Erinnerung an Iblis zu verdrängen). In der Tat hat die Deutung des Romans 'mit dem Skandalon fertig zu werden, daß auch eine stationsweise Liebeserfahrung bis hin zur "Richtigen" vorgestellt und akzeptiert werden muß'[22] – und eben auch noch über die Richtige hinaus. Die bisherigen Deutungen scheinen mir damit nicht 'fertig zu werden' (Bertau ausgenommen, der darin eine Frage mangelnder Qualität sieht), aber welche man auch akzeptierte – zwischen tapferer Bewährung in Minnehaft (Thoran) und 'rechte[m] Gaudi'[23] – Chrestiens Thema wäre weit entfernt.

4. Was für sich genommen nicht weiter auffällig wäre, erhält im Ensemble dieser Inkongruenzen doch auch Gewicht: Eine – worauf schon Walter Haug (wie Anm. 14) hingewiesen hat – recht plakativ ursprüngliche Motivik,[24] bei der z. B. die Nähe des Bewährungsweges zur Jenseitsfahrt[25] noch offen zu Tage liegt und die Umsetzung des Psychischen in mythisierende Bilder ihre Spuren hinterläßt: Valerin, der Entführer, erscheint mit dem Gestus und dem Anspruch des Mannes vor der Ehe, der Vergessenes und Verdrängtes aufruft (die Diskussion um die Vorverlobung in der Nibelungensage mag die Sprengkraft dieses Motivs verdeutlichen).[26] Es mag durchaus offen bleiben, ob solche

---

[22] Bertau, (wie Anm. 19), S. 33.
[23] Welz, (wie Anm. 20), S. 63.
[24] Vgl. etwa Werner Richter, *Der Lanzelet des Ulrich von Zazikhoven*, Deutsche Forschungen, 27 (Frankfurt a.M., 1934), S. 24–80; Lucy Allen Paton, *Studies in the Fairy Mythology of Arthurian Romance*, 2nd edn (New York, 1960), S. 185: 'here [d. h. im *Lanzelet*], accordingly, we find the most primitive extant representation of the Dame du Lac'. Außerdem zum ganzen: Dagmar O' Riain-Raedel, *Untersuchungen zur mythischen Struktur der mittelhochdeutschen Artusepen: Ulrich von Zatzikhoven, 'Lanzelet' – Hartmann von Aue, 'Erec' und 'Iwein'*, Philologische Studien und Quellen, 91 (Berlin, 1978).
[25] Vgl. O'Riain-Raedel (wie Anm. 24), S. 72–78; Arthur C.L. Brown, *The Origin of the Grail Legend* (New York, 1943), S. 36–90, 339–70; Walter Haug, 'Vom Imram zur Aventiure-Fahrt: Zur Frage nach der Vorgeschichte der hochhöfischen Epenstruktur', *Wolfram-Studien* [1] (1970), 264–98.
[26] Vgl. etwa Hans Fromm, 'Kapitel 168 der Thidrekssaga', *DVjs*, 33 (1959), 237–56; Theodore M. Andersson, *The Legend of Brynhild* (Ithaca/London, 1980), S. 259 (Register: Prior betrothal).

möglicherweise ja auch nur scheinbar unbearbeitete Archaik un-mittelbar argumentativ verwertet werden kann. Mindestens aber erinnert sie uns an die Selbstverständlichkeit, daß sich Artustradition in keinem Falle in Chrestien erschöpft, daß es einen auch für andere zugänglichen Fundus wie immer geformter Geschichten und Motive gegeben haben muß, den sein Werk nicht einfach außer Kraft gesetzt hat.

Damit stellt sich von diesem Punkte aus die Frage nach Chrestien als Schöpfer des Artusromans. Es ist bei der Umsetzung in Argumentationen nicht immer deutlich, was hier gemeint ist: Das Baumodell und der in ihm transportierte Sinn gewiß; vielleicht auch die durchaus unabhängig von den Bauformen benannten und verbildlichten Werte und Ideale; aber auch die Artuswelt? Ihre Figuren 'mit ihren spezifischen Rollen Walwein und Keie, mit Erec und Iwein, mit ihren Costumes [. . .]'?[27] Schon Kurt Ruhs eigener Hinweis auf die Erwähnung von Keie und Gawan in ihren 'stereotypen Rollen'[28] bereits vor Chrestien, in der Sensenfallen-Episode der Tristan-*Estoire*[29], zeigt die Notwendigkeit, hier zu trennen und eine mindestens im Inventar bereits geformte Artus-Tradition vor Chrestien zuzulassen. Nicht Namen und Typen und auch nicht Ereignisse oder Verhältnisse (z. B. Erec und Enide als Paar) verweisen dann auf Chrestien, sondern sinnhaltige Zusammenhänge.

Ich konkretisiere meine Fragen an einem Komplex, der für die Darstellung und Diskussion arturischer Ideologie immer eine prägnante Rolle gespielt hat: am Bild des Königs.[30]

Ich rekapituliere nur in Stichworten die Konturen der Artuskonzep-tion Chrestiens:[31] 'höfische Verschiebung des alten feudalen Königs-bildes ins Ethisch-Ästhetische'; Entmachtung des Königs, Reduktion auf die Zeremonien des Hofes, Stilisierung zur Maßstabsfigur für höfische Gesittung, Unantastbarkeit als höfische Instanz, damit verbunden: 'Moralisierung der feudalrechtlichen und ständischen Begriffe'. Der König werde zum *primus inter pares*; aus der Phalanx der

---

[27] Ruh, 'Der *Lanzelet*' (wie Anm. 1), S. 49; ich habe das Zitat um die 'Idealität' der Artuswelt gekürzt, weil gerade sie durchaus in Frage steht, s.u.

[28] *Höfische Epik des deutschen Mittelalters I: Von den Anfängen bis zu Hartmann von Aue*, 2. verb. Aufl. (Berlin, 1977), S. 104: 'er [d. h. der *Estoire*-Dichter] griff eine zu seiner Zeit (um 1150) bekannte Tradition auf und baute sie in seinen Roman ein. Die Szene mit der Sensenfalle gestattet somit einen zwingenden Rückschluß auf die Existenz von Artus-Erzählungen [mit arturischen Typen! K.G.] neben der ''chronikalen'' Tradition.'

[29] Vgl. *Eilhart von Oberge*, hg. von Franz Lichtenstein, QF, 19 (Straßburg, 1877), V. 5099-487.

[30] Ich wiederhole hier Gedankengänge, die ich anderenorts in größerem Zusammenhang vorgetragen habe: 'Der Artusroman und sein König: Beobachtungen zur Artusfigur am Beispiel von Ginovers Entführung', in *Positionen des Romans im Spätmittelalter*, hg. von Walter Haug und Burghart Wachinger, Fortuna Vitrea, 1 (Tübingen, 1991), S. 1-20.

[31] Nach Erich Köhler, *Ideal und Wirklichkeit in der höfischen Epik: Studien zur Form der frühen Artus- und Graldichtung*, 2., ergänzte Aufl., Beihefte zur Zeitschrift für romanische Philologie, 97, (Tübingen, 1970); die Zitate: S. 11.

aktiv Handelnden wird er verdrängt und zur Symbolfigur verklärt – und zwar zur Verpflichtung auf Ideale und Werte, mit denen politische Ansprüche und rechtliche Mechanismen durch Übersetzung in sittliche Maßstäbe bewahrt und gesichert werden sollen.

Ulrich von Zatzikhoven zeichnet – selbstverständlich – ein durchaus höfisches Bild von König Artus.[32] Er tritt in die Erzählung im Bericht eines seiner Ritter, der dem Helden den Artushof schmackhaft machen möchte:

> er saget im, daz dâ wæren
> der besten ritter diu kraft,
> 'die mit ir ritterschaft
> erwerbent lop unde prîs.
> der künic selbe ist sô wîs,
> daz erz wol erbieten kan
> eim iegelîchen man
> nâch sîner werdikheit.
> swer ie durch manheit ûz gereit,
> der sol mîns herren hof sehen.'   (1266–75)

Artus ist 'wîse' (1270), 'der schanden vrîe' (1355), 'der êren stæte' (2946), 'der künic rîch' (2947), 'der êren gernde man' (3406), 'der aller milteste man,/ den diu welt ie gewan' (4947f.); er wünscht, daß Lanzelet, der 'helt', an seinen Hof geholt werde (2286ff.), und Walwein, der Bote, kann sagen:

> swer mînes herren hof niht siht,
> der enist vollekomen niht.   (2469–70)

Artus gebietet Feste, z. B. zu Pfingsten (5574ff.), und er verfügt über die Bräuche, z. B. über die Jagd auf den weißen Hirsch (6697) und den Kuß der schönsten Dame (6733).

Aber König Artus ist nicht auf seinen Hof beschränkt: Er nimmt an einem Turnier teil, das König Lot von Johenis veranstaltet (2627ff.); vor ihm und seiner Schar muß man sich hüten, 'wan dâ ist kraft und manheit' (2885); er greift selbst in das Turniergeschehen ein (3008f.) und befreit an der Spitze seiner 'massenîe' König Lot aus gefährlicher Bedrängnis (3406ff.). Er ist 'unser helt' (3415), dessen 'kraft' gerühmt wird (3418).

Auffällig ist die Verteilung der Epitheta, deren Tendenz sich schon beim Turnier bei Johfrit (633ff.) andeutet, wo man 'degen' heißt, wenn man turniert, und 'ritter', wenn man tanzt:

---

[32] Einiges dazu bei Karin R. Gürttler, *'Künec Artûs der guote': Das Artusbild der höfischen Epik des 12. und 13. Jahrhunderts* (Bonn, 1976), S. 167–76.

> dô nu des genuoc geschach
> und manic degen sîn sper dâ brach
> und diu ros wurdn verhouwen,
> dô muosten aber die vrouwen
> mit den rittern tanzen. (653–57)

Es gibt Artus als Mittelpunkt und Impresario höfischer Geselligkeit – in dieser Rolle häuft er die konventionellen Attribute auf sich; es gibt ihn als Ritter mit 'kraft' und 'manheit'; und es gibt ihn nur und konzentriert als 'künec'. Vom Auftritt des Rivalen Valerin an (4980) tritt alles Gesellige zurück; wo Artus agiert, ist er: der 'künec'. Selbst die Einleitung zum Pfingstfeste erlaubt sich nur ein einziges: 'der êrbære' (5580). Betont werden Macht und Ansehen dieses Königs: als 'der rîche künic' (7137), 'der künic hêr' (7719, 7131), 'der künic mære' (7152, 7689), auf dem Höhepunkt seiner Ratlosigkeit in der Fremde auch: 'Artûs der ellende' (7209).

Erst mit dem Ende der Bedrohung, nach der Befreiung nicht nur Ginovers, sondern auch der beiden Geiseln Walwein und Erec und der Rückkehr Lanzelets, dann aber unverzüglich, tritt uns wieder ein höfischer Artus entgegen: der Veranstalter des Freudenfestes heißt 'Artus der êren stæte' (7762), später wieder 'der miltekeite stam' (8667), 'der êrbære' (8714), 'der milte' (8923, 8997, 9291).

In diesen Rahmen, der ein Artusbild von großer Spannweite und Vielfalt andeutet, das unterschiedlichen Erzählintentionen angepaßt werden kann und so eine programmatische Prägung nicht erhält, ordnen sich die Auffälligkeiten der umfänglichsten und gewichtigsten Episode des ganzen Werkes ein, der von Ginovers Entführung[33] und Wiedergewinnung.

Ginover gerät zweimal in Gefahr, in die Hände des Ritters Valerin vom Verworrenen tan zu fallen: ein erstes Mal, als dieser am Artushof auftaucht und ältere Ansprüche auf Ginover geltend macht. Mit größerem Recht ('billîcher') stehe Ginover ihm zu als Artus, 'wan siu im gemehelt wære,/ ê siu wurde hîbære' (4995f.). Damit ist ein Rechtsanspruch formuliert; er wird verbunden mit dem Angebot, diesen Rechtsanspruch im Kampf zu bestätigen: 'ich wil beherten mîn reht/ mit kampfe als ein guot kneht' (5001f.). Der gerichtliche Zweikampf also wird eingesetzt als ein geläufiges Instrument der Wahrheitsfindung bei unklarer Rechtslage oder widerstreitenden Ansprüchen. Artus geht darauf ein (er muß darauf eingehen), kämpft freilich nicht selbst (womit Valerin auch gar nicht rechnet), sondern stellt den sich nach der Aufgabe drängenden Lanzelet als seinen Kämpfer. Lanzelet siegt,

---

[33] Für die umfangreiche Literatur zu diesem Komplex verweise ich auf meinen Aufsatz 'Der Artusroman und sein König' (wie Anm. 30).

Valerin leistet Verzicht und gibt darauf sein Wort; die Gefahr scheint abgewendet. Valerin aber hält sein Versprechen nicht. Bei günstiger Gelegenheit, der festlichen Jagd auf den weißen Hirsch, überfällt er die wehrlose Hofgesellschaft und raubt Ginover. Viele Ritter werden erschlagen, der König selbst schwer verwundet (6745): er hat für seine Frau sein Leben aufs Spiel gesetzt.

Die Befreiung Ginovers steht ganz im Zeichen von Artus' Entschlossenheit und Tatkraft:[34]
Er spricht die Drohung aus:

> der künec sprach, swie er möhte
> deheine wîle geleben,
> so enwurde der burc niht vride geben,
> unz daz sîn wîp dâ wære.   (6794–97)

Er wählt die drei Gefährten aus, mit denen die Befreiung unternommen werden soll:

> von dem her er ûz las
> die er ze manheit het erkant:
> daz was Karjet und Tristant
> unde Lanzelet: si drîe
> nam er von der massenîe.   (7028–32)

Er setzt sich an ihre Spitze:

> si kômen alle dar an,
> daz der künic niht vermite
> wan daz er selbe vierde rite
> nach dem gougelære.   (7020–23)

Der Erzähler kommentiert:

> dô wart aber wol schîn,
> daz im diu künegîn liep was.   (7026–27)

Wenn die Gruppe zu Dodines und Malduc zieht, steht Artus für sie: 'nu hielt Artus durch nôt/ gein der burcstrâze' (7166f.), und während die Burg befreit und Valerin getötet wird, ist es Artus allein, der zu Ginover vordringt und sie befreit:

---

[34] Zu Unrecht wird die aktive Rolle des Königs von Barbara Thoran (wie Anm. 18) bestritten (vgl. aber S. 67, Anm 52). Daß auch Lanzelet eine maßgebliche Rolle – als Ratgeber! – spielt und daß er nach der Ginover-Befreiung sich bei der Rettung Walweins und Erecs besonders hervortut, läßt sich dagegen nicht ausspielen.

innân des was komen
mîn herre der künic Artûs
in ein wünneclîchez hûs,
dâ Ginovere inne lac. (7398–401)

Hier tritt uns nicht der von Chrestien geschaffene Artus entgegen, der unbewegte Beweger, der nicht durch seine Taten, sondern durch seine Präsenz wirkt, der Idealität in sich verkörpert, ohne sie noch darzustellen, sondern der tat- und kampfkräftige ritterliche Held, der Rechtsansprüche den Regeln entsprechend klärt und sich gegen Gewalt erfolgreich zur Wehr setzt (ganz so, wie er von Geoffrey von Monmouth und Wace gezeichnet worden war und wie er etwa auch in der Gildas-Vita des Caradoc von Llancarfan[35] auftritt: als Heerführer, *Arturus tyrannus*, der an der Spitze einer *innumerabilis multitudo* anrückt und so seine Frau befreit). Verwunderlich kann allein scheinen, daß Artus die Aufgabe des initialen Gerichtszweikampfes nicht selbst auf sich nimmt, aber hier mag die Folie der realen Rechtsverhältnisse durchscheinen oder organisierend zu Hilfe kommen (denn die Geschichte braucht Lanzelet in dieser Situation als Vorkämpfer für die Gemeinschaft: der Stellvertreter ist im Gerichtszweikampf eine wohletablierte Institution).

Chrestien bettet die Ginover-Episode ganz anders in die Handlung ein; dennoch vermag der Vergleich mit seiner Darstellung die Besonderheiten im Agieren des Königs noch schärfer zu beleuchten: Der *Karrenritter*[36] setzt mit der Entführung ein: ein gerüsteter Ritter sprengt grußlos in die Halle, teilt mit, daß sich Damen und Herren des Hofes in seiner Gewalt befänden und bietet einen Zweikampf um die Königin als Preis für die Freiheit der Gefangenen an. Die Situation ist der im *Lanzelet* ähnlich in der Herausforderung an den König: ein Einbruch von Gewalt setzt eine Zwangssituation. Anders als dort aber bleibt ein Entscheidungsspielraum: die Preisgabe der Ehefrau als Pfand im Vertrauen auf den einen als Zweikämpfer geforderten Ritter seines Hofes kann nicht wie ein Rechtstitel beansprucht werden. Verlangt wird von Artus eine 'politische' Entscheidung: Opferung seiner Untertanen und damit Vernachlässigung seiner Herrscherpflichten oder Einsatz der Ehefrau als politisches Handelsobjekt und damit Versagen als Ehemann. Chrestiens König kann sich für oder gegen seine Frau entscheiden; derjenige Ulrichs tritt sofort und fraglos für sie ein. So gesehen hätte Chrestiens Artus sogar die größere Chance auf eine

---

[35] *Vita Gildae auctore Caradoco Lancarbanensi*, hg. von Theodor Mommsen, in MGH, Auct. ant., 13 (Berlin, 1898), S. 107–10. Zu den Zusammenhängen und zu weiterer Literatur: 'Der Artusroman und sein König' (wie Anm. 30).

[36] *Der Karrenritter (Lancelot) und das Wilhelmsleben (Guillaume d'Angleterre) von Christian von Troyes*, hg. von Wendelin Foerster (Halle, 1899), V. 31–315. Zu den Zusammenhängen vgl. etwa Haug (wie Anm. 14), 17–51; Leslie Thomas Topsfield, *Chrétien de Troyes: A Study of the Arthurian Romances* (Cambridge, 1981), S. 105–74.

verdienstvolle Leistung. Aber das sorgsam aufgebaute Dilemma läuft ins Leere; denn die Entscheidung wird Artus aus der Hand genommen durch eine doppelte Folge von List und Betrug. Zuerst provoziert Key den König zum noch inhaltslosen Versprechen, ihm alles zu gewähren, fordert dann die Königin und die attraktive Aufgabe ihres Schutzes für sich und drängt sich so in die Rolle des Zweikämpfers; dann wird der Entscheidungszweikampf, der als Gelegenheit zur erwarteten Bewährung des Artuskämpfers dieser List noch die Schärfe nimmt, überflüssig gemacht, denn Meljagant bereitet einen Hinterhalt und eignet sich Ginover durch Wortbruch und mit Gewalt an.

Das Schema des vorbehaltlosen Versprechens, des *don contraignant*,[37] – bei Ulrich von Zatzikhoven ganz am Rande zur Ermöglichung gefahrloser Rede genützt (4984-91) – wird zum organisierenden Element dieser Szene. Es nimmt den König aus der ihm zunächst auferlegten vollen 'politischen' Verantwortung, 'automatisiert' seine Entscheidung, ethisiert sie aber auch durch die Einführung eines unverbrüchlichen, kategorischen 'moralischen' Prinzips: der Treue zum gegebenen Wort, die unabhängig ist von den Inhalten des Eides. Es ist dieser Prinzipienrigorismus, der den König aus unmittelbarem Machthandeln herauslöst und zur Beispielfigur für die Orientierung an moralischen Gesetzen werden läßt, der die Differenz des Chrestienschen Königs zum Artus Ulrichs von Zatzikhoven ausmacht. (Daran ändert es auch nichts, daß die Wirkungen dieses moralischen Rigorismus hier noch gemildert sind – erst Betrug und Gewalt setzen die ihm inhärenten Gefahren wirklich frei und lassen sie zur Wirkung kommen.)[38]

René Pérennec hat sich mit leichter Ironie dagegen verwahrt, das Artusbild des *Lanzelet* archaisch zu nennen, nur 'weil Artus wie in der *Vita Gildae* [. . .] sich bemüht, seine Frau zu befreien' (ebenso wenig sei es 'dekadent', nur 'weil der Autor nicht begriffen hat, daß im Artusroman König Artus nie selbst handeln darf').[39] 'Man sollte doch', fährt er fort (ebd.), 'nicht vor lauter Belesenheit aus den Augen verlieren, daß im *Lanzelet* Artus sich als Ehemann und König ziemlich normal verhält. Eher sollte man sich darüber wundern, daß er im *Karrenritter* der Entführung der Königin tatenlos zusieht.' Gewiß: genau das soll man tun, darüber soll man sich wundern, dies ist der strukturelle Sinn des Ungewöhnlichen. Im Abweichenden und Auffälligen liegt das Aufmerksamkeitssignal für das literarische Programm. Gerade weil dem so ist, weil die Abweichung programmati-

---

[37] Vgl. Jean Frappier 'Le motif du ''don contraignant'' dans la littérature du moyen âge', in Jean Frappier, *Amour courtois et table ronde* (Genf, 1973) S. 225-64. Zu weiterem vgl. 'Der Artusroman und sein König' (wie Anm. 30), Anm. 13.

[38] Zur Zuspitzung auf die unverstellte Wertentscheidung in Hartmanns *Iwein* vgl. 'Der Artusroman und sein König' (wie Anm. 30).

[39] 'Artusroman und Familie' (wie Anm. 15), S. 32.

sches Gewicht erhält, benimmt sich jemand, der sich nach diesem Ereignis 'ziemlich normal' verhält, eben nicht einfach ziemlich normal, sondern 'programmatisch normal', d. h. er negiert ausdrücklich das Auffällige und dessen Aussage, widerspricht dem, behauptet das Gegenteil. Es sei denn, er hätte vom Besonderen gar nicht gewußt: nur dann wird er sich, ohne auffällig zu werden, 'ziemlich normal' verhalten können.

Was an der Artusfigur zu beobachten ist, gilt für das Verhältnis Chrestiens zu Ulrich (oder seiner Vorlage) generell: Ulrich vertritt eine Art von stoffverhafteter 'Normalität', die auf alle programmatisch aufgeladenen Besonderheiten Chrestienscher Erzählkunst verzichtet – sogar auf solche, die in ihrer den Stoff definierenden Qualität kaum rückgängig zu machen sind, hier also: den Ehebruch der Königin. Auch dafür gilt: Wer nach der Entdeckung der Passion für den Artusroman in Chrestiens *Lancelot* noch einen Lanzelet-Roman ohne das Skandalon der Ginover-Lanzelet-Liebe schreibt, kennt Chrestien entweder nicht oder er negiert ihn mit Bewußtsein (daß er ihn nicht verstanden haben könnte, scheint mir bei einem so sensationellen Vorwurf nicht denkbar).

Nun braucht Ulrichs Vorlage den *Karrenritter* nicht gekannt zu haben, es könnte ihr doch der neue *Typus* des Artusromans bekannt gewesen sein. Feststeht aber, daß alle entscheidenden Errungenschaften des Chrestienschen Artusromanes im *Lanzelet* fehlen: Das Strukturmodell und sein Sinn, die Konsequenz des Episodenbaus, die Angefochtenheit des Helden als Voraussetzung seiner Bewußtwerdung, der Entwurf einer befriedeten Welt, die ein Herrscher von freundlicher Selbstgewißheit ins Bild setzt und garantiert (durch ritterliche Ordnungshüter, die Abweichungen ahnden und die Welt im Sinn der anerkannten Prinzipien reparieren), die Kultivierung von Sexualität und ihre Überführung in eine gleichfalls ordnungsstiftende Macht in der Institution der einen Ehe (nicht in vieren!).

Zu beobachten sind stattdessen: Partikel all dieser Programmpunkte, z. B. eine allgemeine höfische Festlichkeit und Etikettierung der Figuren (die sich noch nicht grundsätzlich von der bei Wace geübten unterscheidet), Ansätze zur Verknüpfung dieser Punkte – und zwar zumeist auf Wegen, die entweder gar nicht oder jedenfalls nicht spezifisch arturisch sind: wie zum einen der eher spielmännischen Mustern folgende Erwerb von Bräuten, zum andern das dynastisch-legitimierende Enfance-Schema, auf das Pérennec zurecht mit Nachdruck hingewiesen hat. Oder es liegen Abläufe zugrunde, die nur in parodistischer Verkehrung identifiziert werden können – und dann ist wieder nach der Berechtigung der Bezugsgröße zu fragen. Wenn z. B., wie Karl Bertau gleichfalls mit vollem Recht betont, alle eschatologische Gerichtetheit durch das Prinzip des glücklichen Zufalls demontiert wird[40] und so 'ein Triumphgesang des Glücks' entstehe, 'der dem Verdienst- und Bewährungsdenken des klassischen Artusromans geradezu ins Gesicht' lache,[41] dann ist vorweg doch wieder zu fragen, ob dieser denn tatsächlich die gemeinte Folie sein könne: er ist es nur dann, wenn andere Möglichkeiten gar nicht erst in Betracht kommen dürfen.

Chrestiens Artusroman tritt so dezidiert und prägnant auf, daß es nicht einmal bei dem von Pérennec versuchsweise eingesetzten künstlerischen Hinterwäldlertum[42] möglich ist, ihn so verwaschen und unengagiert aufzunehmen und zu paraphrasieren wie der (französische) Verfasser des *Lanzelet* dies tut. Ein Gegenmodell kann nicht dadurch entstehen, daß alles Entscheidende und Prägende bloß nicht zur Kenntnis genommen wird; es bedürfte dafür eines sehr viel entschiedeneren (oppositionellen) Bezuges.

Ich fasse zusammen:

— Einzelne Rollen, Figurenkonstellationen, Motive haben Ulrichs *Lanzelet* und seine *welsche* Vorlage mit Chrestiens Artusromanen gemeinsam; nicht unter allen Umständen müssen sie auch daraus übernommen sein.

— Die kompositionellen Prinzipien des Chrestienschen Artusromans sind im *Lanzelet* nicht beachtet; er folgt – wofür man sich auch entscheidet – anderen Bauformen, denen eine dezidierte Gegenposition gegen den 'doppelten Cursus' nicht abzulesen ist.

— Thematik und Ethos scheinen ohne prägnante Berührung mit Chrestiens Themen, aber auch ohne eigentlichen Gegensatz; die Motivik zeigt ihre archaisch mythischen Qualitäten vielfach unmittelbarer und unbearbeiteter als dort: 'an Arthurian romance in its most elementary stage'.[43]

— Ganz ohne Beachtung bleibt der thematische Kern, der dem Stoff seit Chrestien über Jahrhunderte seine Prägnanz gesichert hat: die ehebrecherische, verderbliche Liebe des besten Ritters und der Königin. Die robuste Liebeskarriere Lanzelets taugt gewiß nicht als Gegenmodell und kaum auch als Persiflage (dafür ist vor allem Iblis zu makellos rein beschrieben).

Ein Werk wie den *Lanzelet* kann ich mir deshalb nur unabhängig von Chrestiens Romanen entstanden denken[44] – entweder ohne ihre

---

40 Bertau (wie Anm. 19), S. 38.
41 Bertau (wie Anm. 19), S. 38 zu Welz (wie Anm. 20).
42 'Artusroman und Familie' (wie Anm. 15), S. 11.
43 So mit freilich ganz anderer Argumentation Hendricus Sparnaay, 'Hartmann von Aue and his Successors', in *Arthurian Literature in the Middle Ages: A Collaborative History*, hg. von Roger Sherman Loomis (Oxford, 1959), S. 439.
44 Das heißt also auch – um Mißverständnisse zu vermeiden –, daß ich auch Kenneth G.

Kenntnis oder aber ohne ihre Beachtung (und dies wäre immerhin ein Zeichen dafür, daß er die Szene nicht sogleich konkurrenzlos dominiert hätte). Zugrunde lägen die gleichen halbgeformten Materialien (Episoden, Figuren, Konstellationen, vielleicht auch Verlaufsformen), von denen auch Chrestien ausgegangen sein muß: Artussage vor und außerhalb der Dichtung (es wäre kein Schaden, wenn die neueren Erkenntnisse der Heldensagen-Forschung ein wenig in den Gesichtskreis der Artusliteratur träten). Daß eine Art von linear reihendem Stationenweg spätere Artusromane, z. B. den *Wigalois*, auch die Romane des Pleiers oder den *Gauriel* mit dem *Lanzelet* verbindet, kann nicht dazu ausreichen, darin das Fortwirken eines in ihm geschaffenen 'Modells' zu sehen und dieses selbst dadurch für bestätigt zu halten; ich nähme es gerne als Beleg dafür, daß bei der Organisation epischer Großformen bestimmte Bautypen naheliegen und auch traditionell verfügbar sind, allenfalls: daß sie dem im Stoff enthaltenen Bedeutungspotential inhärent sind.[45]

T. Websters Vorstellung für absurd halte, der normannische Autor des 'welschen buoches' habe den Artusroman – als Vorstufe auch für Chrestien – geschaffen: 'Ulrich von Zatzikhoven's ''welschez buoch'' ', *Harvard Studies and Notes in Philology and Literature*, 16 (1934), 203–28.

[45] Der Aufsatz gibt den Diskussionsstand von 1988 wieder. Später erschienene Literatur konnte nicht mehr eingearbeitet werden.

Iwein *and* Yvain: *Adapting the Love Theme*

TONY HUNT

Until quite recently comparativists exploring the fascinating problems produced by Hartmann's 'Artusepen' felt that they could at least rely on a well established and stable interpretation for his French sources – this interpretation being, of course, the work of Jean Frappier.[1] *Yvain* continued to be regarded as a paradigm of courtly romance, the perfect illustration of the chivalry topos, and a reaffirmation of the social role of marriage.[2] *Mais nous avons changé tout cela!* In the post-Frappier age the very nature of courtly culture is under discussion. Students of the troubadours like Gruber and Gaunt,[3] or of the romances, including myself,[4] now stress the *ludic* nature of courtly culture in which a literary sophistication derived from the schools promotes irony, dialectic and scepticism in the playful competition of a community of poets, writing, it seems, in the full awareness of each other's work.[5] On the other hand, Germanists like Stephen Jaeger[6] stress the ethical components of courtliness and its Ciceronian foundations, even displacing its origins from eleventh-century France to Ottonian Germany and to the figures of the courtier-bishop and the trainee for state administration. This contrast between the notion of playful detachment on the one hand, and that of moral engagement on the other, between manner and matter, is beginning to be reflected

[1] See esp. *Chrétien de Troyes* (Paris, 1957; 2nd edn 1968); *Étude sur Yvain ou le Chevalier au Lion de Chrétien de Troyes* (Paris, 1969); *Chrétien de Troyes et le mythe du graal* (Paris, 1972).
[2] See, for example, P.S. Noble, *Love and Marriage in Chrétien de Troyes* (Cardiff, 1982).
[3] J. Gruber, *Die Dialektik des Trobar: Untersuchungen zur Struktur und Entwicklung des occitanischen und französischen Minnesangs des 12. Jahrhunderts* (Tübingen, 1983). S. Gaunt, *Troubadours and Irony* (Cambridge, 1989).
[4] T. Hunt, *Chrétien de Troyes: Yvain (Le Chevalier au Lion)* (London, 1986).
[5] See my '*Texte* and *Prétexte: Jaufré* and *Yvain*', in *The Legacy of Chrétien de Troyes*, ed. by N.J. Lacy, D. Kelly and K. Busby, 2 vols (Amsterdam, 1987–88), II, 125–41. See also L. Rossi, 'Chrétien de Troyes e i trovatori: Tristan, Linhaura, Carestia', *Vox Romanica*, 46 (1987), 26–62.
[6] C. Stephen Jaeger, *The Origins of Courtliness: Civilizing Trends and the Formation of Courtly Ideals 939–1200* (Philadelphia, 1985).

in literary monographs.[7] Topsfield's study of Chrétien[8] and my modest student guide to *Yvain*[9] have almost nothing in common. This does not mean that one of us is necessarily wrong, but it complicates for non-specialists the problems of coming to terms with France's greatest medieval poet. In seeking to chart a reliable course amongst the various critical currents any investigator would be well advised to reconsider Chrétien's treatment of the love theme. On doing so he would quickly discover how difficult it is to maintain the thesis that *Yvain* is a romance of erotic love, when its most pervasive theme seems more obviously to be friendship (*amicitia*), which underlies the relationships of Yvain and Lunete, Yvain and Gauvain, and Yvain and the lion. In Foerster's text[10] the noun *amor(s)* appears fifty-one times, and the verb *amer* and its derivatives (only four in number) with almost exactly the same frequency. These are very modest figures for a romance of over 6,500 lines. The noun *amor(s)*, of course, poses a tricky problem. When is it simply generic and when does it function as a personification, or at least as an *abstractum agens*?[11] Or, should we also add, as a literary fiction? Of the fifty-one instances twenty-three receive capitalization in Foerster (but typographical distinctions could mean nothing to a medieval audience!). These are located almost exclusively in the scenes of Yvain's first falling in love with Laudine and in the combat of Yvain and Gauvain. There are only two exceptions: 'li Des d'Amors' invoked by the narrator when describing the beauty of the girl in the garden reading to her parents (5377), and, more debatably, on the occasion of Laudine's *pro forma* consultation of her barons with a view to their agreeing to her marriage with Yvain (2139). The French editor Mario Roques, much less meticulous,[12] has twenty-eight instances of capitalized *Amor(s)*, including the three occurrences of the word in the prologue, but he is certainly not consistent. Editors, too, are therefore presented with a problem by the references to love in *Yvain*. The same was undoubtedly true of Hartmann who felt uncomfortable with them, especially since he found Chrétien's Laudine difficult to integrate in what for him was an ethically serious exploration of the problems of knighthood. German editors,

---

[7] See P. Haidu, *Lion – queue – coupée: l'écart symbolique chez Chrétien de Troyes* (Genève, 1972) and, most recently, J.T. Grimbert, *'Yvain' dans le miroir* (Amsterdam/Philadelphia, 1988).

[8] L.T. Topsfield, *Chrétien de Troyes: A Study of the Arthurian Romances* (Cambridge, 1981).

[9] See note 4 above.

[10] I cite from the edition of his 1912 text by T.B.W. Reid (Manchester, 1942; frequently reprinted).

[11] See R. Glasser, 'Abstractum agens und Allegorie im älteren Französisch', *ZfromPh*, 69 (1953), 43–122.

[12] See T.B.W. Reid, 'Chrétien de Troyes and the Scribe Guiot', *Medium Aevum*, 45 (1976), 1–19; T. Hunt, 'Chrestien de Troyes: The Textual Problem', *French Studies*, 33 (1979), 257–71; B. Woledge, *Commentaire sur Yvain (Le Chevalier au lion) de Chrétien de Troyes*, vol. I (Genève, 1986).

equally, have a thorny problem to contend with. *Iwein* lines 8121–36, which strikingly depart from the source by depicting Laudine on her knees begging the hero's forgiveness, are present in only three manuscripts, all of which have weaknesses as textual witnesses, especially towards the end![13] Ludwig Wolff was confident enough to retain them in his critical text, but only at the price of assuming that they stem from a later revision by Hartmann.[14] This textual problem is not, unfortunately, an appropriate subject for a short paper. What can be done, instead, is to show with what care and attention Hartmann has remodelled the love relationship in *Iwein* and, more particularly, to reveal how he has used an *internal* rather than an *external* resource as the technical means of doing so. Quite simply, this internal resource consists of the bringing forward or anticipation ('Vorwegnahme') of details in the source in such a way as to predetermine the audience's interpretation of the material that follows. Whilst Hartmann is not so tyrannical in this respect as the narrator of *La Châtelaine de Vergi*,[15] he certainly seeks to control his audience's response in a way which Chrétien does not.

Before proceeding to my demonstration of this I should perhaps point out that certain aspects of Chrétien's highly ambivalent and even cynical presentation of love[16] obliged Hartmann to resort to the more radical step of straight excision. The evidence of this excision is itself, of course, a useful indication in the assessment of Chrétien's own strategies. There are four instances which it is as well to recall.

First, the prologue. Here Chrétien, writing at a time when there had never been greater interest in exploring the ramifications of love, human and divine, paradoxically sets out a complaint about contemporary lovers whilst praising an Arthurian past which he subsequently shows every sign of undermining. This initial hint of a 'Liebesproblematik' is then reinforced by the reprise of the same complaint when the narrator praises the beauty of the girl who is reading to her parents in the scene at Pesme Avanture (5389ff.). Hartmann cuts both these instances. In the prologue some of the company at court simply 'redten von seneder arbeit' (71) and the girl at Pesme Avanture inspires only a catalogue of courtly virtues: 'zuht unde schœne,/ hôhe geburt unde jugent,/ rîcheit unde kiusche tugent/ güete und wîse rede' (6464–67).

---

[13] See C. Gerhardt, 'Iweinschlüsse', *Literaturwissenschaftliches Jahrbuch*, N.F., 13 (1972), 13–39.

[14] See *Iwein*, ed. by G.F. Benecke and K. Lachmann, 7th edn, rev by Ludwig Wolff, 2 vols (Berlin, 1968), II, 219f. References to *Iwein* are to the text in vol. I of this edition.

[15] See the excellent study of J. Rychner, 'La Présence et le point de vue du narrateur dans deux récits courts: le *Lai de Lanval* et la *Châtelaine de Vergi*', *Vox Romanica*, 39 (1980), 86–103.

[16] See the interesting study of M.-N. Lefay-Toury, 'Roman breton et mythe courtois: l'évolution du personnage féminin dans les romans de Chrétien de Troyes', *Cahiers de civilisation médiévale*, 15 (1972), 193–204, 283–93.

Second, after the hero's marriage Chrétien inserts a short scene of flirtation between Gauvain and Lunete in which he underscores the ambiguity of *cortoisie* by observing that many people mistake the courteous words and attention of a lady for love, but are foolish to do so. There is something slightly tasteless about this apparent defence of good manners, for Chrétien concludes with the proverb 'Fos est liez de bele parole' (2464), 'only a fool is content with fair words', and shows that the subtext is really about sexual satisfaction ('Itant an orent il au mains', 2451). Hartmann removes it, for he had no wish to present courtly rhetoric as deceptive smooth talk or to exploit the ambiguity of *amor* and amorousness.

Third, in Chrétien the principal theme of Gauvain's exhortation to Yvain to ride to the tournaments is uxoriousness and how to intensify love through abstinence ('Biens adoucist par delaiier', 2515). In Hartmann this is all refocussed on the maintenance of chivalry – in its moral and sociological dimensions. Ovidian love casuistry, intertextual references to troubadour love poetry, and the dangers of uxoriousness[17] are replaced by an emphasis on Iwein's obligation to match his conduct to his newly acquired resources of 'wîp unde [. . .] lant' (2782): 'nû muget ir mit dem guote/ volziehen dem muote' (2907–08). Erek's *verligen* is admittedly evoked, but so, even more importantly, is his glorious recovery ('wan daz er sichs erholte/ sît als ein rîter solte', 2795–96).

Finally, the denunciation of Iwein by Lunete after the 'Terminversäumnis' completely ignores Chrétien's single-minded concentration on Yvain as a lover, on the obligations of the *verais amerre*, and concerns itself instead with chivalry and the hero's *untriuwe* in the light of the chivalric, not the amatory, ideal. Iwein lacks 'rîters triuwe' (3173). For this reason it would be shame for the king 'hât er iuch mêre in rîters namen,/ sô liep im triuwe und êre ist' (3188–89). In Lunete's speech there are eleven references to *triuwe* and its derivatives.

These instances of excision show Hartmann striving to assimilate the love theme to the broader issue of chivalric honour, whereas, in my view, Chrétien is doing the exact opposite – resolutely holding them apart! Excision was, obviously, not a solution which could be applied to the love plot itself since this represents a structuring device for the whole romance. It is for this reason that Hartmann devised a technique of anticipation which, if it did not, as we shall see, entirely evacuate awkward features of his source, certainly influenced the audience's reception of them. It is this technique which forms the main subject of the present paper.

---

[17] See T. Hunt, 'Beginnings, Middles and Ends: Some Interpretative Problems in Chrétien's *Yvain* and its Medieval Adaptations', in *The Craft of Fiction: Essays in Medieval Poetics*, ed. by L.A. Arrathoon (Rochester, Mich., 1984), pp. 83–117 (esp. pp. 92ff.).

(1) The most striking example of anticipation, which sets off a sort of chain reaction in the episode of Yvain's first sight of the grieving Laudine, is, paradoxically, the introduction of the love theme itself. In Chrétien explicit references to love (the heroine's) come *at the end* of the whole episode in the form of *Amors* (with a capital) as *dea ex machina* ('Qu'Amors a feire li comande/ ce, don los et consoil demande', 2139–40). Hartmann eschews this sort of fiction and sets the description of the *hero's* love *right at the beginning* of the episode, as the grieving Laudine first emerges. Chrétien is, in fact, strangely silent about Yvain as he watches the distraught widow. In contrast, Hartmann explains fully, and hence authoritatively, the hero's feelings:

> da ersach sî der her Îwein:
> dâ was ir hâr und ir lîch
> sô gar dem wunsche gelîch
> daz im *ir minne*
> verkêrten die sinne,
> daz er sîn selbes gar vergaz
> und daz vil kûme versaz
> sô sî sich roufte unde sluoc.
> vil ungerne er ir daz vertruoc:
> sô wolder dar gâhen
> und ir die hende vâhen,
> daz sî sich niht enslüege mê.
> im tete der kumber alsô wê
> an dem schœnen wîbe
> daz erz an sînem lîbe
> gerner hæte vertragen.
> sîn heil begunder gote clagen,
> daz ir ie dehein ungemach
> von sînen schulden geschach.
> sô nâhen gienc im ir nôt,
> in dûhte des daz sîn tôt
> unclägelîcher wære
> dan ob sî ein vinger swære. (1332–54) (here, and below, my italics)

These twenty-three lines definitively establishing the hero's capacity for 'Mitleid' could scarcely afford a greater contrast with the stark absence of reaction in Chrétien, a vacuum filled with the ironically evasive commentary,

> Mes sire Yvains oï les criz
> Et le duel, qui ja n'iert descriz;

> Que nus ne le porroit descrivre,
> Ne tes ne fu escriz an livre. (1173–76)

This arch literary reflexion is a filler so that Chrétien does not have to commit himself or his hero to finding an appropriate reaction to Laudine's grief at this stage. It is precisely this issue of commitment, or avoidance of it, which so distinguishes Chrétien and Hartmann. By invoking literature ('an livre') Chrétien is content to leave his audience in doubt about the moral reality of what he depicts. Are we dealing simply with self-conscious, literary poses? Chrétien's whole *modus operandi* is characterized by such ambiguities. Perhaps for the first time, literature has become larger than life.

(2) The same process is repeated when the burial of the dead fountain-knight is over. Hartmann is anxious to ensure that we do not mistake the hero's silence for insensitivity. In Chrétien we *still* have no explicit reference to Yvain's love, but rather the depiction of a state which might easily be interpreted as titillating curiosity. Hartmann, however, again anticipates the theme of the hero's love:

> ouch enwas her Îwein niht verzaget:
> im hete *diu minne* einen muot
> gegeben, als sî manegem tuot,
> daz er den tôt niht entsaz.
> Doch hal er die maget [= Lunete] daz
> daz er sîner vîendinne
> truoc *sô grôze minne.* (1418–24)

This predetermining of the audience's interpretation allows Hartmann to remain impressively close to his source in some particularly tricky passages. For example, he now renders almost verbatim Chrétien's cynical account of Yvain's ostensible concern for the funeral procession which masks his real indifference to the mourners (*Yvain* 1271–81; *Iwein* 1432–47). The crucial point, of course, is that Hartmann has by now secured his audience's belief in Iwein's compassionate love – something very far from indifference. From the critical point of view there is an important methodological lesson to be learned here. When studying Chrétien and Hartmann it is no good simply juxtaposing and comparing parallel blocks of text, as it were synchronically. They must also be assessed diachronically, or syntagmatically. In this instance a synchronic section would suggest a complete equivalence of Chrétien's and Hartmann's texts, whereas earlier changes in Hartmann modify the significance of subsequent passages and here completely invalidate the apparent equivalence. This is tellingly illustrated by my next example.

(3) After the second reference to the hero's love we hear of Iwein's rush for the door:

> dô lief er gegen der tür,
> als er vil gerne hin vür
> *zuo ir wolde gâhen*
> *und ir die hende vâhen.* (1479–82)

We interpret the hero's impulse in the light of the earlier account of his compassion for Laudine:

> vil ungerne er ir daz vertruoc:
> sô wolder dar gâhen
> und ir die hende vâhen,
> daz sî sich niht enslüege mê. (!) (1340–43)

Note the last line which is a crucial addition by Hartmann, supplying a quite different, and unexceptionable, motivation compared with Chrétien's lines, which depict mere impetuosity in the hero:

> A mout grant painne se detient
> Mes sire Yvains, a quoi que tort,
> *Que les mains tenir ne li cort.* (1302–04)

So here we have two phenomena: the reslanting or reinterpretation of a detail in Chrétien in accordance with Hartmann's concern for the moral probity of his hero; and the anticipation of this same detail, so that when we encounter it again at the point corresponding to its appearance in Chrétien we interpret it in the light of Iwein's by now well established 'Mitleid' and thus endow it with a quite different significance from that which it has in the French source.

So far, then, we can see that the sudden eruption of *Amors* after the funeral in Chrétien is rejected by Hartmann, who brings forward the theme of the hero's love to the very beginning of the episode where it is presented quite differently, as compassion. Hartmann can afford to render the rest of Chrétien's text closely, thereby safeguarding his status as a translator or adaptor of a prestigious source, because he has already predetermined our understanding of Iwein's love as being of a moral, compassionate nature and not merely erotic.

(4) Hartmann now reinforces this interpretation with another change and anticipation. In Chrétien the admiring hero is obsessed with the paradox of his own love and with Laudine's beauty. His reflexions are concluded by the Nature topos with its Neoplatonic echoes of physical beauty as an expression of moral worth. This comes right at the end of Yvain's monologue (1491ff.). At the beginning of that monologue Yvain

merely thinks selfishly of how much he wishes that Laudine would leave off her weeping and reading (of the psalter) to speak to him (1420–22). Hartmann cuts the religious reference, i.e. the psalter, and, anxious to avoid any impression of callous self-concern or of mere titillation in the hero, brings forward the expression of the grieving widow's outstanding qualities, converting Chrétien's depiction of superlative beauty to the possession of moral qualities which move him deeply:

> dô sî her Îwein eine ersach
> unde ir meinlich ungemach,
> ir starkez ungemüete
> und ir stæte güete,
> ir wîplîche triuwe
> und ir senlîche riuwe,
> dô *minnet* er sî deste mê.   (1599–605; cf. *Yvain* 1411–19)

Already this is the third reference by the narrator to the hero's love. The role of the narrator is, of course, complex. In Chrétien *Amors* is a *dea ex machina* used to smooth over and justify the potentially distasteful elements of sado-masochism. When the narrator tells us that Love often and promiscuously descends to base depths, but is in the present case (i.e. Yvain) well lodged, we may be forgiven for suspecting a measure of irony – for what at this point is noble about Yvain, whose 'Rechtsbrü-che' have been ably catalogued by Anna-Susanna Mathias[18] and whose reaction to the suffering Laudine and whose faith in the fickleness of women can only appear cynical? Precisely the excursus on the conduct of *Amors* draws attention to the problematic status of the hero. As usual, Chrétien's rhetoric has the function of asking rather than answering questions. Iwein, on the other hand, has been firmly portrayed as a man of compassion. And it is not now in women's fickleness that he puts his trust, but in *vrou Minne* who should visit Laudine just as she has visited him, so that Laudine's behaviour may be made more fitted to her 'güete' (1661) – a leitmotif from the beginning. A completely different perspective is adopted by Chrétien: Yvain clings to his cynical belief in the fickleness of women – a literary motif – and the speciously self-justifying argument that it is wrong to resist, and be a traitor to, Love; Iwein, fully recognizing his guilt and helplessness ('ichn trûwe mit mîner vrümekheit/ ir niemer benemen ir leit', 1639–40) hopes that Laudine may be as surprised by Love as he has been – not a touch of antifeminism here, but rather a view of love as a reciprocating and

---

[18] A.-S. Mathias, 'Yvains Rechtsbrüche', in *Beiträge zum romanischen Mittelalter*, ed. by K. Baldinger (Tübingen, 1977), pp. 156–92.

unifying force. In Chrétien rhetoric functions as a substitute for feeling, for he does not wish to commit himself and dispel ambivalence. Furthermore, the importance of the rhetoric lies not in explicit affirmations, but in its allusions to problems. While his rhetoric is thus 'problematisierend', Hartmann's rhetoric is directed by feelings which give moral value to the action. Thus the reprise of the theme of fickleness (1640–44) by the narrator of *Yvain* is transformed by Hartmann into an excursus on the 'güete' of women (1869–88) as he reinforces the motif of their 'unstætekheit' as 'ein guot site' in what is a clearly dissenting commentary on his French source ('er missetuot, der daz seit,/ ez mache ir unstætekheit', 1873–74; 'swer in danne unstæte giht,/ des *volgære* enbin ich niht', 1885–86, a nicely ironical declaration of independence from the source he is 'following'!). The excursus and Iwein's hopes turn out to be self-fulfilling prophecies. Laudine is indeed won over by Love.

(5) This brings me to my fifth example of Hartmann's technique of anticipation. In Chrétien *Amors* surfaces unexpectedly in Laudine at the moment that she has solicited and received her barons' advice and summoned the chaplain to perform the marriage service. This is late in the day! Hartmann brings it forward so that there is nothing implausible or last-minute about it. Pondering Lunete's advice which she has peremptorily rejected,

> Sus brâhte siz in ir muote
> ze suone und ze guote,
> und machte in unschult wider sî.
> dô was gereite dâ bî
> diu gewaltige Minne,
> ein rehtiu süenærinne
> under manne und under wîbe.   (2051–57)

(6) There follows another example of anticipation, which this time stresses what is for Hartmann an extremely important aspect of the love relationship – mutuality. Whilst she is *still* engaged in discussions with her handmaiden, Laudine enquires 'weist aber dû, geselle,/ rehte ob er mich welle?' (2115–16) – there is nothing of this in Chrétien where Laudine is concerned exclusively with her public reputation (1807–10). Lunete in Hartmann's version of the scene explains the feigned arrival of Iwein with the line 'dâ treip in diu liebe darzuo' (2210). Again, Hartmann can proceed to render Chrétien's text of the interview of Laudine and Iwein precisely, because he has already predisposed the audience to believe in the sincerity of their love – we already *know* that Laudine has duly been visited by *vrou Minne* and desires the hero as a

partner. She herself tells him that she does not act out of 'unstæte' (2301). Hartmann now meticulously reproduces the argument about the defence of the fountain. He can afford to reproduce the text he is glossing because he has secured our belief already in the depth of Laudine's feeling. He again confirms it:

> swie selten wîp mannes bite,
> ich bæte iuwer ê.
> ichn nœtlîche iu niht mê:
> ich wil iuch gerne: welt ir mich?   (2330–33)

This is placed before the discussion of the workings of Minne and 'des herzen gebot' (2341ff.) and the hero's description of his love. In other words, in Hartmann the reconciliation is placed *midway* through the interview, before Yvain's declaration of his love (*Yvain* 2015ff.). At the end of the interview comes Laudine's celebrated 'wer hât under uns zwein/ gevüeget dise minne?' (2342–43). Their love is unambiguously established *before* the negotiations with the barons. Chrétien springs *Amors* on us, accompanying it with an Ovidian metaphor about the spurring of a horse (2146–47; cf. *Iwein* 2395–97). The point is that it is all done obliquely with the maximum of ambiguity. At first Chrétien simply says of Laudine,

> Si se fet proiier de son buen,
> Tant que aussi con maugré suen
> Otroie ce, qu'ele feïst,
> Se chascuns li contredeïst.   (2109–12)

This play-acting is again alluded to a little later:

> Tant li prïent, que lor otroie
> Ce, qu'ele feïst tote voie.   (2137–38)

It is at this late moment that the narrator adds a gloss which may be found unconvincing:

> Qu'Amors a feire li comande
> Ce, don los et consoil demande.   (2139–40)

If the editor capitalizes *Amors* here, he must realize that he is creating the only instance in the entire romance where *amors* as an abstraction is applied to Laudine.

This rather long-drawn-out scene is drastically reduced by Hartmann who cuts the seneschal's speech recommending the marriage. Hartmann has no need to supply the motivation of *Amors*, since the mutual love of Iwein and Laudine has already been firmly established.

He therefore enlists the complicity of his audience in commenting briefly on the action of the barons and Laudine,

> sî mohten ir willen unde ir heil
> ir lîhte gerâten.
> ich wæn sî rehte tâten:
> wan dûhtez si alle missetân,
> sî wold in doch genomen hân.   (2398–402)

I have concentrated on six examples of anticipation in the episode of the hero's wooing of Laudine and tried to demonstrate the consequences for the audience's reception of the love theme. Space allows only two further examples to show how Hartmann consistently remodels it.

(7) When Yvain is suddenly struck by the thought that he has outstayed his leave from Laudine, his emotions are merely hinted at. Chrétien says that he could scarcely hold back his tears, but shame made him do so:

> A grant painne tenoit ses lermes,
> Mes honte li feisoit tenir.   (2702–03)

Characteristically, Hartmann cannot accept this apparent shallowness, or absence, of feeling and anticipates the grief which Yvain feels *after* the messenger's denunciation by bringing it forward, so that yet again the audience is predisposed to a favourable interpretation of the hero's *bona fides*:

> sîn herze wart bevangen
> mit senlîcher *triuwe*:
> in begreif ein selch *riuwe*
> daz er sîn selbes vergaz.   (3088–91)

Note that with the phrase 'senlîch[iu] triuwe' Hartmann affirms the very quality which the messenger (Lunete) will deny him in her denunciation. The audience receives this denunciation against the background of a continuing belief in the hero's compassionate nature.

(8) A final example of anticipation. Having extracted the oath of assistance to Yvain from Laudine, Lunete rides out to find the hero and communicate her news. She proudly announces that she has won over her mistress and made her promise to reconcile Yvain with his lady. There is nothing in her words except the thrill and contentment generated by a successful ruse or trick. Hartmann, however, already wishes to evoke the hero's suffering in order to prepare for the more

compassionate treatment which he is to receive from Laudine in Hartmann's version. Lunete therefore declares to Iwein:

> dâ habt ir iuch genietet,
> ein teil von iuwern schulden,
> und von ir unhulden
> von der iu dienete diz lant
> und diu mich ûz hât gesant,
> einer langen *arbeit*. (7960–65)

There is no reference at all in Chrétien to the hero's suffering, but the motif in Hartmann is designed to anticipate the completely changed reaction of his Laudine. Compassion for suffering plays an important role in *Iwein* – of course, *pitié* also plays an important part in *Yvain*, but in chivalric affairs not amatory ones. Laudine *never* expresses any sympathy for Yvain, not even when he declares 'conparé ai mon fol savoir' (6782), which may be an oblique reference to his suffering, but which really remains obscure (it may mean 'I have atoned for my folly', i.e. through acts of chivalric prowess, or 'I have paid for them', namely through personal suffering). However that may be, Hartmann is unambiguous. Laudine asks Iwein for forgiveness because 'grôzen kumber habet ir/ von mînen schulden erliten' (8124–25). This predisposes us to see Iwein as the suffering man. He is overjoyed that his 'kumber' is on the point of ending (8100f.). It was his 'kumber' which led him to resort once more to raising the storm at the fountain (the word 'kumber' occurs five times in 7792–804) and it was Laudine's 'kumber' (1344) which aroused his compassionate love in the first place. Lunete's recognition of Iwein's 'lange arbeit' adds to the motivation of the whole reconciliation and singles out the one factor which enables Hartmann's Laudine to offer her husband a genuine reconciliation. Yet, Hartmann still translates Laudine's vituperative expression of disdain:

> mirn getete daz weter nie sô wê
> ichn woldez iemer lîden ê
> danne ich ze langer stunde
> mînes lîbes gunde
> deheinem sô gemuoten man
> der nie dehein ahte ûf mich gewan:
> und sage dir mitter wârheit,
> entwunge michs niht der eit,
> sô wærez unergangen. (8083–91)

This surprisingly close rendering of such an unsympathetic speech from the source (admittedly attenuated by the addition of *Iwein* 8092–96) leads us to a final reflexion.

The coexistence in *Iwein* of close translations of some of Chrétien's most problematic passages with thorough reinterpretations of them has not attracted the attention it deserves. It is made possible, as we have seen, by Hartmann's technique of anticipation ('Vorwegnahme'). From where did he derive this technique? There is surely a fairly clear parallel between translation and reinterpretation on the one hand, and text and gloss on the other. In Hartmann's time an essential component of literary study in the schools was the work of commentary and glossing, applied not only to theological texts, but to secular poems like Claudian's *De raptu Proserpinae*, Statius's *Achilleis*, Walter of Châtillon's *Alexandreis*, etc. In many parts of *Iwein* Hartmann carefully retains the letter of his source (text) whilst completely reinterpreting its spirit (commentary). It is not unusual in glossed school texts to find the commentary or 'gloss' preceding the section of text to which it applies. This is also the case in some vernacular translations of such texts. For example, a translation with commentary of Ovid's *Ars amatoria* made in France in the thirteenth century frequently preposes the commentary to the translated text[19] and the same is true of the French version of Alan of Lille's *Parabolae* printed by Antoine Vérard in 1492.[20] Hartmann's technique of anticipation as a method of reinterpretation and a means of predisposing his audience to that reinterpretation may well have its origin in the commentary tradition of the schools.

[19] See *L'Art d'amours: traduction et commentaire de l'Ars amatoria d'Ovide*, ed. by B. Roy (Leiden, 1974).
[20] See T. Hunt, 'Les Paraboles Maistre Alain', *Forum for Modern Language Studies*, 21 (1985), 362–75 (pp. 368ff.).

rehte güete *als wahrscheinlich* gewisse lêre: *Topische Argumente für eine Schulmaxime in Hartmanns* Iwein

WIEBKE FREYTAG

Wo Literatur im Hochmittelalter schulmäßig betrachtet wird, weiß man sie nach Thema und Funktion in der Regel dem Sittlichen verbunden. Die humanistisch orientierten Kathedralschulen des 12. Jahrhunderts (und früher) haben reges Interesse für *litterae et mores* entwickelt.[1] Die *Accessus ad auctores* gehen im 12. Jahrhundert bekanntlich so weit, stets nach dem Teil der Philosophie zu fragen, dem die behandelte Dichtung unterzuordnen sei,[2] wobei die *partes philosophiae*, wie außerhalb der *Accessus* üblich und innerhalb ihrer z. B. bei Konrad von Hirsau und Bernhard von Utrecht expliziert, als 'phisica', 'loica' und 'ethica' unterschieden werden.[3] Die allermeisten Werke zählen zur Ethik, daneben tauchen die beiden andern

---

[1] C. Stephen Jaeger, 'Cathedral Schools and Humanist Learning, 950–1150', *DVjs*, 61 (1987), 569–616.

[2] Philippe Delhaye, 'L'enseignement de la philosophie morale au XIIe siècle', *Mediaeval Studies*, 11 (1949), 77–95; dasselbe übersetzt von Annette und Ulrich K. Dreikandt, in *Ritterliches Tugendsystem*, hg. von Günter Eifler, WdF, 56 (Darmstadt, 1970), S. 301–40 (S. 309–19); dazu Paul Klopsch, *Einführung in die Dichtungslehren des lateinischen Mittelalters* (Darmstadt, 1980), S. 48–64; Judson Boyce Allen, *The Ethical Poetic of the Later Middle Ages: A Decorum of Convenient Distinction* (Toronto/London, 1982), siehe dessen Inhaltsverzeichnis.

[3] Bernhard von Utrecht, *Commentum in Theodolum*, in *Accessus ad Auctores: Bernard d'Utrecht: Conrad d'Hirsau, Dialogus super Auctores*, hg. von R.B.C. Huygens (Leiden, 1970), S. 67,228–68,245; Konrad von Hirsau, *Dialogus super Auctores*, ebd., S. 131, 1844–52; *Das Moralium dogma philosophorum des Guillaume de Conches*, hg. von John Holmberg (Uppsala, 1929), S. 77,22 (*Accessus*, ebd., S. 77,14–21); Johannes von Salisbury, *Metalogicon*, hg. von Clemens C.J. Webb (Oxford, 1929), II.2.858c–859a; ders., *Policraticus sive de nugis curialium et vestigiis philosophorum libri VIII*, hg. von Clemens C.J. Webb, 2 Bde. (Oxford, 1909; Nachdr. Frankfurt, 1965), VII.5.645c; vgl. weiter Anm. 5 mit dem Zitat aus der *Vita Monacensis*; früher ist: Cicero, *Tusculanae disputationes*, hg. und übers. von J.E. King, 3. Aufl. (London/Cambridge, Mass., 1950), V.24–25.68–72; Seneca, *Ad Lucilium epistulae morales*, hg. und übers. von Richard M. Gummere, 3 Bde. (Cambridge, Mass., 1920; Nachdr. 1953), *Ep.* 89.9; Isidor, *Etymologiae*, hg. von W.M. Lindsay (Oxford, 1911; Nachdr. 1966), II.24.3f.

philosophischen Gebiete in den *Accessus* nur selten auf.[4] Im Hinblick auf das hier zu Hartmann folgende sei hervorgehoben, daß ein *Accessus* der Handschrift T (12. Jahrhundert, Tegernsee) die *Ars poetica* des Horaz eher der Logik als der Ethik unterordnet und daß eine der Vergil-Viten die zwölf Bücher der Aeneis, wiewohl das Werk bekanntlich allegorisiert worden ist, unter Logik klassifiziert, während sie die *Bucolica* zur Physik, die *Georgica* zur Ethik rechnet.[5]

Die im Schulwissen gegebene Affinität zwischen Poesie und Ethik impliziert nach Bernhard von Utrecht, Konrad von Hirsau und Johannes von Salisbury ein wieder durch die Schule vorgegebenes Verständnis des Ethischen.[6] Denn diese Lehrer sehen die *ethica* durch die bekannte *quadriga virtutum* umrissen, wie es auch sonst begegnet und ähnlich in der *Formula Vitae Honestae* des Bischofs Martin von Bracara verbreitet gewesen ist. Platonisch-stoischen Ursprungs ist diese Quadriga inzwischen längst christlich adaptiert und in der angesprochenen Symbiose von *litterae et mores* wie bei Boethius und Älteren so bei Johannes von Salisbury stellvertretend für alle *virtutes* der Logik überantwortet:[7]

---

4 Folgendes zählen die von Huygens (wie Anm. 3) edierten *Accessus* zur Ethik: die *Psychomachia* des Prudentius (S. 20,27f.), Cato (S. 21,16), Avian (S. 22,15), Maximinian (S. 25,9), Homer (S. 26,17), Theodul (S. 27,16f.), Arator (S. 27,16), Prosper (S. 28,13), Ovids Briefe (S. 29,4; 30,13; 32,63), *Ars amatoria* (S. 33,8), wahrscheinlich auch *De remedio amoris* (S. 34,21–25), gewiß *De Ponto* (S. 35,8f.), *Tristia* (S. 35,11), 'Sine titulo' die *Amores* (S. 36,12), den größeren Teil seiner *Fastes* (S. 38,51), ein ungenanntes Werk Ciceros, das wegen seines Argumentierens auch zur Logik zählt (S. 45,15–17), des Boethius *Consolatio philosophiae* (S. 47, 23f.), die *Ars poetica* des Horaz, die mehr noch zur Logik zählt (S. 50,24–27), seine Briefe (S. 52,78), den *Liber Pamphili et Galatheae* (S. 53,8). Konrad von Hirsau kommt seinem Vorsatz, 'de partibus autem philosophiae, quibus opus omne auctorum subponitur' zu handeln (S. 78,228f.), nur sporadisch nach, indem er Cato (S. 83,366–68), Ciceros *De amicitia* (S. 102,938–40) und Boethius (S. 108,1143) der *ethica* unterstellt. Bernhard von Utrecht zählt Theoduls Werk zur Ethik (S. 67,228), ebenfalls Wilhelm von Conches, *Moralium dogma* (wie Anm. 3), S. 77,20f. 'Phisicae supponitur' heißt es vom *Physiologus* (Huygens (wie Anm. 3), S. 26,6) und von einem kleinen Teil der ovidischen *Fastes* (S. 38,52f.); zur Logik werden ein nicht genauer genanntes Werk Ciceros (S. 45,16f.), eins des Tebaldus (S. 53,7f.) und Horazens *Ars poetica* (S. 50,25f.) gezählt.

5 *Accessus de arte poetica*, in Huygens (wie Anm. 3), S. 50,24–29: 'Ethicae subponitur, quia ostendit qui mores conveniant poetae, vel potius logicae, quia ad noticiam rectae et ornate locutionis et ad exercitationem regularium scriptorum nos inducit. Cum ergo precepta det in omne genus scribendi, rectum ordinem servat, prius removendo quae sunt vitanda, dehinc docendo quae sunt facienda.' Zur Handschrift ebd., S. 2 und 5. *Vita Monacensis*, in *Vitae Vergilianae*, hg. von Jacob Brummer (Leipzig, 1912; Nachdr. Stuttgart, 1969), S. 59,119–22: 'quot sunt partes principales scientiae? in poemate Virgilii tres: physica id est naturalis in bucolicis, ethyca id est moralis in georgicis, loyca id est rationalis in XII libris Aeneidos.' Dies zitiert auch Klopsch (wie Anm. 2), S. 60. Die Vita ist in einer Handschrift des 10. Jahrhunderts überliefert.

6 Zu Bernhard und Konrad siehe Huygens (wie Anm. 3), S. 67,228; 68,242–45; 131,1848–50. Zu Johannes vgl. Anm. 7 und das zugehörige Zitat.

7 Vgl. Martin von Bracara, *Formula Vitae Honestae*, in *Opera omnia*, hg. von Claude W. Barlow (New Haven, 1950), S. 204–50. Boethius, *In Topica Ciceronis commentaria*, PL, LXIV, 1044D–45A. Zitat: Johannes von Salisbury, *Metalogicon* (wie Anm. 3), II.1.857cd.

Logica est ratio disserendi, per quam totius prudentie agitatio solidatur. Cum enim omnium expetibilium prima sit sapientia, ipsiusque fructus in amore boni et uirtutum cultu consistat, mentem necesse est in illius inuestigatione uersari et res plena inquisitione discutere, ut ei de singulis esse possit purum incorruptumque iudicium. Constat ergo exercitatio eius in scrutinio ueritatis, que sicut Cicero in libro de Officiis auctor est, materia est uirtutis primitiue, quam prudentiam uocant; reliquis enim tribus utilitates necessitatesque subiecte sunt. Prudentia uero tota consistit in perscientia ueri et quadam sollertia illud examinandi; porro iustitia illud amplectitur, fortitudo tuetur, temperantia uirtutum precedentium exercitia moderatur. Unde libet prudentiam uirtutum omnium esse radicem; que si precidatur, cetere, uelut rami nature beneficio destituti, marcida quadam ariditate euanescunt. Quis enim amplectetur aut colet quod ignorat?

Wie Bernhard von Utrecht nennt Johannes dabei Sokrates und Cicero als Gewährsleute.[8] Während *litterati* des 12. Jahrhunderts also die *Ethica* material den Kardinaltugenden und formal der Logik verpflichtet sehen, erkennen sie ihren Zweck in der *correctio morum*. In ihr besteht nach den *Accessus* die *utilitas* solcher Autoren, die der Ethik untergeordnet werden als demjenigen Teil der Philosophie, der nach Cicero 'der Darstellung der zu erstrebenden und zu fliehenden Dinge und der Richtschnur des Lebens' verpflichtet ist und in welchem man findet, 'was die Natur als das Höchste im Guten bezwecke, was das Äußerste in den Übeln sei, worauf die Pflichten zu beziehen, welcher Lebensplan zu erwählen sei'.[9] Johannes von Salisbury sieht Vergil den Weg zur *vita beata* weisen, dem christlich philosophischen Lebensziel: 'nostrorum doctissimus poetarum, uite beate monstrans originem'; und ähnlich findet er es bei Boethius.[10]

Wie weit mag ein volkssprachiger Dichter, zumal einer, der wie Hartmann nachweislich Schulautoren kennt und im Kontext seines

Zur patristischen Rezeption der *quadriga virtutum* siehe Joseph Mausbach, *Die Ethik des heiligen Augustinus*, 2 Bde. (Freiburg im Breisgau, 1909), I, 207–18; Sibylle Mähl, *Quadriga virtutum: Die Kardinaltugenden in der Geistesgeschichte der Karolingerzeit*, Beihefte zum Archiv für Kulturgeschichte, 9 (Köln/Wien, 1969), S. 7–15.

[8] Die vier Tugenden bei Cicero, *De inventione*, hg. und übers. von H.M. Hubbell (Cambridge, Mass., 1960), II.53.159; *De officiis*, hg. von C. Atzert, 4. Aufl. (Leipzig, 1963), I.5.15–17 (hier Bezugnahme auf Plato); *De finibus bonorum et malorum libri quinque*, hg. von J.S. Reid (Cambridge, 1925), II.15.48–50. Zu ihn rezipierenden mittelalterlichen, auch volkssprachigen Morallehren siehe Gerhard Traub, *Studien zum Einfluß Ciceros auf die höfische Moral* (Dissertation, Greifswald, 1933), S. 31–78.

[9] Vgl. Anm. 4; Cicero, *Tusculanae disputationes*, übers. von Raphael Kühner, 4. Aufl. (Berlin, o. J.), V.24.68; V.25.71; auch Cicero, *De officiis* (wie Anm. 8), I.3.7.

[10] *Metalogicon* (wie Anm. 3), II.1.858a.

Produzierens sich 'gelehrt' und 'belesen' nennt,[11] den im Schulischen vorgegebenen Verbund von Dichtung und philosophischer Ethik aufgreifen zum erzieherischen Nutzen für sein Publikum und ihm gerade dadurch zeitgemäß erscheinen? Es steht im Grundsatz wohl außer Frage, daß auch volkssprachige Dichter ausgeprägtes Interesse an damals christlich interpretierten ethischen Komplexen zeigen, die sie im höfischen Roman ausdrücklich als ihren eigentlichen Gegenstand zu erkennen geben; so nennt Wolfram eingangs seiner *summa facti* und immer wieder im Verlauf des *Parzival* die *triuwe* als Inbegriff des Guten, Gottfried die *liebe* oder *minne* mit dem ihr notwendig eigenen *leit* und Hartmann im *Iwein* (*Iw.* 1–20) die *güete* in Relation zu *sælde und êre*.[12] In der Terminologie der *Accessus* gesagt, lassen diese Dichter als *causa finalis* bzw. *utilitas* ihrer Werke die *correctio morum* erkennen: so in Wolframs moralisierender Adresse an die *wîsen* unter den Zuhörern, in Gottfrieds Klage über die Diskrepanz zwischen seinem Liebesideal und der herzlosen Praxis seiner Mitmenschen;[13] so auch in Hartmanns Induktion, mit der er das Beispiel des guten Königs Artus auf alle bezieht, damit sie ihm folgen (*Iw.* 18–20). Fraglich aber bleibt, wie sich die materiale und formale Darbietung des Ethischen im höfischen Epos zu den skizzierten Erwartungen der *litterati* verhalten.

Ich wähle die Werkeingänge von Chrestiens *Yvain*[14] und Hartmanns Bearbeitung, sowie Calogrenants Erzählung mit je der ersten Rede Keies und der Königin, um mit Hilfe zahlreicher Parallelen aus Schultexten zu erörtern, wie das Gute, das beide Dichter im König

---

11   Nachweise bei Anton E. Schönbach, *Über Hartmann von Aue: Drei Bücher Untersuchungen* (Graz, 1894), S. 171–91; Fritz Peter Knapp, 'Enites Totenklage und Selbstmordversuch in Hartmanns *Erec'*, *GRM*, 57 (1976), 83–90. Christoph Cormeau, 'Hartmann von Aue', in *Die deutsche Literatur des Mittelalters: Verfasserlexikon*, 2. Aufl., hg. von Kurt Ruh u. a. (Berlin/New York, 1977–), III (1981), Sp. 500–20 (Sp. 502): 'H.s selbstbewußt formulierter Bildungsstand ('A.H.' 1f., 'Iw.' 21f.) läßt an einer fundierten Schulbildung kaum zweifeln; 'Kl.', 'Grg.' und 'A.H.' legen nahe, daß dazu auch philosophische und theologische Grundlagen gehörten.' Wie hier beziehe ich mich im folgenden durch eingeklammerte Zahlenangaben mit der Sigle *Iw.* auf Hartmann von Aue, *Iwein*, hg. von G.F. Benecke und K. Lachmann, 6. Aufl., besorgt von Ludwig Wolff (Berlin, 1962).
12   Wolfram von Eschenbach, *Parzival*, 7. Aufl., hg. von Albert Leitzmann, ATB, 12 (Tübingen, 1961), 4,9f.; siehe den Terminus *triuwe* sonst im Werk nach R.-M.S. Heffner, *Collected Indexes to the Works of Wolfram von Eschenbach* (Madison, 1961), S. 154. Gottfried von Straßburg, *Tristan und Isold*, 8. Aufl., hg. von Friedrich Ranke (Zürich/Berlin, 1964), 211–33; weitere Belege nach Melvin E. Valk, *Word-Index to Gottfried's 'Tristan'* (Madison, 1958), S. 41; und R.A. Boggs, *Hartmann von Aue: Lemmatisierte Konkordanz zum Gesamtwerk*, Indices zur deutschen Literatur, 12–13, 2 Bde. (Nendeln, 1979), I, 89f., 151–53, 342f.
13   *Parzival* (wie Anm. 12), 2,5–3,27. *Tristan* (wie Anm. 12), 191–210.
14   Ich beziehe mich im folgenden mit der in Klammern gesetzten Sigle *Yv.* und Versangabe auf *Chrestien de Troyes: Yvain*, übers. und eingeleitet von Ilse Nolting-Hauff, Klassische Texte des Romanischen Mittelalters in zweisprachigen Ausgaben, 2 (München, 1962).

Artus und manch anderen Personen ihrer Werke sehen, an den verschiedenen Stellen dimensioniert ist. Ohne die untersuchten Probleme der Adaptation des *Yvain* durch Hartmann hier ansprechen zu können, werden damit bewußt schon oft diskutierte Textpartien betrachtet. Dies weil erstens die Ausführungen dazu kontrovers sind (Abschnitt A), zweitens aber eine detailliertere vergleichende Lektüre mehr Hartmanns (Abschnitt B) als Chrestiens (Abschnitt C) beider Terminologie und Vorstellung der *rehten güete* als schulmäßig erweist, und weil schließlich dieser gegenüber der Forschung dann auch im Hinblick auf das Formale ausdifferenzierte Deutungsansatz künstlerisch neue Möglichkeiten der Verknüpfung von *matiere et san* zeigen mag, wie sie der höfische Romanautor nach Chrestiens gewiß maßgeblichem Wort stiftet.[15] Denn Hartmanns und weniger Chrestiens topisches Argumentieren (Abschnitt D), wie es Schulautoren im Kontext des *verum bonum* durchaus vorsehen, scheint der Exemplarität seines höfischen Erzählens einen inhaltlich und mehr noch formal ganz anderen Zuschnitt zu verleihen, als er etwa im *Prosa-Lancelot*[16] zu beobachten ist, oder man es sonst beschrieb. So wenig vorbereitet der heutige Leser darauf auch sein mag, – was Hartmann hier leistet, zeigt den volkssprachigen Autor (und vermutlich sein wohl ständisch beschränktes Publikum) auf dem eingangs skizzierten und im Verlauf der Abhandlung weiter zu präzisierenden Interessen- und Wissensniveau damaliger *litterati*. Hartmann weiß den viel belegten philosophischen Diskurs über das Gute samt den an seiner Darstellung beteiligten *Artes* zur sinnvermittelnden poetischen Bearbeitung seiner Quelle zu nutzen. Sein Wissen speist die kreative Phantasie des Dichters.

A. Der Forschungsstand zu ethischer Materie und ihrer Darbietungsform im Iwein-Prolog

Was die ethische Materie angeht, so sah schon Ehrismann mit dem allerdings nicht zu akzeptierenden Postulat systemhafter Ethik und anderen Versehen die ritterlichen Dichtungen Hartmanns in Beziehung zur Überlieferung der Antike.[17] Ihm folgte am entschieden-

---

[15] Zu *matiere et san*, die Chrestien im Prolog seines *Chevalier de la charrete*, hg. von Mario Roques, CFMA, 86 (Paris, 1958), V. 26, gebraucht, vgl. Walter Haug, *Literaturtheorie im deutschen Mittelalter: Von den Anfängen bis zum Ende des 13. Jahrhunderts: Eine Einführung* (Darmstadt, 1985), S. 107–11.

[16] Vgl. Wiebke Freytag, '*Mundus fallax*, Affekt und Recht oder exemplarisches Erzählen im Prosa-Lancelot', *Wolfram-Studien*, 9 (1986), 134–94.

[17] Gustav Ehrismann, 'Die Grundlagen des ritterlichen Tugendsystems', *ZfdA*, 56 (1919), 137–216 (S. 208f.), allerdings ohne Parallelen zu Hartmanns *Iwein*-Prolog.

sten Traub[18] und trotz der heftigen Kritik, die Ehrismann keineswegs unbillig erfuhr,[19] überwiegen doch zu Recht bis jüngst bei Rocher[20] die Versuche, seine These zu modifizieren und zu ergänzen. Die von Cramer zusammengestellten Übersetzungen der Sentenz zu Beginn des *Iwein*, ihr Verständnis bei Scharmann und die Paraphrase, wie Ruh sie zweimal gibt,[21] zeigen indessen ein Schwanken zwischen allgemein ethischem und ständischem Bezug im Verständnis der mhd. Termini, dem mit den älteren Arbeiten[22] zum Wort 'gut' nicht zu begegnen ist. Maria Bindschedler[23] behauptet für Hartmann im Vergleich zu Chrestien ein überzeitliches Humanum; ich brauche nicht zu begründen, warum nach heutiger Auffassung in mittelalterlicher Literatur mit Derartigem nicht zu rechnen ist, wiewohl die Literaturbetrachtung des 12. und beginnenden 13. Jahrhunderts in den *Accessus* poetische Werke auf den allgemein gültig gedachten Bereich der philosophischen Ethik bezogen hat. Dieser Lehrkomplex ist aber als geschichtliche Gegebenheit zu betrachten und nicht als ein tatsächlich Überzeitliches. Der poetische Text ist gerade in seinem generellen Anspruch als zeitgebunden zu beschreiben, wie schon Xenja von Ertzdorff[24] ausblickend meint. Endres' Kontroverse mit

---

[18]   Traub (wie Anm. 8), S. 81, bezieht lediglich Cicero, *De officiis* (wie Anm. 8) II.5.17, auf *Iw.* 8–11. Wilhelm Weise, *Die Sentenz bei Hartmann von Aue* (Dissertation, Marburg, 1910), bringt keine Quellen zum Eingang des *Iwein*.

[19]   Vgl. Ernst Robert Curtius, *Europäische Literatur und lateinisches Mittelalter*, 3. Aufl. (Bern/München, 1961), S. 506–21, besonders ab S. 508, der allerdings den *Iwein* so wenig erwähnt wie Frederick P. Pickering, 'On Coming to Terms with Curtius', *GLL*, 11 (1957/58), 335–45. Ich ziehe vorrangig andere Texte in Betracht als die bei Ehrismann und Curtius vor allem strittigen (Cicero, *De officiis*; Wernher von Elmendorf; Wilhelms von Conches *Moralium dogma*; mhd. Texte). Zu Recht betont Curtius (S. 520), 'das sogenannte Tugendsystem des Ritters ist wohl kaum ein System gewesen'.

[20]   Daniel Rocher, 'Tradition latine et morale chevaleresque: A propos du ''Ritterliches Tugendsystem'' ', *Et. Germ.*, 19 (1964), 127–41; dasselbe übersetzt von Joachim K. Schmidt in Eifler (wie Anm. 2), S. 452–77. Die Rocher voraufgehenden Arbeiten zum Thema enthält Eiflers Band; ich gehe auf sie nicht ein, da sie das von Ehrismann Angeregte nicht im Sinne des Schulwissens weiterführen.

[21]   Thomas Cramer, '*Sælde* und *êre* in Hartmanns *Iwein*', *Euph.*, 60 (1966), 30–47 (S. 30f.). Theodor Scharmann, *Studien über die Sælde in der ritterlichen Dichtung des 12. und 13. Jahrhunderts* (Würzburg, 1935), S. 4. Kurt Ruh, *Höfische Epik des deutschen Mittelalters* (Berlin, 1967), I, 11: 'Wer sein Streben nach der *rehten güete*, den wahrhaften Gütern und Werten des Lebens, ausrichtet, dem wird *sælde* und *êre* zuteil.' Dagegen heißt es in der 2. Aufl. von 1977, S. 13: 'Wer sein Streben nach der *rehten güete*, dem wahrhaft Guten im Sinne ritterlichen Selbstverständnisses, ausrichtet, dem wird *sælde* und *êre* zuteil'; Ruh betont hier (S. 14) gegenüber dem *Tristan*, daß *sælde* bei Hartmann sich zwar auf das Irdische beziehe, aber 'die Segnung Gottes (beatitudo)' in sich schließe.

[22]   Vgl. Franz Schmidt, *Zur geschichte des wortes 'gut'* (Dissertation, Leipzig/Halle (Saale), 1898), S. 29–33; auch Richard Brodführer, *Untersuchung über die Entwicklung des Begriffes 'guot' in Verbindung mit Personenbezeichnungen im Minnesange* (Dissertation, Leipzig/Halle (Saale), 1917).

[23]   Maria Bindschedler, 'Guot und güete bei Hartmann von Aue', in *Die Wissenschaft von deutscher Sprache und Dichtung: Festschrift für Friedrich Maurer zum 65. Geburtstag*, hg. von Siegfried Gutenbrunner u. a. (Stuttgart, 1963), S. 352–65 (S. 355).

Nagel versucht dies, wenn auch die sich ergebende Alternative nicht einleuchtet, die Alternative von einerseits christlich theologischer Deutung der Sentenz im Sinne augustinisch-bernhardischen Gedankengutes bei Endres und andererseits bloßem Anbinden an einige Hartmann ein wenig nahekommende Reinmar-Verse mit lautem Pochen auf die angeblichen 'gattungsgesetzlichen Bedingungen der Artusepik als einer theologiefreien reinen Diesseitskunst' bei Nagel.[25] K. Gürttler argumentiert demgegenüber, ohne Berührungsmöglichkeiten des höfischen Romans mit religiösen Vorstellungen rundweg auszuschließen, vor allem mit Chrestien für ein standesethisches Implikat der Sentenz.[26] Dem Textverständnis des *Iwein*-Prologs scheinen indes weder Chrestiens Eingangsverse noch die Stellen aus Augustin und Bernhard besonders dienlich, ehestens die aus Reinmar und von Meissburger aus Wolfram beigebrachten und übrigens auch bei Gottfried vorhandenen Textparallelen. Die volkssprachige Literatur bietet, soweit man bisher sieht,[27] vor Hartmann keine engeren Parallelstellen zur Sentenz des *Iwein*-Prologs; sie gibt es erst zu seiner Zeit. Vor Hartmann sind solche Parallelen also vermutlich im Lateinischen zu suchen; schon Hans Neumann betont zum Wort 'gut', daß für die Entwicklung seines Bedeutungsspektrums der Gebrauch des lateinischen *bonus* maßgeblich gewesen sei und zwar 'in theologischer, juristischer und poetischer Literatur'.[28] Zu erwähnen bleibt Grandins lexikologisch interessierte Arbeit zu *guot* und seinen

---

[24] Xenja von Ertzdorff, 'Spiel der Interpretation: Der Erzähler in Hartmanns Iwein', in *Festgabe für Friedrich Maurer zum 70. Geburtstag*, hg. von Werner Besch u. a. (Düsseldorf, 1968), S. 135–57, besonders S. 156.

[25] Rolf Endres, 'Der Prolog von Hartmanns *Iwein*', DVjs, 40 (1966), 509–37, hier S. 522f., 536; ders., 'Die Bedeutung von *güete* und die Diesseitigkeit der Artusromane Hartmanns', DVjs, 44 (1970), 595–612, hier S. 605–10. Bert Nagel, 'Hartmann "zitiert" Reinmar: *Iwein* 1–30 und *MF* 150/10–18', Euph., 63 (1969), 6–39, zitiert ist S. 22; öfter ähnlich. Erwähnt sei George F. Jones, *Honor in German Literature* (Chapel Hill, 1959), S. 84, 115, der die Bibel zum *Iwein*-Prolog heranzieht und Ehrismanns (wie Anm. 17) Theorie insgesamt ablehnt.

[26] Karin Gürttler, '*Künec Artûs der guote*': Das Artusbild der höfischen Epik des 12. und 13. *Jahrhunderts* (Bonn, 1976), S. 63–69.

[27] Ehrismann (wie Anm. 17), S. 146–52. Endres (wie Anm. 25, 1970), S. 605–07, und Gürttler (wie Anm. 26), S. 70–72, den *Welschen Gast* des Thomasin von Zerklaere, 3856–62, 7697f.; die Fassung D des *Herzogs Ernst*, 4509–20; aber auch schon Eilhart, 3100–15. Gerhard Meissburger, '*güete* bei Wolfram von Eschenbach', in *Festgabe für Maurer* (wie Anm. 24), S. 158–77 (S. 158), beginnt mit *Willehalm*, 280,28–281,2: 'ein wîser man gap mir den rât,/ daz ich phlæge, swenne ich möhte,/ sölher güete, diu mir getöhte/ ûzerhalp der valschen wîse:/ des möht ich komen ze prîse.' Er hält dies *praeceptum* allerdings zu Unrecht für 'Wolframs Eigentum' (S. 159); S. 176 weist er *rehtiu* und *wâriu güete* im *Parzival*, 260,10 und 804,16, nach. Zu ergänzen ist *Tristan* (wie Anm. 12), 520–23, 5647–80 u. ö.; diesen Stellen hoffe ich andern Orts nachgehen zu können.

[28] Hans Neumann, 'gut', in *Deutsches Wörterbuch*, begründet von Jacob Grimm und Wilhelm Grimm, IV, 1, 6 (Leipzig, 1935), Sp. 1225–369 (Sp. 1227).

Ableitungen im *Gregorius*,[29] wenn sie es auch beim Nachweis praktisch aller bei Lexer vorkommender Bedeutungen bewenden läßt.

Was die Form, deren Legitimation und Zweck angeht, mit der ein höfischer Epiker vom Guten und von guten Menschen spricht, so ist dem hiermit zur Diskussion anstehenden Fragenkreis wenig vorgedacht. Es sei vor allem an Brinkmann erinnert,[30] der den Bezug zwischen der klaren rhetorischen Form des *Iwein*-Prologs und den *Poetriae* des damaligen Schulbetriebs richtig herstellt, wenn er auch nicht alle Indizien erschöpft. Wichtig und weiterzudenken ist mir das zu *sententia* und *exemplum* Ausgeführte, denn beide Gestaltungsmittel dienen dem Wahren und allgemein Gültigen, wie zu Hartmanns Zeit gelehrt wurde. Dergestalt gebraucht Cicero alle Arten von *exempla* zum Beweis seiner Ausführungen; Johannes von Salisbury zeigt sich überzeugt: 'et exemplorum inductio singularitatem excludat'; 'exemplis saepe magis proficitur quam praeceptis', als er mit Cicero und Horaz den sittlichen Lehrgehalt der Trojadichtung reflektiert.[31] Eine Sentenz ist 'communis sententia, cui consuetudo fidem attribuit, opinio communis assensum accommodat, incorruptae veritatis integritas adquiescit', wie bekanntlich Matthaeus von Vendôme sagt.[32] Was die Forschung darüber hinaus bemühte, um das exemplarische Erzählen im höfischen Epos zu erläutern, entstammt recht verschiedenen Überlieferungszusammenhängen. Ich plane seine genauere Sichtung später und erwähne nur das kürzlich zu Konrads von Würzburg Paris-Urteil Angesprochene.[33] Hier sollen nun die für Sentenz und Exempel

[29] Larry Robert Grandin, 'Guot, güete, unguot, guottât: A Word Study in Hartmann's *Gregorius*', *MLN*, 88 (1973), 927–46. Nicht erreichbar war mir Donald Gutch, 'Die Bedeutungen des Wortes *guot* und seiner Ableitungen in den althochdeutschen und altsächsischen Denkmälern der Karolingerzeit' (unpublizierte Dissertation, Freiburg im Breisgau, 1961).

[30] Hennig Brinkmann, 'Der Prolog im Mittelalter als literarische Erscheinung', *WW*, 14 (1964), 1–21 (S. 9f. zum *Iwein*-Prolog).

[31] Ebd., S. 6. Das zu Einzelnem und Allgemeinem bei Brinkmann Gesagte ist mit den Quellen, die er nennt, nicht zu belegen, scheint jedoch mit andern Gewährsleuten bedenkenswert. Vgl. z. B. Cicero, *Tusculanae disputationes* (wie Anm. 3), I.14–15.32–34, 48–49.116–17. Zum *exemplum* in Lehrbüchern der Rhetorik siehe Fritz Peter Knapp, *Similitudo: Stil- und Erzählfunktion von Vergleich und Exempel in der lateinischen, französischen und deutschen Großepik des Hochmittelalters*, Philologica Germanica, 2 (Wien/Stuttgart, 1975), S. 70–76, 93f. *Policraticus* (wie Anm. 3), II.22.452b; II.25.457b; VII.9.656d. Nach Christian Waas, *Die Quellen der Beispiele Boners* (Dissertation, Gießen/Dortmund, 1897), S. 6, Seneca (wie Anm. 3), VI.5; I.19: 'Longum iter est per praecepta, breve et efficax per exempla.' Weitere Varianten des, wie es heißt, besonders in Predigt und Exempelliteratur gern zitierten Grundsatzes ebd., sowie bei Fritz Peter Knapp (diese Anm.), S. 78, und Klaus Grubmüller, *Meister Esopus: Untersuchungen zur Geschichte und Funktion der Fabel im Mittelalter*, MTU, 56 (Zürich/München, 1977), S. 99f., 306.

[32] Matthaeus von Vendôme, 'Ars versificatoria', I.16, hg. von Edmond Faral, *Les arts poétiques du XIIe et du XIIIe siècle* (Paris, 1924; Nachdr. 1962), S. 113; die Stelle nennt Brinkmann (wie Anm. 30), S. 6.

[33] Wiebke Freytag, 'Zur Logik *wilder aventiure* in Konrads von Würzburg Paris-Urteil', *Jahrbuch der Oswald von Wolkenstein Gesellschaft*, 5 (1988/89), 373–95.

offensichtlich seitens der Rhetorik gegebenen Funktionen im Rahmen topisch angelegter poetischer Rede weiterverfolgt und um etwa vorkommende andere Typen topischer Argumentation ergänzt werden. Jeder weiß, daß die literaturwissenschaftlich mediävistische Diskussion literarischer Topik, soviel topische Materialien und Motive sie mit unumstrittenem Verdienst erforschte, die argumentative und das heißt auch die funktionale Seite dieser sehr literaten Präsentationsform eigentlich unbeachtet ließ.

B. Zur Philosophie des verum bonum im Iwein-Prolog

Welche allgemein gültige Wahrheit mag Hartmann nun mit Exempel und Sentenz meinen?[34] Meines Erachtens ist die kaum zu bezweifelnde *opinio communis*, die er mit *güete*, *rehte*, sowie *sælde*, *êre*, *lop* und schließlich *wârheit* als *gewisse lêre* anspricht (Iw. 1–7), fester Bestand mittelalterlichen Schulwissens über das Gute, ist wie vor Hartmann weniger deutlich bei Chrestien vor allem aus antiken und spätantiken Werken gelernte Ethik und auch nach der Bibel gegebene *doctrina moralis*. Die Termini selbst und ihre Verbindung lassen keinen andern Schluß zu: es handelt sich um jene langlebige, bald so, bald so akzentuierte Philosophie des Guten, die heute zwar in Trivialliteratur oder -film als Lebensgesetz anklingen mag, aber einem philosophischen Kopf wie Musil durchaus Problem ist und Brecht im *Guten Menschen von Sezuan* korrekturbedürftig erscheint.[35] Wohl 1783 hat Goethe sie in der Ode als 'Das Göttliche' gepriesen,[36] und sie erscheint öfter in älterer Dichtung. Als *gewisse lêre* (Iw. 4) vermittelt Hartmann die zu seiner Zeit, wie es nun zu zeigen gilt, eindeutig konturierte und gültige Maxime.

In den mittellateinischen Versionen der aristotelischen *Ethica Nicomachea*, Ciceros Schrift *De finibus bonorum et malorum*, weniger in *De officiis*, öfter in den *Tusculanae disputationes*, dem ersten seiner *Paradoxa Stoicorum*, in Senecas Briefen an Lucilius habe ich die gesuchten

---

[34] Wolfgang Dittmann, 'Dune hâst niht wâr, Hartman! Zum Begriff der wârheit in Hartmanns Iwein', in *Festgabe für Ulrich Pretzel*, hg. von Werner Simon u. a. (Berlin, 1963), S. 150–61 (S. 160f. zum Prolog), sucht Hartmanns Vorstellung von Wahrheit allein aus dem *Iwein* und gelegentlich seiner Vorlage zu beschreiben. Man wird darüber hinausgehen müssen.
[35] *'Gut und glückselig? Ein unbekanntes Textfragment von Robert Musil'*, hg. von Matthias Luserke, *Jahrbuch der deutschen Schillergesellschaft*, 31 (1987), 53–71. Bert Brecht, *Der gute Mensch von Sezuan*, in *Werke*, Bd. VI, hg. von Werner Hecht u. a. (Berlin/Frankfurt, 1989), S. 175–281, besonders S. 208,19; 216,10–13; 220,10–221,5; 279,1–5.
[36] Goethe, *Werke: Hamburger Ausgabe*, hg. von Erich Trunz, 12. Aufl., 14 Bde. (München, 1981), I, 147–49.

Entsprechungen vor allem gefunden,[37] nichts zum *Iwein*-Prolog dagegen (und dies spricht gegen Versuche, allein theologisches Wissen in Hartmanns Sentenz und Exempel entdecken zu wollen) in Augustins *De natura boni* und Hugos von St. Viktor Ausführungen zum *bonum secundum se* und *ad aliquid* oder bei Abaelard.[38] Wie Courcelle nachweist, prägt Boethius in der viel gelesenen *Consolatio philosophiae* wohl in Anlehnung an Plotin, aber mit christlicher Umdeutung des antiken Gedankenguts den Terminus des *verum bonum* samt zugehörigem Wortschatz. Die Beschreibungen der *Consolatio* durch Konrad von Hirsau und einen *Accessus Boetii* aus dem 12. Jahrhundert bestätigen, daß man diesem Text zu Hartmanns Zeit den Terminus und die Philosophie des *verum bonum* entnimmt, und beides begegnet schon in Alcuins *Grammatica*.[39] Boethius könnte auch für Hartmanns Konzept der *rehten güete* maßgeblich gewesen sein, wie die vielen Entsprechungen zwischen beiden Autoren im folgenden zeigen mögen. Wenige Parallelen zum *Iwein*-Prolog gibt es im *Moralium dogma philosophorum* des

---

[37] Aristoteles, *Ethica Nicomachea, Translatio antiquior*, hg. von Renatus A. Gauthier, *Aristoteles Latinus*, 26,2 (Leiden/Brüssel, 1972); *Translatio Grosseteste. Textus purus*, ebd., 26,3; *Textus recognitus*, ebd. 26,4. Vgl. die Übersetzung von Paul Gohlke, *Aristoteles: Die Lehrschriften*, Bd. VII, 3 (Paderborn, 1956), I.4, S. 23–26. Cicero, *De finibus* (wie Anm. 8); *De officiis* (wie Anm. 8). Dies Werk enthält im Vergleich zu den anderen genannten Ciceros weniger enge Parallelen, weil die Frage nach dem Guten nicht zentral ist und das Nützliche oft als übergeordneter Aspekt hinzutritt, den Hartmann indes später im *Iwein* auch aufgreift; *Tusculanae disputationes* (wie Anm. 3); *Paradoxa Stoicorum*, hg. und übers. von H. Rackham (London/Cambridge, Mass., 1960), S. 258–67; Seneca (wie Anm. 3).
[38] Aurelius Augustinus, *De natura boni*, hg. von Iosephus Zycha, CSEL, 25,4,2 (Prag/Wien/Leipzig, 1892), S. 853–89. Handschriften (ebd., S. 854): S, P = 8. Jh.; G, M = 11. Jh.; V, A = 12. Jh.; L = 13. Jh. Im Verlauf des *Iwein* erscheint (wie bei Augustin im ersten Satz) Gott als der Schöpfer des Guten, das Böse als eine nur in Relation zum Guten zu denkende Kraft. – Hugo von St. Viktor, 'De sacramentis', I.4.17–24, PL, CLXXVI, 241C–44D. Die oben erwähnten Termini der *Kategorien* gebraucht der lateinische Aristoteles, *Ethica Nicomachea, Translatio antiquior* (wie Anm. 37), I.4, S. 71,15–74,20 (zit. bis 72,3): 'Bonum autem dicitur et in eo quod quid, et in quali, et in ad aliquid ***; et enim in eo quod quid dicitur, utputa deus et intellectus; et in quali, virtutes; et in quanto, mensuratum; et in ad aliquid, quod utile; et in tempore, tempus (tempestivum); et in loco, dieta; et alia talia; manifestum quod non utique erit commune quid universaliter et unum. *** utique diceretur in omnibus predicamentis, set in uno solum.' *Translatio Grosseteste*, ebd., I.7, S. 146,20–149,2: 'Bonum autem dicitur et in eo quod quid, et in quali, et in ad aliquid'. *Textus recognitus*, ebd., I.2, S. 379,20–381,27. – Petrus Abaelardus, 'De inquisitione summi boni', PL CLXXVIII, 1681B–84D.
[39] Pierre Courcelle, *La Consolation de Philosophie dans la tradition littéraire* (Paris, 1967), S. 169, nennt Plotin, *Enneaden*, I.4.6. Boethius, *Consolationis philosophiae libri quinque. Lateinisch und deutsch*, hg. und übers. von Ernst Gegenschatz und Olof Gigon, 2. Aufl. (Zürich/Stuttgart, 1969), vgl. den Beleg des *verum bonum* in Anm. 56 unten. Mit möglichen Beziehungen zwischen der *Consolatio* und Hartmanns *Erec*, auch dem *Armen Heinrich*, rechnet die Forschung bereits; so der überzeugende Beitrag von Ruth H. Firestone, 'Chrétien's Enide, Hartmann's Enite and Boethii *Philosophiae Consolatio*', *ABäG*, 26 (1987), 69–106, die Früheres nennt. – Konrad von Hirsau (wie Anm. 3), S. 107f.,1115–46; der Terminus *verum bonum* in 1115f., 1135, 1140. Zum Thema von *honor, gloria* und *beatitudo* bei Boethius vgl. *Accessus Boetii*, ebd., S. 47f., besonders 16–26. Alcuin, 'De grammatica', PL, CI, 850C; vgl. Johannes von Salisbury in Anm. 52 unten.

Wilhelm von Conches,[40] das über die engeren Probleme der Ethik
bewußt hinausgeht, wenig zum *Iwein*-Eingang Zitierenswertes auch bei
Wernher von Elmendorf,[41] deutliche Entsprechungen jedoch in
bestimmten Kapiteln des *Policraticus* und *Metalogicon* des Johannes von
Salisbury und auch im *Speculum doctrinale* und *Speculum morale* des
Prinzenerziehers Vincenz von Beauvais, das, Älteres rezipierend,
allerdings Mitte des 13. bzw. erst zu Beginn des 14. Jahrhunderts
entstanden ist.[42] Johannes und Vincenz machen durch Nennung von
Cicero, Seneca, Aristoteles deutlich, wie sehr sie sich an den relevanten
Stellen auf antike Auffassungen, auf Schulwissen beziehen. Nicht
zuletzt könnte ein mittelalterlicher *litteratus* deshalb mit dem in Rede
stehenden ethischen Komplex vertraut gewesen sein, weil mit Boethius,[43] Martianus Capella, Isidor, Alcuin, Johannes Scottus, Remigius
von Auxerre und Abaelard das Schließen am Beispiel der Begriffs-
gemeinschaft von *virtus*, *bonum*, *iustum*, *honestum* und *utile* exerziert
worden ist.[44] Vielleicht waren einem *litteratus* auch die vielen, dem

[40] Wie Anm. 3, S. 78,9–13. Der Begriff des *verum bonum* fehlt bei Wilhelm ebenso wie die
gemüthafte Hinwendung zum rechten Guten und die Verbindung von *honestas* und
beatitudo oder *felicitas*; wo Wilhelm und Hartmann entsprechende Termini gebrauchen,
vermitteln sie kaum dasselbe; vgl. mit dem *Iwein*-Prolog ebd., S. 7,10–18; 69,1–3; 79,23–26;
die *Epistola Nuncupatoria* nennt die Kardinaltugenden nur einmal (ebd., S. 81f.) 'officia
bene beateque viuendi'. Neben dem *honestum* ist das *utile*, das auch Hartmann im weiteren
Verlauf des *Iwein* einbezieht, Wilhelm von Conches ungleich wichtiger als *beatitudo*; S.
77,15–17, sagt er über sein Werk: 'materia ipsius est utile et honestum; [. . .] utilitas est
cognitio utilis et honesti.'
[41] Hg. von Joachim Bumke, ATB, 77 (Tübingen, 1974).
[42] *Policraticus* (wie Anm. 3), besonders VII.8.651a–652c; VIII.14–15.768b–773a; vgl. ders.,
Metalogicon (wie Anm. 3); Vincenz von Beauvais, *Speculum doctrinale* (Duaci, 1624; Nachdr.
Graz, 1964), besonders V.67–71; ders., *Speculum morale*, ebd., besonders I.3.72 und 76;
II.4.1. Vgl. Astrik L. Gabriel, *Vincenz von Beauvais* (Frankfurt am Main, 1967), S. 15 zur
Entstehungsgeschichte des Kompendiums; ebd., S. 24f. zu den vielen Quellen und
pädagogischen Zwecken des Werks.
[43] Vgl. *De syllogismo categorico*, PL, LXIV, 815CD: 'Omne justum bonum est./ Omnis
virtus justa est./ Quoddam bonum justum est.' und 'Nullum bonum malum est./ Omne
justum bonum est, posset colligi;/ Nullum justum malum est; sed ex his per conversionem
colligimus:/ Nullum malum justum est.' Und ähnlich durchgehend im 2. Buch (814B–
30D); siehe auch *De differentiis topicis*, PL, LXIV, 1179B: 'Modus etiam sequitur nomen
principale, ut sit justitia bona est, et quod juste est, bonum est. Nomen etiam principale
sequitur modum, ut si quod juste est, bonum est, et justitia bona est.'
[44] Martianus Capella, hg. von James Willis (Leipzig, 1983), IV.411–13. Isidor, *Etymologiae*
(wie Anm. 3), II.28.3–21. Alcuin, 'De dialectica', PL, CI, 949D–76B; 966AB und 968BC:
z. B. 'Omne justum honestum; omne honestum bonum: omne igitur justum bonum' u. ä.
Remigius Autissiodorensis, *Commentum in Martianum Capellam*, hg. von Cora E. Lutz
(Leiden, 1965), IV.184.12 (S. 47,13–16): 'Constat autem syllogismus propositione,
assumptione, ut est: ''Omne iustum honestum,'' ecce propositio; ''Omne honestum
bonum,'' ecce sumptum vel assumptio; ''Omne igitur iustum bonum,'' ecce conclusio.'
Vgl. weiter die Beispiele ebd. IV.193.15–195.8 (S. 53,26–54,26); IV.197.23 (S. 55,28–34).
Johannes Scottus, *Annotationes in Marcianum*, hg. von Cora E. Lutz (Cambridge, Mass.,
1939), 152.13; 186.10. P. Abaelard, 'Tractatus quartus de ypoteticis', Prologus, in *Abaelard:
Dialectica*, hg. von L.M. de Rijk, 2. Aufl. (Assen, 1970), S. 469,15–25 (zitiert in Anm. 59
unten); siehe dazu de Rijk, ebd., Introduction, S. LXXIf., und ebd., 'Tractatus secundus
de cathegoricis', S. 173–76, 183f., 235–45.

vorher Genannten nicht entgegenstehenden Aussagen zum *bonum*, *iustum*, *honorabile*, *laudabile*, zu *virtus* und *beatitudo* bekannt, mit denen Aristoteles das dritte Buch seiner *Topica* durchgehend versehen hat, um Beispiele für die topische Behandlung der Frage nach dem Besseren von zweien oder mehreren zu geben.[45]

Ich stelle die Terminologie, die Hartmann eingangs des *Iwein* gebraucht, was nie explizit versucht wurde, im folgenden neben diese Texte, ohne alle gefundenen Parallelen vorführen zu können. Wer meint, daß ein Dichter wie Hartmann schlicht aus dem Überschwang seines Herzens schreibt, möge verzeihen, ich halte Hartmanns bekannte, unter ständischem Gesichtspunkt ein wenig paradoxe, gleichwohl im Verknüpfen von Dichten und Muße seit alters legitime und schulmäßige *captatio benevolentiae* für den ernst zu nehmenden obersten Grundsatz seines Schaffens: er schreibt als 'rîter', indes als einer, 'der gelêret was' (*Iw*. 21–25).

Hartmann spricht zunächst von der *güete* als etwas, an das man sein *gemüete* wendet (*Iw*. 1f.). *guoti* oder *daz guot* ist Übersetzung von *bonum*;[46] *güete* gliche wohl eher noch *bonitas*, was nach Isidor mit Bezug auf den Geist, *animus*, gebraucht wird.[47] Was sich der *güete* zuwendet, nennt Hartmann *gemüete*, viel belegte Übersetzungsgleichung von *animus*, die offenbar wie dies neben dem rationalen Vermögen die affektive Strebkraft meint, ein Wollen aus der Empfindung heraus; denn *gemüete* bedeutet nicht nur allgemein 'Stimmung', 'Empfindung', sondern speziell 'Verlangen', 'Lust', 'Begehren', 'Gesuch', 'Ansinnen'.[48] Schon Plato und besonders der zu Hartmanns Zeit übersetzt zugängliche Aristoteles reflektieren das Gute der Kunst wie der *doctrina* und des Handelns als Gegenstand von Verlangen und Begehren, als etwas, 'wonach alles strebt'.[49] Cicero greift neben anderem zu dieser Definition

---

[45] *Topica: translatio Boethii, fragmentum recensionis alterius, et translatio anonyma*, hg. von Laurentius Minio-Paluello und B.G. Dod, Aristoteles latinus, V, 1–3 (Brüssel/Paris, 1969), III.1–6, S. 50–63.

[46] Ich beziehe mich hier und im folgenden bei lateinisch-mhd. Übersetzungsgleichungen auf das im Hamburger Archiv des Lateinisch-Mhd. Handwörterbuches exzerpierte Material. Es ist allerdings häufig spätmittelalterlich; siehe die Aufstellung bei Edeltraut Weigel, 'Ein neues Lateinisch-Mittelhochdeutsches Handwörterbuch: Arbeitsbericht und Probeartikel', *Mittellateinisches Jahrbuch*, 20 (1985), 323–39. Ich danke Frau Weigel herzlich, daß sie mir Einsicht gewährte in die zu den hier interessierenden Lemmata bereits vorliegenden Manuskripte.

[47] *Etymologiae* (wie Anm. 3), X.23: 'Bonus a venustate corporis creditur dictus: postea et ad animum translatum nomen.'

[48] Georg Friedrich Benecke, Wilhelm Müller, Friedrich Zarncke, *Mittelhochdeutsches Wörterbuch*, Bd. II, 1 (Leipzig, 1863), Sp. 257b; Matthias Lexer, *Mittelhochdeutsches Handwörterbuch*, Bd. I (Leipzig, 1872), Sp. 847f.

[49] *Ethica Nicomachea, Translatio antiquior* (wie Anm. 37), I.1, S. 65,4–6: 'Omnis ars et omnis doctrina, similiter autem et operacio et proheresis (eligencia), boni alicuius optatrix esse videtur. Ideoque optime enunciant bonum, quod omnia optant.' *Translatio Grosseteste*, ebd., I.1, S. 141,5–7: 'Omnis ars et omnis doctrina, similiter autem et actus et eleccio, bonum quoddam appetere videtur. Ideo bene enunciaverunt bonum, quod omnia

des *bonum*, und mit Nachdruck spricht Seneca vom *bonum optabile* und vom Wollen als Voraussetzung für das Gutsein, ein Gedanke, der übrigens bei christlichen Lehrern Anklang findet, wenn sie auch andere Aspekte der antiken Überlieferung über das Gute mit der Bibel weglassen oder mit Augustin ganz anders fragen.[50] Alcuin aber lehrt: 'Est enim mentibus hominum veri boni naturaliter inserta cupiditas', und zuvor reflektiert Boethius das Gute wiederholt als das Erstrebenswerte:[51]

> Offenbar also bezieht sich alles übrige auf das Gute. Deshalb wird nämlich das Genügen erstrebt, weil es als das Gute begriffen wird, deshalb die Macht, weil auch sie für das Gute gehalten wird, dasselbe läßt sich von Ehrwürdigkeit, Glanz, Ergötzlichkeit behaupten. Also ist die Summe und die Ursache alles Erstrebenswerten das Gute. Was aber weder der Sache noch der Ähnlichkeit nach irgend ein Gutes in sich enthält, kann man auf keine Weise erstreben. Andrerseits wird auch, was von Natur nicht gut ist, erstrebt, wenn es nur scheint, daß es wahrhaftig gut sei. So kommt es, daß man mit Recht glaubt, daß das Gutsein Summe, Angelpunkt und Ursache alles Erstrebenswerten sei.

Als *quoddam appetibile* gilt das Gute allenthalben und dabei wird, wenn es sich nicht um irrend erstrebtes Scheingut handelt, die Rechtheit als Qualität des erstrebten Guten betont, wie wir es in Hartmanns Sentenz finden in der Formulierung *rehte güete* (*Iw.* 1). Johannes von Salisbury

appetunt.' So auch *Textus recognitus*, ebd., S. 375,4–6. Vgl. die Übersetzung Gohlkes (wie Anm. 37), S. 17: 'Jede Kunst und jede Planung, ebenso jede Handlung und jeder Entschluß scheinen ein Gut vor Augen zu haben. Daher hat man sehr richtig das Gute als das hingestellt, wonach alles strebt.' Vgl. auch *Topica: translatio Boethii* (wie Anm. 45), III.1, S. 50,19: 'omnia enim bona appetunt'; und weiter die Stellen bei H. Reiner, 'Gut', in *Historisches Wörterbuch der Philosophie*, Bd. III, hg. von Joachim Ritter (Darmstadt, 1974), Sp. 937–46 (Sp. 939f.).

[50] *De finibus bonorum et malorum* (wie Anm. 8), I.9.29, 12.42; *Tusculanae disputationes* (wie Anm. 9), V.15.45: 'Denn alles, was so beschaffen ist, daß es gut ist, ist zu erstreben; was aber zu erstreben ist, das ist gewiß billigenswert; was man aber billigt, das muß man für angenehm und willkommen halten: folglich ist ihm auch Würdigkeit beizulegen. Verhält es sich auf diese Weise, so muß es notwendig lobenswert sein; jedes Gut ist also lobenswert. Hieraus folgt, daß das Sittlichgute allein das Gute ist.' – Seneca (wie Anm. 3) *Ep.*, 66.52, 67.3 und 5: 'si virtus optabilis est, nullum autem sine virtute bonum est, omne bonum optabile est' u. ö. in diesem Brief; 80.4: 'Quid tibi opus est, ut sis bonus? Velle'; 94.12; 117.5: 'Expetendum est [. . .] quod bonum est'; 117.17. – Vgl. die von A. Locher und K. Riesenhuber, 'Gut' (wie Anm. 49), Sp. 946–60 (Sp. 948–53, 959), aus Patristik und Mittelalter nachgewiesenen Stellen. Zum im 13. Jahrhundert dominierenden Interesse an ontologischen Fragen des Guten siehe ebd., Sp. 953–60.

[51] Alcuin, 'De grammatica', PL, CI, 850C. Boethius, *Consolatio* (wie Anm. 39), III.10 prosa, S. 138,130–42. Das im Zitat angesprochene Problem der Vielzahl und Hierarchie der Güter, das Boethius aus antiken Schriften kennt, stellt sich für den *Iwein*-Eingang und den später zu betrachtenden Dialog nicht; es wäre indes für weitere Szenen des Werkes wohl zu berücksichtigen.

versteht die 'uera bonitas, ueritas sincera, ratio incorrupta et uera', als
das zwar höchst Geheimnisvolle, doch am meisten zu Erstrebende und
mit Hilfe von *sapientia* und *eloquentia* annähernd Erreichbare; er sieht
den 'ueri bonique appetitum' als ein natürlich anerschaffenes Streben
des Menschen, welchem *Philologia* und *Philosophia* zugleich erzieherisch
zu genügen suchen. Bei ihm entsteht alle Philosophie im Streben nach
dem *summum bonum* und seinem *uerum*:

> Peripatheticorum hinc orta est secta, que in cognitione ueri
> summum bonum uite humane esse constituit. Omnium ergo
> rerum naturas scrutati sunt, ut scirent quid in omnibus rebus
> fugiendum tanquam malum, quid contemnendum tanquam non
> bonum, quid petendum ut simpliciter bonum, quid preferendum
> ut maius bonum, quid ex casu boni nomen sortiatur aut mali. Nate
> sunt ergo due partes philosophie, naturalis et moralis, que aliis
> nominibus ethica et phisica appellantur. Sed quia per imperitiam
> disserendi multa inconuenientia colligebant [. . .] Et hic quidem,
> sicut Boetius in commento secundo super Porphirium asserit, est
> ortus logice discipline.[52]

Damit wird das Gute in der alten wie mittelalterlichen Philosophie als
rectum erstrebt, und dies im Sinne des *verum*, aber auch des *iustum*.
Betrachtet sei zuerst die Intelligibilität und Wahrheit des Guten. Plato
und Aristoteles verstehen das Gute im einzelnen verschieden als wahr,
insofern es dem menschlichen Intellekt faßbar ist und in seiner Substanz
als Gut erkannt werden kann. 'Virtus non aliud quam recta ratio est.
Omnes virtutes rationes sunt', schreibt Seneca, der *virtus* als *unicum
bonum* und das *summum illud hominis bonum* ans rationale Vermögen des
Menschen gebunden sieht: 'Ratio ergo arbitra est bonorum ac
malorum.' Cicero, dem das Gute ebenfalls allein als Sittlichgutes
zugleich das Billigenswerte bedeutet und für den Klugheit die Wahl
zwischen Gutem und Schlechtem ist, widmet sich der Rechtfertigung
des Guten in immer neuen umfänglichen Schlüssen, wobei er den
jeweils angewandten Modus nicht selten mit anspricht und bekanntlich
einen sehr bewußten Umgang mit der Sokratischen Gesprächstechnik
zeigt.[53] Er möchte wie ein gewöhnlicher Mensch, sagt er einmal, das
Gute 'nach mutmaßlichen Schlüssen' als das zu Billigende darlegen,
denn 'über die Erkenntnis des Wahrscheinlichen hinauszugehen', sei er

---

52 *Metalogicon* (wie Anm. 3), IV.29.933ac; II.2.858ab (zitiert).
53 Seneca (wie Anm. 3), *Ep.* 66.35, 66.32f., 71.27f. und 32f., 77.11, 94.8 u. ö. Cicero,
Tusculanae disputationes (wie Anm. 3), V.15.45 (zitiert in Anm. 50); ebd. V.23.67: 'Was aber
ist dem Menschen besser als sein scharfsichtiger und guter Geist? [. . .] das Gut des
Geistes aber ist die Tugend'. Vgl. *De officiis* (wie Anm. 8), I.4.11–7.20: über Erkenntnis und
Wahrheit als Grundlage des pflichtgemäßen, ehrenvollen und glücklichen Lebens. Vgl.
ebd., III.17.71, und Stellen aus Plato und Aristoteles bei Reiner (wie Anm. 49), Sp. 940–44.

nicht imstande.[54] Ciceros Dialoge und Verwandtes, etwa bei Seneca, regen offenbar dialogische Form in verschiedenen späteren Werken an.[55] Auch Boethius trägt durch zunehmend von logisch rhetorischem Schließen bestimmte Diktion der für ihn bedingt gegebenen Intelligibilität des *verum bonum* Rechnung;[56] direkt oder indirekt mag seine *Consolatio philosophiae* hiermit und ebenso mit der Wortverbindung *verum bonum* Hartmann und seinen Zeitgenossen den Weg gewiesen haben beim poetisch philosophischen Umgang mit *rehter güete*.

Johannes von Salisbury stellt folgende Gedankenreihe auf: 'At ueritas materia est prudentie et uirtutum fons; quam qui bene nouerit, sapiens est, qui amauerit, bonus, et beatus qui tenuerit eam.' Wie dieser mit Cicero erklärt Wilhelm von Conches Tugend als vernunftgemäß;[57] auch Wernher von Elmendorf argumentiert im selben Sinne.[58] Eingangs seiner Abhandlung über die hypothetischen Schlüsse erläutert Abaelard, wie das *bonum* durch die 'honestatis sive utilitatis discretio' als ein *verum* dem wissenden Intellekt zugänglich ist und als solches für rechtes Handeln unabdingbar.[59] Ohne daß es wie bei Abaelard um die

---

[54] *Tusculanae disputationes* (wie Anm. 3), I.9.17; hier geht es um den Beweis dessen, daß der Tod kein Übel, sondern ein Gut sei.

[55] Nach Seth Lerer, *Boethius and Dialogue: Literary Method in 'The Consolation of Philosophy'* (Princeton, 1985), Kap. 1, sind dies besonders Fulgentius' *De continentia Virgiliana*, auch Augustins *Soliloquia* und *De magistro*, sowie Boethius' *Consolatio*.

[56] *Consolatio* (wie Anm. 39), III.3 prosa, S. 100,1–6: 'Auch ihr, irdische Geschöpfe, träumt, wenn auch unter einem dürftigen Abbild, von eurem Ursprung, und mögt ihr auch dieses wahre Ziel der Glückseligkeit durchaus nicht erkennen, so ahnt ihr es doch irgendwie in euren Gedanken. Die Absicht eurer Natur führt euch dorthin und zum wahren Guten (*ad verum bonum*), und nur der vielgestaltige Irrtum lenkt euch davon ab.' Der Terminus *verum bonum* noch ebd., III.11 prosa, S. 142,14 (zitiert in Anm. 72). Das im folgenden aus der *Consolatio* Zitierte mag einen Eindruck von den Schlüssen vermitteln, mit denen Boethius das *verum bonum* traktiert; vgl. besonders die in Anm. 81 genannte Stelle. Allerdings treten in der *Consolatio* neben die dialektische Rhetorik zunehmend allegorische Bilder und Mythen wie die von Odysseus, Orpheus und Herkules und deren poetisch philosophisches Implikat und schließlich das Schweigen des Weisen. Dazu Lerer (wie Anm. 55), Kap. 2: zur Dialektik des Dialogs; Kap. 4: zu den allegorischen Mythen; Kap. 5: zum schweigenden Hören auf die Stimme der Philosophie.

[57] *Metalogicon* (wie Anm. 3), II.1.858a. Cicero, *De inventione* (wie Anm. 8), II.53.159f.; nach Holmberg (wie Anm. 3), S. 7. Wilhelm von Conches, *Moralium dogma* (wie Anm. 3), S. 7,11f.: 'Virtus uero est habitus animi in modum nature rationi consentaneus.'

[58] Im Sinne des *rectum bonum* erweist er dessen Gegenteil, Widersinn, Unrecht und Unwert törichter, nicht guter Freundschaft; Wernher (wie Anm. 41), S. 23f., 439–70: 'von tummir minne saltu dich huten./ si lenget sich selden mit guten,/ si kumit dicke zcu leide./ wil tu, daz ich dir daz bescheide?/ manic wunschit siner ammien:/ "muste si eine sucht ligen!" [. . .]/ so denket ein andir an sime mute:/ "eia, rechten gute,/ solde si rumin daz lant;" [. . .]/ so denket ein andir stille:/ "daz mere in ist nicht min wille,/ daz sine me hete zu lebin, [. . .]"/ daz viande vndir in solden,/ daz wunschin di tummen iren holden. [. . .]/ nu lobich nicht vil baz/ der tummen minne denne den haz.'

[59] 'Tractatus quartus de ypoteticis', in *Dialectica* (wie Anm. 44), Prologus, S. 469,15–25: 'Est enim scientia veritatis rerum comprehensio, cuius species est sapientia, in qua Fides consistit. Hec autem est honestatis sive utilitatis discretio; veritas autem veritati non est adversa. Non enim sicut falsum falso vel malum malo contrarium potest reperiri, ita verum vero vel bonum bono potest adversari, sed omnia sibi bona consona sunt et convenientia.

Modalitäten des Urteils ginge, ist auch für Cicero und Johannes von Salisbury in Lob und Ehre ein Urteil über die Güte des gelobten und geehrten Menschen enthalten.[60] Im *Speculum morale* heißt es: 'particulare bonum [. . .] est quoddam appetibile. Et similiter bonum secundum propriam rationem prout est finis appetitus' und weiter: 'est quoddum verum, inquantum est quoddam intelligibile'; oder noch einmal mit Vincenz zur *veritas bonitatis*: sie ist 'accepta veritas', ist benennbar und beurteilt die 'æqualitas rei ad suam regulam'.[61]

Cicero und Seneca verstehen das *bonum* zugleich als den Habitus der Tugend und Gerechtigkeit, als das Gesetzmäßige, wenn sie das Gute nicht nur als *rectum*, sondern auch als *iustum* ansprechen: 'iustum est et honestum, continet ratio; iustitia bonum'.[62] Aristoteles sieht es ähnlich,[63] es gibt daneben in der Antike aber auch andere Auffassungen des Guten, etwa die im Mittelalter oft abgelehnte epikureische, der *voluptas* als erstrebtes *summum bonum* gilt.[64] Ähnlich wie Cicero und Seneca, die Johannes von Salisbury mit anderen Autoren öfter zum Thema nennt, betrachtet letzterer tugendhaftes Leben als Fundament des Gutseins und des Lobs derer, 'qui bene iudicant'.[65] Johannes hält es zwar für möglich, daß jemand 'certe dolis et fallaciis contendit, uolens uideri bonus esse quod non est', wahrhaftes Gutsein, Anerkennung und Glück garantieren ihm aber allein der *amor iusti*, die mit ihm

Scientia autem omnis bona est, et ea que de malo est, que iusto deesse non potest. Ut enim iustus malum caveat, eum prenosse malum necesse est; neque enim vitaret nisi prenosceret. Cuius itaque mala est actio, bona potest esse cognitio, ut, cum malum sit peccare, bonum est tamen peccatum cognoscere, quod aliter non possumus vitare.'

60   Cicero, *De finibus* (wie Anm. 8), II.14.45–47: 'Honestum igitur id intellegimus, quod tale est ut detracta omni utilitate sine ullis praemiis fructibusve per se ipsum possit iure laudari' usw. *Policraticus* (wie Anm. 3), VIII.14.768b und 769b.

61   *Speculum morale* (wie Anm. 42), I.3.76, Sp. 407D: 'ergo veritas includit rationem bonitatis'; 406E–07A: 'veritas dupliciter accipi potest. Uno modo secundum quod veritate aliquid dicitur verum [. . .] Sic enim accepta veritas, non est habitus, quod est genus virtutis, sed æqualitas quedam intellectus, vel signi ad rem intellectam et signatam, vel etiam rei, ad suam regulam.'

62   Seneca (wie Anm. 3), *Ep.* 95.63, 117.8, 94.31–34, 113.17–20. Cicero, *Paradoxa* (wie Anm. 37), I.9, S. 260: 'quod rectum et honestum et cum virtute est id solum opinor bonum'. *De finibus* (wie Anm. 8), II.8.25: 'Quia quod bene, id recte, frugaliter, honeste'; vgl. 22.71; *De officiis* (wie Anm. 8), I.7.20, II.9.36–12.42, II.18.63f.

63   *Ethica Nicomachea, Translatio antiquior* (wie Anm. 37), I.1, S. 67,5; ebd., 3, S. 70,7–71,1; 9, S. 82,7–10: 'Optimum quod iustissimum, bonum sanum esse; delectabilissimum vero, quod quid optat habere. Omnia enim hec existunt operacionibus optimis; has autem vel unam harum optimam inquimus esse felicitatem.' *Translatio Grosseteste* I.2, S. 142,32f.; 4, S. 145,4–146,2; 11, S. 154,2–7; *Textus recognitus* I.1, S. 376,20f.; 3, S. 378,18–379,12; 9, S. 386,27–30.

64   Cicero, *Tusculanae disputationes* (wie Anm. 3), V.30.84f. Zur Ablehnung der epikureischen Auffassung zugunsten der stoischen siehe Mausbach (wie Anm. 7), Bd. II, S. 58–69.

65   *Tusculanae disputationes* (wie Anm. 9), I.46.110: 'Männer von so vortrefflichen Eigenschaften [. . .] nicht nach dem Rufe der großen Menge, sondern nach dem wahren Lobe der Guten bemessend'; *De officiis* (wie Anm. 8), II.12.42. Johannes von Salisbury, *Policraticus* (wie Anm. 3), VIII.13.764c, 14.769a, 768b–69b. Weitere Stellen im 'Index auctorum' in Webbs Ausgabe.

gegebenen *labores* und nicht etwa der *amor commodi*, wie die Epikureer gemeint hätten, eher schon sehe er das Problem wie die *Consolatio Philosophiae*.[66] Boethius versteht Tugend als das Gute, Untugend als das Böse und meint im Kontext von Strafbarkeit, 'quisquam negabit, bonum esse omne, quod iustum est, contraque, quod iniustum est, malum'.[67] Im *Speculum morale* findet sich ebenfalls mit Berufung auf Cicero, auch Augustin und andere Theologen eine lange Abhandlung über die *veritas bonitatis* im zweiten Sinne, nämlich als *habitus* des Gerechtseins und als spezielle, der *iustitia* zuzuordnende *virtus*.[68]

Beide Implikate der Rechtheit des Guten scheint Hartmann im *Iwein*-Prolog anzusprechen, wobei sie in der Sentenz nur im Attribut *rehte*, im Exempel wohl in vollerem Umriß erscheinen; Sentenz und Exempel bedeuten aber in verschiedener Form dasselbe, wie ihre Verbindung durch den relativischen Anschluß mit *des* zeigt. Hartmann meint offenbar die Erkennbarkeit des Guten, seine intelligible *veritas*, wenn er mit Chrestien (*Yv.* 37f.) die *lantliute* des Königs anführt als diejenigen, die seine *güete* und deren Ruhm als *die wârheit* bezeugen (*Iw.* 12f.). Und zugleich erscheint *güete* unter dem Aspekt des Gebotenen als rechtmäßiger Habitus, Tugend, wenn Hartmann sie mit ritterlich löblichem Bemühen des Königs um allgemein vollkommene Lebensführung verbindet (*Iw.* 6–9).

Als Gewinn, den derjenige zu erwarten hat, der sich dem rechten Guten strebend zuwendet, beschreibt Hartmann neben der *sælde* die *êre*, wählt also Übersetzungsgleichungen von *beatitudo* oder *felicitas* bzw. *honos* oder *honestum*. Ähnlich sieht es Seneca: 'Per se enim colligitur unum bonum esse, quod honestum, per se rursus, ad vitam beatam satis esse virtutem. Si unum bonum est, quod honestum, omnes concedunt ad beate vivendum sufficere virtutem; e contrario non remittetur, si beatum sola virtus facit, unum bonum esse, quod honestum est.'[69] Auch dieser Gedanke ist im Schulwissen über das Gute vielfach zu finden, nicht erst seit Cicero wie dann Seneca das *honeste vivere* als Bedingung des *iucunde vivere* sah, das *honestum* gar wie Seneca als *summum bonum*, und dabei im *honestum* die Tugend mit der ihr von außen zukommenden Anerkennung und Achtung meinte.[70] Schon die

---

[66] Ebd., VIII.14.769b, VII.15. 671d–72b.
[67] *Consolatio* (wie Anm. 39), IV.4 prosa, S. 190,69–71.
[68] Vincenz von Beauvais (wie Anm. 42), I.71, Sp. 407B–08C.
[69] Seneca (wie Anm. 3), *Ep.* 85.17; auch 93.3–5, 94.42f., 95.4–6.
[70] *De finibus* (wie Anm. 8), I.18.57–19.63, II.14.45–15.50; *Paradoxa Stoicorum* (wie Anm. 37), I.15; *Tusculanae disputationes* (wie Anm. 9), V.15.45, V.16.48: 'Ferner, wie läßt es sich denken, daß der gute Mann nicht alle seine Handlungen und Gedanken auf das Lobenswerte beziehe. Nun aber bezieht er alles auf das glückselige Leben; glückselig ist also das lobenswerte Leben; und nichts ist ohne Tugend lobenswert; also wird das glückselige Leben durch die Tugend zustande gebracht.' – Seneca (wie Anm. 3), *Ep.* 71.7: ' "Si vis", inquit (sc. Socrates), "beatus esse, si fide bona vir bonus, sine contemnat te

Nikomachische Ethik bringt hierzu Einschlägiges, das an Hartmanns *Erec*
erinnert mit dem Hinweis, daß jemand, der in der Öffentlichkeit Ehre
auf der Grundlage von Tugend und als Zeugnis seines Gutseins sucht,
dies glückselige Ziel auch verschlafen kann, wenn er nämlich sein Leben
tatenlos verbringt und dann das Ärgste erleiden muß.[71] Boethius
verknüpft Tugend mit Ehre, das zuhöchst Exzellente ist auch ihm das
Gerühmteste; er setzt Genügen, Ehre, Glanz und Macht der Substanz
nach dem Glückseligen gleich; er nimmt es, wie schon Cicero
ausführlich darlegt, für klar erwiesen, 'daß die Substanz der Glückseligkeit und des Guten eine und dieselbe ist'.[72] Wilhelm von Conches
nennt die vier Kardinaltugenden 'officia bene beateque viuendi'; er
sagt: 'gloria est alicuius magnifici uel bone artis late patens preconium',
und weiß mit Horaz, daß der Ruhm ein zweites Leben zu geben vermag,

aliquis.'' Hoc nemo praestabit, nisi qui omnia bona exaequaverit, quia nec bonum sine
honesto est et honestum in omnibus par est.' Ebd., 71.4f.: 'summum bonum est, quod
honestum est [. . .] Hoc liqueat, nihil esse bonum nisi honestum, et omnia incommoda
suo iure bona vocabuntur, quae modo virtus honestaverit.' 118.9: 'bonum
honestumque'.
71 *Ethica Nicomachea, Translatio antiquior* (wie Anm. 37), I.3, S. 70,7–71,1; *Translatio
Grosseteste* I.4, S. 145,4–146,1: 'Bonum enim et felicitatem, non irracionabiliter videntur
ex hiis que huius vite sunt estimare (vel existimare) [. . .] Qui autem excellentes et
operativi, honorem (sc. adipiscuntur). Civilis enim vite, fere hic est finis. Videtur autem
magis superficietenus esse eo quod queritur. Videtur enim in honorantibus magis esse,
quam in honorato. Bonum autem proprium quid, et quod difficile aufertur esse
divinamus. Amplius autem videntur honorem querere, ut credant se ipsos bonos esse.
Querunt igitur a prudentibus honorari, et apud eos a quibus cognoscuntur, et in virtute.
Manifestum igitur quoniam secundum hos, virtus melior est. Forsitan autem et magis
utique aliquis finem civilis vite, hanc existimet. Videtur autem inperfeccior et hec.
Videtur enim contingere et dormire habentem virtutem, vel non operari per vitam. Et
cum hiis mala pati, et infortunatum esse plurimum (seu maxime). Ita autem viventem,
nullus utique felicitabit (id est felicem dicet), nisi posicionem custodiat.' *Textus
recognitus* ebd., I.3, S. 378,18–379,12.
72 *Consolatio* (wie Anm. 39), II.6 prosa, S. 74,11–13: 'Ita fit, ut non virtutibus ex
dignitate, sed ex virtute dignitatibus honor accedat.' Dazu ebd., II.7 prosa, S. 84,78–81,
und carmen 1–14; III.4 prosa, S. 106,20: 'Inest enim dignitas propria virtuti, quam
protinus in eos, quibus fuerit adiuncta, transfundit.' III.2 prosa, S. 96,66–68: 'Sed
sequestrari nequit, quin omne, quod excellentissimum sit, id etiam videatur esse
clarissimum.' III.9 prosa, S. 124,46–49: 'Atqui illud quoque per eadem necessarium est
sufficientiae, potentiae, claritudinis, reverentiae, iucunditatis nomina quidem diversa,
nullo modo vero dicrepare substantiam.' III.9 prosa, S. 126,88–93: 'Nam nisi fallor, ea
vera est et perfecta felicitas, quae sufficientem, potentem, reverendum, celebrem
laetumque perficiat. Atque ut me interius animadvertisse cognoscas, quae unum
horum, quoniam idem cuncta sunt, veraciter praestare potest, hanc esse plenam
beatitudinem sine ambiguitate cognosco.' III.11 prosa, S. 142f.,14–19: '(monstravimus)
Tum autem verum bonum fieri, cum in unam veluti formam atque efficientiam
colliguntur, ut, quae sufficientia est, eadem sit potentia, reverentia, claritas atque
iucunditas, nisi vero unum atque idem omnia sint, nihil habere, quo inter expetenda
numerentur'; siehe weiter ebd., 20–31; III.10 prosa, S. 140,129f. – Cicero, *De finibus* (wie
Anm. 8), I.2.5: 'quae autem de bene beateque vivendo a Platone disputata sunt'; I.5.14,
II.15.48–50, 27.88: 'Qui bonum omne in virtute ponit, is potest dicere perfici beatam
vitam perfectione virtutis'; *Tusculanae disputationes* (wie Anm. 9), V, behandelt laut
Überschrift insgesamt diese Gleichung: 'Es wird gezeigt, die Tugend genüge sich selbst
zum glückseligen Leben.'

'secundam uitam dat gloria';[73] ähnlich wie Hartmann es mit der Artussage berichtet (*Iw*. 14–17).[74] Freilich, wie das Leben nach dem Tode so ist nach Augustin und Boethius das höchste Gut, die höchste Ehre wie das höchste Glück allein in Gott, der alles andere außer ihm schuf,[75] und damit kann menschliche Ehre nur als ein sekundäres Indiz geschaffener Güte gedacht sein. Wie Wernher von Elmendorf[76] sieht Johannes von Salisbury mit Cicero Ruhm und Ehre als Widerschein von Tugend; er meint, daß Ehre als Anerkennung der Tugend an Urteil und Urteilsvermögen gebunden ist, wie weit früher Aristoteles sagt. Im *Speculum morale* heißt es, *honor* gebe ein gewisses Zeugnis von der exzellenten *bonitas* eines Menschen: 'Dicendum quod honor testificationem quandam importat de excellentia alicuius'; genauer: 'Dicendum quod [. . .] honor nihil aliud est quam quaedam protestatio de excellentia bonitatis alicuius.'[77]

An ausgezeichnetes, vortreffliches Gutsein, *excellentia bonitatis* (das erinnert an Cicero),[78] ist das Zuteilwerden der Ehre gebunden gedacht worden, und so sieht es doch auch Hartmann in Sentenz wie Exempel:

---

[73] *Moralium dogma philosophorum* (wie Anm. 3), S. 81f., vgl. 66,15f.; 66, 22–67,6. Horaz, *Opera*, hg. von Friedrich Klingner, 3. Aufl. (Leipzig, 1959), Carm. IV.8.28: 'dignum laude virum Musa vetat mori' (nach Holmberg (wie Anm. 3), S. 66, Anm.). Cicero, *Tusculanae disputationes* (wie Anm. 3), I.46.110, bringt Beispiele von Männern, deren Ruhm ihren Tod überdauerte.

[74] Vgl. die Chronik des Herman van Doornik, *Miracula Sanctae Mariae Laudunensis* von 1143. Nach Hubert Lampo und Pieter Paul Koster, *Artus und der Gral*, übers. von Clemens Wilhelm (München, 1985), S. 12–14.

[75] Augustin (wie Anm. 38), S. 855,3–9: 'Summum bonum, quo superius non est, deus est; ac per hoc incommutabile bonum est; ideo uere aeternum et uere inmortale. cetera omnia bona nonnisi ab illo sunt, sed non de illo. de illo enim quod est, hoc quod ipse est; ab illo autem quae facta sunt, non sunt quod ipse. ac per hoc si solus ipse incommutabilis, omnia quae fecit, quia ex nihilo fecit, mutabilia sunt.' Boethius, *Consolatio* (wie Anm. 39), III.9 prosa, S. 128,110–115; III.10 prosa, S. 132,23–134,82, hier 79–82: 'Wir haben jedoch geschlossen, daß sowohl die Glückseligkeit wie auch Gott höchstes Gut sind; also muß die höchste Glückseligkeit dasselbe sein wie die höchste Gottheit.'

[76] Vgl. Wernher (wie Anm. 41), S. 8, 143–48: 'manic is, der sich niene versinnet,/ als man in loben beginnet,/ vnd denket an sime gemute,/ is kume von siner gute/ vnd von siner frumekeit,/ vnd kumez zu groser erbeit.' Cicero, *De officiis* (wie Anm. 8), I.14.45–15.46, 20.67, 18.61, 24.82, III.8.35. *Tusculanae disputationes* (wie Anm. 9), I.45.109: 'so begleitet er (d. h. der Ruhm) doch die Tugend wie ihr Schatten.' Johannes von Salisbury, *Policraticus* (wie Anm. 3), VIII.15.772c: 'gloria, quae est, ut Ciceroni placuit, frequens fama cum laude, a radice uirtutis oritur et ipsius lumine dumtaxat illustratur.' Der Herausgeber nennt hierzu Cicero, *De inventione* (wie Anm. 8), II.55.166; vgl. weiter die Stellen in Anm. 60. *Nikomachische Ethik* (wie Anm. 37), I.3, S. 22: 'Die Vernünftigen und die Tatmenschen aber suchen die Ehre. Das ist ja das Ziel des Lebens in der Öffentlichkeit. Es scheint jedoch für das, was wir suchen, zu oberflächlich zu sein, nämlich mehr von denen abzuhängen, die die Ehre erweisen, als von dem, dem man sie erweist, und wir meinten doch, das Gute sei einem zu eigen und nicht leicht zu entziehen. Auch scheinen jene die Ehre zu suchen, um sich zu vergewissern, daß sie gut sind. Sie suchen also die Ehre bei den Verständigen und ihren Bekannten, und zwar aufgrund einer Tugend.'

[77] Wie Anm. 42, I.3.72, Sp. 393E, 394B.

[78] *Tusculanae disputationes* (wie Anm. 9), V.23.67: 'alles, was schön, sittlichgut und vortrefflich ('praeclarus') ist.' Vgl. auch *De officiis* (wie Anm. 8), I.18.61.

'Artûs der guote' (*Iw.* 5) hat 'gelebet alsô schône/ daz er der êren krône/ dô truoc' (*Iw.* 9–11); *schône* hat er gelebt, also 'schön', 'vollkommen', 'sich auszeichnend' als *der guote*, deshalb wurde ihm soviel *êre* zuteil. – Ehre als rechtmäßige Anerkennung von sittlicher Qualität ist gemäß damaliger philosophischer Ethik etwas, das den Menschen anzieht, 'honestum est quod sua ui nos trahit et sua dignitate nos allicit', und das er methodisch erstreben kann, wie Cicero sagt.[79] Johannes von Salisbury spricht von solchen, 'qui ueram, licet humanarum laudum, gloriam concupiscunt', und betont dabei ihr willentlich zielgerichtetes Handeln: 'dant operam bene iudicantibus non displicere'; ähnlich schreibt Vincenz: 'homines qui volunt honorari, testimonium suae excellentiae quaerunt, ut patet per Philosophum in 8. Ethi.'[80] Allgemein unterscheidet die damalige philosophische Ethik Wollen und Vermögen im menschlichen Handeln, wie etwa *actio recta* und *voluntas recta* bei Seneca oder Boethius.[81] Hartmanns Exempel impliziert dies in den Wörtern *muot* und *kunde strîten* (*Iw.* 6f.), d. h. (in ritterlicher Gesinnung) wollte der gute Artus Ruhm und er vermochte tatsächlich Ruhm zu erringen. Das Ziel des Ringens faßt Hartmann mit *lop*, *êren krône* und *name* (*Iw.* 7–11); der Dichter scheint auch damit im Sinne des gelehrten Diskurses seiner Zeit zu formulieren; denn dort gilt mit je weiterer Bedeutung die terminologische Reihe *laus* (*lop*), *honor* (*êre*), *gloria* (*name*); ich beziehe mich auf den Wortgebrauch bei Cicero, Johannes von Salisbury und im *Speculum morale*.[82]

[79] Wilhelm von Conches, *Moralium dogma* (wie Anm. 3), S. 7,10. Der Herausgeber verweist auf Cicero, *De inventione* (wie Anm. 8), II.52.157f. Vgl. auch Seneca (wie Anm. 3), *Ep.* 118.8f.: 'bonum est quod ad se vocat [. . .] quod petitionem sui movet [. . .] iam et honestum est.' Cicero, *De officiis* (wie Anm. 8), II.12.42f.: Ruhm sei mit Überlegung methodisch zu erwerben; nach Sokrates sei es die kürzeste Straße zum Ruhm, wenn einer es darauf anlegte, daß er so beschaffen wäre, wie er angesehen sein wollte; Ruhm könne man auf Dauer nicht durch Vorspiegelung erwerben, denn er sei Billigung bei den Guten.
[80] *Policraticus* (wie Anm. 3), VIII.14.768b. *Speculum morale* (wie Anm. 42), I.3.72, Sp. 393E. Den Philosophen habe ich nicht identifiziert; ähnlich ist Aristoteles (wie Anm. 71).
[81] Seneca (wie Anm. 3), *Ep.* 95.57; Boethius, *Consolatio* (wie Anm. 39), IV.2 prosa, S. 168,13–18: 'Auf zweierlei beruht alle Wirkung menschlicher Handlungen, auf Wille und Macht; wenn eins von beiden fehlt, kann sich nichts entfalten. Fehlt der Wille, so tritt der Mensch nicht einmal an das heran, was er nicht will, fehlt das Vermögen, so ist der Wille umsonst.' Auf die geschichtlich verschiedene Interpretation von Wollen und Vermögen kann ich hier nicht eingehen. Hartmann hält das Wollen, man sagt mit Abaelard, für wichtiger als das Vermögen; vgl. *Erec*, hg. von Albert Leitzmann, 3. Aufl. besorgt von Ludwig Wolff, ATB, 39 (Tübingen, 1963), 387–95.
[82] Johannes von Salisbury, *Policraticus*, VIII.15.772c (zitiert Anm. 76). Vgl. Cicero, *De inventione* (wie Anm. 8), II.55.166; *De officiis* (wie Anm. 8), III.8.35 (nach Webb, *Policraticus* (wie Anm. 3), S. 335, Anm.). *Speculum morale* (wie Anm. 42), I.3.72, Sp. 394AB: hier die drei benachbarten Begriffe: Zunächst *laus* als Zeugnis 'de bonitate alicuius in ordine ad finem': 'sicut laudamus bene operantes propter finem'. *Honor* dann als Ehre, die den Besten zukommt: 'quae non ordinantur ad finem, sed iam sunt in fine, ut patet per Philosophum in primo Ethi'. Schließlich *gloria*: 'Gloria autem est effectus

Es bleibt noch ein Wort zu *sælde* (*Iw.* 3) zu sagen, das in der Übersetzungsliteratur neben *sælecheit* für *beatitudo* und *felicitas* gebraucht wird. Hartmann versteht es als den erstrebten glückhaften Zustand, der sich für jeden ergibt, wenn er sein Gemüt dem Guten zuwendet. Dies stimmt zu Ciceros Verständnis des glückseligen Lebens als des ungebrochen freudevollen Zustands, der dem Guten durch tugendhaftes Leben erreichbar ist und sich durch die Abwesenheit allen Übels definiert.[83] 'Beata enim vita bonum in se perfectum habet, inexsuperabile. Quod si est, perfecte beata est. Si deorum vita nihil habet maius aut melius, beata autem vita divina est; nihil habet, in quod amplius possit attolli. Praeterea si beata vita nullius est indigens, omnis beata vita perfecta est eademque est et beata et beatissima [. . .] Beatus autem nihil suae praefert', so Seneca.[84] Es berührt sich auch wohl mit Aristoteles und mit Isidors Erklärung des Wortes *beatus* für den, 'qui et habet omnia quae vult bona', auch mit dem Verständnis der *beatitudo* bei Boethius:[85]

> Alle Sorge der Menschen, wie vielfältig auch die Mühe ihrer Bestrebungen sein mag, [. . .] trachtet aber doch nur nach einem Ziele, der Glückseligkeit. Ein Gut aber nenne ich, das nichts weiter zu wünschen läßt, wenn man es erlangt hat; es ist das höchste Gut, in dem alle andern Güter enthalten sind; es wäre das höchste nicht, wenn ihm irgend etwas abginge, da ja dann noch etwas außerhalb verbliebe, was man wünschen könnte. Es ist also klar, daß die Glückseligkeit ein Zustand ist, der durch die Vereinigung aller Güter vollkommen ist.

Johannes von Salisbury möchte dies Ziel aller Menschen wie andere vor ihm besonders auf der *strata regia* der Tugend angestrebt sehen und ebenso der Autor des *Speculum morale*, der aber freilich das

---

honoris et laudis, quia ex hoc quod testificamur de bonitate alicuius, clarescit eius bonitas in notitia plurimorum, et hoc importat nomen gloriæ. Nam gloria dicitur quasi claria, unde Ro.1. dicit quædam Glossa Ambrosii, quod "gloria est clara cum laude notitia".'

[83] Cicero, *Tusculanae disputationes* (wie Anm. 9), V.8.21–23, V.10.28: 'Laß uns sehen, welche wir glückselig nennen müssen. Ich glaube die, welche sich in Gütern befinden, denen kein Übel hinzugefügt ist.' Ausführlicher ebd., V.14.41f.; besonders V.23.67. Vgl. *Paradoxa Stoicorum* (wie Anm. 37), II.17: durch Tugend könne man aus sich selbst der glücklichste Mensch sein.

[84] Wie Anm. 3, *Ep.* 85.19f.; siehe auch *Ep.* 92.

[85] *Ethica Nicomachea, Translatio antiquior* (wie Anm. 37), I.5, S. 75,9–76,15; I.8f., S. 80,12–82,10; I.9f., S. 82,20–83,10. *Translatio Grosseteste*, I.8, S. 149,16–150,2; I.10f., S. 152,22–154,6; I.13, S. 154,21–31. Vgl. ebd. den späteren *Textus recognitus.* Isidor, *Etymologiae* (wie Anm. 3), X.22: 'Beatus dictus quasi bene auctus, scilicet ab habendo quod vellet et nihil patiendo quod nollet. Ille autem vere beatus est qui et habet omnia quae vult bona, et nihil vult male. Ex his enim duobus beatus homo efficitur.' Boethius, *Consolatio* (wie Anm. 39), III.2 prosa, S. 92,2–11; auch III.10 prosa, S. 138,142–140, 150: Erweis der einen Substanz des Guten und der Glückseligkeit.

ungeschmälerte Haben alles Guten, das auch in diesem Werk den ungebrochen freudevollen Zustand der *beatitudo* kennzeichnet, erst im Jenseits für erreichbar hält.[86]

Soweit ich die genannten Texte überblicke, steht Hartmanns Sentenz nicht nur ohne Zweifel Boethius und den genannten von ihm den Terminus des *verum bonum* übernehmenden Autoren nahe, sondern vielleicht auch Ciceros Schlußsatz im ersten seiner *Paradoxa*: 'profecto nihil est aliud bene et beate vivere nisi honeste et recte vivere.'[87] Die Forschung hat bisher, wenn ich recht sehe, zu Hartmanns *rehter güete* weder auf Boethius und seine im Mittellateinischen wie in der Volkssprache bekannte, antikes Denken christlich überformende Prägung des *verum bonum* hingewiesen noch auf diese Stelle aus den *Paradoxa*. In ihrer Formulierung wird das Hartmanns Sentenz terminologisch und gedanklich Entsprechende genauso komprimiert und einprägsam wie bei Hartmann verknüpft; es fehlt, abgesehen von der ungenauen Parallele der Verba *volgen* und *esse*, in Ciceros Satz lediglich ein Äquivalent zu *gemüete* als Strebekraft. Die Ausrichtung des Wollens und Strebens auf das Gute aber ist Cicero sonst geläufig und, wie oben ersichtlich, ein philosophischer Gemeinplatz. Er kann von Hartmann im Sinne des Schulwissens über das Gute leicht und ohne Cicero zu entstellen ergänzt worden sein. Der gelehrte Dichter könnte das Cicero-Wort seit seiner Schulzeit auswendig gewußt haben. Jedoch braucht man hier nichts zu beweisen; Hartmann hat in jedem Fall selbständig ihm und seinen Zeitgenossen geläufiges ethisches Wissen in seine Sprache transponiert.

Es findet sich der Begriffskomplex von *bonum, justum, rectum, honor, gloria, beatitudo, veritas* übrigens auch in der Bibel,[88] wodurch der

---

86 *Policraticus* (wie Anm. 3), VII.8.651bc: 'Illud autem quo omnium rationabilium uergit intentio uera beatitudo est. Nemo etenim est qui non uelit esse beatus; sed ad hoc quod desiderant non una uia omnes incedunt. Vna tamen est omnibus uia proposita sed quasi strata regia scinditur in semitas multas. Haec autem uirtus est; nam nisi per uirtutem nemo ad beatitudinem pergit. Citra uirtutis opera forte quis et procul dubio sine operibus ad beatitudinem trahitur, sed eo nullus nisi uirtutis passibus pergit. Virtus ergo felicitatis meritum est, felicitas uirtutis praemium [. . .] Non enim felix est quis ut recte agat, sed recte agit ut feliciter uiuat.' Johannes bezieht sich sowohl auf die Bibel als auch vor allem auf die Peripathetiker, Stoiker und Epikureer; vgl. ebd., VII.15.671d–72b. – *Speculum morale* (wie Anm. 42), II.4.1, Sp. 842AE.

87 Cicero, *Paradoxa Stoicorum* (wie Anm. 37), I.15. Ausführlicher und etwas anders argumentierend ebd., II.19: 'sic bonus vir et fortis et sapiens miser esse non potest. Nec vero cuius virtus moresque laudandi sunt eius non laudanda vita est, neque porro fugienda vita quae laudanda est; esset autem fugienda si esset misera. Quam ob rem quidquid est laudabile, idem et beatum et florens et expetendum videri debet.'

88 Vgl. *Concordantiarum universae scripturae sacrae thesaurus*, hg. von Étienne Peultier, 2. Aufl. (Paris, 1939), S. 352–54, unter 'diligo'; danach besonders Rom. 2. 10: 'gloria autem, et honor, et pax omni operanti bonum'; Apoc. 7. 12; Eccli. 27. 9; Rom. 2. 7; I Cor. 14. 40; Ps. 98. 4; Ps. 145. 8; Ps. 5. 12; Cant. 1. 3; Amos 5. 15; Prov. 16. 13; Ps. 1. 1; Eccli. 45. 8; Rom. 4. 6; Ps. 126. 5; Ps. 127. 2; Ps. 105. 3; Eccli. 50. 30; Eccli 11. 14f.; Rom. 16. 19; Rom. 13. 3; 2 Par. 6. 8; II Thess. 1, 11; Phil. 2, 13. Die Stellen sind thematisch geordnet.

philosophische Gedanke über die Schultexte hinaus legitimiert worden ist in seinem Anspruch als Lebenslehre. Dies zeigt die zugleich an Schulautoren und Bibelzitaten orientierte Darstellung des Komplexes bei Boethius, Johannes von Salisbury und mehr noch Vincenz von Beauvais. Die Bibelstellen aber, die dem moralischen Philosophem mit einem seiner Termini nahekommen, sind verstreut; sie erfassen es nie als Ganzes. Demnach darf man wohl sagen, daß der Terminus der *rehten güete*, den Hartmann, Reinmar, Wolfram, Gottfried und zuvor lateinische Autoren als das *verum bonum* kennen, wie die ganze Maxime, mit der Hartmann seinen *Iwein* eröffnet, eindeutig ethisches Wissen aus Schulautoren darstellt, dabei der Offenbarungswahrheit keineswegs entgegensteht, diese aber nicht zitiert. Auf Ständisches deutet lediglich das Genetivattribut *rîters* (*Iw.* 6); *strîten* (*Iw.* 7) wird, da Hartmanns Artus nicht kämpft, Metapher sein und 'ringen', 'sich bemühen' oder 'streben' bedeuten. Damit mag resümierend gefolgert werden, daß erstens Hartmann, der gelehrte Ritter, im *Iwein*-Prolog zwar vom ritterlichen König Artus als einer historischen Person spricht, ihn dabei aber als Repräsentanten eines auch in der Sentenz formulierten Allgemeinen nimmt, und daß zweitens dies Allgemeine schulmäßige Philosophie des *bonum, honestum* usw. darstellt, somit ethische *doctrina, scientia moralis* die definitionsgemäß erforderliche *opinio communis* der Sentenz ist wie die im Exemplum vermittelte *gewisse lêre* (*Iw.* 4), – womit Hartmann dem eingangs aus *Accessus* und andern Texten entnommenen schulischen Literaturverständnis seiner Zeit entgegengekommen sein dürfte.

C. Zur Philosophie des Guten in Chrestiens Yvain und Hartmanns Handlungseröffnung

Gegenüber Chrestiens *Yvain*-Beginn bleibt zu betonen, daß dieser zwar auch mit dem von Hartmann wörtlich übernommenen 'Artus, li buens rois de Bretaingne' (*Yv.* 1) beginnt und dies auch in der Absicht, der Figur eine Lehre abzugewinnen; denn es heißt bei Chrestien weiter: 'la cui proesce nos ansaingne/ que nos soiiens preu et cortois' (*Yv.* 2f.). Doch mit den Wörtern 'proesce', 'preu et cortois', die, was Artus lehrt, inhaltlich umreißen, führt Chrestien das Attribut *buens* nicht im Begriffszusammenhang philosophischer Ethik weiter, wie Hartmann es tut. Die richtige Übersetzung von Ilse Nolting-Hauff[89] versteht die

---

[89] Nolting-Hauff (wie Anm. 14), S. 17: 'Artus, der gute König von Britannien, dessen Rittertugend (*proesce*) uns lehrt, ritterlich (*preu*) und höfisch (*cortois*) zu sein.' Vgl. die Belege bei Adolf Tobler und Erhard Lommatzsch, *Altfranzösisches Wörterbuch*, Bd. II (ohne

Wörter als undifferenziertes Bündel ständischer Verhaltenskonventionen, wie sie höfische Literatur auch im Deutschen oft mit *rîterlîch* und *hövesch* zusammenfaßt. Hartmann flicht den Aspekt 'mit rîters muote' (*Iw.* 6) nur einmal, im Vergleich zu seiner Vorlage eher beiläufig ein in seine Schulwissen mit Artus verbindenden Verse (*Iw.* 1–20).

Chrestien erwähnt also eingangs seines *Yvain* nichts vom Konnex des *bonum* mit dem *honestum* samt *laus* und *gloria*, dem *verum*, *iustum* und der *beatitudo*; er gebraucht auch später die Wörter *buen* und *bien*, *mal*, *mauvais* u. ä. sehr oft, ohne das jeweilige gute oder böse Handeln durch Termini der *doctrina moralis* genauer zu präzisieren. Wenn er gelegentlich doch die zugehörigen Begriffe verwendet, zeigt er damit, daß auch er sich auf den Schuldiskurs versteht: so findet man *bien* neben *sage* (*Yv.* 112, 1326f., 6565–75), *bien et bel* (*Yv.* 231, 660), *bien* und *enor* (*Yv.* 779, 1001, 2550–53, 5136), *bien et a droit* (*Yv.* 1772), Gutes, das man sehnlich wünscht (*Yv.* 6659–61), Gutes und Heil (*Yv.* 2551), Gutes und Freude (*Yv.* 1448, 2551, 6803–14), womit der Roman bekanntlich endet. Allerdings sind dies Einzelstellen, die neben den vielen schlichten *buen* und *bien* usw. nicht zuviel Gewicht haben. Chrestien scheint mir kaum denselben Wert wie Hartmann auf solch philosophische Lehre vermittelndes Vokabular gelegt zu haben, wiewohl er es kennt. Jedoch Hartmann wird als aufmerksamer Leser die Stellen, an denen Chrestien das gute Handeln in den genannten Begriffsdoppelungen anspricht, einzuordnen gewußt haben, und er hat das, was er in seiner Vorlage an Reminiszenzen aus dem Schulwissen über das Gute fand, amplifizierend aufgegriffen und zwecks exemplarischer Deutung des Mythos zum werkumfassenden Sinnbezug des erzählten Geschehens auszuweiten verstanden.

Werkumfassend?[90] Bevor das behauptet wird, wäre die Vielschichtigkeit der im ganzen Werk tangierten Diskurse, ihre Verflechtung und die damit implizierten Sinnbezüge des Werks zu erörtern, was wünschenwert wäre, damit auch deutlich wird, wo Hartmanns eigene und vielleicht ausgeprägt ständische Interessen im Verhältnis zu dem hier umrissenen Philosophem liegen. Besonders die juristischen Implikate des Textes wären genauer als bisher zu untersuchen, ob sie gemäß der Gleichung von *bonum* und *iustum* integriert werden, oder ob sie darüber hinausgehen. Wie Galfred beschreibt, blickt Hartmanns Sentenz, ohne schon die Geschichte zu sein, doch auf diese hin und

---

Ort und Jahr), Sp. 921,47–922,19: zu 'cortois'; Bd. VII (Wiesbaden, 1969), Sp. 1922,41–1926,5: zu 'pro/preu' (Adj.); ebd., Sp. 1946,28–1949,14: zu 'proesce'.
[90] Als 'unwandelbarer Leitstern' der Dichtung galt schon Benecke die eingangs wie ausgangs des *Iwein* sich findende Reflexion über *sælde und êre*, und ihm folgt Peter Wapnewski, *Hartmann von Aue*, Sammlung Metzler, M 17, 6. Aufl. (Stuttgart, 1976), S. 78; vorher Hans Schreiber, *Studien zum Prolog in mittelalterlicher Dichtung* (Dissertation, Bonn/Würzburg, 1935), S. 26: 'Das Problem der rechten 'güete' ist im Ablauf des Epos zu lösen.'

steckt zu einem guten Teil deren Sinngefüge ab.[91] Ich muß die Belege aus dem *Iwein*, die den vom Autor offenbar gesuchten gedanklichen Zusammenhang von Sentenz und Geschichte dokumentieren, hier auf ein Beispiel beschränken.

Überdeutlich scheint dieser Zusammenhang gegeben in den Veränderungen, mittels derer Hartmann Laudines und Iweins Heirat neu motiviert durch die *güete* der Frau (*Iw.* 1863–88) und ausdrücklich nicht mehr durch ihren Wankelmut und ihre *folie* (*Yv.* 1638–44). In den langen Gesprächen der Beteiligten verbinden sich, dadurch daß Hartmann die Selbstbezichtigung der Torheit (*Yv.* 1428) durch ihr Gegenteil, *starke sinne* (*Iw.* 1611), ersetzt und das Recht zu hassen (*Yv.* 1432–34) in das Recht der Liebe verwandelt,[92] die Aspekte des *iustum* und *honestum* (*Iw.* 1571–92; 1726–37; 2067) mit dem *utile* (*Iw.* 1918–31; 1978–92), und es entspricht dieses als das affektiv liebend Erstrebte auch dem durch Gott gestifteten *bonum* (*Iw.* 1660–90), das substantiell jetzt als das biblisch paradoxe und gleichwohl höchste sittliche Gebot der Feindesliebe ('Diligite inimicos vestros', Mt. 5. 44; Lc. 6. 27 und 35; 2 Reg. 19. 6) mit nachdrücklicher Wiederholung benannt wird (*Iw.* 1423f., 1541f., 1612f., 1654f.; *Yv.* 1360f., 1449–53), wobei Legitimität und Intelligibilität dieses *bonum* als eines wahrscheinlichen *verum* und *rectum* (*Iw.* 1863–72, 1940, 1954f., 1959–61, 1967) mit schon bei Chrestien angelegten logisch rhetorischen Schlüssen erwiesen ist.[93]

---

[91] Galfred, *Poetria nova*, hg. von Faral (wie Anm. 32), 126–202 (S. 201–03); dies nennen Heinrich Lausberg, *Handbuch der literarischen Rhetorik* (München, 1960), § 279, und Endres (wie Anm. 25, 1966), S. 536. Ähnlich Galfred, *Documentum de modo et arte dictandi et versificandi*, hg. von Faral, ebd., I.7–17 (S. 266–68).

[92] *Iw.* 1625–30, 1647–57. Hartmann läßt seinen Helden offenbar in zweierlei Hinsicht an das Rechtsprinzip der Liebe denken: an der ersten Stelle scheint er das ausgleichende und versöhnende Billigkeitsrecht, den Minnespruch der damals oft geübten Schiedsgerichtspraxis zu meinen, den *amor iudicialis*, wie er auch, als Laudine zur *suone* sich bereit findet, als versöhnendes Rechtsprinzip ihre Überlegungen ausdrücklich prägt (*Iw.* 2015–72). Vgl. Michael Kobler, *Das Schiedsgerichtswesen nach bayerischen Quellen des Mittelalters*, Münchener Universitätsschriften, Reihe der Juristischen Fakultät, Bd. I (München, 1967). Im zweiten Fall handelt es sich um ein naturrechtliches Argument; vorausgesetzt ist hier das im kanonischen Naturrechtsdenken der Zeit begründete Verständnis der Liebe zur Feindin als biblisches *gebot* und *michel reht*. Vgl. Rudolf Weigand, *Die Naturrechtslehre der Legisten und Dekretisten von Irnerius bis Accursius und von Gratian bis Johannes Teutonicus*, Münchener theologische Studien, 3, Kanonistische Abteilung, 26 (München, 1967), S. 193f., 197, 199, 205f., 246 u. ö., zur Auffassung der Liebe als Naturrecht; S. 148, 151, 167f., 190, 192, 208f., 226f., 331 u. ö., zur Auffassung aller Gebote beider Testamente als Naturrecht, darunter auch ausdrücklich das 'Liebet Eure Feinde'. Daß Hartmanns Iwein hier zugleich mit dem Guten, Rechten, Ehrenvollen, Beglückenden und Nützlichen nach sinnlicher Liebeserfahrung strebt, widerspricht nicht dem naturrechtlichen Argument, denn nach Weigand, S. 144, 197, 199, 221, 327 u. ö., ist die vernünftige *discretio boni ac mali*, ist das *honeste vivere* ebenso Naturrecht wie, nach S. 181f., 220f., 222f., 225, 227f., 243, 246, 248, die *sensualitas* und die *maris et femine coniugatio*.

[93] Vgl. *Yv.* 1605–37, 1693–709 und *Iw.* 1610–59, 1665–80, 1796–862, 1890–970, 2015–50, 2084–100 usw. Vgl. Tony Hunt, in diesem Band und weiteres unten in Anm. 98.

Um noch ein weiteres, einfacher zu überschauendes Beispiel zu geben, sei kurz erwähnt, wie verschieden sich Kalogreant in beiden Romanen in seiner Niederlage sieht. Wo Chrestien nämlich allein das Stichwort Schande setzt, flicht Hartmann erneut die ihm als ethische Doktrin vorgegebenen Aspekte und Termini ein. Bei Chrestien heißt es:

> So ließ er mich schmählich ('honteus') liegen [. . .]. Und ich, der ich nicht mehr wußte, was zu tun, blieb voller Gram und Betrübnis zurück. Ich setzte mich ein Weilchen an die Quelle und ruhte mich aus. Dem Ritter zu folgen wagte ich nicht, denn ich fürchtete, eine Torheit zu begehen, wenn ich ihm folgte, und so erfuhr ich auch nie, was aus ihm wurde. Endlich kam mir das Verlangen, meinem Wirt mein Versprechen zu halten und ihn auf dem Rückweg wieder aufzusuchen. Gedacht, getan, doch legte ich alle meine Waffen ab, um leichter ausschreiten zu können, und so kehrte ich mit Schande ('honteusemant') beladen um.[94]

Hartmann legt Kalogreant seine Ehrlosigkeit viermal (*Iw*. 750, 756, 757, 766), also doppelt so oft wie Chrestien, in den Mund und dazu die Unterscheidung von Wille und Werk in bezug auf das Gute: 'mir was der wille harte guot:/ done mohten mir diu werc den muot/ an im niht volbringen' (*Iw*. 759–61), wodurch Kalogreant sich als Gegenbild zu Artus zeigt, von dem es eingangs ja hieß, daß er 'mit rîters muote/ nâch lobe kunde strîten' (*Iw*. 6f.). Außerdem nennt Hartmanns Kalogreant sich wohl wegen der *bona voluntas*, auf die er sich beruft (*Iw*. 759), auch 'ein teil unschuldec' (*Iw*. 758) und berücksichtigt damit den Rechtsaspekt des Guten. Seine Eingeständnisse 'mir was gelückes dâ verzigen' (*Iw*. 748), 'des muost mir misselingen' (*Iw*. 762), 'ich gnâdelôser man' (*Iw*. 780) beziehen negativ den Aspekt der *beatitudo* ein, in 'misselingen', d. h. 'keinen Erfolg haben', 'einen Fehlschlag erleiden', mag auch der Aspekt des *utile* negiert sein.

Hartmann macht also Kalogreant zum Gegenbild des exemplarisch guten und ehrenwerten Artus, und zwar nicht als Autor selbst sprechend wie im Prolog, sondern indem er nun den handelnden Ritter den Sinnbezug zwischen Handlung und durch sie zu vermittelnder Lehre herstellen läßt. Der Autor und seine Personen sprechen in beiden Beispielen im letztlich selben Verständnis der Geschichte.

---

94   *Yv*. 542–60; Nolting-Hauff (wie Anm. 14), S. 41 und 43.

D. Zur topisch argumentativen Darstellung der rehten güete in Dialogen des Iwein

Die eben angeführten Stellen hätten eine Funktion der direkten Rede im Epos zeigen können, um die das in der Forschung zur direkten Rede bei Hartmann bisher Gesagte zu ergänzen wäre, übrigens ganz im Einklang mit der von Diomedes gegebenen und im Schulbetrieb zu Hartmanns Zeit gut bekannten, nur scheinbar banalen Gattungsbeschreibung des Epos als eines Werkes, in dem, wie Diomedes sagt und manche Lehrer des Hochmittelalters wiederholen, der Autor spricht und sprechende Personen eingeführt werden.[95] Autor und Personen sprechen, so meine ich, fast dasselbe; der eine als Betrachter, die anderen als Betroffene widmen sie sich demselben Gegenstand mit denselben Kriterien, nämlich im *Iwein* dem richtigen, erwiesenermaßen Guten, d. h. *rehter güete* im Sinne der damals philosophisch behaupteten Intelligibilität des Guten.

Was heißt aber sprechen? Statt hierüber allgemein mit Schriften aus dem Bereich des Triviums zu handeln, oder nach dem Prolog mit weiteren Erzählerbemerkungen, zu deren Inhalt, Form und Funktion man übrigens einiges nachtragen könnte unter dem Aspekt der Intelligibilität des Guten als des Rechten und des glückhaft Ehrenvollen, seien nun als Beispiele die ersten Reden Keies und der Königin betrachtet, die sich bekanntlich bei Hartmann in einem gegenüber Chrestien deutlich veränderten szenischen Arrangement finden: Keie (*Iw.* 86–92) und nicht mehr Calogrenant (*Yv.* 53–60) steht der übrigen Gesellschaft gegenüber, die Königin wird zu seiner entscheidenden Kontrahentin. In der Tat macht Hartmann die beiden zu Repräsentanten von Gut und Böse,[96] deren Antinomie ihm wichtiger ist als Chrestien,

---

[95] Diomedes, *Ars grammatica*, in *Grammatici Latini*, Bd. I, hg. von Heinrich Keil (Leipzig, 1857; Nachdr. Hildesheim, 1961), S. 482,14–25: 'Poematos genera sunt tria. aut enim activum est vel imitativum [. . .]' (d. h. in Tragödie, Komödie, *satyrica*, *mimica* usw.), 'aut enarrativum vel enuntiativum [. . .]' (d. h. im historischen Gedicht und Lehrbuch), 'aut commune vel mixtum [. . .]' (so in der *species heroica* und übrigens auch der *species lyrica*); es heißt zum *genus mixtum* weiter: 'est vel commune in quo poeta ipse loquitur et personae loquentes introducuntur, ut est scripta Ilias et Odissia tota Homeri et Aeneis Vergilii et cetera his similia.' Dies kennen im 12. Jahrhundert z. B. Bernhard von Utrecht, hg. von Huygens (wie Anm. 3), S. 65,176–82; ein *Accessus Ovidii Epistolarum* (Handschr. T), ebd., S. 32,65–69; vgl. zur Handschrift ebd., S. 2 und 5; *Accessus Lucani*, ebd., S. 44,141–45 ; andere nach Klopsch (wie Anm. 2), S. 45. Diese Gattungsgliederung auch bei Dominicus Gundissalinus; siehe Edgar de Bruyne, *Études d'esthétique médiévale*, 3 Bde. (Brügge, 1946; Nachdr. Genf, 1975), II, 401.

[96] Vgl. H.B. Willson, 'The Role of Keii in Hartmann's *Iwein*', *Medium Ævum*, 30 (1961), 145–58 (S. 154): 'Like the devil and sin itself, he stands condemned for his perversion of order, truth, rightness and justice.' Willson sieht Keie als Kontrastfigur zur *caritas* und mag damit hier die von Hartmann gesuchte Antinomie etwas zu sehr ins Theologische verlagern, wobei indes im weiteren Verlauf der Geschichte doch das sinnstiftende Gute

wenn Hartmann nämlich neben den szenischen Änderungen intensiven Gebrauch macht vom dialektischen *instrumentum*, um das Gute mit schulmäßigem Vorsatz gemäß der oben angesprochenen rationalen Behandlung desselben Gegenstands im Lateinischen[97] argumentativ als das Rechte zu erweisen und das Böse als Unrecht. Beide Dichter können die Rede als Operation logischer Rhetorik aufbauen, darauf ist schon gewiesen worden.[98] Allein, dies ist nicht nur unverbindliches Spiel, in dem der Dichter der 'Freude an genußvoll umständlichen Sophismen und dem spitzfindigen Kanon des Für und Wider [. . .] oft genug die tiefere Logik des sittlichen Urteils' opfert, wie Gruenter es sieht.[99] Bei aller intellektuellen Beweglichkeit und offensichtlich genußvollen gedanklich verbalen 'Akrobatik', selbst bei dem heute durch laxere Einstellung vielleicht komisch anmutenden Mißverhältnis zwischen logisch rhetorischem Aufwand des Dichters und dem Etikettenproblem seiner Personen, bei allen komischen Elementen auch, die die Erzählung von der Jagd auf den unsichtbaren Iwein aufweist, handelt es sich dennoch sowohl in den oben erwähnten langen Dialogen Lunetes und Laudines mit Iwein als auch in der jetzt zu betrachtenden Rede und Gegenrede Keies und der Königin auch um das im Kern ernsthafte Bemühen des Dichters, die *rehte güete* eines bestimmten Handelns im Sinne seines von Anfang des Werks an erkennbaren Vorsatzes nicht einfach zu behaupten, weil es in der Quelle zu lesen steht, oder nur zu glauben, weil Bibel oder geistliche Literatur dies gebieten, sondern sie mit logisch rhetorischen Mitteln als wahrscheinlich recht zu erweisen.

---

biblische Feindesliebe ist. Außerdem Jürgen Haupt, *Der Truchseß Keie im Artusroman*, Philologische Studien und Quellen, 57 (Berlin, 1971), S. 33–46, der zur Stelle zwar wenig bringt (S. 38), aber mit weiteren *Iwein*-Versen richtig beschreibt, wie Hartmann in Keies Herz das Böse in der Auseinandersetzung mit dem Guten obsiegen läßt, so daß Keie mit bösem Herzen Böses spricht. Vgl. weiter Herta Zutt, *König Artus, Iwein, der Löwe: Die Bedeutung des gesprochenen Wortes in Hartmanns 'Iwein'* (Tübingen, 1979), S. 32f., die mit Iw. 38–42 auf den Gegensatz von *bœse* und *guot* im Werkeingang hinweist; auch den nicht so prägnanten Peter Wiehl, *Die Redeszene als episches Strukturelement in den Erec- und Iwein-Dichtungen Hartmanns von Aue und Chrestiens de Troyes*, Bochumer Arbeiten zur Sprach- und Literaturwissenschaft, 10 (München, 1974), S. 252–56; wie Haupt nennt Wiehl mehr Literatur zu Keie.

[97] Vgl. oben um Anm. 4f., 7, 44–49.

[98] Die Opposition als Strukturprinzip des Handlungsentwurfs erörtern Humphrey Milnes, 'The Play of Opposites in *Iwein*', *GLL*, 14 (1960/61), 241–56; John Margetts, 'Gefühlsumschwung in *Iwein*: minne unde haz, luf and envy', in *Großbritannien und Deutschland: Festschrift für John W.P. Bourke*, hg. von Ortwin Kuhn (München, 1974), S. 452–60; Tony Hunt, 'Aristotle, Dialectic, and Courtly Literature', in *Viator: Medieval and Renaissance Studies*, 10 (1979), 95–129, der poetische Beispiele vor allem aus Chrestien auf Texte der *ars dialectica* bezieht. Vgl. vorher auch Rainer Gruenter, 'Über den Einfluß des Genus judiciale auf den höfischen Redestil', *DVjs*, 26 (1952), 49–57, (S. 54f. zum *Iwein*).

[99] Gruenter (wie Anm. 98), S. 54. Hans Joachim Gernentz, *Formen und Funktion der direkten Reden und der Redeszenen in der deutschen epischen Dichtung von 1150 bis 1200* (unpublizierte Habilitationsschrift, Rostock, 1958), S. 292–378: zum *Iwein*; Gernentz stimmt (S. 320) Gruenter zu und sucht weitere ähnliche Textbeispiele, ohne sich allerdings auf die Erfordernisse damaliger Rhetorik und Logik tatsächlich einzulassen.

Der bemerkenswert literate Dichter weiß eine überzeugend gekonnte Mischung aus Scherz und Ernst zu kreieren. Dabei bieten insbesondere die unhaltbaren Gegenpositionen des verwerflichen Bösen einen gewissen Unterhaltungswert, aber wo immer man hier lacht, erinnert es an das bekannte didaktisch motivierte, ablehnende Lachen des Mittelalters, das Suchomski treffend beschrieben hat;[100] so haben es jedenfalls Johannes von Salisbury und andere gesehen, die sich damals im Disputieren auskannten.[101] Hartmann nutzt seine nicht geringen Kenntnisse logisch rhetorischen Argumentierens zur Demonstration des wirkungsvoll schon von Boethius als wahrscheinlich erwiesenen Sieges des Guten über das Böse:

> Dann wirst du [. . .] erkennen, daß die Guten immer die Mächtigen, die Schlechten aber immer die Verworfenen und Schwachen sind, daß niemals die Laster ohne Strafen, die Tugenden ohne Lohn bleiben, daß den Guten immer das Glück, den Schlechten das Unglück zuteil wird.

Mit umfänglicher Argumentation wird dieser Satz bewiesen, so daß Boethius mit Plato enden kann:

> Aus allem diesem erhellt die Macht der Guten und die unzweifelhafte Schwäche der Schlechten. Es zeigt sich die Wahrheit jenes Satzes Platons: daß nur die Weisen tun können, was sie wollen, die Bösen hingegen zwar verüben, was ihnen beliebt, aber das, was sie wünschen, nicht erfüllen können. Denn sie tun Beliebiges, indem sie glauben, durch das, woran sie sich ergötzen, jenes Gut ('beatitudo'), das sie ersehnen, erreichen zu können; aber sie erreichen es keineswegs, weil zur Glückseligkeit Übeltaten nicht gelangen.[102]

Um den höflichen Calogrenant zu beleidigen, wählt Kes bei Chrestien (*Yv.* 71–85) spöttisch doppeldeutige Worte, wenn er den höflichen Gruß mit 'preu' und 'saillant' (*Yv.* 72) bewertet, Termini, die miteinander eher zum kämpfenden Ritter passen[103] als zum höfischen Umgang mit Damen. Man hört Ironie,[104] wenn Kes sich und die anderen

---

[100] Joachim Suchomski, *'Delectatio' und 'utilitas': Ein Beitrag zum Verständnis mittelalterlicher komischer Literatur*, Bibliotheca Germanica, 18 (Bern/München, 1975).
[101] Siehe unten Anm. 124.
[102] Vgl. *Consolatio* (wie Anm. 39), IV.1 prosa, S. 166,25–29; IV.2 prosa, S. 168,4–178,161; zitiert: 178,153–61.
[103] Zu *preu* und *saillant* (*Yv.* 72) vgl. Tobler/Lommatzsch (wie Anm. 89), Bd. VII, Sp. 1922,41–1926,5; ebd., Bd. IX, Sp. 119,7–31. Beide Wörter heißen 'ritterlich vorbildlich', 'herausragend', aber auch 'tapfer im Kampf' bzw. 'gewandt', 'gelenkig', 'rasch hervorspringend', *saillant* auch 'leichtfertig'.
[104] Vgl. zur *ironia*, die vom Gegenteil des Gemeinten spricht, die umfangreichen Hinweise Lausbergs (wie Anm. 91), nach dem Register, S. 729–31.

unaufmerksamen Ritter träge (*Yv.* 80–82), Calogrenant aber den Höfischsten und Ritterlichsten von allen (*Yv.* 74, 78f.) nennt, beides aber im selben Atemzug als bloße Einbildung in Frage stellt und mit Emphase widerruft (*Yv.* 75f., 83–85). In der spöttisch verzerrenden Doppeldeutigkeit der Wörter, in der Ironie, dem direkten Vorwurf der Einbildung und dem ausdrücklichen Widerruf des Kompliments liegt hier die beleidigende Aggression des Redners. – Hartmann läßt Keie (*Iw.* 113–35) seine unangebrachte Attacke nicht auf diese leicht durchschaubare Weise vorbringen, sondern verschlagener mit sophistischer Argumentation, wie sie dem *litteratus* des 12. und beginnenden 13. Jahrhunderts aus dem Dialektikunterricht bekannt geworden sein wird,[105] mit Trugschlußstrukturen, die kunstgerecht[106] das Faktum der Höflichkeit des Kalogreant zerreden, um die Unhöflichkeit der übrigen dagegen fälschlich aufzuwerten: 'sophisticum dicimus quicquid melius apparet quam sit'.[107] Denn entgegen dem allen Anwesenden augenscheinlichen Ereignis endet Keie mit der impertinenten Behauptung, daß Kalogreant genausogut hätte sitzen bleiben können wie die übrigen Ritter.

Dabei beginnt Keie mit einer scheinbar lobenden Beurteilung der sittlichen Qualität des Kalogreant: 'daz undr uns niemen wære/ sô höfsch und als êrbære/ als ir wænet daz ir sît' (*Iw.* 115–17). Dem würde man zustimmen, wenn Keie das 'ir wænet daz' weggelassen hätte.

---

[105]   Hierzu vgl. L.M. de Rijk, *Logica Modernorum*, Bd. I: *On the Twelfth-Century Theories of Fallacy* (Assen, 1962); *Anonymi Aurelianensis I commentarium in Sophisticos Elenchos*, hg. von Sten Ebbesen, *Cahiers de l'Institut du Moyen Âge Grec et Latin (CIMAGL)*, 34 (1979), V–XIX; hier S. XVII eine Liste von Kommentaren des 12. Jahrhunderts; Sten Ebbesen, *Commentators and Commentaries on Aristotle's Sophistici Elenchi: A Study of Post-Aristotelian Ancient and Medieval Writings on Fallacies*, 3 Bde. (Leiden, 1981); auch *Incertorum auctorum Quaestiones super sophisticos elenchos*, hg. von Sten Ebbesen, Corpus philosophorum Danicorum medii aevi, 7 (Kopenhagen, 1977); und weitere Veröffentlichungen Ebbesens zur mittelalterlichen Geschichte der Elenchik seit 1972 in den *CIMAGL*. Von Abaelard ist bisher keine Schrift über die sophistische Argumentation gefunden, siehe de Rijk, *Abaelard: Dialectica* (wie Anm. 44), S. XIII. Vgl. weiter mit allgemeiner informationsreicher Einleitung Clemens Kopp, *Die 'Fallaciae ad modum Oxoniae': Ein Fehlschlußtraktat aus dem 13. Jahrhundert* (Köln, 1985); Kopp, 'Ein kurzer Fehlschlußtraktat: Die *Fallaciae breves (ad modum Oxoniae)*. London, British Museum, Royal MSS 12 F XIX, 104rb–105vb', *Miscellanea Mediaevalia*, 15 (1982), 262–77; ders., 'Die *Fallaciae breves (ad modum Oxoniae)*: ein Werk Walter Burleys?', *Miscellanea Mediaevalia*, 18 (1986), 119–24.

[106]   Die Zugehörigkeit zu den Artes wird der Sophistik bestritten, da sie nicht auf Wahrheit zielt; vgl. *Glose in Aristotilis Sophisticos Elencos*, hg. von de Rijk (wie Anm. 105), I, Prologus, S. 192,22–24. Anders argumentiert zwischen 1160 und 1180 der *Anonymus Aurelianensis I*, hg. von Ebbesen (wie Anm. 105), S. 2–5, daß sie mit Aristoteles als Teil der Logik doch *ars* sei, wobei er (S. 4) sich u. a. auf Gorgias beruft, der (siehe das gleichnamige Werk Platos) in den *Sophistici Elenchi* des Aristoteles in einem besonderen Verständnis doch 'artem sic disputandi tradiderit, id est sophisticam'. Für die Bezeichnung der Sophistik als *ars* sprechen ebenfalls Johannes von Salisbury, *Metalogicon* (wie Anm. 3), II.5.861cd; die *Summa Sophisticorum Elencorum*, hg. von de Rijk (wie Anm. 105), Introduction, S. 269,5–17; auch die *Fallaciae ad modum Oxoniae*, hg. von Kopp (wie Anm. 105), S. 10f.

[107]   *Anonymus Aurelianensis I* (wie Anm. 105), S. 11.

Kalogreants Meinung über sich selbst ist bisher durch nichts erkennbar, und Keie führt die unbewiesene Aussage darüber als argumentatorische Falle ein, wie man sehen wird. Der Schluß aus Ungesichertem ist sophistisch: 'que [sc. ars] sillogizat ex aperte falsis et dicitur sophistica (ars disserendi)'; 'Sophistica est que sillogizat ex his que videntur probabilia, non autem sunt'.[108] Nichtsdestoweniger unterstreicht Keie die angebliche Gültigkeit seines ersten Satzes dreifach, indem er ihn als deren Überzeugung allen übrigen Rittern (*Iw.* 118f.), dem Kalogreant selbst (*Iw.* 121) und sogar der Königin (*Iw.* 122) unterstellt, 'sî tæte iu anders gewalt' (*Iw.* 123). Keie tut so, als ob er Kalogreant vor einem möglichen Fehlurteil der Königin in Schutz nehmen müßte und deshalb sein anscheinend lobendes Urteil im folgenden noch beweise.

Dieser Beweis ist aber keiner, weil beide Prämissen nicht taugen: Keie wiederholt als deren erste (*Iw.* 124f.) nur einen Teil der Behauptung, wobei er sich variierend auf den Kalogreant betreffenden Teil des zu beweisenden Satzes (*Iw.* 116f.) bezieht und die relationale Komponente des gesamten Urteils (*Iw.* 115–17) über Kalogreants sittliche Qualität im Verhältnis zu der der übrigen anwesenden Ritter zunächst unbeachtet läßt. Keie begründet nämlich nun das Scheinlob mit der Feststellung, daß Kalogreant erstens sehr wohlerzogen sei und sich zweitens selbst überaus vollkommen dünke (*Iw.* 124f.). Dabei entspricht die keineswegs unzutreffende Benennung der mannigfaltigen 'zuht' des Kalogreant dem 'höfsch' und 'êrbære' aus dem zu beweisenden Satz, und dies Urteil ist durch das höfliche Handeln des Ritters, das alle gesehen haben, durchaus gerechtfertigt, ganz im Gegensatz zum zweiten Urteil, das mit 'ir dunket iuch' dem immer noch unbewiesenen 'ir wænet daz ir sît' des zu billigenden Satzes gleichkommt. Der das unbewiesene Erstgesagte nur in andern Worten wiederholende Gedankengang zeigt ganz die Struktur eines bestimmten Trugschlusses, nämlich der *fallacia de petitione principii*.[109]

---

[108] *Glose in Aristotilis Sophisticos Elencos*, hg. von de Rijk (wie Anm. 105), I, Prologus, S. 191,10f.; *Summa Sophisticorum Elencorum*, hg. von de Rijk (wie Anm. 105), Introduction, S. 269,27f.; ausführlicher ebd., S. 277,25–278,4. Ähnlich die *Fallacie Vindobonenses*, hg. von de Rijk (wie Anm. 105), Prologus, S. 497,5f.

[109] Zum Terminus siehe Aristoteles, *De sophisticis elenchis: translatio Boethii, fragmenta translationis Iacobi, et recensio Guillelmi de Moerbeke*, hg. von Bernardus G. Dod, Aristoteles latinus, VI, 1–3 (Leiden/Brüssel, 1975), S. 12,26–13,2; 69,10–16; 104,4–10. Vgl. das einfache Beispiel der *Glose in Aristotilis Sophisticos Elencos*, hg. von de Rijk (wie Anm. 105), I.5, S. 219,1–8; *Summa Sophisticorum Elencorum*, hg. von de Rijk, ebd., S. 383,4–385,35; *Fallacie Vindobonenses*, hg. von de Rijk, ebd., S. 537,3–538,11; *Fallacie Parvipontane*, hg. von de Rijk, ebd., II.9, S. 601,3–602,28; den *Anonymus Aurelianensis I*, hg. von Ebbesen (wie Anm. 105), S. 173f., der erläutert, daß derartiges Argumentieren mit der zu beweisenden Sache selbst formal nicht dem Syllogismus entspricht und somit ein *paralogismus* sei; auch Boethius, *Elenchorum Sophisticorum Aristotelis interpretatio*, I.4, PL, LXIV, 1011C; dies wörtlich bei Johannes von Salisbury, *Metalogicon* (wie Anm. 3), IV.2.930b; siehe weiter die *Fallaciae ad modum Oxoniae*, hg. von Kopp (wie Anm. 105), S. 131–35; Vincenz von Beauvais, *Speculum doctrinale* (wie Anm. 42) III.96, Sp. 279CD: 'De petitione principii notandum est, quod

Diese bietet als eine ihrer Prämissen eine schon im zu beweisenden Satz selbst enthaltene und somit immer noch unbewiesene Aussage. Sie besteht dadurch eigentlich nur aus zwei Sätzen, was dem erforderlichen Dreisatz des korrekten Syllogismus nicht genügt, weshalb solch ein Sophisma auch auf Unkenntnis des logischen Schlusses zurückgeführt werden kann, die fehlerhaft zu bloßer *phantasia* verleitet.[110] Sophismen erschließen nicht Wahrheit, noch Wahrscheinlichkeit, sie sollen täuschen durch scheinbare Schlüssigkeit bei fehlendem Beweisgrund sowie verdecktem Widerspruch.[111] Dies auch hier in Keies tückischer Rede, die irreführend verborgene Kontradiktionen zwischen dem zutreffenden und dem unbewiesen behaupteten Teil der Aussagen enthält. Zuerst widerspricht das unbewiesen behauptete starke Eigenlob löblicher Wohlerzogenheit des Ritters.[112] Darauf wird in der zweiten Prämisse dieses Trugschlusses das Kontradiktorische verstärkt mit einer weiteren ungerechtfertigten Unterstellung: 'deiswâr ir hât iuch an genomen/ irne wizzet hiute waz' (*Iw.* 126f.). Keies Beteuerung 'deiswâr' zeigt seine Absicht zu täuschen, denn auch dieser Satz ist ja keineswegs wahr, sondern läuft in weiterhin sophistischem Operieren mit Unbewiesenem aus dem ersten Satz ebenfalls dem positiven Urteil über Kalogreant entgegen, so daß dadurch nun entweder dieses aufgehoben sein müßte,

---

principium nihil aliud est hic, quam principale propositum, quod debet probari. ''Fiunt ergo paralogismi secundum hoc, quando ad probandum aliquod, sumitur idem, siue aliquid minus notum.'' Et hoc quinque modis, vt distinguitur in 8. Topicorum, quod iam supra posuimus' (gemeint sind offenbar Ciceros *Topica*, Kap. 8). Vgl. Ebbesen, *Commentators* (wie Anm. 105), Bd. I, S.10: 'the fallacy of *petitio principii* arises when the point to be proved is in some way or other used as a part of the premisses'; auch ebd., S. 669; C.L. Hamblin, *Fallacies* (Bungay, Suffolk, 1970), S. 32–35; Jan Pinborg, *Logik und Semantik im Mittelalter* (Stuttgart-Bad Cannstatt, 1972), S. 66–69.

110 Vgl. *Anonymus Aurelianensis I*, hg. von Ebbesen (wie Anm. 105), S. 172f.: 'manifestissima est reductio praedictorum, ''secundum elenchi definitionem'', id est secundum omissionem eorum quae exiguntur ad hoc ut fiat elenchus [. . .] id est quare dicantur secundum elenchi ignorantiam. Et vere hoc manifestum est, ''nam fit phantasia'', id est deceptio, ''secundum rationis'' etc. ''dividentibus sic deminutio'' etc. ''communis'', id est communiter dicendum in his qui peccant secundum ignorantiam elenchi.' Vgl. Aristoteles, *De sophisticis elenchis* (wie Anm. 109), S. 15,5–8; 16,14–17; 17,22–27; Aristoteles, *Topica: Translatio Boethii* (wie Anm. 45), I.1, S. 6,1–23: allgemein über den *litigiosus syllogismus* als falschen Schluß des Sophisten; siehe weiter Vincenz von Beauvais, *Speculum doctrinale* (wie Anm. 42), III.96, Sp. 279BD.

111 Vgl. *Anonymus Aurelianensis I*, hg. von Ebbesen (wie Anm. 105), S. 2: 'Dicit namque Alexander: ''Nemo arbitretur quod huius speciei syllogismorum ratio insit philosophis'' ' und weiter ebd. über die Sophistik: 'non est veritatis inquisitiva'. Ebd., S. 66: 'sophistica enim argumenta nec scire nec credere, sed suspicari solum faciunt. Unde dicit ''quot coniectant'' id est quot suspicari faciunt. Vel ideo dicit ''coniectant'' quia non semper hoc possunt facere, sed in mente habent ut faciant.' Ebd., S. 11: 'Elenchus est syllogismus contradictionis, id est factus ad contradictionem.' Zur Identität Alexanders siehe Ebbesen, ebd., S. VIII. Vgl. auch Vincenz von Beauvais, *Speculum doctrinale* (wie Anm. 42), III.90, Sp. 275BE.

112 Vgl. Boethius, *Consolatio* (wie Anm. 39), I.4 prosa, S. 22f., 113–16: 'Scis me haec et vera proferre et in nulla umquam mei laude iactasse. Minuit enim quodam modo se probantis conscientiae secretum, quotiens ostentando quis factum recipit famae pretium.'

oder aber der Hinweis auf Kalogreants *wænen* über sich selbst als irrig entlarvt sein sollte. Keie intendiert natürlich das erste und konzentriert sich deshalb in dieser Prämisse allein auf die unbewiesene Behauptung, die er von Anfang an betreibt, wenn er das vorher dem Kalogreant unterstellte *dünken* und *wænen* (im Sinne des gegensätzlichen philosophischen Begriffspaars *opinio* und *scientia*)[113] jetzt *ab opposito* als ein *niht wizzen* nimmt; denn *wænen*, also bloße *opinio*, ist nicht *scientia*, ist *niht wizzen*. Damit könnte er, wenn seine Hörer ihm folgten, Kalogreants 'hiute' von allen Anwesenden gesehenes Handeln mit einem vermeintlichen moralischen Defizit bedenken und diskreditieren: insofern nämlich Wissen und Weisheit für den Philosophen Attribute des Guten sind und umgekehrt, 'bona omnia sapientiae accessoria sunt',[114] kann einer, der nicht weiß, was er tut, auch nicht gut sein und kein Lob für sittlich tadelloses Handeln beanspruchen.

Es ist offensichtlich: diese in sich widerspruchsvolle und in folgerichtiger Argumentation unzulässige *petitio principii* ist ein absichtliches Scheinlob, das tatsächlich in seinen Widersprüchen das Loben unterbinden soll, indem hier nämlich die Halbwahrheit des ersten Satzes keineswegs zur ganzen Wahrheit geführt oder demaskiert wird, sondern sie vielmehr in variierender Wiederholung sich fortschreibt zu zwei als solche kaschierten Widersprüchen und einem markanten Übergewicht des falsch Unterstellten. Die Konzeption der sophistischen Rede zielt von vornherein und ganz gekonnt auf das *suspicari*: Keies scheinbar lobende Aussagen fördern eigentlich die boshafte Verunglimpfung des ehrenwerten Kalogreant. Mit einem halben Zugeständnis an die Anwesenden und ihren gewiß nach dem höflichen Gruß guten Eindruck von Kalogreant lassen sie gerade den guten Eindruck zugleich fraglich werden, wie nicht nur die Widersprüche der *fallacia de petitione principii* offenbaren, sondern auch die weitere Rede zeigt; denn das Mischen von Wahrem und Falschem, das heimtückische Verdrehen dessen, was sich ereignet hat, endet noch nicht.

---

[113] *Anonymus Aurelianensis I*, hg. von Ebbesen (wie Anm. 105), S. 45: ' "Scire", ergo ut ait Alexander, "est rem cognoscere sic se habere ut se habet et ex quibus causis et quod aliter se habere non possit". Rusticana etenim est cognitio quae non ex causis, sed ex aliena inditione et sensuali provenit perceptione, nec dicenda scientia sed potius opinio. Est autem aliud scire, aliud credere, aliud opinari, sicut aliud scientia, aliud fides, aliud opinio: plus enim est credere quam opinari, plus est vero scire quam +opinari nec + credere – Est enim opinio existimatio proveniens ex coniecturis, fides est credulitas ex certis causis non proveniens, "scientia", vero, ut dicit Alexander, "est demonstrativus habitus rerum semper aut frequenter eodem modo se habentium".' Vgl. schon Aristoteles, *Topica: Translatio Boethii* (wie Anm. 45), II.8, S. 44,17–25; siehe weiter den Gebrauch von *opinio* und *scientia* bei Boethius, *Consolatio* (wie Anm. 39), V.5 prosa, S. 260,51–57; V.6 prosa, S. 268,94–97; ferner Irene Ruttmann, *Die Bedeutungskomponente des Trügerischen in mhd. 'wân' und 'waenen'* (Frankfurt am Main, 1965), S. 4–6: zu den Wörterbuchbefunden, S. 162–75: zum *Iwein*, S. 171: zu *Iw.* 117; auch Freytag (wie Anm. 16), S. 155–59.

[114] Johannes von Salisbury, *Policraticus* (wie Anm. 3), VII.8.653b.

Erneut sophistisch nimmt Keie das bisher ausgeklammerte relationale Urteil des ersten Satzes (*Iw.* 115–17) auf und sucht es umzukehren mit einer Aussage nach Art der *fallacia secundum non causam ut causam, quando non causa ponitur ut causa, propter quam sequitur impossibile;*[115] das eben geäußerte Scheinzugeständnis wird damit zurückgenommen.[116] Keie behauptet zunächst, daß keiner der sitzengebliebenen Ritter so träge gewesen sei, daß er nicht genauso wohlerzogen wie Kalogreant aufgesprungen wäre, wenn er die Königin gesehen hätte (*Iw.* 128–31), was ein höflicher Mensch nicht leichthin wird bestreiten wollen, also als wahrscheinlich annimmt (wobei er sich aber doch auch sagen muß: so ist es nicht gewesen). Die Wahrscheinlichkeit dieser ersten Prämisse wird jedoch in der zweiten dadurch hinfällig, daß Keie nun ganz offen fragt, ob das Nichtsehen der Königin tatsächlich der Grund für das Sitzenbleiben der Ritter gewesen ist, oder ob es nicht andere Gründe dafür gegeben hat: 'sît unser keiner sîne sach,/ od swie wir des vergâzen,/ daz wir stille sâzen' (*Iw.* 132–34). Hiernach überzeugt die erste Prämisse nicht mehr, in der das höfliche Aufstehen vom Sehen der Königin abhängig gemacht bzw. das Sitzenbleiben durch Nichtsehen begründet wurde (*Iw.* 128–31). Somit hat Keie selbst in seiner zweiten Prämisse das in der ersten geäußerte womöglich Wahrscheinliche in Frage gestellt, und wegen dieses offen kontradiktorischen Ansatzes kann auch das Weitere nicht stimmen. Jedoch, obwohl der Redner seinen ersten mutmaßlichen Beweisgrund aufhebt und keinen neuen bietet, versucht er dennoch folgenden Trugschluß: Nachdem er das (faktisch nicht gegebene) Aufspringen der übrigen Ritter für möglich oder auch nicht möglich erklärt hat, folgert er nach dem Modus der *fallacia secundum non causam ut causam*[117] aus diesem anfangs nicht

---

115 Aristoteles, *De sophisticis elenchis* (wie Anm. 109), S. 13,22–14,10; 19,6–10. Vgl. die *Glose in Aristotilis Sophisticos Elencos*, hg. von de Rijk (wie Anm. 105), I.5, S. 221,1–15; *Summa Sophisticorum Elencorum*, hg. von de Rijk, ebd., S. 386,4–388,9; ähnlich die *Fallacie Vindobonenses*, hg. von de Rijk, ebd., S. 539,3–540,4; *Fallacie Parvipontane*, hg. von de Rijk, ebd., II.9, S. 605,3–606,11; *Fallaciae ad modum Oxoniae*, hg. von Kopp (wie Anm. 105), S. 144–49; Vincenz von Beauvais, *Speculum doctrinale* (wie Anm. 42), III.97, Sp. 279E; vgl. auch Boethius, *Elenchorum Sophisticorum Aristotelis interpretatio*, I.4, PL, LXIV, 1011C; dies fast wörtlich bei Johannes von Salisbury, *Metalogicon* (wie Anm. 3), IV.23.930b. Zur *fallacia secundum non causam ut causa* siehe auch das Zitat in Anm. 117; Ebbesen, *Commentators* (wie Anm. 105), Bd. I, S. 10: ' "Non-cause as cause" consists in inserting irrelevant matter among the premisses and presenting the conclusion as due to that irrelevant matter'; auch ebd., S. 660; Hamblin (wie Anm. 109), S. 37f., und Pinborg (wie Anm. 109), S. 68.

116 Es handelt sich um Widerlegung des erst *ex probabilibus* Zugestandenen, eine *redargutio;* siehe *Anonymus Aurelianensis I*, hg. von Ebbesen (wie Anm. 105), S. 67f.; auch die *Fallaciae ad modum Oxoniae*, hg. von Kopp (wie Anm. 105), S. 6f.: 'Redargutio est praenegati concessio vel praeconcessi negatio, et hoc vi argumentationis'; Vincenz von Beauvais, *Speculum doctrinale* (wie Anm. 42), III.91, Sp. 276B. In seiner *Topik* warnt Aristoteles besonders vor der offenen Unschlüssigkeit sophistischer *redargutio;* vgl. Aristoteles, *Topica: Translatio Boethii* (wie Anm. 45), II.5, S. 38,21–39,2.

117 Vgl. noch den *Anonymus Aurelianensis I*, hg. von Ebbesen (wie Anm. 105), S. 143f.: 'Causa dicitur proprie id cuius motu aliquid habet esse, scilicet generatione vel corruptione

Unwahrscheinlichen, doch im selben Atemzug Widerrufenen, das eben demzufolge keine tragfähige Prämisse für einen guten Schluß bieten kann, fälschlich, daß auch Kalogreant hätte sitzenbleiben können. Er sagt (*Iw.* 132–35), 'weil wir aber nun die Königin nicht gesehen haben und demzufolge – oder warum immer sitzen geblieben sind, deshalb könntet auch Ihr sitzen geblieben sein'.

Das ist in der Tat genauso inkonsequent gedacht wie jenes Beispiel es vorführt, mit dem der Anonymus Aurelianensis I den dritten Modus der *fallacia secundum non causam ut causam* erläutert, der 'per destructionem consequentis et alicuius propositionum quae proponuntur' versucht *ad impossibile* zu führen: 'si Socrates currit et Plato sedet, Socrates movetur; ergo si Socrates non movetur et Socrates currit Plato non sedet'.[118] Ab dem *ergo* stimmt hier nichts mehr: der zweite Konditionalsatz über Sokrates kann nicht richtig sein, weil der erneut zitierte erste, der in seiner Aussage über Sokrates wahrscheinlich ist, entgegengesetzt lautet; die Schlußfolgerung 'Plato non sedet' kann sich unmöglich aus 'Plato sedet' und den voraufgehenden widersprüchlichen Aussagen über Sokrates ergeben; nichts des über Sokrates Gesagten ist irgendwie relevant für die Umkehr des über Plato Gesagten; überhaupt werden hier nicht nur zwei Sachverhalte teilweise widersprüchlich beurteilt, sondern sie werden auch ohne jeden sachlichen Zusammenhang willkürlich zu einem Trugschluß verknüpft, d. h. ohne daß ein beiden Gemeinsames da wäre, wie es der Syllogismus erfordert: 'decipit exemplum eo quod non causa apposita nihil consecutionis sit effectiva'.

Auch Keie verknüpft willkürlich zwei Sachverhalte, das träge Sitzenbleiben der Ritter und das höfliche Aufspringen Kalogreants, ohne daß er ein vermittelndes Faktum beibrächte, über das man die

---

vel aliquo alio motu. Dicitur etiam aliter, sed minus proprie, causa quicquid est ex quo aliud suae veritatis evidentiam potest recipere, et hoc modo accipitur in hoc loco. Quandoque enim inducimus aliquid tamquam causam ad propositum demonstrandum, ut ex eo et alio, vel aliis, propositum demonstremus, cum tamen illud inductum non valeat ad probandum propositum, et ita, cum non sit causa propositi, quod non est causa ponimus ut causam. Tunc ergo ponimus non causam ut causam. Sed si hoc est, videtur quod omnis paralogismus in quo ponitur aliquid cum alio vel aliis non cooperativum ad conclusionem fit secundum non causam ut causam, et ita omnis paralogismus delinquens in forma videtur esse secundum non causam, cum in huiusmodi syllogismo praemissa non habeant efficaciam ad conclusionem [. . .]. Dicimus igitur quoniam paralogismus est secundum hanc fallaciam quandocumque ponitur aliquid non cooperativum ad inferendum conclusionem cum alio vel aliis quae sunt causa conclusionis, id est ex quibus potest sequi conclusio, <et> ponitur velut ex eo et illis aliis inferatur conclusio. Palam ergo quoniam non causam ut causam ponere est aliquam propositionem conclusioni cum eius causa vel causis praeponere, quae ad conclusionem nihil sit necessaria sive videatur sive non. Non enim dicitur "ut causa" quia videatur causa, sed quia conclusioni praeponitur, quod causae non est proprium.

Fallacia vero secundum non causam est deceptio proveniens ex eo quod putatur causa conclusionis quod non est.'

[118] Dies Beispiel und seine folgende Erläuterung hat der *Anonymus Aurelianensis I*, hg. von Ebbesen (wie Anm. 105), S. 146.

Beurteilung dieser Tatbestände umkehren könnte. Es hätte vielleicht im Sehen bzw. Nichtsehen gefunden werden können; Keie jedoch destruiert diese mögliche Prämisse durch seine Frage ('oder warum immer'), so daß alles über die übrigen Ritter Gesagte als *non causa* gelten muß (wie im Beispiel das widersprüchlich über Sokrates Gesagte *non causa* ist), wodurch dann bei Gebrauch dieses nicht zum Beweisgrund Dienlichen als Prämisse auch die Schlußfolgerung unmöglich wird. Man fühlt sich durch Keies sophistischen Umgang mit Sitzen und Stehen an Schulbeispiele erinnert wie das eben Zitierte oder eines für die *aequivocationis fallacia* (äquivok ist *sedens*): 'Quicumque surgebat, stat,/ sedens surgebat,/ ergo sedens stat'; oder eines für die *fallacia compositionis et divisionis*: 'Sedentem ambulare est possibile'.[119] Keie will für Sitzengebliebene mögliches Aufgestandensein glauben machen und umgekehrt; die Tatsachen stehen eindeutig dagegen: Kalogreant ist aufgesprungen und die anderen sind sitzen geblieben. Wie unwahr Keies sophistische Rede ist (die als solche aber ja auch nicht Wahrheit bezwecken will, sondern deren Manipulation), zeigt sich einfach daran, daß sie nicht dem Geschehen entspricht; denn eine Aussage ist wahr, wenn sie den Tatbestand trifft, mit dem sie gilt, wie Aristoteles z. B. mit Erklärungen in der *Topik* zum Gebrauch von *sedere* als *proprium* allein für einen, der sitzt, nicht aber für einen Nicht-Sitzenden ('quando quis solus sederit tunc quando proprium erit, non solo autem sedente ad non sedentes proprium'), und auch Boethius mit dem Satz 'jemand sitzt' ausführt:[120]

'Denn wenn irgendwer sitzt, so muß die Meinung, welche aussagt, daß er sitzt, notwendig wahr sein, und ebenso umgekehrt: wenn man die wahre Meinung hat, daß jemand sitzt, so muß er auch notwendig sitzen. Beiden Fällen wohnt also Notwendigkeit inne, hier dem Sitzen, dort der Wahrheit; aber es sitzt nicht jemand, weil die Meinung wahr ist, sondern sie ist vielmehr wahr, weil das Sitzen vorausging.' Und bald darauf: 'Schließlich, wenn jemand in anderer Richtung denkt, als es sich wirklich verhält, so ist dies nicht nur kein Wissen, sondern eine falsche Meinung, völlig verschieden vom Wissen der Wahrheit. Wenn darum etwas in der Weise zukünftig ist, daß sein Eintreffen nicht sicher und notwendig ist, wie könnte er dann vorauswissen, daß es eintreffen wird? So wie das Wissen selbst mit Falschem nicht vermischt sein

---

119 Die Beispiele sind 1. aus den *Fallaciae ad modum Oxoniae*, hg. von Kopp (wie Anm. 105, 1985), S. 46; 2. aus den *Fallaciae breves* (*ad modum Oxoniae*), hg. von Kopp (wie Anm. 105, 1982), S. 266.
120 Aristoteles, *Topica: Translatione Boethii* (wie Anm. 45), I.5, S. 11,18f. Vgl. Abaelard, 'Topica', in *Dialectica* (wie Anm. 44), III.1, S. 390,8–13, zur Auffassung der *contrarietas* im Falle von 'sedet, non sedet'. – *Consolatio* (wie Anm. 39), V.3 prosa, S. 238,34–41; 240,60–70.

kann, so kann auch das, was von ihm erfaßt wird, nie anders sein, als es erfaßt wird. Das nämlich ist die Ursache, weshalb das Wissen der Falschheit entbehrt, weil jede Sache sich mit Notwendigkeit so verhält, wie das Wissen sie begreift.'

Derartiges scheint Hartmann inspiriert zu haben beim poetischen Beschreiben seines falsch redenden Keie: 'von sînem valsche er was genant/ Keiîn der quâtspreche'.[121] Auch weil er gleich 'dem hunde' sehr bedrohlich 'grînen kan' (Iw. 875–78), gehört er zu den Sophisten, denn diese schimpft man damals 'Zähne fletschende Hunde'.[122] Er redet mit soviel Falsch, Bosheit und unfreiwilliger Komik, wie er bekanntlich auch bei den meisten anderen Dichtern handelt. Im Iwein paßt ins Negative gewendet das Proverbium 'talis hominibus fuit oratio qualis vita', das Seneca gebraucht und Cicero dem Sokrates zuschreibt,[123] das indes auch in der Poetik des Hochmittelalters sein Pendant hat. Wer Keies Reden durchschaut, mag lachend oder empört ablehnen, wie Johannes von Salisbury es schildert; er mag hier 'hilaritatis et iocularis letitiae materia' sehen oder als ernsthafter Mensch Verachtung fühlen: 'quia qui sophistice loquitur odibilis est', schon laut Altem Testament.[124] In jedem Fall wird er, sofern er dem tückischen 'uenenum' der sophistischen Rede, wie Martianus Capella, seine Kommentatoren und Johannes bildhaft sagen,[125] wohlgerüstet mit Verstand zu entgehen weiß, ihren ex

---

[121] Erec (wie Anm. 81), 4663f. Vgl. Haupt (wie Anm. 96), S. 34f. Hermann Mushacke, 'Keiî der kâtspreche' in Hartmanns von Aue 'Erec' und 'Iwein' (Dissertation, Rostock/Berlin, 1872), war mir nicht zugänglich.

[122] Iwein, der sich voller Ironie davon distanziert, möchte Keie nicht knurrend wie ein Hund gegenübertreten, 'sô in der ander grînet an' (Iw. 878). Vgl. den Anonymus Aurelianensis I (wie Anm. 105), S. 66f.: 'Sequitur "qui decertant" – id est decertando et cum lite disputant –"et" –id est– "corrixantur" – Eorum officio dantur intelligi [. . .] (es folgt eine Worterklärung) proprie itaque morem exprimit sophistarum eos canibus comparans quorum proprium est corrixari circa ossa et cadavera dum alter alteri ringitur (d. h. 'die Zähne fletscht'). Et est verbum frequentativum. Inde tractum est ut dicantur corrixari qui sibi nullatenus consentiunt velut sophistae.'

[123] Seneca (wie Anm. 3), Ep. 114.1; Cicero, Tusculanae disputationes (wie Anm. 9), V.16.47: 'Denn so' (d. h. 'durch jene Sokratische Schlußform') 'sprach jenes Haupt der Philosophie: Wie jedes Menschen Seele gestimmt sei, so sei der Mensch beschaffen; wie aber der Mensch selbst beschaffen sei, so sei auch seine Rede beschaffen; seiner Rede aber entsprächen die Thaten, den Thaten das Leben.' Vgl. auch Horaz, Ars poetica (wie Anm. 73), 108–11. Matthaeus von Vendôme (wie Anm. 32), I.45, S. 120: 'verborum proprietas vultibus personarum loquentium et fortunae intrinsecae debet conformari.' Galfred, hg. von Faral, ebd., S. 236, 1263–66: 'quibus quae sit hominis natura patenter/ Describo: color iste magis meliusque colorat./ En alium florem, personae quando loquenti/ Sermo coaptatur redoletque loquela loquentem.'

[124] Policraticus (wie Anm. 3), VII.12.663d–64a; Metalogicon (wie Anm. 3), IV.22, 929d; Webb weist den Satz als Schriftwort nach: Eccli. 37. 23.

[125] Policraticus (wie Anm. 3), VII.12.663d: 'Vt uenenum eius effugias, patientiam indicas auribus, morem geras insano qui nulli parcit et, si eum forte uis reprimere, benignissime obsecra ut in docendo aut disputando sententiae plus apponat et eam uerborum deductione compenset. Nam qui uerba rebus et res temporis opportunitati contemperat, modestissimam totius eloquentiae regulam tenet. Illa uero copia laudem parit cui ueritas

negativo erwiesenen Dienst am Wahren und Guten erkennen; denn darin liegt im damaligen Schulbetrieb[126] der für die Philosophie keineswegs geringe, womöglich gar staatsdienliche Nutzen solch lustig-lächerlichen Unsinns:

> Non mediocris tamen utilitas est in deprehendendis importu-nitatibus sophisticis, sine quarum notitia quisquis ad examinatio-nem ueri et rerum uentilationem progreditur quasi miles inutilis est qui aduersus exercitatum et instructum hostem procedit exarmatus [. . .] ubi se colloquentium intentio ad philosophiae sobrietatem erigit, importunitates sophisticae delitescunt. Et, si forte ab alterutra parte emerserint, sic a sapientibus corripiuntur sicut in re publica inter contrahentes dolus malignantium cohercetur. Ceterum uerba rebus, res temporibus contemperare, et interuenientes fallacias prudenter arguere non paucorum dierum est aut leuis opera.[127]

Mit anderen Autoren hat Cicero in *ratio et oratio*, wie sie Menschen (im Gegensatz zu den Tieren) zugleich mit den Gaben der *iustitia*, *aequitas*, *bonitas* eignen, die natürlichen Grundlagen menschlicher Gemeinschaft gesehen: zusammen fördern diese Qualitäten und Fähigkeiten das allgemeine Wohl.[128] Zu Hartmanns Zeit denken *litterati* offenbar ähnlich,

---

uirtuti et omnibus officiis amica consentit.' Vgl. die giftige Schlange in der linken Hand der allegorischen Figur der Dialektik bei Martianus Capella (wie Anm. 44), IV.328 u. ö. und die Erklärung von Gift und Schlange als Zeichen der sophistischen Falschheit durch Johannes Scottus (wie Anm. 44), 151.19; 152.4; Remigius von Auxerre (wie Anm. 44), IV.152.3–9, S. 13,11–14,3; vgl. die Giftmetapher (*Yv.* 86–91) und *eiter* (*Iw.* 156).

126 *Summa Sophisticorum Elencorum*, hg. von de Rijk (wie Anm. 105), S. 492, 10–22: 'Utiles enim sunt hee solutiones (d. h. 'sophisticorum elencorum'), ut dicit Aristotiles, ad philosophiam, quoniam postquam habemus eas, melius scimus et intelligimus ea que sunt in philosophia'; auch den *Anonymus Aurelianensis I* (wie Anm. 105), S. 58: 'Temptativus vero a fine dicitur. Ad hoc enim repertus est huiusmodi syllogismus, ut per ipsum temptemus eos quia affectantes doctoris officium scholas magistrandi causa exeunt, et ad veritatis inquisitionem habet fieri. Erat enim consuetudo maiorum, quando aliquis exibat scholas ut alios doceret, primo mittere eum ad sophistam, qui statutus ut singulos huiusmodi experiretur, inde proprios redditus habebat. Quaesito autem ab eo quam artem maxime profiteretur, sophista cum suis exercitatoribus huiusmodi paralogismis disputabat cum eo ut ignorantiam eius manifestaret. Ille ergo qui facile capiebatur nesciens illis resistere repellebatur et derisioni habebatur. Qui vero prompte et expedite omnibus respondebat tamquam probatus imperatori praesentabatur, ut iussu imperatoris aucto-ritaretur in arte quam profitebatur. Prius tamen ante imperatorem iurabat ut quoad sciret ac posset ad utilitatem rei publicae suos discipulos erudiret; deinde ne quis eius scriptis contradiceret, sed ea quisque authentica reputaret, populo eius auctoritas publicabatur.'

127 Johannes von Salisbury, *Policraticus* (wie Anm. 3), VII.12.664ab. Vgl. Boethius, *Elenchorum sophisticorum Aristotelis interpretatio*, II.1: 'De utilitate cognoscendi sophisticas orationes et apparatu ad eas diluendas', PL, LXIV, 1025BD.

128 *De officiis* (wie Anm. 8), I.16.50f. Mit Bezug auf Cicero *in primo de Oratore* ähnlich Vincenz von Beauvais, *Speculum doctrinale* (wie Anm. 42), III.99, Sp. 280DE; vgl. auch Isidor, *Etymologiae* (wie Anm. 3), II.1.1: 'Rhetorica est bene dicendi scientia in civilibus quaestionibus, (eloquentia copia) ad persuadendum iusta et bona.'

wie neben Johannes von Salisbury dies Beispiel im *Iwein* zeigt. Bald unterstützt von Iwein und Kalogreant, rettet die 'guote künegîn' (*Iw.* 230) das durch Keies Invektive in seiner harmonischen *vreude* bedrohte Artusfest, indem sie sich der schweren, gleichwohl für die Gemeinschaft wichtigen Aufgabe annimmt, Keies Sophismen zu widerlegen. Hartmann verleiht ihr durch entschiedenes Erweitern ihrer Reden so viel mehr Gewicht als Chrestien, daß hier ein kleiner Exkurs zur Darstellung der Frau bei beiden Autoren Stoff genug fände.[129] Als *bona* und, so möchte man die bekannte Definition des Rhetors ins Weibliche verkehren, auch *dicendi perita*,[130] kennt sie sich auch aus in der *dialectica* als der 'bene disputandi scientia; quod quidem ita accipiendum est, ut uis habeatur in uerbis'.[131] Wissend ist sie Keies falsch redender Bosheit verbal wie sittlich gewachsen; 'et qui sciens [. . .] immutans quicquid non bene dictum uidetur; et qui circumstantes attendit rationes, in singulis uerum facilius discernit a falso, et habilior redditur ad intelligendum et docendum, quod philosophantis propositum expetit et officium exigit.'[132]

Die Königin kennt die Mittel zur Widerlegung von Trugschlüssen, wie sie zum Lehrstoff des Gebietes gehören: ein Sophisma wird durch einen formal korrekten, in seinen Prämissen sachgerechten und also wahrscheinlichen oder gar wahren Syllogismus aufgehoben, der den Fehler des Sophisten aufzeigt und richtigstellt, indem er mit Argumenten aus bestimmten Sachbereichen operiert, eben den *loci communes* der Rede. So empfehlen es Aristoteles, Boethius, auch Johannes von Salisbury, ähnlich Vincenz von Beauvais und schon zwischen 1160 und 1180 der wohl nordfranzösische Anonymus Aurelianensis I, der den wahrschein-

---

[129] Hartmanns Königin zeigt mehr Bildung und Initiative als ihre Kollegin bei Chrestien, sie dominiert die Szene, weil sie für das Rechte und Gute einzustehen weiß, und gleicht eher Hartmanns Laudine als seiner Enite, der Hartmann wohl nicht so viel vernünftiges Denken und Handeln zutraut; vgl. Kathryn Smits, 'Enite als christliche Ehefrau', in *Interpretation und Edition deutscher Texte des Mittelalters: Festschrift für John Asher*, hg. von K. Smits u. a. (Berlin, 1981), S. 13–25 (S. 18f.); dieselbe, 'Die Schönheit der Frau in Hartmanns *Erec*', *ZfdPh*, 101 (1982), 1–28 (S. 11f., 17).

[130] Vgl. Catos Etymologie von *rhetor* bei Quintilian, *Institutionis oratoriae libri XII*, hg. und übers. von Helmut Rahn, 2 Bde. (Darmstadt, 1972), XII.1.1, und Isidor, *Etymologiae* (wie Anm. 3), II.3.1f.; dies übernimmt z. B. Alcuin, *Dialogus de rhetorica et virtutibus*, PL, CI, 245D; Vincenz von Beauvais, *Speculum doctrinale* (wie Anm. 42), III.100, Sp. 281D. Ähnlich Horaz, *Ars poetica* (wie Anm. 73), 445; vgl. weiter Lausberg (wie Anm. 91), § 32f.

[131] Johannes von Salisbury, *Metalogicon* (wie Anm. 3), II.4.860b; Johannes bezieht sich nach Webb auf Augustin, *Dialectica*, I, PL, XXXII, 1409, und schließt den Sophisten ein: 'Item non bene disputat qui id quod intendit uere et probaliter, nequaquam probat. Pace dixerim demonstratoris et sophiste, quorum neuter bene procedit ad propositum dialectici.'

[132] Johannes von Salisbury, *Metalogicon* (wie Anm. 3), II.13.870c. Johannes hat vorher (ebd., II.12.869d) die gemeinten *circumstantie* mit Bezugnahme auf 'Boetius in quarto Topicorum' als 'quis, quid, ubi, quibus adminiculis, cur, quomodo, quando' aufgezählt.

lichen Syllogismus zur Aufhebung eines Sophismas wie folgt beschreibt:[133]

'ex probabilibus': in hoc tam syllogizandi modus quam syllogismi materia denotatur, in quo tam probabilitas materiae quam formae est intellegenda, ut utraque tam sophistici quam temptativi syllogismi species removeatur. Per probabilitatem enim formae removentur sophisticus sive litigiosus et temptativus syllogismus, quorum hic ex principiis, ille ex probabilibus syllogizat apparenter. Per hoc quod habet probabilitatem materiae removentur illi quorum hic ex apparentibus principiis, ille ex apparentibus probabilibus syllogizat.

Zuvor hat der Anonymus die *probabilia* der Materie mit Bezug auf die *Topik* des Aristoteles durch die *loci communes* benannt:

Quae autem sint probabilia praesentis negotii non est determinare, quae tamen Aristoteles in Topicis hac descriptione manifestat: 'probabilia autem sunt quae videntur' et cetera. Sed notandum quoniam cum et verum et falsum sit probabile, tamen in eo differunt quoniam probabile excedit utrumque et exceditur ab utroque. Item differunt iudicio, nam utrum verum vel falsum sit aliquid ex re ipsa de qua dicitur iudicium sumitur. Si enim res se habet, ut dicitur, verum est, si non, falsum. Utrum vero probabile sit quod dicitur ex opinione, natura, consuetudine dinoscitur, aut ex similitudine vel, si mavis, ex adiunctione. Est enim probabile quod unicuique natura suggerit, ut patrem vel matrem diligere

---

[133] Aristoteles schließt seine *Topik* bekanntlich mit einem den Trugschlüssen gewidmeten Buch, das Boethius, Jacobus (siehe den Editor, S. XXXIII–XXXV) und Wilhelm von Moerbeke gesondert übersetzten: *De sophisticis elenchis* (wie Anm. 109). Zu den Fehlern der Trugschlüsse als Ansätzen zur Korrektur siehe ebd., S. 15,5–8; und zu den einzelnen Typen weiter bis 19,21; 64,16–18. Auch *Glose in Aristotilis Sophisticos Elencos*, hg. von de Rijk (wie Anm. 105), II.17, S. 242,18f.: 'Recta solutio est manifestatio falsi sillogismi secundum quod falsum.' Ähnlich die *Summa Sophisticorum Elencorum*, hg. von de Rijk (wie Anm. 105), S. 430,3–5. Beispiele von Fehlschlüssen werden mit der entsprechenden *solutio* angeführt; siehe z. B. die *Fallaciae breves (ad modum Oxoniae)*, hg. von Kopp (wie Anm. 105, 1982), 264–73. – Boethius, *Elenchorum sophisticorum Aristotelis interpretatio*, II.2: 'De apparenti solutione respondentis', PL, LXIV, 1025D–28A; und zur Kontradiktion, die man im Sophisma nachweisen sollte: ebd., II.5, PL, LXIV, 1034AB. – Johannes von Salisbury, *Metalogicon* (wie Anm. 3), I.19.850b: 'Verborum autem significatio diligentius excutienda est, et quid sermo quilibet in se, quid ab adiunctis in contextu possit, sollertius perscrutandum, ut sophismatum umbras, que uerum obnubilant, discutere possit. Dicendi autem ratio pensanda est ex circumstantiis dictorum, ex qualitate persone, ex qualitate auditorum, ex loco et tempore, aliisque uario modo apud diligentem exploratorem considerandis.' – *Speculum doctrinale* (wie Anm. 42), III.98, Sp. 280BC: 'Modus autem soluendi paralogismos est uniuscuiusque fallaciam siue locum sophisticum assignare, et in consequentia [besser: inconsequentia] conclusionis ostendere, sicut iam superius tactum est, ex 8. libro Topicorum, in capitulo de falsa oratione.' Zur *falsa oratio* siehe ebd., III.87f., Sp. 273A–74B. – *Anonymus Aurelianensis I* (wie Anm. 105), S. 57.

filium. Est etiam probabile quod suggeritur a consuetudine, ut amico benefaciendum et inimico nocendum. Similiter ex opinione sive ex auctoritate, ut lunam esse rotundam. Nullus enim noscit sic esse, sed sic opinantur plures, vel forsitan invenitur scriptum ab aliquo auctore qui fortassis hoc habebat ex sola opinione. Item probabile est ex adiunctione vel similitudine, ut contrariorum esse eundem sensum quemadmodum eorundem est eadem disciplina. Quoniam itaque tot sunt species probabilis, et dialecticus syllogismus fit ex probabilibus, tot modis fit dialecticus syllogismus. Ut ergo volens dialectice syllogizare abundet in probabilibus, considerandum est quid suadeat natura, quid hominum consuetudo teneat, quid plurium opinio ferat, considerandum etiam et in similitudine.[134]

Dazu sollte man bedenken, daß die *loci communes* zwar besonders Juristen und Philosophen oder Theologen, Redner und Logiker als *sedes argumentorum* interessiert haben werden, die Handbücher zur Topik auch von solchen verfaßt wurden, daß aber schon Aristoteles einmal mit Aiax, Ulixes, Achilles und Nestor, also mit poetischen Beispielen den Gebrauch eines Topos erläutert, daß Cicero und mehr noch Isidor die *Topica* auch den *poetae* empfehlen,[135] selbst *Poetriae* des Hochmittelalters die Topik durchaus einbeziehen. Insbesondere Matthaeus von Vendôme (der auch einmal 'Boetius in *Cathegoricis sillogismis*' zitiert) und mit ihm Gervais von Melkley berücksichtigen die *circumstantiae* recht genau als *loci* poetischer Deskriptionslehre.[136] Im 13. Jahrhundert

---

[134] Ebd., S. 56. Zitiert wird hier, wie der Editor anmerkt, Aristoteles, *Topica* I.1.100b.21–23. Man kennt auch im Mittelalter verschiedene Aufstellungen der argumentatorischen Topoi; vgl. nur Vincenz von Beauvais, *Speculum doctrinale* (wie Anm. 42), III.46–48, Sp. 245E–47D; ebd., III.106f., Sp. 285E–86E. Sie sind wenig untersucht; zur Forschungssituation vgl. Lothar Bornscheuer, 'Topik', in *Reallexikon der deutschen Literaturgeschichte*, hg. von Klaus Kanzog und Achim Masser, Bd. IV, 2. Aufl. (Berlin/New York, 1984), S. 454–75.
[135] Aristoteles, *Topica: translatio Boethii* (wie Anm. 45), III.2, S. 54,22–55,10. Isidor, *Etymologiae* (wie Anm. 3), II.30.17: 'Memoriae quoque condendum est Topica oratoribus, Dialecticis, poetis et iurisperitis communiter quidem argumenta praestare; sed quando aliquid specialiter probant, ad Rhetores, poetas, iurisperitosque pertinent; quando vero generaliter disputant, ad philosophos attinere manifestum est.' Cicero, *Topica*, hg. und übers. von H.M. Hubbell (Cambridge, Mass./London, 1949; Nachdr. 1960), VII.32 (zu *similitudo*); XVIII.67 (zum *locus qui efficitur ex causis*), erklärt einzelne *loci* als besonders für Dichter geeignet. Er zitiert auch ein Beispiel aus der Poesie (ebd., XVI.61) und hebt (ebd., XX.78) dazu den Beweiswert des Zitats in topischer Argumentation hervor: 'et oratores et philosophos et poetas et historicos, ex quorum et dictis et scriptis saepe auctoritas petitur ad faciendam fidem.' Boethius scheint auch an die Dichter zu denken, nennt sie aber nicht ausdrücklich; vgl. *In topica Ciceronis*, PL, LXIV, 1116BC.
[136] Matthaeus (wie Anm. 32), I.74–117 (S. 135–151); II.38 (S. 165,48); Gervais von Melkley, *Ars poetica*, hg. von Hans-Jürgen Gräbener, Forschungen zur romanischen Philologie, 17 (Münster, 1965), S. 201,1–204,12 (dazu S. CVII): 'Consequenter utile est noscere rationem coniecturalis probationis rhetorice, que consistit in locis vel argumentis' (ebd., S. 201,1–3). Und nach einigen Beispielen, Anweisungen und Aufzählung der

sehen bedeutende Gelehrte die *ars poetica* neben den sprachwissen-
schaftlichen Disziplinen als Teil der Logik.[137] Es bleibt genauer zu
prüfen, wie die *enarratio poetarum* des Triviums diesen Aspekt berücksichtigt, wofür es in der Tat manche Belege gibt. Ihrer Intention
nach ist Topik bei Aristoteles, Cicero, ausführlicher bei Boethius u. a.
zugleich *ars inveniendi* und *ars iudicandi*, wobei die *inventio* des
Arguments natürlich dem Urteil über die *causa* dient.[138] Wie schon im
Ansatz verschieden Topik darüberhinaus auch immer erklärt wird, sie
ist Inventions- wie Urteilslehre und in den beiden zusammengehö-
renden Funktionen, wie es scheint, auch für Dichter relevant gewesen,
offenbar selbst für gebildete volkssprachige Autoren.

Während Chrestien seine Königin lediglich bildhaft die übervolle
Giftigkeit des Beleidigers konstatieren und ihm einen Verweis für die
ungezogene Schmährede erteilen läßt (*Yv.* 86–91), sucht Hartmanns
künegîn Keies Aggression mit topisch wahrscheinlich schlüssiger Argumentation zu entschärfen (*Iw.* 137–58). Sie legt dar, daß Keies Verhalten
wohl mehr für ihn selbst als für die anderen schädlich ist (*Iw.* 138f.), und
entwickelt dies folgerichtig mittels sechs Aussagen, deren erster sie in
Parenthese das zu Beweisende bzw. zu Folgernde einschiebt: 'und
enschadest niemen mê dâ mite/ danne dû dir selbem tuost' (*Iw.* 138f.).
Von den sechs Argumenten der Rede gehören je zwei in ihrem
topischen Ansatz zusammen; die Königin spricht nämlich erstens in
zweierlei Hinsicht von der Wertlosigkeit der *site* selbst (*Iw.* 137–45; ohne
138f.), dann wendet sie sich zweitens deren Konsequenzen zu und
konstatiert mittels zwei Aussagen die Unschädlichkeit der schlechten
site Keies für die andern (*Iw.* 146–52), um schließlich drittens wieder in
einem Doppelschritt mit einem Blick auf das seelisch Verursachende,
das allbekannt hinter dieser *site* steht, und mit Chrestiens Bild des
Platzens deren Schädlichkeit für Keie selbst nahezulegen (*Iw.* 153–58).
In diesen Zweiergruppen ist das zweite Argument stets im ersten
impliziert und aus ihm entwickelt, so daß der Gedankengang, wie mir

---

attributa persone wie *negotio* abschließend: 'De huiusmodi igitur locis, quin valde necessarii
sunt, rhetoricas consulamus et in istis contenti simus Cicerone.' Gervais zitiert im
Zusammenhang des *enthymema* breit aus Ciceros *Topica* und erläutert verschiedene ihrer
Spezies, die er wie Cicero als *ex contrariis conclusa* versteht; siehe ebd., S. 157,1–181,11.
Galfred, *Poetria nova*, hg. von Faral (wie Anm. 32), 1274f. (S. 236); 1740–42 (S. 250); S. 242–
45 registriert Faral (ebd.) zu einem Textbeispiel der *Poetria nova* (1462–565) verschiedene
circumstantiae rei.

137   Hier nenne ich nur Vincenz von Beauvais, *Speculum doctrinale* (wie Anm. 42), III.109,
Sp. 287D; so auch 280C.

138   Aristoteles, *Topica: translatio Boethii* (wie Anm. 45), VIII.1, S. 156,3–8; *Topicorum
Aristotelis translatio anonyma* (12. Jahrhundert), ebd., S. 288,3–8. Cicero, *Topica* (wie Anm.
135), II.6f.; Martianus Capella (wie Anm. 44), V.442; Boethius, *In topica Ciceronis*, PL,
LXIV, 1044C–48A; Johannes von Salisbury, *Metalogicon* (wie Anm. 3), II.5.860d–861b;
II.6.862b; III.5.892b; und weitere; vgl. die Darstellung der Topik unter *inventio* und
argumentatio bei Lausberg (wie Anm. 91), § 260–62; 348–430, besonders 366–409.

scheint, dreigliedrig ist. Mit dem zu beweisenden Satz und einer ihm zugeordneten Doppelaussage sowie mit zwei weiteren als Prämissen gegebenen Doppelaussagen zeigt er eine erkennbar syllogistische Struktur, nämlich die rhetorisch erweiterte Form des hypothetischen Syllogismus, die zu Hartmanns Zeit *epichirema* heißt.[139] Welchen Zuschnitt haben die sechs Argumente im einzelnen? Wie könnten sie sich vorsichtig mit den topischen Suchformeln für rhetorisches Argumentieren beschreiben lassen, vorsichtig angesichts des Wenigen, was bisher über mittelalterliche Traktate zur Topik bekannt ist, aber auch vorsichtig wegen des sehr kleinen Ausschnitts aus dem *Iwein*, der kaum Festlegung auf eine bestimmte Terminologie erlaubt, wie z. B. auf die der aristotelischen oder ciceronischen *Topica*, die in *De Inventione* oder der *Rhetorica ad Herennium*, bei Quintilian, Martianus Capella oder wem immer.

Betrachten wir die Antwort der Königin im einzelnen. Fraglich ist die beiläufig eingeschobene Behauptung, daß Keie mit seiner *site* niemandem mehr schade als sich selbst (*Iw.* 137–39). Redegegenstand ist also die *site* des Keie und zwar im Hinblick auf ihre Schädlichkeit, dies in einem ungleich relationierenden Sinn, d. h. die Schädlichkeit der *site* für Keie selbst wird größer eingeschätzt als diejenige für andere. Dies gilt es in der Rede argumentativ zu bekräftigen. Da mit Keie und anderen Personen ganz bestimmte Geschehenszusammenhänge zur Debatte stehen, handelt es sich bei dieser *quaestio* oder *dubitabilis propositio* um ein rhetorisch zu behandelndes und nicht im eigentlichen Sinne dialektisches Problem; die Frage oder zu bestätigende Behauptung der Königin ist eine hypothetische, im Rahmen ihrer *circumstantiae* zu betrachtende *causa*.[140] Um sie im folgenden in jedem Punkt gemäß ihrer

---

[139] Vgl. die Beschreibung der weiten Schlußform ohne den Terminus bei Cicero, *De inventione* (wie Anm. 8), I.37–39, 67–72, sowie auch die Darstellung von sieben Modi des Schließens in Ciceros *Topica* (wie Anm. 135), 13–14.54–57, wo sich aber nur der Terminus Enthymem findet (in einer nicht im mittelalterlichen Sprachgebrauch vorherrschenden Auffassung). Quintilian (wie Anm. 130), V.14.5–19 u. ö. im folgenden, bringt beide Termini; er spricht in Anlehnung an Cicero von vier, fünf oder sechs Teilen des *epichirema*, hält aber die dreiteilige Grundform aus *intentio, adsumptio, connexio* für wesentlich (V.14.5f.). Als *longior syllogismus* beschreibt das *epycherema* Remigius von Auxerre (wie Anm. 44), IV.152.9 (S. 14,4–9); ähnlich vorher Fortunatian, Cassiodor und Isidor (abweichend Victorin und Iulius Victor); vgl. *Rhetores Latini minores*, hg. von Karl Halm (Leipzig, 1863; Nachdr. Frankfurt am Main, 1964), S. 118,30–119,2; 247,40–42; 411,35–412,2; 500,9–17; 512,22–32. Als verkürzten und erweiterten Syllogismus kontrastiert Enthymem und Epichirem auch Vincenz von Beauvais, *Speculum doctrinale* (wie Anm. 42), III.105, Sp. 285CD; vgl. weiter H. Schepers, 'Epichirem', in *Historisches Wörterbuch der Philosophie* (wie Anm. 49), Bd. II, Sp. 577–79; auch Lausberg (wie Anm. 91), § 371.

[140] Vgl. Vincenz von Beauvais, *Speculum doctrinale* (wie Anm. 42), III.43, Sp. 244BC: 'Quæstionis duæ sunt species. Vna scilicet Thesis, quæ de re cæteris circunstantiis nuda quærit ac disserit: vt "voluptas ne summum bonum sit?" Hæc à nobis propositio, vel propositum dicitur: et tales maxime à dialecticis ad disputationem sumuntur. Altera vero Hypothesis, quæ scilicet personis, temporibus, factis, cæteris que circunstantiis implicita

Behauptung klären zu können, bestimmt die Königin lehrbuchgemäß ('A diffinitione ergo incipimus')[141] gleich mit dem zu beweisenden Satz den fraglichen Redegegenstand. Zweifach beschreibt sie Keies gewohntes Handeln, seine *site*, mit der er 'iemer' allen begegnet, dem 'ingesinde' wie den Gästen (*Iw*. 140-45). Mit der Handlungsbeschreibung wählt die Königin die *notio*; diese ist nach Cicero und anderen eine Art der *definitio*,[142] keine universal substantielle, sondern eine nur durch *proprietates* beschreibende, 'non enim dixit quid est homo, sed quid agat', wie Isidor die *notio* erklärt. Auch Vincenz von Beauvais behandelt diese Nebenform des Definierens, die wie alle Definitionen als Argument *a toto* dienen kann.[143]

Die deskriptive Definition (*Iw*. 140-45) inkriminiert die fragliche *site* folgendermaßen: erstens in beiden Sätzen allein schon durch Benennen des Handelns mit *hazzen* und *nît* (*Iw*. 140-42), weil die Wörter auch damals moralischen Unwert implizieren. Hartmann hätte dies leicht mit dem Beispiel des die Menschheit hassenden 'nidis vater Lucifer'[144] bekräftigen können oder mit einer Sentenz über die moraltheologische Einschätzung der *mala consuetudo*.[145] Beidem kommt im Endeffekt nahe,

---

est [. . .] hæc à nobis dicitur causa.' Vgl. auch Boethius, *In Topica Ciceronis*, PL, LXIV, 1048D; vorher (1048BC) erklärt Boethius das topische Argument mit Cicero, *Topica* (wie Anm. 135), II.8.

[141] Johannes von Salisbury, *Metalogicon* (wie Anm. 3), II.6.862cd; auch Martianus Capella (wie Anm. 44), V.475; Boethius, *Liber de diffinitione*, PL, LXIV, 891B.

[142] Cicero, *Topica* (wie Anm. 135), XXII.83: 'Cum autem quid sit quaeritur, notio explicanda est et proprietas et divisio et partitio. Haec enim sunt definitioni attributa; additur etiam descriptio [. . .] Notio sic quaeritur: sitne id aequum quod ei qui plus potest utile est. Proprietas sic: [. . .] Divisio et eodem pacto partitio sic: [. . .] Descriptio, qualis sit avarus, qualis assentator ceteraque eiusdem generis, in quibus et natura et vita describitur.' Vgl. ebd., V.26f.; VI.28; dazu Boethius, *In Topica Ciceronis*, PL, LXIV, 1057BC; 1092B-93C, besonders 1093B; 1106BC; auch Martianus Capella (wie Anm. 44), V.475. Hartmanns Königin wendet eine derartige *descriptio* der Natur und Lebensweise Keies an und kein eigentlich logisches Definitionsverfahren. Vgl. Abaelard, 'Topica', in *Dialectica* (wie Anm. 44), III.1, S. 338,23-33; Johannes von Salisbury, *Metalogicon* (wie Anm. 3), II.6.862d, 863bc, behält sie den *suprema* vor, 'quia genere, et infima, quia differentiis carent, diffiniri non possunt. Eis tamen descriptio applicatur que fit ex proprietatibus'.

[143] Isidor, *Etymologiae* (wie Anm. 3), II.29.3; II.30.2; ähnlich II.29.8; dies nach Cicero, *Topica* (wie Anm. 135), II.8; ebd., II.9: Sed ad id totum de quo disseritur tum definitio adhibetur, quae quasi involutum evolvit id de quo quaeritur; siehe dazu Boethius, *In Topica Ciceronis*, PL, LXIV, 1052D; 1056BC: 'Ergo locus qui dicitur ex toto, id est, quoties argumentum ex alicujus diffinitione termini qui est in quæstione tractatur, sive subjecti, sive prædicati.' Ausführlich dazu ebd., 1059A-60B. *Speculum doctrinale* (wie Anm. 42), III.47, Sp. 246DE.

[144] *Summa theologiae*, V. 53, in *Die religiösen Dichtungen des 11. und 12. Jahrhunderts*, hg. von Friedrich Maurer, 3 Bde. (Tübingen, 1964-70), Bd. I, S. 310; vgl. Hartmut Freytag, *Kommentar zur frühmittelhochdeutschen Summa theologiae*, Medium Aevum, Philologische Studien, 19 (München, 1970), S. 60-62.

[145] Zur Beteiligung der *consuetudo* an der allegorisch dargestellten destruktiven Wirkung des Teufels oder der *malitia* vgl. *St. Trudperter Hohes Lied*, hg. von Hermann Menhardt (Halle, 1934), 1,11-16 und 19-22; 4,12-17. Zur moraltheologischen Einschätzung der *mala consuetudo* vgl. Mausbach (wie Anm. 7), Bd. II, S. 78, Anm. 2; 87; 181, Anm. 2; 186; 220f.; Vincenz von Beauvais, *Speculum morale* (wie Anm. 42), III.7, Sp. 1013B-18D.

was die Königin über Keies Verhalten denkt; biblisch theologische
Wendungen und Wertungen werden von ihr jedoch zunächst nicht
herangezogen. Um Keies Tun und Reden im Sinn ihres abschließenden
Urteils als wahrscheinlich 'bœse site' (*Iw.* 234) zu disqualifizieren, läßt
Hartmann die Königin zweitens im definierenden Satz ergänzen, wen
die *site* betrifft, daß nämlich Keies *hazzen* immer dem gilt, 'deme dehein
êre geschiht' (*Iw.* 141). Dieser Zusatz offenbart wiederum das Falsche
der *site*, denn wer sich erinnert, versteht sogleich, daß Keie bezüglich
der *êre* nicht im Sinne der philosophischen Maxime des *Iwein*-Eingangs
handelt, weil er ihre philosophisch anerkannte Funktion als Bestätigung
rehter güete nicht gebührend achtet, sich vielmehr im Affekt des Hasses
davon abwendet, während das Gute aber in der philosophisch
konzipierten Eingangspartie als *optabile* gilt, die Ehre als folgend und
anziehend.

Daß Keies *site* nicht recht, also 'bœse site' (*Iw.* 234) ist, begründet die
Königin jedoch auch nicht mit dieser Überlegung, sondern indem sie
das Falsche in Keies gewohntem Urteilen und Handeln nun als
unlogische Kontradiktion aufzeigt, und zwar mit einer paradoxen
Paronomasie:[146] 'der bœste ist dir der beste/ und der beste der bœste'
(*Iw.* 144f.). Die Pointe markiert die mangelnde Plausibilität der von Keie
geübten *site* und der ihr zugehörigen Trugschlüsse; denn *a
repugnantibus*[147] zeigt sich hier eindeutig der Fehler der *site*; denn solche
Gleichung widersprechender Begriffe bildet nach Aristoteles' *Categoriae*
keine sinnvolle Aussage.[148] Man könne nicht, heißt es dort, vom selben
Gegenstand zugleich Gegensätzliches behaupten, wie vom selben

---

[146] Vgl. nur *Anthologia Latina*, hg. von Franz Buecheler und Alexander Riese, Bd. I, 2
(Leipzig, 1906), Nr. 485 'De figuris vel schematibus', S. 15,108–111: 'Paronomasía./
Supparile est, alia aequisono si nomine dicas./ ''Mobilitas, non nobilitas.'' ''bona gens,
mala mens est.''/ ''Dividiae, non divitiae.'' ''tibi villa favilla est.'' '
[147] Zum *locus a repugnantibus* vgl. Cicero, *Topica* (wie Anm. 135), IV.21 (er gibt nur ein
Rechtsbeispiel); XII–XIII.53 (in Anm. 150 zitiert). Martianus Capella (wie Anm. 44), V.474,
492: 'a repugnantibus argumentum, cum ostenditur duo sibi cohaerere non posse, verbi
causa, ut et parasitus quis sit et ridiculus non sit, quae per negationem simul esse non
posse praedicantur hoc modo: ''non et parasitus est Gnatho et ridiculus non est''. eius loci
exemplum est in re magis ipsa quam forma verborum: ''is igitur non modo a te periculo
liberatus, sed etiam honore amplissimo ornatus arguitur domi suae te interficere
voluisse.'' ' Boethius, *In Topica Ciceronis*, PL, LXIV, 1077D–78C, der Ciceros Beispiel
ausführlich erklärt und resümiert (1078C): 'Argumentum, ab eo quod in ipso est de quo
agitur, id est de eo quod recte acceptum est. In ipso vero est velut affectum contrarietatis
modo, ut superius dictum est. Est autem argumentum a repugnanti. Maxima propositio,
repugnantia convenire non posse.' Abaelard, 'Topica', in *Dialectica* (wie Anm. 44), III.1, S.
374,23–384,9: sehr ausführlich über die Arten des von ihm unter *locus a contrariis*
subsumierten Gemeinplatzes.
[148] *Categoriae vel praedicamenta: Editio composita*, hg. von Laurentius Minio-Paluello,
Aristoteles latinus, I, 2 (Brügge/Paris, 1961), S. 74,7–75,10; vgl. Klaus Jacobi, ' ''gut'' und
''schlecht'': Die Analyse ihrer Entgegensetzung bei Aristoteles, bei einigen Aristoteles-
Kommentatoren und bei Thomas von Aquin', *Miscellanea Mediaevalia*, 15 (1982), 25–52;
siehe auch Abaelards Abhandlung 'De contrariis' (in der vorigen Anmerkung).

Menschen 'Sokrates ist gesund' und 'Sokrates ist krank'; derartiges verhielte sich wie Bejahung zu Verneinung, eine der Aussagen müsse falsch sein. Da Aristoteles dabei auch *bonum* und *malum* als *contrarium ex necessitate* erwähnt, scheint mir die Königin in der bewußt kontradiktorischen Gleichung von *besten* und *bœsten* ein Schulbeispiel zu steigern. Es ist demnach nicht nur, wie schon die Termini *hazzen* und *nît* besagen, moralisch verwerflich, es widerstrebt auch nicht nur der *gewissen lêre* des Prologs, wie der aufmerksame Leser erkennt, sondern es entbehrt erwiesenermaßen der Logik, wie die Kontradiktion (*Iw.* 144f.) zu erkennen gibt, wenn Keie durch seine Trugschlüsse die Besten zu den Bösesten und umgekehrt zu machen versucht. Die fragliche *site* ist somit beschrieben und definiert in ihrer irrationalen und falschen Wertlosigkeit.

Nachdem die Königin ihre Antwort auf Keies Sophismen mit dieser umfänglich definierenden Handlungsbeschreibung eröffnet hat, dabei die fragliche *site* bereits durch die Termini *hazzen* und *nît* und begründet *a repugnantibus* als gewiß falsche *site* zu erkennen gegeben hat, nutzt sie das hiermit Gesagte im folgenden argumentierend aus. Um nämlich nun die Unschädlichkeit der *mala consuetudo* oder *bœsen site* für die andern und deren wahrscheinliche Schädlichkeit für Keie selbst darzustellen, betrachtet sie das Gesagte, wie es im hypothetischen Syllogismus nach Abaelard geschehen sollte,[149] zunächst *a consequentibus*.[150] Das heißt, sie argumentiert im zweiten Teilschritt ihrer syllogistischen Ausführungen mit dem aus der Definition der *site* Folgenden (*Iw.* 146–52).

Was die Konsequenz des beschriebenen Handelns angeht, so hält die Königin Keie folgendes tröstlich entgegen: 'daz man dirz immer wol vertreit', d. h., daß man dir dein Handeln nie übel nimmt, 'daz kumt von dîner gewonheit', ist Konsequenz der *site*. Die Wendung 'daz kumt von' kennzeichnet den auf das aus der *gewonheit* Folgende gerichteten Gedankengang. Die Konsequenz des *wol vertragens* ergibt sich aus dem, worin Keies Gewohnheit definitionsgemäß besteht, nämlich: 'daz dus

---

149 'Topica', in *Dialectica* (wie Anm. 44), III.1, S. 259,1–5. Johannes von Salisbury, *Metalogicon* (wie Anm. 3), III.6.904d, hält diese Auffassung mit Boethius für zu eng.
150 Zu den *loci a consequentibus* und *ab antecedente* bzw. zur notwendigen Korrelation der beiden Aspekte vgl. Cicero, *Topica* (wie Anm. 135), XII–XIII.53: 'Deinceps est locus dialecticorum proprius ex consequentibus et antecedentibus et repugnantibus. Nam coniuncta, de quibus paulo ante dictum est, non semper eveniunt; consequentia autem semper. Ea enim dico consequentia quae rem necessario consequuntur; itemque et antecedentia et repugnantia. Quidquid enim sequitur quamque rem, id cohaeret cum re necessario; et quidquid repugnat, id eius modi est ut cohaerere numquam possit. Cum tripertito igitur distribuatur locus hic, in consecutionem, antecessionem, repugnantiam, reperiendi argumenti locus simplex est, tractandi triplex.' (Es folgt die Beschreibung der sieben Schlußformen.) Boethius, *In Topica Ciceronis*, PL, LXIV, 1066AC; 1075B–77D; 1124A–29B; 1137A–41B; Martianus Capella (wie Anm. 44), V.490f.; Abaelard, 'Topica', in *Dialectica* (wie Anm. 44), III.1, S. 364,31–369,12.

die bœsen alle erlâst/ und niuwan haz ze den vrumen hâst' (*Iw.* 149f.; wie *Iw.* 140f.). Die *gewonheit*, die, wie vorher gesagt, allein die *vrumen*, Rechtschaffenen und Guten treffen will, impliziert, wenn man sie im Hinblick auf ihre für die *vrumen* gegebene Konsequenz betrachtet, daß diese Keies gewohnt böses Verhalten nicht übelnehmen. Eine ethisch einwandfreie Reaktion, wie Hartmann gut mit Blick auf die Bibel hätte feststellen können, denn jeder kennt das Gebot der Sanftmut (Mt. 5. 5; Lc. 6. 22), der verzeihenden Liebe: 'Liebet eure Feinde; tut Gutes denen, die euch hassen; segnet die, welche euch fluchen; bittet für die, welche euch beleidigen!' (Lc. 6. 27f.), oder daß man die linke Wange darbieten solle, wenn man auf die rechte geschlagen worden ist (Mt. 5. 39; Lc. 6. 29). Hartmanns Königin sieht die *vrumen* zwar im Sinne biblischer Ethik reagieren, bemüht aber gar nicht die Bibel, um die Reaktion der *vrumen* als richtig zu erweisen. Sie hebt vielmehr deren logische Rechtheit durch ein Zusatzargument hervor, das sie in dem *a consequentibus* Gegebenen findet, indem sie nun die besondere geistige Qualität der *vrumen* als der Personen in den Blick nimmt, die Keie mit seiner falschen *site* zu treffen sucht.

Wie Boethius Vernunftgründe vorbringt, die dagegen sprechen, daß die Weisen die Bösen hassen, und vielmehr für weises Mitleid mit den Bösen plädiert,[151] so vermag Hartmanns Königin mit anderen vernünftigen Argumenten das *wol vertragen* als Reaktion auf Keies Anwürfe zu rechtfertigen: Da die *vrumen* gemäß der philosophischen Korrespondenz von *bonitas* und *sapientia* natürlich 'al die wîsen' sind (*Iw.* 152; so auch *Yv.* 1325–27, *Iw.* 1499–510), können sie keinen Anlaß sehen, Keie etwas übelzunehmen; denn sie wissen, daß das Gegenteil des Gesagten dort zutreffen muß, wo aus Bosheit widersprüchlich und 'verkehrt' geurteilt wurde. Sie stellen das widersprüchlich Falsche in Keies *site* konsequent richtig, indem sie Keies Fehlurteil umkehren, offenbar nach dem Grundsatz 'contrariorum enim contraria sunt consequentia'.[152] Wenn man weiß, daß Keies Schelten fälschlich den *besten* zum *bœsten* zu machen versucht und umgekehrt, dann muß

---

151 *Consolatio* (wie Anm. 39), IV.4 prosa, S. 196,160–198,167: 'Daher rührt es, daß bei den Weisen überhaupt gar kein Platz für den Haß übrigbleibt. Denn wer wäre ein so völliger Tor, daß er die Guten hassen möchte? Die Schlechten aber zu hassen, entbehrt der Vernunft; denn wenn die Lasterhaftigkeit, wie ein körperliches Siechtum, eine Krankheit des Geistes ist und wenn wir die körperlich Kranken keineswegs des Hasses, sondern eher des Mitleids für würdig halten, so sind noch weit mehr diejenigen nicht zu verfolgen, sondern zu bedauern, deren Geist die Ruchlosigkeit bedrängt, die schlimmer ist als alles Siechtum.'

152 Cicero, *Tusculanae disputationes* (wie Anm. 9), V.17.50: 'Wenn man bekennt, daß eine hinlänglich große Kraft in den Lastern zum elenden Leben liege; muß man nicht gestehen, daß die Tugend dieselbe Kraft zum glückseligen Leben besitze? Denn aus Entgegengesetztem folgt Entgegengesetztes.' Vgl. zur Gegenfolgerung *e contrario* aus Position und Negation bei Aristoteles, *Topica* (wie Anm. 45), III.4, S. 75,4–10; auch I.9, S. 15,24–16,7; II.7f., S. 41,1–44,7; besonders II.8, S. 43,9–44,7.

folglich richtig derjenige, den Keie zum *bœsten* zu machen versucht, der *beste* sein und umgekehrt. Keies falsches Schelten zeichnet demnach paradoxerweise die *besten* aus, sie hat die im *Iwein*-Eingang gemäß philosophischer Lehre beschriebene Funktion des Lobs[153] und kann deshalb *wol vertragen* werden. Auf diese Weise im *locus a consequentibus* durchdacht, gilt Keies Schelten bei den *wîsen* also als verträglich und für sie, die Betroffenen, nicht schädlich, wiewohl das Schelten als solches falsch und böse ist.

Dies gleicht einem Kernsatz christlicher Philosophie nicht nur bei Augustin. Mit Boethius ist das Böse als solches ohne Sein und ohne Fähigkeit, sein Ziel zu erreichen: 'wie sehr also auch die Schlechten toben, dem Weisen wird sein Kranz nicht herabfallen noch welken; denn fremde Bosheit entwendet edlen Seelen nicht ihre eigene Zier'.[154] Oder mit Hugo von St. Viktor[155] ist das *malum*, mag es auch *secundum se* nichts anderes als *malum* sein, doch *ad aliquid* betrachtet ein *bonum*. In diesem Sinne und auch wieder nah einem biblischen Paradox ('vertitque [sc. Dominus] maledictionem eius in benedictionem tuam, eo quod diligeret te', Deut. 23. 5), sagt die Königin: 'dîn schelten ist ein prîsen' (*Iw.* 151). Bibelwort, philosophische Ethik und logische Operation des Dichters bzw. seiner fingierten Person gehen hier Hand in Hand bei der Formulierung eines Gedankens, der, Chrestien, Hartmanns Quelle, erweitert. Der Dichter könnte Anregung zu dem Paradox 'dîn schelten ist ein prîsen' (*Iw.* 151), das als Zitat und zugleich als logisch integrierter Teil der Argumentation seiner Königin zu sehen ist, nicht nur in der Bibel, sondern ebenso bei Boethius und dem Bischof Martin von Bracara empfangen haben oder im *Policraticus* des Johannes von Salisbury: 'Nolo, inquit sapiens, ab his laudari quorum laus uituperium est, nec ab his culpari uereor quorum criminatio laus est.' Der *Accessus Lucani* sagt über Lucans Intention, Nero zu loben: 'Recte autem intelligentibus haec laus est vituperatio.'[156]

153   Vgl. die Nachweise oben um Anm. 76, 79–82, 84f.

154   Mausbach (wie Anm. 7), Bd. I, S. 105–10; weiteres bei H. Reiner, 'Bosheit', in *Historisches Wörterbuch der Philosophie* (wie Anm. 49), Bd. I, Sp. 953f. Boethius, *Consolatio* (wie Anm. 39), IV.1f. prosa, S. 164,9–178,161; vgl. besonders S. 178,153–58: 'Ex quibus omnibus bonorum quidem potentia, malorum vero minime dubitabilis apparet infirmitas veramque illam Platonis esse sententiam liquet solos, quod desiderent, facere posse sapientes, improbos vero exercere quidem, quod libeat, quod vero desiderent, explere non posse.' Gigon weist hierzu (S. 296) auf Platos *Gorgias*, besonders 466B–68E. Boethius, *Consolatio* (wie Anm. 39), IV.3 prosa, S. 180,14–16, ist oben zitiert.

155   'De Sacramentis' I.4.20, PL, CLXXVI, 241C: 'Quod vero ad aliquid et non secundum se bonum dicitur, non substantialiter bonum dicitur, quia ipsum bonum non est, sed accidentaliter et denominative'; ebd., 242CD: 'Ex eo enim quod bonum non est et alicui bonum est, illud etiam sequi necesse est quod bonum est et alicui bonum est: [. . .] ex malo bonum [. . .] et malum bonis ad bonum.'

156   *Consolatio* (wie Anm. 39), I.3 prosa, S. 12,38f., spricht von Philosophen seinesgleichen, 'deren oberster Grundsatz ist, den Schlechten zu mißfallen'. Martin von Bracara (wie Anm. 7), S. 244,37f.: 'Laetior esto quotiens displices malis et malorum de te

Nun geht es endlich nach dem fundierten Erweis der Unschädlichkeit von Keies *bœser site* für andere darum, deren Schädlichkeit für Keie selbst wahrscheinlich zu machen. Freilich mildert die Königin dies Negative und sucht die *site* zuerst gewissermaßen als das für Keie kleinere Übel darzustellen, indem sie mit Chrestien (*Yv.* 86: 'ja fussiez crevez') behauptet, daß die *site* des Scheltens fürwahr Keies 'Platzen' verhindere: 'dune hetest ditz gesprochen/ dû wærst benamen zebrochen' (*Iw.* 153f.). Wie kommt sie darauf? Gibt es außer Chrestiens Text noch Anhaltspunkte für diese Überlegung im topischen Wissen der *litterati*? Und inwiefern kann man überhaupt von wahrscheinlich doch vorhandenem Schaden durch die falsche *site* für Keie reden, wenn sie doch Schlimmeres verhindert? Offenbar indem die Königin (*Iw.* 153f.) die fragliche *site* im Hinblick auf ihre Wirkung betrachtet, die sie verursacht, und von da aus zur Ursache als dem eigentlichen Übel gelangt. Das heißt, im Rahmen des *locus rerum efficientium*, und hier speziell in dessen Sonderfall, dem *locus rerum effectarum ab efficientibus causis*, wird ausgehend von den verursachten Dingen oder Wirkungen der Blick auf das Verderbliche der falschen *site* frei, denn das Verursachte weist, wie Cicero in seiner *Topica* ausführt, auf die Ursache selbst zurück. Damit ermöglicht dieser *locus* nach Cicero Rednern, Philosophen und Dichtern, prächtig, in bewundernswerter Redefülle zu vermelden, was eine Sache (soweit bekannt) in Zukunft alles bewirken könne, denn Kenntnis der Ursachen führe zu Kenntnis der Ereignisse.[157] Dieser Gemeinplatz, 'cum denuntiant quid ex quaque re sit futurum', wie Cicero sagt, erlaubt der Königin, auf rhetorisch seriöse Weise über das zu spekulieren (*Iw.* 153f.), was aus welchen bestimmten und allgemein anerkannten Gründen hätte geschehen können, und sie reicht diese Gründe sofort nach zur Stütze ihrer Annahme (*Iw.* 155–58). Während sie mit der Konjunktion 'wand' die im Rahmen des gewählten *locus* erforderliche Angabe der *causa efficiens* einleitet, beruft sie sich auf das Wissen aller: 'wand wir daz wizzen vil wol/ daz [. . .]' (*Iw.* 155f.). Was alle wissen, gilt seit Aristoteles' Topik

---

existimationes malas veram tui laudationem adscribe.' Johannes von Salisbury, *Policraticus* (wie Anm. 3), VIII.14.768c, S. 328,17–19. *Accessus Lucani*, hg. von Huygens (wie Anm. 3), S. 43,123f.

[157] Cicero, *Topica* (wie Anm. 135), XIV.58: 'Proximus est locus rerum efficientium, quae causae appellantur; deinde rerum effectarum ab efficientibus causis.' Ebd. XVIII.67: 'Coniunctus huic causarum loco ille locus est qui efficitur ex causis. Ut enim causa quid sit effectum indicat, sic quod effectum est quae fuerit causa demonstrat. Hic locus suppeditare solet oratoribus et poetis, saepe etiam philosophis, sed eis qui ornate et copiose loqui possunt, mirabilem copiam dicendi, cum denuntiant quid ex quaque re sit futurum. Causarum enim cognitio cognitionem eventorum facit.' Vgl. dazu Boethius, *In Topica Ciceronis*, PL, LXIV, 1066C; 1067C; 1079B–80B; Alcuin, *De Dialectica*, PL, CI, 971AC; Vincenz von Beauvais, *Speculum doctrinale* (wie Anm. 42), Sp. 247C.

meist als wahrscheinliches Argument,[158] wie für Cicero und Boethius so auch für Johannes von Salisbury: 'Probabilis autem uersatur in his que uidentur omnibus aut pluribus aut sapientibus; et his uel omnibus uel pluribus uel maxime notis et probabilibus aut consecutiuis eorum.'[159]

Daß die *site*, unter dem Aspekt der *causa efficiens* gesehen, für Keie selbst wahrscheinlich schädlich sein dürfte, wird dabei nur durch das unschöne Bild nahegelegt, mit dem die Königin nach Chrestien sagt, was Keie erfüllt und ihn zum Schelten bewegt. Indem sie nämlich Chrestiens Bild aufgreift und die Metapher 'venin' (*Yv.* 89) durch 'eiter[s]' (*Iw.* 156) variiert, argumentiert sie im *locus rerum effectarum ab efficientibus causis* metaphorisch vergleichend oder mit Hilfe eines Bilds, wie auch Alanus innerhalb eines Exordialtopos seines *Anticlaudianus* mit Bildern argumentiert.[160] Sie spricht also im Hinblick auf Keies *site* (als Wirkursache betrachtet) *a simili* oder *a comparatione*, und dabei sind befremdliche Unmöglichkeiten oder Übertreibungen erlaubt,[161] um ihren Kontrahenten auf die für ihn selbst wahrscheinlich recht bedenkliche Wirkung seiner *site* hinzuweisen. Durch Bilder, durch *similitudo* oder *comparatio*, vermag ein Redner lediglich Hinweise zu liefern, keine eigentlichen Beweise, deshalb ist die Stringenz des letzten Komplexes dieser Rede (*Iw.* 153–58) geringer als im ersten Beweiskomplex (*Iw.* 146–52), was wohl Rücksicht oder Mitleid[162] der guten und

---

158 Aristoteles, *Topica* (wie Anm. 45), I.1, S. 5,17–6,1: 'probabilia autem quae videntur omnibus aut pluribus aut sapientibus, et his vel omnibus vel pluribus vel maxime notis et (praecipuis) probabilibus'; I.10, S. 15,17–21; u. ö. sehr ähnlich.

159 Cicero, *Topica* (wie Anm. 135), XVIII.70, XX.76; Boethius, *In Topica Ciceronis*, PL, LXIV, 1167D–68D; Johannes von Salisbury, *Metalogicon* (wie Anm. 3), II.3.859d.

160 Alain de Lille, *Anticlaudianus*, hg. von R. Bossuat (Paris, 1955), S. 55: 'Cum fulminis impetus uires suas expandere dedignetur in uirgulam, uerum audaces prouectarum arborum expugnet excessus, imperiosa uenti rabies iras non expendat in calamum, uerum in altissimarum supercilia rerum uesani flatus inuectiones excitet furiosas, per uitiosam nostri operis humilitatem inuidie flamma non fulminet, nostri libelli depressam pauperiem detractionis flatus non deprimat, ubi potius miserie naufragium, misericordie portum expostulat, quam felicitas liuoris exposcat aculeum.' Hier wird die *captatio benevolentiae ab adversariis*, ein Topos des Exordiums, *a similitudine* begründet.

161 Zum *locus a comparatione* oder *similitudine* bzw. *a simili* vgl. Aristoteles, *Topica* (wie Anm. 45), I.13, S. 19,9–17; Cicero, *Topica* (wie Anm. 135), III.15; IV.23; besonders X.41–45, wo nach den geschichtlichen und erdachten Beispielen von Merkwürdigkeiten, Unmöglichkeiten, Übertreibungen, *mirabilia*, die Rede ist, wie sie Rednern und Philosophen im Rahmen dieses *locus* zugestanden werden als Argument: 'In hoc genere oratoribus et philosophis concessum est, ut muta etiam loquantur, ut mortui ab inferis excitentur, ut aliquid quod fieri nullo modo possit augendae rei gratia dicatur aut minuendae, quae ὑπερβολή dicitur, multa alia mirabilia. Sed latior est campus illorum. Eisdem tamen ex locis, ut ante dixi, et (in) maximis et minimis (in) quaestionibus argumenta ducuntur.' Boethius, *In Topica Ciceronis*, PL, LXIV, 1071D–72C; 1080B–81C; 1115C–19A; 1159B–64A; Martianus Capella (wie Anm. 44), V.487; Abaelard, 'Topica', in *Dialectica* (wie Anm. 44), III.2, S. 424,17–432,5: 'A comparatione'; S. 439,18–441,19: 'A simili'.

162 Vgl. Arthur T. Hatto, 'Die Höflichkeit des Herzens in der Dichtung der mittelhochdeutschen Blütezeit', in *Strukturen und Interpretationen: Festschrift für Blanka Horacek*, hg. von Alfred Ebenbauer u. a., Philologica Germanica, 1 (Stuttgart/Wien, 1974), S. 85–101.

redegewandten Königin nahelegt (und dem Dichter die Möglichkeit gibt, später neue und härtere Aspekte in den Disput einzubringen). Doch gestützt auf *opinio communis*, ist diese bildhafte Gedankenfolge auch nicht unklar oder ohne jede Wahrscheinlichkeit, vor allem vermag sie den Ernst, mit dem die Königin Keies Fehlverhalten verurteilt, nachdrücklich zu unterstreichen, denn das ziemlich groteske, aber nicht eben rätselhafte Bild ist leicht zu entschlüsseln. Wenn die Königin vom möglichen Platzen der ganzen, 'bitters eiters vol' sich vorzustellenden Person spricht, denkt sie vielleicht an Vergils Neider, der in den *Bucolica* mit böser Zunge zu schaden versucht, *ultra placitum* lobt und platzt:[163] 'Pastores, hedera crescentem ornate poetam,/ Arcades, invidia rumpantur ut ilia Codro;/ aut, si ultra placitum laudarit, baccare frontem/ cingite, ne vati noceat mala lingua futuro.' Ihr Bild könnte auch biblisch sein und Keie gleichsam miteins als den über und über eiternden Hiob auf dem Mist und den bitteres Unrecht redenden Simon Petrus apostrophieren oder Keies giftig bittere Kehle mit einem Psalmwort als offenes Grab und Unglück zu erkennen geben; das Bild scheint wie anderes aus dem Signifikantenbereich 'Krankheit' und 'Bitteres' für das Böse zu stehen,[164] wobei es dessen Defizienz betont, aber auch die Tücke und Schädlichkeit für den mit seinem Mangel Belasteten. Gleich den 'zwen eiterslangen in tuben bilde', Melot und Marjodo, in denen 'der eiterine nit' dem Tristan 'mit valsche und mit aswiche' begegnet,[165] ist das Bild in Hartmanns Kontext zu verstehen: 'bitters eiters vol' steht für das in ihrer Definition benannte *malum* der *site*, für *hazzen* und *nît* (*Iw.* 140–42). Das Bild *eiter* impliziert mit dem Attribut *bitter* zugleich das Schadhafte, das Keies Herz ausfüllt und seiner Ehre widerstrebt (*Iw.* 156–58), *bitter* hat nämlich nicht selten die Konnotation des Heillosen,[166] des Mangels dessen, was im *Iwein*-Prolog *sælde und êre* heißt. Damit dürfte der Schaden, der Keie aus seiner *site* nach topisch begründeter Ansicht wahrscheinlich erwachsen wird, deutlich genug zu erkennen sein. Mehr an- als ausgesprochen rundet die bildhafte Betrachtung der Gewohnheit im *locus rerum effectarum ab efficientibus causis* das vorher in der *definitio* und *a repugnantibus* sowie im *locus a consequentibus* Gesagte stimmig ab, so daß Keie mit seiner *site*, die

---

163 Vergil, *Opera*, hg. von Friedrich A. Hirtzel (Oxford, 1900; Nachdr. 1959), VII,25–28.
164 Vgl. Iob 2. 7f.; Act. 8. 21–23; Rom. 3. 13–17 gleich Ps. 13. 3; auch Ez. 13. 21; Osee 13. 8.
165 Gottfried von Straßburg (wie Anm. 12), 15060, 15078, 15088f.; Tristan erkennt Melot und Marjodo sofort und warnt Isolde: 'vor den habet iuwer sinne,/ sæligiu küniginne!/ wan swa die husgenoze sint/ gantlützet alse der tuben kint/ und alse des slangen kint gezagel,/ da sol man criuzen vür den hagel/ und segenen vür den gæhen tot./ sæligiu vrouwe, schœne Isot,/ nu hüetet iuch genote/ vor dem slangen Melote/ und vor dem hunde Marjodo!' (15091–101); vgl. weiter den ganzen Passus 15047–116.
166 Zu *bitter* siehe Friedrich Ohly, 'Geistige Süße bei Otfried', in *Typologia Litterarum: Festschrift für Max Wehrli*, hg. von Stefan Sonderegger u. a. (Zürich/Freiburg im Breisgau, 1969), S. 95–124 (S. 123–25).

nach allem nicht gut und nicht recht ist, in *hazzen* und *nît* besteht, im logisch falschen Reden über die *vrumen* sich auswirkt, ohne diesen zu schaden, vielmehr wahrscheinlich zum Schaden an der Ehre seines eigenen Herzens, nun gänzlich dem im Prolog gegebenen Ziel von *rehter güete, sælde* und *êre* entgegensteht. Durch die Argumentation der Königin wird also deutlich, daß Keie die Aussage der Eingangssentenz *ex negativo* exemplifiziert.

Eine in sich klare Argumentation bedarf nach Cicero nicht unbedingt einer wörtlichen Schlußfolgerung.[167] So endet auch die Königin, ohne daß sie aus den beigebrachten Argumenten noch die *conclusio* zöge, im Sinne des eingangs ihrer Entgegnung eingeschobenen Beweiszieles (*Iw.* 137–39). Man wird dies wohl umso eher verstanden haben, als ihre Argumentation wider das Böse dem theologisch geprägten Grundsatz genügt, nach dem das Böse auf den Bösen selbst zurückfällt:

> Wenn dies so ist, kann auch kein Weiser an der unentrinnbaren Strafe der Bösen zweifeln. Denn da gut und böse wie Strafe und Lohn einander entgegengesetzt sind, muß sich notwendigerweise das, was wir bei der Belohnung des Guten entstehen sehen, auf der Gegenseite bei der Bestrafung des Bösen wiederholen. Wie also den Guten die Güte selbst zur Belohnung wird, so ist den Bösen die Schlechtigkeit selbst Strafe.[168]

Keies böse Gewohnheit, über ehrenwerte Ritter falsch zu reden, dürfte sich nach allem nicht empfehlen. Gibt es nicht auch ein biblisches Gebot gegen das falsche Zeugnis (Exod. 20. 16), das Hartmann aber nicht erwähnt? Das in Sentenz und Exempel des Prologs, in andern Szenen der Vorgeschichte und in den betrachteten Dialogen implizierte Sinnangebot des *Iwein* ist im Stichwort *rehte güete* und seinen Implikaten, wie sie in philosophischen Texten und der Bibel zu finden sind, unübersehbar vorgegeben. Zu diesem Stichwort kann in den Texten, in denen es begegnet, wie bei Boethius das topische Argumentieren gehören, mit dem Hartmann es als wahrscheinlich *gewisse lêre* der betrachteten Partien seiner Romanerzählung zu explizieren weiß. Wie logisch rhetorische Verfahren es in anderen *artes* und Wissensgebieten der Zeit bezwecken, so scheint die logisch rhetorische Sprachkunst des Dichters mit durchaus unterhaltenden Reizen dem sich vergewissernden und harmonisierenden Interpretieren des Vorgegebenen zu dienen, sei es Interpretation der poetischen Quelle, sei es der überlieferten Normen, damit das Werk mit schulmäßig angelegtem Nachweis der Rechtheit des Guten, des Unrechts des Bösen, die von

---

167 Vgl. Cicero, *De inventione* (wie Anm. 8), I.40.72–74.
168 Boethius, *Consolatio* (wie Anm. 39), IV.3 prosa, S. 182,32–39; vgl. dazu Mausbach (wie Anm. 7), Bd. I, S. 119–22.

ihm erwartete Wahrheit und Lehre biete und dadurch exemplarisch wirke. Es versteht sich, daß dies der Schule verpflichtete Dichtungskonzept mit dem Aufgreifen weiterer poetischer Quellen als Chrestien und anderer Wertvorstellungen als derjenigen antiker und biblischer Ethik, das Angebot des Textes verbreitert, wie es im *Iwein* geschieht, ohne daß hier Raum für weiteres wäre.

Der aventiure bilde nemen:
The Intellectual and Social Environment of the Iwein Murals at Rodenegg Castle

MICHAEL CURSCHMANN

A few brief reminders should suffice to introduce the subject of this paper;[1] more than fifteen years after the re-discovery of the Iwein paintings at Rodenegg castle near Bressanone (Brixen) most Arthurian scholars have come into contact with them in one way or another.[2] One enters the surprisingly small (7 by 4 meters) ground-level room of the *palas* from the east. On the right, i.e. on the north wall, a knight on horseback, designated as YWAIN, encounters the wild man in the forest and proceeds to the magic fountain where he conjures up a storm. In the next two scenes he appears in single combat with the lord of this land, designated as ASCHELON, whom he wounds with a blow to the head. The west wall accommodates three scenes: between images of Iwein in hot pursuit through the castle gate being trapped by the falling portcullis that cuts his horse in half and of Iwein being saved by the maiden Lunete with a ring that will render him invisible, the badly damaged middle portion shows as the centerpiece of the whole composition the lady of the land with the dead or dying defender in her lap, in basic deposition or lamentation iconography. Finally, the south wall, too,

---

[1] My remarks at the conference were intended to suggest new approaches and to provoke discussion. Further research and detailed documentation are clearly needed, and this may well lead to substantial modifications, but in keeping with my original intent I have left the text virtually unchanged and added only a few indispensable bibliographical footnotes.

[2] It is, however, difficult to obtain a clear overview over the whole cycle from the accounts published so far. The best series of photographs may be found in Volker Schupp's article, 'Die Ywain-Erzählung von Schloß Rodenegg', in *Literatur und bildende Kunst im Tiroler Mittelalter*, ed. by Egon Kühebacher, Innsbrucker Beiträge zur Kulturwissenschaft, Germanistische Reihe, 15 (Innsbruck, 1982), pp. 1–27. Anne-Marie Bonnet, *Rodenegg und Schmalkalden: Untersuchungen zur Illustration einer ritterlich-höfischen Erzählung und zur Entstehung profaner Epenillustration in den ersten Jahrzehnten des 13. Jahrhunderts*, tuduv-Studien, Reihe Kunstgeschichte, 22 (Munich, 1986), provides useful schematic reconstructions of individual scenes.

comprises three scenes – scenes through which, in juxtaposition to the initial sequence of adventures on the opposite wall, a new relationship, the relationship between the hero and the lady, identified as LAVDINA, unfolds: he watches from above what is either the public display or the burial of Aschelon's body in Laudine's commanding presence; he escapes detection by the furious mob of the town; and guided by Lunete (LVNETA) he appears in total submission before the grief-stricken widow. Obviously this is the story of Iwein as structured and textualized by Chrétien de Troyes and adapted for German audiences by Hartmann von Aue, told in abbreviated and remarkably individualized pictorial fashion. The *tituli* record the names of the protagonists in their German (Bavarian) form, as one would expect it in that part of the world at that time, but there is no further indication as to the specific version of Chrétien's tale which the designer of this picture-story knew and in what form he knew it (or knew of it). In any event, that is not what concerns me at the moment.

Considerably more relevant to my own concerns is the matter of the date. During much of the scholarly discussion that quickly surrounded these pictures[3] they were thought to have been painted in the very early years of the thirteenth century, and that caused a great deal of confusion among literary historians attempting to fit them into the famous relative chronology of the classical period and of Hartmann von Aue's literary output in particular. In the last few years, it has become increasingly clear, however, that this cycle was painted quite a bit later: possibly 'in den 20er Jahren des 13. Jahrhunderts', as Anne-Marie Bonnet has put it (p. 62).[4] As we shall see, this later date makes it very much easier to account for this artistic undertaking in literary-historical terms, while it in no way alters the fact that we have in this picture cycle an extraordinary document without known precedent: the oldest surviving, and indeed known, representation in the monumental arts of the

[3] James Rushing has recently given us the first comprehensive account of all known pictorial representations of the Ywain/Iwein story as well as of the attendant scholarly discussions: James A. Rushing, Jr., *Adventures Beyond the Text: Iwain in the Visual Arts* (dissertation, Princeton University, 1987). The chapter on Rodenegg is on pp. 15–62. Bonnet's discussion of earlier work covers only the period until 1978; a brief but lucid, up-to-date review (and bibliographical documentation) specifically of the controversy surrounding the date of the murals is by Peter and Dorothea Diemer, ' "Qui pingit florem non pingit floris odorem": Die Illustrationen der Carmina Burana (Clm 4660)', *Jahrbuch des Zentralinstituts für Kunstgeschichte*, 3 (1987), pp. 43–75 (55–58).
[4] In an earlier detailed stylistic study of the artistic environment, Bonnet allows for an even later date: Anne Marie Birlauf-Bonnet, 'Überlegungen zur Brixener Malerei in den ersten Jahrzehnten des 13. Jahrhunderts', *Wiener Jahrbuch für Kunstgeschichte*, 37 (1984), 23–39 and 187–98: 'in den zwanziger bis dreißiger Jahren des 13. Jahrhunderts' (p. 38). Cf. also Schupp, esp. pp. 9 und 11. I myself hold with the Diemers that it should be possible, 'eine Hypothese aufzustellen, welche auch den Kriterien von Literaturchronologie und Rezeptionsbedingungen in der höfischen Gesellschaft angemessen Rechnung trägt, ohne das erste Viertel des 13. Jahrhunderts zu überschreiten' (p. 57).

High Middle Ages of a profane narrative subject in the context of profane architecture; vernacular literature visualized monumentally for a member of the secular upper-class who commanded the services of a first-rate artist; adventures from Arthurian romance, the beautiful lies of secular fiction, painted by people trained undoubtedly to furnish the faithful with images of the truth. How did all this become possible all of a sudden? That is the question to which I wish to propose a couple of answers in the form of 'unvorgreifliche Gedanken' that follow from two sub-questions: one, what is it that may have prompted people like the masters of Rodenegg to conceive of and initiate such a project in the first place? Two, what was it in the intellectual climate of that particular time that enabled them to carry it out – what, in other words, authorized their undertaking in intellectual terms and permitted the participation of what must surely have been a well established ecclesiastical workshop?

I

Our first question calls for the identification of an impulse strong enough to cause Arnold II or Arnold IV of Rodeneck to take a major, indeed unheard-of, initiative toward self-representation through literature. Such an impulse is most likely to derive from their social-feudal status. The Rodenecks were *ministeriales*, documented as such since 1126: nobles whose status and land tenure derived from administrative service to a regional overlord, in this instance the Bishop of Brixen, rather than from birth, as was the case with the old and free nobility. And it is worth remembering in this connection that similar status is generally ascribed to the (unknown) family that commissioned, only one generation later, a second picture cycle on the very same subject for the so-called Hessenhof in the town of Schmalkalden in Thuringia. This is not likely to be entirely coincidental, and one wonders of course why patronage of such revolutionary transfer of subjects from the current literary vogue into a major medium of visual representation did not involve the secular or ecclesiastical princes of the realm who were in fact the chief literary patrons of the day – people like the landgrave Hermann of Thuringia in the north or the bishop and patriarch Wolfger von Erla in the south. Why, to put this more generally, the conspicuous absence of the old nobility while the emerging service élite takes the lead in this movement towards representative appropriation and display of literary subjects? I am not talking here about the role of this new class of often successful, wealthy and powerful social climbers in the propagation of Arthurian narrative in general or the fact that Hartmann, Chrétien's chief adaptor in Germany, was himself a member of this group. I am talking about this rather specific phenomenon that such families go well beyond the usual forms of literary patronage and adopt such subjects as part of their permanent, every-day visual environment, as representative 'Hausbesitz', so to speak. And I submit that we shall not understand this unless we remind ourselves that the old nobility had in many instances enjoyed, sometimes for centuries, comparable proprietary associations with certain literary subjects, albeit in rather different form.

These subjects were indigenous, as it were, and much older, predating Arthurian romance by centuries; and the form in which they were 'owned' was oral: informal narrative prose as well as song (musically performed poetry) recounting events from the heroic age of the Germanic tribes for the 'rich and powerful', according to the prologue to *Þiðdreks saga*[5] and other sources. In the course of time some families had virtually identified themselves with certain segments of these native traditions: we know that from personal names, e.g. OHG Sigifrid, Cundheri or Kysalheri, as well as place names like Günthering or – these two villages lie six miles apart near Straubing in Lower Bavaria – Geiselhöring and Gundhöring. In this way the dominant families in a given region voiced their claim to historical identification with momentous events of the past celebrated in contemporary poetry and storytelling. Speaking of the Carolingian period in Bavaria, Wilhelm Störmer writes, 'Es kann kaum ein Zufall sein, daß in einem kleinen Raum westlich Münchens zwischen Ammersee, Amper und Glonn in der Zeit Herzog Tassilos III., des letzten Agilolfingers, und Karls des Großen sowie seiner Nachfolger nahezu alle Nibelungennamen bei adeligen Grundbesitzern und Ortsnamengebern erscheinen.'[6] The 'adeligen Grundbesitzer' in question here are not members of the highest nobility, but this kind of ancestral Nibelungen consciousness clearly also reaches into the first families of Bavaria, the families of the Huosi, Agilolfingi, etc., and from there it could even be projected back into the tradition itself: Pilgrim von Allershausen, bishop of Passau during the last quarter of the tenth century, was a member of the Huosi clan who ended up as a character in the very same poetic tradition which his family had begun to espouse centuries earlier.

Its historical consciousness and political propaganda connected the old nobility – high or low – with literary traditions which they regarded as family traditions and, we must assume, propagated accordingly. That

---

5   *Þiðdriks saga af Bern*, ed. by Henrik Bertelsen (Copenhagen, 1905–11).
6   Wilhelm Störmer, 'Nibelungentradition als Hausüberlieferung in frühmittelalterlichen Adelsfamilien?' in *Nibelungenlied und Klage: Sage und Geschichte, Struktur und Gattung*, ed. by Fritz Peter Knapp (Heidelberg, 1987), pp. 1–20 (p. 7). My other examples are also taken from Störmer.

is the social dimension of traditional oral heroic poetry and prose as well as the model of identification that explains, at least in part, why a new class of upwardly mobile would-be nobles would turn to a new kind of literature to manufacture similar connections in pursuit of their own social aspirations. The Germanic past and that body of more or less poetic narrative that connected it with the present had been pre-empted by the old families, but the advent of written narrative poetry devoted to new subject matters created the opportunity for equivalent acts of identification and self-representation. In this instance, the appropriation of names alone would not have served that purpose; these characters and the world in which they moved simply lacked historicity. The thing to be appropriated became the story as such, or to put it more precisely: exemplary patterns of action and behaviour derived from the story as created, in this case, by Chrétien de Troyes. The old nobility had linked itself to historical truth guaranteed and perpetually renewed in oral tradition. No doubt that sense of linkage had weakened gradually in the process of literarization which took hold even of these traditions in the course of the twelfth century; certainly literary patronage among the same families had gradually turned to the production of written texts based increasingly on imported literary models. But, for the reasons I have just discussed, *ministeriales* like the masters of Rodenegg castle or the Hessenhof in Schmalkalden eventually took this development into a new dimension: their particular acts of appropriation in effect recognized the truth of fiction as a means of social identification.

II

This brings us to the second part of the initial question: what is it that legitimizes this undertaking not only in social but particularly also in intellectual terms? And, as a matter of practical consideration, what accounts for the participation of a first-class workshop whose proper business undoubtedly was church art? The chronologically parallel example of the Berlin *Eneide* notwithstanding, a major secular commission still seems to call for special justification at that time. Apart from the fact that Heinrich von Veldeke's adaptation of Virgil, so splendidly illuminated by the Prüfening workshop, was a text sanctioned as *historia*, the Rodenegg project involved a cycle of wall paintings in a quasi-public place and not a cycle of miniatures in a quasi-private book. Actually, whatever religious scruples the South Tyrolean Rodenecks might have harboured themselves and whatever ideological resistance to their project they might have had to expect from outside had just been countered quite effectively by the appearance of Thomasin von

Zerclaere's didactic verse tract *Der welsche Gast*.[7] Here Thomasin talks at length about the educational function of vernacular romance in contemporary aristocratic society, and these are some of the more pertinent lines from the passage that follows his reading list for young people:

> ich enschilte deheinen man,
> der aventiure tihten chan:
> diu aventiure die sint gût,
> wan si bereitent chindes mût.
> swer niht fûrbaz chan vernemen,
> der sol da bi ouch bilde nemen.   (1699–1704)

> von den gemalten bilden sint
> der geboure unde daz chint
> gefrewet ofte. swer niht enchan
> versten, daz ein biderb man
> an der schrift versten sol,
> dem si mit den bilden wol.
> der phaffe sehe die schrift an.
> so sol der ungelerte man
> die bilde sehen, sit im niht
> die schrift zerchennen geschiht.   (1709–18)

> ich schilt die aventiure niht,
> swie uns ze liegen geschiht
> von der aventiure rat,
> wand sie bezeichnenûnge hat
> der zuht und der warheit:
> daz war man mit lûge chleit.   (1733–38)

The tri-literate Thomasin was, let us remember, a native of the adjacent Friuli region, canon of Aquileia, and closely associated with the court of the patriarch Wolfger von Erla, one-time benefactor of Walther von der Vogelweide. Although it lies about a hundred miles to the south-east and the Bishop of Brixen was a suffragan of Salzburg, there were close ties between Aquileia and Brixen and, by extension, Rodenegg. Bishop Conrad, a cousin of Arnold II, visited the Patriarch in 1214/15, for example. Not coincidentally certain stylistic and icono-graphic similarities between the Rodenegg paintings and those in the crypt of the cathedral of Aquileia have been noted repeatedly, particularly with reference to the central lamentation scene.[8] Above all,

---

7 *Thomasin von Zerclaere: Der welsche Gast*, ed. by F.W. von Kries, GAG, 425, I–IV, 4 vols (Göppingen, 1984–85).
8 Cf. esp. Rushing, pp. 42f.

however, we must realize that when Thomasin addresses the German nobility, for whom he wrote his didactic verse tract in 1215/16, he addresses first of all the German-speaking population directly to the west and northwest, the very people, in other words, who lived in places like Rodenegg. If we assume, as we must, that the owners of Rodenegg were sufficiently 'literate' to have at least a passing acquaintance with some German version of the story of Iwein, it is at least as likely that they, or some of the people with whom they conferred in matters of literature and the arts, knew Thomasin's work in one form or another.

The lines I have quoted somewhat out of context are part of an extended (and not entirely coherent) metaphor composed of ancient clerical topoi some of which had served traditionally to define the distinction between clergy and laity and their respective ability to discern the truth. The ultimate purpose of this metaphorical disquisition is the (grudging and conditional) admission of secular courtly narrative into the canon of wholesome, if not salvific, writing and 'reading', and in this connection recent scholarly debate has focused on the *integumentum* question, that is to say, whether Thomasin, in proposing this informal compromise between church doctrine and lay practice, actually expected his audience to understand vernacular romance in pretty much the same allegorical terms that twelfth-century commentators applied to Virgil and the classics and whether in so doing he might even tell us something rather profound about the poetics of romance as such.[9] However that may be, there is absolutely no reason to assume that patron or painter of the Rodenegg Iwein understood their own undertaking in those integumental terms. That is not my point at all. It is rather that Thomasin's language *per se* encourages, even fosters the creation of actual, visual images of romance *aventiure*, once other factors such as socio-literary ambition or the legitimization of secular narrative as 'literature' in the clerical sense have already come into play.

The general sanction of *aventiure* as (indirect) purveyor of (partial) truth (1736f.) which informs the passage as a whole as well as the catalogue of exemplary literary characters, including *Iwain* (1654), that precedes it culminates in the equation of *aventiure* with *bild*, while at the same time the notion of *bild* advances abruptly from abstract *exemplum*, *Vorbild*, in line 1704 to concrete painting (*gemalten bilden*, 1709) for

---

[9] See esp. Christoph Huber, 'Höfischer Roman als Integumentum? Das Votum Thomasins von Zerklaere', *ZfdA*, 115 (1986), 79–100. On Thomasin's use of topoi and the ontological status of romance texts see my article, 'Hören – Lesen – Sehen. Buch und Schriftlichkeit im Selbstverständnis der volkssprachlichen literarischen Kultur Deutschlands um 1200', *PBB* (Tüb.), 106 (1984), 218–57 (pp. 238–48). Rushing is the first to have pursued the possible connection between Thomasin and Rodenegg, albeit in rather general terms (pp. 52–55). My own argument is more specific and more in the direction of what Rushing calls 'wildest speculation' (p. 54).

the instruction of those who cannot read (1717f.). With regard to secular vernacular literature, this association is as powerful as it is novel. Irrespective of what Thomasin himself may have meant or what intentions he may thereby have attributed to authors like Chrétien or adaptors like Hartmann, the way he said it offered a suggestion of immense practical interest to anyone wanting to adopt Arthurian adventure and characters as prominently visible 'Hausbesitz'. His quasi-official authorization, in the immediate wake of the Fourth Lateran Council, of courtly romance as morally defensible, even beneficial, literary fare established at the same time 'a theoretical framework [. . .] for discerning a morally didactic function in secular pictures' (Rushing, p. 53), but in effect it went even further: it defined *aventiure*, the prime narrative constituent of this secular literature, as image to be painted and object to be viewed. Of course the equation of *aventiure* with *bild* is grounded in metaphor, but precisely in this time-honored metaphorical usage *bild* also stands for a very concrete notion which the church had used for centuries to identify and establish the process by which the illiterate laity might be able to gain limited access to the truth and to justify its own expansive and expensive picture programmes in holy places. Beginning with Gregory the Great's canonical dictum that pictures are desirable as scripture substitute for the illiterate, the church had always been entirely concrete about this, and although Thomasin manipulates the old topos to create a new metaphor for the relative value of secular narrative, there is no reason why his audience, the very same illiterate laity, could and would not have taken him at his literal word. Especially, if we imagine them as medieval vernacular readers: a group in which perhaps only one had truly 'read' Thomasin and the rest were only in conversational contact with the text, so to speak, so that a memorable figure of speech could easily move out of context and metaphor could actually become a prescription for reality.

As we have come to realize fully only during the last two decades or so, wall-painting in various forms had been a truly major industry in the South Tyrol since the Carolingian period. That, too, is part of the explanation why it was here, of all places, that the first Arthurian picture cycle we know of was designed – eloquent witness to, among other things, the tremendous popularity of this new literate, fictional narrative throughout the ranks of the lay élite. But it takes a look beyond the artistic and literary predilections of the time to uncover the most potent impulses behind the Rodeneck Iwein: the strong desire among the recently or soon to be ennobled to rival some of the more established families in owning, and being publicly identified with, a segment of that literature. And, secondly, the authorization of this undertaking through the didactic voice of a cleric who wrote, in the vernacular, at what was without a doubt the most influential ecclesiastical court of the region at large. The primary recipients of this message were people like the master of Rodenegg and they derived from it not only moral-theological authorization but also inspiration to establish and manifest their personal ownership through paintings on their walls. At the same time, the general atmosphere of tolerant compromise and moralistic concern with the education of the laity which Thomasin's tract reflects and articulates also ensured that a distinguished ecclesiastical workshop would not feel led too far astray, if it devoted its artistic energies to this secular commission: to transpose Iwein's adventures into the language of pictures, fashioning a picture programme that is neither Hartmann's nor Chrétien's but constitutes in effect a major pictorial variant of the story: the Rodenegg Iwein.

Wolfram von Eschenbach vor dem Conte du Graal

RENÉ PÉRENNEC

Das 'vor' statt des üblichen 'und'[1] soll andeuten, daß der situativen Komponente der Adaption Rechnung getragen wird.

Nicht, daß das 'und' ausgedient hätte. Im Gegenteil: man wünscht sich Aufsatz- und Buchtitel, in denen das 'und' eine additive – und nicht nur eine kontrastierende – Funktion hätte, d. h., um das Beispiel des *Erec* zu nehmen, Arbeiten zum *Erec et Enide*-Roman Chrétiens und zum *Erec* Hartmanns, denen folgende Gleichung zugrundeliegen würde: deutscher *Erec* = französischer *Erec* + Hartmann von Aue + deutscher Kontext. Tatsache ist aber, daß die allermeisten Vergleiche auf Differentialanalysen, also auf einer Subtraktion vom Typ: Hartmanns Leistung = deutscher *Erec* minus Chrétienscher *Erec* beruhen. Die Logik letzterer Gleichung führt dazu, die Leistung des deutschen Nachdichters da besonders hoch zu veranschlagen, wo die Vorlage keine Handhabe zum Vergleich bietet, also vor allem im Romanschluß. Und tatsächlich wird in der von J. Bumkes Forschungsbericht zu den romanisch-deutschen Literaturbeziehungen im Mittelalter (1967) gedeckten Sekundärliteratur[2] sowie in Arbeiten aus den zwei letzten Jahrzehnten[3] der Romanschluß im deutschen *Erec* in der Regel als der Ort angesehen, wo religiöse bzw. sozialgeschichtliche Implikationen der Rezeption des französischen Stoffes durch Hartmann deutlich werden. Viel mehr als eine Epiphanie von Zusammenhängen, deren Manife-

---

[1] Zum Beispiel: Bodo Mergell, *Wolfram von Eschenbach und seine französischen Quellen, Teil II: Wolframs Parzival* (Münster, 1943); Jean Fourquet, *Wolfram d'Eschenbach et le Conte del Graal* (Paris, 1966). – Zitate nach: *Les Romans de Chrétien de Troyes, V–VI: Le conte du Graal (Perceval)*, hg. von Félix Lecoy, CFMA, 100 und 103, 2 Bde. (Paris, 1972–75); *Wolfram von Eschenbach*, hg. von Karl Lachmann, 6. Ausg. (Berlin/Leipzig, 1926) (*Parzival*); Wolfram von Eschenbach, *Willehalm*, hg. von Werner Schröder (Berlin/New York, 1978).
[2] Joachim Bumke, *Die romanisch-deutschen Literaturbeziehungen im Mittelalter: Ein Überblick* (Heidelberg, 1967).
[3] Vgl. z. B.: Bernd Thum, 'Politische Probleme der Stauferzeit im Werk Hartmanns von Aue: Landesherrschaft im *Iwein* und *Erec*', in *Stauferzeit: Geschichte, Literatur, Kunst*, hg. von R. Krohn, B. Thum und P. Wapnewski (Stuttgart, 1979), S. 47–70; Ursula Schulze, '*âmîs unde man*. Die zentrale Problematik in Hartmanns *Erec*', PBB (Tüb.), 105 (1983), 14–47.

station an der Textoberfläche durch die Übertragungsarbeit gehemmt worden wäre, erscheint mir der *Erec*-Schluß als eine Rückbindung an ein Literaturverständnis (literarische Kommunikation als Abbild der Kommunikation innerhalb der Glaubensgemeinde) und an einen ideologischen Raster (das 'augustinische' Königsideal), über die bis zu diesem Punkt die deutsche Nachdichtung – im Kontakt mit der Vorlage – hinausgewachsen war (poetische Autonomie durch werkinterne Relationen/Erweiterung und Festigung des laikal-aristokratischen Selbstverständnisses durch die gruppenübergreifende Ritter-König-Diskussion). Die Tendenz des angefügten Schlusses ist eigentlich eher regressiv.[4] Die Leistung Hartmanns ist nicht an diesem Schluß – gewiß einem Zeugnis handwerklicher Solidität und Kompetenz – zu messen, sondern an der weniger auffälligen Arbeit, deren es bedurfte, um das Innovatorische an der Chrétienschen Schöpfung wiederzugeben oder unter Beachtung des neuen Kontexts zu adaptieren, also um das zu transportieren, was die Vorlage schon leistete – was die Theorie der 'adaptation courtoise', die auf die Unzulänglichkeiten der Differential-analyse hinweist und das Gemeinsame an Vorlage und Nachdichtung bzw. Bearbeitung stark betont, ihrerseits ebenfalls übersieht, da sie prinzipiell die Konvertibilität der Inhalte, d. h. das Vorhandensein eines westeuropäischen literarischen 'Binnenmarktes' postuliert,[5] wo doch diese Konvertibilität nicht immer gegeben war und in bestimmten Fällen, wie der Vergleich zwischen Hartmanns *Erec* und Hartmanns *Iwein* lehrt, weniger eine Voraussetzung als ein Ergebnis gewesen ist.

Nichts also gegen 'Chrétien de Troyes *und* das deutsche Mittelalter'. Plädiert wird lediglich für ein volleres Ausschöpfen des Potentials des 'und'. Wenn ich mich aber in diesen Überlegungen zum *Parzival* und zum *Conte du Graal* doch für das 'vor' entscheide, so liegt es daran, daß Adaption in diesem Fall auch Konfrontation bedeutet. Bei Hartmann ist die Adaptionsarbeit auf Integration ausgerichtet. Widerstandsformen – und dazu gehört auch der Hartmannsche Humor – bilden sich vom *Erec* zum *Iwein* zurück. Bei Wolfram halten sich dagegen Übernahmebereit-schaft und Renitenz die Waage. Hier ist an K. Bertaus Auffassung anzuknüpfen, wonach Wolfram ein Gegenüber braucht und dazu neigt, den Gegenstand der Erzählung – auch das, was er um- oder hinzugedichtet hat – vom anderen Ende her zu betrachten: den Glaubenskrieg aus der Perspektive der Nicht-Christen (dies bis zu einem gewissen Grade) oder – und das bleibt auch heute überraschend – das vom großen Weltgeschehen verursachte Blutbad aus der 'Fluß-

---

4 Vgl. Verf., 'Zu den romanisch-deutschen Literaturbeziehungen um 1200', in *DAAD Dokumentationen & Materialien, 12* (Deutsch-französisches Germanistentreffen, Berlin, 30. 9. bis 4. 10. 1987, Dokumentation der Tagungsbeiträge), S. 18–35.
5 Vgl. Jean Fourquet, 'Réflexions sur le *Nibelungenlied*', *Et. Germ.*, 20 (1965), 221–32 (S. 231).

perspektive' (*Willehalm* 439,1–3).[6] Ich füge nun folgende Überlegung bei: ist nicht die Nachdichter-Position die ideale Voraussetzung für die Entfaltung einer solchen künstlerischen Grundhaltung? Der Nachdichter, der an der Grenze zwischen zwei Welten steht, bekommt die Möglichkeit, nach zwei Seiten hin Alterität zu demonstrieren.

Im *Willehalm* – der Exkurs sei um der besseren Perspektivierung willen gestattet[7] – hat Wolfram diese Möglichkeit weidlich ausgenutzt. Seine Wiedergabe von *Aliscans* darf als subversiv bezeichnet werden, denn er stellt in den Vordergrund, was in der Quelle und in der Tradition der Karlsepik ausgeblendet wird: großes Geschehen bedeutet großes Leid. Zugleich muß man aber bedenken, daß er den Kriegsschauplatz und die 'Kriegsziele' erweitert hat. Insofern ist die 'Destruktion der Fabel' (K. Bertau) auch ein Angriff gegen die eigene Konstruktion. Außerdem agiert in einer bestimmten Textschicht ein hinterwäldlerischer Erzähler, der die besondere Form von Holzhackerei, die auf Alischanz geübt wird, staunend wahrnimmt, oder Rennewarts Schwert lobt, das noch imponierender sein soll als die größte Flachsschwinge, die in Nördlingen aufzutreiben wäre (295,12–17). Zur Destruktion kommt also die Demontage, und die betrifft auch die Leidthematik: von der Nördlinger 'Flachslinie' aus gesehen dürften sowohl die Glaubenskriegsthematik als auch die Klage über die traurigen Folgen des Kampfes abstruses Pathos sein. Eine andere Formulierung, diesmal mit engerem Bezug auf die Schaltfunktion, die jeder Nachdichter als Vermittler ausübt: Wolfram sorgt dafür, daß er den größtmöglichen Manövrierraum bekommt. Einerseits verdeutscht er die Vorlage auch in dem Sinne, daß er die völlig provinzialisierte französische Karlsepik wieder auf Reichsniveau hebt. Diese Verdeutschung ist aber andererseits mehr eine Fränkisierung, eine Karolingisierung, als eine Germanisierung der Fabel. Orts- und Ländernamen sprechen eine deutliche Sprache. Der deutsche Teil des *rîches*, von dem sich behaupten läßt, daß er vom großen Krieg betroffen ist, ist mit dem linksrheinischen Raum identisch ('Ache', 'Arraz', 'Iper', 'Lahrein', 'Nanzei', vgl. vor allem 126,13–15; 437,14–19). Ob auch der süddeutsche rechtsrheinische Raum zu den 'tiuschen landen' gehört, aus denen – so heißt es – die Christen Unterstützung erwarten können (210,27–30), bleibt ungewiß. Rückendeckung dürfte aber die *Fabel* von dort nicht erwarten, denn dieser Raum (mit dem Bodensee, dem Spessart, dem Schwarzwald, Kitzingen, Nördlingen) stellt die Beobachtungswarte dar, auf der man sich im Anblick des Kampfgetümmels und des ganzen epischen Aufwands die Augen reibt. Damit wird nicht behauptet, daß die Nördlingen-Perspektive *die* richtige Perspektive ist, denn es ist anzunehmen, daß

---

[6] Karl Bertau, *Über Literaturgeschichte: Literarischer Kunstcharakter und Geschichte in der höfischen Epik um 1200* (München, 1983), S. 115f.

[7] Dieser Aspekt des *Willehalm* soll an anderer Stelle ausführlicher behandelt werden.

auch dort Wolframs Deutsch als zu *krump* empfunden werden konnte; es ist vielmehr so, daß Wolfram das eine gegen das andere ausspielt unde vice versa, denn er kann sich auf diese Weise den Spielraum verschaffen, den man ja braucht, wenn man sich alles vom anderen Ende her ansehen will.

Der Autor des *Parzival* hat prinzipiell dieselbe Einstellung. Die Grundtendenz ist auch hier, war schon hier, das oppositionelle Nachdichten. Am Anfang ist der Protest, und deshalb eignet sich der Protest (gegen die Primogenitur) zum Werkanfang. Aber die Voraussetzungen zu einem offensiven Nachdichten waren hier anders. Das liegt an der Gralsutopie. Der Erzähler kann freilich die Artus- und Gralswelt aus der Kleiner-Mann-Perspektive betrachten, er kann Wildenberc gegen Munsalvaesche ausspielen. An der Gralsutopie selbst ist – anders als an dem Krieg, der ja der Glaubenskrieg auch ist – gar nichts auszusetzen. Dies hätte dem oppositionellen Nachdichten die Flügel beschneiden können. Dennoch kam Wolframs grundsätzlicher Erzählhaltung der Umstand entgegen, daß die Gralsutopie – so wie sie Chrétien konzipiert hatte – episch nicht gestaltbar war. So konnte sich das offensive Nachdichten auf einer anderen Ebene entfalten, sich gegen das richten, wovon die Gralsutopie bei Chrétien Abschied nehmen wollte, ohne daß sie eine Karte des ersehnten Neulands entwerfen konnte. Meine These also: die konzeptionelle Aporie der Chrétienschen Gralsutopie kam Wolframs agonaler Erzählhaltung entgegen.

Im Vergleich mit anderen, späteren Graldichtungen zeichnet sich Chrétiens Gralskonzeption durch ihre Unentschiedenheit aus. Sie entfernt sich von der bisherigen Minne-und-Aventiure-Thematik, ohne damit brechen zu wollen. Im Perceval-Teil bleibt der Stellenwert der Geschlechterliebe unbestimmt. Außerdem wird die Funktion des Kampfes nicht umdefiniert; es läßt sich nur feststellen, daß die Kampfschilderungen gleichsam verkümmern, so, als wäre der ritterliche Kampf nicht mehr die richtige Ingredienz, ohne daß eine Ersatzlösung bereitläge. Die Utopie entfaltet sich nicht, und man darf wohl annehmen, daß Chrétien dieselbe Feststellung machte und es anders versuchte, mit einem neuen Helden und mit einem neuen Kompositionsprinzip. Im Perceval-Teil sieht es so aus, als hätte Chrétien an seinem strukturalen Rezept festhalten wollen: Diskontinuität des Geschehensablaufs als Aufforderung zur eigenen Sinnfindung, Sinnfindung als Nachvollzug von Relationen. Der Gauvain-Teil liest sich dagegen wie ein Fortsetzungsroman. Es scheint aber, daß Chrétien sein 'Erneuerungsprogramm' nicht ganz aus den Augen verloren hat. Was zuerst nur parodistisch anmutet (Gauvain und das Fräulein mit den eng anliegenden Ärmeln, Gauvain und die Orgueilleuse de la Lande: Parodie auf den Minnedienst), oder burlesk (das Fräulein von Escavalon als Kampfgefährtin Gauvains), oder ironisch (der Inzest als Inbegriff der Harmonie zwischen den Geschlechtern: Gauvain und seine Schwester als ideales Brautpaar in den Augen von Gauvains Mutter, 8788–90), hat durchaus einen ernsthaften Kern, hat – trotz der Verengung auf die Mann-Frau-Beziehung – mit der Gralsutopie von einer Erneuerung des Minne-und-Aventiure-Koordinatensystems zu tun, enthält die utopische Vorstellung von einer Unmittelbarkeit, 'Un-vermittelt-heit' der Liebe. Nur: die Erneuerung des Minne-und-Aventiure-Romans scheint lediglich als Vorführung eines sonderbaren Rituals oder als Burleske darstellbar zu sein, so, als hätte Chrétien sich damit abfinden müssen, daß nur das Negativbild seines Entwurfs zu gestalten war.[8]

Man muß m. E. die Aporie der Chrétienschen Konzeption im Perceval-Teil sowie die indirekte Annäherung an die Gralsutopie im Gauvain-Teil im Auge behalten, wenn man Wolframs Reaktionen auf seine Vorlage verstehen will. Dieses Verhalten Wolframs versuche ich jetzt am Beispiel der Gestaltung der Blutstropfenszene zu beschreiben.

Der Blutstropfenszene sind u. a. die Episoden der Begegnung mit Blancheflor und des Besuchs auf der Gralsburg vorgeschaltet. Hier bot sich somit die Möglichkeit, den Zusammenhang von Minnehandlung und Aventiure zu umreißen. Und so geschieht es auch im *Conte du Graal*, andeutungsweise, durch Transparenz: das Bild, das auf dem Schnee entsteht, erinnert an Blancheflors Gesicht und – schemenhaft – an die Lanze der Gralsburg, an 'den weißen Speer' und 'das weiße Speereisen', 'aus dessen Spitze ein Blutstropfen herausquoll'.[9] Dabei ist aber zweierlei zu bedenken:

— Der Konnex entsteht auf der Ebene der Vision: Minnevision, visionsartiger Anblick der Lanze auf der Gralsburg. Beide Paradigmen, Minne und Suche, sollen offenbar die Qualität des Faszinosums besitzen. Wie kann aber ein Epiker in dieser Höhe weiterdichten, wie kann er in solchen Regionen eine Welt entstehen lassen?

— Die so suggerierte Relation mutet ambivalent an. Die Terme lauten nicht: Frau und Gral, sondern eigentlich: Frau und Lanze. Das Blut auf dem Schnee, von einem Angriff hinterlassen, der letzten Endes als ein etwas bewegtes Spiel erscheint, könnte Leben versprechen. Aber gilt das auch für das Blut an der Lanze, das Schuld, Schuld am

---

[8] Ausführlicher dazu: Verf., *Recherches sur le roman arthurien en vers en Allemagne aux XIIe et XIIIe siècles*, GAG, 393, I–II, 2 Bde. (Göppingen, 1984), II, 101–83.

[9] *Conte du Graal*, 3184–89: 'et tuit cil de leanz veoient/ la lance blanche et le fer blanc,/ s'issoit une gote de sanc/ del fer de la lance an somet/ et jusqu'a la main an vaslet/ coloit cele gote vermoille.'

Mitmenschen, zu indizieren scheint? Wie lassen sich dann Geschlechterliebe und diese Schuld vermitteln?

Es will *scheinen* – das ist die Funktion der doppelten *sanblance* –, daß die Blutstropfenszene die Erneuerung des Koordinatensystems Minne/ Aventiure in der Form einer Sublimierung des einen Paradigmas (das Sich-selber-vergessen als Bild der totalen Hinwendung zum Andern) und einer Problematisierung des anderen Paradigmas (Hinweis auf die Schattenseite der Aventiure, auf die damit verbundene Gewalttätigkeit) andeuten soll, dies unter Beibehaltung einer gedanklichen Klammer zwischen den erneuerten Paradigmen. 'Verdichten' ließ sich aber das neue Konzept nur – als Halluzination.[10]

Wie lassen sich so flüchtige Andeutungen von Relationen in eine Übertragung hinüberretten, in eine Übertragung, die zudem den Anspruch erhebt, die Geschichte 'endehaft' zu erzählen? Die ungewöhnliche Ausgangssituation erklärt wohl zum Teil, warum sich in Wolframs Fassung der Blutstropfenszene der Text sich in drei Schichten spaltet:

(1) Darstellung: etwa wie in der Vorlage, mit dem nicht unerheblichen Unterschied, daß die Blutstropfenszene nicht mehr auf den Gralsburgbesuch transparent ist.

(2) Handlungsbezogener Diskurs. Der Erzähler teilt sofort mit, *vor* der Schilderung der Minne-Faszination, daß Parzivals 'nôt' 'von sînen triuwen [. . .] geschach' (282,23), und er schließt an seine Darstellung die Bemerkung an: 'er pflac der wâren minne/ gein ir gar âne wenken' (283,14–15). Und nach einiger Zeit wird – zum ersten Mal, wenn ich recht sehe – der Zusammenhang von Minne und Gralsuche hergestellt, dies in der Form eines Erzählerkommentars: 'sîne gedanke umben grâl/ unt der küngîn glîchiu mâl,/ iewederz was ein strengiu nôt' (296,5–7). Wolfram hat die Blutstropfenszene und die Gralsburgepisode nicht zusammen-*gesehen*; wohl aber hat er das Gefühl gehabt, daß er an dieser Stelle die Fäden zusammenknüpfen, *grâl* und *wîp* aufeinander beziehen sollte.

(3) Diskurs als Exkurs über die Macht der Minne und den Topos der Minneknechtschaft, Rhetorisierung, Theatralisierung des Minne-zaubermotivs, wo Chrétien auf die Frische des Märchens gesetzt hatte, um diesen Zauber zu suggerieren.

---

[10] Die Annäherung an eine epische Erfüllung der Gralsutopie gelang – im *Perlesvaus* und in *La Queste du Saint Graal* – nur über eine durchgreifende, die Geschlechterliebe ausschließende Radikalisierung des Sublimationsmoments und eine Entmetaphorisierung des *militia Christi*-Begriffs, die den ritterlichen Kampf entproblematisierte.

Die zwei Diskursformen lassen sich nicht auf einen Nenner bringen.[11] Wenn Parzival auf Veranlassung von 'Frou Minne' 'von sînen witzen schiet' (293,7), so ist einerseits sein Verhalten kaum dazu geeignet, die *untriuwe*-stiftende Kraft dieser Instanz (vgl. 291,19–27) zu beweisen. Vor allem aber: worin soll die besondere Qualität der Liebe Parzivals zu Condwiramurs, d. h. die Gralswürdigkeit des Helden in diesem Bereich, denn bestehen, wenn Parzivals Zustand von der Minne-verfallenheit des Bruders von Condwiramurs, Kardeiz, nicht unter-schieden (293,5–13) oder auf 'genetisches Erbgut' zurückgeführt wird (300,16–19)? Was legitimiert eigentlich die Anwartschaft *dieses* Sprosses einer 'ungezalt[en] sippe' (300,16) auf das Gralkönigtum? So entsteht der Eindruck, daß der Angriff auf die literarische Minne-Maschinerie, an deren Zelebrierung der Dichterkollege Heinrich von Veldeke maßgeblich beteiligt gewesen sein soll (292,18–23), einer Frustration entsprungen sein könnte, daß literarische Konventionen deshalb aufs Korn genommen werden, weil ein Durchbruch zu neuen, adäquateren Darstellungsformen nicht gelingen will, oder, anders formuliert, daß 'Frou Minne' dafür herhalten muß, daß eine Legitimierung von Parzivals Sonderstatus mit rein erzählerischen Mitteln nicht zu be-wältigen ist.

Verstärkt wird dieser Eindruck durch die nicht wenigen Stellen, wo der Erzähler oder eine Gestalt die verheerenden Folgen einer Minne-und-Abenteuer-Konzeption herausstellt, die den Ritter dazu führt, einer Frau zuliebe oder 'niwan durch prîses hulde' (538,4) sein Leben aufs Spiel zu setzen. Diese verkürzte Konzeption wird im *Parzival* als ein gängiges Romanrezept hingestellt. Einer der Söhne von Gurnemanz, Lascoyt, soll 'umb einen sparwære' den Tod gefunden haben; sein Bruder Gurzgri, der die Kombination von Minne und Aventiure vorexerzieren wollte und auf seinen Ritterfahrten von seiner Frau begleitet wurde, starb beim Schoydelakurt-Abenteuer (178,11–26). Was hier hineinzitiert wird, ist nicht der Hartmannsche Roman bzw. der Roman 'Chrétienscher Prägung', in dem Minne und Abenteuer ein Koordinatensystem bilden, das als Rahmen für eine Werte-Diskussion dient, sondern eine reduzierte Form dieses Romans, in der *prîs* verdinglicht wird.

Diese Reduktion mag zuerst als ziemlich unfaire Manipulation empfunden werden, insofern Wolfram zu Zwecken der Kritik eine Minne-und-Abenteuer-Konzeption in seinen eigenen Text hinein-projiziert, die allenfalls dem Rat Gaweins im *Iwein* entspricht, aber keineswegs der Gesamtkonzeption des *Iwein* oder des *Erec* (bzw. derer Vorlagen) gerecht wird – und das tut er ausgerechnet bei der

---

[11] Siehe Elisabeth Schmid, *Studien zum Problem der epischen Totalität in Wolframs 'Parzival'* (Erlangen, 1976), S. 36.

Übertragung eines Romans, der von der gegenläufigen Tendenz getragen ist, nämlich von dem Wunsch, auf der Basis der *Erec-* und *Yvain*-Konzeption einen qualitativen Sprung zu wagen.

Es ist aber gleichzeitig zu bedenken, daß im *Parzival* eine Alternative zu dem 'klassischen' Konzept nirgends episch realisiert wird, so daß auch hier der Gedanke naheliegt, daß die Kritik die Stelle der Positivbestimmung vertritt, die ausbleiben muß, weil Wolfram an den Grundprämissen seiner Vorlage festhält – eine Art Quellentreue, die besonders eindrucksvoll dadurch dokumentiert wird, daß er die '*templeise*-Lösung' (kriegerischer Einsatz als Ausdruck der ausschließlichen Liebe zu Gott) erwog und (außer für Statisten) für inadäquat befand.

Die hier zur Diskussion gestellte These läßt sich nun folgendermaßen präzisieren:

Angesichts der Aporie, welche die Gestaltung einer 'humanen' Gralsutopie darstellt, wird die Erneuerung der Minne-und-Aventiure-Definition auf die Diskursebene verlagert, nach zwei Modi:

— positiv, als Affirmation des paradigmatischen Wandels (Parzivals Sehnen ist auf *grâl* und *wîp* gerichtet, 'der wirt [in] von sünden schiet/ unt im doch rîterlîchen riet' (501,17–18), Parzival hat doch letzten Endes den Gral 'erkämpft' (vgl. 798,24–26)) oder als Mitteilung von 'mære[n] umben grâl' (Frimutel soll die Verbindung von Minne und Aventiure musterhaft vorgelebt haben),

— negativ, als Warnung (Trevrizents Lehre) bzw. als Angriff auf eine Reduktion der höfischen Thematik.

Die These kann wie folgt ergänzt werden:

Möglich blieb eine Darstellung, mit der sich das unerreichbare Ziel perspektivieren ließ, d. h. eine Form der Benutzung des 'alten' Minne-und-Abenteuer-Schemas, die, weil sie weniger aggressiv als die Attacken auf 'Frou Minne' war, eine fortlaufende Erzählung und eine Staffelung der Handlungsteile erlaubte. Es spricht einiges dafür, daß Wolfram eine solche Abstufung bewußt angestrebt hat. Bekannt ist die 'Kulissen-Regie' in den Gawan-Büchern, die auf der Linie des 'klassischen' Schemas bleibt und dazu einlädt, sich den im Hintergrund agierenden Parzival als 'post-arthurischen' Helden vorzustellen. Aber auch die Gahmuret-Bücher erfüllen m. E. primär eine ähnliche Funktion. Mit seiner Analyse des onomastischen Materials des *Parzival* hat J. Fourquet nachgewiesen, daß die Gahmuret-Bücher nach dem 6. Buch entstanden sind, wie die Gawan-Bücher also. Fourquets Deutung dieses Sachverhalts kombiniert materielle (die Vorlage war aus irgendeinem Grund Wolfram abhanden gekommen) und kompositorische Gründe (Wolfram machte aus der Not eine Tugend und konnte durch die Abfassung des Gahmuret-Teils die Dualität der Gawan- und

Parzival-Handlung in der Ternarität eines 'Dreiweltengedichts' aufheben (Gralwelt, Artuswelt, Orient)).[12] Eine bestechende Erklärung, der aber die Vorstellung zugrunde liegt, daß Wolfram die Gawan- und die Parzival-Handlung als zwei feste Größen betrachtete, deren gediegene Proportionen ein architektonisches Problem stellten. Dies mag für den Gawan-Teil stimmen, der sich abschließen ließ, vorausgesetzt, daß man – allerdings unter Mißachtung des 'Gesetzes', wonach Gauvain prinzipiell nicht heiratet – die Gawanhandlung an die normale Laufbahn eines selbständigen Romanhelden anglich. Kann aber die Parzivalhandlung in Wolframs Augen je eine solche feste Größe dargestellt haben? Die Parzival-Auftritte nach dem 9. Buch machen noch keinen Romanschluß aus, die Schlußpartie des Parzival-Teils erweist sich, klopft man sie ab, als Attrappe. Den Grund für die entstehungschronologische Nähe der Gahmuret-Bücher zu dem Gawan-Teil würde ich mir also eher so vorstellen: Wolfram wird relativ früh gespürt haben, daß ein eigentliches Weiterdichten nur im Umfeld oder im Vorfeld des schon Bestehenden möglich war. Im Umfeld durch den Ausbau der Gawanhandlung, im Vorfeld durch die Anfügung einer nach dem 'alten' Schema operierenden Fabel. Pointiert formuliert: Wolfram wird gefühlt haben, daß die Geschichte nur per Dekret 'endehaft' zu erzählen war und daß man einem ehrlichen Ende am besten dann näher kommen konnte, wenn man die Anfänge mehrte, mit 'verwandten' Geschichten, die sich in eine gemeinsame Perspektive einordnen ließen. Zu dem darstellbaren und schon dargestellten Anfang des Parzival-Romans kam als Vorspann die Schilderung eines abgeschlossenen Geschicks, das keinen anderen Anspruch erhob als den, eine Vorstufe zu sein. Daß dies nicht die einzige Funktion der Gahmuret-Bücher ist, daß diese Bücher die Voraussetzung für die Entfaltung einer die Erde umspannenden Romanwelt bilden, daß Welt- und Adelschronistik die Modelle abgaben, an denen sich die Gestaltung des Gahmuret-Teils orientierte, soll unbestritten bleiben. Der entscheidende *Anstoß* zur Abfassung der Gahmuret-Bücher dürfte aber die Erkenntnis des aporetischen Charakters der Chrétienschen Gralromanskonzeption gewesen sein.[13]

Das bleibt zugegebenermaßen eine Spekulation. Zum Ausgleich seien deshalb zuletzt zwei praktische Konsequenzen der hier vorgetragenen These erwähnt.

Die eine betrifft den Umgang mit der Forschungsliteratur, genauer: die Verwertung zweier Gruppen von Interpretationen, die beide eine Bereicherung für die Wolfram-Forschung bedeuten, obwohl sie in der

---

[12] J. Fourquet (wie Anm. 1), bes. S. 148–52.
[13] Dieser Abschnitt enthält eine 'zeitversetzte' Antwort auf eine Frage von Uwe Ruberg (zur Verträglichkeit meiner Vorstellungen mit der universalistischen Tendenz des Werkes) und auf eine Bemerkung von Arthur Hatto (zur Genese des *Parzival*).

Beurteilung des geistigen bzw. ideologischen Standorts des *Parzival* völlig divergieren. Auf der einen Seite wird (aus der Sicht der Theorie der 'adaptation courtoise') die – stark minderheitliche, aber fundierte – Auffassung vertreten, daß in Wolframs Nachdichtung das ritterlich-höfische Wertesystem stabilisiert, ja zementiert wird,[14] während auf der anderen Seite mit nicht weniger guten Argumenten und auf ebenso breiter textlicher Basis an der These festgehalten wird, daß Wolframs *Parzival* eben diese Werte hinterfragt.[15]

Nun: wenn es stimmt, daß beim Prozeß des Nachdichtens polare Relationen des Perceval-Teils des *Conte du Graal* (kurz: Glanz und Schuld) quasi wie beim Vorgang der prismatischen Brechung so auseinandergefaltet werden, daß die Terme jetzt nebeneinander stehen, als Affirmation und Kritik, dann hätte man für das irritierende Forschungsbild die eher beruhigende Erklärung, daß beide Interpretationsrichtungen jeweils einen Teil des so entstandenen Spektrums korrekt beschreiben.

Wenn die Nachdichtung die strukturalen Relationen des Perceval-Teils aufspaltet und die Terme vergrößert, dann ist andererseits die Vorstellung nicht abwegig, daß die Beschäftigung mit dem *Parzival* der Interpretation des *Conte du Graal* förderlich sein könnte. Ich glaube, ein Beispiel für eine solche Reversibilität der Interpretationsarbeit geben zu können. Es handelt sich um die Ither/Chevalier Vermoil-Episode.

Kontrastive Analysen führen dazu, einen großen Unterschied, wenn nicht einen Gegensatz, in der Schuldauffassung bei Chrétien und Wolfram anzunehmen. Bei Chrétien hätte man es mit einer globalen, existentiellen Schuld zu tun, während im *Parzival* Schuld primär spezifisch als ritterliche Schuld definiert werde. Es scheint in der Tat, daß bei Wolfram der Modus der Verleihung der 'Ritterwürde' an den Helden sich nach einer solchen Definition richtet: da *ritterschaft* leicht Mord bedeuten kann, fungiert die Ermordung Ithers als Schwertleite. Das begleitende Ritual wird überflüssig, sobald die Sache im Kern erfaßt und dargestellt wurde.[16] Eine Kontrollanalyse der entsprechenden Textteile bei Chrétien scheint ebenfalls die Differenz zu bestätigen: Perceval wird feierlich zum Ritter geschlagen, Gornemant stimmt dabei eine Lobeshymne auf die *chevalerie* an (1632–36) und bis zum Ende des

---

[14] J. Fourquet (wie Anm. 1), S. 147 f.: 'Le détail de ses réactions révèle sa foi dans la victoire du bien sur le mal, au plan religieux, et son admiration pour la table des valeurs courtoises, sur le plan de la vie chevaleresque.' – Michel Huby, 'Réflexions sur *Parzival* et le *Conte del Graal*. ''schildes ambet ist mîn art'' ', *Et. Germ.*, 34 (1979), 390–403 und 35 (1980), 1–17.

[15] Vgl. z. B. Dennis Green, 'Homicide and *Parzival*', in D.H. Green und L.P. Johnson, *Approaches to Wolfram von Eschenbach: Five Essays*, Mikrokosmos, 5 (Bern/Frankfurt/Las Vegas, 1978), S. 11–82.

[16] Joachim Bumke, 'Parzivals ''Schwertleite'' ', in *Taylor Starck Festschrift*, hg. von W. Betz, E. S. Coleman und K. Northcott (London/The Hague/Paris, 1964), S. 235–45.

Torsos äußert sich keine einzige Stimme kritisch zu der Ermordung des Chevalier Vermoil.

Hier scheint also ein klarer Fall umakzentuierender, wenn nicht gar uminterpretierender Nachdichtung vorzuliegen. Man kann aber den Text Chrétiens anders befragen und zwar bei der Frage ansetzen: könnte es nicht sein, daß der Erzähler zu der Ermordung des Chevalier Vermoil schweigt, weil er uns eine Interpretationsvorgabe geliefert hat, ohne daß wir es gemerkt hätten? Um diese Interpretationsvorgabe zu entdecken, könnte man von Wolfram ausgehen und weiterfragen: werden nicht ebenfalls im *Conte du Graal*, aber *in einem anderen Textteil*, Schwertleite und Totschlag miteinander in Verbindung gebracht? Es stellt sich dann heraus, daß aus dem Bericht der Mutter über den Tod der Brüder Percevals eine solche Relation herausgelesen werden kann: 'An un jor andui li vaslet/ adobé et chevalier furent,/ et an un jor meïsmes murent/ por revenir a lor repeire,/ [. . .] qu'as armes furent desconfit./ As armes furent mort andui' (466–73). Der insistente Verweis auf die 'Zeiteinheit' ('an un jor') legt nahe, daß Percevals Brüder noch am Tage ihrer Schwertleite erschlagen wurden, was übrigens von der handschriftlichen Überlieferung gestützt wird,[17] und daß das zeitliche Zusammenfallen von Schwertleite und Tod mehr als Zufall sein könnte. Wer diesen Zusammenhang beim Lesen der Chevalier Vermoil-Episode in Erinnerung hat, kann die Verbindungslinie ziehen: Ritterweihe stellt sich als eine Alternative dar, sie bedeutet Selbstmord oder Mord. In diesem Punkt gehen also Wolframs und Chrétiens Darstellung gar nicht so weit auseinander. Zu der Symmetrie-Relation kommt bei Chrétien eine polare Relation hinzu. Der Standpunkt der Mutter kann nicht absolute Gültigkeit beanspruchen, selbst wenn die Chevalier Vermoil-Episode der Veuve Dame recht zu geben scheint. Auch Gornemants Worte sind zu beherzigen: 'la plus haute ordre [. . .]/ que Dex a fete et comandee,/ c'est l'ordre de chevalerie' (1633–35). Dem Gralroman soll – wie dem *Erec* und dem *Yvain* – die Funktion zufallen, die Lévi-Strauss dem Mythos zuschreibt: die Vermittlung zwischen extremen Positionen. Diesmal aber hat Chrétien den Bogen seines 'synthetischen Mythos' überspannt. Wie man sich den Zusammenhang von Licht und Blut vorzustellen hat, das bleibt dem Leser/Hörer praktisch gänzlich überlassen. Was dem verjüngten 'wilden Denken' als unlösbare Aufgabe anvertraut wird, formuliert Wolframs naturgemäß mehr reflektierende Nachdichtung klarer, widersprüchlicher – widersprüchlicher, da klarer: *ritterschaft* kann Wiederholung der Kainstat sein, ist aber zugleich das schönste *ambet*.

---

[17] *Der Percevalroman (Li Contes del Graal) von Christian von Troyes*, hg. von Alfons Hilka (Halle, 1932), zu V. 470 Hilka (= Lecoy 468): 'Et an un jour meïsmes murent', Lesart von *F*: 'an un jour meïsmes morurent'; *P*: 'an un jor mesmes morurent'; *R*, *S*: 'an un jor andoi morurent'; zu V. 474 Hilka (= Lecoy 472), Lesart von *U*: 'Qu'armez furent et desconfit'.

Damit kein Mißverständnis aufkommt: ich gehe in keiner Weise davon aus, daß Wolfram eine Vorlage bearbeitet hat, die den Tod der Brüder Percevals erwähnte und daß er in seiner Darstellung der Ermordung Ithers diesen Passus indirekt verwertet hat. Gemeint ist vielmehr folgendes: Wenn man Wolfram eine außerordentliche Feinfühligkeit und Rezeptivität gegenüber seiner Quelle bescheinigen darf – und man darf das wohl –, dann ist als nächster Schritt denkbar, daß man diese Einsicht instrumentalisiert und die Arbeitshypothese aufstellt, daß Wolframs Text 'Vibrationen' der Vorlage verstärkt und insofern als Kommentar zu dem *Conte du Graal* benutzt werden kann.

Damit hätte man eine etwas breitere Basis sowohl für die internationale germanistische Diskussion als auch für die interdisziplinäre Zusammenarbeit.

Heteroglossia and Clerical Narrative:
On Wolfram's Adaptation of Chrétien

ADRIAN STEVENS

The twelfth-century clerics who established the courtly romance in France and Germany as a narrative genre sometimes had enough self-confidence to present themselves as the modern successors of the classical authors they had studied in their schools, and to think of themselves as renewing in their works the rhetorical artifice that defined Latin literary culture.[1] Chrétien de Troyes announced in the prologue to his *Cligés* that chivalry (*chevalerie*) and learning (*clergie*) had been translated from Greece to Rome, and from Rome to the France of his own time:

> Par les livres que nos avons
> Les fez des ancïens savons
> Et del siegle qui fu jadis.
> Ce nos ont nostre livre apris
> Qu'an Grece ot de chevalerie
> Le premier los et de clergie.
> Puis vint chevalerie a Rome
> Et de la clergie la some,
> Qui ore est an France venue.   (25–33)[2]

---

[1] On the question of the relationship between Latin and vernacular literary texts, see Adrian Stevens, 'Zum Literaturbegriff bei Rudolf von Ems', in *Geistliche und weltliche Epik des Mittelalters in Österreich*, ed. by David McLintock, Adrian Stevens and Fred Wagner, GAG, 446 (Göppingen, 1987), pp. 19–28; and Adrian Stevens, 'The Renewal of the Classic: Aspects of Rhetorical and Dialectical Composition in Gottfried's *Tristan*', in *Gottfried von Strassburg and the Medieval Tristan Legend: Papers from an Anglo-North American Symposium*, ed. with an introduction by Adrian Stevens and Roy Wisbey (Cambridge/London, 1990), pp. 67–89.

[2] Chrétien de Troyes, *Cligés*, ed. by Alexandre Micha, CFMA, 84 (Paris, 1957). On Chrétien's attitude towards Latin literature, and his use of rhetoric and dialectic, see Lucie Polak, *Chrétien de Troyes: Cligés*, Critical Guides to French Texts, 23 (London, 1982), pp. 16–21, 70–86; and Tony Hunt, *Chrétien de Troyes: Yvain*, Critical Guides to French Texts, 55 (London, 1986), pp. 80–93.

(Through the books we possess we learn of the deeds of
the people of past times and of the world as it used to be.
Our books have taught us how Greece ranked first in
chivalry and learning; then chivalry passed to Rome along
with the fund of transcendent learning that has now come
to France.)[3]

Gottfried von Straßburg in the literary excursus of his *Tristan* argues that
the Germans, too, were successful in extending and perpetuating the
classic by adapting it to the vernacular. He celebrates the artistic and
cultural distinction that accrues to German narrative poetry as the result
of its having been successfully grafted, like its immediate French
models, onto the stem of classical Latin literature. But from the clerical
narrative tradition which, according to Gottfried, originated in Germany
with Veldeke and continues through Hartmann, Bligger von Steinach
and Gottfried himself, Wolfram, notoriously, is excluded. The clear
insinuation of Gottfried's excursus is that Wolfram was unschooled.[4]
Even if this leaves open the possibility that Wolfram may have been, to
use Clanchy's term, practically literate,[5] able to read German and
French, and perhaps a little Latin, he remains in Gottfried's eyes
technically illiterate, an *illiteratus* incompetent in the essential poetic
disciplines of grammar, rhetoric and dialectic which could be mastered
only by an intensive study of the trivium.[6]

For his own part, Wolfram is careful to disclaim any affinity with
clerical ideals of literary composition. He is, to borrow Chrétien's
distinction, a representative not of *clergie* but of *chevalerie*, and he makes
no bones about his allegiance to the profession of arms: 'schildes ambet
ist mîn art' (115,11).[7] In keeping with his strongly stated knightly image,

---

[3] All translations of Chrétien are taken from *Chrétien de Troyes: Arthurian Romances*, trans.
with an introduction and notes by D.D.R. Owen, Everyman Classics (London, 1987)
(henceforth referred to as Owen); ibid. p. 93.
[4] On the question of Wolfram's literacy, see D.H. Green, 'Oral Poetry and Written
Composition: (An Aspect of the Feud between Gottfried and Wolfram)', in D.H. Green
and L.P. Johnson, *Approaches to Wolfram von Eschenbach: Five Essays*, Mikrokosmos, 5 (Bern/
Frankfurt am Main/Las Vegas, 1978), pp. 163–271.
[5] See M.T. Clanchy, *From Memory to Written Record: England 1066–1307* (London, 1979),
esp. pp. 197–98, 262–63.
[6] On the relationship between literacy and illiteracy in medieval society, see Clanchy,
From Memory to Written Record, pp. 175–201; and Herbert Grundmann, 'Litteratus –
Illiteratus', *Archiv für Kulturgeschichte*, 40 (1958), 1–63.
[7] The German text of *Parzival* used here is that in *Wolfram von Eschenbach*, ed. by Karl
Lachmann, 6th edn (Berlin/Leipzig, 1926; repr. 1965). On Wolfram's self-presentation as
an *illiteratus*, see Hugo Kuhn, 'Wolframs Frauenlob', *ZfdA*, 106 (1977), 200–10; and the
general question of the relationship between German and Latin as literary languages
Dietmar Jürgen Ponert, *Deutsch und Latein in deutscher Literatur und Geschichtsschreibung des
Mittelalters*, Studien zur Poetik und Geschichte der Literatur, 43 (Stuttgart, 1975).

Wolfram refuses to countenance the possibility of his version of the Grail story being classified as a book:

> ich spræche iu d'âventiure vort.
> swer des von mir geruoche,
> dern zels ze keinem buoche.
> ine kan decheinen buochstap.
> dâ nement genuoge ir urhap:
> disiu âventiure
> vert âne der buoche stiure.
> ê man si hete für ein buoch,
> ich wære ê nacket âne tuoch,
> sô ich in dem bade sæze,
> ob ichs questen niht vergæze.   (115,24–116,4)

The much-debated line 'ine kan decheinen buochstap' (115,27) is perhaps best understood as a programmatic acknowledgement by Wolfram that he is an *illiteratus*, somebody who, in the strong Latin sense of the term, is unlettered.[8] But to be an *illiteratus* is not necessarily to be in modern usage illiterate. Even if he had never formally studied Latin and been taught how to write, Wolfram may have learned to read vernacular texts, including both Chrétien's *Conte du Graal* and his own *Parzival*. There is no need to assume that when he says his narrative proceeds without the support of books ('âne der buoche stiure', 115,30), he means that he is unable to read a manuscript copy of the *Conte du Graal*. The books he mentions are more likely in this context to be the classical works read in the schools by clerics, the *literati* whose practice as poets, even when they write in the vernacular, originates in and is shaped by their Latin literary education: 'dâ', i.e. in the study of letters of which Wolfram professes to be ignorant, 'nement genuoge ir urhap' (115,28). Courtly narrative, Wolfram reminds his audience, is in a fundamental sense clerical narrative. As a knight without the usual background of clerical training he is, and knows himself to be, an outsider among courtly authors.

If Gottfried for this reason refused to incorporate Wolfram into his literary canon, others were neither so dismissive nor so polemical. Rudolf von Ems ranks Wolfram with Hartmann and with Gottfried himself;[9] Wirnt von Gravenberg, although well aware that Wolfram was a layman in a predominantly clerical literary culture, praises his untutored artistry: 'leien munt nie baz gesprach',[10] and Ulrich von

---

[8] See Kuhn, 'Wolframs Frauenlob', p. 205, and Ponert, *Deutsch und Latein*, p. 40; also Green, 'Oral Poetry', pp. 265–71.

[9] See Xenja von Ertzdorff, *Rudolf von Ems: Untersuchungen zum höfischen Roman im 13. Jahrhundert* (Munich, 1967), pp. 114–59.

[10] Wirnt von Gravenberc, *Wigalois*, ed. by J.M.N. Kapteyn, Rheinische Beiträge und

Türheim reflects ruefully on the fact that Wolfram's reputation as an author stands much higher among the public at large than that of his learned rivals:

> sin lop fur uns alle wac,
> der dehein buch gemachet hat.[11]

In his own eyes and in the eyes of the clerical establishment, Wolfram had managed the paradox of producing a book that was not a book. *Parzival* was a book in the pragmatic sense that it existed in manuscript form, and was apparently so much in demand that it was being copied and distributed long before Wolfram had completed it (already at the end of Book VI he talks of women seeing the written text: 'diu diz mære geschriben siht', 337,3). But if *Parzival* was a book in physical fact, it was not a book by conventional definition, since it was not written by a cleric in accordance with the Latin-based norms that governed the composition of literary texts. In adapting Chrétien's *Conte du Graal*, Wolfram was accommodating a clerical poem to a lay perspective. Such relationship as his *Parzival* had to the classics, 'der buoche stiure', was indirect, mediated through clerical authors writing in the vernacular. One consequence of this is that in the literary context of 1200 *Parzival* is a radically modern work, free of all but the remotest classical influences and deeply rooted in the lay aristocratic culture of its time.

Perhaps because it is so detached from 'der buoche stiure', Wolfram's text engages in a dialogue with the feudal world that is in some respects more wide-ranging than anything to be found in the works of courtly fiction that precede it. Bakhtin goes so far as to suggest that *Parzival* can be seen as an authentic novel,[12] and the basis for his startling claim is Wolfram's willingness to incorporate into his fiction the heteroglot reality of his age, the rich multiplicity and variety of languages in actual use in the society in which he lived and to which he presented his adaptation of Chrétien. A novel is constructed, as Bakhtin puts it, 'on concrete social speech diversity'.[13] Its determining generic feature is that it embodies and dramatises a 'plenitude of actual social-historical

Hülfsbücher zur germanischen Philologie und Volkskunde, 9 (Bonn, 1926), l. 6346. On Wirnt's characterization of Wolfram as a non-clerical author, see Hedda Ragotzky, *Studien zur Wolfram-Rezeption: Die Entstehung und Verwandlung der Wolfram-Rolle in der deutschen Literatur des 13. Jahrhunderts*, Studien zur Poetik und Geschichte der Literatur, 20 (Stuttgart, 1971), pp. 37–43.

[11] Ulrich von Türheim, *Rennewart*, ed. by Alfred Hübner, DTM, 39 (Berlin/Zürich, 1938), ll. 4538–39.

[12] See M.M. Bakhtin, 'Discourse in the Novel', in *The Dialogic Imagination: Four Essays by M.M. Bakhtin*, ed. by Michael Holquist, trans. by Caryl Emerson and Michael Holquist, University of Texas Press Slavic Series, 1 (Austin, Texas, 1981), p. 377.

[13] *The Dialogic Imagination*, p. 412.

languages'.[14] Each of the languages which constitutes its heteroglossia is a 'point of view, a socio-ideological conceptual system of real social groups and their embodied representatives. [. . .] Any point of view on the world fundamental to the novel must be a concrete, socially embodied point of view, not an abstract, purely semantic position; it must, consequently, have its own language'.[15]

To apply the generic term novel to *Parzival* is, for an English-speaking reader, a stumbling block. Historically, the word novel in English is associated with a polemical bias against romance. The novel, according to the Oxford English Dictionary, is a narrative form 'in which characters and actions representative of the real life of past or present times are portrayed'; whereas in romance 'the scene and incidents are very remote from those of ordinary life'. But Russian, like German, has less of a problem with novels than English. It borrows the French *roman*, a comparatively neutral term for a fictional narrative, as is evidenced by the fact that it can be translated into English both as 'novel' and as 'romance'. For Bakhtin, *Parzival* is a *roman*; for his American translators it is sometimes a novel and sometimes a romance.[16] In English, novel and romance are mimetic concepts; for Bakhtin, who does not operate within Aristotelian categories of reference, the *roman* is defined by its generic relationship to language, or rather to the languages of heteroglossia. The fact that a given work is on Bakhtin's definition heteroglot will make it in some measure true to the life of its time, although not necessarily in a mimetic sense. As seen from Bakhtin's perspective, realism is essentially a matter of linguistic register. The languages which fictional narrative incorporates may be imaginative, abstract, theoretical or even fantastical, and as such remote from the everyday and the mundane, while still forming part of the social world inhabited by the author and his original audience. Wolfram's *Parzival*, like Goethe's *Faust* and many of the major works of European literature, uses registers which range freely from the fantastic to the familiar, and consequently contains elements which a mimetic theory would associate both with romance and with the novel.

Significantly, Wolfram's willingness to introduce into *Parzival* registers which were non-literary in the purist sense that they were not sanctioned by the authority of 'der buoche stiure' is subjected to dismissive criticism in Gottfried's *Tristan*. In relating how the wound Tristan received at the hands of Morolt was healed by Isolt's mother,

---

14   *The Dialogic Imagination*, p. 412.
15   *The Dialogic Imagination*, pp. 411–12.
16   See *The Dialogic Imagination*, pp. 376ff. On Bakhtin's theory of the link between heteroglossia and the novel, see Tzvetan Todorov, *Mikhail Bakhtin: The Dialogical Principle*, trans. by Wlad Godzich, Theory and History of Literature, 13 (Manchester, 1984); and David Lodge, *After Bakhtin: Essays on Fiction and Criticism* (London/New York, 1990).

Gottfried demonstratively refuses to include in his account the sort of detail which would necessitate the use of technical medical vocabulary. Viewed from the classicising angle adopted by Gottfried, the language of medicine is a jargon incompatible with refined literary usage:

> Ob ich iu nu vil seite
> und lange rede vür leite
> von miner vrouwen meisterschaft,
> wie wunderliche guote craft
> ir arzenie hæte
> und wies ir siechen tæte,
> waz hülfez und waz solte daz?
> in edelen oren lutet baz
> ein wort, daz schone gezimt,
> dan daz man uz der bühsen nimt.   (7935–44)[17]

The rhetorical convention of decorum which Gottfried invokes demands rigorous selectivity (the choice of 'ein wort, daz schone gezimt', 7943), and the exclusion of any linguistic register which might be considered incompatible with politeness and good taste.[18] Subject matter which cannot be accommodated to the constraints of decorum is better omitted from courtly narrative composed in the clerical manner, even though it might be thought to contain information relevant to the story:

> als verre als ichz bedenken kan,
> so sol ich mich bewarn dar an,
> daz ich iu iemer wort gesage,
> daz iuwern oren missehage
> und iuwerm herzen widerste.
> ich spriche ouch deste minner e
> von iegelicher sache,
> e ich iu daz mære mache
> unlidic unde unsenfte bi
> mit rede, diu niht des hoves si.   (7945–54)

While Wolfram is by no means indifferent to decorum, which is not only a literary but a social convention, his attitude towards it is a good deal more elastic than Gottfried's. Where Gottfried is hostile to what Bakhtin calls the 'brute heteroglossia of the real world',[19] and attempts to purify his text of what he sees as the unacceptably rustic dialects of

---

[17] Gottfried von Strassburg, *Tristan und Isold*, ed. by Friedrich Ranke (Berlin, 1962).
[18] On the rhetorical convention of decorum, see Heinrich Lausberg, *Handbuch der literarischen Rhetorik* (Munich, 1960), section 258, pp. 144–45, and sections 1055–62, pp. 507–11.
[19] *The Dialogic Imagination*, p. 385.

the tribe ('rede, diu niht des hoves si', 7954), Wolfram is much given to interweaving polite and impolite linguistic registers and juxtaposing courtly language with its common, extraliterary counterpart. Unlike Gottfried, he delights in medicine and has no scruples about appropriating for his text the register of herbal remedy. In Book XIII of *Parzival*, in a passage which has no parallel in Chrétien, he assures his audience that the combined skills of all the doctors in the world could not have cured Gawan of the wounds he sustains in the service of Orgeluse. Orgeluse alone has the remedy for his ills, and that remedy is sexual:

> dar zuo al der arzte kunst,
> ob si im trüegen guote gunst
> mit temperîe ûz würze kraft,
> âne wîplîch geselleschaft
> sô müeser sîne schärpfe nôt
> hân brâht unz an den sûren tôt.
> ich wil iuz mære machen kurz.
> er vant die rehten hirzwurz,
> diu im half daz er genas
> sô daz im arges niht enwas:
> Diu wurz was bî dem blanken brûn.   (643,21–644,1)

The authentic hart's eye ('rehten hirzwurz', 643,28, wild dittany, according to Hatto),[20] which Gawan finds, the herb that shows brown against white ('bî dem blanken brûn', 644,1) is, of course, Orgeluse's pubic hair.[21]

Bakhtin speaks appositely of Wolfram's propensity for 'bringing high discourses low through a series of degrading comparisons'.[22] The metaphorical references to Gawan's sharp distress ('schärpfe nôt', 643,25) and to the bitter death ('sûren tôt', 643,26) he would have suffered without 'womanly companionship' ('wîplîch geselleschaft', 643,24) are, in the generic context of romance narrative, routine enough: stock items selected from the familiar literary inventory of courtly love. But the abrupt switch to the register of herbal cure defies comfortable anticipation, and the earthy innuendo which links hart's eye with Orgeluse's pudenda is a deliberate flouting of propriety. Wolfram's relaxed and humorous tolerance of vulgarity distinguishes him not only from Gottfried but from Chrétien, whose *Conte du Graal*, in observing

---

[20] Wolfram von Eschenbach, *Parzival*, trans. by A.T. Hatto, Penguin Classics (Harmondsworth, 1980), p. 322.
[21] See the commentary on this passage in *Wolframs von Eschenbach Parzival und Titurel*, ed. by Karl Bartsch, 4th edn, rev. by Marta Marti, vol. 3 (Leipzig, 1932).
[22] *The Dialogic Imagination*, p. 386, n. 51.

the niceties of clerical stylisation, draws significantly on 'der buoche stiure'. Chrétien's account of the meeting of Perceval and Blancheflor, to cite one striking example, owes much to his reading of Ovid. The *Ars amatoria* functions as a subtext against which each stage in Blancheflor's progress towards the eventual seduction of Perceval can be knowingly read off. Ovid proposes the sequence: *visus* (seeing, watching, exchanging glances); *colloquium* (love talk); *osculum* (kissing); *tactus* (touching, embracing, caressing); *coitus* (intercourse).[23] Chrétien, urbanely cynical, subverts this progression to the extent that he casts Blancheflor in the role Ovid originally devised for the male lover. Although technically still a virgin at the time of her meeting with Perceval, Blancheflor is no innocent. At her first entrance she is compared to a sparrowhawk ('espreviers', 1797),[24] traditionally the symbol of the knightly seducer. When Perceval remains dumb in her presence, much to the displeasure of the assembled nobles, who think that he and Blancheflor make a splendid match (1852-76), it is Blancheflor who makes the first move by initiating conversation (1877-82). After the two of them have retired to their separate beds for the night, Perceval at once falls into the untroubled sleep of a man who knows nothing of the pleasures of love (1935-44). It is Blancheflor who is restless and disturbed:

> Mais s'ostesse pas ne repose,
> Qui en sa chambre estoit enclose;
> Cil dort a ese, et cele pense,
> Qui n'a en li nule desfense
> D'une bataille qui l'asaut.   (1945-49)

> (However, his hostess, shut in her room, finds no rest: he sleeps at ease, but she, involved in a struggle in which she is defenceless, is deep in thought.)[25]

The studied ambiguity of Chrétien's formulation makes it possible to interpret Blancheflor's sleeplessness literally (and innocently), as the result of her 'knowing she has no defence against the army which will attack her'.[26] But students of Ovid and of clerical romance are likely to surmise that Blancheflor's hopeless struggle is not only against the besieging army of Anguingueron, seneschal of Clamadeus des Isles, but

---

[23] See Rüdiger Schnell, 'Ovids *Ars amatoria* und die höfische Minnetheorie', *Euph.*, 69 (1975), 132-59.
[24] Chrétien de Troyes, *Le Roman de Perceval ou Le Conte du Graal*, ed. by William Roach, Textes Littéraires Français, 71, 2nd edn (Geneva/Paris, 1959).
[25] Owen (see note 3 above), p. 400.
[26] So L.T. Topsfield, *Chrétien de Troyes: A Study of the Arthurian Romances* (Cambridge, 1981), p. 247.

against love experienced as overwhelming passion. Putting a scarlet silk mantle over her shift, Blancheflor makes her way to where Perceval lies peacefully asleep, resolved to tell him 'part of what she had on her mind':[27]

[. . .] et si li dira
De son pensé une partie. (1958–59)

What she will tell Perceval about directly is Clamadeus and the siege; but what is also (and even more urgently) on her mind may be deduced from the careful description Chrétien supplies of her physical and emotional state. As she approaches the unsuspecting Perceval, Blancheflor is 'in such fear that she trembled in every limb and was bathed in perspiration':[28]

A tel paor que tuit li membre
Li trambloient, li cors [li] sue. (1962–63)

Trembling and sweating are, in the Ovidian tradition, two of the characteristic symptoms of passion; and so, too, are the laments and deep sighs to which Blancheflor gives vent when she kneels down beside Perceval's bed and wets his face with tears because, as Chrétien ironically expresses it, 'she lacks the courage to do any more'[29] ('N'a hardement que plus en face', 1970). But when Perceval is finally awakened, it is to find Blancheflor 'holding her arms tightly clasped round his neck':[30]

[. . .] qui le tenoit
Par le col embrachié estroit. (1975–76)

Finding himself in this delicate situation, Perceval for the first time in the story behaves with what might be called natural courtesy:

Et tant de cortoisie fist
Que entre ses deus bras le prist
Maintenant et vers lui le trait,
Se li dist: 'Bele, que vos plait?
Por coi estes venue chi?' (1977–81)

(He was courtly enough to take her at once in his two arms and draw her towards him, saying: 'What do you want, my fair one? Why have you come here?')[31]

---

27 Owen, p. 400.
28 Owen, p. 400.
29 Owen, p. 400.
30 Owen, p. 400.
31 Owen, p. 401.

Perceval's questions to Blancheflor are innocent, but the reader (or audience) is expected to be more experienced and to supply a sexual *double entendre* in keeping with the Ovidian subtext. That subtext lends a finely salacious ambiguity to Blancheflor's response

> 'Ha! gentius chevaliers, merchi!
> Por Dieu vos pri et por son fil
> Que vos ne m'en aiez plus vil
> De che je sui chi venue.
> Por che se je sui pres que nue
> Je n'i pensa[i] onques folie
> Ne mauvestié ne vilonnie,
> Qu'il n'a el monde rien qui vive
> Tant dolente et tant chetive
> Que je ne soie plus dolente.'   (1982–91)

> ('Ah, noble knight, have pity on me! I beg you in the name
> of God and His Son not to think the worse of me for
> having come here. Despite my being almost naked, I had
> no foolish, wicked or base intention; for there's no living
> soul in all the world who is so grief-stricken or wretched
> that I am not more so.')[32]

Read literally, Blancheflor's concern is to preserve her honour and reputation against Clamadeus. But sophisticated clerical narrative of the type Chrétien produces is not intended to be interpreted only on a surface level. The study of grammar and rhetoric that was an integral part of the trivium inculcated the theory that all canonical texts, whether secular or religious, have the generic capacity to signify something more (and more illuminating) than they explicitly state. Texts were seen by the schoolmen as rhetorical constructs. Composed of figures, they have hidden figurative meanings, what Bernard Silvester called 'misterium occultum' and Thomasin von Zerclære (who was speaking of courtly romances) 'tiefe sinne'.[33] Isidore of Seville offers a beguiling but wholly

---

[32] Owen, p. 401.

[33] Bernard uses the phrase 'misterium occultum' in his commentary on Martianus Capella, in which he expounds the theory of hidden figurative meanings, and argues that such meanings are a feature of both sacred and profane texts. I quote from Hennig Brinkmann, *Mittelalterliche Hermeneutik* (Darmstadt, 1980), p. 169: 'Figura [. . .] est oratio quam involucrum dicere solent. Hec autem bipartita est: partimur namque eam in allegoriam et integumentum. Est autem allegoria oratio sub historica narratione verum et ab exteriori diversum involvens intellectum, ut de lucta Iacob. [. . .] Integumentum vero est oratio sub fabulosa narratione verum claudens intellectum, ut de Orpheo. Nam et ibi historia et hic fabula misterium habent occultum.' For the phrase 'tiefe sinne', see Thomasin von Zirclaria, *Der wälsche Gast*, ed. by Heinrich Rückert with an introduction and index by Friedrich Neumann, Deutsche Neudrucke, Reihe Texte des Mittelalters (Berlin, 1965), l. 1108. On the argument that courtly romances could be read, at least by

conventional argument for the use of the figures. 'The things which are to be understood are concealed in figured garments', he writes, 'so that they may exercise the mind of the reader and not be made vulgar by being exposed naked to public view': 'ea quae intelligenda sunt, propterea figuratis amictibus obteguntur, ut sensus legentis exerceant et ne nuda atque in promptu vilescant.'[34]

There is no doubting that Blancheflor would like to be rid of Clamadeus, but her plea to Perceval is dressed in figures which conceal a more fundamental desire. The undeclared, hidden meaning of her words may be deduced from the way in which she associates her appeal for mercy ('merchi', 1982, a stock euphemism for sexual gratification in the courtly love lyric) with the fact that she is all but nude ('pres que nue', 1986). Her desire for Perceval is something that she, as a virgin and a representative of the nobility, cannot confess openly because it is, as she herself intimates, mad, wicked and base (cf. 'folie', 'mauvestié', 'vilonnie', 1987–88). As she is only too well aware, it exposes her to the risk of humiliation and disgrace (cf. 'Que vos ne m'en aiez plus vil', 1984). But Blancheflor's use of figures and of figurative meanings enables her, just, to preserve her respectability; she contrives, to rephrase Isidore slightly, not to make herself vulgar by exposing herself naked to public view. To penetrate to the underlying indecorous and uncourtly significance of her speech, the reader is obliged to supply privately the heteroglossia which Chrétien's sophisticated courtly narrative suppresses publicly in the interests of politeness and decorum. What Gottfried describes as 'rede, diu des hoves si' is a form of language that is highly stylised in the sense that it is highly selective; calculated to maintain appearances, it nevertheless has a dramatic capacity for intimating meanings often violently at odds with its surface control and elegance.

Chrétien's Ovidian subtext continues to subvert the literal meaning of his courtly text by adding to it an implicitly indecent commentary. Moved by Blancheflor's plea Perceval, much to her secret gratification, loses no time in kissing her and drawing her into his bed:

> [. . .] Et il le baisoit
> Et en ses bras le tenoit prise,

clerics, as integuments, see Christoph Huber, 'Höfischer Roman als Integumentum? Das Votum Thomasins von Zerklære', *ZfdA*, 115 (1986), 79–100. On the wider aspects of the question of figurative writing and allegorical interpretation, see Jon Whitman, *Allegory: The Dynamics of an Ancient and Medieval Technique* (Oxford, 1987), and Philip Rollinson, *Classical Theories of Allegory and Christian Culture*, Duquesne Studies, Language and Literature Series, 3 (Pittsburgh/Brighton, 1981).

[34] Isidore, *Etymologiae*, ed. by W.M. Lindsay (Oxford, 1911), I.37.1–2. Linda M. Paterson, *Troubadours and Eloquence* (Oxford, 1975), argues that the Provençal poets who cultivated the *trobar clus* intended their songs to provoke a search for hidden figurative meanings.

> Si l'a soz le covertoir mise
> Tot soavet et tot a aise;
> Et cele soffre qu'il le baise,
> Ne ne quit pas qu'il li anuit.
> Ensi jurent tote la nuit,
> Li uns lez l'autre, bouche a bouche,
> Juisqu'al main que li jors aproche.   (2058–66)

(Then he kissed her and, holding her tightly in his arms, drew her gently to lie at ease under the coverlet. She let him kiss her and was not, I think, unhappy to do so! Thus they lay all night long, side by side and mouth to mouth until the morning and the approach of daylight.)[35]

Kissing and touching, the third and fourth stages in Ovid's sequence of seduction, merge in a way that has no counterpart in Wolfram's presentation of the scene. Whereas Chrétien sustains an urbane and finely ironic literary dialogue with Ovid, reversing the roles presented in the *Ars amatoria* by casting the girl as the calculating seducer, Wolfram ignores the Roman author, and with him 'der buoche stiure', and concentrates instead on a systematic dismantling of his French source. Condwiramurs, unlike Blancheflor, is a genuine innocent uncompromised by Ovid's literary paternity, while Parzival is considerably less precocious than Perceval in matters of love and lovemaking. Significantly, when Wolfram offers a description of the beauty of Condwiramurs, he remains firmly within a vernacular frame of reference, asserting that Condwiramurs surpasses not only Jeschute and Cunneware de Lalant but also Enite and the two Isaldes (187,12–21). When she retires for the night Condwiramurs is not kept awake by the assaults of love; she does not suffer the characteristic Ovidian symptoms of love sickness, trembling and sweating, as she approaches Parzival's bed; she does not embrace the hero as she kneels beside him, nor does she tell Parzival, as Blancheflor so revealingly tells Perceval, that she is nearly naked. For his part Parzival, once he is aroused from sleep by Condwiramurs's tears, does not follow Perceval's example by promptly taking her into his arms. On the contrary, he offers to vacate his bed in her favour, and when Condwiramurs joins him on the explicit condition that he will not struggle with her, there is no suggestion of any form of erotic contact, much less of the kiss (the Ovidian precursor to full intercourse) which in Chrétien is prolonged uninterrupted all through the night:

---

35   Owen, p. 402.

ûf rihte sich der junge man,
zer küneginne sprach er sân
'frouwe, bin ich iwer spot?
ir soldet knien alsus für got.
geruochet sitzen zuo mir her'
(daz was sîn bete und sîn ger):
'oder leit iuch hie aldâ ich lac.
lât mich belîben swâ ich mac.'
si sprach 'welt ir iuch êren,
sölhe mâze gein mir kêren
daz ir mit mir ringet niht,
mîn ligen aldâ bî iu geschiht.'
des wart ein vride von im getân:
si smouc sich an daz bette sân.   (193,21–194,4)

In short, the result of Wolfram's reworking of the scene is that
Chrétien's suggestive Ovidian subtext is expunged; honour and
decency rule unchallenged, and Parzival and Condwiramurs maintain a
degree of chastity which Perceval and Blancheflor do not begin to
match.

But if the protagonists are naïve and innocent, the same cannot be said
of Wolfram the narrator or of the reactions he expects from his audience.
Wolfram's text is no less worldly wise than Chrétien's, but it presents its
awareness of human fallibility and corruptness in a quite different,
unclerical manner. Wolfram does not leave his audience, as Chrétien
does, to unclothe in discreet privacy the figures generated by the
rhetorical structure of his text; his narrative is explicit and heteroglot
rather than allusive and decorous. Where Chrétien maintains a mask of
literary tact, presupposing the complicity of an 'hypocrite lecteur' who
will move suavely and knowingly from surface politeness to hidden
indecency, Wolfram makes discourse of an explicitly common kind an
integral part of his text. This common (and on occasion vulgar) discourse
is designed to join him and his audience in a community of experience
which separates them from the superlative (and unworldly) innocence
of Parzival and Condwiramurs. A fallen narrator tells the idealised story
of his protagonists in a fallen world to fallen readers and listeners. That
fallen world, the Germany of 1200, resounds to the Babel of heteroglossia; its heteroglot nature is both an indication and a condition of its
corruptness. But if heteroglossia includes the worldly registers of the
Fall, it includes also the spiritual registers of its repair, and the two are
ironically and humorously interwoven in the narration of the love and
marriage of Condwiramurs and Parzival.

When Condwiramurs makes her way to Parzival's bed, there is,
Wolfram emphasises, no breach of feminine propriety. Her motives,

unlike those of Blancheflor, are not suspect. She is kept awake solely by the distress of war and the death of supporters dear to her. The purpose of her nocturnal exploit is not, as Wolfram and his audience might in their worldly way be inclined to suppose, to find the kind of love which makes virgins into women, but to enlist Parzival's help in raising the siege of Pelrapeire:

> Daz kom als ich iu sagen wil.
> ez prach niht wîplîchiu zil:
> mit stæte kiusche truoc diu magt,
> von der ein teil hie wirt gesagt.
> die twanc urliuges nôt
> und lieber helfære tôt
> ir herze an sölhez krachen,
> daz ir ougen muosen wachen.
> dô gienc diu küneginne,
> niht nâch sölher minne
> diu sölhen namen reizet
> der meide wîp heizet,
> si suochte helfe unt friundes rât.   (192,1–13)

Even Condwiramurs's appearance is seductive not in her own eyes or in Parzival's, but in the eyes of the narrator and his audience. Besieged, she puts on the armour of love, yet without being conscious of doing so:

> an ir was werlîchiu wât,
> ein hemde wîz sîdîn:
> waz möhte kampflîcher sîn,
> dan gein dem man sus komende ein wîp?   (192,14–17)

Only when viewed from the corrupt perspective of experience does Condwiramurs's dress take on an erotic significance; but that significance, uppermost in the minds of narrator and audience, is lost on Condwiramurs herself. In an unreflecting display of modesty she puts on a long samite mantle over her shift, and grief alone guides her footsteps to the sleeping Parzival:

> ouch swanc diu frouwe umb ir lîp
> von samît einen mantel lanc.
> si gienc als si der kumber twanc.   (192,18–20)

When she kneels on the rug by Parzival's bed, no thoughts of sex enter her mind. She, like Parzival, is entirely ignorant of physical love:

> ûffen teppech kniete si für in.
> si heten beidiu kranken sin,

> Er unt diu küneginne,
> an bî ligender minne.   (193,1–4)

For his part, Parzival is so lacking in the narrator's and the audience's assumed knowledge of (and taste for) sexual pleasure that even later, on his wedding night, he displays the kind of polite restraint which, Wolfram remarks, would not at all satisfy many of the women typical of modern German society:

> er lac mit sölhen fuogen,
> des nu niht wil genuogen
> mangiu wîp, der in sô tuot.   (201,21–23)

The humour of this commentary is a function not only of the clearly implied distinction between the innocence of Parzival and Condwiramurs and the experience of Wolfram and his listeners, but of the abrupt lowering of stylistic register, the unprepared shift from the decorous to the bawdy.[36] Free of the constraints of 'der buoche stiure', Wolfram regularly indulges in the kind of explicit indecency which the clerkly Chrétien, with his aversion to heteroglossia, decorously avoids.

---

[36] On the relationship between bawdy and humour in Wolfram, see Karl Bertau, 'Versuch über tote Witze bei Wolfram', in Karl Bertau, *Wolfram von Eschenbach: Neun Versuche über Subjektivität und Ursprünglichkeit in der Geschichte* (Munich, 1983), pp. 60–109.

Dialogic Transpositions:
The Grail Hero Wins a Wife

ARTHUR GROOS

Discussing the relationship between Chrétien de Troyes's *Li Contes del Graal* and Wolfram von Eschenbach's *Parzival* sometimes seems as difficult as playing rugby in a cow pasture: it's hard to make it to the goal-line without either getting tackled or stepping in something. To begin with, classical conceptions of translation, such as metaphrase, imitation, and paraphrase,[1] seem inadequate for dealing with the transposition of Chrétien's narrative to Wolfram's, and do not account for differences so extensive that nineteenth-century scholars scurried off in quest of alternative sources, that hobgoblin of the philological mind. Modern advances in defining the characteristics of each work as well as the process that links them have brought the problem into sharper focus. Recent scholarship has posited fundamental differences in style that are grounded in extrinsic factors ranging from genesis to reception, from the author's social class and education – clerical for Chrétien, knightly for Wolfram – to the relative social composition and literary sophistication of French vis-à-vis German audiences.[2] Furthermore, medieval 'translation' corresponds only partially with modern expectations, allowing greater freedom in characterization, amplification, and choice of style.[3]

Such approaches, however, may preclude other considerations, especially when they assume the transposition of one unified authorial style into another unified authorial style without examining the implications of this assumption. Although rhymed verse tends to mask differences that later become much more apparent in prose, all Arthurian romance seems capable of creating what Mikhail Bakhtin calls

---

[1] See George Steiner, *After Babel* (Oxford, 1975), pp. 254–56.
[2] See Karl Bertau, 'Versuch über den späten Chrestien und die Anfänge Wolframs', in *Wolfram von Eschenbach: Neun Versuche über Subjektivität und Ursprünglichkeit in der Geschichte* (Munich, 1983), pp. 24–59.
[3] Carl Lofmark, 'Der höfische Dichter als Übersetzer', in *Probleme mittelhochdeutscher Erzählformen*, ed. by Peter Ganz and Werner Schröder (Berlin, 1972), pp. 40–62.

dialogic or polyphonic discourse.[4] That is: romance narratives can incorporate a variety of view-points – those of the author, a narrator, any number of characters – and inscribe them in varieties of discourse ranging from differing linguistic registers to distinct genre styles. The traditional approach, which reduces a narrative or its transposition to a single, undifferentiated authorial style in a single, undifferentiated genre thus ignores a primary feature of romance: its ability to juxtapose, play with, and ultimately integrate competing voices.

A principal difference between Chrétien's and Wolfram's Grail stories consists, I would suggest, in their relationship to this dialogic potential, specifically in Wolfram's transposition of a comparatively homogeneous to a much more heterogeneous narrative, of a still monologic romance to a more nearly dialogic one. Note that I have tentatively defined the two works in terms of a third factor, a diversified concept of genre, rather than in terms of each other, in order to avoid suggesting that Wolfram's narrative is simply more 'detailed' than his counterpart's. Each text, rather, reflects differing options with respect to romance's potential for polyphonic discourse, and thus represents a different subgenre as well. Chrétien's clerical rhetoric provides an apparently unifying principle that exploits small-scale possibilities for dialogic discourse. Wolfram's decentered narrative, with its more highly differentiated role for the narrator, delights not only in dialogic structures within and between episodes, but also relates Parzival's adventures to those of other figures, and ultimately engages in dialogue with other texts. In Bakhtin's terms: Chrétien's text exemplifies a 'first-line' development of medieval romance, using narrative to exploit some stages in the heteroglossic interaction of discourse; Wolfram creates from it 'the first German novel to be profoundly and fundamentally double voiced'.[5]

I

The following discussion will attempt to exemplify this thesis by discussing a central event in the Grail story, Perceval's winning of Blancheflor, and Parzival's of Condwiramurs.[6] Chrétien and Wolfram present essentially the same event, an archetypal episode of the romance mode: the hero's rescue of a damsel in distress. Chrétien

[4] The Dialogic Imagination: Four Essays, trans. by Caryl Emerson and Michael Holquist (Austin, 1981).
[5] Dialogic Imagination, p. 377; see also p. 400.
[6] Citations will be from Der Percevalroman (Li Contes del Graal), ed. by Alfons Hilka, Christian von Troyes: Sämtliche erhaltene Werke, vol. V (Halle/Saale, 1932); and Wolfram von Eschenbach, ed. by Karl Lachmann, rev. by Eduard Hartl, 6th edn (Berlin/Leipzig, 1926; repr. Berlin, 1965).

presents his version of this engaging episode with the elegant structure
and sophisticated elaboration of themes characteristic of his learned
rhetorical style. The events of the first two days at Belrepeire suggest a
pattern of anticipation and fulfillment, particularly through a reception
on the first day that culminates in the presentation of Perceval and
Blancheflor as a potentially ideal couple, and the hero's winning of her
favor on the second day through a series of encounters that culminates
in his victory in a pitched battle. The narrator elaborates this pattern,
among other things, by intimating a metonymic relationship between
public and private behavior, board and room, or – more precisely – food
and sex. On the first evening, both are inadequate: the inhabitants of the
castle dine on meager provisions (1910–17); Perceval retires alone to a
bed that promises every comfort one could imagine – except, the
narrator assures us, female companionship (1938–40). On the second
evening, absence becomes presence: the arrival of a barge loaded with
supplies (2525ff.) provides the opportunity for a lively feast; and
Perceval and Blancheflor disport themselves freely (2575).

While the plot thus suggests a self-contained structure of anticipation
and fulfillment, the presentation of the heroine's and hero's actions
complicates this expectation. Blancheflor's nocturnal visit at the end of
the first evening creates an ironic discrepancy between the narrator's
assurance of propriety and the ambiguity of her behavior – scanty attire,
symptoms that resemble Ovidian love sickness,[7] and patently
manipulative actions. This discrepancy introduces a competition
between the narrator and a figure within the story, which not only
subverts the narrator's authority, but also reverses sex roles, allowing
Blancheflor to play the predatory male and Perceval her innocent prey.
Moreover, Blancheflor's sudden shift to hypercorrect behavior the next
morning, which begins with an apology for the 'inadequate lodging',
appropriates the narrator's metonymic play with public and private
metaphors of food and sex, transforming it into a synecdochic one, part
of a sophisticated ploy to induce the hero to reject her public
suggestions, and thus to undertake what her private visit has aroused
him to do.

The narrator's apparently more straightforward presentation of
Perceval's actions articulates basic themes of his development, such as
the relation between socialization and natural ability. Here, too, ironic
discrepancies between the hero's actions and the expectations of socio-
literary conventions also open possibilities for polyphonic discourse. On
two occasions, Perceval applies the rules of behavior impressed on him
by Gornemant (1649, 1644–47), remembering not to talk too much (1857–
61) and never willingly to slay a vanquished knight (2238–42).

---

7   See Adrian Stevens in this volume.

Both occasions seem to represent an advance over his foolish attempts to apply his mother's advice, since the new strictures are passive, helping him avoid inappropriate action.[8] Nonetheless, the immediate contexts – significant for their relationship to the dominant concerns of love and prowess in courtly romance – suggest that the hero's application of Gornemant's advice remains mechanical and inappropriate. On the first occasion, the narrator makes Blancheflor's importance clear by introducing her with the catalogue description of feminine beauty typically reserved for heroines in Chrétien's romances.[9] Perceval's silence immediately establishes an ironic disjunction between two types of discourse, Gornemant's advice and the genre expectations for the hero, a disjunction emphasized by the bystanders, who wonder whether the strange knight is dumb while also observing that he and their lady seem made for each other (1862–74). On the second occasion, Perceval remembers Gornemant's admonition to spare a vanquished opponent while Anguingueron is enumerating the unstrained qualities of mercy. The discrepancy between an abstract rule and the actual context in which he applies it draws attention to the gap between the foolish hero and sophisticated courtly society.

In contrast to such prescribed behavior, the hero also makes choices pertaining to love and chivalry that can only be attributed to the emergence of an innate heritage that is helping him bridge that gap. The narrator emphasizes prior to Blancheflor's nocturnal visit that the hero knew and thought nothing of the pleasures of a lady's company in bed (1941f.). The action that night does not progress beyond lying 'boche a boche' (2065, 2068) and exchanging kisses, a relatively innocent natural activity that he practiced on his mother's handmaids (725–28) even before his mother's advice permitted him (546–49) to apply it to the Tent Maiden (693–95). But when, on the ensuing morning, Perceval explicitly demands Blancheflor's 'druërie' (2104) as his reward for breaking the siege, he suddenly progresses to a socially complex form of love relationship – mentioned here for the first time in the romance – that he cannot have known previously. There is a similar progression in chivalric behavior immediately after Perceval's mechanical offer of mercy to Anguingueron: the victorious hero returns to the castle, countering the townspeople's annoyance over his failure to kill the seneschal with an eloquent defense of his moral integrity (2347f.).

As these examples suggest, the momentum of Chrétien's narrative often derives from rhetorical opposition, such as natural or ignorant

---

[8]   See Peter Haidu, *Aesthetic Distance in Chrétien de Troyes: Irony and Comedy in 'Cligès' and 'Perceval'* (Geneva, 1968), p. 156.
[9]   Cf. Alice M. Colby, *The Portrait in Twelfth-Century French Literature: An Example of the Stylistic Originality of Chrétien de Troyes* (Geneva, 1965).

versus sophisticated chivalric behavior, progressing by alternating
between them. Indeed, this structuring principle of rhetorical dialectic
extends to the third day at Belrepeire, creating new variations that
frustrate the closure implied by the previous pattern of anticipation and
fulfillment. Whereas the hero's recourse to Gornemant's precepts
seemed to provoke their dialectical opposite, leading from precondi-
tioned to instinctual aristocratic behavior, the narrator now begins to
negate the role of advice itself by shifting attention to the hero's
antagonist. Rejecting the sound advice of a squire (2390–92) and
accepting that of a misguided 'mestre' (2395), who misinterprets every
important motif introduced by the narrator during the previous day,
Clamadeu intensifies the hostilities, and thereby hastens his own army's
defeat. Nonetheless, he rejects the closure implied by this defeat as well
as by the providential arrival of supplies in the beleaguered city, and, in
an inversion of the motif of advice, challenges the hero to single combat
without listening to anyone's counsel, a challenge that the hero accepts,
also without listening to the advice of his mistress and townspeople.
Although Perceval thereby regains control of his destiny in a way that
stands in pointed contrast to Blancheflor's initial manipulation of his
actions, he causes an extension of the combat so anticlimactic that the
narrator refuses to elaborate his summary of the duel (2678–81).

This generation of events out of a spirit of rhetorical dialectic seems to
represent a major organizing principle of Chrétien's narrative. The most
common forms of dialogic discourse, such as that between the narrator
and characters, are local, deriving from individual moments or from the
elaboration of themes and their reversal from one character or moment
to another. The most extensive dialogic potential of this rhetorical
dominant lies in repeating the hero's role as fool, and in the ironic
conflict between his simplistic actions and sophisticated social or literary
conventions as he proceeds from episode to episode. Repetition of such
moments generates a series of episodes and a thematic dialectic, but
does not create a concomitant impression of their larger unity.
Perceval's treatment of the defeated Anguingueron and Clamadeu
provides a good example.

The hero offers both men the choice of presenting themselves to
Blancheflor, then Gornemant, then Arthur – a choice that surveys his
knightly adventures in reverse order and anticipates his eventual return
to the latter's court. The arrival of the seneschal and his lord there three
days after their defeat allows the fool to repeat his prophecy about Kay's
punishment (2866–71), and thus to anticipate once more Perceval's
eventual return. The process will subsequently be repeated after the
defeat of Li Orguelleus, whom the hero also orders to Arthur's court as a
condition of his mercy (3950–80) and whose arrival again triggers the
fool's prophecy (4074–76). But there is no immediate indication of the

relative importance or interrelationship of these two parallel events, except for the fact that Li Orguelleus is given only one choice, which could reflect either distance from Blancheflor and Gornemant or proximity to Arthur. The extent and structure of the series remain uncertain.

A principal reason for this uncertainty seems to be that Chrétien's emphasis on exploiting the rhetorical possibilities of individual episodes or themes avoids the organization and orchestration of interrelation-ships that characterize more overtly dialogic forms of narrative. Again, another of Bakhtin's concepts provides a point of departure:[10] the chronotope, i.e., the differentiation of discourse through the articulation of time and space. In *Li contes del Graal* chronotopic markers usually denote a change from one episode to another, rather than distinguish or create relationships between them. The events before and after Perceval's sojourn at Belrepeire are clearly delineated by one-day time periods: the first day in the woods, the progression from abusing the Tent Maiden the following morning to his knighting by Gornemant on the morning after that (635/1597). His visit to the Grail castle, the encounters with the cousin and the Tent Maiden, Li Orguelleus's arrival at court, and the 'Blutstropfenepisode' each encompass a day or have a clear reference to morning or night (2975, 3356f., 3998, 4160–64), while the festivities that celebrate his integration into the Arthurian world last two days, emphasizing the conclusion of his first series of adventures. Large-scale chronological references, however, remain confusing. The adventures between Perceval's first and second Arthurian visits last a few weeks at most, though it is difficult to reconcile ambiguous and conflicting evidence.[11] The time period mentioned by the fool's prophecy (1264), which links the initial and concluding Arthurian episodes, varies in the manuscripts from forty days (the most common number) to a fortnight and even a week, none of which accords entirely with the cumulative time elapsed in individual episodes and with other points of reference, the celebration of Pentecost at court (2785) and the snowfall after Perceval's departure from the Grail castle (4162).

References to space also serve primarily to delineate individual episodes. Geographical change from one place to another is indicated by a path or road (861, 3422, 3644) or by the transition from forest to meadow or plain (630–39, 1306f., 1703f.). To be sure, the fact that

---

[10]   See, for example, 'Forms of Time and of the Chronotope in the Novel: Notes toward a Historical Poetics', in *Dialogic Imagination* (see n. 4 above), pp. 84–258.

[11]   See Hermann J. Weigand, *Wolfram's 'Parzival': Five Essays with an Introduction* (Ithaca, 1969), pp. 18–74, especially 21–33. The most recent study, Margaret Sauer, *Parzival auf der Suche nach der verlorenen Zeit*, GAG, 323 (Göppingen, 1981), presents further considera-tions on pp. 153–66 and some results (the basis of which is not entirely clear) in tables after p. 362.

Perceval's journey after leaving the Tent Maiden proceeds along the coast to the castles at Carduel, Goort, and Belrepeire, each located above or facing the sea (843/863; 1322/1332; 1708f.), intimates some coherence to these episodes. But it is uncertain whether the wild landscape at Belrepeire reflects the local effects of the siege or marks the climax to the series. The ensuing episode at the Grail castle breaks the pattern, since Perceval's journey moves inland to a river valley – a puzzling direction, since he intends to return to his mother. The articulation of space after this becomes less precise: Perceval leaves the Grail castle on a path leading into the forest (3422f.), where he meets his cousin, who then directs him to a paved road (3644) in the woods (3832), where he encounters the Tent Maiden and Li Orguelleus.

Chrétien thus seems to employ changes of time and space primarily to differentiate episodes from each other, only hinting at interrelationships between them, such as the importance of events at Belrepeire, the only prolonged episode in the hero's first series of adventures (it lasts a month, if we subtract the surrounding one-day episodes from the forty days prophesied by the fool), or the Grail castle's apparently unique location. The vagueness accords with the treatment of other potential structuring principles, such as genealogy and kinship,[12] implying the absence of large-scale relationships. Inasmuch as Chrétien's highly controlled rhetorical style seems to raise expectations of just such an organization, readers have not hesitated to fill in his absences with a wide variety of conjectures.

II

Wolfram transposes Chrétien's episode at Belrepeire into a narrative that subverts the hero's relationship to the heroine, altering the thematic elaboration of events and substantially increasing their dialogic potential. The modest expansion of Chrétien's 1275 lines (1699–2973) to 1338 lines (179,13–223,30) still retains the clear-cut pattern of anticipation and fulfillment for events of the first and second day. This pattern is further emphasized by one of Wolfram's most obtrusive additions, a first-person narrator, who comments at length on the lack and then on the abundance of provisions in the beleaguered city. These two commentaries are clearly interrelated. Surveying the initial deprivation of the inhabitants, the narrator observes that his lord 'wær ungern soldier dâ gewesn' (184,5) and that the inhabitants are starving, 'in trouf

12 See Elisabeth Schmid, *Familiengeschichten und Heilsmythologie: Die Verwandtschafts-strukturen in den französischen und deutschen Gralromanen des 12. und 13. Jahrhunderts*, Beihefte zur Zeitschrift für romanische Philologie, 211 (Tübingen, 1986), pp. 35–71.

vil wênic in die kolen' (184,18). The arrival of provisions the following day reverses this condition and the narrator's opinion:

den burgærn in die kolen trouf.
ich wær dâ nu wol soldier.   (201,4-5)

Such kitchen humor fulfills a subversive intertextual function, uncoupling – so to speak – the metonymy between food and sex in Chrétien's narrative, and directing our attention to the public consumption of food.

The reason for this change is that Parzival's adventures do not culminate in *druerie*, but in marriage and kingship. As a result of this shift, perhaps the most important and far-reaching in the entire romance, the narrator does not lead us immediately from the public dining-hall to the privacy of the bedchamber, but pauses to emphasize Parzival's ability to distribute and manage provisions, first dealing with scarcity, then with abundance. The divergences from Chrétien are instructive: on the first night, Blancheflor commands the table to be set, and all sit down to supper and eat briefly but eagerly (1921f.); Condwiramurs apportions the meager supplies to her people on the advice of Parzival, with the result that they have scarcely anything to themselves (191,1-5). On the second day, the arrival of a barge with provisions creates a great commotion among Chrétien's townspeople and merchants, who rush to purchase all the supplies and prepare a feast, freeing the hero to disport himself in private with his *amie* (2574f.). Wolfram's hero, who has just received the townspeople's fealty as their *hêrre*, immediately exercises his rule through the queen's marshal, who imposes order and brings the merchants to the new regent for negotiations (200,24-201,1). Moreover, Parzival then serves his people with his own hands, beginning with small portions in order to observe moderation and not overstuff their shrunken stomachs.

Parzival thus demonstrates a new and sovereign control over the appetite that ruled his own behavior as recently as his sojourn at Gurnemanz's castle, confirming his mentor's assessment that the hero is destined to be a ruler, 'volkes hêrre' (170,22). This shift in focus, already apparent in the change from 'Ritterlehre' to 'Fürstenlehre', from Gornemant's brief chivalric rules delivered at Perceval's dubbing to Gurnemanz's general advice on deportment and future kingship, is a consequential one.[13] The narrative conventions for knights-errant are not identical with those for kings and rulers. The christological overtones of Parzival's feeding of the multitude and serving of his

---

[13] On the absence of a *swertleite* at this juncture in Wolfram's narrative, see Joachim Bumke, 'Parzivals "Schwertleite" ', in *Taylor Starck Festschrift*, ed. by Werner Betz and others (London/The Hague/Paris, 1964), pp. 235-45, and my 'Parzival's *swertleite*', *GR*, 50 (1975), 245-59.

people, for example, together with references to divine providence (185,18; 200,16), appropriate the discourse of medieval political theology on the ideal ruler as an *imago Christi* or *christomimetes*,[14] presaging a unique reign for 'der reine' and 'der unlôse niht ze hêr' (201,9/18).

Given this radical alteration of the hero's and heroine's relationship from private *druerie* to public rule and marriage, it is not surprising that the bedroom scenes following the first and second day's distribution of food also have a different focus. To be sure, there is still a 'doppelter Cursus' of anticipation and fulfillment in the portrayal of the hero's and heroine's adventures at night, but it is sexless – a dry run with a different agenda. Wolfram's narrator immediately establishes a first-person authority to guarantee the maidenly propriety of Condwir-amurs's visit to the hero's chamber: 'Daz kom als ich iu sagen wil./ ez prach niht wîplîchiu zil' (192,1–2). Rejecting the private sexual motivation of Chrétien's *pucele*, he attributes the queen's nocturnal visit to a public obligation, the search for *auxilium* and *concilium*:

> dô gienc diu küneginne,
> niht nâch sölher minne
> diu sölhen namen reizet
> der meide wîp heizet,
> si suochte helfe unt friundes rât.   (192,9–13)

A brief comparison of the two heroines' actions confirms this change in motivation. Blancheflor, sweating with Ovidian anticipation of her 'avanture' (1954), dresses in a *short* silk coat – 'un mantel cort de soie' (1952) – before proceeding to wake the hero with tearful embraces. Condwiramurs, driven ('twanc', 192,5/20) by anguish over the death of friends and vassals, dresses in a *long* silk coat, 'von samît einen mantel lanc' (192,19), and stops in supplication before the hero's bed. The narrator intrudes with an editorial comment to emphasize that neither hero nor heroine is capable of doing what their counterparts do in Chrétien's narrative:

> si heten beidiu kranken sin,
> Er unt diu küneginne,
> an bî ligender minne.   (193,2–4)

There is irony in this nocturnal encounter, but it differs from Chrétien's.[15] Having emphasized the innocence of the approaching queen, the narrator also alerts his audience to the erotic potential of the encounter with metaphors of the 'Minnekrieg' and a rhetorical question:

[14] See Ernst Kantorowicz, *The King's Two Bodies: A Study in Medieval Theology* (Princeton, N.J., 1957), pp. 42–86.
[15] See Adrian Stevens in this volume.

> an ir was werlîchiu wât,
> ein hemde wîz sîdîn:
> waz möhte kampflîcher sîn,
> dan gein dem man sus komende ein wîp?   (192,14–17)

But the actions of the principals and the suspicions of the audience will remain distinct, confirmed by Condwiramurs's agreement to a *bîligen* without *ringen* (194,1–2). In contrast to Chrétien's narrative, where the lovers spend the night kissing until dawn, Parzival and Condwiramurs continue their discussion, the hero's earnest promise of aid coinciding with the narrator's ironic marking of time with a dawn-song motif, 'diu naht het ende und kom der tac' (196,2).[16] The following night will confirm the lack of physical love intimated by the hero's and heroine's ignorance, not the innuendos shared by the narrator and audience.

The second night in Wolfram's narrative accordingly alters the retreat to private joy in the midst of general feasting that Chrétien describes. It is a formal wedding night: Parzival and Condwiramurs have been publicly asked about consummating their relationship, and have assented.[17] In the bedroom, the narrator intrudes with a lengthy excursus, first on the behavior of women, then of men in a particular type of relationship. Parzival's *mâze* resembles that of 'der getriuwe stæte man':

> er denket, als ez lîht ist wâr,
> 'ich hân gedienet mîniu jâr
> nâch lône disem wîbe,
> diu hât mîme lîbe
> erboten trôst: nu lige ich hie.
> des hete mich genüeget ie,
> ob ich mit mîner blôzen hant
> müese rüeren ir gewant.
> ob ich nu gîtes gerte,
> untriwe es für mich werte. [. . .]'
> sus lac der Wâleise.   (202,5–19)

The moderation of the constant and loyal servant is that of a courtly lover, who – after having served in pursuit of his lady's consolation for years – still treats her with solicitude at the moment of reward.[18]

---

[16] Wolfgang Mohr, 'Spiegelungen des Tagelieds', in *Mediaevalia litteraria: Festschrift für Helmut de Boor zum 80. Geburtstag*, ed. by Ursula Hennig and Herbert Kolb (Munich, 1971), pp. 287–304; John Greenfield, 'The "Tageliet" in Wolfram's *Parzival*', *Neoph.*, 71 (1987), 154–57, discusses only Parzival's and Condwiramurs's reunion in Book XV.

[17] See Marlis Schumacher, *Die Auffassung der Ehe in den Dichtungen Wolframs von Eschenbach* (Heidelberg, 1967), pp. 37–47.

[18] It is the exact opposite – to cite the scene that may be the target of Wolfram's humor – of the eagerness of Gunther, whose wedding in the *Nibelungenlied* also comprises two

Wolfram's excursus suggests that Parzival and Condwiramurs combine the features of two very different kinds of relationship, marriage and courtly love. Parzival accordingly is Condwiramurs's 'hêrre' as well as 'amîs' (200,5–7); she is his 'frowe unde wîp' (302,7). To be sure, this combination of love and marriage is no more unusual in Arthurian romance than is their conflict in the Tristan legend, both types of narrative reflecting a complex interplay in the high Middle Ages between secular and clerical systems of discourse as well as generational conflicts within secular society.[19] But the complete inactivity of this wedding night also suggests something about Wolfram's couple that makes them unique.

Parzival and Condwiramurs seem to lack the already existing passion that characterizes most romance heroes and heroines, including their randy counterparts in Chrétien's narrative. As late as their first night together, Parzival remains bothered by 'Lîâzen minne' (195,11), while Condwiramurs mourns for Liaze's brother Schenteflurs, killed in the siege of her castle (195,1–6). In spite of the opportunity traditionally afforded to romance heroes and heroines by their first meeting (as Gahmuret and Belakane amply demonstrate), Parzival and Condwiramurs have not fallen in love,[20] and do not even seem eager to consummate their marriage now.

To be sure, Condwiramurs considers herself married and dresses as well as acts accordingly on the following morning, wearing a woman's *gebende* and ceding her possessions to her husband (202,21–28). In this respect, she shares the attitude of Sigune, who considers that her love for Schionatulander makes him her husband in the sight of God even though she remains a virgin (440,7f.). The parallel with the 'Minneheilige' Sigune hints at a religious and ascetic component in Parzival's and Condwiramurs's marriage that knightly couples in romance narratives usually lack. Unlike Erec and Enite, who can scarcely wait to consummate their marriage with two or three nights of lovemaking, 'jâ enwirde ich nimmer vrô,/ ich engelige dir noch bî/ zwô naht oder drî' (1873–75), Wolfram's hero and heroine remain chaste for two days and three nights:

> si wâren mit ein ander sô,
> daz si durch liebe wâren vrô,
> zwên tage unt die dritten naht.   (202,29–203,1)

evenings and whose lust finds the same metaphorical expression in the desire to rumple his bride's shift.

[19] Cf. George Duby, *The Knight, the Lady, and the Priest*, trans. by Barbara Bray (New York, 1983).

[20] See, for example, Martin Jones, 'Formen der Liebeserklärung im höfischen Roman bis um 1300', in *Liebe in der deutschen Literatur des Mittelalters*, ed. by Jeffrey Ashcroft, Dietrich Huschenbett, and William Henry Jackson (Tübingen, 1987), pp. 36–49.

They thus repeat the Biblical example of Tobias, who remains continent for three nights, enacting a typology with Adam and Eve that imitates their prelapsarian ignorance of lust (Tobias 8.1–10). Parzival and Condwiramurs, of course, do not so much imitate the Biblical model as accidentally recapitulate it. One is tempted to conclude that they unconsciously retain a modicum of primal innocence, a positive 'Adamic' element that shapes their love and forms a counterpart to the negative 'Adamic' overtones of Parzival's knighthood.[21] Indeed, they experience pleasure in each other's company, but do not seem motivated by the lust that characterizes postlapsarian sexual relations.[22] For this reason, the narrator adds a motif to his source, stating that Parzival and Condwiramurs consummate their marriage after he remembers the advice of his mother and Gurnemanz:

> von im dicke wart gedâht
> umbevâhens, daz sîn muoter riet:
> Gurnemanz im ouch underschiet,
> man und wîp wærn al ein.   (203,2–5)

Sex is for them an act of will rather than a natural inclination, and therefore a learned activity. Of course, it is licit within the bounds of matrimony, and Wolfram, who seldom employs the Biblical 'one flesh' metaphor to describe marriage, invokes it while recalling Gurnemanz's advice (173,1).[23]

In order to suggest the unusual nature of Parzival's and Condwiramurs's relationship, then, Wolfram subverts the private *druerie* of Chrétien's couple into a public marriage and rulership in which several different types of discourse interact dialogically. Most obviously, the hero and heroine combine the roles of husband and wife with that of lover and lady found in romance. At the same time, their inaction as husband and wife coexists with more extreme clerical conventions regarding marriage, a discourse increasingly important in the sacralization of this relationship in the twelfth century, and one that is often invented *post hoc* in ecclesiastical encomia of rulers.[24] The marriage of this hero and heroine not only combines the secular roles of king and queen with those of knight and lady, but also satisfies the demands of clerical culture, reconciling chivalric narrative and the religious *vita*, and thus suggesting its central role in realizing the general theme of Wolfram's romance, 'got unde der werlde gevallen'.

[21] See Wolfgang Mohr, 'Parzivals ritterliche Schuld', *WW*, 2 (1951/52), 148–60; repr. in *WW, Sammelband II: Ältere deutsche Sprache und Literatur* (Düsseldorf, 1962), pp. 196–208.
[22] It is described at length in St. Augustine's *De civitate Dei*, Book XIV, the fundamental locus for the Middle Ages.
[23] Schumacher, *Die Auffassung der Ehe* (see n. 17 above), pp. 115–18.
[24] On the 'Tobiasnächte' as a characteristic of rulers, see Peter Browe, *Beiträge zur Sexualethik des Mittelalters* (Breslau, 1932), p. 116.

III

The increased role of the narrator and the intertextual subversion of Chrétien's narrative by the theme of marriage and kingship do not exhaust the dialogic elaboration of Parzival's sojourn at Pelrapeire. Bakhtin's concept of the chronotope, the differentiation of discourse through parameters of time and space, a possibility utilized only tentatively in *Li contes del Graal*, suggests a more important point of comparison. Wolfram's transposition introduces several types of chronotopic differentiation, which not only organize and orchestrate the episodes in Parzival's first set of adventures, but also create dialogic relationships with the adventures of other figures as well as with other Arthurian romances.

One type of chronotopic differentiation involves characters, providing them with a specific name, a place of origin, and a family as well as a genealogy, transforming the largely functional and therefore anonymous figures in Chrétien's adventure romance into particularized characters interacting in a family romance. At the hero's reception at Belrepeire, for example, Blancheflor appears in the company of two lords ('prodome', 1790); she later mentions an uncle, a holy prior, who has sent six loaves of bread and a bottle of boiled wine (1910–14). Wolfram assumes their identity, making it necessary to double the number of clerics, and proceeds to particularize them. Kyot of Katelangen and Manpfilyot have names, a specific social class and kinship relationship with Condwiramurs, a personal history that explains their change of estate, and an appearance that indicates they live outside the beleaguered city:

> Von Katelangen Kyôt
> unt der werde Manpfilyôt
> (herzogen beide wâren die),
> ir bruoder kint si brâhten hie,
> des landes küneginne.
> durch die gotes minne
> heten se ûf gegebn ir swert.
> dâ giengen die fürsten wert
> grâ unde wol gevar. (186,21–29)

Both dukes are interesting in their own right rather than as anonymous agents of a rhetorical narrative principle. Whereas Chrétien states that an uncle provides a meager amount of food – schematically designated as 'bread and wine' – for the night's meal, beginning the pattern of deprivation that will characterize the entire evening, Wolfram lets Kyot speak for himself, volunteering twice as many loaves and vessels of wine as Chrétien's nobleman, but extending this schematic doublet to a longer and more nourishing shopping list and invoking sibling rivalry to goad his brother into sending an equal amount (190,10–17).

The adaptation of a series of events in Chrétien's narrative, such as Perceval's sending defeated knights to Arthur's court, illustrates how chronotopic elaboration of character also organizes narrative. Wolfram has characteristically given the fool a name, Antanor (152,23), but deletes him from these scenes, eliminating the mechanical repetition of an open-ended prophecy. Instead, he separates Kingrun's and Clamide's arrival into two distinct episodes, with Orilus' appearance comprising a third. As is typical of the switch from the impersonal rhetoric of adventure romance to the multi-voiced dialogism of family romance, the relationship of the characters structures Chrétien's uncertainly connected events. Kingrun, Clamide, and Orilus form a series with a principle of intensification, progressing from a seneschal to his king and then to the brother of the injured woman; simultaneously, Kay's responses reveal increasing anxiety as he proceeds from jocular shop-talk to self-justification and then to judicious absence from dinner. Moreover, Parzival gives the defeated Kingrun a choice of three people to whom he can surrender, Gurnemanz, then Condwiramurs, then Arthur (198,3–199,12); Clamide a choice of two, Gurnemanz, then Arthur (214,5–215,12); and Orilus only one, Arthur (267,9–268,2) – a clear progression. This is not a mechanical and potentially infinite linear series, but a graduated one that simultaneously builds and narrows to a climax.

A second type of chronotopic differentiation organizes episodes rather than characters, providing them with unique chronological and spatial attributes. In contrast to the time references in Chrétien's narrative, which provide a point of transition between episodes but relate them to each other inconsistently and even contradictorily, Wolfram's allusions form a unified pattern. The period that elapses between Parzival's robbery of Jeschute and her reconciliation with Orilus, 'mêr danne ein ganzez jâr' (139,20), accommodates other references to Arthur's celebration of Pentecost (216,14) and the snowfall after Parzival's failure at the Grail castle (281,12). Within this larger time frame, most episodes are clearly delineated by references to morning and evening.[25] Book III

---

[25] Parzival's first day in the woods, the encounters with Jeschute, Sigune, and the fisherman, and the first episode at Arthur's court begin in the morning (128,13; 129,15; 143,16), cf. also the reference early in the sojourn with Gurnemanz (166,20). Parzival takes leave of Condwiramurs one morning (223,15), riding until he meets the Fisher King in the evening (225,2), sleeps at the Grail castle, where he wakes up early the following day and again at mid-morning (245,2/28). During the second day he encounters Sigune, then Jeschute and Orilus, after whose defeat Wolfram – emending the chronotopic vagueness

encompasses seventeen days, with the sojourn with Gurnemanz lasting a full fourteen days (176,29) rather than the one in Chrétien; the chronology of Books V–VI is equally clear, comprising only three days. As in Chrétien's text, there is a break in the continuity of episodes at the end of Book IV; but the consistency of Wolfram's large-scale chronological organization enables us to estimate its duration and confirm the importance of Parzival's stay with Condwiramurs. If the events of Book III encompass seventeen, those of Books V and VI three days, then the remainder of the time spent in Book IV accounts for most of the period 'more than an entire year' anticipated by the narrator after the first Jeschute episode – by far the most extensive stay in Parzival's career.

The organization of space also differs substantially from Chrétien's narrative. Whereas Perceval's journey proceeds along the sea coast from Arthur's court at Carduel to Belrepeire, then suddenly shifts inland to the Grail castle, Parzival takes an inland route, organized by the direct and gradual upward progression from Arthur's court, now located at Nantes, to the mountains of Munsalvaesche. And whereas Chrétien's narrative uses changes in space to delineate episodes without suggesting any clear large-scale pattern, Wolfram's relates them chronotopically through three fantastic journeys that confirm the geographical suggestion of a graduated progression. The increasing speed and distance of the hero's superhuman rides from Nantes to Graharz (161,17–21), Graharz to Brobarz (189,22–26), and Brobarz to Munsalvaesche (224,22–30), the only such travels in the narrative, also differentiate these stations chronotopically from each other, with the extended sojourns at Graharz and Brobarz providing distinct intermediate stages between the Arthurian and Grail worlds.

Those two worlds are also differentiated by a contrasting organization of time and space. Chrétien's narrative intimates a disjuncture between the normal world of Arthurian adventure and the Other World of the Grail castle, which does not obey the laws of space and time, appearing suddenly ('parut', 3051) between a broad, unfordable river and the woods (3034). Wolfram's narrative invests this difference with an extensive chronotopic organization: whereas the Arthurian world is localized in a pleasance or *locus amœnus* landscape at a fixed time of year (May or Pentecost), the Grail world is placed in a rugged and inaccessible landscape and in a dynamic mode of telling time, the liturgical calendar – a contrast of chronotopes that is emphasized in the famous commentary on the incompatibility of

---

of his source – explicitly raises the issue of where the heroes will find accommodation that night (271,14–22). The third day is devoted to Parzival's love trance and ensuing events.

Arthur, 'der maienbære man', and the snowfall from the Grail realm at the beginning of Book VI (281,14–22).[26]

Such chronotopic differentiation and orchestration of both figures and episodes contribute to a further large-scale organization of the narrative, the interrelation of the hero's adventures and the adventures of other characters, as well as between Wolfram's *Parzival* and other Middle High German narratives – dialogism in the traditional sense of intertextuality. One brief example of each will have to suffice.

The most obvious dialogical relationship between Parzival's marriage to Condwiramurs and the adventures of another figure involves Gahmuret's winning of Belakane, a diachronic parallel across generations not in Chrétien's narrative. Both father and son win their wives by breaking the siege of a castle, and Wolfram's episodes are clearly conceived with reference to each other. Belakane and Condwiramurs are described – alone of the women in *Parzival* – in an introductory portrait with the 'rose in the dew' topos of Mariological poetry (24,6–11; 188,9–14).[27] The queens have been left defenseless by the deaths of Isenhart and Schenteflurs respectively; their castles, bordered by land on one side and sea on the other, are beset by two armies. Gahmuret and Parzival enter the besieged cities unopposed, are introduced to the queens in a manner that intimates their predestination as hero and heroine, and after a sleepless night set forth and single-handedly break the siege, whereupon the queens publicly proclaim them as their future lords and husbands.

But while a father-son typology emerges triumphantly in Parzival's knightly activities, as references to him as Gahmuret's progeny during the battles with Kingrun and Clamide attest (197,1; 212,2), Gahmuret's sexually prominent nature (*art*), mentioned only at the beginning of Book IV (179,24), exerts a weaker compulsion. The attraction to Liaze prevents Parzival from falling in love with her relative and look-alike Condwiramurs, a pointed contrast to the rapacious glances exchanged by Gahmuret and Belakane on their first meeting. The absence of Gahmuret's sexual proclivity on Parzival's wedding night has already been explicitly foreshadowed by the narrator's comment on the missed opportunity with Jeschute (139,15–19). And although Parzival has offered service for reward at Pelrapeire, just as his father did at Patelamunt, the anticipated love-service will be subsumed by the new pattern of public and private sovereignty, enabling him – unlike Gahmuret – to combine knight-errantry and kingship, love and marriage.

[26] See my 'Time Reference and the Liturgical Calendar in Wolfram von Eschenbach's *Parzival*', *DVjs*, 49 (1975), 43–65.
[27] See Anselm Salzer, *Die Bilder und Beiworte Mariens in der deutschen Literatur und lateinischen Hymnenpoesie des Mittelalters* (1886-94; repr. Darmstadt, 1967), pp. 183–92.

The conclusion of Book IV, briefly describing Parzival's year-long sojourn, the most extensive in the romance, therefore shows the hero as both knight and regent, frequently participating in tournaments up to the borders of his kingdom (222,20–28), while also rebuilding his ravaged domain and establishing loyalty through regal largesse (222,12–19). Moreover, the relationship between the royal couple and lovers is so total that Condwiramurs can be said to have 'den wunsch ûf der erde' (223,2), a clear expression of the fact that their achievement anticipates the accession to supreme dominion at the Grail, the 'wunsch von pardîs' (235,21).

On an even broader level, Parzival's winning of Condwiramurs differs from Chrétien's treatment of the same episode through its dialogic relationship with another narrative, Hartmann von Aue's *Erec*.[28] Wolfram invests the ties of consanguinity between Gurnemanz and Condwiramurs with a new significance by involving them in Hartmann's history of Erec's adventures as well as in the current enmity of Erec's extended family, thus creating an intertextual battle between romances. As we learn at the end of Book III, Gurnemanz lost two sons in the adventures that Hartmann's hero resolved at the beginning and conclusion of his narrative, Lascoyt having perished in the Sparrow Hawk contest and Gurzgri in the *joie de la curt* at Brandigan (178,11–26). The third son, Schenteflurs, has recently died defending Condwiramurs against Kingrun and Clamide, who is presented by Wolfram as king of Brandigan (184,20) and as a cousin of Mabonagrin (220,9), the warning example of destructive private love in *Erec*.

Wolfram's appropriation of Hartmann's narrative history and the extension of its destructive consequences into his own narrative suggest that Erec's success did not permanently restore the social order by breaking the adventure at Brandigan. Indeed, the damage described there is officially resolved only in Wolfram's narrative by Clamide's suit for Arthur's forgiveness (220,11–24). Moreover, two of Erec's relatives through marriage, Orilus (husband of Erec's sister Jeschute) and Clamide (cousin of Mabonagrin and husband-to-be of Orilus' sister Cunneware), continue to inflict suffering and disorder in Wolfram's narrative. Parzival's triumph over these representatives of immoderate chivalry thus makes him a perfect match for the chaste Condwiramurs, whose beauty – according to the narrator – outshines that of Jeschute, Enite, and Cunneware (Erec's sister, wife, and sister-in-law), not to mention both Isoldes (187,14–19). There are, of course, numerous other parallels, which will have to be pursued in a larger context. Suffice it to

[28] For a more conventional interpretation of the broader issues of the relationship, see Rüdiger Schnell, 'Literarische Beziehungen zwischen Hartmanns *Erec* und Wolfram's *Parzival*', PBB (Tüb.), 95 (1973), 301–32.

say that Wolfram's version of Hartmann's *Erec* presents only one set of intertextual relationships in the interplay between *Parzival* and Arthurian romance. Their variety suggests that Wolfram's dialogic imagination creates a pervasive intertextual dynamic, which, for lack of a better term, we might provisionally call – Parzivlage.

IV

Some medievalists may prefer to deny the relevance of a modern critical concept such as dialogic discourse to medieval narrative on *a priori* grounds. They might, however, reconsider Wolfram's own statement about his relationship to Chrétien in his epilogue, a place traditionally reserved for source attributions and protestations of fidelity:

> Ob von Troys meister Cristjân
> disem mære hât unreht getân,
> daz mac wol zürnen Kyôt,
> der uns diu rehten mære enbôt.   (827,1–4)

Wolfram mentions two options in narrating the Grail story, revealing that he has chosen to follow Kyot rather than Chrétien. Whether Kyot actually existed is immaterial; at the very least, he represents an imaginary source that Wolfram projects retroactively from his own narrative, and we can use the implied differences between Chrétien's and Kyot's narratives to tell us something about Wolfram's. Unlike Chrétien's fragment, Kyot's version is complete and definitive, 'endehaft' (827,5). More importantly: unlike Chrétien's story, which may not do the subject justice, Kyot's narrative is not only right ('reht'), but provides Wolfram with a pluralistic model of discourse, as the highly unusual plural 'mære' suggests.[29]

Indeed, the description of Kyot's sources in Book IX both confirms this impression and requires that we extend our model to include non-literary discourse as well. Wolfram explicitly describes a variety of sources, secret stories about the Grail, 'diu verholnen mære umben grâl' (452,30), placing the central narrative in a more variegated context than a pure romance narrative. The 'sources' for Wolfram's 'source' – we might call them 'Kyots gesammelte Werke' – consist of two representative types of non-literary discourse, scientific and historical. The first

---

[29]   Closing references to a work *qua* narrative cited by Käthe Iwand, *Die Schlüsse der mittelhochdeutschen Epen*, Germanische Studien, 16 (Berlin, 1922), pp. 66–79 and 120–34, are usually singular, with the exception before Wolfram of Veldeke's *Eneide*. Later references, such as Rudolf von Ems's *Willehalm von Orlens* (15601f.) or Pleier's *Tandareis* (18304f.), are clearly derived from Wolfram. Another exception, in *Diu Klage* (Iwand, p. 127), may derive from the pluralistic source-conception of Latin historiography.

source description (453,11–455,1) relates how Kyot found a written Arabic text in Toledo (the contemporary center for the recovery of Greek science from Arabic translations), and describes the genealogy as well as the astronomical investigations of its heathen author, Flegetanis. The second source description (455,2–22) summarizes Kyot's quest to locate in Latin sources the Grail family alluded to by Flegetanis. Seeking historical chronicles, 'der lande chrônicâ' (455,9), Kyot proceeds through Britain, Ireland, and France – the countries of Arthurian and Tristan romances as well as *chansons de geste* – before finally finding 'diu mære' in Anjou, a country without a literary tradition. We should note the repeated emphasis on plural sources, explicitly derived from the tradition of Latin historiography. Kyot's chronicles, like Wolfram's summary of his own narrative, 'diu rehten mære' (823,11ff.), consist of a typical series of lives of rulers and their immediate families from the founder to the present hero Parzival, 'des disiu mære sint' (455,22).

Wolfram's retroprojection of Kyot's collected narratives as source of the diverse 'mære' he faithfully 'translates' requires us to reject the idea that he has simply transformed Chrétien's narrative from – for example – an adventure romance to a family romance (sub-genres within one narrative tradition[30]), replacing the nameless structure- and episode-generating figures (Mother, Tent Maiden, Cousin, etc.) by named characters with an interrelated genealogy and family history. Instead he insists on recognizing the pluralistic unity of *Parzival*: a variegated romance narrative that also subsumes – unlike his source – historiographical and scientific discourse.

This pluralistic approach clearly represents a radical departure from the relatively young tradition of Middle High German secular narrative, with a normative ideal defined primarily in terms of stylistic elegance, such as Gottfried defends in the literary excursus of *Tristan*. It is not surprising that Gottfried criticizes Wolfram for deviating from this unified stylistic norm, and also for being a 'vindære wilder mære,/ der mære wildenære' (4665f.),[31] for choosing and elaborating unusual types of discourse (we note the plural) that do not provide the edifying entertainment characteristic of literature, but come equipped with 'ketenen' (4667), the learned footnotes of non-fiction, and need commentators, 'tiutære' (4684), even glosses derived from the forbidden arts (4690). It is equally understandable that Gottfried refuses, in an aside aimed at the extensive medical descriptions of Book IX, to narrate the cure of Tristan's festering wound on the grounds that it would

---

[30] On this differentiation, see Mikhail Bakhtin, *Problems of Dostoevsky's Poetics*, ed. and trans. by Caryl Emerson, Theory and History of Literature, 8 (Minneapolis, 1984), pp. 101–06.

[31] Cited from Gottfried von Strassburg, *Tristan und Isold*, ed. by Friedrich Ranke, 9th edn (Zürich, 1964).

offend noble ears by introducing non-courtly discourse on medicine, an applied art, 'rede, diu niht des hoves si' (7954). But in demonstrating the capability of vernacular literature to appropriate and integrate disparate varieties of discourse, many of them hitherto the prerogative of learned clerical culture, Wolfram's narrative dramatically points toward the future, not only of Middle High German literature, but of the modern novel as well.

Clinschor
Wolfram's Adaptation of the Conte du Graal: The Schastel Marveile Episode

TIMOTHY McFARLAND

I

The necromancer Clinschor is Wolfram's creation, one of the most decisive innovations in his adaptation of the Gauvain episodes of the *Conte du Graal*.[1] It is all the more remarkable therefore that we may owe this figure to a fairly elementary misunderstanding of Old French syntax on Wolfram's part, as Wolfgang Mohr has suggested.[2] The passage of Chrétien's text in question occurs in the course of Gauvain's conversation with the boatman in whose house he has just spent the night (7494–637). This is the first time that any significant information has been given, either to the protagonist or to the reader, about the mysterious castle above the river, inhabited by many noble women and maidens, which Gauvain had seen on the previous evening (7232–57). We learn that the aged, rich and noble queen who was responsible for building the castle had brought a learned astronomer with her for the purpose of constructing the enchantments in the hall; no mention is as yet made of a bed (7527–52). These marvels are to provide the test in which only the knight who excels most in ethical qualities can prevail

[1] The editions cited are: *Chrétien de Troyes: Le Roman de Perceval ou le Conte du Graal*, ed. by William Roach, 2nd edn (Geneva/Paris, 1959); *Wolfram von Eschenbach*, ed. by Karl Lachmann, 6th edn (Berlin/Leipzig, 1926). On Clinschor: Norbert Richard Wolf, 'Die Gestalt Klingsors in der deutschen Literatur des Mittelalters', *Südostdeutsche Semesterblätter*, 19 (1967), 1–19; Walter Blank, 'Der Zauberer Clinschor in Wolframs *Parzival*', in *Studien zu Wolfram von Eschenbach: Festschrift für Werner Schröder zum 75. Geburtstag*, ed. by Kurt Gärtner and Joachim Heinzle (Tübingen, 1989), pp. 321–32. Blank's essay appeared after my paper had been written; it is referred to in the footnotes where appropriate.
[2] First suggested in Wolfgang Mohr, 'Parzival und Gawan', *Euph.*, 52 (1958), 1–22 (p. 20, n. 13); repeated and discussed further in 'König Artus und die Tafelrunde: Politische Hintergründe in Chrétiens *Perceval* und Wolframs *Parzival*', in Wolfgang Mohr, *Wolfram von Eschenbach: Aufsätze*, GAG, 275 (Göppingen, 1979), pp. 170–222 (p. 202).

(7553–62). The magical art which the astronomer employs for this purpose must be associated with his astronomical learning, and like much of the magic in Chrétien's narratives it appears to be intrinsically neither good nor evil.

At the core of Wolfram's adaptation of this material is his decision to transpose this relationship of power between the old queen and her learned clerk, and to make the latter rather than the former into the builder and the master of the castle which he calls Schastel Marveile. Such an inversion of natural hierarchical authority was made possible, and perhaps suggested by the astronomer's command of the art of magic which enabled him to construct, 'par art et par enchantement' (7545) the great magic bed. The offence against order evident in the state of affairs in *Parzival* is reinforced by the sharper formulation: the astronomer with a good clerical education and magical skills has become a priest who has turned to the forbidden study of necromancy, 'ein phaffe der wol zouber las' (66,4), as he is described in passing by Kaylet to Gahmuret, and whose skill in astronomy is no longer explicitly mentioned.

It is true that the reversal of the original relationship between queen and learned clerk might naturally suggest itself to anyone who, upon reading (or hearing) Chrétien's lines: 'Uns clers sages d'astrenomie,/ Que la roïne i amena' (7548–49), mistook the 'que' for a nominative instead of an accusative;[3] it is also possible to imagine that such a momentary misreading might set a fertile and imaginative process in motion. It is preferable to see the change as reflecting such a fleeting stimulus to Wolfram's creativity, rather than to assume a serious and lasting misunderstanding of Chrétien's text; for this to be the case, Wolfram would have had to misunderstand the twenty lines preceding the two lines cited above, and a good deal more in the text of *Perceval* besides.

We may take it that Wolfram had his own well-considered reasons for introducing a clerical necromancer into the text of *Parzival* at this point. Magicians are no rarity in the courtly romance, and Merlin occupies a central position in the Arthurian tradition. It is therefore natural that Clinschor should be interpreted first and foremost intertextually, as an instance of one of those many literary motifs in the Arthurian romance which are derived from Celtic narrative traditions.[4] My primary aim in this paper however is to suggest that Wolfram's treatment of Clinschor and the theme of necromancy in *Parzival* may also be seen as standing in some relationship to the phenomenon of clerical necromancy as Wolfram might have experienced it in the courtly world of his time. We

3   See Mohr (n. 2 above).
4   See Blank (n. 1 above), pp. 322–30.

are now aware that the courtly romance, in spite of being a formally complex and highly artificial literary genre, is nevertheless capable of accommodating and reflecting upon various aspects of contemporary chivalric and aristocratic life, especially in the hands of Hartmann and Wolfram. Such reflections go well beyond the general treatment of universal topics such as chivalry and religion, and have been shown to include (among many other possible examples) such issues as the tournament, the significance of complex kinship relationships, the problems facing women rulers, and manifestations of the poverty movement.[5]

Each of these topics presents its own problems of interpretation; and just as formidable are the problems confronting any attempt to suggest that Wolfram's Clinschor might be seen in the context of the practice of necromancy in courtly society around 1200. Firstly the historical topic itself is controversial, and it cannot be my intention to attempt to adjudicate, in a paper of this scope, between the differing interpretations offered by historians to account for the full range of evidence – theological, judicial and literary – at their disposal.[6] Secondly the figure of Wolfram's Clinschor is shadowy and absent, a true *maleficus absconditus*; we do not see him at work and cannot compare his practice with that described in other contemporary sources. Instead I want to suggest that it may be profitable to consider this figure in *Parzival* in the light of the suggestive and widely discussed explanatory model put forward by Peter Brown to account for changing attitudes towards magic and sorcery in certain societies.[7] First, however, it is necessary to glance at the way in which Wolfram has adapted Chrétien's text so as to shift the emphasis and to direct narrative tension to a different end; and secondly to delineate those aspects of Wolfram's presentation of Clinschor which seem important in this connection.

[5] On these topics, see William Henry Jackson, 'The Tournament in the Works of Hartmann von Aue: Motifs, Style, Functions', in *Hartmann von Aue: Changing Perspectives: London Hartmann Symposium 1985*, GAG, 486, ed. by Timothy McFarland and Silvia Ranawake (Göppingen, 1988), pp. 233–51; Elisabeth Schmid, *Familiengeschichten und Heilsmythologie: Die Verwandtschaftsstrukturen in den französischen und deutschen Gralromanen des 12. und 13. Jahrhunderts*, Beihefte zur Zeitschrift für romanische Philologie, 211 (Tübingen, 1986); Volker Mertens, *Laudine: Soziale Problematik im 'Iwein' Hartmanns von Aue*, Beihefte zur Zeitschrift für deutsche Philologie, 3 (Berlin, 1978); Marianne Wynn, *Wolfram's 'Parzival': On the Genesis of its Poetry* (Frankfurt/Berne, 1984).

[6] Among recent accounts, Richard Kieckhefer, *Magic in the Middle Ages* (Cambridge, 1990) offers a balanced perspective. The present essay has benefited most from Edward Peters, *The Magician, the Witch and the Law* (Philadelphia, 1978).

[7] Peter Brown, 'Sorcery, Demons and the Rise of Christianity: from Late Antiquity into the Middle Ages', originally in *Witchcraft: Confessions and Accusations*, ed. by Mary Douglas (London, 1970), pp. 17–45; cited here from the reprinted version in Peter Brown, *Religion and Society in the Age of Saint Augustine* (New York, 1972), pp. 119–46.

II

In the *Conte du Graal* the episode of the enchanted castle is introduced in the passages referred to in the opening paragraph of this essay, in which Gauvain catches his first glimpse of the castle and asks his host the boatman about it the next morning. On the preceding day, and soon after the beginning of the second Gauvain sequence of adventures, Gauvain had been told by Greoreas that he was approaching the borders of Galvoie, which no knight could cross and return alive (6603–04), thereby introducing for the first time the imagery of the other-world journey which is to characterise this episode in Chrétien's version. A little later the boatman had warned him against spending the night on the river bank because it was a savage place, full of great marvels (7462–65). Although these remarks anticipate what is to come in a significant and atmospheric way, they convey little information, and it is indeed the case that Gauvain has not been in any way prepared for this challenge, of which nothing has been mentioned earlier in the romance. After denouncing Perceval at Arthur's court the Ugly Maiden had summoned knights to attempt the adventures of the Chastel Orgueilleus and of the peak of Montesclaire (4685–714), but makes no mention of what is to be Gauvain's greatest challenge. From the ferryman we learn a good deal about the inhabitants of the castle, most especially that the queen who built it is now, along with all the other inmates, longing for the end of the enchantments which she herself established; for this a perfect knight must arrive, who will become master of the castle, but this, the boatman says, is not possible: it is 'une grant folie/ Qui ne porroit avenir mie' (7583–84). But we do not learn the identities of the royal ladies, nor do we know why they are there.

At the equivalent point in Wolfram's *Parzival*, after his conversation with the ferryman, (i.e. by 560,13) Gawan knows more than Chrétien's hero. On the preceding evening the boatman had told him the name of Clinschor while warning him of the special and sinister nature of his lordship: 'gar âventiure ist al diz lant:/ sus wert ez naht und ouch den tac' (548, 10–11). The next morning, in the course of attempting to fend off Gawan's insistent questions, the ferryman and his daughter repeatedly emphasise the evil nature of the place: 'hêr, dâ ist nôt ob aller nôt' (556,16). When finally the land, the castle and its magic contents are named ('Terre marveile', 'Lît marveile', 'Schastel marveil', 557,6–9), Gawan knows that he is confronted with the greatest of all chivalric challenges, the one named solemnly by Cundrie before the Arthurian court over four and a half years previously: 'al âventiure ist ein wint,/ wan die man dâ bezalen mac,/ hôher minne wert bejac' (318,20–22).

From Cundrie he had also heard that four women of royal rank were among those imprisoned in the castle (318,16). But did he hear the names of these four women, his own closest female relatives, in the account given by the Greek Clias (334,11–22)? Wolfram is careful to draw attention to Gawan's own travel preparations and leave-taking in a passage (335,1–30) which is placed directly after the passage about Clias, and a more unforced reading of the Schastel Marveile episode is possible if we conclude that he did absorb this information than if we do not. In assuming that he did hear these names, I follow the careful analysis of D.H. Green, according to which we can infer that as soon as the ferryman names the castle Gawan knows that this is where four of his own close kinswomen were incarcerated.[8] The reader of *Parzival* does not know as much as Gawan, for he has no way of recognising the names mentioned by Clias, and neither the reader nor Gawan could possibly recognise at this point in the fleeting mention of Clinschor (548,5) the clerical necromancer with whom, according to Kaylet, King Arthur's unnamed mother had eloped two years before the tournament at Kanvoleis (66,1–8). Nevertheless we are to come to realise in due course that Gawan has enjoyed one certain and a second probable advantage, both of which were denied to Parzival at Munsalvaesche: firstly, he was able to approach his great castle challenge knowing that it represented the supreme test of chivalric excellence available in his world, and secondly he did so, as I believe, in the knowledge that his own relatives were there awaiting his help.

Of the many differences between the two accounts of the hero's success in withstanding the perils and enchantments of the castle, only two which relate to the differences in the narrative situation are relevant to our concerns. In Chrétien's account Gauvain, having survived his ordeal, is immediately congratulated by the boatman (7871–84), who, however, shortly afterwards also tells him that he will never be able to leave the castle again (8014–24). This arouses great distress and rage in him until the aged queen restores his good humour with her insistent questions about the court of King Arthur (8199–210), and on the following day she is persuaded to let him leave the castle on condition that he promises to return before nightfall (8326–49). Underlying the whole episode in Chrétien's treatment is the motif of the other-world journey, which the poet employed in structurally analogous but thematically different situations in *Lancelot* and *Yvain* as well as here in the *Conte du Graal*.[9] By making the old queen into the agent of Gauvain's

---

[8] D.H. Green, *The Art of Recognition in Wolfram's 'Parzival'* (Cambridge, 1982), pp. 151–54. For a reading which assumes that Gawan has not heard Clias and therefore does not know the identity of his relatives, see Wolfgang Mohr, 'Parzival und Gawan' (n. 2 above), pp. 20–22.

[9] See Walter Haug, 'Das Land, von welchem niemand wiederkehrt': Mythos, Fiktion und

permitted return to the land of the living, Chrétien is reminding us that there is no power in the castle higher than hers, however much she may have been longing for an end to this situation. Wolfram necessarily eliminated this motif from his adaptation, and rationalises the queens' reluctance to let Gawan depart in pursuit of Orgeluse by attributing it to their *triuwe* and to their concern for his health and for their own fate (593,19–595,16).

Secondly, Wolfram introduces Clinschor's name in this section of the narrative only at the two significant moments when he is describing the magic bed (566,23–26) and the magic column in the watch-tower (589,10–12).[10] In both cases he also draws our attention to the distant origin of these devices; this is left vague in the case of the bed, but the column is from the lands of Feirefiz where, Arnive tells us, it was stolen from Secundille in Thabronit (592,18–20). At the point where Gawan leaves the castle to follow Orgeluse, he and the reader still know very little about the magician who is responsible for the suffering to which the hero has just put an end.

In both texts it is the hero's later conversations which provide the significant information which has heretofore been lacking. In Chrétien's fragmentary text, it is Gauvain's long and important exchange with Guiromelans (8544–917) which tells him and the reader what they have not known before – that the castle is called the Roche de Canguin (8817), that its mistress is Arthur's mother Ygerne (8742), Gauvain's own grandmother, whom he had considered to be long dead (8735–38), and that his mother, also held to be dead, and his sister, whom Guiromelans wishes to marry, are also there (8748–63). In the short remaining part of Chrétien's fragment we learn nothing more about this, but it is clear that the thrust of the narrative is directed towards the point at which Gauvain will reveal his identity to the relatives whom he has liberated, and that they will all be joyfully reunited with Arthur and his court. This was clearly understood and given narrative form by the poet of the so-called First Continuation, which Wolfram may have considered to be by Chrétien.[11] The eventual recognition of and reunion with relatives assumed to be dead is the culmination of this strand of the action.

In *Parzival*, as we have seen, Gawan probably knows that the noble ladies are his relatives, even if he does not yet know which of the two young princesses is Itonje and which is Cundrie, and has to ask Bene to tell him (631,4–8). Occasional pieces of information offered by the

Wahrheit in Chrétien's 'Chevalier de la Charrete', im 'Lanzelet' Ulrichs von Zatzikhoven und im 'Lancelot'-Prosaroman, Untersuchungen zur deutschen Literaturgeschichte, 21 (Tübingen, 1978).
10   For these two motifs, see Blank (n. 1 above), pp. 324–29.
11   See *Der Percevalroman (Li contes del graal) von Christian von Troyes*, ed. by Alfons Hilka (Halle, 1932), Einleitung, pp. xxviii–xxix, Anmerkung.

narrator in the course of the events in the castle make it possible for the reader to learn who they are as well (586,22–25; 590,17–20).[12] Wolfram is concerned to direct his audience's attention towards two further matters: firstly to following the elaborate diplomatic activity surrounding the big surprise with which Gawan is preparing to astonish all the other members of his family both inside and outside Schastel Marveile;[13] and secondly towards what Gawan himself still has to learn: not who his relatives are, but the reason why they are in the castle at all. This is where the greatest difference between the two versions is to be found.

In the *Conte du Graal*, there is nothing further to learn on this score after listening to what Guiromelans has to tell Gauvain (8726–63). His account makes it clear that in the general disorder and danger in the years after the death of Uther Pendragon, his widow Ygerne had withdrawn to this magically defended fortress with other noble ladies for protection and safety. Here they have lived in total isolation from the world, and it is only when Gauvain surmounts the perils and passes their elaborate entry test that they learn that, thanks to the restoration of order under Arthur, the world outside is now safe enough for them to leave their castle. Ygerne's withdrawal to an inland refuge is similar to the retreat of Perceval's parents to their manor house in the wild forest at the same time (427–58), and the withdrawal of the wounded Fisher King to his hunting castle (3507–33) appears to conform to a similar pattern.[14]

Gawan discovers why his relatives have been imprisoned, that is to say he learns about Clinschor, in the course of his three long conversations with Gramoflanz, Orgeluse and (a little later) Arnive. The last of these is the most important as it gives Clinschor's personal history. But the other two mention him as well, and it is of interest that we learn of the political and diplomatic ramifications of the current situation before we learn the history of Clinschor himself. Gramoflanz tells Gawan (605,22–606,3) that he would have attempted the challenge of Lit Marveile, were it not that Clinschor had preserved peace with him during his hostilities with Orgeluse: 'wan daz der wîse Clinschor/ mir mit vriden gieng ie vor' (605,29–30). Orgeluse herself then explains that, as an act of appeasement and in the hope of luring Gramoflanz to his death in attempting the challenge, she had made over to Clinschor the booth of precious goods given her by Amfortas (617,4–618,12). The terms 'nigrômanzî' (617,12) and 'zouber' (617,13) are here used with reference to Clinschor for the first time in the Gawan narrative.[15] It is

[12] See Green (n. 8 above), pp. 155–56.
[13] See Sidney M. Johnson, 'Gawan's Surprise in Wolfram's *Parzival*', *GR*, 33 (1958), 285–92; see also Mohr (n. 2 above) and Green (n. 8 above), pp. 165–75.
[14] See Mohr, 'König Artus' (n. 2 above), pp. 180–84.
[15] For the negative connotations of *nigrômanzî* as the black art, concerned with the

significant that they occur in a political, courtly context. When the practice of necromancy is attributed to a neighbouring lord who is seen as cultivated, polished and intelligent, 'hövesch unde wîs' (618,1), it becomes an additional uncomfortable, complicating factor in the state of hostility and war between the duchess of Logrois and the king of Rosche Sabbins. In this triangle Gawan has now taken Clinschor's place, thereby setting the stage for the extended diplomatic activity which constitutes the denouement of the Gawan story in books XIII and XIV.

The full account of Clinschor's life and motives which Arnive provides in Book XIII (655,28–659,16) has no counterpart in the *Conte du Graal*, and it is the culmination of this strand of the Schastel Marveile episode. Before commenting in greater detail on the picture of the necromancer presented here, let us draw the conclusions of the comparative analysis so far presented. For Chrétien the late revelation of the kinship relationships obtaining between Gauvain, the royal ladies in the castle and King Arthur is the point towards which the narrative movement of the episode is directed. For Wolfram the kinship relations are also of supreme importance, as almost every book of *Parzival* demonstrates, and he handles them with as much narrative virtuosity here as anywhere. But for the protagonist Gawan, whom the reader is constantly accompanying, they do not in themselves constitute the principal element of narrative tension as they do in Chrétien's version. Wolfram has replaced Chrétien's single strand of gradually revealed information (about kinship relationships) with two strands. The astonishment at the recognition of long-lost relatives is displaced from Gawan to the imprisoned ladies and then to King Arthur. For Gawan, as for the reader, the principal element of narrative tension is now about Clinschor, and this doubling of the process of gradual revelation of important information (a central feature of Wolfram's narrative technique) may be considered the central feature in his restructuring of the narrative here.

The changes in Wolfram's adaptation of the material are designed to lead his hero and his audience to realise by gradual stages in the narrative process that he is assigning central importance to a theme absent from the *Conte du Graal*, namely that the womenfolk of the house of Mazadan have suffered their great misfortune and imprisonment as the victims of demonic sorcery, and not primarily as a result of their own human sinfulness and weakness like Amfortas and Parzival. We may therefore wish to ask why Wolfram should have attached so much

conjuration of demons and with *maleficium*, see most recently Eberhard Nellmann, 'Wolfram and Kyot als *vindære wilder mære*', ZfdA, 99 (1988), 31–67 (pp. 56–58). *zouber* is used pejoratively in *Parzival*, exclusively with reference to Clinschor, including the early reference in Book II (66,4); it is not used with reference to Cundrie's beneficent magic or astrology.

significance to sorcery as a source of evil in courtly society and as an
explanation for misfortune that he was prepared to recast a major
episode of the work in order to depict it. It is in the light of this question
that we should now look at the sorcerer himself.

III

Students of *Parzival* are accustomed to locate the figure and the history
of Clinschor, as told to Gawan by the aged queen Arnive in book XIII
(655,28–659,16), within the context of the narrative strategy which
appears to shape Wolfram's adaptation of Chrétien's Gauvain material.
By various means the German poet contrives to draw attention to the
many implicit and explicit structural and thematic parallels between the
Parzival and Gawan histories, so that the Gawan material is perceived to
be providing a kind of constant gloss, an implicit commentary on the
Parzival material. Within this pattern countless individual narrative
details, and the broad comparability of major narrative elements, all
signal to the reader that he should be prepared to look for, and to
respond to, significant similarities and significant differences between
the two histories. These include the differences between the heroes'
upbringing – Gawan at court, Parzival in isolation – and the landscapes
they traverse, the contrasting circumstances in which they win their
wives, the way their paths intersect, and, perhaps most important of all,
their central castle challenges.[16]

Within this framework, which is as much a narrative technique as it is
a structural feature, Clinschor occupies a position analogous to that of
the maimed Amfortas. Like the Grail king, Clinschor is the lord of the
castle which constitutes the hero's main chivalric challenge and within
which the hero's maternal relatives are suffering and waiting for release.
As in the case of Amfortas, Clinschor's trangression against the moral
code of his world was to do with *minne*, and like Amfortas he has been
punished for it with impotence. The history of Clinschor's adultery with
the queen of Sicily and his subsequent castration (656,25–657,25)
motivates his envious hatred of humanity from *scham* (658,3–5); but it
also serves to integrate the figure more securely into the narrative
process of glossing the history of Parzival, by providing a kind of savage
parody of the fate of Amfortas. Clinschor's fate clearly expects a
different order of audience response from that demanded for and
accorded to the agonies of Amfortas: this jarring change of register is

---

[16] For the classical statements of this view, since elaborated and developed further by the
same author's subsequent critical work, see Mohr, 'Parzival und Gawan' (n. 2 above); see
also Marianne Wynn, 'Parzival and Gâwân – Hero and Counterpart', *PBB* (Tüb.), 84
(1962), 142–72, revised version in the same author's *Wolfram's 'Parzival'* (n. 5 above).

signalled when Arnive expresses her doubts about the propriety of even mentioning castration in her decorous narrative (657,3–7), and it is firmly established for the reader or listener by the contemptuous metaphor of the *kapun* and by Gawan's hearty laughter (657,8–11).

The details of his personal history confirm that Clinschor is to be seen in a more unrelievedly negative light than some other medieval sorcerers, and they have to compensate us for the lack of more circumstantial evidence of his necromancy. We learn virtually nothing of the details of Clinschor's magical practices, although we do of course see their spectacular products in full operation when Gawan confronts the challenge of Schastel Marveile. Orgeluse tells Gawan that Clinschor's necromancy enables him to exert power over men and women, and that he uses it to inflict unhappiness, *kumber*, on noble people (617, 11–16). Arnive knows that his power extends to all spirits, 'mal unde bêâ schent,/ die zwischen dem firmament/ wonent und der erden zil', except for those whom God is willing to protect (658, 26–30). Taken together, these two statements make it clear that Clinschor is a practitioner of demonic and not of natural magic, and that he is a necromancer in the sense that his capacity to inflict misfortune on men and women is derived from his power to conjure up spirits who must do his bidding.

His evidently universal hatred of humanity and his desire to hurt it wherever he can is based on shame and envy (658,3–8), and it is these characteristics which make him appear, among all the figures in *Parzival*, as the one who is most Lucifer-like in his behaviour, and the one whose humiliating misfortune has led to a response of *haz* and *nît* most like the response of Lucifer described by Trevrizent (463,4–9). There are other features which reinforce this impression, of which the most striking is his invisibility itself. His magic is operative although he is personally absent from Schastel Marveile, or at least permanently out of sight. But he has even greater centres of power in many other lands (656,6–9). In Schastel Marveile he has been defeated by a Christian knight who put his entire trust in God to deliver him (568,1–14), and who was defended from all serious harm. Faced with such an opponent, like Lucifer faced with a triumphant saint, Clinschor will yield the castle to him completely and keep peace with him henceforth (659, 1–10). But there is no reason to believe that he is permanently defeated, or that he has surrendered his power to make people suffer, or that he has lost his strongholds elsewhere, compared with which the wonders of Schastel Marveile, including its great column, are merely 'kleiniu wunderlîn' (656,7). A final feature which reinforces the analogy with Lucifer is the circumstance that Clinschor too is an apostate who has fallen away from God, a clerk in holy orders and a nobleman from a Christian country, who has journeyed to Persida in order to devote himself to the black art:

'ein phaffe der wol zouber las' (66,4). It is impossible to over-emphasise the importance, for our understanding of Wolfram's moral priorities, of the distinction which is to be drawn between such a Christian renegade, who is is not a heathen in the ordinary sense of the term, and all of those figures created by Wolfram in Book I of *Parzival* and in *Willehalm* who were born heathen and have remained so, like Belakane or Terramer. It is striking, and surely significant, that we are presented with this Lucifer-like apostate as the principal personal embodiment of active spiritual evil in *Parzival*, at a point in the narrative time only a few days before the appearance of Feirefiz.

It is to this association with Lucifer and the demonic that we should look in order to explain one of the most unusual features of Clinschor: the absence of any mention by Wolfram of any knowledge or practice of astrology or astronomy on his part. The fact that Clinschor is never seen at work casting spells may have come to Wolfram's aid here, for in historical terms the practice of demonic necromancy without the aid of astrology is unheard of in this period. The point of this unusual and sharp separation of astrology and necromancy must have been lost on Wolfram's successors in the thirteenth and early fourteenth centuries, who had no qualms about making an astrologer of Clinschor, both in the *Wartburgkrieg* and in the German verse legend of St Elisabeth. Chrétien's learned clerk is an astronomer; and the reason why Wolfram was so careful is undoubtedly because, as Wilhelm Deinert noted, the subject of astronomy and astrology is assigned in *Parzival* to the sphere of sacred learning.[17] It is central to Wolfram's presentation of the Grail and its history through the figure of Flegetanis and the learned studies of Kyot (453,11–454,30).[18] Astrology is practised at Munsalvaesche by Cundrie la surziere.

Among the many structural and thematic parallels linking the Parzival and Gawan histories in *Parzival*, we must see Clinschor as being antithetically juxtaposed to Cundrie as well as to Amfortas. She had studied magic in the same oriental centres as did Clinschor, not as a Christian apostate, but as a student of a branch of learning long pursued in those regions. Whereas Cundrie was sent by Secundille with her brother and the booth of precious wares as a diplomatic gift to Amfortas, Clinschor stole the magic mirror-column in Schastel Marveile from the same Secundille and brought it back to serve his own evil purposes. Clinschor uses his acquired skills to injure mankind through necromancy; Cundrie, whose brother Malcreatiure is described as 'der würze unt der sterne mâc' (520,3), places her special affinity with, and

---

[17] Wilhelm Deinert, *Ritter und Kosmos im 'Parzival': Eine Untersuchung der Sternkunde Wolframs von Eschenbach*, MTU, 2 (Munich, 1960), pp. 118–21.
[18] See most recently Nellmann (n. 15 above), pp. 54–67.

knowledge of, the plants and stars in the service of the attempts to heal Amfortas; her astronomical knowledge is used for divining the appropriate moment for significant events and for expounding Parzival's summons to the Grail (781,1–782,30). She must therefore be seen as exemplifying what Wolfram sees as the positive forms of magic: astronomy and the natural magic of the healing arts. Her cognomen 'la surziere' refers to this and carries no negative connotation. Taken together, the approval which Wolfram bestows on the skills of Cundrie and his abhorrence for the demonic magic (or *zouber*) of Clinschor give us a pointer towards what may have been his attitude towards the study of magic in his time.

On the basis of the foregoing it seems to me that Wolfram has given the figure of Clinschor a sharp and distinctive profile, not as a piece of 'characterisation', but by virtue of the important place which he occupies in so many different patterns of significance in the text. To establish these links within *Parzival* is more my concern in this paper than to compare him as a literary figure with other major magicians of medieval vernacular literature, such as Merlin or the striking figure of Roaz von Glois in Wirnt's *Wigalois*. Instead I should prefer merely to mention two of the great legendary magi of medieval Europe who appear in negative contexts in other German texts of the period, namely the Simon Magus of the 'Faustinianus' episode in the *Kaiserchronik*, and Pope Sylvester II, who is briefly but significantly mentioned as the 'zouberære Gêrbreht' in Walther's anti-papal polemic in the 'Unmuts-ton' (L 33,22).[19] In both of these figures sorcery is associated with simony in a figure who represents the antitype of the true Pope. The ecclesiastical problem of simony and the nature of the papacy were not of course Wolfram's concerns; what seems to me to be relevant in both cases is the role of the sorcerer as a manifestation, a figure, of evil spiritual power in a binary opposition of this kind. In this they reveal some affinity to the role assigned to Clinschor in the grand pattern of *Parzival*.

IV

The difference between the value accorded in *Parzival* to the beneficent magic of Cundrie with its place in the world of the Grail on the one hand, and the threatening necromancy of Clinschor on the other might encourage us to think that Wolfram looked more kindly on some forms

---

[19] *Kaiserchronik*, ed. by Edward Schröder, *MGH*, *Deutsche Chroniken*, I, i (Hannover, 1892), vv. 2054–4082; *Die Gedichte Walthers von der Vogelweide*, ed. by Karl Lachmann, 13th edn, rev. by Hugo Kuhn (Berlin, 1965).

of magic than on others, and indeed that might have been a not uncommon position in his time; nevertheless it would be inadvisable to draw too firm a conclusion about his personal convictions from a constellation that reflects the exigencies of the narrative situation to a certain extent, however much the treatment of the theme may be Wolfram's own. I would however wish to suggest that the position accorded to Clinschor and what he stands for in the Gawan parts of *Parzival* are a clear indication that Wolfram took the phenomenon of sorcery seriously and was concerned to communicate a specific perception of how it could bring about human misfortune and unhappiness.

The general context within which this must be seen is the revival of learning in the twelfth and thirteenth centuries, which brought with it an influx of Arabic texts on a great variety of subjects, including magical texts of various kinds. Subsequently there is an increase in the number of surviving defences of magic, learned distinctions between different kinds of magic, and above all an increased awareness of it, interest in it, and practice of it, all of which must be seen in some sense as an adjunct of the revival of learning. Edward Peters maintains that, in the controversies surrounding this increasing interest in magic, the courts played a central role.[20] He detects power struggles between old-established élites and new groups, and he relates these conflicts to an increasing number of accusations of magical practices and witchcraft, a process which he sees as culminating in developments at the French court around 1300, in which huge numbers of such accusations were made. But much of the material with which he documents this development is from the twelfth and early thirteenth centuries. In the famous strictures in the second book of the *Policraticus*, he claims, John of Salisbury is denouncing 'a new set of vices, the vices peculiar to the court society that was just taking shape around' him.[21]

In relating the increasing occurrence of sorcery accusations to social factors as well as to theological ones, Peters is adopting a model first developed by Peter Brown in an article concerned with sorcery in the world of late antiquity.[22] The model which he developed to explain it is however of a more general relevance, and Peters claims that it can also be applied with advantage to the phenomenon of the increase of magic in medieval Western society. Brown is concerned with the intense rash of accusations of sorcery in mid-fourth century Roman society, and the greatly reduced number of such accusations in the following two hundred years. He stresses that it is mistaken to regard such accusations

---

[20] Peters (n. 6 above), p. 46. For a more cautious view, emphasising that there are more sources from the courts than from elsewhere, see Kieckhefer (n. 6 above), pp. 96–97.
[21] Peters (n. 6 above), p. 112; for John, see especially pp. 46–50.
[22] Brown (n. 7 above).

merely as cynical smears and slanders, and suggests that sorcery may, in certain epochs, be seen as an explanation for personal misfortune, an explanation eagerly embraced by people who consider themselves victims, and as one of the ways in which men have attempted to come to terms with the problem of evil. He then asks why, in societies that accept the reality of sorcery and witchcraft, this particular explanation of misfortune and unhappiness should appeal to men and women more in some periods than in others.

The complex answer he provides to this question has both a social and a theological dimension. On the social side, he locates the flourishing appeal of sorcery in a situation in which two systems of power are clashing within one society – a vested traditional authority on the one hand, and new, less easily defined sources of parvenu power associated with specific skills and forms of prestige on the other. He finds that, in late Roman society, accusations of sorcery are normally made by representatives of the old type of power, officially established but threatened and losing confidence. As the new power structure of the Late Empire became established and unified after 400 A.D., these tensions relaxed and the accusations of sorcery died down.[23]

On the theological side, he argues that, as the increasingly unified society of the Late Empire came to see itself as more completely Christian, the universal doctrine of the punishment of the human race for the sin of Adam, as argued persuasively by St Augustine, came to be seen generally as a most comprehensive and sufficient explanation, not merely for human sin, but for all varieties of human misfortune and unhappiness.[24] In this scheme of things, sorcery, while still real enough, is seen to be less a convincing underlying *explanation* of human misfortune than one of its manifestations, one of the ways in which the devil is sometimes enabled to attack and torment humanity. This latter 'Augustinian' approach is the more orthodox Christian standpoint and may be perceived to have held sway in periods in which Pauline and Augustinian views on the fall of man were dominant. Peters stresses that this attitude is closely related to the conviction that God intervenes directly in human affairs to eradicate evil. This doctrine, which has been called the theory of immanent justice, held sway in Europe between the sixth and the twelfth centuries, and this too had diminished the prestige of the sorcerer.[25]

Brown was examining a period which saw a marked decline in the number of accusations of sorcery as the new society of the Later Empire and the new religion became established. Peters claims that it is possible

23 Brown (n. 7 above), pp. 124–31.
24 Brown (n. 7 above), pp. 131–36.
25 Peters (n. 6 above), p. 11, and Chapters 2 and 3, passim.

to see the process described by Brown operating in reverse, as it were, in the Middle Ages from the twelfth century on. For now the hold of the orthodox view of the fall of man as a universal explanation for all human misfortune can be seen to weaken, and alternative explanations leading to accusations of sorcery can become more attractive as the new learning disseminates knowledge of magic and accords it a fresh glamour. With the increasing popularity of magic goes an increasing belief in the power of the devil, and a corresponding loss of confidence in the power of God to intervene directly, or in the power of faith alone to triumph over evil.[26]

The great value of Brown's model, and of the application of it by Peters to the period in which *Parzival* was produced, is that it enables us to see that in certain periods there were available two rival, alternative explanations for human suffering and misfortune. One of these is the belief that the orthodox doctrine of original sin is an adequate explanation for all human ills, whereas the other has recourse to the assumption of malevolent and demonic intervention and gives rise to accusations of sorcery.

The availability of two ways of explaining misfortune as advanced in this model is strikingly analogous to dominant themes in the two balanced narrative worlds of *Parzival*. At Munsalvaesche we and Parzival are confronted with the suffering which Amfortas endures as a consequence of sin, and the theme is worked out subsequently, in the history of Parzival himself, and in the explanations of Book IX, in terms of a broadly Augustinian discourse of original sin, suffering and grace. At Schastel Marveile, however, we are in a different world. Here we gradually come to realise, as Gawan does himself, that his relatives are suffering as the consequence of sorcery, and not primarily as a result of their own sins. If this is so, then Wolfram is here confronting us, in the two major and contrasted spheres of his narrative world, and in specific relation to the castle challenges of the two heroes, with two contrasted views of the causes of human suffering and misfortune which were familiar to his time. Whereas the situation at Munsalvaesche reflects the traditional and dominant view, that at Schastel Marveile affirms that much human suffering is ultimately due to the malevolent activity of spirits, if not of Satan himself, mediated through the practices of sorcerers and witches. This view, although always possible and always present in some form in the Middle Ages, was gaining a renewed currency in Wolfram's time, not least in the courts of Europe. As we all know, it was to gain in strength for the next four hundred years until the epoch of the great witch-crazes of the sixteenth and seventeenth centuries was reached.

[26] Peters (n. 6 above), pp. 117–18.

Although Wolfram juxtaposes the worlds of these two castles in a way which points up rich patterns of meaning linking them, it does not follow that he sees them as being equal in importance or interest. The weight and position of Book IX, and the sustained intensity of its discourse, is sufficient to remind us of the primacy of Munsalvaesche and of the greater depth of the theological issues at stake. Nor is there much room for doubt about Wolfram's attitude towards the practice of necromancy and the conjuration of spirits. His presentation of Clinschor as a sorcerer motivated by envy and hatred of humanity and thus analogous to Lucifer is in accordance with Augustine's denunciation of diabolical magic, linking it with *idolatria* and *superstitio*, in the second book of the *De Doctrina Christiana*.[27] Gawan's success in overcoming the challenge of Lit Marveile must be seen as illustrating the orthodox conviction that a sufficiently firm faith in the power of divine protection can render sorcery ineffective (568,1–14). Clinschor's power over all human beings and spirits beneath the firmament is powerless against those whom God expressly wishes to protect (658,26–30). For all his courtliness and wisdom, the castrated lover who turns to the black arts for vengeance is in himself a comic figure, as is demonstrated by Gawan's laughter when first told of his discomfiture.

This might lead us to think that sorcery is not a central problem for Wolfram, and that he is not inclined to take it too seriously. On the other hand he has given the subject a prominent place in *Parzival*, which it did not have in its source, and he has substantially reshaped Gawan's culminating chivalric adventure in order to accommodate it. Why should he have done this?

The most convincing explanation is that it is a response to his perception of the study and practice of sorcery as a real and potent presence in the world, and more specifically perhaps in the courtly society of his time. The work of Brown and Peters makes clear, as we have seen, that any society in which charges and accusations of sorcery flourish or increase must be regarded as one in which the belief that the Catholic doctrine of original sin offers a sufficient explanation for human misfortune has lost at least part of its hold. We cannot know whether Wolfram would have seen the interest in magic, especially necromancy, as a growing trend in his own age as our historians do, but there can be little doubt that he was aware of it as something in which certain groups of clerics and some members of courtly society were taking a particular interest. He took pains to make it clear that Clinschor belongs to both these groups; he is first mentioned as a cleric in Book II (66,4) but he is

[27] Augustine, *De Doctrina Christiana*, II, xvii–xxiv (27–37), in *Aurelii Augustini Opera*, IV, 1, ed. by Joseph Martin, Corpus Christianorum, Series Latina, 32 (Turnhout, 1962), pp. 52–60. For an English translation, see Augustine, *On Christian Doctrine*, trans. by D. W. Robertson (Indianapolis, 1958).

also a nobleman, indeed a duke, and in good standing with his peers before his disgrace (656,19–24). After his return from Persida he re-establishes himself in political life by using his necromancy as a means of gaining political power and influence. He is feared by his neighbours Orgeluse and Gramoflanz's father Irot, and both of these rulers attempt to appease him – Orgeluse with her gift of oriental treasure (617,4–23) and Irot with the gift of the rock and the land upon which he builds his castle (658,9–18). Clinschor thus makes use of magic as a political weapon, perhaps as a means of regaining something of the honour and status he had enjoyed before his disgrace.

The practice of magic for political purposes in courtly and high clerical circles may therefore be seen to be one of Wolfram's themes. Although it is not impossible that he had particular people in mind, it is unlikely that we will ever know who they might have been. Let us however conclude with a final hypothesis which is concerned with just these circles. It is in the writings of three of Wolfram's contemporaries, Alexander Neckham, Konrad von Querfurt and Gervase of Tilbury – all of them clerical courtiers from Northern Europe writing between about 1190 and 1214 – that the legend of Virgil the Neapolitan magician is first attested in its fully developed form. It is now believed that these clerics were the inventors of the notion, which can no longer be considered a Neapolitan folk tradition.[28] That Wolfram is alluding to this legend in making Clinschor into the 'nephew' or kinsman of Virgil (656,14–18) is quite clear, but it is less clear why he should do so.

A possible explanation presents itself, however, if my reading of Wolfram's treatment of the Clinschor theme is correct. Men like those named above, intellectuals and courtiers and statesmen, were dabbling fashionably in the new discoveries in magic and it must have seemed that they wished to dignify and legitimate this interest by claiming for it the patronage and protection of the great poet and prophet. If this is so, then Wolfram is here alluding, with savage irony, to these self-proclaimed 'kinsmen of Virgil' and exposing their pretensions by associating them with his own diabolical necromancer Clinschor. He is contrasting what they might see as an interest in science, novelties and classical culture with his own rigorous condemnation of necromancy.

This offers a possible explanation for the presence of such a seemingly pejorative reference to Virgil in *Parzival*. It also liberates us from the uncomfortable impression that Wolfram might really have believed that Virgil was a malevolent sorcerer of the Clinschor kind. Wolfram knew Veldeke's *Eneit* well and must therefore have known a good deal about

---

[28] See Domenico Comparetti, *Virgilio nel medio evo*, new edn by Giorgio Pasquali, 2 vols (Florence, 1937–41), introduction to vol. 2, pp. xx–xxiii; J. W. Spargo, *Virgil the Necromancer: Studies in Virgilian Legends* (Cambridge, Mass., 1934), pp. 4–18.

Virgil, even if not at first hand. And finally this reading would confirm that the theme of sorcery in *Parzival* is to be understood as standing in a complex, but real, relationship to the phenomenon of sorcery in Wolfram's world and that it can therefore be set alongside his treatment of contemporary chivalry and warfare, kingship, nobility and kinship, love, marriage and religion and many other things.[29]

---

[29] I hope to give fuller and more adequately documented treatment shortly to the view of Wolfram's reference to Virgil presented here in outline.

Versuch einer vergleichenden Ästhetik: Die Kunst des Porträts bei Chrétien und einigen deutschen Bearbeitern des 12. und 13. Jahrhunderts

JEAN-MARC PASTRÉ

Wie die Ästhetik des Mittelalters ausdrücklich bezeugt, besteht die hauptsächliche Funktion der Beschreibung der Frau im Lob ihrer Schönheit.[1] Es wäre trotzdem irreführend zu denken, daß die Kunst der Frauendarstellung im Mittelalter dieselbe Benutzung von ähnlichen Topoi in ganz Europa aufweist. Von Hartmann im *Erec* und im *Iwein* und von Wolfram im *Parzival* wiederaufgenommen, dienten Chrétiens Frauenporträts als Prüfstein für die deutschen Bearbeiter. Ihre Reaktion auf die neue französische Mode zeigt nämlich ihre Bedenken diesbezüglich, und der Abstand, den die komparatistische Analyse ihrer Porträts an den Tag legt, drückt den Unterschied zwischen der damaligen französischen und der deutschen Ästhetik exemplarisch aus.

Wenn Chrétien die schöne Enide vorstellt, erwähnt er, daß das Kleid, das sie über ihrem Hemd trägt, so sehr abgenutzt ist, daß es an den Ellenbogen Löcher hat, daß aber unter der ärmlichen Kleidung der Körper schön ist.[2] Diese Art und Weise, den Körper der Schönen darzustellen, ist um so zurückhaltender, als Chrétien gleich darauf die detaillierte Beschreibung des Gesichts Enides folgen läßt (*EE* 427–36); erst später, nachdem Erec angekündigt hat, daß er das junge Mädchen heiraten will, beschreibt Chrétien den Körper Enides ausführlicher (*EE* 1471–77). Hartmann verkehrt die Motive, schiebt die Schilderung vom Gesicht der Enite auf und betont gleich, wie Erec ihren Körper ansieht. Hartmann verändert übrigens die Motive der Löcher im Kleid und des schönen Körpers, den man unter dem Hemd sieht. Beim

---

[1] Matthäus von Vendôme, *Ars versificatoria*, I.67, in Edmond Faral, *Les Arts Poétiques du XIIe et du XIIIe siècle* (Paris, 1924; Nachdr. Paris, 1958), S. 109–193 (S. 134).
[2] *Les Romans de Chrétien de Troyes, I: Erec et Enide*, hg. von Mario Roques, CFMA, 80 (Paris, 1953) (= *EE*), V. 409–10: 'povre estoit la robe dehors,/ mes desoz estoit biax li cors'. Hartmanns *Erec* zitiert nach: *Erec von Hartmann von Aue*, hg. von Albert Leitzmann (Halle, 1939) (= *E*).

Bearbeiter sind beide, Kleid und Hemd, an vielen Stellen zerrissen, so daß ihr Körper, von dem man sagte, daß niemals ein junges Mädchen einen so vollkommenen Leib gehabt habe, schwanenweiß hindurchschimmert (*E* 324–32). Merkwürdigerweise lenkte Hartmann dabei die Aufmerksamkeit auf die physischen Reize des jungen Mädchens, etwa wie man es beim Porträt der Camille im französischen *Eneasroman* findet: ihre Kleidung in dunklem Purpur liegt eng an der Haut an, und da sie ihren Mantel an einer Seite offen läßt, ist ihre rechte Körperhälfte sichtbar.[3] Es kam also darauf an, die physische Anziehung zu betonen, die Enite auf Erec ausübte. Das entspricht perfekt dem Gesetz der poetischen Wahrscheinlichkeit: Der traditionellen Theorie der Ursachen nach läßt sich nämlich die Schönheit durch die von ihr hervorgerufenen Wirkungen definieren. Wie Andreas Capellanus und Matthäus von Vendôme hervorheben, weckt die Schönheit die Liebe und schürt das Begehren.[4] Die physischen Reize der Enite wecken eine sinnliche Liebe, die dann zum *verligen* führt. Hartmann unterstreicht also das Motiv, büßt aber dabei etwas von der Feinheit ein, die es in der französischen Quelle hatte. Indem Chrétien zunächst das schöne Gesicht des Mädchens und erst danach die Blicke Erecs auf den Körper der Braut beschrieb, zeigte er zuerst die objektive Reinheit der beiden jungen Leute, dann die subjektivere Begierde, die der junge Erec empfindet, und darüber hinaus, wie er später ihre gegenseitige Liebe mißbrauchen wird.

Ganz anders ist das von Hartmann entworfene Porträt der Enite, wenn die Königin sie dem Hofe vorstellt und der Menge der Ritter entgegenführt (*E* 1698–743). Diesmal wird Enites Gesicht geschildert, wobei Hartmann zwei Züge Chrétiens wiederaufnimmt, die Gesichtsfarbe, die heller glänzt als die Lilienblüte, zu der sich ein natürliches, frisches Rot gesellt, und den Mund (*EE* 427–32, 436). Nie sah man eine edlere Frau, fügt Hartmann hinzu (*E* 1707). Das, was der Hof von ihr sieht, ist aber gar nicht mehr das, was Erec anfangs von ihr sah: Den Körper sieht man nämlich nicht mehr, da die herrlichen Kleider ohne Löcher sind, und so geht man von der Betrachtung des Körpers zu der des Gesichts über.

Die doppelte Beschreibung der Schönheit drückt den gesellschaftlichen Aufstieg und die innere Krönung der Person aus. Gerade das betonte Hartmann gleich beim ersten Porträt des Mädchens, als er abschließend schrieb: 'und wære si gewesen rîch, / sô engebræste niht ir

---

[3] *Eneas: roman du XIIe siècle*, hg. von J.-J. Salverda de Grave, CFMA, 44 und 62, 2 Bde. (Paris, 1925-29), V. 4011–12 und 4045–46.

[4] Edgar de Bruyne, *Études d'esthétique médiévale*, 3 Bde. (Brügge, 1946), II, 173ff.; III, 172ff. Matthäus von Vendôme, in Faral (wie Anm. 1), I.40 (S. 119); *Andreae Capellani Regii Francorum De Amore Libri Tres*, hg. von E. Trojel (Kopenhagen, 1892; Nachdr. München, 1972), I.1.1 (S. 3).

lîbe/ ze lobelîchem wîbe' (*E* 333–35). Die Schönheit genügt also nicht, und sie zu lange beschreiben hieße wahrscheinlich für Hartmann, ihr eine zu große Bedeutung einzuräumen. Indem der Bearbeiter diese Komponente des höfischen Wertsystems der sozialen Stellung unterordnete, veränderte er übrigens den Standpunkt Chrétiens, der die Schönheit nicht dem Reichtum unterordnete, sondern der Weisheit, der ersten der höfischen Tugenden in den Augen von Enides Vater.[5] Viel mehr als ein ästhetischer Wert, den es zu beschreiben gilt, ist so für Hartmann die Schönheit ein dem Rang der Enite gebührendes Merkmal, und aus diesem Grunde wirkt das Porträt der Enite zum Teil mehr funktionell als ornamental. Hartmann ordnet diese Schönheit übrigens sehr streng einer Hierarchie zu, indem er gegen Ende des Werks behauptet, daß die Dame im Zelt in den Augen Erecs nach Enite die schönste sei, d.h., daß Enite als höchster Maßstab im Epos wirkt (*E* 8926–36), während Chrétien seinen Maßstab anderswo anlegt und von der Dame sagt, sie sei viermal schöner als die Lavine des *Eneasromans* (*EE* 5837–43).

Diese Unterordnung des Ästhetischen unter das Funktionelle bringt es also mit sich, daß dieses Porträt so wenig ornamental ist. Chrétien dagegen beachtet beide Funktionen im gleichen Maße, wenn er die glänzenden Haare der Enide, ihre strahlende Stirn, ihre Augen, die wie Sterne leuchten, und das Gesicht, das so klar ist, daß man sich darin wie in einem Spiegel sehen kann, erwähnt. Hartmann folgt Chrétien also in dieser Darstellungsweise nicht, und das obschon Enide auffallenderweise nach den antiken Epen, nach den Porträts der Gaïte und der Cardiones im *Athis et Prophilias* und nach jenen des französischen *Trojaromans* eine der Personen der Artusepen ist, bei der man die präziseste Beschreibung des Gesichts findet. Außerdem sind diese Details oft bemerkenswert, weil sie damals selten auftraten, wie etwa der Vergleich mit Sternen, der bei Alanus ab Insulis im *De Planctu Naturae* vorkommt,[6] oder der den Trobadors vertraute Vergleich mit dem Spiegel[7] oder noch das Motiv der goldenen Haare, die noch mehr glänzen als der sie schmückende Goldreifen, das im *Roman de Thèbes*

---

5 *EE* 537–38: 'Molt est bele, mes mialz asez/ vaut ses savoirs que sa biautez'. Siehe Karl-Heinz Bender, 'L'essor des motifs du plus beau chevalier et de la plus belle dame dans le premier roman courtois', in *Lebendige Romania: Festschrift für Hans-Wilhelm Klein*, hg. von A. Barrera-Vidal, E.P. Ruhe und P. Schunck (Göppingen, 1976), S. 35–46. Ders., 'Beauté, mariage, amour. La genèse du premier roman courtois', in *Amour, mariage et transgressions au moyen âge*, hg. von Danielle Buschinger und André Crépin, GAG, 420 (Göppingen, 1984), S. 173–83.

6 PL, CCX, 432C. Siehe Nancy C. Zak, *The Portrayal of the Heroine in Chrétien de Troyes's 'Erec et Enide', Gottfried von Strassburg's 'Tristan', and 'Flamenca'*, GAG, 347 (Göppingen, 1983), S. 29 und Anm. 61. Siehe auch Alice M. Colby, *The Portrait in Twelfth-Century French Literature: An Example of the Stylistic Originality of Chrétien de Troyes* (Genf, 1965).

7 Zak (wie Anm. 6), S. 29. Siehe auch Tony Hunt, 'Redating Chrestien de Troyes', *BBSIA*, 30 (1978), 209–37.

zunächst erscheint und das Chrétien schon im *Philomena* benutzt hatte.[8] Erst zwanzig Jahre später wird ein Gottfried von Straßburg für das hervorragende Porträt der Jungfrau Isolde solche Formeln wiederaufzunehmen wissen.[9]

Nicht ohne Grund nimmt Hartmann von diesem Porträt nur den Mund und die rosen- und lilienfarbene Gesichtsfarbe auf: 'als der rôsen varwe/ under wîze liljen güzze,/ und daz zesamene vlüzze,/ und daz der munt begarwe/ wære von rôsen varwe,/ dem gelîchete sich ir lîp' (*E* 1701–06). Zwar hätte der Bearbeiter ähnliche Angaben bei Minnesängern wie Morungen finden können,[10] er erwähnt sie aber deshalb, um die Handlung zu veranschaulichen, die er nach Chrétien darstellt (*EE* 1707–14): Als Enite zuerst von der Tür her unter die Ritter trat, wurde sie verlegen; ihre Rosenröte schwand, blaß und rot wurde sie abwechselnd, wie wenn die Sonne in vollem Glanze strahlt und plötzlich eine dünne Wolke davortritt (*E* 1708–35). Hier begegnet man einer der Konstanten der Ästhetik der ersten deutschen mittelalterlichen Epen, wo Porträts dazu dienen, das menschliche Handeln vorzugsweise in seinen expressiven Zügen darzustellen. Das ist noch die romanische Auffassung, die sich hier vor allem in den Angaben ausdrückt, die den Wechsel der Farben als Wirkung der Gefühle erscheinen lassen. Grundsätzlich von funktioneller und narrativer Natur, weicht sie erst später und übrigens ziemlich selten der wirklichen Beschreibung der Schönheit des Gesichts, also einer echten Ästhetik des Porträts.[11] Schematisch aufgebaut und auf Kontrasteffekten fußend, erklärt diese erste deutsche Darstellungsweise, warum Hartmann bei Enites erstem Auftreten schreibt, daß ihr Körper durch die schäbige Kleidung schimmerte wie eine Lilie, wenn sie weiß unter schwarzen Dornen blüht (*E* 336–38). Seiner Vorlage fügt er also diesen normativen Gegensatz von Schwarz und Weiß, von Licht und Finsternis, von der schmählichen Armut und der unbefangenen Schönheit hinzu, den er damit begründet, daß Enites Hemd nicht mehr weiß ist wie bei Chrétien, sondern nach langem Tragen schmutzig geworden ist. Ähnlich führt

---

[8] *Philomena: conte raconté d'après Ovide*, hg. von C. de Boer (Paris, 1909), V. 140–41. Siehe P. Graf, *Strahlende Schönheit als Leitlinie höfischer Vollendung: Eine Untersuchung zur Gestalt und Funktion des Schönen in den Romanen Chrétien de Troyes'* (Dissertation, München, 1974); P.M. Schon, 'Das literarische Porträt im französischen Mittelalter', *Archiv für das Studium der neueren Sprachen und Literaturen*, 202 (1965–66), 241–63.

[9] *Tristan und Isold*, hg. von Friedrich Ranke (Berlin, 1930), V. 10977–85, 10996–11005. Siehe J.M. Pastré, 'La beauté d'Isolde', in *Tristan et Iseut, mythe européen et mondial*, hg. von Danielle Buschinger, GAG, 474 (Göppingen, 1987), S. 326–40.

[10] F. Nickel, *Heinrich von Morungen und die Troubadours* (Straßburg, 1980), und E.J. Morrall, 'Light Imagery in Heinrich von Morungen', *London Medieval Studies*, 2,1 (1951), 116–24.

[11] J.M. Pastré, 'Pour une esthétique du portrait: les couleurs du visage dans la littérature médiévale allemande', in *Les couleurs au moyen âge*, hg. von J. Subrenat, Senefiance 24 (Aix-en-Provence, 1988), S. 284–300.

Hartmann, nachdem er die Lichtangaben des von Chrétien entworfenen Porträts gestrichen hat, diesmal aber nach der Vorlage (*EE* 1780–82), das breit ausgeführte Bild der strahlenden Enite nur deswegen ein, weil er die Tatsache veranschaulichen will, daß alle sie als die allerschönste ansehen, und daß Artus sie also auf den Mund küssen darf, denn ihr Glanz stellt alle anderen Damen in den Schatten, so wie der Mond alle Sterne überstrahlt (*E* 1763–83). Auf stilistischen Requisiten fußend, ist diese Darstellungsweise nur da zu finden und hat nur dann Genauigkeit, wenn sie etwa die Gesichtsfarbe mit Rose und Lilie oder mit der Sonne vergleicht, und so entpuppt sie sich mehr als eine poetische Rhetorik denn als eine richtige Ästhetik des Porträts.

Nicht zufällig sind übrigens die Angaben der Gesichtsfarbe und der Haut – die einzigen also, die Hartmann übernimmt – gerade jene, die auf die ältesten Auffassungen zurückgehen. So ist in Isidors *Etymologien* die weiße Farbe der Haut das Hauptelement der Schönheit, von dem sich alle anderen Züge ableiten lassen. Darin und in dem Grad seiner Ausdruckskraft liegt für ihn in erster Linie die Schönheit des Gesichts, genauso wie Enite am Hofe abwechselnd weiß und rot wird, und das gerade, weil das Antlitz die Synthese des Menschen, der Spiegel der Seele und das Symbol der Gefühle ist.[12] Dazu hängt für Isidor die Schönheit von einer gewissen Röte der Farbe ab, die auf die Qualität des Blutes zurückführt, was auch der Grund dafür ist, warum die Schönheit bei jüngeren Menschen, deren Blut gesünder ist, am deutlichsten in Erscheinung tritt.[13] Niemand wird staunen, wenn in seinem funktionellen Schematismus Hartmann als seltene Farben für das Porträt Enites nur das Weiß, das Rot und, als Folie, das Schwarz beibehält, also gerade die drei Farben, auf denen das normative Farbensystem des Mittelalters beruht.[14]

Chrétien zeichnet nun ein zweites Porträt der Enide, nämlich wenn die jungen Leute sich auf dem Wege nach Cardigan befinden. Erec kann nicht umhin, Enide zu küssen und ihre blonden Haare, ihre lachenden Augen, die helle Stirn, die Nase, das Gesicht, den Mund und das Kinn zu bewundern, wobei sein Blick nicht davor zurückscheut, über die weiße Kehle, über die Seiten, über Arme und Hände bis zu den Hüften herunterzugleiten (*EE* 1466–77). Dadurch wollte Chrétien die physische Anziehung veranschaulichen, die Enide auf Erec ausübt, der sie später anderer Eigenschaften wegen wird lieben lernen müssen.[15] Nach der

---

[12] 'Facies dicta ab effigie. Ibi est enim tota figura hominis [. . .]. Vultus vero dictus, eo quod per eum animi voluntas ostenditur: secundum voluntatem enim, vultus in varios motus mutatur'. Zitat nach de Bruyne (wie Anm. 4), I, 85.

[13] 'Pulcher ab specie cutis dictus, quod est rubens pellis. [. . .] Venustus, pulcher, a venis, id est a sanguine'. Zitat nach de Bruyne (wie Anm. 4), I, 83.

[14] M. Pastoureau, *Figures et couleurs* (Paris, 1986).

[15] Zak (wie Anm. 6), S. 32–33.

Tradition des *Trojaromans*, wo etwa die Brüste, Schultern, Arme und Hände der Polyxena erwähnt wurden, zählt Chrétien die Körperteile auf und zwar eingehender als der Dichter des *Eneasromans* im Porträt der keuschen Nebenfigur Camille. Zurückhaltend, wie es die meisten deutschen Bearbeiter sein werden, faßt Hartmann die Stelle drastisch zusammen: Erec betrachtet seine Braut, beide wechseln beständig liebevolle Blicke (*E* 1486–87, 1490–91). Hartmann streicht also einfach dieses allzu realistische und verführerische Bild der Schönheit. Indem er dabei vermeidet, wie etwa zwanzig Jahre zuvor Rahewin im Porträt Barbarossas, die Stirn, das Kinn und den eigentlichen Körper Enites zu erwähnen, verzichtet er in der Tat auf die Körperteile, die seit Augustin als rein dekorativ aufgefaßt wurden. Mehr als das: Hartmann unterläßt es sogar, die Hände zu erwähnen, da sie für Augustin neben ihrer objektiven Nützlichkeit und ihrer funktionellen Schönheit auch die äußerliche, freie und unabhängige Schönheit bezeugen. Aus extremer Vorsicht und aus einem starken Gefühl für Anstand erwähnt Hartmann die Hände nur für ihre *utilitas magna*, also auf Kosten ihrer *species decentissima*,[16] etwa wenn die weißen Hände der Enite das Pferd Erecs mit Umsicht versorgen (*E* 354–55), während bei Chrétien das Mädchen Erec einfach an der Hand ins Haus führt (*EE* 473–74), wobei Hartmann ganz eindeutig den Gegensatz zwischen der Schönheit des Mädchens und der Niedrigkeit der Funktion eines Pferdeknechtes betont.

Ähnlich verfährt Hartmann im *Iwein*.[17] Vom so geschickt funktionellen Porträt der Laudine übernimmt der Bearbeiter nur die unauffälligste Angabe der schönen blonden Haare, die sie sich rauft (*I* 1310–11, 1329–30, vgl. 1671–74). Statt die Körperteile, denen sie Gewalt antut, wieder aufzuzählen, erfindet Hartmann das Motiv vom Kopfschmuck und von den Kleidern, die sie zerreißt, so daß dabei – also genau wie im *Erec*, wo er das Motiv eingeführt hatte – hie und da ihr Körper zu sehen ist, der so herrlich ist wie ihre Haare (*I* 1331–34). Vom funktionellen Schematismus aufs einfachste reduziert, d.h. auf ihren kollektiven Sinn, sollen Gesicht und Körper durch ihre Schönheit so wirksam sein, daß Iwein sich gleich ganz und gar in Laudine verliebt (*I* 1335–39). Ebensowenig wie im *Erec* wollte also Hartmann die rein dekorativen Körperteile Laudines aufzählen, obschon Chrétien sie sowohl kontextgemäß als auch ihrer Schönheit wegen beschrieben hatte: ihre Augen, die schönsten, die er je sah, aus denen soviele Tränen quellen; das Gesicht, das sie sich zerkratzt, das so schön und mit so frischen

---

[16]   E. de Bruyne (wie Anm. 4), I, 80ff.

[17]   Stellenangaben nach: *Iwein: Eine Erzählung von Hartmann von Aue*, hg. von G.F. Benecke und K. Lachmann, neu bearbeitet von Ludwig Wolff, 7. Ausg., 2 Bde. (Berlin, 1968) (= *I*); *Chrestien de Troyes: Yvain*, übers. und eingeleitet von Ilse Nolting-Hauff, Klassische Texte des Romanischen Mittelalters in zweisprachigen Ausgaben, 2, 2. Aufl. (München, Nachdr. 1983) (= *Y*).

Farben versehen ist; und für den Körper den Hals, den sie sich mit den Händen zusammenpreßt, den kristallklaren und spiegelglatten Hals; schließlich die Hände, die sie sich verletzt (Y 1462–87). Dabei verändert Hartmann den Standpunkt Chrétiens. Während letzterer das Mitleid, die Traurigkeit und die Wut Yvains darstellte, der sieht, wie sich diese Schönheit selbst zerstört, läßt Hartmann Iwein sich fragen, warum Laudine sich an ihrem unschuldigen Körper rächt (I 1668–74) – einerseits also die Schilderung der von der Bewunderung und von der Liebe geweckten Gefühle, anderseits abstraktes Fragen über die Beweggründe eines solchen Benehmens; auf der einen Seite ein ornamentales und funktionelles Porträt, wie es Galfred von Vinsauf in seiner *Poetria nova* empfahl, auf der anderen ein funktioneller Schematismus aus früheren Zeiten.

Der Lehre der Personendarstellung nach sollte der Künstler etwas anderes anstreben als eine realistische Nachahmung der Natur und nicht alles wiedergeben, was das Auge sah. Der Künstler sollte nämlich die innere Natur der Person aufzeigen und nur das vom äußeren Aspekt behalten, was für sein Vorhaben nötig war.[18] Durch eine bewußte und affektbezogene Stilisierung unterschied sich diese expressive Schönheit von einer rein formellen. Wie etwa in der karolingischen Ästhetik begnügt sich Hartmann damit, eine Schönheit darzustellen, die einem von fern und auf einmal auffällt, während für die spätere französische Kunst, so wie sie Galfred vertrat, das Bildnis seine Schönheit dem musternden Blick des Beobachters, *diligenter intuenti*,[19] beim näheren Hinsehen offenbaren sollte. Wie zum Beispiel für die Crescentia der *Kaiserchronik*[20] wird die Schilderung der Schönheit der christlich gemeinten Darstellung des menschlichen Tuns und Treibens untergeordnet: In ihrem funktionellen Schematismus hängt sie mit der augustinischen Ästhetik zusammen, die ziemlich rigoros und etwas mißtrauisch der Frauenschönheit gegenübersteht und sich deswegen vor dem wirklichen Porträt scheut. Den Zisterziensern und den Karthäusern aus der Jahrhundertmitte folgend, strebt Hartmann in seiner Ästhetik der Personendarstellung eine einfache und schlichte Kunst an, die sich auf das Notwendigste beschränkt. Die *necessitas* und die *simplicitas* der *superfluitas* und der *curiositas* vorziehend, und mißtrauisch dem gegenüber, was allzu rege Empfindungen hervorrufen

---

[18]   E. de Bruyne (wie Anm. 4), I, 176ff.; II, 32ff. P.E. Schramm, *Die deutschen Kaiser und Könige in Bildern ihrer Zeit* (715–1152) (Leipzig, 1928).

[19]   Galfred von Vinsauf, *Documentum de modo et arte dictandi et versificandi*, II.3.2, in Faral (wie Anm. 1), S. 284: 'similis est picturae vili quae placet longius stanti, sed displicet proprius intuenti'; E. de Bruyne (wie Anm. 4), I, 230 und III, 40.

[20]   J.M. Pastré, 'L'esthétique du portrait dans les chroniques allemandes du moyen âge', in *Chroniques nationales et chroniques universelles*, hg. von Danielle Buschinger, GAG, 508 (Göppingen, 1990), S. 121-33.

könnte, will diese Kunst zwar erfreuen, aber in den Grenzen anständiger, würdiger und nüchterner Porträts.[21]

Bei seiner Bearbeitung des *Perceval* verfährt Wolfram nicht anders für das Porträt von Condwiramurs und Orgeluse, den beiden weiblichen Hauptfiguren seines Epos.[22] Obschon so dargestellt, wie der Dichter sie sieht, und daher weniger funktionell als im *Yvain*, zeugt das Porträt der Blancheflor von einer großen Sorgfalt und weist im Vergleich mit den übrigen Porträts von Chrétien neue Details auf: Dem Porträt der Argia und der Deipyle im *Roman de Thèbes* entnommen, ist die Stirn hoch und glatt, wie handgemacht aus Stein, Elfenbein oder Holz; die Augenbrauen sind getrennt, die Augen wie in den antiken Epen klar und lachend und dazu weitgeöffnet – eine Angabe, die Chrétien damals als einziger gebrauchte; auch ist die Nase gerade und fein (1805–29). Mehr auf das Plastische, auf die Beschreibung, und weniger auf die Rhetorik ausgerichtet, zeigt dieses absichtlich keusche, auf das Gesicht reduzierte Porträt, daß Chrétien mehr als in seinen früheren Werken unter den von der Tradition gelieferten Merkmalen gerade jene aussucht, die eindeutig eine reine und unbefangene Schönheit erkennen lassen: Die deutschen Bearbeiter fingen also etwa da an, wo Chrétien aufhörte.

Das, was Wolfram daraus machte, erinnert an Hartmann. Ebensowenig wie Hartmann übernimmt er die Haare, die Stirn, die Augenbrauen und die Nase des jungen Mädchens, ordnet jedoch ebensowie dieser die Schönheit Condwiramurs' einer Hierarchie zu, da sie schöner ist als alle anderen Frauen im Epos (187,12–15; 188,6–7). Genauso wie Hartmann behält Wolfram zwar vom Gesicht nur ein paar markante Züge bei, er verändert sie aber sehr eigenartig. Mehr noch als Hartmann beachtet er die Vorschläge Isidors über die Ausdruckskraft des Gesichts, wenn er ein freundliches Antlitz und Augen voller Sanftmut beschreibt (186,17–20): Für Isidor waren die Augen nämlich die schönsten Organe, weil sie am hellsten und am expressivsten waren, die Wahrzeichen des Geistes und des höheren Lebens der Seele, und ihm war nichts schöner als Augen, die die Regungen der Seele verraten.[23] So etwa schilderte Rahewin den Blick Friedrichs und nicht die Form oder die Farbe seiner Augen. Erst spät greifen aber die deutschen Dichter zu solchen Merkmalen. Zwar erwähnt Veldeke Kamilles schöne Augen[24] und später Herbort von Fritzlar den Glanz von Medeas und von Helenas

---

[21] E. de Bruyne (wie Anm. 4), II, 133–39.

[22] Stellenangaben nach: *Wolfram von Eschenbach*, hg. von Karl Lachmann, 6. Ausg. (Berlin/Leipzig, 1926; Nachdr. 1965); *Chrétien de Troyes: Le Roman de Perceval ou le Conte du Graal*, hg. von William Roach, 2. Ausg. (Genf/Paris, 1959).

[23] E. de Bruyne (wie Anm. 4), I, 85.

[24] Heinrich von Veldeke, *Eneasroman: Mittelhochdeutsch/Neuhochdeutsch*. Nach dem Text von Ludwig Ettmüller ins Neuhochdeutsche übersetzt von Dieter Kartschoke, Reclam UB, 8303 (Stuttgart, 1986), V. 5161–63.

Augen ('luter vnd clar'),[25] nur Wolfram und Gottfried (10996–11005)
würdigen aber den Augenausdruck ihrer weiblichen Figuren. Auch
führen beide Lichtmerkmale in Fülle ein, diese wesentliche Eigenschaft
der visuellen Schönheit, so wie sie die neue französische Darstellungsweise schon nach der Mitte des 12. Jahrhunderts auffaßte. Erst
ein halbes Jahrhundert später gelangte sie nach Deutschland: So hat
etwa Condwiramurs ein helles, strahlendes Gesicht. Wolfram überbietet
schließlich das Topos der Rosen- und Lilienfarbe des Gesichtes, indem
er die Gesichtsfarbe des jungen Mädchens mit der im Tau kaum
aufgegangenen Rose (188,10–13) vergleicht, wobei er das Motiv der
kaum aufgeblühten Rose, das Herbort für sein Porträt Polyxenas (3280–
85) der Medea Benoîts von Sainte-Maure entnommen hatte, mit dem
Motiv der im Tau badenden Rose paart, das Walther von der
Vogelweide in einem seiner Lieder eingeführt hatte.[26] Indem Wolfram
wie nebenbei hinzufügte, daß das Mädchen den wahren 'bêâ curs'
(187,22–23) hatte, ahmte er die Darstellungsweise Hartmanns nach, der
zunächst nur allgemein den Körper neben dem Gesicht, dem Teint, dem
Mund oder den Haaren erwähnte. Orgeluse, die zukünftige Gattin
Gawans, der zweiten Hauptgestalt im Epos, ist ihrerseits ebensosehr die
strahlende Blume der Schönheit und nach Condwiramurs die schönste
(508,18–30).

Ganz anders verhält es sich mit den Porträts der Jeschute und der
Antikonie. Als Nebenpersonen wurden die beiden von Chrétien nicht
oder kaum porträtiert. Für diese tatsächlich oder anscheinend in einer
Liebesaffäre verwickelten Personen erfindet Wolfram gerade die
Merkmale, die er nach Hartmann für keusche Gestalten vermied, die
weder der geringste Verdacht noch die geringste Schmach beflecken
sollten. So erscheint die in ihrem Bett liegende Jeschute, die bei Chrétien
einfach als 'pucelete endormie' (671) bezeichnet wird, als eine herausfordernde Schönheit mit einem roten Mund, der das Feuer der Liebe
erahnen läßt, eine wahrhafte Qual für liebende Augen (130,3–25) und
eine zu starke Versuchung, als daß Parzival widerstehen könnte, die
schlafende Schöne auf den Mund zu küssen. Die Einführung dieser
Feuermetapher war in der Tat nicht ohne tiefere Absicht. Sie dient
Wolfram auch dazu, die wenig zurückhaltende Antikonie zu
beschreiben, deren brennender Mund den scheuen Begrüßungskuß
Gawans in einen liebevollen Kuß verwandelt (405,16–21). Gottfried
diente sie dazu, Isolde im zweiten Porträt des *Tristan* zu schildern, wie
sie bei ihrem Geliebten in der Minnegrotte schläft und dabei von dem

---

[25] *Herbort's von Fritslâr liet von Troye*, hg. von Ge. Karl Frommann, Bibl. d. ges. dt. Nat.-
Lit., 5 (Quedlinburg/Leipzig, 1837), V. 600 und 2492.
[26] Walther L 27,29: 'dîn munt ist rœter danne ein liehtiu rôse in touwes flüete' (*Die
Gedichte Walthers von der Vogelweide*, hg. von Karl Lachmann, 13., aufgrund der 10. von
Carl von Kraus bearbeiteten Ausg. neu hg. von Hugo Kuhn (Berlin, 1965), p. 36).

sie begehrenden Marke beobachtet wird (17568–69). Ähnlich verhält es sich mit den vollen Lippen der Antikonie: Wie die der verführerischen Amurfina in der *Crône*[27] und wie die der später von Konrad von Würzburg beschriebenen Helena,[28] deuten sie in der deutschen Tradition immer auf ein galantes Abenteuer. Zwar kamen solche Angaben in der lateinischen Tradition häufig vor[29] und dies schon im 11. Jahrhundert bei dem Dichter Maximian;[30] zwar begegnet man ihnen auch in der französischen Tradition, zum Beispiel auf Blancheflor angewendet, deren volle und rote Lippen für den Kuß gemacht sind,[31] aber Konrad Fleck hat sich wohl gehütet, diesen allzu sinnlichen Zug in seiner Bearbeitung zu übernehmen.[32] Auch das Motiv des halb offenen Mundes der Jeschute hat eine heikle Konnotation; im französischen *Narcisus*, wo es zuerst zu finden ist, wird es ausdrücklich als Verführungmittel gedeutet.[33]

Auch dazu dienen die kleinen, weißen, gleichmäßigen Zähne der Jeschute. Die Zähne, in den lateinischen[34] und französischen[35] Quellen sehr sparsam erwähnt, wurden in den deutschen Epen erst im 13. Jahrhundert angeführt: Veldeke verwendete dieses Merkmal für Kamille nicht, obwohl er es im *Eneasroman* vorfand (3999–4000). Herbort dagegen wies schon auf die weißen Zähne der Creusa (3257) und die gesunden Zähne der Helena (2494) hin, Wolfram häuft aber als erster so viele Merkmale, die die deutschen Dichter nach ihm im *Wigalois*,[36] im

---

[27] Heinrich von dem Türlin, *Diu Crône*, hg. von G.F.H. Scholl, StLV, 27 (Stuttgart, 1852), V. 8187–88.

[28] J.M. Pastré, 'Typologie und Ästhetik: Das Porträt der Helena im *Trojanerkrieg* Konrads von Würzburg', *Jahrbuch der Oswald von Wolkenstein Gesellschaft*, 5 (1988–89), 397–408.

[29] Sidonius, *Epist.* I.2.2: Theodoric (*Sidoine Apollinaire*, hg. und übers. von André Loyen, 3 Bde. (Paris, 1960–70), II (1970), *Lettres*, S. 5); Matthäus von Vendôme, *Ars versificatoria* (wie Anm. 1), I.56.24–26 (S. 130); Johannes de Hauvilla, *Architrenius*, hg. von Paul Gerhard Schmidt (München, 1974), I.445–52 (S. 142).

[30] E. de Bruyne (wie Anm. 4), II, 175: 'modicum tumentia labra'.

[31] *Le Conte de Floire et Blancheflor*, hg. von Jean-Luc Leclanche, CFMA, 105 (Paris, 1980), V. 2893–94. Siehe auch *Le Roman de la Rose par Guillaume de Lorris et Jean de Meun*, hg. von Ernest Langlois, SATF, 5 Bde. (Paris, 1914–24), V. 537; *Philomena* (wie Anm. 8), V. 153–54; *Le Roman de Thèbes*, hg. von Léopold Constans, SATF, 2 Bde. (Paris, 1890), V. 8430–32, Salemandre. Siehe auch Colby (wie Anm. 6), S. 50–53.

[32] Konrad Fleck, *Flore und Blanscheflur*, hg. von Emil Sommer, Bibl. d. ges. dt. Nat.-Lit., 12 (Quedlinburg/Leipzig, 1846), V. 6895–99.

[33] Ausgabe: Alfons Hilka, 'Der altfranzösische Narcisuslai, eine antikisierende Dichtung des 12. Jahrhunderts', *ZfromPh*, 49 (1929), 633–75.

[34] Weder bei Ovid noch in der *Alda* (*Guilelmi Blesensis Aldae Comoedia*, hg. von Carolus Lohmeyer (Leipzig, 1892)), aber bei Sidonius (wie Anm. 29); Matthäus von Vendôme, *Ars versificatoria* (wie Anm. 1), I.56.27-28 (S. 130); *Architrenius* (wie Anm. 29), I.453–61 (S. 142).

[35] *Li Romanz d'Athis et Prophilias*, hg. von Alfons Hilka, 2 Bde. (Dresden, 1912–16), V. 511–12, 2629; *Floire et Blancheflor* (wie Anm. 31), V. 2895–96; *Philomena* (wie Anm. 8), V. 158; Adam de la Halle, *Le Jeu de la Feuillée*, hg. von Ernest Langlois (Paris, 1911), V. 121; *Li Romans de Garin le Loherain*, hg. von Paulin Paris, 2 Bde. (Paris, 1833–35), I, S. 298, V. 3–4.

[36] Wirnt von Gravenberc, *Wigalois, der Ritter mit dem Rade*, hg. von J.M.N. Kapteyn,

Flore und Blanscheflur (6841–42) und in der *Crône* (8191–92) übernehmen. Neben dem Gesicht besagen die erwähnten Körperteile der Jeschute noch mehr. Da es ihr zu warm war, hatte sie die Decke zurückgeschlagen, so daß ihre Hüfte sichtbar wurde, was wieder an das Porträt der etwas herausfordernden Camille im *Eneas* erinnert (4011–12, 4045–46). Es diente als Signal, ein Kleid ausgeschnitten zu zeigen, wie im zweiten Porträt Isoldes, wo Gottfried ihr Brustbein nannte (17602). Im ersten Porträt dagegen, dem der scheuen Isolde, begnügte sich Gottfried mit allgemeinen Bemerkungen,[37] wie man sie vor ihm bei Benoît,[38] bei Chrétien für die Tochter des Edelmanns, der Calogrenant beherbergt,[39] bei Veldeke für Kamille oder bei Herbort fand. Letzterer ersetzt die von Benoît auf den Körper bezogenen Angaben[40] durch vage Anspielungen bei seinem Porträt der scheuen Polyxena, so sehr hütet er sich davor, diese Körperteile im Detail und mit Namen zu nennen; für ihn beschränkte sich der Körper auf die allgemeine Silhouette (3286–90), so wie Veldeke für Kamille nur von einem wohlgeformten, schlanken und sehr weiblichen Körper sprach (5177–79). In der Nachfolge von einigen französischen Dichtern[41] erwähnt also Wolfram als erster und sehr zweckmäßig die kleine Hüfte der Jeschute so wie die Taille der unbefangenen Antikonie, die zwischen Hüfte und Brust schmaler ist als ein Hase am Spieß (409,26–29), Merkmale, die sich die Märendichter und Konrad von Würzburg für Helena nicht entgehen ließen.[42]

Im Anschluß daran geht Wolfram zur Beschreibung dessen, was die *Poetriae* den Körper nannten, über, und erwähnt die langen Arme und die weißen Hände der Jeschute (130,25). Die französischen Autoren führen die Arme selten an.[43] Außer Veldeke, der die Arme nennt, um das Porträt der männerscheuen Kamille zu vervollständigen, ohne Risiko mißverstanden zu werden (5175), nennen sie die deutschen

Rheinische Beiträge und Hülfsbücher zur germanischen Philologie und Volkskunde, 9 (Bonn, 1926), V. 917–19.

[37] Isolde ist groß, schlank, wohlgerundet und wohlgebildet in jeder Hinsicht, V. 10894.
[38] *Le Roman de Troie par Benoît de Sainte-Maure*, hg. von Léopold Constans, 6 Bde. (Paris, 1904–12), V. 5545, Polyxena: groß, schlank und gerade.
[39] *Yvain* (wie Anm. 17), V. 229: groß, schlank und gerade.
[40] *Roman de Troie* (wie Anm. 38), V. 5557–61: Schultern, Brüste, Arme und Hände.
[41] *Philomena* (wie Anm. 8), V. 164: Philomena; *Athis et Prophilias* (wie Anm. 35), V. 2635–37: Gaïte; *Floire et Blancheflor* (wie Anm. 31), V. 2907: Blancheflor; *Le Jeu de la Feuillée* (wie Anm. 35), V. 147: Maroie. Siehe auch Colby (wie Anm. 6), S. 60–61.
[42] *Gesammtabenteuer: Hundert altdeutsche Erzählungen*, hg. von Friedrich Heinrich von der Hagen, 3 Bde. (Stuttgart/Tübingen, 1850): LVIII, *Das Rädlein*, V. 63; XIII, *Frauentreue*, V. 87–88. Konrad von Würzburg, *Der trojanische Krieg*, hg. von Adelbert von Keller, StLV, 44 (Stuttgart, 1858), V. 20000–01, 20009: eine feine und wohlgeformte Taille und schmale Hüften.
[43] *Roman de Troie* (wie Anm. 38), V. 5561: Polyxena; *Partonopeus de Blois*, hg. von G.A. Crapelet, 2 Bde. (Paris, 1834), V. 7467: Mélior; *Les Romans de Chrétien de Troyes, II: Cligés*, hg. von Alexandre Micha, CFMA, 84 (Paris, 1957), V. 2696: Fénice. Siehe Colby (wie Anm. 6), S. 57.

Bearbeiter sehr zielgerichtet: Herbort vermeidet es, für die keusche Polyxena den von Benoît erwähnten Zug beizubehalten, aber er benutzt ihn in einer sehr typischen Weise, um die weißen Arme der Helena zu beschreiben (2495). Auch bewundert Marke die schönen Arme Isoldes sowohl in der Minnegrotte (17599–603) als auch im Obstgarten (18196, 18204). Nackte Arme gehörten also bei den deutschen Dichtern zu den Reizen der Schönen und drückten das aufreizende Gebaren von wenig zurückhaltenden Frauen aus, wie das sehr anschaulich die Porträts der Amurfina in der *Crône*, der Helena bei Konrad und die derbsten Mären aus dem 13. und 14. Jahrhundert zeigen.[44] Die Erwähnung der Hände unterliegt dem selben Prinzip. Außer der lateinischen Tradition[45] kommen sie viel seltener vor als die Arme[46] und werden genauso wenig von den deutschen Bearbeitern übernommen. Wie Hartmann hegten sie ein sichtbares Mißtrauen gegenüber müßigen Händen und beschrieben nur tätige Hände, was dem damals herrschenden teleologischen Prinzip entsprach, wonach Gliedmaßen Funktionen haben, die ihnen der Körper zuschreibt. Isolde hält so im *Tristan* ihren Mantel mit Hand und Finger elegant zu (10935–44), und bei Wolfram schneidet Cunneware mit ihrer weißen und zarten Hand dem Bruder seine Speise (279,13). Außer Veldeke in bezug auf Kamille findet man sonst erst bei Wolfram und Gottfried solche Merkmale, aber immer in heiklen Situationen, wie etwa wiederum die von Marke bewunderten Hände Isoldes in der Minnegrotte (17599–603) und im Obstgarten (18204), Elemente, die die Schwankmären später wiederaufnehmen, wobei die deutschen im Detail am genauesten sind und klar zeigen, daß weiße und lange Hände Gegenstand der Begierde waren.[47]

Wolfram war sicher glücklich, bei der zweiten Begegnung mit Parzival die doch schon sehr realistische Beschreibung der Jeschute ergänzen zu können. Um den ärmlichen Zustand des jungen Mädchens zu betonen, erwähnte Chrétien die schönen Brüste, die unter den Fetzen, die die Schöne trug, hervorschauten, und ihre von Hitze, Wind und Frost aufgerissene Haut (3722–29). Etwas ungeschickt übernimmt Wolfram

---

[44] *Gesammtabenteuer* (wie Anm. 42): XX, *Der Gürtel*, V. 54–55; XL, *Die Meierin mit der Geiß*, V. 23; XXIV, *Der schwangere Mönch*, V. 128. J.M. Pastré, 'Quelques portraits de femme dans les fabliaux allemands du moyen âge', in *Le Portrait en littérature*, hg. von J. Bailbé (Rouen, 1987), S. 53–61. *Diu Crône* (wie Anm. 27), V. 8203: Amurfina. *Trojanerkrieg* (wie Anm. 42), V. 19994–97: Helena.

[45] *Architrenius* (wie Anm. 29), II.45–46 (S. 145); Sidonius (wie Anm. 29).

[46] *Athis et Prophilias* (wie Anm. 35), V. 2631: Gaïte; *Floire et Blancheflor* (wie Anm. 31), V. 2909–10: Blancheflor; *Roman de Troie* (wie Anm. 38) V. 5561: Polyxena; *Philomena* (wie Anm. 8), V. 163: Philomena; *Jeu de la Feuillée* (wie Anm. 35), V. 132–33: Maroie. Siehe Colby (wie Anm. 6), S. 57–58.

[47] *Gesammtabenteuer* (wie Anm. 42): XX, *Der Gürtel*, V. 54–55; XXIV, *Der schwangere Mönch*, V. 128; *Neues Gesamtabenteuer*, hg. von Heinrich Niewöhner (Berlin, 1937): 19, *Der Wirt*, V. 182–183; 23, *Die Meierin mit der Geiß*, V. 24–25.

aus *Erec* die schwanenweiße Haut, die durch die Kleiderfetzen hindurch sichtbar ist, so wie ihre runden, schimmernd weißen und hohen Brüste, die wie gedrechselt aussehen (257,8–13; 258,25–29). Die in dieser Hinsicht wiederum sehr zurückhaltenden deutschen Dichter sprachen sonst kaum davon. Herbort nahm die Erwähnung weder von Polyxenas (5559–60) noch von Helenas (5135–36) Brüsten wieder auf, obgleich dies einer der seltenen von Benoît genannten Züge war. Wie gesagt, hütet sich Hartmann wohlweislich, die Brüste zu erwähnen, die sich Laudine bei Chrétien zerkratzt. Die französischen und lateinischen Autoren beschreiben diesen Körperteil zwar oft,[48] doch hieß das für die meisten deutschen Dichter, in ein allzu naturalistisches Porträt zu verfallen. Von Wolfram wurde das aber nicht sehr geschickt gehandhabt, da jene glänzend helle Haut Jeschutes den Umständen widerspricht, die er doch von Chrétien übernimmt. Indem er seiner Vorlage anschauliche Merkmale hinzufügt, legt er nämlich ein unzeitgemäßes Vergnügen an den Tag, die physischen Reize einer erniedrigten Unschuldigen zu beschreiben, ein Schauspiel, das aber bei Chrétien kein anderes Ziel hatte, als beim Publikum Mitleid zu erwecken.

Interessant an diesen Porträts ist außerdem, was sie in bezug auf die deutsche und französische Ästhetik aussagen.

In der Nachfolge der lateinischen Tradition bemühten sich schon ab der zweiten Hälfte des 12. Jahrhunderts die französischen Dichter, das vollständigste Porträt von ihren Figuren zu zeichnen, und dies aus zwei Gründen. Es ging zunächst darum, die objektive Gegebenheit der Natur, die das Schöne darstellt, wiederzugeben, das heißt minutiös die von der logischen Klarheit der *descriptio* aufgedrängten Details aufzuführen und die der Kürze anhaftende Unklarheit zu vermeiden. Diese neue Länge der Porträts erschien deshalb nicht als mißglückt, sondern als Folge der Präzision, die selber ein Attribut der intellektuellen Klarheit war.[49] Genau wie bei der gotischen Baukunst wollte diese Ästhetik, daß auch im Kunstwerk alles zu sehen ist; in der Dichtkunst bedeutet dies eine diskursive Kenntnis, eine präzise und methodische Detailanalyse, eine mühsame Wiederherstellung nach rationalen, zu Prinzipien der Kunst erhobenen Verfahren.[50] Es ging darum, besonders für das Porträt, die ästhetischen Werte hervorzuheben, die der beschriebene Gegenstand besitzen mußte, um die

---

[48] Alwin Schultz, *Das höfische Leben zur Zeit der Minnesinger*, 2 Bde. (Leipzig, 1889), I, 217; *Architrenius* (wie Anm. 29), II.17–21 (S. 144); Galfred von Vinsauf, *Poetria nova*, V. 591–92, in Faral (wie Anm. 1), S. 215; *Roman de Troie* (wie Anm. 38), V. 5559–60: Polyxena; *Philomena* (wie Anm. 8), V. 159–60: Philomena; *Cligés* (wie Anm. 43), V. 834–37: Soredamors. Siehe Colby (wie Anm. 6), S. 59.

[49] E. de Bruyne (wie Anm. 4), II, 48–49. R. Assunto, *Die Theorie des Schönen im Mittelalter* (Köln, 1963), S. 99.

[50] Alanus von Lille, Richard von Sankt Victor, siehe Assunto (wie Anm. 49), S. 39, 95, 159.

Gefühle zu erwecken, die die Rede hervorrufen will. Für das Porträt von fiktiven Figuren hatte nach dieser Auffassung das Bild dem universellen Schönheitsideal zu gleichen: Es handelte sich nicht um das Porträt einer Schönheit, sondern der Schönheit überhaupt, wobei die beschriebene Person notwendigerweise den von ihr vertretenen spezifischen Typ darstellen mußte.

Im Gegensatz zu den französischen Autoren bedienten sich die deutschen Dichter erst spät dieser neuen Art und Weise der Personendarstellung, genauso spät wie sich die Gotik in der Baukunst in Deutschland durchsetzte. Die Kapetinger-Monarchie, die zur Rivalin des Heiligen Römischen Reiches zu werden und das politische und geistige Erbe Karls des Großen für sich zu beanspruchen begann, hatte in Abt Suger seinen Ideologen gefunden. Aus diesem Grunde verbreiteten sich jedoch die neuen ästhetischen Ideen nur langsam außerhalb Frankreichs. Am längsten hielt das kaiserliche Deutschland an der romanischen Auffassung fest, deren erste Blüte mit der Epoche zusammengefallen war, in der sich das Heilige Römische Reich seiner größten Machtentfaltung erfreute. Erst nach Beginn des 13. Jahrhunderts entstanden in Deutschland die ersten gotischen Bauten.[51] Die deutschen Dichter beschränkten sich auch lange auf die Darstellung dessen, was notwendig war und legten die Porträts auf Expressivität an, die auf einem funktionellen Schematismus und auf der instrumentalen Funktion des Porträts beruhte. Wenn dabei ein Merkmal genügte, um darauf aufmerksam zu machen, worum es sich handelte, erfüllte es seinen Zweck. Das gerade war die Grundlage der karolingischen Kunst, wo der Künstler aus dem Kodex der herkömmlichen Merkmale schöpfte und wo jede Gestalt sowohl in der Malerei als auch in der Literatur ihr festgelegtes Schema hatte. Die Porträts waren nicht nach der Natur, sondern nach dem traditionellen Kodex gemalt; so *sieht* man nicht, ob sie ihrem Modell ähneln, man *weiß* dagegen, *wen* sie darstellen, und das genügt.[52] Ähnlich verhält es sich mit dem literarischen Porträt fiktiver Personen: Man weiß, *was* sie darstellen, und das genügt: Die strahlende Schönheit der keuschen Jugend für Enite, die rührende Schönheit einer trauernden Witwe für Laudine, die sanfte und liebenswürdige Schönheit für Condwiramurs und die herausfordernde Schönheit für Jeschute und Antikonie. Während die französischen Porträts von einem ästhetischen Optimismus zeugten, wenn sie die Reize von an sich vollkommen keuschen Schönheiten beschrieben, blieb die deutsche Tradition der Vorsicht eines Cassiodor verhaftet, für den das Porträt das christliche

---

[51] Assunto (wie Anm. 49), S. 90–93.
[52] E. de Bruyne (wie Anm. 4), I, 284. J.M. Pastré, 'Pouvoir et culture: le portrait de Barberousse', im Druck in *Cours princières et châteaux: pouvoir et culture du XIe au XIIIe siècle en France du Nord, Angleterre et Allemagne.*

Ideal ausdrücken sollte, ein christliches Leben, das sich in der Zurückhaltung des ganzen Körpers äußern und anders aussehen mußte als das, was die Heiden bewunderten.[53] Auch für Boethius trat für den menschlichen Körper die Schönheit an dritter Stelle auf, nämlich nach der Gesundheit und der Kraft, wobei ihm die Schönheit der Lebewesen allzu vergänglich und eitel vorkam.[54] Diese Aussage zeugt von dem Mißtrauen gegenüber der körperlichen Schönheit, besonders der weiblichen Schönheit, die ein Bernard von Clairvaux in seiner Unterscheidung von drei ästhetischen Menschentypen hegte. Außer dem 'in recto corpore recta anima', das das klassische Ideal neuplatonisch christianisiert, gibt es das 'in recto corpore curva anima' und das 'in curvo corpore recta anima'. So etwa ordnete Hartmann der positiven Häßlichkeit des durch die Entbehrungen geheiligten Gregorius die Schönheit der noch in seiner Sünde verhafteten Gestalt zu, und nicht zufällig ist dieses doppelte Porträt des Gregorius gleichzeitig das Porträt eines Mannes und das erste ausführliche Porträt der deutschen mittelalterlichen Literatur. Nimmt man ein paar seltene Fälle aus,[55] so ist das detaillierte Porträt der weiblichen Hauptpersonen in den deutschen Epen das Symbol für die Sinnlichkeit und die Verführung, wobei klar hervortritt, wie die damalige deutsche Ästhetik sich von der französischen unterscheidet und wie sehr sich Hartmann und Wolfram von Chrétien abheben, obschon beide gerade dessen Werke bearbeiteten.

[53] E. de Bruyne (wie Anm. 4), I, 73.
[54] E. de Bruyne (wie Anm. 4), I, 5–6.
[55] Blancheflur bei Konrad Fleck und Dulciflor im *Wigamur*.

Guillaume d'Angleterre, Gute Frau, Wilhelm von Wenden:
Zur Beschäftigung mit dem Eustachius-Thema in Frankreich und Deutschland

VOLKER HONEMANN

Karl Stackmann zum Ende des WS 1989/90

Daß der *Guillaume d'Angleterre* ein Werk des Chrétien de Troyes ist, davon hat sich die Romanistik bis auf den heutigen Tag geradezu halsstarrig nicht überzeugen können, obwohl die Argumente für Chrétien bei weitem überwiegen. Den Untersuchungen Foersters und seines Schülers Müller, die den Stil des *Guillaume* mit dem der Chrétien sicher zugewiesenen Werke verglichen,[1] sowie der Analyse Wilmottes[2] haben die Gegner der Zuschreibung an Chrétien wenig entgegenzusetzen vermocht.[3]

Ich nehme den *Guillaume d'Angleterre* also als Werk des 'Crestiiens' (de Troyes), der sich im Prolog zweimal nennt (1 und 18) und stelle ihn ein in eine literarische Reihe thematisch verwandter Texte des 8. (?) bis späten 13. Jahrhunderts, bestehend aus der lateinischen *Eustachius-legende*, dem *Guillaume* (kurz vor 1170?), der *Guten Frau* eines unbekannten alemannischen Autors (wohl um 1235) und dem *Wilhelm von*

---

[1] Wendelin Foerster, *Kristian von Troyes: Wörterbuch zu seinen sämtlichen Werken*, Romanische Bibliothek, 21 (Halle/S., 1914), S. 29*–33*, 69*f. (mit Verweis auf eigene frühere Arbeiten); Rudolf Müller, *Untersuchung über den Verfasser der altfranzösischen Dichtung Wilhelm von England*, (Dissertation, Bonn, 1891).

[2] Chrétien de Troyes, *Guillaume d'Angleterre*, hg. von Maurice Wilmotte, CFMA, 55 (Paris, 1927), S. X (mit Verweis auf eigene Studien).

[3] Daß der *Guillaume* nicht in der Werkliste des *Cligés*-Prologes erscheint, besagt nicht viel, da hier auch andere Werke Chrétiens fehlen. Der 'Streit um die Verfasserschaft dauert an', konstatiert Beate Schmolke-Hasselmann, 'Chrétien de Troyes', in *Lexikon des Mittelalters*, Bd. II, 1983, Sp. 1897–1904, hier 1898f. Fast jede der neueren Arbeiten über den *Guillaume* beginnt mit einer Diskussion des Problems der Verfasserschaft, vgl. Emanuel J. Mickel, 'Theme and Narrative Structure in *Guillaume d'Angleterre*', in *The Sower and his Seed: Essays on Chrétien de Troyes*, hg. von Rupert T. Pickens, French Forum Monographs, 44 (Lexington, Kentucky, 1983), S. 52–65, hier S. 52f. mit Anm. 1, wo Mickel zurecht notiert: 'It is curious that the prevalent opinion is against the text's authenticity, even though nearly all the evidence points to the contrary conclusion.' Siehe weiterhin Sara Sturm-

311

Wenden des Ulrich von Etzenbach (um 1289/90).[4] Diese Texte sollen im folgenden in einigen Punkten miteinander verglichen werden. Dabei ist unwichtig, ob sie tatsächlich miteinander 'verwandt' sind im Sinne der vergleichenden Erzählforschung des 19. und frühen 20. Jahrhunderts – darüber hat sich schon 1904 Gordon Hall Gerould in seiner umfangreichen Studie *Forerunners, Congeners and Derivatives of the Eustace Legend*[5] ausgesprochen, mit allen Meriten und Schwächen dieser Forschungsrichtung, die den Ursprung der Erzählung von Eustachius und seiner Frau denn auch in diesem Falle im fernen Orient aufspürte.

Was hier interessiert, ist etwas anderes. Die vier soeben genannten Texte teilen miteinander die grundsätzliche Thematik, die ich im Anschluß an Käthe Leonhardt folgendermaßen formuliere: Ein in glücklichen Verhältnissen lebendes Ehepaar höheren Standes verläßt aus religiösen Gründen heimlich seine Heimat. Die Familienmitglieder werden getrennt, Vater, Mutter und die beiden Kinder erleiden separate Schicksale. Später wird die Familie wieder vereint.[6] Dieses Thema ist früh in der *Eustachiuslegende* formuliert, die im Hoch- und Spätmittelalter in einer Fülle von Ausprägungen, sowohl lateinisch wie in den Volkssprachen, verbreitet war.[7] Das in ihr verarbeitete Erzählmaterial

Maddox, 'Si m'est jugiee et destinee: On *Guillaume d'Angleterre*', ebd. S. 66–80, hier S. 66 und Anm. 1, 2, 12, 15.

[4] Folgende Ausgaben werden verwendet: *Eustachiuslegende* (E): Acta Sanctorum [. . .] Septembris tomus sextus (Paris/Rom, 1867), S. 123–37 (griech. und lat. Text. Der Held heißt hier, wie in der griechischen Fassung, stets Eusthatius.); *Guillaume d'Angleterre* (*GdA*): Wie die neuere Forschung zu diesem Text (s. o. Anm. 3) benütze ich die Ausgabe von Wilmotte (oben Anm. 2); *Gute Frau* (*GF*): 'Die Gute Frau', hg. von Emil Sommer, *ZfdA*, 2 (1842), 385–481, mit Korrekturen: *ZfdA*, 4 (1844), 399f. (Sehr zu bedauern ist, daß die weit bessere Edition von Denis Mackinder-Savage: *'Die Gute Frau': A Textual and Literary Investigation*, 2 Bde., (Dissertation, Auckland, 1978) bisher nur als Mikrofilm verfügbar ist.); Ulrich von Etzenbach, *Wilhelm von Wenden* (*WvW*), hg. von Hans-Friedrich Rosenfeld, DTM, 40 (Berlin, 1957).

[5] *PMLA*, 19 (1904), 335–448, hier S. 354–70.

[6] Käthe Leonhardt, *Quellengeschichtliche Untersuchungen zum Wilhelm von Wenden des Ulrich von Etzenbach*, (Dissertation, Jena, 1931), S. 16. – Vergleicht man die Legende mit den drei volkssprachlichen Texten, so fällt auf, daß alle von der Legende in zwei Punkten abweichen: Die Kinder sind Zwillinge, und sie werden erst *nach* dem Aufbruch in die Fremde, unter elenden Umständen, geboren, nachdem die Mutter ihrem Ehemann hochschwanger gegen dessen Willen gefolgt ist. Woher diese Abweichung rührt und was mit ihr, abgesehen von einer Intensivierung des Leidens in der Fremde, bezweckt wird, ist unklar. Für den weiteren Verlauf hat diese Abweichung nur wenig Gewicht.

[7] Zum Hl. Eustachius (Fest: 20.9.) und seiner Legende siehe allgemein: Odilo Engels, 'Eustachius', in *Lexikon für Theologie und Kirche*, 2. Aufl., Bd. III, Sp. 1201; F. Werner, 'Eusthatius/Eustachius', in *Lexikon der christlichen Ikonographie*, Bd. VI (1974), 194–99 sowie Angelo Monteverdi, 'La legenda di S. Eustachio', *Studi Medievali*, 3 (1909), 169–229, 392–498. Die griechischen Fassungen der Legende verzeichnet: *Bibliotheca hagiographica graeca I* (Brüssel, 1957), S. 201 (Nr. 641a–d – 643), die lateinischen: *Bibliotheca hagiographica latina I* (Brüssel, 1898–99), S. 414f. (Nr. 2760–2771; 2762 = *Legenda aurea*); Ergänzungen: dass., *Novum Supplementum*, hg. von H. Fros, Subsidia Hagiographica, 70 (Brüssel, 1986), S. 315f. Die 11 (?) bekannten altfranzösischen Versfassungen verzeichnet Holger Petersen in: *La Vie de Saint Eustache*, hg. von H.P., CFMA, 58 (Paris, 1928), S. XIIIf. Hinzu treten Prosafassungen, vgl. *La Vie de Saint Eustache: Version en prose française du XIIIe s.*, hg. von

war damit allgemein verfügbar. Daß die Autoren der drei genannten volkssprachigen Texte mit dem Eustachius-Thema auf die eine oder andere Weise vertraut waren, ist deshalb mehr als wahrscheinlich. Im übrigen wird man, wie etwa im Falle der Udo-Legende, auch hier 'gut daran' tun, 'die Verfügbarkeit literarischer Motive für grundsätzlich unbegrenzt zu halten'.[8]

Es soll deshalb im folgenden nicht darum gehen, die Abhängigkeit der drei Romane von der Legende oder eines Romanes vom anderen zu untersuchen, sondern darum,

(a) durch Vergleich gemeinsamer Erzählelemente mehr über die Eigenart der einzelnen Texte zu erfahren, und

(b) zu ermitteln, inwieweit die religiösen, literar- und sozialhistorischen Umstände, unter denen die drei Romane entstanden sind, sich auf die Gestaltung einzelner Motive wie der Werke insgesamt ausgewirkt haben.

Bevor ich in den Vergleich eintrete, ist noch eine Bemerkung zur *Eustachiuslegende* nötig. Sie unterscheidet sich von unzähligen anderen Legenden nicht nur durch ihre ungeheure Beliebtheit – die Zahl der erhaltenen Versionen wird von kaum einer anderen Legende übertroffen. Sie ragt aus der Masse des Legenden-Erzählgutes auch hervor durch die vielen Motive, die der Verfasser der Legende dem spätantiken Reise- und Abenteuerroman, vor allem dem *Apollonius von Tyrus*, entnommen hat,[9] und dadurch, daß der Autor der Legende die

Jessie Murray, CFMA, 60 (Paris, 1929). Das Alter der französischsprachigen Fassungen ist nicht befriedigend geklärt. – Auch die mittelhochdeutsche Überlieferung ist außerordentlich reich. Die Eustachiuslegende fehlt in keiner der großen Legendensammlungen des deutschen Mittelalters, vgl. Werner Williams-Krapp, *Die deutschen und niederländischen Legendare des Mittelalters*, Texte und Textgeschichte, 20 (Tübingen, 1986), S. 409f. Zusätzlich sei auf die verlorene Eustachiuslegende des Rudolf von Ems (ca. 1225–30, vgl. *Alexander*, V. 3287–89) und auf den Text im *Spegel der Conscientien*, Druck Lübeck 1487, Bl. tIV^v–tVI^v hingewiesen. Hinsichtlich der uns interessierenden Fragen bestehen zwischen den wichtigsten lateinischen Texten, der *Vita et Passio Sancti Eustathii* (*BHL*, I, 2760) der Acta Sanctorum, der identisch ist mit dem Text des Boninus Mombritius, *Sanctuarium* (Paris, 2. Aufl., 1910), S. 466–73 (ohne die dort in [. . .] gesetzten Ausschmückungen), der kürzeren *Passio* (*BHL*, I, 2761, Ausgabe: *Bibliotheca Casinensis III*, (Monte Cassino, 1877), *Florilegium Casinense* S. 351–54) und der Version der *Legenda Aurea* keine wesentlichen Unterschiede. Ich lege daher die früheste lateinische Fassung, die der Acta Sanctorum, zugrunde. Untersuchungen über deren Verbreitung scheinen zu fehlen. Ein Vergleich der beiden lateinischen Fassungen (*BHL*, I, 2760 und 2761) mit der altfranzösischen *Estoire d'Eustachius* (auch: *Le Roman de Placidas*) bei Andreas C. Ott, 'Das altfranzösische Eustachiusleben [. . .] der Pariser Hs. Nationalbibliothek fr. 1374', *Romanische Forschungen*, 32 (1913), 481–607, hier S. 486–90.

[8] Fidel Rädle, 'De Udone quoddam horribile. Zur Herkunft eines mittelalterlichen Erzählstoffes', in *Tradition und Wertung: Festschrift für Franz Brunhölzl zum 65. Geburtstag*, hg. von Günter Bernt, Fidel Rädle und Gabriel Silagi (Sigmaringen, 1989), S. 281–93, hier S. 293.

[9] Vgl. dazu *Lexikon des Mittelalters*, Bd. I (1980), Sp. 771–74. Mit dem Apollonius hat die Legende vor allem das Motiv der Trennung und Wiedervereinigung der Familie sowie das

komplizierte Abfolge der Ereignisse erzählerisch sehr differenziert umgesetzt hat. Die *Eustachiuslegende* läßt sich deshalb, zumindest in der Fassung der *Vita et Passio* als 'Legendenroman' bezeichnen. Der Text ist sehr umfangreich (elf Folio-Spalten in der Edition der Acta Sanctorum), und er ist ungewöhnlich komplex. Neben dem Leben des Heiligen ist noch das seiner Frau und das seiner Kinder zu verfolgen. Bedingt durch die Trennung des Ehepaares voneinander und von den Kindern ergibt sich die Notwendigkeit dreisträngigen, mehrfach den Schauplatz wechselnden Erzählens, dazu die eines reichen Nebenpersonals. Der Autor der *Vita et Passio* hat außerdem die Beziehung der Protagonisten zu Christus stark betont (direkte Reden!), und er läßt den Leser immer wieder am Gefühlsleben der Personen Anteil haben.

Mit Blick auf die drei Romane ist ein weiteres zu beachten: Eustachius und seine Frau Theopista sind noch Heiden und tragen als solche auch 'heidnische' Namen (Placidas bzw. Trajana).[10] Sie sind aber, dies macht die Legende mit Nachdruck deutlich, in allen Tugenden derart ausgezeichnet, daß ihnen zum Christentum nur noch die Taufe fehlt. Von Placidas heißt es gleich eingangs: 'Operibus vero justitiae et cunctis virtutibus erat praeditus et meritus. Subveniebat oppressis, patrocinabatur gravatis judicio, plures etiam a judicibus injuste damnatos suis opibus relevabat, nudos vestiebat, esurientes satiabat.' (*E* 123F).[11] Seine Frau lebt wie er 'sub daemonum cultura [. . .], sed similem moribus Mariti' (*E* 123F bzw. 124A). Der Schritt hin zum Christentum ist damit für beide nur klein. Ungeachtet dessen aber muß Eustachius – und mit ihm seine Frau – um des neugewonnenen Christenglaubens willen leiden. Nachdem der Erzähler der Legende schon eingangs bemerkt hatte, Gott wolle den Placidas aus der Finsternis des Götzendienstes retten (*E* 124A), erklärt Christus dem Helden bei ihrer ersten Begegnung: 'Oportet [. . .] te humiliari' (*E* 126A und B, zwei Stellen), wofür eine eigentliche Begründung nicht gegeben wird. Christus erläutert sein Vorhaben lediglich dahingehend, daß Placidas/Eustachius, 'exaltatus [. . .] usque modo negotiis hujus seculi et temporalibus opibus' (*E* 126B), erniedrigt werden müsse 'de alta tua vanitate' und geprüft werden

---

– sehr gängige (Crescentia!) – der bewahrten Unschuld gemein. Aber auch Einzelzüge, wie z. B. die zur Wiedererkennung nötige Narbe, fehlen nicht. Zur Bedeutung des antiken Romans für die Legende im allgemeinen siehe Max Wehrli, 'Roman und Legende im deutschen Hochmittelalter', in *Worte und Werte: Bruno Markwardt zum 60. Geburtstag* (Berlin, 1961), S. 428–43, hier S. 432ff.

10 Der heidnische Name der Ehefrau wird in den meisten Versionen (so z. B. auch in der *Legenda Aurea*) nicht angegeben, vgl. Acta Sanctorum (wie Anm. 4), S. 125 mit Fußnote y (S. 129). Es überrascht, daß die (sprechenden) Namen nicht ausgelegt werden, auch nicht in der an Etymologien reichen *Legenda Aurea*.

11 Placidas übt also unwissentlich bereits die christlichen Werke der Barmherzigkeit.

solle, damit es Gott möglich sei, ihn 'rursus exaltari in spiritualibus divitiis', ja ihn wiederum 'in propriam gloriam' einzusetzen (ebd.). Dieses Versprechen wiederholt Christus und präzisiert es, als die Boten des römischen Kaisers nach Eustachius suchen: 'Confide, Eustathi, in praesenti enim tempore remeabis ad tuum priorem statum, et accipies Uxorem tuam et Filios. In resurrectione vero majora horum videbis, et aeternorum bonorum delectationem reperies, et nomen tuum magnificabitur in generationem et generationem' (E 130C–131D). Eustachius kann so von vornherein des glücklichen Ausgangs für sich und seine Familie in dieser Welt sicher sein. Daß Christi Versprechen bald darauf eingelöst wird – Eustachius wird wieder 'magister militum' (E 132A) und findet Frau und Kinder wieder (E 133E–F) – braucht deshalb kaum erwähnt zu werden. Das der Vereinigung bald folgende Martyrium der Familie ist angesichts dieser Konstruktion des Legendengeschehens geradezu akzidentiell. Bekehrung zum christlichen Glauben und Prüfung durch Leiden um des Glaubens willen sind damit in der Legende nicht miteinander verknüpft, sondern nur nebeneinander gestellt. Eine rein christliche, auf das Element der Bekehrung verzichtende Inszenierung des Themas war damit leicht möglich.

Eine solche bietet nun Chrétien, indem er Anfang und Schluß der Erzählung anders faßt. Bei ihm ist es ein vorbildlich lebendes christliches Ehepaar königlichen Standes (damit sozial gegenüber der Legende angehoben), das ins Elend aufbricht.

Während aber Eustachius vom Herrn geprüft und am Ende wieder in seine vorherige Stellung eingesetzt wird wie Job (dieser Vergleich wird zweimal angestellt, E 126B und 128A), bietet Chrétien eine ganz andere Motivierung für den Weg ins 'essil' (GdA 83). Zwar fordert auch hier Gott den Helden zum Verlassen der Heimat auf – er tut dies dreifach durch den Mund eines Himmelsboten (GdA 83, 116, 204) –, aber er gibt keinen Hinweis darauf, warum er dies fordert. Jedenfalls vermögen der vom Kaplan angeregte Verzicht Guillaumes auf Besitz, der ihm nicht rechtmäßig gehört (GdA 96f.) und die Verteilung des Privateigentums an die Armen (GdA 147ff.) die göttliche Stimme nicht zu besänftigen. Bei ihrem dritten Erscheinen wiederholt sie den 'Willen Gottes, daß du in die Fremde gehst' (GdA 207) und erklärt, Gott sei 'schwer ergrimmt und beleidigt, daß du so lange zögerst' (GdA 208f.). Guillaume und seine Frau Gratiiene 'müssen' letztlich deshalb in die Fremde, weil dies Gottes Wille ist – und der ist unerforschlich. Eine Deutung des göttlichen Handelns, wie sie dem Eustachius zuteil wird, fehlt. Guillaumes eigene Interpretation des Geschehens als Folge seiner 'covoitise' (GdA 886–924) ist unzureichend – schließlich hat er ja seinen Besitz weggegeben –, auch wenn Kritik an der Besitzgier, vor allem im Kontext der breit ausgestalteten Kaufmanns-Thematik, ein wesentliches, durch die sozioökonomischen Veränderungen des 12. Jahrhunderts beeinflußtes Thema des *Guillaume d'Angleterre* ist.[12]

Unerforschlich bleibt auch Gottes Wirken am Ende des Werkes. Guillaume und Gratiiene werden miteinander vereint, Guillaumes Neffe verzichtet, wie er schon früher angekündigt hatte (*GdA* 2222-26) auf die Herrschaft über England und übergibt sie Guillaume, der mit den Seinen zur großen Freude der Bevölkerung in London einzieht (ganz wie Eustachius als Triumphator in Rom, *E* 134A) und wiederum als König herrscht. Im Nachhinein läßt sich auch hier das Geschehen als göttliche Prüfung begreifen – aber Chrétien verliert darüber kein Wort. Während so die Legende einen geradezu 'rationalen', dem Menschen die Gründe für sein Wirken erläuternden Gott präsentiert, ist es bei Chrétien ein unerforschlicher, in seiner 'Kommunikationsfähigkeit' auf das Erteilen von Befehlen reduzierter Gott, der auch auf Verzweiflungsausbrüche des Menschen nicht reagiert und ihn über sein und seiner Familie Schicksal in dieser Welt völlig im Unklaren läßt.

In stark veränderter Gestalt erscheint bei Chrétien das Motiv, das in der Legende dem heidnischen Ritter Placidas den Einbruch des Christengottes in seine Existenz signalisiert, das des wunderbaren Hirsches. Signum seiner Rolle als Bote Gottes ist das Kreuz zwischen den Stangen seines Geweihs mit dem Bild des Gekreuzigten, das dann zu Placidas spricht.[13] Die Legende läßt den Hirsch, nachdem er Placidas in die Einöde entführt hat (*E* 124B–C), noch ein zweites Mal, nach der Taufe des Eustachius, auftreten (*E* 126A); Christus sagt nun dem Ritter seine Zukunft voraus. Bei Chrétien ist der Hirsch der Attribute des Wunderbaren fast restlos entkleidet. Er erscheint im *Guillaume* nicht weniger als dreimal, zuerst als merkwürdig zahmes, den Pfeil von Guillaumes Sohn Marin ruhig erwartendes und dann, tödlich getroffen, einen Schrei ausstoßendes Jagdtier (*GdA* 1744-55). Seine Tötung bringt die Söhne zwar zunächst selbst dem Tode nahe, führt sie dann aber an

---

[12] Siehe dazu Guillaumes Selbstanklage, als der Adler ihm die Börse entwendet hat (*GdA* 886–924: 'Covoitise' als 'rachine de tos maus' (896), der ihr Verfallene gleicht Tantalus).– Schmolke-Hasselmann (wie Anm. 3), Sp. 1899 sieht im 'Verhältnis von Habgier und Verzicht' gar die 'zentrale Thematik' des Werkes. Ähnlicher Meinung ist Sturm-Maddox (wie Anm. 3), die aber auch erwägt, ob nicht die himmlische Stimme und die Aufforderung, das Land zu verlassen, damit zusammenhängt, daß Guillaume seiner hochschwangeren Frau den Besuch des Morgengottesdienstes untersagt hatte (S. 70f.). Für Mickel (wie Anm. 3) besteht die Verfehlung des Königspaares darin, daß es sein Schicksal in die eigene Hand nehmen will – was dem Text nicht zu entnehmen ist. Die sozialhistorische Interpretation von Katharina Holzermayr, 'La Métamorphose du Roi Guillaume', *Médiévales*, Centre de Recherche, Université Paris, 4 (1983), 91–101 geht aus von der These, daß 'chevalerie' Chaos bedeute und Guillaume bürgerlich-kaufmännische Ordnung lernen müsse. In der Habgier sieht auch sie ein wesentliches Moment (S. 94). – Festzuhalten ist, daß der Erzähler keine Deutung anbietet. Guillaume erhält von Gott keine Auskunft darüber, warum er ins 'essil' muß.

[13] Zum Hirschmotiv vgl. Hippolyte Delehaye, 'La légende de saint Eustache', *Académie Royale Belgique. Bulletin de la Classe des Lettres*, No. 4 (1919), 175–210, hier 203–07.

den Hof des Königs von Catanasse (*GdA* 1883ff.), wo sie später als Ritter
– unwissentlich – gegen ihre Mutter kämpfen. Ein zweites Mal erscheint
das Hirsch-Motiv, als der Kaufmann Gui (= Guillaume) im Hafen der
Landesherrin, seiner Frau, gestrandet und von ihr zum Mahle geladen,
am Feuer eindämmernd von einer Hirschjagd als einem früher oft
geübten Vergnügen träumt (*GdA* 2565–74). Gratiiene macht am näch-
sten Tag den Traum wahr. Gui/Guillaume darf zur Jagd gehen, verfolgt
einen Hirsch über den die Landesgrenze bildenden Fluß und gerät so in
eine Konfrontation mit zwei Rittern des Königs von Catanasse, seinen
Söhnen (*GdA* 2621ff.). Aufgrund der von ihm erzählten Geschichte
erkennen sie ihn als ihren Vater.

Chrétien nimmt so dem Hirsch bzw. dem Hirschmotiv zwar
weitgehend das Wunderbare, baut aber das Motiv des Tieres, das den
Menschen, der es verfolgt, hinführt zu einem für ihn wichtigen
Geschehnis, kräftig aus. Für das Wiederfinden der Söhne, das in der
Legende dem Zufall, also dem unausgesprochenen Willen Gottes,
überlassen war (*E* 132B: 'Contigit autem, ut [. . .]'), wird hier ein
Zeichen gesetzt, das die Verbindung zwischen den noch getrennten
Mitgliedern der Familie herstellt.[14] Chrétien führt darüber hinaus
zusätzliche Elemente des Wunderbaren in seine Geschichte ein.[15] Wohl
aus einer frühen Version des *Escoufle*[16] stammt das Motiv vom Adler, der
zuerst die Geldbörse stiehlt und Guillaume so ins tiefste Unglück stürzt,
ihm damit aber auch seine Ausrichtung auf das Irdische deutlich macht
(*GdA* 876–84). Der Adler tritt dann aber deutlich als Bote Gottes auf,
wenn er die Geldbörse im richtigen Moment und am richtigen Ort fallen
läßt, als nämlich Guillaume den ihn noch nicht erkennenden Söhnen
seine Lebensgeschichte erzählt und dabei eben an dem Punkte
angekommen ist, wo der Adler ihm die Börse stiehlt (*GdA* 2777–804)!
Der Erzähler führt das plötzliche Wiedererscheinen der Börse ausdrücklich als ein Wunder ein ('Et maintenant sont avenues/ Miracles
[. . .]', *GdA* 2805f.), über das Guillaume und seine Söhne sehr
erschrecken. Einer der Söhne erklärt darauf, Gott habe solcherart und
soeben das von Guillaume Erzählte wunderbar bestätigt.

Diese Bestätigung aber war eigentlich nicht notwendig. Guillaume
hatte bereits vor dem Erscheinen der Börse die beiden Rockschöße
erwähnt, in die er Lovel und Marin nach der Geburt gewickelt hatte
(*GdA* 479–84 bzw. 2790f.) und die den beiden von ihren Ziehvätern auch

---

14 Ähnlich schon Sturm-Maddox (wie Anm. 3), S. 73f.
15 Zur Unterscheidung Wunder-Wunderbares siehe Wehrli (wie Anm. 9), S. 430f. und
434.
16 *L'Escoufle: Roman d'Aventure*, hg. von Henri Michelant und Paul Meyer, SATF (Paris,
1894). Der räuberische Vogel tritt erst in der Mitte des Werkes auf (4543ff.); er stiehlt, wie
im *Guillaume*, eine Börse von roter Farbe (*GdA* 879f.); im *Escoufle* hält er die Börse für ein
Stück Fleisch (4548f.).

ausgehändigt worden waren (*GdA* 1484f. bzw. 1510f.). Erst *nach* dem Fall der Börse bestätigen Lovel und Marin, daß sie die Rockschöße besitzen, erkennen sich daran als Brüder und die Wahrheit des von Guillaume erzählten (*GdA* 2825 bzw. 2849). Bald darauf werden die Schöße dann als Beleg für die 'aventure' (*GdA* 2898), die den Söhnen wiederfahren ist, dem König von Catanasse vorgezeigt. Der spektakuläre Fall der Börse ist damit als Wiedererkennungszeichen eigentlich entbehrlich. Es liegt daher nahe anzunehmen, daß die Bedeutung des Zeichens hier eine andere ist: Das sichtbare Eingreifen Gottes soll dem Helden Guillaume anscheinend signalisieren, daß seine Leidenszeit nun zu Ende ist.[17]

So, wie Chrétien hier ein weiteres Tier als Träger des Wunderbaren einführt, wählt er auch sonst andere und zusätzliche Zeichen. An die Stelle der Narbe am Nacken des Eustachius, an der er von den Boten des Kaisers erkannt wird (*E* 131E, zweifache Erwähnung) und die seiner Frau als Hinweis dient (*E* 133D), setzt Chrétien den Ring, dessen Geschichte ebendann, als Gratiiene dabei ist, Gui als ihren verlorenen Ehemann Guillaume zu erkennen, vom Erzähler nachgetragen wird (*GdA* 2443–87). Hinzugefügt wird als andeutendes, zur Wiedererkennung aber nicht ausreichendes Motiv mit eigener Geschichte das Horn.[18]

Verglichen mit der *Eustachiuslegende* baut Chrétien also das Moment des Wiederfindens und -erkennens erheblich aus. An die Stelle der einfachen 'Setzungen' der Legende (vgl. *E* 132B–C) tritt eine kunstvolle Regie. Sie läßt Gott die Vereinigung der Familie auf eine Weise bewirken, die für den menschlichen Verstand weitgehend nachvollziehbar ist – was in scharfem Kontrast zur Gestaltung der Kernproblematik durch Chrétien steht, der fehlenden Erörterung des Problems, *warum* Guillaume und Gratiiene überhaupt ins 'essil' müssen.

Ähnlich wie das Thema der Wiedererkennung hat Chrétien auch ein weiteres Motiv gestaltet, das der Bewahrung der ehelichen Treue. Die Legende erklärt knapp: 'Domini vero gratia obumbravit Mulierem, ut non se illi [dem Schiffer, der sie als Lohn für die Passage behalten hatte] commisceret alienigena in omni illi tempore' (*E* 130B); bald darauf stirbt der Schiffer (ebd.). An späterer Stelle referiert der Erzähler das Faktum

---

[17] So auch Sturm-Maddox (wie Anm. 3), S. 72f. Beweisen läßt sich diese Deutung freilich nicht.

[18] Als die Hofgesellschaft das Gemach des verschwundenen Königspaares plündert, findet 'Uns petis enfes' (*GdA* 412) das Elfenbeinhorn und bewahrt es auf; später kauft es Gui teuer von diesem zurück (*GdA* 2069–103); Gratiiene sieht es bei der Besichtigung der Handelsgüter des gestrandeten Kaufmannes Gui, schaut es lange an und küßt es, legt es schließlich aber wieder zurück (*GdA* 2422–38) und nimmt an seiner Stelle den Ring. Nachdem Gratiiene in V. 2412ff. bereits vermutet hat, daß Gui ihr Mann ist, erkennen sich bald darauf beide gleichzeitig (2543–46).

der bewahrten Treue (*E* 132B), bald danach wiederholt es Theopista selbst, als sie Eustachius ihre Leidensgeschichte erzählt: 'Et testis est mihi Christus, quia nec ipse polluit me, nec alter; sed usque hodie servavit Dominus castitatem meam.' (*E* 133E). Wird hier das Eingreifen Gottes in aller Kürze, aber unmißverständlich klar gemacht, so gestaltet Chrétien dieses für mittelalterliches Empfinden und im Bereich der Ehe eines Königspaares besonders heikle Thema aus. Gleolais, der Herr des Landes, in das das Schicksal Gratiiene verschlagen hat, ist alt und hinfällig. Seinem Ansinnen, sie zur Frau zu nehmen, begegnet Gratiiene zunächst mit dem Argument des enormen Standesunter- schiedes – einem Argument von einiger Raffinesse, weil das, was Gratiiene vorbringt (sie sei die Tochter eines gemeinen Mannes), die tatsächlichen Verhältnisse auf den Kopf stellt. Schließlich gelingt es ihr, indem sie ein Gelübde vorschützt, das sie noch ein Jahr binde, eine Frist für den physischen Vollzug der Ehe zu erlangen. Gleolais kann somit die Ehe schließen und Gratiiene als Landesherrin einsetzen (*GdA* 1095– 297). Aus der stets drohenden Gefahr, die Gott und Guillaume geschuldete eheliche Treue brechen zu müssen, erlöst sie vor Ablauf der Jahresfrist der Tod des Gleolais, wie sie dem Kaufmann Gui mitteilt (*GdA* 2647-53);[19] verwitwet wird sie später – wie die Mutter des Gregorius – von einem unverheirateten Nachbarn, dem König von Catanasse, bedrängt.

Wesentlich erscheint hier, daß das Problem der Bewahrung der ehelichen Treue bei Chrétien von der Ebene der Einhaltung christlicher Gebote auf die des Gefühles einerseits und der Bewahrung von Herrschaft andererseits verlagert ist. Gleolais ist bereit, Gratiienes Wunsch zu respektieren. Sie wiederum – dies führt der Erzähler breit aus (*GdA* 1118ff.) – ist durchaus nicht abgeneigt, Herrin seines Landes zu werden. Der Zwiespalt zwischen 'Le terre veut' (*GdA* 1197) aber: 'Que de son cors li eüst faite/ carnelment nule conpagnie' (*GdA* 1194f.) bringt sie auf die Erfindung der Jahresfrist. Daß sie hier lügt, und noch dazu im Kontext eines frommen Gelübdes, scheint Chrétien nicht gestört zu haben. Die komplizierte Lösung, die er hier gewählt hat, rührt im übrigen nicht zuletzt daher, daß er die Rolle der Frau gegenüber der Legende ganz erheblich ausweitet. Sie macht, unabhängig von ihrem Mann, Karriere in der Welt – Ausdruck einer gegenüber der Legende stark veränderten, das neue Frauenbild des 12. Jahrhunderts reflektierenden Sichtweise?

In der Ausgestaltung der Rolle Gratiienes liegt jedenfalls ein zusätzli- ches Erzählziel, dem Chrétien aber noch weitere zur Seite gestellt hat, so das der – verglichen mit der Legende viel ausführlicher behandelten –

---

[19] Erst durch diesen Bericht erfahren wir vom Tod des Gleolais. Das Faktum erscheint Chrétien offenbar als so nebensächlich, daß er es erst an so später Stelle nachträgt.

Geschichte der beiden Kinder,[20] das der Kaufmanns-Problematik,[21] das – spiegelbildlich gedoppelte – sozialen Auf- und Abstiegs (Gui, der König inkognito, steigt vom niedrigsten Diener eines Kaufmanns zu dessen Teilhaber auf; Gratiiene, die Königin, heiratet einen Ritter und Landesherrn, dem sie diese Ehe als extremen sozialen Aufstieg präsentiert).

Der *Guillaume d'Angleterre* erscheint so, verglichen mit der *Eustachiuslegende*, die nur ein einziges Ziel kennt, die Demonstration des wunderbaren Wirkens Gottes in seinen Geschöpfen, durchaus vieldeutig, was auch deshalb möglich ist, weil das Werk die Legende um ein Mehrfaches an Umfang übertrifft.

Wenden wir uns nun der *Guten Frau* zu. Die Erzählung entspricht vom Umfang her ziemlich genau dem *Guillaume d'Angleterre* (3058 VV. gegenüber 3310). Aber sie muß das im *Guillaume* enthaltene Erzählmaterial auf etwa der halben Strecke bewältigen, weil sie verglichen mit diesem – und erst recht mit der *Eustachiuslegende* – andere, ebenfalls recht vielfältige Erzählziele verfolgt.[22]

Die erste Hälfte der Erzählung von der *Guten Frau* (1–1440), die im *Guillaume* keine Entsprechung hat, enthält nur éin Motiv, das in der zweiten Hälfte benötigt wird. In der Schlacht gegen den unerwünschten Brautwerber wird der Held an der Hand verwundet. Der krumme Finger, den er davon zurückbehält, kommt ihm, wie der Erzähler vorausdeutend bemerkt, später sehr zustatten (*GF* 1194): In dem Bettler, der sich beim 'jârtac/ ze sant Dênîse' (2695f.) vor die Königin von Frankreich (zu dieser Stellung hat es die Gute Frau inzwischen gebracht) drängt, erkennt diese, seines 'krumben vingers' wegen, ihren Mann (*GF* 2681–88). Der Verfasser der *Guten Frau* greift also das Wiedererkennungszeichen der *Eustachiuslegende* auf (während der Körper des *Königs* Guillaume ohne erkennbaren Makel geblieben war).

Das Thema der Wiedererkennung der Ehegatten ist damit in der *Guten Frau* in geradezu lakonischer Knappheit behandelt,[23] knapper noch als

---

[20] Hängt dies damit zusammen, daß Chrétien den *Guillaume* möglicherweise für eine Familie Lovell schrieb, deren Vorfahr dann der Lovel des Romans gewesen wäre? Der *Guillaume* wäre dann eine 'ancestral romance', was M. Dominica Legge, 'The Dedication of *Guillaume d'Angleterre*, in *Medieval Miscellany presented to Eugene Vinaver* (Manchester/ New York), 1965, S. 196–205 als sicher annimmt. Vgl. dazu auch Beate Schmolke-Hasselmann, *Der arthurische Versroman von Chrétien bis Froissart: Zur Geschichte einer Gattung*, Beihefte zur Zeitschrift für romanische Philologie, 177 (Tübingen, 1980), hier S. 186, 194f. und 200, die sich dieser Ansicht anschließt.

[21] Dazu vgl. Holzermayr (wie Anm. 12).

[22] Als Beispiel sei nur das für den ersten Teil der *Guten Frau* wesentliche Motiv des Standesunterschiedes zwischen der Heldin und ihrem Geliebten genannt.

[23] Im Gegensatz dazu wird der Frage, wie den Großen Frankreichs und dem Volke das plötzliche Auftauchen eines Ehemannes, der noch dazu sofort ihr König werden soll, große Aufmerksamkeit geschenkt (*GF* 2705–90, 2867–84, 2981–3018). Bedingt – und notwendig – ist dies durch die Ehekarriere der Guten Frau.

in der Legende, wo Theopista ihren Gemahl an den 'signa' erkennt, ihn bittet, ihr seine Lebensgeschichte zu erzählen, dies aber sofort selbst tut und darauf von Eustachius erkannt wird (*E* 133D–E). Entsprechendes gilt für die Wiedervereinigung mit den Kindern: Kaum fragt die Gute Frau nach ihnen und erzählt ihr Gemahl, wie er sie verloren hat (*GF* 2908–54), da melden sich auch schon Graf und Bischof, die die Kinder gefunden und aufgezogen haben (*GF* 2955–65).

Die zweite Hälfte des Romans setzt ein mit dem Aufbruch der Guten Frau und ihres – noch immer namenlosen – Mannes ins 'ellende' (*GF* 1477ff.). Der Autor hat ihn gegenüber der Legende wie dem *Guillaume* völlig anders begründet. Der Anblick von zwölf Armen bei einer Mühle läßt den Helden nachdenken über die unendlichen Wohltaten, die Gott ihm erwiesen hat. Seiner radikalen Feststellung: 'êre unde guot/ daz ist ein mortgalle/ zem êwigen valle' (*GF* 1532ff.) und der daraus abgeleiteten Konsequenz: 'sô suln wir êre unde ruom/ durch got vil schiere ûf geben' (*GF* 1564f.) stimmt die Gute Frau sogleich zu; die beiden verzichten auf 'bürge unde lant' (*GF* 1586) und machen sich heimlich ins 'ellende' auf. Ein äußeres Eingreifen Gottes fehlt hier. Weder erscheint ein Bote Gottes noch spricht dieser zu den Eheleuten. Offensichtlich kann der Verfasser auf derartige Manifestationen verzichten, genauso wie er auch keine Begründung der Art liefert, die beiden seien von Gott gezüchtigt worden wie Job oder sie folgten dem Rat eines Kaplans. Die Protagonisten der *Guten Frau*, unter denen hier (und fast *nur* hier) der Mann die Führung innehat,[24] handeln autonom, bedürfen deshalb auch keines geistlichen Beraters mehr. Sie sind selbst fähig, ihre ethisch-moralische Position in der Welt einzuschätzen und daraus die ihnen angemessen scheinenden Konsequenzen zu ziehen.[25] Dabei ist aber zu beachten, daß – anders als in der Legende und im *Guillaume d'Angleterre* (wo Theopista und Gratiiene wie ihre Ehemänner den göttlichen Befehl gehört hatten und gleichermaßen von ihm betroffen sind (*E* 125E und *GdA* 238–46)) – die Schicksale der Protagonisten in der *Guten Frau* nicht parallel verlaufen. Äußerer Beleg dafür ist zunächst, daß der Guten Frau eben *kein* Mühlenerlebnis zuteil wird, und weiterhin, daß sie, nach Jahren des Dienens, eine außerordentliche gesellschaftliche Karriere macht, ihr Ehemann aber bis zur Wiedervereinigung in Armut dahinvegetiert. Der Autor der *Guten Frau* hat dies auf der theologischen Ebene begründet, wenn er den Ehemann

---

[24] Auch in den übrigen hier behandelten Werken ist es der Mann, der in Fragen der Religion entscheidet.

[25] Daß eine solche, die Güter der Welt absolut negierende Handlungsweise und deren Darstellung mit der Frömmigkeits- und insbesondere Armutsbewegung des 13. Jahrhunderts zusammenhängt, haben Mackinder-Savage (wie Anm. 4), S. 66–73 und Gudrun Aker, *Die 'Gute Frau': Höfische Bewährung und asketische Selbstheiligung in einer Versezählung der späten Stauferzeit* (Frankfurt am Main/Bern, 1983), S. 66–97 eindrucksvoll beschrieben.

mehrfach als 'genâde[n]lôs' bezeichnet (*GF* 1793, 1827, 1933). An einer
wichtigen Stelle des Werkes, als die Gute Frau eben die Börse
empfangen hat und deshalb annehmen muß, daß ihr Mann tot ist,
erklärt der Erzähler: 'disiu vrouwe unde ir kint,/ diu hâten gemach sint:/
[nämlich seitdem sie ihr Schicksal völlig in Gottes Hand gelegt hat (*GF*
1903–07)] ir sæliger man leit/ kumber unde arbeit./ daz kunde nieman
bewarn,/ er muose tuon unde varn/ als ein genâdelôser' (*GF* 1927–33,
mit 1927 beginnt in der Handschrift ein neuer Abschnitt). Ist dies so zu
verstehen, daß allein der Mann – von dem vor seinem Aufbruch ins
'ellende' keine christlichen Wohltaten berichtet werden – 'schuldig' ist –
nämlich des Verfallenseins an 'êre' und 'guot', an denen seine Ehefrau
als Frau in der Gesellschaft des 13. Jahrhunderts ohnehin weit weniger
Anteil haben konnte als ihr Mann? Der Text gibt hierauf keine
eindeutige Antwort, doch würde eine derartige Interpretation immerhin
erklären helfen, warum die Gute Frau im weiteren Verlauf der
Handlung ganz in den Vordergrund tritt.

Der Verfasser der *Guten Frau* hat im übrigen keinerlei Versuch
unternommen, die radikale Abkehr des Helden von einem vorbildlichen
höfischen Leben zu *erläutern*. Vorbildlich war dieses Leben gewesen
etwa im Sinne der Romane Hartmanns; von kirchlicher Frömmigkeit
des Paares (z. B. Gebet, Gottesdienstbesuch) war bei dessen Beschreibung nicht die Rede gewesen, ganz im Gegensatz zum *Guillaume
d'Angleterre*. Äußere Zeichen der Frömmigkeit spielen aber auch später,
im 'ellende', kaum eine Rolle,[26] so daß hieraus nicht etwa auf ein
Versäumnis des jungen Paares geschlossen werden darf. Dem Verfasser
des Werkes ist derartiges augenscheinlich unwichtig, was zählt, ist die
vollständige Abkehr vom 'werltlîche[n] tuon' (*GF* 1563), der bewußte
Anschluß an das Christuswort: 'swer sich durch mich/ nideret ûf der
erde,/ der kumt ze hôhem werde' (*GF* 1592ff.). Das Mühlenerlebnis ist
dabei als eine Art dichterischen Bildes aufzufassen, das den Helden
geradezu heimsucht. Statt daß er sich über die Wohltaten seiner Frau
freut (denn sie ist es, die die Armen ernährt), trifft ihn der Blitzschlag
göttlicher Erkenntnis und zeigt ihm, daß er sein Leben von Grund auf
ändern muß.

Während hier der Verfasser der *Guten Frau* auf ein äußeres Zeichen
für das Wunder der Bekehrung verzichtet, gestaltet er andernorts
Zeichen um. Das aus dem *Guillaume* bekannte Adlermotiv
beispielsweise wird folgendermaßen variiert: Auch in der *Guten Frau*
stiehlt der Vogel die Börse (*GF* 1849ff.), und auch hier fällt sie wieder

---

[26] *GF* 1649f. wird beiläufig erwähnt, daß die Gute Frau zur Kirche geht; als Königinwitwe
'daz jâr si alsô vertreip/ mit almuosen und mit gebete' (*GF* 2592f.). Davon zu
unterscheiden sind die individuellen Formen des Umgangs mit Gott, Anrufungen in Leid
oder Freude (*GF* 1841ff., 1857ff., 1998ff., 2706ff., 2862ff.) oder Reflexionen über Gottes
Wirken (*GF* 1903ff.).

vom Himmel, aber in den Schoß der Guten Frau. Diebstahl und Fall der Börse sind in eine Szene zusammengezogen. Gleich nachdem er die Börse entwendet hat, wird der Adler von den Krähen und Weihen erspäht. Sie verfolgen ihn, und als eine ihm in den Nacken stößt, läßt er die Börse fallen (GF 1865–77). Mit dieser Umgestaltung erreicht der Verfasser der *Guten Frau*, daß die Szene nun weitgehend 'realistisch' wirkt, was das Verhalten des Adlers angeht, und das ist es, worauf es ihm offenbar ankommt. Wie im *Guillaume* aber läßt der Vogel die Börse am rechten Ort und zum richtigen Zeitpunkt fallen. Die Gute Frau, die sich nicht im mindesten überrascht zeigt (GF 1872ff.), erkennt die Börse sofort, ja geradezu 'automatisch', als die ihres Mannes und meint daraufhin für einen Moment, er sei zugrunde gegangen. Die Börse verweist so auf die verzweifelte Lage des Mannes, die auch die Frau in Verzweiflung stürzt. Aber diese Verzweiflung läßt sie zu Gott flehen, der ihr Trost sendet. Das Adlermotiv wird so stark verändert. Seine Bedeutung bleibt in der *Guten Frau* allerdings, im Vergleich zum *Guillaume d'Angleterre* und erst recht zum *Escoufle*, gering.

In anderer Form erscheint auch das in der *Guten Frau* gedoppelt auftretende Motiv der von der Frau erwünschten, vom Mann aber erlittenen Josefsehe. Wie Theopista und Gratiiene übersteht die Gute Frau ihre erstaunliche Karriere als Gräfin von Blois und schließlich als Königin von Frankreich, ohne die ihrem Mann gelobte Treue brechen zu müssen. Dieses Moment ist dem Autor so wichtig, daß er es im Epilog noch einmal anspricht: 'Ze êren guoten wîben' will er gedichtet haben, 'daz si merken unde schouwen/ bî dirre guoten vrouwen,/ daz niemer wîbe missegât/ diu truwe gên ir manne hât' – so die letzten Verse der Erzählung (GF 3054–58).[27] Von der Begründung her kehrt der Autor der Guten Frau im ersten Fall zur Legende zurück. Dem Ansinnen des Grafen von Blois gegenüber wird die eheliche Treue der Guten Frau durch den 'kameræere' Christus bewacht (GF 2019–28), dem ihr Mann sie scheidend anvertraut hatte (GF 1779f.). Im zweiten Fall hat die Regie Gottes bereits vorgesorgt. Die dem König entlaufene frühere Königin von Frankreich hatte diesen mittels der Nigromantie eines Meisters von Toledo unfähig gemacht, 'mit den wîben/ mannes werc [ze] trîben' (GF 2443f.), was die Gute Frau natürlich als 'guot heil' ansieht, 'daz si got der guote/ vor schanden behuote' (GF 2492–94). Die eheliche Treue der Guten Frau wird so gar nicht wirklich geprüft; weibliches Taktieren, wie Gratiiene, hat sie nicht nötig. Das Eingreifen Gottes (der auch für den rechtzeitigen Tod der beiden Männer sorgt) macht dergleichen überflüssig.

So knapp der Autor die Reaktion der Guten Frau beschreibt, so ausführlich schildert er die der betroffenen Männer. Sowohl der Graf

---

[27]   Daß dies eine unzureichende, weil viel zu 'enge' Lehre ist, bedarf keiner Erörterung.

von Blois (*GF* 2035–51) wie der König von Frankreich (*GF* 2455–62, 2479–84) äußern sich wortreich über das Problem des Versagens im Ehebett. Ist solch direktes Ansprechen auch physischer Sachverhalte damit zu erklären, daß die *Gute Frau* rund ein halbes Jahrhundert nach dem *Guillaume d'Angleterre* und damit auch nach den Werken der Hartmann, Wolfram und Gottfried entstand? Festzuhalten bleibt, daß auch im Falle des Motives der bewahrten Treue die *Gute Frau* eine Fassung bietet, die ganz ohne äußere, spektakuläre Zeichen auskommt, aber das Wirken und Vorausplanen und -handeln Gottes (von dem nicht explizit die Rede ist!) klar erkennen läßt.

In vielen anderen Zügen kommt die *Gute Frau* der *Eustachiuslegende* entschieden näher als dem *Guillaume*. Hier wie dort erhalten beispielsweise die Kinder keine eigene Geschichte – die *Gute Frau* berichtet über sie noch weniger als die Legende. Nähe zu dieser signalisiert auch das Schicksal des Helden. Er wird, wie Gregorius, durch sein Bettlerleben völlig entstellt. Wie Eustachius – und im Gegensatz zu Gui(llaume) – gelingt *ihm* natürlich keine Karriere, er bleibt Bettler. Das aber hat, wie schon bemerkt, auch mit einer der erzählerischen Hauptintentionen des Verfassers zu tun, der Demonstration einer weiblichen 'Erfolgsgeschichte'. Unterstrichen wird dies dadurch, daß die einzige Stelle des Werkes, an der Gott unmittelbar in das Geschehen eingreift, die ist, an der die Gute Frau Bedenken hat, die Hand des Königs von Frankreich zu akzeptieren. Nachdem sie Gott um Beistand angerufen hat, erklärt ihr im Schlaf eine Stimme: 'Es enmac dehein rât sîn,/ du muost werden künegîn/ da ze Frankrîche/ und dar nâch êweclîche/ ze himele tragen krône:/ daz gît dir got ze lône' (*GF* 2313–18). Über die Ansätze des *Guillaume d'Angleterre* geht die Gute Frau hier weit hinaus; ihre Karriere übertrifft die der Gratiiene.[28] Von der Legende unterscheiden sich beide Werke in einem Punkte aufs deutlichste: Theopista muß ihr Leben als Hüterin eines Gartens fristen.

Ein letzter Blick sei noch auf das Ende der Erzählung von der *Guten Frau* geworfen: Wie Eustachius und Theopista, Guillaume und Gratiiene gelangen die Protagonisten nach Jahren der Entbehrung wieder zu Besitz und gesellschaftlichem Ansehen. Die Gute Frau nimmt am Ende sogar eine höhere gesellschaftliche Position ein, als zu Anfang des Romans. Während in der Legende dies irdische Glück rasch abgelöst und überhöht wird durch das zum ewigen himmlischen Glück führende Martyrium, fehlt im *Guillaume*, wie erst recht in der ethisch weit rigoroseren *Guten Frau* eine Begründung für das neue Glück auf Erden. Weder Chrétien noch der Verfasser der *Guten Frau* lösen den

---

[28] Inwieweit dies durch den genealogischen Rahmen bedingt ist (in Pro- und Epilog wird die *Gute Frau* als Familiengeschichte der Karolinger deklariert), braucht hier nicht erörtert zu werden.

Widerspruch zwischen dem Anlaß für den Aufbruch ins 'essil' bzw. 'ellende' und dem irdischen Happy End auf. Besonders gilt dies für die *Gute Frau*: 'Ere unde guot' sind für den neuen König von Frankreich offenbar nicht mehr 'mortgalle/ zem êwigen valle' (*GF* 1532–34) – aber darüber, daß der Held der Erzählung nun ein neues Verhältnis zu den Gütern dieser Erde gewonnen hätte, sagt der Verfasser am Ende des Werkes ebenso wenig wie Chrétien.

Eine gegenüber dem *Guillaume d'Angleterre* und der *Guten Frau* stark veränderte Variante der Beschäftigung mit dem Eustachius-Thema bietet der *Wilhelm von Wenden*. Angesichts mehrerer neuerer und neuester Arbeiten zu diesem Werk kann ich mich hier kurz fassen.[29] Ulrich von Etzenbach, der Autor des *Wilhelm*, scheint sich an die Grundkonstellation der Legende angelehnt zu haben. Willehalm und Bene, die Protagonisten seines Werkes, sind Heiden. Sie leben in einer heidnischen, genauer: slawisch-heidnischen Umwelt, in der man das – bereits bestehende – Christentum und seinen Kampf gegen die Heiden, der Willehalm später die Teilnahme an einem Kreuzzug ermöglicht, nicht kennt. Wie Placidas und Trajana führen sie, was der Autor vor allem am Beispiel Willehalms zeigt, ein vorbildliches Leben (vgl. *WvW* 140–46, 336, 385, 439, 655–88). Schon hier aber weicht der *Wilhelm* von der Legende ab: An die Stelle eines beiden Eheleuten zuteil werdenden Bekehrungserlebnisses setzt Ulrich – ähnlich wie der Verfasser der *Guten Frau* – eine nur Willehalm betreffende Begegnung mit christlichen Pilgern. Dies von ihm vernommene 'süeze wort/ Krist' (*WvW* 503f.) verändert Willehalm auf einen Schlag, was Ulrich ausführlich beschreibt (*WvW* 506–24). Es ist das süßeste Wort, das er je gehört hat, sein hartes heidnisches Herz (!) unterwirft sich diesem Wort, er trägt es beständig im Sinn und im Munde, es beschwert seinen 'muot' (*WvW* 518) – und deshalb will er wissen, wie er dahin kommen könnte, 'dâ er volliclich vernæme/ und man im bescheinde/ waz Krist der name meinde' (*WvW* 520–22). Vergleichen läßt sich dieses Erlebnis mit der Mühlenszene der *Guten Frau*: War es dort der Anblick

29   Rainer Kohlmayer, *Ulrichs von Etzenbach 'Wilhelm von Wenden': Studien zu Tektonik und Thematik einer politischen Legende aus der nachklassischen Zeit des Mittelalters*, Deutsche Studien, 25 (Meisenheim am Glan, 1974); Achim Masser, 'Zum *Wilhelm von Wenden* Ulrichs von Etzenbach', *ZfdPh*, 93 (1974), Sonderheft Spätmittelalterliche Epik, 141–55; Rainer Kohlmayer, 'Formkunst und Politik in den Werken Ulrichs von Etzenbach', *ZfdPh*, 99 (1980), 355–84 (zum *Wilhelm von Wenden* S. 369–75); Walter Haug, *Literaturtheorie im deutschen Mittelalter* (Darmstadt, 1985), S. 330–34; Jan-Dirk Müller, 'Landesherrin per compromissum. Zum Wahlmodus in Ulrichs von Etzenbach *Wilhelm von Wenden* V. 4095–401', in *Sprache und Recht: Beiträge zur Kulturgeschichte des Mittelalters: Festschrift für Ruth Schmidt-Wiegand zum 60. Geburtstag*, hg. von Karl Hauck u. a. (Berlin/New York, 1986), Bd. I, S. 490–514; Hans-Joachim Behr, *Literatur als Machtlegitimation: Studien zur Funktion der deutschsprachigen Dichtung am böhmischen Königshof im 13. Jahrhundert*, Forschungen zur Geschichte der älteren deutschen Literatur, 9 (München, 1989), hier S. 175–206.

menschlichen Elends, das radikal zur Erkenntnis eigener Sündhaftigkeit führte, so ist es nun das Anhören eines Namens, und zwar des Namens schlechthin, das Willehalm die Mangelhaftigkeit seiner heidnischen Existenz erkennen lassen soll.[30] Dies freilich will dem Leser des *Wilhelm von Wenden* kaum einleuchten, zu deutlich hatte Ulrich schon vor der 'Bekehrungsszene' seinen Helden als vorbildlichen Menschen dargestellt. Ulrich hatte ihn als 'von Parrit sante Willehalm' (*WvW* 74) eingeführt und seine 'heilekeit' schon vor seinem Aufbruch hin zu Christus betont (*WvW* 752). Diese Präsentation des Protagonisten als eines Heiligen spielt aber im Verlauf der Erzählung keine Rolle, sie ist Ausdruck der 'extremen Idealität', mit der Ulrich seine Akteure ausgestattet hat.[31] Sie zeigt an, daß es auch im *Wilhelm von Wenden* der Mann ist, der 'in spiritualibus' die Führung innehat – wie Eustachius, Guillaume und der Ehemann der Guten Frau. Unterstrichen wird dies im *Wilhelm von Wenden* noch dadurch, daß Bene bis kurz vor Ende des Werkes Heidin bleibt.[32]

Willehalms Führungsrolle tritt auch beim Aufbruch in die Fremde zutage: Bene folgt ihm gegen ihren Willen – nicht, weil sie wie ihr Mann wissen will, was es mit Christus auf sich hat, sondern als treue Ehefrau. Bei der Gestaltung dieses Aufbruchs ist Ulrich äußerlich dem Modell der Legende bzw. den beiden älteren Romanen gefolgt. Die Art der Ausführung ist jedoch von einer geradezu erstaunlichen Inkonsequenz und Widersprüchlichkeit:[33] Willehalm verkauft die beiden Kinder an christliche (!) Kaufleute (*WvW* 2296–311), obwohl er, wie an anderer Stelle betont wird, reichlich mit Geld versehen zur Suche nach dem Christengott aufgebrochen ist, so daß er dann die während des Verkaufs schlafende Bene in Pension geben und für sich eine Schiffspassage ins Heilige Land buchen lassen kann (*WvW* 2556–72).[34]

---

[30] Die unterschiedliche Gestaltung der äußeren Umstände des Bekehrungserlebnisses (von der Erscheinung Gottes über die göttliche Stimme und die Ein-Sicht hin zum Hören des Namens) wäre gesondert zu untersuchen. Daß Ulrich als Zeichen den *Namen* Gottes wählt, ist sicher nicht unabhängig von der seit dem 12. Jahrhundert zu belegenden, durch Franz von Assisi besonders geförderten Namen-Jesu-Verehrung, vgl. *Lexikon für Theologie und Kirche*, 2. Aufl., Bd. VII, Sp. 783.

[31] Vgl. dazu Behr (wie Anm. 29), S. 179 und 182.

[32] Ihre Bekehrung ist eine allmähliche, die über die Schmähung der heidnischen Götter angesichts des Verlustes ihrer Kinder (*WvW* 4596ff.) zur Beherbergung christlicher Pilger (*WvW* 4627ff., Christenlehre 4817ff.) und die Teilnahme am christlichen Gottesdienst (*WvW* 6847ff.) zur Taufe führt (*WvW* 7942ff.). Der Christengott hat sich als der erfolgreichere erwiesen, er hat ihr Mann und Kinder wiedergegeben (vgl. *WvW* 7825ff.).

[33] Auf diese hat Kohlmayer (wie Anm. 29, 1974), S. 60 ausführlich hingewiesen, weshalb hier einzelne Beispiele genügen.

[34] Es ist interessant zu sehen, wie sehr sich im *Wilhelm von Wenden* die Vorstellung vom 'Höfischen Leben' gegenüber dem *Guillaume d'Angleterre* und der *Guten Frau* geändert hat. Man ist fein geworden und auf Distanz gegangen und braucht deshalb vermittelnde Chargen. Willehalm zieht zuerst seinen Kämmerer ins Vertrauen, der die Pilgerkleidung besorgt. Als Bene entdeckt, daß Willehalm heimlich betet, spricht sie darüber zuerst mit ihrer Kammerfrau – nicht etwa mit ihrem Ehemann (*WvW* 591–613 bzw. 767–812).

Bene, die Heidin, erscheint ihrem Manne als Last, derer er sich rasch entledigt, um heimlich seinem Ziel, dem Land des Christengottes, näher zu kommen. Um das zu erreichen sind offensichtlich alle, auch schlimme Mittel recht, so neben dem Verkauf der Kinder auch die nur als verantwortungslos zu bezeichnende Desertion seinen Pflichten als Herrscher und damit den Untertanen gegenüber (*WvW* 1143–51). Im Unterschied zu den anderen hier behandelten Werken ist also Willehalm selbst für den Verlust seiner Familie verantwortlich. Willehalm und Bene durchlaufen so auch, anders als Eustachius und Theopista, keine Zeit hiobgleicher Prüfungen; ihr Leid wird reduziert auf eine höchst irdische Trennung der Familienmitglieder, die allen, auch den Kindern, deren Schicksal hier ausführlich – ähnlich wie im *Guillaume d'Angleterre* – dargestellt wird, eine eigene 'Erfolgsgeschichte' zugesteht.

Daß Bene beim Verkauf der Kinder schläft, weist auf ein geradezu dominierendes Merkmal von Ulrichs Roman hin; sein extremes Harmoniebedürfnis, das sich vor allem darin äußert, daß mögliche Konflikte vermieden werden. Das von Chrétien wie vom Verfasser der *Guten Frau* ausführlich behandelte Problem der Bewahrung ehelicher Treue hat Ulrich dadurch aus der Welt geschafft, daß der Herzog des Landes, in dem Bene lebt, ohne Erben stirbt, Bene nach Jahren der Anarchie gebeten wird, das Land zu regieren und nach einem Jahr als Fürstin eingesetzt wird.[35] Als solche soll sie sich zwar verheiraten, es wird aber keine Frist gesetzt. Bene kann deshalb fünf Jahre lang auf ihren Mann warten (*WvW* 4791ff.).

Konfliktvermeidung betreibt Ulrich auch bei der Gestaltung des Wiedererkennens: Mehr als noch in der *Guten Frau* ist Bene daran interessiert, den Großen ihres heidnischen Landes den wiedergefundenen Christenfürsten Willehalm als Herrscher akzeptabel zu machen.[36]

Ein letzter Blick sei auf die Ebene der Wunder und Zeichen gerichtet, mit denen die Legende die irdischen Geschehnisse umfängt und überhöht. Ulrich von Etzenbach hat auf sie rigoros verzichtet. So christlich und fromm sein Werk zu sein vorgibt, so leer ist es in dieser Hinsicht: Keine Spur von einer göttlichen Stimme oder gar einer Erscheinung Gottes, kein Adler als Werkzeug göttlichen Willens, kein Horn und auch kein Ring, an dem Bene ihren Ehemann wiederer-

---

35   Zu den Umständen siehe im einzelnen Müller (wie Anm. 29). Probleme dieser Art, nämlich solche der Ausübung und Legitimierung von Herrschaft sind es, die Ulrich vor allem interessieren, vgl. dazu auch Behr (wie Anm. 29), S. 191.
36   Ulrichs ins Extrem gesteigerte Bedürfnis, eine 'heile Welt' zu präsentieren, führt auch zu der moralisch wie juristisch gleichermaßen fragwürdigen Lösung des Konfliktes zwischen den Raubritter-Söhnen und der Landesherrin, ihrer Mutter, vgl. *WvW* 6765–86.

kennen könnte.[37] Lediglich die Rockschöße von Willehalms Gewand, in die er die neugeborenen Kinder wickelt, hat Ulrich, Chrétien folgend, als häufig genanntes Erkennungszeichen beibehalten (*WvW* 2252, 5150, 5570, 6589, 7053). Im übrigen aber nimmt er Ansätze Chrétiens auf, die in seinen historisch-genealogischen Kontext passen. Die Kinder verraten schon durch ihr Aussehen ihre edle Abkunft.[38] Die feudale Ideologie des Geblütsadels – das ist es, was Ulrich hier, Chrétien übertrumpfend, vorführt.

All dies weist darauf hin, daß es Ulrich von Etzenbach nicht darum ging, den Weg eines heidnischen Ehepaares und seiner beiden Kinder hin zu einem durch harte Prüfungen errungenen christlichen Glauben darzustellen. Sein Hauptanliegen ist vielmehr die Beschreibung der Konstituierung von Macht innerhalb einer Feudalgesellschaft,[39] eingebunden in die genealogisch-politische Situation in Böhmen am Ende des 13. Jahrhunderts. Ulrichs Wahl des Eustachius-Themas, die wohl bedingt war durch den Namen der Gemahlin Wenzels II., Guta von Habsburg, und die dem Ehepaar 1289 geborenen Zwillingskinder, erweist sich so als arger Mißgriff: Indem er die Vorgaben des Eustachius-Themas zu nutzen versucht, tut er dessen Ethos Gewalt an. Es ist deshalb kein Zufall, daß das äußerlich 'frömmste' Werk unserer Reihe zugleich das geistlich gesehen leerste und oberflächlichste ist. An die Stelle des wunderbar sich dem Menschen zeigenden, ihn bis ins Detail über sein künftiges Schicksal informierenden Gottes der Legende ist hier der zwar beständig angebetete und mit frommen Werken überhäufte, aber ferne und völlig sprachlose Gott getreten. Der fast beliebige Wechsel ganzer Völker vom Heiden- zum Christentum am Ende des *Wilhelm von Wenden* (*WvW* 8209–13) zeigt, wie wenig Ulrich an einer tiefgehenden Formulierung des Eustachius-Themas interessiert war. Verglichen damit nimmt Chrétiens Gestaltung, die mit der Ulrichs einige Parallelen aufweist,[40] bei aller Frische und Leichtigkeit das Thema doch ernst: Der heitere Schluß (mit der Kaufmannsszene) läßt das

---

[37] Bene bedarf bei Ulrich aber auch keiner äußeren Erkennungszeichen, denn *ihr Herz* sagt ihr (*WvW* 5947ff.), daß der durch die Strapazen der Kreuzfahrt entstellte und dadurch unkenntlich gewordene Pilger ihr Mann Willehalm ist. Die in den Romanen Konrads von Würzburg zu bemerkende Psychologisierung ist so auch hier zu erkennen.

[38] Vgl. *GdA* 1344–1434 mit besonderem Hinweis auf das Wirken von 'nature' (= Abstammung), die verhindert, daß die Kinder zu 'vilains' werden; Lovel und Marin können Gosselins und Foukiers Kinder nicht sein (1431–34). Im *Wilhelm von Wenden* wird frühzeitig die (hohe) 'geburt' der beiden Kinder deutlich (5069), später bemerkt der reiche Bürger, der sie aufnimmt, sogleich, daß sie edler Abstammung sind (5343f.). Als er sie an den Hof des Königs Honestus mitnimmt, erkennt dieser sofort, daß diese Kinder nicht die leiblichen Söhne des Kaufmanns sein können (5479–85). Schon die *Eustachiuslegende* kennt das Motiv: Die Söhne des Eustachius fallen in dem Dorfe, in das sie das Schicksal verschlagen hat, dadurch auf, daß sie 'grandi statura et decora facie valde' sind (*E* 132A).

[39] Behr (wie Anm. 29), S. 192.

[40] So z. B. hinsichtlich der hohen Wertschätzung und Bedeutung des Geldes.

geistliche Anliegen, die Demonstration des Wirkens eines unerforschlichen Gottes in seinen Geschöpfen, unbeschädigt. Vom Ernst der *Guten Frau*, die weltlichen Ruhm und Besitz uneingeschränkt als Übel beschrieben hatte, und so dem Thema eine radikale, durch das diesseitig-glückliche Ende des Schlusses nicht aufgehobene Zuspitzung verliehen hatte, ist das konfliktfrei-oberflächliche Christentum des *Wilhelm von Wenden* sehr weit entfernt. Ein schärferer Bruch in der Auffassung ein und desselben Themas, noch dazu im Abstand von nur etwa 60 Jahren, läßt sich kaum denken.

Index

The names of scholars are included in the index only if their work is the subject of discussion in one of the contributions. Medieval men and women are indexed under their Christian names.

331

ARTHURIAN STUDIES